Chris,
Please enjoy this
glimpse into my past
and only other fender bender.
Sincerely,
Carolyn Benne...ter

# The Powell

# Mountain Matter

*by*

*Carolyn Bennett-Hunter*

Copyright 2017 by Carolyn Bennett-Hunter

# INDEX

## Other Books by Carolyn Bennett-Hunter:

*City Beyond the Deep*

*The Widow's Four*

*The Oceanview Matter*

# ACKNOWLEDGMENTS

My heartfelt thanks to the family and friends who carefully proofed the pages of this book, including, but not limited to paralegal friends Julie Cohen and Jacky Withem, and film producer friend Sherry Collins, for their extraordinary efforts, unique insights and many helpful suggestions!

In particular, I am in debt to my wonderful husband David for his tireless hours of proofing, advice regarding all things mechanical – including any weapons mentioned herein – and his unique perspective on how some of the male characters in this book might have reacted under similar circumstances.

My deepest appreciation to attorney friend Rachel Bertoni for not only proofing, but for her skills in reviewing several brief speaking parts that were originally "machine translated" from English into Italian but now have the human touch. I am also appreciative to learn that there is a difference between tenants "by the entirety" and tenants "in common" as it relates to matters of probate.

Of special mention is the moral support and encouragement from long-time dear friend Sherry Collins as this project progressed on an almost daily basis. And, I can't tell you how excited I am that Sherry has agreed to be featured as Sherry "Collingsworth" in this book!

Imagine my surprise when Susan "Rives" (whose real last name cannot be revealed) flew all the way from her home to mine for the first book signing of this book's predecessor – "The Oceanview Matter" – and to learn that Susan is as thrilled with and excited about these books as I am! Both Susan and my friend Janette "Manza" (whose real last name also must be kept confidential) have volunteered to be main characters in this book, as well. I hope they will enjoy the adventure!

Many thanks to former classmate and email friend Bert Higa for again sharing his aeronautic expertise, and for looking over the Learjet sequence in chapter four, as well as the air show sequence in chapter seven. Bert was a chief inspector at an aircraft repair station for commercial airliners, inspected propulsion systems for orbiting spacecraft, and worked for many years as an airplane mechanic. Bert is now semi-retired but actively participates in piloting small planes on humanitarian aid missions of mercy to third world countries.

Special thanks to church friend Kent Garrett for confirming the factual accuracy of the Learjet sequence in chapter four, and for his extremely helpful suggestions regarding the air show sequence in chapter seven, as well. I especially appreciate his educating me as to what verbatim phraseology is, how and when it is used by pilots and air traffic controllers, and as to some of the finer points relating to ejection seats. While I do believe the aerobatic plane that I actually rode in back in 1974 was equipped with an ejection seat, it made sense to omit it from this story. Kent is a retired Air Traffic Controller and commercial pilot with experience flying many different types of airplanes.

Special thanks to friend Brenda Anderson for sharing with me her knowledge about flight suits and taking the time to explain to me that they have pant legs (and not booties) on them. Brenda is an experienced parachute jumper who has been jumping for ten years now and aspires to someday become a certified instructor.

Thank you very much to Mazda Mokalla of Shutterbug for his tremendous help sizing the photos ultimately used in the cover art.

Deepest thanks and appreciation to my husband's distant cousin and dear friend Laurey Lee for her help with "touching up" the photos used on the cover of this book, and for finalizing the lettering and other cover artwork. I could not have managed this without her!

Unlike the old days when it was necessary for writers to make repeated trips to the local library while researching various topics, a vast realm of knowledge is literally at one's fingertips in today's modern electronic age. I am especially grateful for the marvelous "Wikipedia" feature on my computer.

Thanks again to Richard from BestBuy for again showing me the latest voice-activated smartwatches with independent internet access that are available now, in 2016, and for patiently explaining to me their capabilities.

# FOREWORD

Seven long years had passed since the recovery of Joyce Troglite and Veronica Jensen's skeletal remains from the isolated bunker tunnel cave at Oceanview Academy in 2016.

It was finally 2023, and the skeletal remains of several young coeds were unexpectedly discovered at a long-abandoned winery near Powell Mountain University, where Carolyn had attended her first year of college back in 1974 and 1975. Among the personal effects of one victim was Carolyn's missing wallet, the one she reported lost or stolen in 1975. Could the victim prove to be someone Carolyn knew who mysteriously vanished without a trace 48 years ago?

Carolyn's overdue visit to the Killingham Lighthouse Bed and Breakfast to relax and enjoy some time with her friend Susan was suddenly cut short when she received news of the gruesome discovery. Would the infamous Powell Mountain Killer turn out to be responsible, or someone else?

Was a well-loved community icon and local woodcutter possibly responsible for all of the murders, or just one of them? Was that particular crime scene really staged as alleged by the Deputy DA assigned to prosecute the case? Was the judge presiding over the eventual trial somehow involved?

Carolyn Bennett-Hunter and her friend Sherry Collingsworth join forces with Susan Rives and Janette Manza to solve a whole new matter – the Powell Mountain Matter – multiple cold cases that have haunted law enforcement officials for almost 50 years.

Again, you will be kept guessing until the very end what really happened in this incredible story that spans a lifetime and manages to incorporate many of the author's own real life experiences and other true events into the plot, as well. Sometimes truth is stranger than fiction, after all. Romance, mystery, suspense and an occasional dose of fun will keep you entertained.

Any semblance to events, true crimes, places, organizations or persons either living or dead within the pages of this book are purely coincidental.

# 1. The Fifth Floor

Carefully winding its way past aging redwood trees and thickly overgrown underbrush, the Bennett family car slowly climbed the steep two-lane highway toward Powell Mountain University. The white Dodge Dart of which Mr. Bennett was so proud suddenly began to hesitate and sputter. Steam could be seen escaping from around the edges of its over-heated hood.

"Looks like it might be the radiator," remarked Mrs. Bennett.

"Do you think?" snapped her husband in an irritated tone as he pulled over, came to a stop and shut off the engine to wait for it to cool. His wife had an innate talent for stating the obvious.

"How much farther is it?" questioned their daughter Carolyn.

"The handbook mentioned that it should take only forty-five minutes to get from St. Diablo to Powell Mountain University," recalled Carolyn's mother.

"Well, we've already been driving for over an hour since leaving St. Diablo," reminded Carolyn. "Not to mention the ten hours it took to get from Ashton to there, when it should have taken about nine!"

"Your father does like to drive slower than most people," pointed out Mrs. Bennett. "But, I think that should be nine-and-a-half."

"Maybe if your daughter didn't eat so slowly, it might not be so late already!" retorted her husband. He frequently spoke to his wife about their daughter Carolyn in the third-person, even when Carolyn was present.

Carolyn merely rolled her eyes as she thought of the time her father had received a traffic citation for impeding traffic - to the tune of 120 cars - after failing to pull off the road for everyone else to pass. She and her friend Susan Rives had been in the backseat at the time. It was bad enough that a majority of the angry drivers had honked their horns and uttered profanities at them while they passed! But, when Mr. Bennett later decided to pull into a popular cattle ranch restaurant for lunch, most of those same people were already there, including the officer who had given Mr. Bennett the citation! It had been most embarrassing, to say the least. That was in the spring of 1973, during the last half of Carolyn's junior year at Oceanview Academy. Then, after spending her senior year at Ashton Academy during the 1973-1974 school year, Carolyn's first year of college was finally about to begin.

Usually a man of few words, Mr. Bennett was close to losing his temper. It had taken him the better part of a year to finish paying off the tuition debt from Carolyn's junior year at Oceanview Academy. Thank goodness his daughter had agreed to return home to complete her senior year of high school at Ashton Academy! Not only was the local school in Ashton more affordable, but having Carolyn back at home made it possible for her father to keep better track of her extracurricular activities, as well. Yet, despite everything, Mr. Bennett had somehow allowed himself to be talked into sending his only daughter to still another expensive coed parochial boarding school in the middle of nowhere! Undoubtedly, he would be faced with yet another enormous financial obligation because of it.

"What if there aren't any good rooms left in the dormitory by the time we get there?" worried Carolyn.

"Well, at least Susan Rives won't be in one of 'em!" retorted Mr. Bennett with a smug grin as he opened his car door to get out. He had already checked to be sure of that before agreeing to any of this. Carolyn's father had never cared much for her friend Susan and was not about to allow them to be roommates again. It was nothing definitive that he could put his finger on – and neither of the girls had really done anything seriously wrong that he knew of – but it still was his opinion that Susan was a bad influence on Carolyn.

"Susan is going to Ocean Bay University this year," Carolyn informed him matter-of-factly.

"I really don't think keeping in touch with her is such a good idea," replied Mr. Bennett. He had done his best to intercept Susan's letters to prevent Carolyn from keeping in touch with her.

"Why?" questioned Carolyn. "I just don't understand what you have against her." Carolyn was still quite angry about coming across two of Susan's letters in her father's desk drawer while looking for a paperclip only two weeks prior – and the letters had already been opened! Clearly, her father had not yet managed to get them to the incinerator.

Understandably, the incident involving Susan's letters had been another breaking point between Mr. Bennett and Carolyn, and had caused the tension between them to resurface in full force.

"Your father just doesn't think Susan was a very good influence on you," explained Carolyn's mother. She was always doing that - answering other people's questions for them - and it annoyed Mr. Bennett greatly.

After breathing in deeply and quickly letting it out, Mr. Bennett climbed from the car and slowly stood up to stretch. His carrot red colored hair was neatly combed back with an abundance of men's hair tonic and virtually glistened in the late afternoon sunlight.

"It might still be too hot," warned Mrs. Bennett.

"I'll take my chances," responded her husband. Hopefully, enough time had passed to allow him to safely open the hood without getting burned.

"At least it's cooler along here, under the trees," noted Carolyn's mother. "It really is pretty up here, too."

Mr. Bennett merely nodded as he finished stretching and walked toward the front of his vehicle. He knew how important it was to his wife that their daughter attend her first year of college at a parochial school where religion would be included in the agenda. Still, it would be expensive and he had no idea how he would ever afford it. On top of that, the last thing he needed was another unexpected car repair expense. Just then, a young doe and her two fawns ran across the road beside him.

"Oh, look!" exclaimed Carolyn as she, too, opened her door to climb from the car and noticed the deer.

"There doesn't seem to be much traffic up here, does there?" asked Mrs. Bennett. She had not looked in time to see the small family of deer, but was clearly entranced by the scenic forest surrounding them.

"No, there doesn't," agreed her husband.

"Everyone else is probably there already," interjected Carolyn as she folded her arms and began to look around. "It is pretty here, though. I wonder if there are any mountain lions?"

"Guess we'll find out," muttered Mr. Bennett as he tested the hood but found that it was still too hot to touch.

All at once, a battered old pickup truck appeared from around the last bend in the road and slowed as it approached. The tattered American flag clipped to its radio antenna flapped gently in the breeze, and the brightly colored flower stickers adorning it reminded Carolyn of an old hippy van she had seen once several years ago.

"Need some help?" questioned an affable black man in his late fifties, who had just rolled his window down and pulled to a stop in front of the Bennett family car.

The unassuming but friendly black man appeared at first glance to be a lumberman, and his truck was obviously used on less-than-desirable roads. Mr. Bennett, who was fastidious about checking his car tires for unwanted gravel and rocks at every possible opportunity, scowled with disapproval at the rock-infested tires on the stranger's outlandishly decorated truck.

"Name's Woody," grinned the stranger.

"We were just on our way to meet our daughter's new dean," volunteered Mrs. Bennett. "But now, we might not get there in time."

"In time for what?" questioned the stranger as he opened the door to his truck and climbed out. Woody was unexpectedly diminutive in size, only five feet, six inches tall, weighed about 115 pounds, and walked with a slight limp. Nevertheless, Woody's muscular arms were clearly used for demanding physical labor of some sort.

Mr. Bennett shook his head with disapproval. His wife was always doing that – freely giving out more information than necessary to perfect strangers.

"To get our daughter checked in before all the good dormitory rooms have been claimed," smiled Mrs. Bennett. "They are first-come, first-serve."

"I'll probably end up in the attic!" complained Carolyn as she approached her mother and the stranger.

"Woody, this is our daughter Carolyn," introduced Mrs. Bennett. "And we are the Bennetts."

"Excuse me," interrupted Mr. Bennett. "I see you have a trailer hitch on the back of your truck."

"Got a winch on the front, too," informed Woody proudly as he cordially shook hands with both Carolyn and then her mother before turning his full attention to Mr. Bennett. "Hey, it kud be just over-hot."

"Even without opening the hood, I'm pretty sure from how it sounded that it's a broken fanbelt," assessed Mr. Bennett.

"Kudn't hurt to look," suggested Woody. "Mind if I see?"

"It's probably still too hot," assumed Carolyn's father.

Carolyn and her mother watched with surprise as Woody removed an old shop rag from his back pocket and expertly used it to open and prop up the hood to the Bennett family car. "Sure enuf, 'tis a broken fan belt."

"My husband was an airplane mechanic during the Korean war," revealed Carolyn's mother.

Mr. Bennett merely rolled his eyes and shook his head. Once his wife began volunteering information to people, there really was no stopping her.

"Hey, kin I give you a tow?" offered Woody. "I'm goin' right past the school. Still gots another delivery to make tonight."

"What kind of delivery?" delved Mr. Bennett.

"Why, firewood, of course!" chuckled Woody as he took out a white corncob pipe, filled it with an odd-looking tobacco mix, and proceeded to light it up. "I'm known 'round these parts as Woody the Woodcutter. Ya see, after a loggin' accident took my left foot a few years back, they just wudn't let me work up on the lumber crew anymore. So, now I mostly chop firewood for folks."

"Firewood, huh?" pondered Mr. Bennett. He suspected that Woody's tobacco might consist of marijuana – which was definitely illegal everywhere in 1974 – but refrained from mentioning it. There was no reason to alarm his family.

"Three dollars a cord," revealed Woody as he walked over to his truck, untied and pulled back one corner of the tarp covering his load. "Includes delivery and stacking."

"I see," Mr. Bennett nodded with approval. Despite everything, it was always refreshing to come across someone like Woody who was willing to do an honest day's work. "Do you live around here?"

"Since 1956," responded Woody straightforwardly. "And now, I gots a wife 'n three kids. Matthew, he's ten next month; Mark is six. Den ders da baby, she be almost three. We wuz gonna call her Luke, but gotta girl, so we named her Luella."

"What do you charge for a tow?" inquired Mr. Bennett as he watched Woody grab and start to fasten his tow chain to the front under chassis of his precious car.

"No charge," responded Woody. "Let's see, the first thing I gotta do here is get the pull nice 'n even across it. And we gotta take it slow, especially on dem hairpin turns. 'Tis a mighty steep climb."

Tow hooks were generally not offered as a standard accessory on most vehicles until around 1987 or later, depending upon the make and model, so the possibility of tow-related damage in 1974 was a very real consideration. Yet, being stranded in the remote mountainous area with his family was an even less attractive prospect. Mr. Bennett did not appear very happy about the likelihood of tow-related damage to his vehicle but could see he was out of options.

"Or, I kin stop at Mike's Auto Shop - if they're still open - and maybe he kin send out a dolly? But, that kud be tomorrow," estimated Woody.

"We can't just stay here!" fretted Carolyn's mother. "What if there are wild animals out here?"

"Oh, there wud be, yes," assured Woody with an amused smile, "but they be the least of yer worries."

"Maybe we could just leave the car here and come back for it tomorrow?" suggested Carolyn.

Mr. Bennett inhaled and quickly let out a deep breath of air as he pulled a twenty-dollar bill from his wallet and handed it to Woody. "Thank you, sir."

"No, sir," declined Woody. "'Tis right on my way. Really, 'tis no trouble at all."

"I insist," persisted Mr. Bennett as he forced the twenty-dollar bill into Woody's hand. "I trust they do have phones at the school?"

"Uh, yes, sir," informed Woody as he shoved the twenty-dollar bill into the front pocket of his red plaid flannel shirt, rolled up his sleeves, and re-lit his white corncob pipe for another toke. "But, Mike's Auto Shop will be de first stop and der's a phone right in front."

"That'll be fine," agreed Carolyn's father as he watched Woody finish preparing for the tow.

"Can't we just have him drop us off at the dormitory first?" Carolyn whispered to her mother.

"Excuse me," interjected Mrs. Bennett as she approached her husband. "Can't Woody just drop Carolyn and me off at the dormitory first? We need to get there as soon as possible."

"'Tis still five miles from here to Mike's, and den two more to da school," revealed Woody with a shrug of his shoulders. He wasn't trying to eavesdrop but had easily overheard Mrs. Bennett's request to her husband.

"We'll get there when we do," advised Carolyn's father. He was not the least bit sympathetic with her plight. In fact, perhaps if they arrived there late enough, the rooms might all be taken and he would be spared the financial burden of paying for it after all.

Carolyn noticed the twinkle in her father's eyes at once, which was how he smiled on the rare occasions when he did, and knew he had no intention of hurrying things along on her account.

Only those who knew Mr. Bennett well knew for sure when he was amused by something, and that was fine with him. His usual poker face had come in handy more than once. His wife, on the other hand, was easily read and normally spoke whatever was on her mind at the time.

Carolyn's mother was not only tall and slender but also well-endowed in all the right places. Her short dark hair was arranged in a stylish wedge haircut, with steep-angled layers cut all around the sides and back. The fashionable baby blue pullover sweater she wore was revealing but modest at the same time. The blue denim bell-bottomed slacks she wore were definitely in style, which was important to her, though Mrs. Bennett much preferred pedal pushers to wear at home or when out riding her bike, as bell-bottoms would often get caught in the chain of her bicycle. Her clean white tennis shoes and matching white handbag were now in peril of becoming dirty from the red clay soil on which she stood.

Carolyn, on the other hand, was wearing a pair of dark brown waffle stompers with thick wool socks, and ready for just about any type of terrain. She had read about Powell Mountain University being in a rugged area and wanted to be prepared. Thankfully, Powell Mountain University allowed its students to wear blue jeans when not in class. If only Oceanview Academy had been as progressive during her junior year of high school! Carolyn's bright red pullover sweater and warm hooded navy blue jacket were almost too warm at the moment, but would be ideal for evenings.

Both Carolyn and her mother had smooth alabaster skin and purposely waited in the nearby shade while Woody finished hooking up the Bennett family car to the back of his truck.

"One of y'all needs to ride in de car to steer it," explained Woody as Carolyn and her mother climbed into the cab of his truck.

"Yes, indeed," agreed Carolyn's father as he walked back to the driver's side door of his vehicle, opened the door, and climbed inside.

"Just honk if ya needs me to stop," called Woody with an amused smile as he watched Mr. Bennett slam shut the door to his car and settle himself behind the wheel. "Got her in neutral?"

Mr. Bennett merely nodded in response.

"Brakes off?" added Woody.

Mr. Bennett nodded again, but clearly was losing patience with the entire situation.

"He doesn't look very happy," whispered Carolyn to her mother.

"He'll get over it," assured Mrs. Bennett.

"He might," chuckled Woody as he waited to close the passenger door of his truck for Mrs. Bennett and her daughter before circling back around to climb into the driver's side.

"We're lucky he stopped to help us," commented Mrs. Bennett.

"That's for sure," agreed Carolyn.

"Not to worry, ladies," assured Woody as he climbed in, sat down and carefully pulled his left leg with the artificial foot inside. "We'll get you der in time."

"We sure do appreciate your help!" responded Carolyn.

"My pleasure," smiled Woody as he closed the driver's door, inserted his key into the ignition and started up the engine of his truck.

"If you don't mind my asking," snooped Carolyn's mother, "but can you still drive okay with your foot like that?"

"Mother!" scolded Carolyn.

"She's fine," grinned Woody as he shifted into gear and started off with a jolt. "No worries, ma'am. Mostly just needs de right one for driving, anyway. Septin' when I shifts."

Carolyn turned at that moment and was in time to see the scowl of displeasure on her father's face from where he sat in the white Dodge Dart behind them, and could not help but chuckle about it.

"You do manage to get around quite well with it," continued Mrs. Bennett.

"Dat's de other reason dey call me Woody the Woodcutter," informed Woody. "Because of my wooden foot."

"Hmm," nodded Carolyn's mother. "So, do any of your children go to school around here?"

"Goodness, no," laughed Woody as he shifted into a lower gear and slowed down for the first hairpin turn. "And 'tis doubtful dey ever will. Dat school up der on de hill, it be for dem dats privileged. And, de cash kin get perty skinny for folks like me, 'specially around here. Der be Crusaders here in these parts, ya know."

Carolyn understood immediately what Woody was alluding to, though Mrs. Bennett didn't seem to understand at first.

"Crusaders?" questioned Mrs. Bennett.

"The Crusading Knights of Powell Mountain," explained Carolyn, embarrassed by her mother's naiveté.

"The CKPM?" Mrs. Bennett suddenly comprehended, and was clearly disturbed by the revelation.

"Dat school up der is mostly for da white folk, anyway," added Woody. "Or any other rich folk, too, I suppose."

"Oh, I see," nodded Mrs. Bennett, suddenly embarrassed. She had indeed heard of the white supremacist organization known as the Crusading Knights, but was astonished to learn of their presence in the isolated Powell Mountain area.

"Dat's okay," grinned Woody. "My kids and der kids will most likely go to St. Diablo High, and from der to da Junior College down in Ocean Bay. Dat is, if dey be so inclined to pay der own way. But, I plans to help all me kids and der kids if I kin sumday."

"You must be very proud of them," replied Carolyn's mother.

"Yes, um," responded Woody as he successfully completed negotiating another hairpin turn. "Indeed I am."

"Do you support your entire family just by cutting firewood, then?" questioned Carolyn's mother.

"Yer mama sure duz ask a lot o' questions," Woody commented as he winked and smiled at Carolyn.

"Yes, she certainly does," grinned Carolyn.

"Wise woman," replied Woody. "Specially with dat Powell Mountain Killer still on de loose 'round these parts."

"The Powell Mountain Killer?" repeated Mrs. Bennett with a sudden look of trepidation on her face.

"Good thing old Woody here stopped to give y'all a ride," reminded Woody as he slowed to allow a scurrying chipmunk to safely cross the road.

It was several minutes before Carolyn's mother spoke again. The thought of leaving her only daughter in a place where victims of the Powell Mountain Killer had recently been discovered was a sobering reality. Perhaps bringing Carolyn here was a mistake, after all.

"I wudn't worry too much, ma'am," assured Woody as he slowed to enter the driveway leading into a small parking area in front of Mike's Auto Shop. "Yer daughter looks like she has good sense. Just gotta stay in groups, and never go off alone."

"Indeed!" agreed Carolyn's mother.

"Well, here we be," indicated Woody as he pulled into the parking lot in front of Mike's Auto Shop and came to a stop. "But, they's closed."

"What now?" questioned Carolyn.

"We should go ahead and just leave the car here," opined Mrs. Bennett.

As if on cue, Mr. Bennett suddenly shifted his vehicle into park and put on the emergency brake before climbing out. He immediately began unhooking his vehicle from the tow chain leading to the trailer hitch on Woody's rear bumper.

"I got it," advised Woody as he hurriedly climbed from his truck and hobbled over to help.

"Already done," replied Mr. Bennett as he handed the tow chain to Woody. "Thank you for your help."

"Ain't nobody here," pointed out Woody.

"I'll wait with the car while you take them up to the school," informed Mr. Bennett.

"But, dey's closed, sir!" objected Woody.

"I'll just call Mike from this pay phone," determined Mr. Bennett. "There's a phone number on the door to call after hours."

"I kin't just leave you here by yerself, sir," argued Woody. "'Tisn't safe."

"Perhaps you can stop back by here and check on me, on your way back then?" requested Mr. Bennett as he handed Woody a ten-dollar bill to appease him.

"Yes, sir!" agreed Woody with a big grin. "I won't be long."

Powell Mountain University was a magnificent sight indeed. Located high above the vineyards of St. Diablo on the valley floor fifteen miles below, it was carefully nestled within a large expansive recess in the otherwise steep mountainous terrain surrounding it. Though much flatter than most of the dense, old growth forest in which it stood, the campus of Powell Mountain University was anything but flat. Several series of steps and staircases led everywhere, and were located in front of and inside most of its various buildings.

The imposing gray and tan brick structure now used as its Administration Building had originally been constructed in 1874 and had been part of the Powell Mountain Resort, an exclusive getaway retreat for the very rich and accessible only by horse and buggy back in those days. The black spired rooftops on most of its older buildings gave the entire place a medieval appearance. Tiny cement figures engaging in lascivious acts of pleasure, frolicking, eating grapes, or playing small harps, still adorned the Administration Building's front soffits but were slated for eventual removal due to their inappropriate subject matter.

The resort's hotel, bowling alleys and cottages ultimately became dormitories, classrooms and faculty homes in 1882 after being purchased by the Protestant sect who founded Powell Mountain University. Additional buildings were fashioned from lumber harvested at or near Powell Mountain University shortly thereafter.

Practical courses such as blacksmithing, home economics, dairy management and chicken farming had helped Powell Mountain University first establish its independence within the isolated mountain community surrounding it. Crop farming, however, had been out of the question due to the harsh winter weather conditions prevalent on Powell Mountain during some months of the year. Bible history, along with superior science and pre-medical courses, finally allowed the college to meet the local Regent Board of Education standards for accreditation in 1932. The introduction of seminary and post-graduate degree programs in 1951 had given the university added curbside appeal. Then in 1956, physical education, aviation, film and even television programs were eventually introduced into the curriculum to increase its diversity for prospective students.

By 1974, Powell Mountain University had succeeded in attracting a host of quality professors and other professionals from around the world and could accommodate up to eight hundred students each year. Of particular interest to Carolyn was the modern secretarial program it offered. Truly, the isolated co-ed boarding university on

Powell Mountain had become a prestigious community of quality learning that fostered spiritual values in a beautiful mountain setting.

Ten miles farther up the old Powell Mountain Road was Powell Lake, where students from Powell Mountain University would occasionally go for recreation on their days off. After winding up and over the uppermost crest of Powell Mountain, and past a dilapidated winery that had seen better days, Powell Mountain Road gently descended into the valley beyond where Powell Lake was located. Sunbathing, swimming, and skydiving were but some of the activities available there. Also, due to the inaccessible terrain at Powell Mountain University, the aviation courses it offered could only be held at the Powell Lake Airport – the only airport on Powell Mountain.

Both sides of Powell Mountain were quickly plunged into twilight shadows when the afternoon sun reached its zenith at the towering tree line each day.

"It sure gets dark early up here," noted Carolyn as Woody pulled up in front of the girls' dormitory to drop her and her mother off.

"'Tis all dem trees, ma'am," grinned Woody.

"Even though we're quite a bit farther north than we would be in Ashton, that is a pretty tall tree line," recognized Mrs. Bennett as she reached for the door handle on Woody's truck to open it.

"Please, allow me, ma'am," insisted Woody as he hurriedly climbed from the cab and hobbled over to open its passenger door.

"Thank you so much!" acknowledged Carolyn's mother as she took Woody's hand and allowed herself to be helped onto the curb below.

"Sorry dat runnin' board's so high," apologized Woody.

"Nonsense," interjected Carolyn as Woody proceeded to help her, too, from the cab. "We just appreciate your help!"

"Dis here's me card," offered Woody as he handed one to Carolyn and then another one to Mrs. Bennett. "Ya kin call on me any time." Woody then took out, replenished, and relit his white corncob pipe before taking a long drag from it. Often, Woody would just leave the pipe in his mouth while going about his daily routine, but he would usually stow it in his ashtray while driving.

Woody's business card was simple and to the point. It simply indicated, "Woody's Salvage Yard and Woodcutting" with the address and phone number beneath it. No hours were mentioned on the card indicating when it might be open for business.

"Will you be at this number later tonight, then?" questioned Mrs. Bennett. She was grateful for a way to contact Woody if needed.

"Not 'till I unload all dis wood up at Mike's, and den go check on yer man," replied Woody with his usual charismatic charm. "And I'll be sure Mike kums down to de shop fer his customer."

Mrs. Bennett merely nodded in acknowledgment, and was not her usual talkative self at that moment. Normally she would have asked whether "Mike" was the same Mike who owned Mike's Auto Shop, though it was rather obvious. Thoughts of the CKPM and trepidation about the Powell Mountain Killer were foremost on her mind.

It was also concerning to both Carolyn and her mother to see the last light fading when it was only eight o'clock in the evening. Even this far north, they had expected it to stay light until at least eight thirty.

Carolyn and her mother had only their purses and coats with them as they stood on the curb watching Woody drive away. Everything Carolyn had brought with her was still in the white Dodge Dart.

"Let's hope your father gets here soon," said Carolyn's mother as they began climbing the wide stone steps leading up to the girls' dormitory. "He has the checkbook."

"Guess we better see if there's even any rooms left before we get too worried about it," countered Carolyn. She was anxious to find out, but did not want to get her hopes too high and then be disappointed.

"I'm sure it will work out," comforted her mother as she put a reassuring hand on Carolyn's upper arm.

The Dean of Girls at Powell Mountain University was not at all what Carolyn or her mother had expected. In fact, Nancy Forrest was only 28 years old, pleasant natured, and rather attractive. Dressed in loose fitting bell-bottomed blue jeans, white tennis shoes, and a simple but modest green blouse, Ms. Forrest did not seem like much of an authority figure at all.

"Please, sit down," invited Dean Forrest with a pleasant smile. Her alabaster skin glowed with health, and her short dark hair was parted down the middle and feathered back on each side. Carolyn noticed at once that Ms. Forrest even had on some makeup!

"I'm sorry we're late," apologized Mrs. Bennett.

"We had car trouble," interjected Carolyn. "Radiator and fan belt. Thankfully, we got a tow with a man named Woody."

"Woody the Woodcutter?" smiled Ms. Forrest. "A rather interesting character to say the least, but most folks around here think the world of him. Old Woody would give just about anyone the shirt off his back if they asked."

"He sure went out of his way for us," replied Carolyn.

"Yes, he did," acknowledged Mrs. Bennett. "In fact, on his way back from delivering a load of firewood to Mike, Woody plans to return to Mike's Auto Shop to check on my husband. That's where he's waiting now with our car."

"Where do you folks plan to stay tonight?" Dean Forrest suddenly became serious. "There's no way Mike would be able to repair your car until tomorrow."

"Actually, we had planned on heading back after dropping Carolyn off here," responded Mrs. Bennett. "We had no idea it would be this late by now, or that the car would break down!"

"Perhaps they can stay in my room?" suggested Carolyn hopefully. "That is, if there are still any rooms left."

"There is only one room left at this point," responded Dean Forrest with a slight grin. "Unlike the other rooms where there are only two girls per room, the attic can hold up to six girls. Right now, it already has four."

"The attic?" repeated Carolyn with astonishment. She had only been kidding earlier about ending up in the attic, and yet that is exactly where she would be staying!

"You are joking?" objected Carolyn's mother.

"It's actually a rather nice room," assured Ms. Forrest. "But, we obviously can't have a man staying up there."

"I see your point," smiled Carolyn's mother.

"But, *you* are certainly welcome to sleep in the room with Carolyn and her new roommates," offered the Dean. "That last bed has not yet been claimed by anyone and should be available tonight."

"What about my husband?" questioned Mrs. Bennett.

"I can see if the Dean of Boys has a place for him over there," volunteered Ms. Forrest.

"In the boys' dormitory?" snickered Carolyn.

"The parents of the last girl who checked in here had to drive all the way back down to St. Diablo to find a hotel for the night, but they had a vehicle in which to get there," explained the Dean, who actually seemed to be enjoying their predicament.

"There's nothing here on campus at all, or even nearby?" pressed Mrs. Bennett.

"Everything up here on the mountain is booked already, by other parents," answered Ms. Forrest. "There is one guest facility on campus. It is a duplex, and both rooms are full."

"Maybe Woody could put both of you up for the night," suggested Carolyn as she pulled out and studied his business card again.

"You know, he probably would if you just ask him," grinned Dean Forrest. "That's not a bad idea."

"I hear there are Crusading Knights around here," Carolyn's mother suddenly blurted. "Would we be in any danger from them if we stayed there?"

Becoming serious again, Ms. Forrest confirmed, "Actually, the Crusading Knights of Powell Mountain do have a rather strong hold here on the mountain. You may recall me telling you that *most* folks around here think the world of Woody."

"But not all?" deduced Carolyn at once.

"Not all," replied the Dean. "Though, I don't think you need to be concerned. It's been a couple years since the CKPM tried to burn anyone from their home around here."

"You are kidding?" said Carolyn hopefully.

"I wish I were," lamented Ms. Forrest. "But, like I said, that was a while ago, and should be the least of your worries."

"Is it true that the Powell Mountain Killer is still frequenting this area?" continued Mrs. Bennett. "I heard on the news last month that he was finally captured. Otherwise, my husband and I would never have agreed to let our daughter come here in the first place!"

"Calm down, Mrs. Bennett," chided Dean Forrest. "Did Woody tell you about that?"

"He mentioned it," interjected Carolyn. "And he seemed quite concerned for our safety."

"As we should all be. Still, you can't believe everything you hear on the news," sighed Ms. Forrest. "The Powell Mountain Killer was never caught, not that we are aware of. But, I'll tell you the same thing I tell all my girls. Stay in groups, use good sense, and never go anywhere alone. As far as we know, all of the girls who went missing had one thing in common – they each wandered off alone."

"Exactly how many girls have disappeared?" prompted Carolyn.

"No one really knows for sure," admitted the Dean. "The disappearances date as far back as 1956, but there are at least fifteen known cases in recent times."

After an awkward moment of silence, a loud buzzer suddenly sounded from the office wall.

Mrs. Bennett was so started by the sound that she let out an involuntary shriek.

"Front doorbell," explained the Dean. "Curfew is at nine o'clock and anyone trying to get in after that must ring the buzzer for me to unlock the door."

"It's already after nine o'clock now?" questioned Mrs. Bennett. It certainly didn't seem like an entire hour had passed since being dropped off in front of the girls' dormitory!

"It's 9:01," clarified Dean Forrest as she got up and headed for the front door and paused to look through the peephole.

"Don't you have hall monitors?" wondered Carolyn aloud.

"Just someone at the front desk," answered Dean Forrest. "That's odd. It's Woody."

"Woody the Woodcutter?" Carolyn's mother was surprised.

"Where did the front desk person go?" quizzed Carolyn.

"Off duty at 9:00," explained the Dean as she unlocked and opened the door. "Woody! What can I do for you?"

"Howdy, ma'am," nodded Woody. "Mr. Bennett will be stayin' at Mike's and sends his best. Most of de young lady's stuff is here in de back of me truck. He said to call him at dis number." Woody then handed a battered scrap of newspaper to the Dean on which a phone number was scribbled.

Ms. Forrest then handed the paper to Carolyn's mother and shook her head ever so slightly. She was clearly displeased by the entire situation but managed to remain pleasant in spite of the circumstances.

16

"I'll help him unload," volunteered Carolyn as she rushed outside. Then, turning to Woody, Carolyn said, "Thank you so much!"

"My pleasure," grinned Woody as he and Carolyn proceeded to unload and carry her suitcases and boxes of things up the front steps.

"You may go ahead and bring them inside," instructed the Dean. Then, for Carolyn and her mother's benefit, the Dean explained, "Men are normally not allowed into the girl's dormitory under any circumstances after curfew."

"But, they are allowed inside during regular hours?" inquired Carolyn's mother.

"Usually just to announce themselves at the front desk before sitting down over there in the visiting room to wait for the person they're here to see," elaborated the Dean. "There are no phones in the rooms, so someone would need to go upstairs and knock on the particular girl's dormitory room to announce her visitor. The girl would then either come down here to see her male visitor, or have the messenger inform him she is not available."

"There's no intercom system, then?" Carolyn smiled with relief.

"Like the one at Oceanview Academy where the Dean is able to listen in on each of the rooms?" grinned Ms. Forrest. "No, we have nothing like that here."

"Did you go to Oceanview Academy, too, then?" queried Mrs. Bennett.

"Indeed, I did," smiled the Dean. "Anyway, that's our visiting room. And, normally we request that the visits be kept to around 15 minutes. Then, if the young lady chooses to leave with the young man, where they go after that is up to them. After all, the students here are 18 years old and being legal adults means that how we deal with them is not quite the same as how an underage boarding academy might. In fact, some of our students live off campus and are even married with families of their own already. But, if any student is reported doing something questionable or that is against university policy, they will be called into account for it. We have a zero-tolerance policy for drinking, smoking, using drugs, or inappropriate displays of physical intimacy."

"Does that include holding hands?" grilled Carolyn.

"Of course not!" laughed the Dean. "Hand holding is absolutely fine, and so is wearing blue jeans."

"Hey, I'll let Mister Bennett know y'all wud be callin' him soon," interrupted Woody as he turned to leave. He had been patiently waiting for a polite moment to bid them farewell.

"Oh, yes, thank you very much!" added Mrs. Bennett.

"Yes, thank you again!" called Carolyn as she watched Woody hobble out the front door, down the dormitory steps, and toward his pickup truck below.

Nancy Forrest then closed and locked the deadbolt behind him before turning her attention back to Mrs. Bennett and her daughter.

"So, anyone coming back after curfew would have to be let inside by you?" clarified Carolyn.

"I'm afraid so," responded the Dean. "Once the front desk attendant's shift is ended for the day, I'm it."

"How early does the front desk open in the morning?" asked Mrs. Bennett.

"Eight o'clock sharp. But, it's getting late now, so we can sit down tomorrow with your husband to answer any other questions," informed Nancy Forrest as she grabbed one of Carolyn's suitcases and began climbing a nearby stairway. "Follow me."

"Wait!" called Carolyn's mother. "I need to call my husband."

"Oh yeah," realized the Dean as she paused on the stairs. "You can use my desk phone while Carolyn and I take up the first load. Or, one of the pay phones on the wall over there, if you'd prefer."

"What about finances?" grilled Mrs. Bennett.

"That can wait until tomorrow, too," sighed Ms. Forrest as she resumed her climb.

"Good thing we wear the same size," mentioned Carolyn to her mother as she grabbed a suitcase and followed after the Dean.

"Indeed," mumbled Mrs. Bennett as she took out the scrap of newspaper and tried to decipher the phone number written on it.

"Just how many floors up is it?" Carolyn finally asked.

"It's on the fifth floor," grinned Ms. Forrest.

"Isn't there an elevator?" asked Carolyn.

"No, I'm afraid not," regretted the Dean as she patiently waited for Carolyn to catch her breath before continuing.

"Looks like I'll certainly be getting my exercise," noted Carolyn. "I'll probably need to leave a half hour early just to make it to my first class each day."

"You just might," agreed the Dean as they continued their ascent up the seemingly unending flights of stairs.

The next morning, sunlight inundated the huge fifth-floor attic dormitory room, streaming relentlessly through both of its large, east facing windows. No blinds or curtains adorned either of them, and an outdated window screen was long missing from one. There were absolutely no other windows whatsoever in the 60-foot-long by 40-foot-wide room. All six of the beds were single-sized and on the short side, as far as Carolyn was concerned. Being five feet, ten inches in height, Carolyn had endured a similar short mattress problem at Oceanview Academy during her junior year of high school.

Sarah Tremaine and Rachel Pierson slept in beds arranged against the southeast corner of the large area, just past the window on that end. Ruby Gomez slept in a bed at the very southwest corner of the attic dormitory room, right beside its only exit door and closest to its closet wall. That half of the room was referred to as the "south side" of the fifth-floor attic dormitory space.

Six small dressers with walnut veneer were arranged in a row across the center of the room from east to west, and acted as an area divider. Three of the dressers were turned facing the south side of the room, and back-to-back behind them were three other dressers facing toward the north side of the room, though there was still sufficient space beside the row of dressers for the north side occupants to easily walk around them. The entire west wall consisted of nothing but long narrow closets with rolling track doors. There were no ceiling lights whatsoever, and the only lighting available came from the freestanding lamps that sat on each of the small study desks. One such desk sat beside each of the six beds, available for the students to use when doing their homework. The room's expansive dark gray linoleum floor was highly shellacked and appeared as if it could be slippery when wet. The remainder of the room, including its closet doors, was painted entirely in a drab shade of light gray.

Karlin Gomez, who was Ruby's younger sister, slept in one of the three beds arranged against the northern wall, closest to the western wall of closets. Carolyn's bed was in the very northeast corner of the room, closest to the other large window. The empty bed in the very middle of the northern wall was used by Mrs. Bennett.

Sleep had managed to elude both Carolyn and her mother for most of the night. Introductions to her new roommates the previous evening had been hastily made by the Dean in-between the half-dozen trips it had taken to bring up Carolyn's things. There had not been time to unpack or put anything away the night before, so all of the boxes and suitcases still sat in the vast open floor space beside Carolyn's bed.

Due to the abundance of space available in the large room, Carolyn was also able to find a place for her cedar chest at the foot of her bed – something that had not fit in her room at Oceanview Academy when staying there during her junior year of high school. At least she would not have to send it back home with her parents this time!

Suddenly realizing that she had to use the restroom, Carolyn sat up and glanced around the room. As if able to read Carolyn's thoughts, Karlin mentioned, "The restrooms are down on the fourth floor."

"There are no restrooms on the fifth floor at all?" interjected Carolyn's mother, who also needed to use the facilities most urgently.

"I wish!" chuckled Karlin.

Each wearing one of Carolyn's nightgowns, Carolyn and her mother sprang up simultaneously and traversed the entire length of the spacious fifth-floor dormitory room without hesitation. Ruby grinned with amusement as she watched Mrs. Bennett and Carolyn dash past her sleeping area by the door before racing out onto the fifth floor's hallway landing and down the flight of stairs separating them from the nearest restroom below.

"Where is it?" demanded Mrs. Bennett when they reached the fourth-floor landing.

"Over there!" noticed Carolyn as she sped in that direction.

Several yards farther down the fourth-floor corridor was a junction that led directly into a well-lit open doorway. Unlike the hard, dark gray linoleum stairs that led from ground level to the attic, the hallways on each of the other floors were mercifully covered with carpet. Sadly, the well-worn and fading dark gray carpet had seen better days and reminded Carolyn a good deal of the worn-out rug with bald spots that had been in Dean Dixon's small apartment office back at Oceanview Academy.

Lacking a door or even a restroom sign, the rounded arch above the entrance to the fourth-floor shower and toilet facilities was adorned with cheap-looking floral plaques that had been glued onto it for decoration and then painted with the same light gray paint as everything else. No doubt the plaques had been in style during some bygone era, but were now unsightly and pulling away from the arch where the glue holding them on was beginning to fail. In fact, they appeared ready to fall on some unsuspecting person below at any given moment.

"Better watch for those!" cautioned Carolyn's mother as she dashed past her and into the nearest toilet stall.

Even the metal toilet stalls were gray, but it was a different gray than the walls or the gray tile floor that covered the entire shower and toilet area. The toilets themselves were entirely black, though, so there was no way of determining at a glance whether or not they had been recently cleaned. At least they were not equipped with antiquated pull chains like the toilets at Oceanview Academy had been!

"Carolyn?" called Mrs. Bennett from the sink area as she washed her hands. "Are you still in here?"

"Yes, I'm still here," replied Carolyn from the toilet stall as she exited. Why did her mother always feel the need to call out her name in public restrooms where her voice echoed throughout the facility? It was embarrassing! Did her mother really think she wasn't going to wait for her?

"My mother does that, too," grinned Karlin as Carolyn approached the row of black sinks to wash her hands. Mrs. Bennett, however, was already over by the shower area, looking it over.

Carolyn merely smiled at Karlin and nodded as she washed her hands. She could tell already that she and Karlin would be good friends.

There were four toilet stalls and four black sinks, with a large square mirror mounted on the wall above the sinks. The counter space surrounding the sinks was covered with dark gray tiles that had also seen better days.

"At least they have paper towels," approved Carolyn with relief as she reached over to pull one from the dispenser with which to dry her hands. Her memories of the self-renewing blue cloth dispenser at Oceanview Academy had always left doubt as to its cleanliness and prompted most of the students there to merely shake their hands dry rather than be forced to touch it!

"What high school did you go to?" asked Karlin as she, too, dried her hands with a paper towel.

"Oceanview Academy during my junior year, but I ended up staying at home in Ashton for my senior year," revealed Carolyn.

"My cousin went to Oceanview," responded Karlin. "That place sure has a lot of rules."

"Indeed!" laughed Carolyn as she studied herself in the mirror.

"The lighting here is terrible," pointed out Karlin. "Did you bring a makeup mirror?"

"I wish," answered Carolyn.

"You're welcome to use mine anytime you want," offered Karlin as they started toward the door. "When I'm not using it, that is."

"You just have to see these showers!" called Mrs. Bennett from the other side of the room, her voice again echoing quite loudly.

Karlin and Carolyn walked over to where Mrs. Bennett was standing at the entrance to one of the shower stalls.

"Wow!" exclaimed Carolyn when she saw them. "These are great! They're nothing like the showers at Oceanview Academy!"

"Tell me about it!" laughed Karlin. "I understand you guys had those large showers with a single shower pole in the middle that had multiple heads on it pointing in every direction?"

"And no shower curtains!" interjected Carolyn's mother. "That was the first thing I noticed when we got there, and even complained to Dean Dixon about it, but she only laughed at me!"

"My mother even thought at first that the showers there were under construction," explained Carolyn to her new friend Karlin.

"Well, that would be a logical conclusion to come to with no shower curtains!" justified Mrs. Bennett. "I still can't believe those people would condone such immodesty in the showers but then make such a big deal about kids merely holding hands!"

Carolyn was surprised by her mother's comment and raised an eyebrow. She had no idea her mother even knew about the "no hand holding" policy that had been strictly enforced at Oceanview Academy.

Carolyn thought at once of a young man named Lenny Owens that she had met while at Oceanview Academy in 1972. After filling out personality questionnaires, her and Lenny's names had been analyzed by a computer and found to be the most compatible. That was how she had come to be Lenny's date for the first official date night there.

Lenny and Carolyn had instantly been drawn to one another and eventually their friendship had blossomed into much more. During the date night, which happened to consist of watching a Walt Disney movie, it soon became obvious that assigned faculty members were carefully perusing the audience in search of policy violators. Lenny and Carolyn had let go of one another's hands at once the moment the lights unexpectedly came on during the movie, so had not been noticed. Another less fortunate pair who had been caught holding each other's hands were called out and each sent to his or her respective dormitory room without being allowed to watch the remainder of the movie. They were then put on "all boy" and "all girl" social status for the rest of that week. She would not be allowed to speak to any members of the male sex for an entire week, with the exception of teachers during open class period. The young man in turn was not allowed to speak to any member of the female sex for the rest of that week, particularly the one with whom he had been caught. Further incursions would have led to possible suspension and finally to expulsion from school.

"Hillview Academy was just the same," revealed Karlin. "It's another coed parochial boarding school run by the Church. Same rules and everything."

"No kidding?" Carolyn was surprised. She had no idea there were other schools like Oceanview Academy anywhere in the world.

"I thought Oceanview just had that kind of showers because it was left over from the old military base it was converted from," mentioned Carolyn's mother.

"Hillview was once a military base, too," informed Karlin.

"I had no idea," responded Carolyn's mother.

"The Church apparently purchased several old military facilities around the same time," recollected Karlin. "Just after World War II."

"Oh, okay," nodded Mrs. Bennett. "When the war was over. That makes sense."

"Good thing this place was supposed to be a resort!" laughed Karlin as she walked into the shower stall and pushed open a second door inside. "That's the shower in there. This is just a dressing room."

"Each shower has its own dressing room?" beamed Carolyn.

"Now, that's more like it!" approved Carolyn's mother with a big smile. "It's even got benches and lockers for your stuff."

"No locks, though," pointed out Karlin. "Still, it's actually quite private. There's even a shelf for your towel closest to the shower stall."

"And with only ONE shower head on it," observed Mrs. Bennett with a nod of satisfaction.

"There are no curtains here, either," chuckled Karlin as she turned to leave.

"But, no need for curtains with an entire stall like this," realized Mrs. Bennett. "Very nice!"

"I think I'm gonna like it here," decided Carolyn.

"Wait until you see the cafeteria!" tempted Karlin as the three of them exited the fourth-floor restroom area and headed back upstairs.

"Carolyn had a job serving breakfast in the boys' food line at Oceanview Academy," revealed Mrs. Bennett as they reached the fifth floor and went inside.

"Really? That was one of my jobs at Hillview Academy!" responded Karlin.

"What job was that?" grilled Ruby as her sister walked past her sleeping area with Carolyn and Mrs. Bennett.

"Serving food at Hillview," replied Karlin with a toss of her head. It was clear that she and her older sister were anything but friends.

Both Karlin and Ruby Gomez were Hispanic, and both were very well-built and attractive. Karlin, however, was much more exotic in appearance than her older sister Ruby and had always been more popular with the boys. The sibling rivalry between them was evident. Each wore her black wavy hair parted in the middle with curls on the sides and back. Karlin and Ruby also wore the same size clothes, but were not inclined to share them with one another.

"I think I was half asleep when you guys came in last night," mentioned Rachel Pierson as she approached to shake hands with

Carolyn and her mother. "I'm Rachel Pierson, and I'm a freshman, too."

Rachel was an attractive, well-tanned, dishwater blonde with short hair that she wore parted on one side and feathered back. Rachel's genuine farm-girl smile and country appeal gave her a wholesome look.

"And I'm Sarah Tremaine," the other girl introduced herself as she also shook hands with Carolyn and her mother. "Freshman."

"Nice to meet you both," greeted Mrs. Bennett. She was pleased to see that at least two of Carolyn's roommates appeared wholesome and desirable for her daughter to be residing with.

"Good morning," nodded Carolyn, but with less enthusiasm.

Sarah Tremaine was a studious, mild-mannered girl with long, straight, strawberry blonde hair that she parted in the middle and kept off her pale face with barrettes on each side. Unlike most other kids in 1974, Sarah had chosen not to get the sides of her hair feathered back, and it was all one length. Sarah wore no makeup whatsoever and was extremely thin and frail looking. If the dress she had on now was any indicator of her fashion sense, she would more than likely turn out to be a typical dweeb. Nevertheless, Sarah was pleasant enough.

"What are your majors?" grilled Mrs. Bennett.

"Physical Education," informed Rachel proudly.

"Chemistry with a minor in Biology," answered Sarah.

"Nursing," revealed Ruby Gomez. "And I'm a junior."

"And what about you?" questioned Mrs. Bennett as she turned to Karlin. "You did say you were a freshman, too?"

"All she thinks about is boys and having fun!" accused Ruby with a condescending smirk.

"That's not true!" objected Karlin. "Most of my classes are secretarial, and I'm still making up my mind if that will be my major or not. And yes, I'm a freshman."

"I'm taking the secretarial classes, too," advised Carolyn with a smile. "And I'm a freshman."

"Then all of you should know," informed Ruby, "that I will be in charge, since I'm an upper classmate, and you will answer to me."

"Excuse me?" responded Carolyn with surprise.

"Oh, Ruby just thinks she has to be in charge of everything because she's older," snickered Karlin.

"Like what time the lights go out each night," clarified Ruby. "There will be no studying past ten o'clock here in this room."

"Did the Dean put her in charge?" Carolyn whispered to Karlin.

"She wishes!" snorted Karlin.

Surprised by the interaction between Ruby and her younger roommates, Mrs. Bennett was speechless.

"Come on, we'd better get going or we'll all be late for orientation," urged Ruby as she finished dressing.

"My husband and I still need to finish up some details with the Dean first," mentioned Carolyn's mother.

"Sorry!" laughed Ruby. She had almost forgotten that Carolyn's mother was not one of the freshman girls she considered to be under her tutelage. "Guess we'll see you down there."

"Pay no attention to her," directed Karlin as they watched Ruby put on her sweater, grab her purse and hurriedly leave the fifth-floor dormitory room.

Rachel and Sarah merely raised their eyebrows with surprise as they, too, grabbed their purses and followed after Ruby.

"They are all going to the cafeteria first, of course," explained Karlin. "Your husband could be there."

"Let's just hope he's somewhere here on campus," answered Mrs. Bennett as she quickly dressed back into her clothes from the previous day. Karlin and Carolyn proceeded to dress, as well.

"Woody the Woodcutter towed us over to Mike's Auto Shop last night," clarified Carolyn. "Broken fan belt."

"That's why we were so late getting here," elaborated Carolyn's mother. "And of course, the auto shop was closed."

"I've heard of Woody," said Karlin as she quickly put on her makeup. "An older black gentleman, isn't he?"

"That's him," confirmed Carolyn. "Said he cuts firewood for folks around here and then delivers it."

"Sweet man," added Mrs. Bennett. "He even gave Carolyn and me a ride over here from the auto shop, and then made a second trip with all of Carolyn's things."

"But just left your husband there?" Karlin seemed surprised.

"Mr. Bennett has a mind of his own," assured Mrs. Bennett.

"My dad's like that, too," laughed Karlin. "I think that's where Ruby gets it from."

"Well, Mr. Bennett does have the checkbook," revealed Carolyn's mother, "so we'll probably need to wait for him here."

"Nonsense! I have my cafeteria card already," indicated Karlin as she pulled a small green plastic credit card with yellow lettering on it from her purse. "I'll buy breakfast for you ladies today, and then Carolyn can buy breakfast for me the next two times. Fair enough?"

"I guess that would be okay," agreed Mrs. Bennett, though reluctant to place herself in debt to her daughter's new roommate.

"Where have you been?" demanded Mr. Bennett as Carolyn and her mother entered Dean Forrest's office.

"Having breakfast," replied his wife with an innocent shrug of her shoulders. "We had no idea when you would get here."

"Well, I did try to call, but you had already taken off for breakfast," fumed her husband, who had not yet eaten. "They even sent someone all the way up there to that room to try to find you!"

"You two can work this out later," interrupted Dean Forrest.

"Sorry!" apologized Mrs. Bennett.

"Your husband has made all the financial arrangements already," informed Dean Forrest. "So, everything else will take place at orientation. They will issue Carolyn a cafeteria card, since she was not here yesterday, along with computerized worship service cards to turn in each time Carolyn attends one of the worship services."

"You're kidding?" frowned Carolyn.

"They have three services each day, but not all of them are mandatory," continued the Dean. "The important thing is that all cards have been turned in by the time the semester is over, or the administration office will withhold your grades."

"How can they do that?" scowled Carolyn.

"You don't want to find out," grinned Ms. Forrest. "Just make sure you attend as many of them as you can while the semester is young, and then you won't have to worry about it later, during finals."

"That sounds prudent," agreed Mr. Bennett.

"They will also make job assignments today at orientation, most likely based on what classes you sign up for," continued the Dean.

"We should go there first then," suggested Carolyn, "before the classes I need are all full."

"Some of us still have not eaten!" snapped Mr. Bennett.

"Well, you're not alone," sympathized Ms. Forrest. "Why don't you come to the cafeteria with me while Carolyn and her mother go get her registered? Then, I can walk you over there after we eat."

"That would be fine," agreed Carolyn's father, more calmly.

"Excellent," smiled Nancy Forrest as she got up to leave. "And, I've already discussed the dorm's house rules with Carolyn and her mother. So, I can go over those with you as we walk to the cafeteria."

"Uh, what about the paychecks?" Carolyn suddenly asked.

"There are mail slots here in the lobby," indicated the Dean as they walked from her office toward the front door. "All incoming mail and paychecks are placed in the slot assigned to each student. Slot 5-E will be yours, since you are the fifth student to check into the room on the fifth floor."

"What are the numbers on the other slots?" wondered Mrs. Bennett aloud. "This one says 4-23-B."

"Four is the floor, 23 is the room number and B designates the second student to check into that room," elaborated Nancy Forrest.

"Shouldn't Carolyn's number be 5-1-E then?" continued Mrs. Bennett.

"Not necessary," responded the Dean. "Since the room on the fifth floor is the *only* room on that floor, there is no need for the 1 in the slot number. Carolyn's slot is merely 5-E."

"Seriously?" Mr. Bennett was becoming irritated again, especially with the direction the conversation was headed.

"So, to answer your question, Carolyn," concluded Ms. Forrest, "yes, you will receive your paycheck, and it will be placed in your slot here on the first floor. There is even a bank window over at the campus store where students may cash their paychecks."

"Hold on!" objected Carolyn's father. "You mean to tell me that the money will not be applied directly to her tuition account?"

"That is correct," smiled Dean Forrest. "This isn't Oceanview Academy, sir, and these students are adults now. They are perfectly capable of learning to handle their own money."

"See ya," beamed Carolyn as she and her mother quickly headed toward the Administration Building.

"And what about that cafeteria card?" frowned Carolyn's father as he watched his wife and daughter leave. "Is there a limit on it?"

"No limit," responded Nancy Forrest rather matter-of-factly as she and Mr. Bennett headed down the flight of stairs in front of the girls' dormitory. "These students may be adults, but they are still growing kids and access to proper nutrition is imperative. That way, they do not have to worry about what to eat while they are busy trying to study and excel in their courses."

"What's to stop them from buying food for all their friends?" grilled Mr. Bennett.

"Probably nothing," sighed the Dean, "but for the fact that each student has their own card already, so there would be no need."

"So, who ends up paying for it, then?" scowled Mr. Bennett.

"It just goes onto the student's bill," explained Ms. Forrest with a mischievous grin. Clearly, this was not what Mr. Bennett had expected.


"That's a lot of classes," pointed out Carolyn's mother as she studied the list of courses her daughter would be taking.

"English Literature, Bible History, Bookkeeping, Physical Education, and Advanced Shorthand?" questioned Carolyn. "That's only five classes. And, they are studying the life of Christ in the Bible History class and Badminton for PE. Those shouldn't be too hard."

"You and your father always did love playing Badminton after school each day when you were in junior high school," reminisced Mrs. Bennett.

"Yes, we did," agreed Carolyn.

"So, are you all registered?" asked Mr. Bennett as he and Dean Forrest approached.

"The only thing she still needs to do is get her work assignment," replied Mrs. Bennett.

"That would be at the last table over there on the end," directed Dean Forrest as she made her departure.


Alone in her new fifth-floor dormitory room, Carolyn sat on her small bed, gazing out the giant window beside it. The entire campus could be seen from that spot, including the black spired rooftops of the Administration Building and many of the other older buildings, as well. The medieval-looking campus reminded Carolyn of something from *Grimms' Fairy Tales,* especially with the dense, old growth forest surrounding it. Would she be happy here?

It had been a long day already, so Carolyn had elected to forego the evening worship service so she would have time to unpack her things. According to her calculations, it would be possible to skip at least a dozen of the worship services offered and still be able to turn in the required number of computerized "worship service cards" before semester's end.

Strange that she had been placed in a second-year shorthand course, especially being a freshman, but her timed speed was only 10 words per minute slower than the other second-year students. Whereas, taking the first-year class would not have been an adequate challenge to her skills, as Mrs. Ritter had put it.

Mrs. Ritter had been a widow for many years. She wore her yellow-streaked gray hair straight back in a harsh bun and wore thick horn-rimmed glasses with heavy black frames. She wore no makeup whatsoever and wore modest clothes that had probably been in style around 1930. Her baggy nylon stockings had thick black seams running up the back, and her jet black shoes reminded Carolyn of corrective orthopedic footwear.

In spite of everything, Mrs. Ritter was a cheerful person who smiled often, revealing an unsightly set of bucked teeth when she did. She had been instantly drawn to Carolyn and was impressed with her shorthand skills. It was Mrs. Ritter's personal recommendation to the Industrial Education Department that had landed Carolyn a job as Secretary to the five Industrial Education Professors working there.

Ronald Krain, who was the head of the entire Industrial Education Department, would be Carolyn's main boss. Carolyn would also be modeling part time for a life drawing class held in the same building as the Industrial Education Department. Unlike life drawing classes offered in public schools, this one would involve wearing clothes.

"There you are!" greeted Karlin as she entered the large fifth-floor dormitory room and sauntered over to the north side that she shared with Carolyn. "Did your parents make it off okay?"

"Yeah, they did, thanks," replied Carolyn, who was still deep in thought. "They're on their way home now."

"It was sure nice of that woodcutter man to help you guys out like that," continued Karlin. "Not many people would do that."

"Tell me about it!" agreed Carolyn. "I don't know what we would have done if Woody hadn't stopped."

"Especially with that Powell Mountain Killer on the loose!" added Karlin as she began undressing to put on something more comfortable.

"All right, that's enough of that!" objected Ruby as she entered the room and saw her younger sister tossing her dirty clothes on the vacant bed beside her.

"Excuse me?" responded Karlin from across the room.

"Just because there's an empty bed there, that doesn't give you a license to just start using it as your own personal laundry pile," chastised Ruby.

"Well, you know what?" challenged Karlin.

"What?" demanded Ruby as she came over to confront her.

"That extra desk is gonna be our ours, too, since it's here on this side of the room and no one's using it yet!" informed Karlin with a defiant nod. "It'll make a great makeup table."

Ruby then studied Carolyn to see whether she was in agreement with the situation.

"Hey, sounds fair to me," opined Carolyn with a slight smile and a shrug of her shoulders.

"Well, don't get too used to it," cautioned Ruby. "We could still very well get a sixth roommate up here, you know."

"Duly noted," replied Karlin with a roll of her eyes as she pulled on a white t-shirt and then climbed into her favorite pair of blue jeans.

"You're lucky they let you wear those things here," reminded Ruby as she headed back over to the south side of the room to settle herself at her desk where she planned to look over her new school books.

"Don't we know it!" interjected Carolyn. "From what Karlin tells me, Hillview was just as bad as Oceanview. We couldn't wear blue jeans or white t-shirts there either."

"Humph!" grunted Ruby as she sat down at her desk and turned on the small desk lamp there.

"What's wrong with her?" whispered Carolyn.

"She just resents having to share a room with her younger sister," replied Karlin.

"Only until the room I asked for becomes available!" reminded Ruby from where she sat on the other side of the room. Apparently, Ruby's hearing was quite excellent.

"Whatever!" snorted Karlin. "And the sooner the better, too!"

"Hey, then we'll have two extra beds and desks in here," chuckled Carolyn with an amused grin.

"You never know who might lay claim to 'em, though," replied Karlin as she glanced at the southeast corner of the room where Rachel and Sarah dwelt.

"I wonder where they are, anyway?" mused Carolyn.

"Probably at study hall, where all studious bookworm bores should be," guessed Karlin.

"I heard that," muttered Ruby as she shook her head with exasperation.

"Hey, let's go visit my friend Eula," suggested Karlin.

"Eula?" repeated Carolyn.

"Eula King," added Karlin. "You'll love her! She lives down on the fourth floor."

"Let's go," agreed Carolyn as she followed her new friend Karlin from the room. Both of them were anxious to escape Ruby's presence so they could freely chat and get to know one another better without having to be concerned with what they said.

"Eula's room is just three doors down from the restroom and showers," revealed Karlin as they scurried down the stairs and onto the fourth floor. "She just has one roommate, and Stacia's cool. I think you'll like her, too."

After only two quick knocks, the door to Eula and Stacia's room suddenly opened. "It's about time you made it down here to see your old roommate!" grinned Eula as she gave Karlin an affectionate hug.

Eula was slim in all the right places but powerfully built and dressed to show it off. Her tight red sweater clung tenaciously to her ample bosom, and her tight black sweat pants did nothing to hide her shapely derriere. Eula's waist was surprisingly small, and it was obvious that she lifted weights. Eula's huge afro was perfectly groomed, and not a hair was out of place. The makeup on her gorgeous, dark-complexioned face included false eyelashes, though they were totally unnecessary.

"You two were roommates?" Carolyn was surprised.

"Yep, at Hillview," nodded Eula.

"This is Carolyn Bennett," introduced Karlin. "She went to Oceanview Academy."

"Then we all got lots in common, honey," laughed Eula as she motioned for Karlin and Carolyn to sit on the bed across from hers.

"Where's Stacia?" queried Karlin.

"Anastacia, as she prefers to be called, is down at study hall," informed Eula.

"She's a bookworm, too?" questioned Carolyn.

Eula and Karlin both began howling with laughter. When they finally were able to stop, Eula revealed, "Stacia is anything but a bookworm. She's only down there because of some guy she likes."

"Ah hah," perceived Carolyn. "Smart gal."

"Too bad they didn't have coed study hall back at Hillview," lamented Karlin.

"There was some guy there at Hillview that Karlin liked, but he always stayed in his room and studied for his stupid chemistry class," recalled Eula.

"That sounds familiar," realized Carolyn with a frown as she thought of Lenny Owens.

"What was his name again?" Eula asked Karlin.

"Kyle Monagan," sighed Karlin.

"Oh, yes, Kyle Monagan," mimicked Eula. "That's all I ever heard about, all year long. Did everything I could to get the two of them hooked up, but when Kyle wasn't busy studying for his chemistry class, Karlin was busy studying for her English Literature class."

"Just like two ships passing in the night," interjected Carolyn wistfully. "Reminds me of a guy I was crazy about at Oceanview who was always busy studying for his chemistry class. Meanwhile, I was over in my room studying for English Literature class."

"Incredible," mumbled Eula as she shook her head.

"Just like two ships passing in the night? That was from a poem by Henry Wadsworth Longfellow," recognized Karlin.

"Yes! *The Theologian's Tale*, from *Tales of a Wayside Inn*, published in 1873," elaborated Carolyn excitedly.

"Oh, my god!" chucked Eula. "You're seriously kidding me?"

"Ships that pass in the night, and speak each other in passing," began Karlin.

"Only a signal shown and a distant voice in the darkness," continued Carolyn.

"So on the ocean of life, we pass and speak one another, only a look and a voice, then darkness again and a silence," concluded both Karlin and Carolyn together.

"I think I'm gonna be sick," threatened Eula. "You two seriously need to loosen up and have some fun. Just wait until we get old Ruby out of that room up there. That gargantuan fifth floor is gonna become our own personal dance studio!"

"You dance?" Carolyn appeared worried.

"You don't?" responded Eula.

"Uh, not really," confirmed Carolyn.

"Oh, honey, I can see we got our work cut out for us," decided Eula, "but you is gonna learn to dance."

"What for?" Carolyn shrugged her shoulders.

"Because it's FUN!" informed Eula.

"It is," agreed Karlin.

"And then, we can all steal away to some Saturday night disco place and meet some decent fellas," planned Eula.

"I don't know," objected Carolyn.

"You ain't gonna be one of them stick-in-the muds, are ya?" challenged Eula.

"Of course not," assured Carolyn. "It's just that I'm hoping to avoid becoming as well acquainted with Dean Forrest as I was with Dean Dixon back at Oceanview."

"Indeed," smirked Eula. "So, what's your major?"

"Secretarial," informed Carolyn, "though I do love English Literature."

"I can't believe how much you two are alike," opined Eula.

"So, what's your major?" questioned Carolyn.

"Physical Education, with an emphasis on gymnastics," revealed Eula. "I was hoping to brush up on my ballet while I was here, but they just don't seem to offer dance classes of any kind at this place."

The three new friends then laughed heartily together.

"Hey, did you hear the announcement at worship service tonight?" Eula suddenly became serious.

"I kind of slipped out early," confessed Karlin.

"Better not let 'em catch you doing that, either," warned Eula, "or they might not count your computer card for that session."

"That's a scary thought," mentioned Carolyn.

34

"Oh, there's scarier things than that," continued Eula. "Anyway, it was right at the very end when some guy came in and handed the speaker a note. That's when he made the announcement."

"What announcement?" urged Karlin.

"That they found another body," answered Eula. "Probably the Powell Mountain Killer again."

"Another body?" Carolyn became alarmed.

"Just past the old Shady Brook Winery, up on Powell Mountain Road," described Eula. "They didn't go into details."

"When did this happen?" grilled Carolyn.

"Who knows," shrugged Eula. "I'm sure the police are investigating it."

"Anyone we know?" pressed Karlin.

"No, but she was a student here," recalled Eula. "I think they said she was a junior."

"How horrible!" exclaimed Carolyn.

"It certainly is," agreed Eula, "but what we gotta remember to do is stay together, and don't be goin' off alone anywhere! As long as we do that, we will be fine. Trust me!"

# 2. Return to Oceanview

**B**rilliant afternoon sun streamed through the passenger side window of the 2023 white Dodge Dart as Carolyn Bennett-Hunter and her friend Sherry Collingsworth pulled to a stop at the Ocean Bluff Gas Station. At least two other cars were in line ahead of them.

"Didn't you say there were only 317 people living here?" questioned Sherry as she pressed the button to lower her window so she could get a better look at their surroundings.

"That was seven years ago," reminded Carolyn. "Even 2016 seems like a lifetime ago. There's 7,423 people living here now."

Sherry then noticed the population sign toward which Carolyn had nodded with her head. "Hopefully, this visit will be a bit less adventurous than your last one!" Sherry had heard Carolyn speak often of the life-threatening adventure in 2016 when the skeletal remains of Joyce Troglite and Veronica Jensen had been recovered after 43 long years.

"Fill her up?" questioned the gas station attendant as they reached their turn at the pump.

"Yes, please. Regular," indicated Carolyn as she handed the young man her credit card.

"Humph," snorted the young man as he grabbed the credit card, scanned it, and hurriedly gave it back to Carolyn before filling the tank.

While credit cards were still generally accepted at gas stations and other places of business, most younger customers in 2023 preferred to pay using an app on their smartwatch that would wirelessly send a signal of approval to the pump. The gas station attendant usually tried to be patient with older folks from the baby boomer generation that insisted upon using old fashioned credit cards, but he was currently in an irritable mood due to the large volume of extra customers showing up for the annual Oceanview Festival.

"Look at all the booths and concession stands!" noticed Sherry. "Do we have time to look around while we're here?"

"It's almost 4:30 now, and check-in time is by 5:30," reminded Carolyn. "We don't want them giving our room away to someone else before we even get there! We can always come back."

"Just how much farther is this place?" asked Sherry. "We've been driving all day!"

"At least half an hour more," replied Carolyn, "and it is a rather dicey stretch of road. It's nothing more than a two-lane highway that winds along the bluffs."

"It's always nice to avoid driving on a road like that at night," decided Sherry. "Let's wait until tomorrow to return."

"I agree," smiled Carolyn as she grabbed her receipt from the gas station attendant, started up the engine, and pulled away.

Carolyn was still tall and slender, even at 66 years of age. Her long blonde hair perfectly matched her natural color and her daily exercise routine had helped her maintain a shapely physique.

"It's too bad your hubby couldn't make it," mentioned Sherry, "but I'm glad I got to come in his stead. It should prove interesting to finally meet Jim Otterman and all the other characters you've been telling me about for all these years."

Carolyn merely smiled and shook her head. She wondered if Jim Otterman was still as enamored with her as he had been in 1972-1973, and in 2016. Hopefully, Jim was so deeply in love with his wife Sheree by now that he was finally over his feelings for Carolyn!

"Is your hubby going to take care of all those animals by himself?" queried Sherry.

"Well," Carolyn sighed deeply, "there's only about six cats left back there now, so they shouldn't be too much trouble for David to manage. I sure will miss them, though!"

"And David, too?" teased Sherry.

"David most of all," grinned Carolyn. "He really did want to come, but had made a prior commitment to take some paying clients on a guided fishing expedition for the day. Sadly, our retirement only pays out about half of what we made when we were still working."

"Don't you work as a receptionist for some animal shelter now?" questioned Sherry.

"Actually, I do, but the pay's not even worth mentioning," verified Carolyn. "Apparently, there's just no rest for the wicked!"

"Sounds like a labor of love," chuckled Sherry.

"Indeed," nodded Carolyn.

Carolyn and Sherry both laughed as the white Dodge Dart brought them ever closer to the Killingham Lighthouse Bed and Breakfast where Carolyn had made a room reservation the previous day. Thankfully, her friend Sheree Otterman had answered the phone and confirmed that a newly remodeled room was indeed available in the attic as Carolyn had been advised in an email from Sheree's daughter Ann. Rooms were hard to come by during the annual Oceanview Festival each year on March 23rd so Carolyn had made the reservation immediately.

As they wound past windswept ocean cliffs overgrown with aging cypress trees, Sherry could not help but admire the scenic ocean below. "I would have liked to have gone to school out here!"

"You really think so?" chuckled Carolyn.

"It couldn't have been all that bad," opined Sherry.

"Remind me to show you the student handbook they used back in 1972 and '73," grinned Carolyn.

Sherry had graduated from Ocean Bay High School in the spring of 1972, just three months before Carolyn began her stint at Oceanview Academy in the fall of 1972, but was so young looking for her age that you would never guess she was two years older. She and Carolyn first met when working together at a large law firm back in 1989, doing legal secretarial work, and had remained dear friends ever since. Sherry had a vivacious personality, and a zest for life. Her smile was contagious to those around her, and her sincere and genuine interest in others was part of her charm. Though only five feet, five inches tall, Sherry was well rounded in all the right places and wore a modest yet appealing wardrobe. Like Carolyn, Sherry concealed her age well, and neither of them appeared at first glance to be much more than 55 years of age. Sherry's dark brown hair was shoulder length with delicate bangs that swept to one side. Her makeup was adequate but not too heavy, and her adventurous side revealed itself in all sorts of interesting ways when Sherry was otherwise busy creating documentaries and quality films appropriate for family entertainment.

"What about your friend Lenny?" Sherry suddenly asked.

"Lenny Owens?" Carolyn seemed surprised that Sherry would ask about him.

"Do you think he might be there?" asked Sherry innocently with a mischievous smile.

"I seriously doubt it," assured Carolyn. "No one has seen or heard a thing from him for years."

"When was the last time you actually saw him?" pressed Sherry.

"I did see him briefly in 1979," revealed Carolyn, "but it was at a revival meeting. We really didn't have much chance to talk. Besides, I've been happily married to David for 40 years now!"

"Just checking," smiled Sherry. "Hey, what's that place over there? Do we have time to stop? It looks intriguing."

"The Ocean Bluff Mental Institution?" questioned Carolyn with a raised eyebrow.

"Really, that's it?" Sherry seemed surprised. "Isn't that the place you told me about where Birdboy was committed?"

"Actually, his real name was Jon Roth, and yes, it was there. That was back in 1973. Birdboy was his alternate personality," replied Carolyn as they approached the huge wrought iron gate leading into Ocean Bluff Mental Institution and slowed to a stop at its entrance.

"And then he became the theology instructor at Oceanview Academy after they finally let him out?" recalled Sherry, still finding it hard to believe.

"Indeed, they did," confirmed Carolyn.

"And, wasn't Sheree Wilkins institutionalized there, too, at the same time?" quizzed Sherry.

"Indeed, she was," replied Carolyn rather distantly as she thought of Sheree. "Sheree's the one who was married to Jon Roth when he was still alive, but now she's married to Jim Otterman."

"The Ottermans? Aren't they the ones who run the bed and breakfast where we're going to stay?" Sherry suddenly deduced.

"They are," Carolyn could not help but grin at the expression on Sherry's face.

"Oh dear! Are you sure about this?" questioned Sherry.

"Sheree's fine now," assured Carolyn. "You'll like her."

"If you say so, but I'd still like to make a quick stop here at the institution while we're here. What if we don't get a chance to come back later?" pointed out Sherry.

"I guess I can just send Sheree a text to let her know we're slightly behind schedule," nodded Carolyn as she proceeded through the huge wrought iron gate leading into Ocean Bluff Mental Institution. "I'm sure she'll hold the room."

"That works. Wow! Just look at this place!" exclaimed Sherry as the new white Dodge Dart made its way down the long sweeping driveway and around the circular entrance drive before coming to a halt at the front doors.

The Ocean Bluff Mental Institution was a large two-story brick building first established in 1887. Its white spiraled steeples and clock tower gave it a medieval appearance. Housed on the first floor of the building was its administration department where new patients and visitors alike were received. Situated on a high elevation of land overlooking the city below on one side and a vast expanse of ocean on the other, Ocean Bluff Mental Institution was a magnificent sight. The ample grounds with its fine trees, beautiful flowers and well-trimmed hedges were a veritable park. White wrought iron benches were strategically placed along its various walkways for visitors and less serious patients who were free to stroll through the gardens and enjoy the sound of crashing waves on the rocky hillside below.

"I never realized until this very moment how much this place reminds me of Powell Mountain University! That's where I spent my freshman year of college," explained Carolyn as she quickly sent a text message to Sheree Otterman at the Killingham Lighthouse Bed and Breakfast before opening the car door and starting for the front entrance of the Ocean Bluff Mental Institution. It had been only seven years earlier that Carolyn had come here with her friend Susan Rives to try to obtain information about Jon Roth, so it truly seemed like déjà vu.

"Your college looked like this?" grilled Sherry.

"Most of the buildings there must have been built around the same time period as this one," realized Carolyn out loud.

The huge white double doors to Ocean Bluff Mental Institution were ornately curved on top with a large metal plaque centered over them that read: "When the waves reach to our heads we begin to listen to anything; no advice is too contemptible for us; no person too insignificant for us to be willing to listen." by Johann Peter Lange - 1872.

"Wow, that's profound," remarked Sherry as Carolyn lifted the huge brass lion-head door knocker and let it fall against the huge brass plate beneath it. After a few moments, footsteps could be heard inside.

A gruff-looking woman in her mid-forties answered the door. "What do you want?" She had gray-streaked hair, thick horn-rimmed glasses, and wore a white knee-length nurse's uniform that had not been in style for fifty years.

"Nurse Redden?" asked Carolyn, rather cautiously.

"Oh yes, I remember you," acknowledged the woman. "It was in March of 2016." She had a keen alertness about her intense blue eyes that was disconcerting. "Please come in."

The nurse's clean rubber-soled shoes made little sound as she walked on the hard linoleum floor. "We can go in here."

Carolyn and Sherry were led to a small sitting room with an antique Queen Anne style couch and matching chairs, all of which appeared to have been there since 1887 when the institution first opened. Nevertheless, the furniture was well kept and in excellent condition. A small coffee table displayed leaflets advertising the Ocean Bluff Mental Institution and its few amenities. Carolyn picked one up, studied it, and then carefully put it back onto the coffee table. She had picked one up just like it seven years ago for possible future reference but had never looked at it again.

"What can I do for you?" asked Nurse Redden as she studied them with an even, hard gaze and tilted her head slightly back to see them more clearly through her bifocals.

"My name is Sherry Collingsworth," volunteered Sherry with a pleasant smile as she extended her hand in greeting.

"And?" prompted Nurse Redden without bothering to shake hands. Clearly, she was not interested in social formalities and merely stood there with her hands on her hips gazing down at them where they sat on the less-than-comfortable couch.

"I'm here to do a documentary on the phenomenon of why young people continue to go surfing and boogie boarding in shark infested waters, even when they know of the danger it poses," elaborated Sherry in her usual enthusiastic and friendly way.

"What's that got to do with a mental institution?" asked Nurse Redden. "Are ya thinkin' folks like that must be crazy, then?"

"Probably they are," chuckled Sherry.

"What can I really do for you?" probed Nurse Redden suspiciously as she turned to Carolyn. "That Jon Roth fellow is dead now, in case you were still looking for him."

"I know. I was there with Sheree Roth and Ray Dixon the day he shot himself in the head," Carolyn informed her with an even gaze.

"You don't say," responded Nurse Redden as she suddenly decided to sit down beside them.

"I also know now that Jon Roth was *your* cousin," revealed Carolyn with a genuine poker face.

After an awkward moment of silence, Nurse Redden seemed to soften. "Our mothers were sisters, yes."

"So, being a blood relative yourself, YOU could have given his daughter Ann the information she was seeking that day," pointed out Carolyn. "Back in 2016, when we brought her here to see you."

"Yes, I remember when it was!" snapped Nurse Redden.

"I also know now that Helen was *your* mother," continued Carolyn. "And I'm very sorry for your loss, by the way."

"My mother was 50 years old when she had me," described Nurse Redden. "She was 97 years old when she finally died. A definite blessing in her case, I'm afraid."

"Perhaps someday you can aspire to be as kind to others as she once was," wished Carolyn as she got up to leave.

Stunned by the entire exchange between Carolyn and Nurse Redden, Sherry was speechless but also stood to leave.

"Just how did you come across all this information?" Nurse Redden suddenly looked up and asked.

"From Ann," revealed Carolyn with a slight smile. "She not only has Ginny's journal, but Helen's diary, as well."

Nurse Redden suddenly looked as if she had been punched in the stomach and slowly took off her glasses with one hand to wipe away a stray tear with the other.

"Hey, I'm sorry," apologized Carolyn as she came over to sit beside Nurse Redden and put a comforting hand on her back. Carolyn's attitude toward Nurse Redden had softened considerably.

"Wanna clue me in on what's going on here?" urged Sherry as she came over and sat down on the other side of Nurse Redden.

"Ann and I have been email friends for years now," replied Carolyn. "It was in 2016 that Ann first learned from Ginny's journal that Helen had *two* daughters. One of them was Virginia Borden, and the journal had Ginny Eggersol written in parentheses beside it."

"Have you actually seen the journal?" demanded Nurse Redden.

"Sheree originally *gave* it to me to keep for her," replied Carolyn, "and yes, I have read it. Ann has it now."

"That's not possible! Ginny Eggersol's parents were killed in a plane crash several years before she died," argued Nurse Redden.

"Ginny mentioned in her journal that she learned of her adoption when she was 12 years old," added Carolyn. "Apparently,

Ginny had found the paperwork in her father's desk and pressed the issue until the Eggersols finally let her know about Helen."

"I actually had a sister and she never even told me," mumbled Nurse Redden as tears began to stream down her cheeks. "All those times Ginny came here to visit Jon and Sheree, and she never breathed a word about it!"

"Ginny had Helen and Edith's entire family tree drawn up in the journal," recalled Carolyn. "It showed the complete family line, all the way from Lizzie Borden's illegitimate son Jon down to Edith and Helen. Apparently, the real father never stepped forward, so Jon Borden took on and kept his mother's maiden name after learning his true identity."

"Are we talking about Lizzie Borden? The lady who murdered her parents with a hatchet back in the 1800s?" interjected Sherry with alarm.

"Actually," clarified Carolyn, "Lizzie Borden was tried but finally acquitted for the hatchet murders of her father and stepmom. That was back in Massachusetts in 1892. And, according to Ginny's journal, the family who adopted her illegitimate son came out West on a wagon train after that."

"Oh, my stars," muttered Nurse Redden as she shook her head.

"It was from Helen's diary that we learned some interesting facts about Jon Roth's illegitimate half-brother," added Carolyn. "That's one reason I've decided to finally come back out and pay them all a visit."

"But, Jon Roth was an only child," informed Nurse Redden.

"Well, according to your mother," responded Carolyn, "Jon Roth, Sr. – that would have been Jon Roth's father – once had a torrid love affair with a woman named Linda Dixon."

"What?" exclaimed Nurse Redden. "That can't be right! Linda Dixon died in childbirth while giving birth to the son of Mark Killingham!"

"I think you'll find that Mark Killingham was not the baby's father," differed Carolyn, "if you should ever happen to read your mother's diary. Apparently, Ann found the diary in a secret compartment of the old trunk that once belonged to Helen."

"Oh, my God!" exclaimed Nurse Redden. "I can't believe it!"

"It said that though they never married, Mark Killingham met and fell in love with Linda Dixon when she was six months pregnant," continued Carolyn. "And, rather than tarnish the stellar reputation of Jon Roth, Sr. - the man who had fathered her child - Linda Dixon went to her grave without revealing the secret to anyone but her midwife."

"My Aunt Edith?" questioned Nurse Redden suspiciously.

"Yes, indeed," confirmed Carolyn. "Linda's deathbed confession to Edith Roth of the affair she'd had with her husband was something Edith later shared only with her sister Helen."

"Making Ray Dixon my cousin, too?" realized Nurse Redden with astonishment.

"Pretty much," smirked Carolyn. Though not entirely unsympathetic, Carolyn was secretly glad to finally see Nurse Redden taken down a peg or two.

"We better get going," reminded Sherry uncomfortably. "Will you be all right, ma'am?"

"Never better," Nurse Redden responded unconvincingly.

"You should have warned me about all of this," chastised Sherry as she and Carolyn exited the facility and headed for the white Dodge Dart to resume their journey to the Killingham Lighthouse Bed and Breakfast.

Carolyn merely shrugged her shoulders in response but made no comment.

"I know this is a stupid question," continued Sherry as they climbed into the car, "but Ray Dixon and Ray Killingham are the same person, right?"

"That's right," replied Carolyn as she fastened her seatbelt and started up the engine. "We originally knew him as Ray Dixon when he was working for his aunt Cathy, our Dean."

"Dean Dixon?" clarified Sherry with a furled eyebrow.

"The same," grinned Carolyn as they drove toward the large wrought iron gate leading from Ocean Bluff Mental Institution. "It was when Ray married my friend Susan that he finally decided to change his name to Killingham, since he never figured on finding out who his real father actually was."

"Does he know now, then?" pressed Sherry.

"If my calculations are correct, Ann should be telling him about it right about now," estimated Carolyn. "At least that's what she said she was going to do in her last email. She felt that the eve of March 23rd was an appropriate day to finally tell him what she learned."

"So, the information about Ray's identity is new?" questioned Sherry as she took out her purse, removed a compact, powdered her nose, and touched up her lipstick.

"The trunk was only recently acquired, following Helen's death," replied Carolyn.

"You're kidding?" Sherry was surprised. "That woman we just saw only recently lost her mother?"

"According to Ann, yes," answered Carolyn.

"So, if Ann is Jon Roth's daughter," pointed out Sherry, "wouldn't that make her a descendent of Lizzie Borden, too?"

"It would," grinned Carolyn with amusement.

"And we're still staying there?" quizzed Sherry with trepidation.

"Ann can explain to you in great detail just why Lizzie Borden was perfectly sane," chuckled Carolyn. "And why she had more than compelling motive to commit the crimes that she did."

"Are there are locks on the doors there?" pressed Sherry.

"Seriously?" laughed Carolyn. "You don't need to worry, we'll be fine. Trust me!"

"Isn't that what your friend Susan always told you?" razzed Sherry with a raised eyebrow.

"Touché!" laughed Carolyn as they continued their way down the narrow, winding highway.

The sprawling ocean view below them was frequently framed by eucalyptus and aging cypress trees growing along the windswept cliffs as they passed. Gently interspersed between some of them was a hearty mat of creeping succulent ice plants with hot pink blooms. Occasional junipers and creeping cypress shrubs also grew there at impossible angles, caused by constant exposure to excessive wind.

The last rays of sun shimmered like delicate fingers of light across the vast ocean as Carolyn and Sherry searched for the road leading into the Killingham Lighthouse Bed and Breakfast.

Meanwhile, over at the Killingham Lighthouse Bed and Breakfast, a family meeting was just concluding at the new annex while its proprietors awaited the arrival of their remaining customers. Both parties still expected to check in had reservations to stay there during the annual Oceanview Festival, slated to begin the following day on March 23, 2023.

Among the proprietors were Ray Killingham and his wife Susan (formerly Rives), Jim Otterman and his wife Sheree (formerly Roth and Wilkins before that), and finally Sheree's daughter Ann and her husband Ted Jensen.

Ray Killingham appeared to be in excellent physical condition despite his age; he was 81 years old. Dressed in raggedy blue jeans, worn out steel tipped cowboy boots, and a dirty white t-shirt, Ray wore thick, horn-rimmed glasses. Even after wiping the grease and grime from his work-worn hands, they still had a dirty appearance. The crewcut on his well-tanned leathery head was visible only when he removed his ten-gallon cowboy hat, which was usually just indoors. The years had not been kind to him. Faded tattoos of naked women adorned his muscular but leathery-looking arms. A good shower wouldn't have hurt him much, either, but helping to maintain the elaborate grounds of the Killingham Lighthouse Bed and Breakfast had proven to be a rather dirty job. Ray's stint in Vietnam had left him with post-traumatic stress disorder, though thankfully recurrences were rare. Falling in love with and marrying Susan Rives had turned out to be the best thing that had ever happened to him.

Like her former high school roommate Carolyn Bennett, Susan Rives was now 66 years old, but still quite shapely for her age. Her ample cleavage, small butt, and long muscular legs were nicely proportioned for a person of her size. Susan's exotic facial features and hazel colored eyes hinted of Latin heritage. Her medium brown hair was parted in the middle and hung loosely over her shoulders with long bangs hanging down to one side in the front. Susan had decided to wear an elegant pair of sterling silver posts with dolphins on them that day that had once been a gift from her brother Damien. While grateful for the financial security her marriage to Ray had provided, Susan was beginning to feel trapped by her continuous duties at the bed and breakfast and badly in need of a change in scenery. Added to that was the knowledge that her older husband Ray would likely begin declining physically in the foreseeable future and would probably need constant care and supervision beyond what she could provide.

Mayor Otterman and his wife Sheree lived at the newly refurbished annex building, located within a short walking distance of the Killingham Lighthouse Bed and Breakfast, just north of Oceanview Academy. The annex building was what the old servants' quarters had come to be called, and served as overflow accommodations for guests of the Killingham Lighthouse Bed and Breakfast when its other rooms were already booked to capacity. The red-headed, freckle-faced man had been hopelessly in love with Carolyn Bennett during their junior year of high school, relentlessly attempting in vain to win her affections.

Still barely five feet, eight inches tall, skinny and gangly looking, with slouched bony shoulders, Jim's fair complexioned skin was continuously sunburned, especially around his freckled ears and face. Jim had once switched from glasses to contact lenses in an attempt to make himself more appealing to Carolyn, but finally reverted back to wearing glasses again. Jim had also quit wearing greasy looking hair tonic in high school, again in a useless attempt to make himself more desirable to Carolyn. Jim's curly but well-trimmed red hair still continued to have its own mind without the use of hair tonic.

Sheree Otterman had been very insecure in high school, had worn various braces, glasses, and thought of herself as unattractive. Nevertheless, she was actually quite pretty now and Jim had finally decided to marry her at Carolyn's suggestion. Sheree would then have someone to care for her following the untimely suicide of her former husband Jon Roth. Sheree had secretly managed to learn of new her husband Jim's sizable fortune, inherited following his parents' demise during an avalanche in Switzerland when they were skiing the Alps back in 2004. Not only had Jim Otterman inherited their fortune, but also his dad's multi-million-dollar brokerage firm. Though employees had been hired to run it for him, it still was necessary for Jim to show up once or twice a year for board meetings.

Jim still maintained his aging Cessna as a patrol plane for occasional flights over the beach as he had done when previously serving as town Sheriff, and would take up guests wishing to participate in occasional skydiving adventures. Jim's plane of choice was now an eight-passenger Learjet aircraft, which made his periodic trips to the home office of his mortgage brokerage firm more enjoyable.

Sheree's daughter Ann Roth had been as skinny and pale complexioned as Sheree had been. Even at 23 years of age, Ann's dark straight hair and large hooked nose had given her a rather homely appearance. Still, Ann's avid love for animals and zest for life seemed to emanate a natural beauty from within. Neither Ann nor her mother had really been very sorry to see Jon Roth end his own life, as his mental illness and volatile temper had made their lives unbearable. Ann was quite content now to be married to Ted Jensen, the love of her life since high school.

When not working to maintain the elaborate Silver Creek Golf Course next door to the Killingham Lighthouse Bed and Breakfast, Ted Jensen and his wife Ann lived over on campus in the home that had once belonged to Ginny Eggersol, who had been the English Literature instructor at Oceanview Academy in 1972 and 1973. It was late one foggy night in 1976 when a drunk driver ran Ms. Eggersol off the dangerous bluff-top highway, causing both cars to crash into the rocky shoreline below, and killing both of them instantly. Following that, the home had belonged for a while to Miss Neilson, who had been the Religious Spiritual Care Coordinator at Oceanview Academy in 2016.

Ann Jensen was delighted, of course, to be near her mother Sheree and stepdad Jim Otterman, and was generally kept quite busy helping Marine Biology Professor John Murray and his wife Jeon maintain and operate the Killingham Wildlife Center on campus near the dairy where her colony of feral cats still lived. Many of the aging felines were part of the original group, though their numbers had dwindled considerably since being successfully captured and neutered.

Ted Jensen's love of surfing and boogie boarding was surpassed only by his love for Ann. While originally befriending Ann in an attempt to covertly learn more about the 1973 death of his aunt Veronica, Ted had fallen helplessly in love with Ann in the process.

It was now the eve of March 23, 2023, and Ann had just finished sharing the exciting news of her discovery in Helen's diary about her Uncle Ray's true identity. The family meeting was drawing to a close as the two remaining parties expected to check in at the Killingham Lighthouse Bed and Breakfast were anticipated to arrive any moment.

"And the point of all this?" asked Ray.

"To reassure all of you that there is no mental illness to worry about from the Borden line," replied Ann.

"What about Birdboy?" pressed Ray.

"I'm glad you asked," answered Ann. "In doing my genealogy, the only evidence I've found of mental illness actually came from the Roth side of the family, though that was several generations ago. You're welcome to come over and look at my book any time you wish. I'm still working on getting it online."

"Hey, we're all related," reminded Susan.

"How do you figure?" frowned Ray.

"Adam and Eve?" teased Susan. "Remember them?"

"There's also a theory called the 'six degrees of separation' where everyone and everything in this world is only six or fewer steps away from anyone else in the world, by way of introduction or personal contact of some kind, so that a chain of friend-to-friend statements can be traced back to connect them with each other by no more than six degrees of separation," elaborated Ann.

"Well, I'm a Killingham now!" informed Ray with finality. He had no interest in learning anything more about the Roth family. It was a big enough step for Ray to abandon the Dixon name he had been raised with for Susan's sake when he married her six years ago. Susan had insisted that Ray's stepdad – old man Killingham – would have wanted it that way, especially after raising him on his own like he had for all those years. So, Ray was not about to change his name again, and definitely not to Roth!

"Anyway, we're going to have a baby!" beamed Ann.

"And we plan to name her Elizabeth Ann Jensen," added Ted with a twinkle in his eyes.

"And you know for certain it's a girl?" pressed Jim.

"Ultrasound," grinned Ted proudly.

"Well, congratulations," acknowledged Jim.

"Then, after Lizzie is born, we plan to name our next children Emma and Alice," revealed Ann with a mischievous twinkle in her eyes.

Jim's eyes opened wide for a moment. "Did you know that Elizabeth Andrew Borden's sisters were named Emma and Alice?"

"You know, I think they were," teased Ann.

"How 'bout that," Ray shook his head and laughed sardonically.

"Guess we'll need to keep our doors locked, our weapons handy, and never turn our backs on 'em," laughed Susan with a wicked grin.

"I hate to ask this, but what was the third thing you were going to tell us?" urged Jim.

"Oh, yes," Ann smiled mischievously. "Have you looked at your guest register lately?"

"Our guest register?" frowned Jim. With everything being online now like it was, Jim never bothered much with it anymore and usually just let Sheree or Susan handle all the reservations.

"When Susan and I were up there putting new sheets on the beds in those two new rooms in the attic today," described Ann, "we just happened to pull up the guest register on our smartwatches to see who would be staying in them. Imagine our surprise when it was someone we knew!"

Jim suddenly pulled up his sleeve, activated his smartwatch to revive it from sleep mode, and commanded, "Guest register for today."

Almost immediately, the current day's guest register was displayed on Jim's smartwatch. Since the screen on his smartwatch was so tiny, Jim normally preferred using his laptop for such things.

"Doctor and Mrs. Lenny Owens?" read Jim after putting on his glasses. "Is this for real? Is this some kind of a sick joke or something?" Jim then looked over in time to see Susan give him a crooked smile.

"Too bad there's only one bathroom up there," chuckled Sheree. "That means the two couples will have to share it."

"Well, we eventually will have to have a second one put in," assured Jim with a troubled look on his face.

"Look at the other name," suggested Sheree rather smugly.

Jim then became quiet when he glanced again at the guest register displayed and saw who it was. Jim deliberately put his smartwatch back into sleep mode and rolled down his sleeve. It was suddenly as if a cloud of despair had descended upon him.

"Who did it say?" demanded Ray. "I don't have my smartwatch with me."

"Carolyn Bennett-Hunter and her husband will be staying in the other room," said Sheree matter-of-factly. Sheree had been with Susan and Ann when they had pulled up the register previously and had been waiting ever since to see how Jim would react.

"Oh, this oughta be good," chuckled Ray. "Do you want us to see if we can switch one of them with someone in the lighthouse?"

"Not a chance!" responded Sheree as she gave Jim a pointed grin. "Just how would you feel if you had a nice room at the lighthouse and suddenly found out you were being moved over to the old servants' quarters instead?"

"Hold it!" commanded Jim. "I know I should have shared this with all of you at the time, but we had already been through so much."

"What are you talking about?" Sheree became serious.

"Just two short months after the day we recovered Joyce's and Veronica's remains," began Jim, "I learned of some other tragic news." Jim was always careful not to mention the tragedy involving Jon Roth when talking about that day, especially in front of Sheree or Ann.

After an awkward silence, Jim continued. "Lenny Owens had some sort of medical situation on March 23, 2016. It was most likely a heart attack, but the man at the hospital absolutely would not share any further details with me."

"How awful!" exclaimed Ann.

"Not on that exact same day?" Susan could not believe it.

Everyone else was dumbfounded.

"Lenny died just a few short weeks later," added Jim.

"And you didn't think any of us would have wanted the chance to say goodbye to him?" demanded Susan.

"Well, I can't go back and change it now, can I?" retorted Jim. "I feel bad enough as it is."

"Let him finish," insisted Sheree.

"Well, Lenny's funeral service was almost two months to the day after that," added Jim. "That's really all I know."

"And what about Carolyn? You didn't think she would want to know?" demanded Susan.

"Frankly," replied Jim, "I didn't expect to ever see her again."

"Well, as you now know, I've been emailing and skyping with Carolyn regularly for seven years," pointed out Ann. "I could certainly have told her! In fact, I'm the one who let her know about the new rooms we have available upstairs."

"And that's another thing!" snapped Jim. "Why was I never told that you were keeping in contact with Carolyn?" Jim did not like being kept in the dark about such things.

"You're one to talk!" accused Sheree.

Then, unexpectedly, the sound of someone's vehicle pulling up outside could be heard. "Someone must be early," pointed out Susan.

Jim suddenly felt his heart rate increase exponentially and experienced a high level of anxiety when he heard the car doors shut and the sound of steps on the pavement outside.

Jim was well aware that the fight-or-flight response is a physiological reaction that occurs in response to a perceived harmful event, attack, or threat to survival, and was irritated at himself for reacting so irrationally.

A brisk knock on the front door could be heard.

"Carolyn will have to be told about Lenny," reminded Sheree rather evenly as she approached and opened the door.

A tall, dark, handsome young man in his early forties smiled and nodded at Sheree. Beside him was a tall, attractive blonde woman who bore a striking resemblance to what Carolyn had looked like in her forties. The two made a remarkable pair.

"Dr. Owens, I presume?" questioned Sheree.

"Yes, ma'am," confirmed the stranger. "And this is my lovely wife, Lila."

Lila's shapely physique and timeless presence seemed to command the attention of others, yet she also had a shy and demure quality about her, too. Jim was astounded at how much she reminded him of Carolyn, and could not help but be drawn toward her.

"Hello," greeted Lila with a warm, inviting smile.

"Please, come in," invited Sheree, after covertly jabbing her husband Jim in the side with a warning elbow.

"You wouldn't be related to a Lenny Owens who once went to school over there at Oceanview, would you?" asked Susan.

"He was my father," revealed the man. "I'm Lenny, Jr."

"This should be interesting," Susan suddenly smiled a crooked smile. "My name was Susan Rives when I went to school there, and I knew your father and his cousin Pete quite well. In fact, my friend Carolyn – who also knew them – should be arriving any minute."

Jim Otterman approached and warmly shook Lenny Jr.'s hand before taking Lila's hand and briefly holding it as he finished the introductions. "I'm Jim Otterman. This is my wife, Sheree, our daughter Ann, and her husband Ted."

"And that is my husband Ray," added Susan.

"I'm afraid you all have me at a disadvantage," admitted Lenny, Jr. "But, it is very nice to meet all of you."

Just then a second vehicle could be heard approaching.

"You'll be all right," assured Sheree as she gave her husband Jim a challenging look. "Trust me!"

After taking a deep breath, Jim went ahead and opened the door, and waited for Carolyn and her husband David to park and get out of their vehicle. "That's odd."

"What is it?" questioned Sheree as she came over to stand beside her husband Jim.

"That's not Carolyn at all," informed Jim.

"Well, the room's Carolyn's," advised Sheree with finality. "Whoever else it is will just have to be disappointed."

"I think I know that woman," remarked Susan from behind them. "But, it can't be who I think it is."

The proprietors watched in silence as a middle-aged Hispanic woman climbed from the aging yellow Volkswagen Beetle now parked in the only remaining parking space.

Just then, Sheree noticed a text message on her cell phone that she had not noticed previously due to having it set on mute. Perhaps if she had a smartwatch like everyone else, she might have noticed the message sooner.

"Janette?" exclaimed Susan as she ran from the door and approached the woman.

"Susan!" shouted the stranger as they ran toward one another and embraced.

"Janette Manza, I don't believe it!" greeted Susan. "What in the world are you doing here?"

"I'm here to spend the weekend with you and Carolyn, of course," smiled Janette with her irrepressible smile.

Though the years of housekeeping duties at Ashton Valley Medical Center had taken their toll on Janette, she was determined not to let her aching back or bad knees get in the way of spending time with two of her dearest friends.

"Let me get that for you," offered Jim as he opened the passenger door, reached in and grabbed Janette's large suitcase from the backseat of her car. "You drove all the way here from Ashton alone?"

"Sure did," responded Janette. "At least I didn't have as far to come as Carolyn did. Ashton's only four hours away."

"1965?" questioned Jim as he paused to study Janette's car.

"Yeah, it is," verified Janette. "You know your cars."

"I dabble," smirked Jim.

"His first love is planes," revealed Sheree as she approached. "Hey, I just got a text from Carolyn. She's been delayed but will be along shortly. Carolyn said to just have Janette go ahead and check into her room."

"You'll be staying in the same room with Carolyn and her husband David?" questioned Jim, curious about the arrangement.

"I will be staying in Carolyn's room, yes," confirmed Janette. Unsure whether she should mention that Sherry Collingsworth would be coming in David's place, Janette decided not to say anything about it just yet.

"You guys, this is Carolyn's dear friend Janette Manza from Ashton," introduced Susan. "I still remember the time she and Carolyn came up to Ocean Bay to spend the weekend with me in 1979."

"Oh, girl, you're telling me!" laughed Janette. "That was when Jorge took us up that zigzag mountain in his little yellow sports car, just so he could scare the hell out of us on the way back down!"

"You were screaming even louder than Carolyn, as I recall," laughed Susan.

"And all you did was laugh at us!" recalled Janette.

"Hey, it's so good to see you again!" beamed Susan as she gave Janette another hug. "You're gonna love it here. Trust me!"

"Uh oh, should I be worried?" asked Janette.

"You've apparently heard Susan's expression 'trust me' before," grinned Ray as he extended his hand in greeting. "I'm Susan's husband Ray. Pleased to meet you."

"Likewise," nodded Janette as she shook his hand.

"And this is Jim Otterman and his wife Sheree," introduced Susan. "They run the overflow annex here where you'll be staying. Jim's also town Mayor, when he's not busy over here telling the rest of us what to do."

"We won't be staying in the actual lighthouse?" questioned Janette with disappointment.

"Don't worry, we do tours every day," grinned Susan. "You'll get to see it tomorrow. Trust me!"

"I'd better get to see the inside of that lighthouse, girl!" razzed Janette with a big grin. "The outside is sure beautiful."

"Thanks," nodded Susan.

"And I'm Carolyn's friend Ann," mentioned Sheree's daughter as she extended her hand to Janette. "This is my husband Ted."

"Aren't you the one whose aunt was found over in that cave?" quizzed Janette as she focused her attention on Ted.

"Indeed I am," confirmed Ted as he shook Janette's hand.

Ted was well-built and muscular, and the grip on his handshake unexpectedly firm. His well-tanned arms had clearly spent a good deal of time in the sun, though he did appear to have some Polynesian heritage. His shoulder-length hair was kinky but not unduly frizzy, and his large, round, seductive brown eyes were both captivating and serious at the same time.

"I think I might still need that hand for something," razzed Janette as she exaggeratedly shook her hand back and forth afterwards.

"Sorry about that!" apologized Ted.

"Sometimes he just doesn't know his own strength," flirted his wife Ann as she gave him an affectionate hug.

"And it can't be?" added Janette as she noticed Lenny Owens, Jr. and his wife Lila silently taking everything in. "Are *you* Lenny Jr.?"

"Yes, I am," replied Dr. Owens with surprise. "Did you go to school at Oceanview, too?"

"Oh, heavens, no," laughed Janette. "I've just been real good friends with Carolyn for a very long time, and she's certainly told me all about Lenny Owens. Senior, that is. Is he here, too?"

"My father passed back in 2016," informed Lenny, Jr. "But, I can see that his memory lives on, and I'm definitely looking forward to chatting more with each of you, especially Carolyn when she arrives."

"I'm so sorry!" apologized Janette. "My condolences. I had no idea. Carolyn never mentioned …."

"Carolyn doesn't know yet," interrupted Jim.

"She'll be pretty upset by the news," guessed Janette.

"Well, she has been married to David for 40 years now," reminded Susan. "I think she'll be fine."

"What she won't get over is the fact that I knew about it and never bothered to tell her at the time," added Jim.

"You must know Carolyn quite well, then," nodded Janette as she studied Jim more carefully.

"How long have *you* known Carolyn?" quizzed Jim.

"We first met back in 1976, I think it was," reflected Janette. "So, I've known her almost as long as you and Susan have."

"Let me show you all to your rooms," offered Sheree, suddenly realizing that she had not yet done so.

"Is there a place to eat around here?" Lila finally spoke up.

"That's a good question," interjected Janette. "I'm famished!"

"We were all just getting ready to eat," offered Ann. "Why don't you folks join us? Our other guests are all eating out, anyway, so we should have plenty."

"We'd love to," accepted Lila without hesitation. "Just as soon as we've seen the room, of course."

"I'm in!" agreed Janette.

Lenny, Jr. merely nodded his assent. Like his father, he was a man of few words.

It was almost seven o'clock by the time Carolyn and Sherry found the entrance road leading to the Killingham Lighthouse Bed and Breakfast. Sunset would be at 7:23 that night. Expecting a steep, narrow, unpaved road that would switch back and forth as it descended through the dense coastal forest and continuing until reaching the sandy beachfront below, Carolyn was surprised to find the entire road widened, paved and well lit.

What once had been an abandoned rundown trailer park at the end of it was now the new Silver Creek Golf Course. The original Silver Creek Trailer Park Store was now used as its golf pro shop. "Look! There's even a small delicatessen sandwich shop built onto one end of it!" exclaimed Carolyn with surprise.

"Looks like they have ice cream there, too!" approved Sherry as she noticed a picture of an ice cream cone on the sign. "Doesn't look like they're still open tonight, though."

"Well, it is seven o'clock already," reminded Carolyn as she glanced at her watch.

"We still have those sandwiches from the ice chest," suggested Sherry. "We can always eat 'em in our room, once we get there."

Carolyn absently nodded as she studied the other improvements Jim had made to the surrounding area. Silver Creek Road, as it now was named on a beautiful new well-lit sign, among them.

An electric security gate that opened by the swipe of an app on their smartwatches, or by a security card for patrons who didn't have them, had been left in "guest" mode for the late arrivals. Carolyn pulled to a stop beside the gate and pressed the "guest' button, immediately causing the gate to open automatically.

"Nice!" admired Carolyn, grateful to see the gate open without having to get out of her vehicle.

The barrier chain that had previously been threaded through metal eyelets atop short metal posts along the cliff-side edge of the steep road ahead of them had been replaced by a short but sturdy brick wall. "This is the part of the road that leads up from the golf course to the lighthouse and then over to the annex," informed Carolyn.

"Wow! Can you imagine how dangerous the drop-off beside it would be without that wall?" commented Sherry as she glanced out at the sprawling ocean view beside them to admire the colorful rays of setting sun on its water.

"Tell me about it!" replied Carolyn rather distantly as she recalled how it had been seven years earlier, before the improvement.

After proceeding through the security gate and up the steep road to the lighthouse, Carolyn slowed to admire some newly planted begonias that were in full bloom by the lighthouse entrance.

The unusually shaped white structure was trimmed all in bright red. The building itself was octagonal in shape and approximately thirty feet in diameter. Atop the building was a long, pointed tower which projected upward at least sixty feet from its center and was only about fifteen feet in diameter at the very top, but entirely round. Randomly placed windows could be seen spiraling their way up its exterior, presumably to provide natural lighting to as many interior locations as possible. An octagonal-shaped lookout tower at the very top had large picture windows on all but the side which had a single arched exit door leading to an exterior catwalk that encircled the entire upper tower at that level. The catwalk was about three feet wide, could only be accessed through the arched exit door, and was protected by a sturdy wrought iron railing that had been painted entirely white. The tower's conical shaped roof came to a perfect point on top and was covered entirely with bright red ceramic tiles. At ground level was a covered entryway to the front door, also covered with bright red ceramic tiles. The cement porch and steps leading up to it were painted bright red, to match the ceramic tiles, and a large brass bell mounted beside the front door was graced with a long brass chain with which to ring it.

"That's new," commented Carolyn as she noticed a freestanding sign out front that read, "Killingham Lighthouse Bed and Breakfast."

"Nicely lit, too," added Sherry. "What a beautiful lighthouse!"

"I think those other small structures beside it are for the generators and yard maintenance stuff," recalled Carolyn.

"And that must be the annex over there, where we're staying?" questioned Sherry as she noticed the old servants' quarters a short distance away.

"Yes, ma'am," smiled Carolyn as she continued their drive over to the annex. "He did absolutely everything I suggested," marveled Carolyn. "Even the golf course, every bit of it."

"The golf course was *your* idea?" doubted Sherry rather skeptically.

"Actually, it was. Ask Jim about it if you don't believe me," recommended Carolyn as she reached the annex.

"Oh, I believe you," replied Sherry. "This is just a lot to take in all at once."

"Then consider yourself duly warned," suggested Carolyn.

"About what?" frowned Sherry.

"I don't know," chuckled Carolyn. "About whatever might come up once we get there. Who knows."

"Point taken. Hey, that must be Jim's private parking space," grinned Sherry when she noticed the sign above it that simply said "Jim" in large reflective letters that were almost as impossible to miss as Jim's bright red 2023 AWD Jeep Cherokee.

"Almost makes you wonder what kind of plane he's flying these days," speculated Carolyn as she paused to search for a parking space. Suddenly, both Carolyn and Sherry were startled by a tap on the driver's side window.

"Jim?" muttered Carolyn as she pressed the button to automatically lower her window.

"Greetings," smiled Jim, pleased with himself for successfully sneaking up on Carolyn's vehicle on foot without being noticed. "You'll be parking in my spot while you're here. Just give me a moment."

"Now, that's service," acknowledged Sherry as she and Carolyn watched Jim get into his new bright red Jeep.

"I wonder where he plans to park?" mused Carolyn as Jim started up his engine, backed out, and quickly drove toward the lighthouse.

"And Jim is married now?" teased Sherry with a mischievous grin as she gave Carolyn a sidelong glance.

"You are kidding?" scoffed Carolyn as she pulled into Jim's parking space and turned off the engine to her new white Dodge Dart.

"I should have known you'd be driving a white Dodge Dart," called Jim as he hurriedly returned on foot.

"Thanks," nodded Carolyn as she climbed from the car.

"My pleasure," beamed Jim as he quickly reached for Carolyn's hand to assist her to her feet.

"How's Sheree?" quizzed Carolyn as she snatched her hand away from him.

"I think I'm just fine," called Sherry from the other side of the car. "Last I checked, anyway."

"Oh, Jim, this is my friend Sherry – with a 'y' in her name, like the drink," introduced Carolyn.

"Pleased to meet you," greeted Sherry as she came around the car and warmly shook hands with Jim.

"Now, this will be confusing," commented Jim. "My wife is Sheree, too, but with two 'e's in her name."

"Almost makes you want to go and pour a glass of sherry, doesn't it?" laughed Sherry as she flirted shamelessly with Jim.

Carolyn merely rolled her eyes and shook her head, keenly aware that Jim was still enamored with her, even after all these years.

"She's really crazy about me," Jim whispered jokingly to Sherry, in reference to Carolyn.

"Actually, it's his wife, Sheree, who's crazy about him," corrected Carolyn rather smugly. Carolyn never had shown any interest in Jim whatsoever, not in high school, not in 2016, and certainly not now!

"Come on inside," invited Jim. He refused to be daunted by Carolyn's obvious lack of enthusiasm for him. "Everyone has started eating already, but there are two places at the table saved just for you. We had assumed, of course, that your husband would be the other guest. You are still married, aren't you?"

Carolyn began to chuckle and shake her head at Jim's inappropriate optimism. "Very much so! For 40 years now."

"And yet he's not here," pointed out Jim with a hint of sarcasm.

"Her husband is busy working to keep Madam Carolyn and her many animals in the style to which they've become accustomed," interjected Sherry with a wry grin.

"Carolyn already knows that money is no object here," rebutted Jim, just a little too over-confidently for Sherry's liking.

Sherry then leaned close to Carolyn and started to whisper, "You were right. He is a pompous little …."

"Carolyn!" screamed Janette and Susan as they got up and rushed over to hug her.

"Oh, my God, it's really you, girlfriend!" exclaimed Janette as she gave Carolyn a warm hug.

"Welcome back!" beamed Susan as she, too, hugged her friend. Somewhat saddened that Carolyn had not been able to make it out for her wedding to Ray, Susan nevertheless had considered Carolyn as her first choice for a matron of honor.

"Well, I usually stay at home and lock my doors on March 23rd," mentioned Carolyn half seriously, "but what else can possibly go wrong now, right?"

Jim was still feeling uneasy about sharing the news of Lenny's death with Carolyn but knew it was unavoidable. Sheree's even glare added to his trepidation. Could she tell how much he still cared for Carolyn, even after all these years?

"Jim, come join us," invited Ray.

Everyone else was already seated at the table.

"May we please bless the food before we eat?" questioned Sherry Collingsworth.

"Absolutely," agreed Jim. "Any volunteers?"

"Dear Lord," began Janette without hesitation as the others hurriedly closed their eyes and grabbed hands. "Thank you for this food. Please bless the hands that prepared it and help it to make us healthy and strong. And thank you for everyone's safe arrival here tonight. Amen."

"Amen," chorused the others.

After a leisurely dinner of shish kabob with rice pilaf and cucumber, tomato and onion salad, Ann hurriedly rushed to the kitchen to retrieve a huge platter of homemade baklava for dessert.

"Now, that's what I'm talkin' about!" grinned Janette when she saw it. "The last time I had that was in Ashton."

"You're *from* Ashton," reminded Carolyn with a sly smile.

"Or, 'Little Armenia' as your dad used to call it," laughed Janette as she slapped her knee. "Lots of good food, just like this."

"Thank you," smiled Ann. She was quite proud of her baklava and grateful for the compliment.

"I seem to remember seeing an old Armenian woman sitting on her porch down the street from Carolyn's parents' house with a huge shotgun on her lap one afternoon back in 1973," grinned Susan.

"That was the day we drove out to Ashton University to see the farm animals with Jorge and managed to get my dad's white Dodge Dart stuck between a ditch and a pig feeder," roared Carolyn.

"A pig feeder?" howled Sheree as she, too, began to laugh.

"You did warn me about these people," whispered Sherry as she gave Carolyn another sidelong glance but then joined in the merriment.

"And, you should have seen how mad Mr. Bennett was when he realized that the chrome strip on the side of his car had come off," recalled Susan.

"That's absolutely true," corroborated Carolyn. "I've never seen him that mad."

"But, we did try our best to refasten the strip with paperclips and string that we found in the glovebox," continued Susan, "in the hope that it would hold, at least until after we'd left."

"I take it that didn't happen?" questioned Sherry.

"No. We were inside the house eating dinner at the time – I think it was corn on the cob," recalled Susan.

"It was," interjected Carolyn.

"And while we ate, Mr. Bennett went out and began walking around the car to inspect it like he usually did, for rocks in the tires, that kind of thing," elaborated Susan.

"Then, at the very moment he was standing beside the place where we had repaired it," contributed Carolyn, "the thing suddenly came loose with a loud boing."

"It just missed hitting him in the face, too!" howled Susan.

The entire room erupted into uncontrollable laughter.

When she was finally able to speak again, Carolyn suggested to Susan, "Hey, why don't you tell them about the time we crawled under the girls' dormitory and knocked on the floor?"

"Oh, yeah! And the dorm was put on 'demon alert' after that because some girls had been having a séance in their room at the time," Susan managed to say before breaking into a new round of laughter.

"You two certainly had quite the adventures there at that school, didn't you?" remarked Lenny, Jr.

"We certainly did," replied Carolyn, but suddenly became serious as she thought of Lenny, Sr.

"Tell me," inquired Carolyn, "just how is your dad doing these days, anyway? Will he be joining you here for the festival?"

Everyone in the room immediately became serious.

"There's something I need to tell you," volunteered Jim. He had already promised the others that he would be the one to tell Carolyn about Lenny's passing, and there was no getting out of it.

Carolyn suddenly turned to Lenny, Jr. and – for just a moment – it was as if she were looking at his father again. They looked so much alike! "What aren't they telling me?"

"Jim knew that Lenny Owens had passed in 2016," blurted Sheree, "but didn't feel the rest of us were up to learning about it at the time, especially after everything else we had been through already."

"Jim didn't even tell *us* about it until earlier today!" snapped Susan. She, too, was clearly quite upset about it.

Carolyn silently sat and stared at Lenny, Jr. as unbidden tears began to flow down her cheeks.

"We all had a right to know about our friend Lenny!" interjected Susan. "Especially Carolyn!"

"When did he pass?" questioned Carolyn.

"Almost two months to the day after his heart attack," informed Lenny, Jr. "Even with extensive surgery after that to repair the damage, Dad just didn't make it."

"That was two entire months we could have had to go visit him and say our goodbyes!" Susan reminded Jim with an accusing glare.

"His heart attack was on March 23, 2016," acknowledged Jim as he hung his head in shame. "I'm so sorry! I should have told all of you when it happened. Then, when time had passed, how could I tell you then? You'd react just like you are now!"

Jim then got up and fled from the table to be alone.

"It was on March 23, 2016, when the bodies of Joyce Troglite and Veronica Jensen were finally discovered in an abandoned bunker tunnel along the beach," described Ted. "Veronica was my aunt."

"They had been missing for 43 years," added Susan, for Janette, Lenny Jr. and Lila's sakes. "And, it was quite an emotional time for all of us."

"March 23rd never was a very good day, was it?" asked Ray as he thought of his experiences in Vietnam. It had been on March 16, 1968, that at least two entire villages of innocent civilians were gunned down by a platoon of rogue American soldiers. Many of the women were gang-raped and some of their bodies mutilated beyond recognition before the welcome release of death. The tragedy had generally come to be known known in America as the 'My Lai Massacre.' A woman carrying Ray's unborn child had been among the civilians that lived in that village. The day before it happened, Ray had been unexpectedly deployed to participate in another mission over in Da Nang, which was about 70 kilometers north of Sơn Mỹ village. If only he had been there to try to stop it! But, since Ray and his common-law wife were not technically married – at least not in the eyes of the American government – the red tape he was forced to endure before being allowed to come identify the body was unbelievable. It was on March 23, 1968, that her body was finally released to him for burial.

"My brother Damien died on March 23, 2009," revealed Susan rather sadly. "He was in the kitchen fixing breakfast for his six-year-old daughter when he suddenly slumped over the table and died right in front of her."

"It was on March 23, 1993, that my elderly cat Pippin died in my arms from a massive stroke," mumbled Carolyn. "It was an earthquake that day that triggered it."

"Maybe that day is cursed," commented Lila.

"It also marks the anniversary of one of the most destructive earthquakes of all time," announced Ann as she pulled up a website on her smartwatch.

"It says here that 'several earthquake catalogues and historical sources describe the Ardabil earthquake as a destructive earthquake that struck the city of Ardabil (in Iran), on March 23, 893. The magnitude was unknown but the death toll was reported to be very large.' It also says that 'the USGS in their list of earthquakes with 50,000 or more deaths give an estimate that 150,000 were killed, which would make it the ninth deadliest earthquake in history,'" read Ann.

"The earthquake we had here on March 23, 2016, was nothing to scoff at," reminded Sheree, "and being in that cave when it happened was absolutely terrifying!" Sheree purposely did not mention that it was there in the cave on that same day that her previous husband Jon Roth had shot himself in the head right in front of her, Carolyn and Ray.

"If it weren't for the earthquake that day, we probably never would have found the skeletal remains of Joyce or Veronica, though," reminded Carolyn. "Excuse me, I need some air."

"May I join you?" offered Lenny, Jr., whose wife Lila nodded her silent agreement for him to go ahead.

"I'm afraid I wouldn't be very good company right now," apologized Carolyn as she grabbed the napkin to take with her so she could wipe her eyes and blow her nose.

"Nevertheless," countered Lenny, Jr., "you certainly can't go out there alone at night."

"Okay, thanks," Carolyn finally agreed as she headed outside and began walking toward the beach access steps that Jim had commissioned contractors to install the previous year.

The well-lit steps gradually descended to the beach after switching back and forth several times down the side of the bluff. Enclosed handrails on the steps ensured the safety of guests while negotiating them. Built to last, the steps and their handrails were made of synthetic wood. Though more expensive than regular wood, synthetic wood was constructed of recycled plastic with wood fibers, and pressure treated to withstand water damage and other rigors of time.

Just as she reached the beach, Carolyn caught the edge of her shoe on the bottom stair and started to lose her balance.

"I got you," advised Lenny, Jr. as he reached over to grab Carolyn's arms from either side and steadied her. "Why don't we sit down for a while? How 'bout that log?"

Carolyn then nodded her head in assent. "Thanks!"

"Glad I could help," responded Lenny, Jr.

"Oh, my goodness!" exclaimed Carolyn when she saw the log. "I can't believe it's still here."

"That log?" questioned Lenny, Jr. as he and Carolyn made their way toward it and sat down.

"It's a special log. It's been here a long time," revealed Carolyn. "The first time I saw it was in 1972."

"Humph," acknowledged Lenny, Jr.

The crisp scent of salt water filled the air as the sound of ocean waves could be heard gently licking the shoreline. The outline of two large freestanding offshore boulders could be seen against the fading purple twilight. "The tide's definitely on its way in," noticed Carolyn.

"I take it you and my dad were an item back in high school?" Lenny, Jr. finally asked.

"Kind of," replied Carolyn as she dabbed fresh tears from her cheeks. "I'm sorry, I shouldn't be reacting like this. I've been married to a wonderful man named David for 40 years now, and love him with all my heart. I don't know what's wrong with me."

"Well, you're human. And, it's not every day we learn that someone we once cared about has unexpectedly passed," replied Lenny, Jr. as he put a comforting hand on Carolyn's back. "I can't believe how much you remind me of my mom."

"Excuse me?" replied Carolyn as she pulled away to study Lenny, Jr. more carefully.

"She has the same color eyes, hair and skin that you do," smiled Lenny, Jr.

"You're kidding me?" responded Carolyn. "I'll bet your grandfather was none too pleased about that!"

"That's what I understand," answered Lenny, Jr., "but gramps is long gone, too."

"I'm so sorry," consoled Carolyn. "Death is never easy."

After several awkward moments of silence, Carolyn mentioned, "See those initials carved down here on the end of this log?"

"LO and CB," Lenny, Jr. read with surprise. "Lenny Owens and Carolyn Bennett?"

"Your dad sat right where you are now when he carved them," revealed Carolyn. "That was more than fifty years ago. We were just sitting here, holding hands and watching the sunset together."

"And there's even a heart around it," noticed Lenny, Jr.

"I'm afraid the heart was my doing, but after the fact," interjected Jim from behind them. "Originally, I had planned on changing the L to a J, as in Jim, but just couldn't bring myself to do it. I knew if Carolyn ever saw it like that, she would be furious."

"JO for Jim Otterman, of course!" realized Lenny, Jr. "You're that guy my Uncle Pete wanted to beat the pulp out of in the cafeteria one night, but it was my dad who stopped him. I remember Uncle Pete telling me about that one time."

"Guilty," admitted Jim.

"What?" grilled Carolyn. "I never heard anything about that!"

"It was the weekend you went away with Susan and her friend in the bright yellow sports car," reminded Jim.

"Why in the world was Pete going to beat you up?" demanded Carolyn. "I just can't imagine Pete doing something like that!"

"It had to do with you," confessed Jim, "and the fact that I just wouldn't leave you alone. Pete was always very protective of his cousin Lenny, though a guy that size certainly didn't need protecting, at least not from my point of view!"

"I see some things never change," remarked Lenny, Jr., with a renewed understanding of his Uncle Pete's desire to beat the pulp out of Jim Otterman all those years ago!

"Hey, I owe you both a huge apology and came to tell you how sorry I am," Jim attempted to get the conversation back on track. "I had no right to just get up and leave like that."

"And?" prompted Carolyn. She was not going to make it easy for Jim to say what he had come to say.

"And I'm very sorry for not telling you or the others about Lenny passing when he did, or about him being ill before that," added Jim. "You all had every right to know about it and the chance to go and say your goodbyes. There's nothing I can do or say now to make it right, but I am sorry and I hope that someday you can find it in your heart to forgive me."

"I do forgive you," answered Carolyn, "but I'm going to need time to get over it. This probably will be my last trip to the Oceanview area. Perhaps I shouldn't have come back at all."

"Then you wouldn't have met me," reminded Lenny, Jr. "Or found out about my dad, apparently."

66

Carolyn then smiled and nodded. "You're right, of course. Thanks."

Jim then sat down on the log on the other side of Carolyn and the three of them continued to sit in awkward silence for several minutes, watching the ever-darkening ocean sprawled out before them.

"There was a phone call from your husband," Jim finally spoke up. "You need to call him back tonight, no matter how late it is."

It was finally March 23, 2023. Morning sunlight filled the annex dining room as its guests finished consuming a scrumptious breakfast of quiche, fruit and lamb sausage.

"Where's Carolyn?" asked Sherry.

"She looked like she could use some more rest," replied Janette, "so she's still up there."

"The lighthouse tour begins in five minutes," announced Susan from the doorway. "Don't worry, Carolyn's seen it before."

"Sherry, Janette, Margaret, Hilda, Lila and Lenny, Jr. Anyone else?" questioned Ann as she began to clear the table.

"Our husbands were supposed to join us, but decided to go sky diving instead," informed Hilda.

"Mr. Otterman took 'em up at daybreak," advised Margaret.

"The other guests have all gone into town," relayed Ann as she made another trip from the kitchen to grab more of the dishes so she could clear them from the table.

"Let's go, then," directed Susan. "This way."

As the tour group made its way from the annex over to the lighthouse, Lenny, Jr. happened to notice Carolyn walking down on the beach. "Lila, do you mind?"

"Go ahead," smiled his understanding wife. "I know you don't like tours like this much, anyway."

"You won't know what you're missing!" advised Janette. "I can't wait to see that lighthouse!"

"Well, the lighthouse was originally built in 1872 by the first Killinghams to come here from Ireland," began Susan. "The first small out building beside it has a commercial grade heat pump with stand-by generator inside. It's actually a turbine generator unit."

"Very impressive!" admired Sherry.

"The next small out building houses a diesel powered backup generator, but hasn't been actively used since 1961, other than to start it up periodically to make sure it still works," added Susan as they walked toward the lighthouse.

Several members of the tour group chuckled at that.

"The military actually took over this complex, during World War II, and used it as a defensive seaside outpost. The lighthouse was often used to send light signals by Morse code to ally vessels at sea," narrated Susan. She had given the spiel so many times by now that she could practically recite it in her sleep.

"Can they do that?" questioned Janette. "They can't just make someone leave their home like that, can they?"

"They can and they did," replied Susan. "That was when the Killingham family set up shop over there where the golf course is today. It originally was used as a trailer park."

"Wow!" exclaimed Janette. "Unbelievable."

"At first it was just supposed to be temporary, until the military people left," continued Susan. "Then, it became a lucrative business venture, especially with the ice cream shop. People love ice cream."

"Definitely on my bucket list for today!" grinned Sherry.

"Here, here!" added Margaret and Hilda.

"But the Killingham family still moved back over here to live after the military people left?" asked Lila.

"They did indeed," chuckled Susan as she reached and opened the front door of the lighthouse for her tour group to enter. "We'll be heading up the spiral staircase straight ahead of you."

"Just look at this place!" exclaimed Janette. "And you live here? This is a dream come true, girl!"

"Yes, indeed," nodded Susan, unconvincingly.

"Don't tell me you're bored with all this?" Janette whispered to Susan. "This is the life!"

"Later," whispered Susan in return. "Okay, folks, there are two rooms on each of the four levels. They are currently occupied by other guests, so unless a door is open, we ask that you respect their privacy. Those who have gone out for the day are encouraged to leave the door to their room open so tour groups can get a look inside."

"Look at the beautiful hardwood floors and the Queen Anne furniture in those rooms!" appreciated Sherry.

"The bed quilts and matching throw rugs were all made by hand," revealed Susan proudly. "And so were the wooden rocking chairs and seat cushions. All made by Killinghams."

"Where are the restrooms?" questioned Lila.

"There's one toilet at each level, each shared by the two guest rooms on that level," informed Susan. "Each room does have its own sink, but the showers are all downstairs."

"This is incredible!" exclaimed Janette. "Too bad we couldn't have stayed over here!"

"Who used to live over there in the annex when they first built all this?" quizzed Margaret.

"Servants, mostly," smiled Susan as she started up the final leg of the spiral staircase. "There was a butler, a maid, a nanny, a gardener, a cook, and even a tutor for the children. From what I was told, the original Killingham family named each of their eight daughters after various flowers, and each of these guest rooms is named after its original occupant."

"How clever," remarked Hilda. "That one down there has a sign by the door that says it's 'The Daisy Room.'"

"And right across from it is 'The Violet Room,'" smiled Susan.

"Oh, okay, they're *all* names of flowers," realized Janette.

"Indeed, they are," grinned Susan. "There's also 'The Lavender Room' and 'The Rosemary Room' up near the top. 'The Rosemary Room' is reserved for staff."

Again, the members of the group chuckled.

"Finally, up here in 'The Tower Room' is where the main lighthouse lamp used to be, when this was used as a lighthouse," informed Susan as she motioned toward the perfectly round wooden table in the center of the room. The table was surrounded entirely by a perfectly round wooden bench, both of them made from the same highly shellacked yellow pinewood that covered the inner ceiling and walls.

"How come there's no lamp in it?" questioned Janette. "Who ever heard of a lighthouse without a lamp!"

"The lighthouse was actually decommissioned by the military at the end of World War II," explained Susan. "And you can't have a lighthouse without proper approval. A valid permit is required to be in compliance with federal regulations, and since they're the ones who voided the permit and decommissioned the lighthouse in the first place, it hardly seems likely they might change their minds."

"How sad," remarked Sherry.

"Indeed," agreed the others.

"Any other questions before we end the official tour?" prompted Susan. "If not, you're free to look around on your own, and please be careful to use the handrails."

"Yes, ma'am!" grinned Janette with a salute.

"And please respect the privacy of our other guests who are staying here," called Susan as the group disbanded.

Down on the beach, Carolyn slowly made her way toward the old bunker tunnel. She had intended never to visit it again, but somehow felt herself compelled to see it.

"Hey, wait up!" called a voice from behind her. It was Lenny, Jr. "Mind if I join you?"

"Lenny, Jr.," acknowledged Carolyn. "Please, by all means."

"I'm not much for lighthouse tours, anyway," grinned the tall, handsome young man as he caught up with Carolyn.

"How tall are you, anyway?" questioned Carolyn.

"A whole inch taller than my old man," grinned Lenny, Jr. "I'm six feet, six inches tall."

"Of course, Lenny always seemed taller than he was because of his afro," recalled Carolyn with a smile.

"Strange, but I don't remember him having one when I was growing up," recalled Lenny, Jr. "He always kept his hair close-cut and professional looking for the workplace."

"When did he finally cut off the afro?" wondered Carolyn.

"I think it was about the time he took up varsity fencing in college," guessed Lenny, Jr. "Probably, it got in the way."

"So, this is where your friends used to boogie board?" asked Lenny, Jr. as they approached the bunker tunnel. Even the outer opening was now gated and completely off limits to anyone without a key.

"Right there on the sand is where Steve Fredrickson died from his injuries after being attacked by a shark," reflected Carolyn. "I was with him when he died."

"How horrible!" exclaimed Lenny, Jr.

"At least he died doing something he loved," replied Carolyn as she slowly sat down on the sand.

The sound of ocean waves could be heard crashing against the ragged shoreline nearby, interrupted occasionally by cries from a lone seagull as it circled overhead in search of small prey below. It was almost mesmerizing to watch the panoramic scene sprawled out before them, complete with brilliant tentacles of light moving across the water's surface while the rising sun slowly made its way toward the sky above. All at once, the seagull loudly cawed again as it flew by and heavily dropped a clam shell onto the hard surface of a large rock below. Gentle rays of sunlight reflected against the moist shell as it fell open. The seagull then circled and landed to devour its prey.

"It is beautiful here," recognized Lenny, Jr. "I can see why my dad loved it here so much. It really is too bad gramps never let him return."

"I'm probably to blame for that," admitted Carolyn. "He made it quite clear that no son of his was going to be dating a white girl."

"And yet he married one anyway," pointed out Lenny, Jr. with a wry grin.

"You'd never know your mother is the same color as I am," smiled Carolyn. "Interestingly, my dad wouldn't let me come back to Oceanview, either, but for the same reason in reverse."

"Would this be your dad's handwriting, then?" inquired Lenny, Jr. as he removed a tattered old letter from his coat pocket and handed it to Carolyn.

"Oh, my God!" exclaimed Carolyn when she saw it.

"You are the Carolyn Bennett to whom this is addressed, I presume?" inquired Lenny, Jr. as she took the letter from him with trembling hands. The return address indicated it was from Lenny Owens and the letter was postmarked August 26, 1979.

"I can't believe it!" mumbled Carolyn as she stared at the letter. In her late father's distinctive handwriting were the words "Return to Sender, Not at This Address."

"Looks like your father held onto it for a couple of months before he actually sent it back, though," noted Lenny, Jr. as he pointed out the date on the return stamp.

"Lenny really did write to me, just like he said he would," marveled Carolyn. "I wonder if there were other letters, too?"

"I'm pretty sure we'll never know," advised Lenny, Jr. "The only reason I came across this particular letter is because it was in a box of things my mom was going to get rid of."

"Why would she do that?" queried Carolyn.

"My mom plans to get married again and was going through some of my dad's old things to clean out and get rid of them," explained Lenny, Jr. "When she found the box this was in, along with some of his other important papers, she just gave them all to me. This was the only item like this one, believe me!"

"And how did you just happen to have it with you today?" prompted Carolyn.

"I didn't even know if any of my dad's old friends would be here, particularly you, but I brought it just in case," smiled Lenny, Jr. "After all, it is addressed to you. It's yours. I'm sure my dad would have wanted you to have it."

"I don't have anything to open it with," realized Carolyn. "I don't want to just tear it open."

Lenny Jr. reached into his pocket and retrieved a small Swiss Army knife that he handed to Carolyn. "That was my dad's, too, but I want it back."

"Oh my goodness!" exclaimed Carolyn. "This is the same knife he used to carve our initials on that log!"

"You don't say?" smiled Lenny, Jr.

Carolyn carefully opened the letter and then sighed with frustration as she handed the Swiss Army knife back to Lenny, Jr. "My glasses are back in the room!"

Lenny, Jr. merely laughed and shook his head.

"You have your father's laugh, too," noticed Carolyn.

"Would you like me to read it to you?" questioned Lenny, Jr. "Only if you want me to, that is. I'm actually dying of curiosity."

"Sure, that would be nice," agreed Carolyn.

"Hey, you two!" called Jim Otterman as he approached them on foot from the airport end of the beach. "I thought I saw someone down here. The bunker tunnel is strictly off limits to all guests, you know."

"You may go ahead and read the letter if you like," whispered Carolyn to Lenny, Jr., "but just not out loud with Jim around. I can read it later for myself."

Lenny, Jr. hurriedly read the letter in silence before carefully folding it and handing it back to Carolyn.

"What's that?" demanded Jim as he started to reach for the letter.

"It's Carolyn's," informed Lenny, Jr. as he stood up to his full six foot, six inches of height for the express purpose of intimidating Jim Otterman, without success.

"Humph!" snorted Jim as he turned to leave. "I don't know what you two have going on, but you are both married, you know!"

"Are you for real?" gasped Lenny, Jr. "Seriously?"

"At least we're both happily married to other people, and have no reason to even think of something like that!" retorted Carolyn, rather angrily. "Sometimes I wonder if you even realize that *you* are married!"

"Look, I didn't come down here to argue with you," snapped Jim. "I came to tell you that the Learjet is fueled up and ready go to."

"Well, don't let us stop you," urged Carolyn.

"I spoke with your husband this morning when he called the front desk, since you didn't bother to turn your cell phone back on this morning," chastised Jim, "and he told me what's going on."

"Oh?" replied Carolyn with surprise.

"Just when were you planning on telling everyone that you had to leave so soon?" demanded Jim. "Susan, Sherry and Janette are devastated, not to mention Ann!"

"I was planning on mentioning it at lunch," answered Carolyn.

"You were waiting until lunch to begin a 5½ hour drive in your car by yourself?" scoffed Jim. "What were you thinking?"

"Well, it's not like I have much choice in the matter," responded Carolyn. "They'll just have to see me when I get there!"

"Wrong!" countered Jim. "I'm how you're getting there."

"I don't think so," differed Carolyn.

"Carolyn's college roommate went missing back in 1975," explained Jim for Lenny, Jr.'s benefit. "A wallet that Carolyn reported lost or stolen at the time was just discovered with what appears to be the girl's skeletal remains. Carolyn is now wanted for questioning up at the St. Diablo Sheriff's Office."

"Is this true?" questioned Lenny, Jr.

"It's true that I lost my wallet the day Karlin disappeared," admitted Carolyn, "but none of us ever knew what had become of her until now. Plus, we probably never will find out what really happened to her."

"We will," promised Jim. "I'm flying you, Susan, Sherry and Janette up to the Powell Lake Airport, just as soon as you all are ready. They're packing their things now as we speak."

"What?" Carolyn was stunned.

"Naturally, Sheree has to stay here to run the annex, and Ray will need to take care of the lighthouse alone while poor Ted takes care of the entire grounds and the golf course all by himself!" fumed Jim.

"What about Ann?" questioned Carolyn.

"Gee, I don't know," snapped Jim, "maybe she'll take care of all the animals by herself while she's not busy filling in for Susan giving tours at the lighthouse!"

"Just what is your problem, sir?" demanded Lenny, Jr. as he took a step closer to Jim.

"What do you mean?" barked Jim, refusing to be intimidated.

"Look, whatever you may have had against my dad," replied Lenny, Jr., "that was between you and him! But, you have no right to treat Carolyn or me like this, and frankly, if my Uncle Pete were here right now and wanted to beat the crap out of you, I can't say I'd do a thing to try to stop him!"

After an awkward silence, Jim finally softened and asked, "How is Pete, anyway?"

"Well, Pete is married with four kids, eleven grandkids, a huge mortgage on his house, and working two jobs just to pay for it all. How do *you* think he is?" Lenny, Jr. had never encountered someone like Jim Otterman before but was certain he had no desire to do so again!

"Perhaps I can do something to help him?" offered Jim.

"Are you for real?" laughed Lenny, Jr. sardonically.

"Oh, money is no object for Jim Otterman," assured Carolyn sarcastically. "He seems to think he can just go around buying off whomever or whatever he wants."

"First of all," Lenny, Jr. informed Jim, "some of us have no need for your money! Secondly, Pete would not even accept help from *me*! So, I'm pretty sure there's no way in hell that he would accept a single dime from the likes of *you*!"

"What does Pete do for a living, anyway?" queried Carolyn.

"He's a computer technician by day and a cab driver by night," revealed Lenny, Jr.

"Wow!" pondered Carolyn. "And what do you do?"

"He's a veterinarian," Jim answered for him.

"At least when I get an unruly patient who won't shut up, all I have to do is muzzle him!" commented Lenny, Jr. as he glared at Jim.

74

"And I'd gladly help you!" added Carolyn as she scowled at Jim.

"Look, I'm sorry, okay?" Jim finally apologized and shrugged his shoulders. "We do need to head back, though."

"I think I'd prefer to walk over and take a look at Oceanview Academy while I'm down this way, where my dad went to school," declined Lenny, Jr. "And then after that, I'd like to stop by that wildlife center Ann told me about."

"Ann also helps John and Jeon Murray maintain and operate the Killingham Wildlife Center," mentioned Jim. "It's on campus over near the dairy where her colony of feral cats still lives."

"I definitely want to see that!" advised Carolyn.

"There just isn't time right now," insisted Jim. "I'm sure Ann will be delighted to take you there when we get back. Right now, we need to get up to St. Diablo. At least with the Learjet, it will take less than half an hour to make the flight, but the only place to land is at Powell Lake Airport."

"That's a little over 10 miles past Powell Mountain University," remembered Carolyn.

"And, down a steep, windy mountain road," reminded Jim. "Plus, another forty-five minutes beyond that to get down to St. Diablo."

"And I suppose someone will be magically waiting there with a car to drive us from Powell Lake all the way down to St. Diablo?" challenged Carolyn.

"Yes, they will," assured Jim. "And, your husband is well aware of our travel plans. I didn't want to have to do this, but you have just been served with a subpoena to be at the St. Diablo Sheriff's Office by two o'clock this afternoon." Jim then pulled an official looking envelope from his pocket and handed it to Carolyn.

"You can't do that!" objected Carolyn as she shoved the envelope away.

"Technically, I can," differed Jim. "Even though I'm Mayor now, they never officially released me from my position as Sheriff."

"Sheriffs can serve subpoenas," acknowledged Lenny, Jr.

"Incredible!" marveled Carolyn. "I sure didn't see that coming. Guess I have no choice then?"

"I could arrest you," offered Jim with a smug grin.

"You wouldn't dare!" fumed Carolyn.

"Of course, then I'd have to confiscate all your personal possessions, including your handbag and everything that's in it," threatened Jim with a mischievous smile.

"Fine, let's go!" snapped Carolyn. "It won't be necessary to arrest me!" There was no way she was going to allow Jim to get his hands on Lenny's letter, that much was certain!

"I thought you might listen to reason," smirked Jim.

"And I hadn't intended to tell the others about *The Powell Mountain Matter* until it was time for me to leave," added Carolyn, "because I didn't want to spoil their holiday."

"I think you've already managed to do that," sniggered Jim as he turned to head back to the lighthouse.

"Good luck to you," bid Lenny, Jr. as he bent to kiss Carolyn on the cheek. "And thank you for letting me read that letter. I think you'll find it quite informative."

"Thanks," sniffed Carolyn as she quickly wiped a tear from her cheek. She would have to wait until later to read the long overdue letter from Lenny that she now had in her handbag.

"*The Powell Mountain Matter*," repeated Jim. "I like it!"

"Excuse me?" questioned Carolyn as she watched Lenny, Jr. head toward the narrow switchback trail that would lead him from the beach to the bluff-tops above. "You do need another set of access steps down here, by the way."

"Consider it done," answered Jim as he began walking the other way, toward the lighthouse.

"Why would you say you like *The Powell Mountain Matter*?" pressed Carolyn as she turned to walk alongside Jim Otterman toward the lighthouse.

"Think about it," replied Jim. "When I was actively serving as Sheriff, I spent over forty years working on *The Oceanview Matter*, but then once it was solved, my life seemed to lose all purpose."

"I don't understand," admitted Carolyn.

"I'm tired of being Mayor of this town," informed Jim. "I'm a Sheriff at heart. Solving crimes and doing investigative work is what I'm all about."

Carolyn appeared troubled by Jim's statement.

"Well, don't you see?" persisted Jim as they continued their trek. "Now my life will have meaning and purpose again – at least while I'm solving this case – and whatever monetary or other resources are needed are completely at my disposal to do it!"

Carolyn sighed deeply and shook her head.

"And," added Jim, "I promised your husband David that I would watch over you and stick to you like glue until *The Powell Mountain Matter* is resolved."

"My husband knows I can't stand you!" blurted Carolyn, though sorry at once for doing so.

"Perhaps that's why he realized he has nothing to worry about," grinned Jim.

"So, just why were you so upset back there?" quizzed Carolyn. "Wait a minute! You certainly weren't jealous of the fact that I was sitting there chatting with Lenny, Jr.? Seriously? He's literally young enough to be my son!"

Jim then blushed, ever so slightly, but didn't reply.

"You were!" perceived Carolyn as she started to laugh. "Unbelievable!"

"Well, he is a virtual carbon copy of his tall, dark and handsome father," pointed out Jim as he kicked a rock from his path and caused a small cloud of sand to erupt behind it.

"A little light on the carbon part, though," chuckled Carolyn.

"What's that supposed to mean?" grilled Jim.

"Apparently, his mother has the same color hair, eyes and skin as I do," revealed Carolyn with a sly grin.

"No kidding?" Jim feigned surprise.

"I thought you knew everything, what with all your fancy surveillance equipment and all," razzed Carolyn.

"Amazing," marveled Jim. "And all this time I had thought she was the cleaning lady."

"You creep, you already knew!" realized Carolyn as she smacked Jim in the arm with her fist.

"I could still arrest you for assaulting an officer," threatened Jim with a wicked smile.

"I hate you!" advised Carolyn. "I really do!"

"At least you feel something for me," chuckled Jim, undaunted by Carolyn's statement.

Carolyn merely glared at Jim in return.

"Don't worry," assured Jim when they arrived at the lighthouse. "Your friends will be with us. Surely they can keep me in line."

"That's what I'm afraid of," worried Carolyn. "Then you might threaten to arrest one of them, too!"

"Only if they break the law," qualified Jim with an even grin.

"Well, I certainly am going to confirm with my husband that he's on board with all of this!" advised Carolyn.

"Hey, it's not like we're gonna crash or something, just 'cause it's March 23rd," assured Jim. "We'll be fine. Trust me!"

# 3. Weekend at Ocean Bay

Now that Ruby was no longer residing in the fifth-floor dormitory room, there seemed to be no one to boss everyone around anymore, or to tell them when to turn off the lights each night. Karlin and Carolyn subsequently spent many evenings studying into the wee hours of the morning.

Finally, frustrated with the constant interruption in their sleep, their roommates Sarah and Rachel confronted them.

"Hey, you two," acknowledged Rachel as she approached them one evening. "It's almost midnight."

"So?" Karlin shrugged her shoulders. "Go to bed."

"Well, it's kind of hard to do with you two constantly staying up so late," complained Rachel.

"Exactly," agreed Sarah as she joined them on the north side of the large dormitory room. "Some of us would like to get some rest around here. I was actually dozing off in my history class yesterday, and all because the two of you kept me up half the night before!"

"Well, cry me a river!" retorted Karlin, somewhat defiantly.

"Just because Ruby's not here anymore to try to help you get the sleep you need each night," explained Sarah, "doesn't mean you can just keep the rest of us up whenever you please."

"But, we haven't made a sound!" argued Carolyn. "And these tiny little desk lamps are hardly enough to even light up a closet!"

"They're brighter than you realize," responded Rachel in her southern farm-girl accent.

"Perhaps we can hang up a divider?" suggested Carolyn.

"We ain't hanging up any divider," interjected Karlin. "Everyone knows that study hall ends at eight each night, and dorm curfew is at nine! How else are we supposed to get all our homework finished each day?"

"Perhaps you two might consider using more of your free time more wisely," recommended Sarah. "Every day after class, you come up here with Eula and practice your dancing, if that's what you call it!"

"Then that would mean that you are not over in study hall making good use of your time, or you wouldn't be aware of that!" pointed out Karlin rather snidely.

"I go down to study hall all the time," differed Sarah. "You certainly don't think I could be majoring in chemistry with a minor in biology and still manage to get all my homework done up here in this noisy place!"

"Now there's a riveting social life," scoffed Karlin.

"Is that all you two think about?" Rachel came to Sarah's defense.

Sarah was extremely pale, thin and frail looking, while Rachel was a well-tanned, robust southern girl and capable of holding her own. In fact, she was in Eula King's advanced physical education class where they were currently studying jujitsu.

"At least we're not a couple of boring dweebs," rebutted Karlin.

"You know what?" fumed Rachel.

"What?" answered Karlin.

"Perhaps Dean Forrest might like to know what's been going on up here," threatened Rachel.

"Yeah!" agreed Sarah.

"Then perhaps she might also like to know how YOU ditched out of PE class just to study for your history exam the other day," reminded Karlin with a triumphant smile. "And, Eula will be able to confirm that. She was up here with us and saw you!"

"She wouldn't?" tested Rachel.

"Would," smirked Karlin with an even gaze.

"And you!" Karlin turned to Sarah. "You knew about it and said nothing!"

"Aiding and abetting a crime," Carolyn chimed in with a smile of amusement on her face.

"That's right," sniggered Karlin. "What do you think Dean Forrest might have to say about that?"

"That's blackmail!" snapped Sarah, who normally was mild-mannered and soft-spoken.

"Yes, it is," beamed Karlin triumphantly.

"Well, now that we all understand one another," added Carolyn, "I really need to get back to my Advanced Bookkeeping assignment."

"You just wait!" threatened Rachel as she stormed back over to the south side of the large dormitory area, climbed back into bed, and pulled the covers up over her head.

"With baited breath!" called Karlin.

Sarah merely turned and went back to her bed without further comment. Clearly, things had come to a definite head between the north and the south sides of the fifth-floor dormitory room.

"You'd think they would be able to put all of this onto a computer or something," mumbled Carolyn when it was finally one o'clock in the morning. "Just look at this!"

"That's insane," agreed Karlin, who was struggling to complete a paper for her English Literature class. "At least I have only one book for this class. Why are there so many books for your class, anyway?"

"Well, there are the debit book, the credit book, the accounts payable book, the accounts receivable book, the client book with tabbed subsections for each of seventeen different fictitious corporations, as well as the tax withholding section for each of them," described Carolyn. "In fact, we're not even allowed to use a calculator. That's considered cheating."

"How would they even know?" questioned Karlin.

"Because there's also a calculation book, where you write down all the number calculations you've made," added Carolyn. "And, it all must be done by hand with a number two pencil. That has to be turned in with it, as well."

"They look at that, too?" Karlin was astonished.

"Indeed they do," corroborated Carolyn. "And, the books must all balance by the end of the semester, in order to pass the class."

"That's stupid!" opined Karlin. "I'm sure glad I didn't sign up for that class!"

"Well, it was the only class left that fit into my secretarial course that would meet my math requirement," explained Carolyn with less enthusiasm than one might have before an appendectomy.

"Someday they will have all of this stuff computerized," predicted Karlin. "Just wait and see!"

"Well, that will be then," responded Carolyn with a deep sigh of frustration. "This is now. And at this rate, I'm going to be up all night!"

"Hey, you just stay up as late as you like," replied Karlin. "But, you probably do need to get *some* sleep before morning."

"That's the most sensible thing I've ever heard you say!" commented Rachel from the other side of the room.

"Amen!" agreed Sarah.

"Oh, heck, I'm not staying up any later for this!" Carolyn finally decided. "This is just too much to ask of anyone."

"Perhaps it'll look less ominous in the morning?" opined Sarah.

"I sure hope so," wished Carolyn as she shut out the light and then walked over to the large window on her side of the room. Tired though she was, sleep just would not come. What if she did fail her Advanced Bookkeeping class because she couldn't get all the books to balance? And why was there always so much homework?

Carolyn gazed absentmindedly at the campus below and then at the roof of the fourth floor immediately below them. The roof stretched across a total of fifteen sets of other rooms that were housed in the east wing of the fourth floor, with a hallway down the middle. Fifteen more sets of rooms with a hallway down the middle of them were located on the west wing, though not visible from the fifth-floor dormitory room due to there being no windows on the west side of the room where its closets were located.

"There is a set of fire escape stairs at the far end," Karlin whispered to Carolyn, startling her momentarily. "It leads all the way down to ground level."

"I thought you were asleep," grinned Carolyn.

"Not yet," replied Karlin. "You know, that might be a way back inside sometime, if we ever happen to miss the nine o'clock curfew."

"What about them?" Carolyn nodded toward Rachel and Sarah's side of the room.

"Then we make good on our promise and go to Dean Forrest about Rachel ditching class that day," reminded Karlin. "We got 'em where we want 'em. No worries."

"What if the Dean does send someone to do one of those impromptu room checks that she sometimes does, just to make sure that everyone is here?" questioned Carolyn.

Karlin then quietly tiptoed over to her bed, grabbed her coat, and neatly tucked it under the covers, making it look like someone was there. She then grabbed a brunette wig from a drawer in her makeup table and carefully placed it on the pillow. "What do you think?"

"Wow!" marveled Carolyn in a whispered voice. "You'd never know it wasn't you."

Karlin then reached for yet another small drawer in her makeup table, stealthily slid it open, and pulled out a dishwater blonde wig that she handed to Carolyn. "Just your color."

Carolyn then held the wig up to her head and tried to see in the mirror how well it matched her hair, but in the deep shadows it was hard to tell.

"Always be prepared," grinned Karlin. "Just in case. They'll never know the difference. Trust me!"

"I don't know," objected Carolyn. "We could get into terrible trouble for something like that."

"Only if we're found out, and they're sure not gonna tell," persisted Karlin.

"Well, let's just hope we never have the opportunity to test that theory!" responded Carolyn.


Proud of his Industrial Education Department, Professor Ronald Krain was pleased to learn that one of Mrs. Ritter's more accomplished secretarial students would be working as his new secretary, taking shorthand. Writing letters by hand had become cumbersome for him, not to mention processing timecards, student grades and purchase orders for items used by the various branches of his department.

Born in 1910 in Houston, Texas, Ronald Krain was 64 years old and just one year from retirement. He had begun his stint with the Industrial Education Department eighteen years ago, when he was 46 years of age. That was in 1956, the same year he had joined an organization called The Crusading Knights of Powell Mountain.

Professor Krain had been raised on his father's cattle ranch, where he had learned a variety of industrial education skills. His first assignment in the Industrial Education Department at Powell Mountain University had been as its woodworking professor. His extensive knowledge of not just woodworking, but also welding, automotive repair and architectural planning made him the perfect choice to become head of the entire department when his predecessor finally retired in 1961. Since that time, Ronald Krain had been sure to exclusively hire fellow Crusading Knights to fill each of the other teaching positions under his domain. Interestingly, each of their last names began with a K. Willy Kox, Jim Kraven and Fred Kollins were the three Ks that he had personally hired thus far to teach automotive, welding and woodworking, respectively. Al Sandut, who taught both architectural and life drawing, however, was not a member of The Crusading Knights of Powell Mountain and his cultural heritage was somewhat of a concern to his cohorts.

"Ms. Bennett?" greeted Professor Krain when he saw her. Pleased by her long, golden blonde hair, pale complexion and green eyes, he greeted her with a pleasant smile. "I'm Ronald Krain, Head Professor of the Industrial Education Department. You can just call me Mr. Krain, though."

"Pleased to meet you, sir," nodded Carolyn as she studied her new boss.

Mr. Krain was just over six feet fall, with a medium build, slightly stooped shoulders, and graying red hair. Like Carolyn's father, Mr. Krain was a believer in using greasy men's hair tonic, and lots of it. He did not appear to wear glasses, but his big ears and long pointy noise with large nostrils reminded Carolyn somewhat of a scarecrow.

"You look like you might have some French in you?" quizzed Professor Krain.

"Actually, yes," confirmed Carolyn. "Bennett is a French name, but I'm also Swedish, Irish, Welsh and Cherokee."

"Well, we won't hold that last one against you," laughed the Professor. "Krain is French, too, by the way."

"I see," nodded Carolyn, politely. She was actually quite proud of her Cherokee heritage and not quite sure she appreciated Mr. Krain's last remark, though she held her silence about it.

"That will be your desk over there," indicated her new boss. "You will be my receptionist, answer the phone, greet visitors, take letters, and eventually process timecards, student grades and purchase orders for items used by the various branches of this department."

"Where's the timeclock?" asked Carolyn.

"Oh, we don't need one of those around here," replied Mr. Krain. "Just keep track of your time on a piece of paper and give it to the receptionist at the end of the week to process. That would be you." Mr. Krain then laughed at his own joke, much too heartily for Carolyn's liking. Overall, Mr. Krain was a loud, irritating man with a rather superior impression of himself.

"Hey, Ronald, who's this?" questioned another similar-looking man as he entered the small office. Except for the fact that he wore large wire-rimmed glasses, his overall physical description was nearly identical to that of his cohort.

"Jim, how are you?" greeted Mr. Krain. "Carolyn, I'd like you to meet Professor Jim Kraven, our welding professor here."

"Pleased to meet you, sir," acknowledged Carolyn as she extended her hand to him.

"You can just call me Professor Kraven," chuckled the man as he shook Carolyn's hand. "Good choice," he added with a meaningful glance at Mr. Krain. "A beautiful, fare-complexioned damsel like yourself is always a welcome sight here in the Industrial Education Department at Powell Mountain University, especially amongst a crusty old group of aging codgers like us."

Both men then laughed. Carolyn forced a smile but failed to see the humor in Professor Kraven's remark. Working with a crusty old bunch of aging codgers like them was the last place she wanted to be!

Carolyn was then taken on a tour of the entire building by Professor Krain. Professor Willy Kox from the automotive department was about ten years younger than the other two men, slightly friendlier, but otherwise resembled them in every noticeable way.

Professor Al Sandut, who taught both architectural and life drawing, was actually rather tall and good looking. His exotic accent had been acquired in his native country of India, though his English was excellent. Carolyn could not help but notice that Professor Krain did not treat him with the same amount of respect and conviviality with which he had treated Professors Kraven or Kox.

Finally, Carolyn was taken to the woodworking shop where she was introduced to Professor Fred Kollins. Like Professors Krain, Kox and Kraven, he wore a small white lapel pin on his shirt collar that was shaped like a knight riding on a horse and holding a sword.

"What are those lapel pins you all have on?" asked Carolyn.

"All of us except Professor Sandut," corrected Mr. Krain with a meaningful raising of one eyebrow.

"Should we tell her?" worried Professor Kollins as he glanced at Professor Krain.

"Why not," Mr. Krain shrugged his shoulders. "I think we can trust her. We can trust you, can't we?"

"Of course," replied Carolyn.

"What we are about to reveal to you is to be kept confidential and you must tell absolutely no one," directed her new boss. He apparently had no qualms about sharing sensitive information with his new secretary.

"Absolutely no one," repeated Carolyn, though she was actually quite concerned about being placed in such a position.

"Very well," proceeded Professor Krain. "We are all Crusading Knights of the Powell Mountain Order."

Though shocked by the revelation, Carolyn suddenly understood why Professor Sandut had been treated differently and was not wearing one of the small white lapel pins on his shirt collar like the other professors were. She merely nodded with understanding, forced a smile, and hoped fervently that her new boss would not be able to detect her disapproval.

"Excellent!" approved Professor Krain. "Now that that's out of the way, let's get you situated. You'll be working each day from the time your last class gets out until dinner time, whenever you decide that should be."

"Sometimes my last classes end at different times," advised Carolyn, rather nervously.

"I'm well aware of that," smiled Professor Krain. "There really is no set time you need to be here. The main thing is that you do come in each day for a couple of hours or so, and somehow manage to finish up whatever work we have for you. Think you can do that?"

"I'll do my best, sir," promised Carolyn.

"We'll start by having you take a letter," decided Mr. Krain.

"Take it where?" asked Carolyn, not realizing at first that he intended to dictate a letter while she took down what he said in shorthand, later to be transcribed at her leisure.

"Take it where?" howled Professor Krain as he slapped his knee. "That's a good one!"

"Oh, you want me to take down a letter in shorthand?" Carolyn finally comprehended and then smiled.

"I like you. You're hired," grinned her new boss. "And, I hope you'll accept my apology that we weren't able to get you started over here until now, but my wife and I were on an extended holiday over in Texas. Kind of a clan gathering of sorts, if you get my meaning."

"I see," nodded Carolyn. "Though, it is too bad that I've had to miss out on two weeks of work already."

"Here," offered Professor Krain as he opened his wallet and handed Carolyn a twenty-dollar bill. "This should hold you over."

"Wow, thanks!" beamed Carolyn. "I'll pay it back."

"Nonsense," differed the Professor. "Consider it a gift. It's the least I can do. And who knows, perhaps your first paycheck might not even be for that much."

Carolyn then smiled and nodded with gratitude, but inside she had inexpressible concerns about her new boss and was deeply troubled by his affiliation with the Crusading Knights organization.

Karlin and Carolyn had gone down to Eula and Stacia's room for a visit, and to listen to some Aretha Franklin albums on Eula's new turntable. Not only had Eula managed to teach Carolyn to dance during the past two weeks, but was now determined to teach her to sing.

"You got talent, girl!" informed Eula.

"I never have been able to sing very well," differed Carolyn.

"Nonsense," persisted Eula. "Can you get off work early today? That's kind of too bad that you don't have your afternoons free anymore."

"But, at least now I can start saving up to try to get a car," reminded Carolyn. "It's a forty-five-minute drive down to St. Diablo."

"Nevertheless, they are having tryouts for the upcoming talent show, and you need to be there!" insisted Eula. "You can sing that new song we've been working on!"

"The contestants will be performing for the entire school!" objected Carolyn. "I can't do something like that!"

"You can and you will," replied Eula. "We can sing a duet. I'll be singing with you! In fact, Karlin should sing, too. The three of us would be dynamite together."

"Perhaps we can just stop by and see where you work on the way to dinner tonight?" proposed Karlin.

"There's some guy named John that's in the last period auto class," explained Eula. "She's just hoping to see him there!"

"Can you blame me?" grinned Karlin. "Plus, he says he might have a line on how we can get a car for only a hundred bucks."

"Hey, that's not a bad idea," recognized Eula. "We could all pitch in on it."

"There's something you should know," Carolyn suddenly said as she became serious.

"What is it?" queried Karlin.

"You can't mention this to anyone," qualified Carolyn. "My boss told me that I couldn't say a thing about it, but I don't think it would be a very good idea for either of you to come over there."

"That old codger isn't trying to pull some hanky-panky on you, is he?" demanded Eula.

"No, it's nothing like that," assured Carolyn. "In fact, he even felt so bad about delaying my job until now that he gave me twenty bucks today."

"You're kidding?" Eula was surprised. "I just wonder what that's gonna cost ya?"

"Nothing," assured Carolyn. "He said it's a gift, and was the least he could do after preventing me from working until now."

"Humph," mumbled Eula, unconvinced.

"We're not gonna say anything!" promised Karlin.

"Okay, mum's the word," agreed Eula.

Stacia had been silent until now but finally nodded. Being from the Dominican Republic, Stacia McFerson was dark complexioned with straight black hair that she wore parted in the middle and combed into a shoulder-length pageboy style. Her out-of-date clothing was allegedly the result of an overly strict home life and limited finances. Still, Eula had already begun teaching Stacia how to apply makeup and given her more attractive clothes to wear. In fact, Stacia had not even known how to dance until joining Eula, Karlin and Carolyn for one of their regular dance sessions during the past two weeks and quickly realized how much she loved it.

"Very well," responded Carolyn. "The professors over there are all members of the Crusading Knights of Powell Mountain."

"You're kidding!" exclaimed Karlin.

"All of them?" grilled Eula with a frown.

"All except Professor Sandut," clarified Carolyn.

"That would make sense," nodded Eula. She was well aware of the tall, dark, handsome art professor and actually had a crush on him. In fact, Life Drawing was one of her elective courses that she had needed to drop because of insufficient time for it.

88

"Are you sure about this?" questioned Karlin.

"They proudly *told* me they are all Crusading Knights," revealed Carolyn. "And they all wear those little white lapel pins on their collars that are of a knight riding a horse, holding a sword."

"That's horrible!" exclaimed Karlin.

"Sounds like they're the real deal," recognized Eula. "You probably shouldn't have accepted his money like that."

"Well, I'm sure not gonna give it back!" advised Carolyn.

"Excuse me," interrupted Stacia, "but just who are the Crusading Knights? I've never even heard of them."

"They are a white supremacist group who believes that other races should be eradicated from the face of the earth!" explained Eula.

"Like the Nazis?" Stacia was horrified.

"Kind of like that," replied Eula.

"I can sure tell they don't like Professor Sandut very much," added Carolyn. "They certainly don't treat him the same way they treat each other. And he's the only professor over there that isn't wearing one of those little white knight pins on his lapel."

"I'll just bet!" fumed Eula. "That cinches it! Karlin and I definitely will be stopping by to visit you over there! And, hopefully some of those old creeps will be around to see it when we do!"

"What if they don't want Carolyn to work there anymore after that?" pointed out Karlin.

"In that case, I wouldn't *want* to work there!" advised Carolyn. "In fact, all three of you should definitely stop by tomorrow, about four o'clock. Professor Krain usually never leaves until five."

"It's a date," grinned Eula.


Back in Ashton, Mr. Bennett had just come inside from watering his expansive back yard. "It must be a hundred degrees out there!"

"Good thing we decided to get that swamp cooler last summer," remarked his wife as she hurried to get him a glass of freshly squeezed lemonade.

"Was there any mail today?" questioned Mr. Bennett as he sat in his recliner, put his feet up and reached for the television remote.

"There was a letter from Carolyn," responded his wife as she hurried to the living room where he was seated and handed him the glass of lemonade.

"How's she doing, anyway?" asked Mr. Bennett as he put the glass to his lips and took a long cool drink.

"Carolyn apparently plans to pitch in with two other girls to buy some old car so they can have a way to get to town when they want to," informed Mrs. Bennett.

"What!" exclaimed Mr. Bennett, rather angrily. "Why would they need to go to town? Everything they need is right there on that campus! There's even a grocery store there! Not to mention her little green food card with no limit on it at that cafeteria!"

"Calm down, sweetheart," entreated his wife. "Right now they're just thinking about it. I don't think she's actually invested in it yet. But, perhaps you should give her a call."

"I knew sending her there was a mistake!" fumed Carolyn's father. "I don't know why I let you talk me into this!"

"Perhaps you should calm down first before you call her, though," added his wife. "Maybe we should just go ahead and get her a decent car. It doesn't have to be a really expensive one, but at least then she won't spend what little money she has on some old piece of junk that could end up costing her even more in the long run."

"I don't know," hesitated Mr. Bennett. "It might be a good lesson for her."

"What if she does get stranded alongside that road and the Powell Mountain Killer happens along?" questioned his wife. "How would you feel then?"

Mr. Bennett sighed deeply and pursed his lips as he considered his wife's suggestion. "I hate to admit it, but you may be right."

"Oh, thank you!" beamed Carolyn's mother as she bent down to give her husband a hug.

"Yeah, yeah!" acknowledged Mr. Bennett as he gently pushed her away. "You're gonna make me spill my lemonade."

"Sorry!" grinned Carolyn's mother. She was very excited and could not wait for Carolyn to learn the good news. Unknown to her husband, she had spoken with Carolyn on the phone earlier that same afternoon and had promised to do her best to persuade Mr. Bennett of the merits of such an investment.

Up on the fifth floor of the girls' dormitory at Powell Mountain University, a quick, rapid knock could be heard at the door.

90

"Who is it?" questioned Carolyn, suddenly concerned that she and her friends might get caught dancing to disco music in their room.

Even though nothing was really wrong with dancing or with disco music per se, the combination of them together was greatly frowned upon by those in charge at Powell Mountain University. In fact, disco dancing was considered to be on a par with smoking, drugs or alcohol by many of the other students, as well. And, while not specifically mentioned in the student handbook, disco dancing was generally thought of as worldly and undesirable and likely to promote inappropriate social behavior by those who participated in it.

"Here," offered Karlin. "Just toss a blanket over that pile of record albums. Nobody will know what it is. They'll just think it's a pile of dirty laundry or something."

"It could be Stacia," chuckled Eula. "Hey, we're not really doing anything wrong!"

"Technically true," agreed Carolyn, "but let's just not take any chances, shall we?"

After the three girls quickly hid the stack of disco albums and turned off Eula's turntable – which was now kept on the fifth floor beneath Karlin's "makeup table" – Karlin started across the large room to answer the door.

"Your headphones!" warned Carolyn.

"Oh yeah, thanks," grinned Karlin as she quickly took off her headphones, rolled up the cord, and secreted them under the blanket with the record albums.

As an added precaution, those listening to disco music on the fifth floor had taken to wearing headphones attached by long cords to the turntable, so that the music would not be heard elsewhere. While there were only two headphone jacks available on Eula's turntable, that was enough for at least two of them to plug in headphones and listen simultaneously. Carolyn's headphone cord was fifty feet long and much resembled a curly black phone cord.

Karlin hurried over to open the door.

"There's a phone call for Carolyn," informed a rather curt young woman from the front desk below. She clearly was displeased at having to climb so many flights of stairs, just to announce a phone call, and then been made to wait. "Hopefully, they won't hang up before you can get there. That has happened before, you know."

"Thanks!" beamed Carolyn as she hurried past her and began racing downstairs.

"Slow down! You're gonna end up falling and breaking your neck!" called the Dean's assistant.

Ignoring the precaution, Carolyn speedily made her way to the first floor. The three antique-looking rotary-dial wall phones designated for student use were separated by ornately shellacked wooden dividers. True, the dividers did provide some small measure of seclusion, but noise in the lobby and prying ears were always a concern when trying to have a private conversation. Matching wooden stools were placed by each phone, one with a slightly shorter leg that caused it to wobble. Next to the phones were the open wooden mail slots where any personal student mail would be placed each afternoon.

Quickly locating the particular phone that was off the hook, Carolyn snatched it up and said, "Hello?"

"Carolyn?" came a familiar voice at the other end. "This is your father."

"Oh, hello!" greeted Carolyn. "How are you? And how are Mom and Socky doing?"

"We're all fine," assured Mr. Bennett.

"Is everything all right?" Carolyn suddenly asked. It was not like her father just to call her out of the blue for no particular reason.

"Your mother tells me you intend to buy a car," replied Mr. Bennett. He usually got right to the point when having a conversation, and when finished, he usually just hung up without bothering to say goodbye. Such unnecessary social formalities were just not his way.

"I was hoping to," answered Carolyn.

"For how much?" quizzed her father.

"Well, my roommate, Karlin, knows a guy in automotive class who says they're getting ready to auction off the class car," described Carolyn. "It's a green Mustang."

"Just what is a class car?" pressed Mr. Bennett.

"It's the car that the automotive class is rebuilding as their class project," answered Carolyn. "And, just as soon as they are finished with it, it will be sold at auction for a hundred bucks."

"So, it could end up costing you even more than that?" assumed Mr. Bennett.

"There's a two-hundred-dollar ceiling on what they will charge, though," clarified Carolyn. "And, my friends Eula and Karlin both want to go in on it with me."

"Meaning that it would belong to all three of you?" sniggered Mr. Bennett with amusement.

"Yes," confirmed Carolyn, rather uncomfortably.

"Just where did this car come from?" interrogated Mr. Bennett. "For all you know, it might have been in a head-on collision."

"Not this car," assured Carolyn. "It came from Woody's Salvage Yard. And, the proceeds from the sale will then be used to buy the next class project."

"Another old junker from the woodcutter's salvage yard?" disapproved Mr. Bennett.

"Actually, yes. And he delivers auto parts, too," revealed Carolyn. She decided against mentioning to her father that she had seen an invoice from Woody's Salvage Yard the previous day where she worked, for a delivery he had made to the automotive class.

"Have you checked to see what the upkeep and maintenance on it will be?" grilled Mr. Bennett.

"No, not yet," admitted Carolyn.

"What about insurance?" reminded Mr. Bennett, rather smugly. "It is against the law to drive without it."

"Actually, I was hoping you could just add the car to your policy," explained Carolyn. "I was going to ask you about it. And, you already have me on there as a driver, anyway."

After an awkward silence, Mr. Bennett responded, "No, absolutely not. If you are financially able to have your own car, then you will need to get your own insurance."

"But ...," began Carolyn.

"Did you tell her?" interrupted Mrs. Bennett as she picked up the extension line to join in the conversation.

"Not yet," replied Carolyn's father.

"Tell me what?" questioned Carolyn.

"We've decided to help you out," informed Mrs. Bennett.

Irritated at his wife for imposing herself upon the conversation, Mr. Bennett merely hung up the phone. It would now be up to his wife to fill Carolyn in on the good news.

"Dad, are you still there?" asked Carolyn.

"I think he might have hung up already," apologized Mrs. Bennett. "But, he did say we could go ahead and get a second car that you will be able to use while you're up there."

"Really?" beamed Carolyn. "That's great! It sure didn't sound like that when I was talking to him just now."

"Well, you know how your father is," reminded her mother. "I think he was just getting ready to tell you about it, though."

"I can't tell you how much this means to me," said Carolyn.

"Just don't get too used to it. Once school's out, I'll be using it here to get to work in after that," explained Carolyn's mother.

Up until 1974, the Bennett family had been a one-car family, so getting a second vehicle was definitely a big deal.

"And he's okay with that?" confirmed Carolyn.

"Absolutely!" assured Carolyn's mother. "The last thing we want is to see you stranded by some old junker and then have the Powell Mountain Killer happen along!"

"Oh, thank you!" replied Carolyn. She could hardly wait to tell Karlin, Eula and Stacia about it.

"Anyway, we will be driving up this weekend with both cars, and then will leave the new one with you," described Mrs. Bennett.

"What kind of car is it?" pressed Carolyn excitedly.

"It's a 1974 green Ford Mustang," responded her mother.

"That's incredible!" marveled Carolyn. "That's the same kind of car they will be auctioning off from the automotive class."

"But, this one will be brand new," reminded Mrs. Bennett proudly. "In fact, the salesman told us that the new hatchback model will be a classic. They just came out with it this year."

"Hatchback?" repeated Carolyn, to be sure she had heard correctly. "Like a Pinto?"

"Yes, like that!" verified her mother.

"Well, I think the one from the automotive class might be a couple years old, then," realized Carolyn. "It's definitely not a hatchback."

"We love you so much, Carolyn, and are so proud of you," added her mother. "And, we want you to be safe."

"I love you, too," responded Carolyn. "And, I can't wait to see you this weekend!"

Several weeks had passed since the new green Ford Mustang had found a home with Carolyn at Powell Mountain University. Sadly, between classes, work and homework assignments, it had yet to be driven all the way down the mountain and into town. The extent of its road life included trips to the campus market and weekend daytrips over to Powell Lake for the afternoon. Worse still, the twenty dollars that had been given to Carolyn by Professor Krain had been needed to pay for an assigned parking space, and covered only the first four months.

"I can't believe they charge you five dollars each month for parking!" marveled Karlin. "That's practically highway robbery!"

"How much does Ruby pay for her spot?" questioned Carolyn. "I thought she told me it was just 'a couple of dollars' each month."

"I'm pretty sure it's the same as you," responded Karlin. "But, it's still highway robbery!"

"Hey, you two!" greeted Eula as she entered the fifth-floor dormitory room after two short knocks. "You got mail, girl!"

"For me?" questioned Carolyn as she watched her friend Eula toss an envelope onto her small desk. "Not that I don't miss them, but my parents are the only ones who ever write."

"Not this time, honey," smirked Eula as she sat down on Carolyn's bed. "Who's Susan Rives, anyway?"

"Isn't that your roommate from high school, back at Oceanview Academy?" recalled Karlin as she came over and sat down beside Eula. "I wonder what she's up to these days, anyway?"

Carolyn hurried to open the envelope. "She wants me to come down this next weekend, and to bring along a couple of my friends!"

Eula and Karlin gave one another a "high five" hand greeting at that point before Eula asked, "What about Stacia? She definitely has to come!"

"And now that you have a car," pointed out Karlin with a sly smile, "we're golden!"

"Wait a minute," interjected Carolyn. "What about Rachel and Sarah? There's absolutely no way they'll agree to cover for us for an entire weekend. Not only that, it's Thanksgiving weekend."

"I have no plans to go home for Thanksgiving," declared Karlin.

"Actually, I was just planning to stay here, too," admitted Carolyn. "There's no way my family can afford for me to come all the way home now, especially after buying the car."

"Then we're in luck," grinned Eula. "I wasn't going home, either. You just leave Rachel and Sarah to me."

"What do you have in mind?" quizzed Carolyn.

"Oh, ye of little faith," chided Eula. "I got this covered! We're gonna have the time of our lives this next weekend!"

"This next weekend?" repeated Stacia as she entered the room, anxious and ready to practice more disco dancing. "What happens this next weekend?"

"We're goin' to Ocean Bay," informed Eula in sing-song voice as she got up and did a little happy dance.

"Look at you, girl!" commented Stacia as she got up and walked over to Eula's *not-so-secret-anymore* turntable. "Sounds like we better do some practicin'!"

"Aren't you going home for Thanksgiving, either?" questioned Carolyn.

"My family's back in the Dominican Republic, and the next time I get to see them will be next summer," advised Stacia.

"I wonder just how far it is from here to Ocean Bay, anyway?" mused Carolyn

"Well, it's about forty-five minutes from here to St. Diablo," reminded Karlin. "And probably at least two more hours from there down to Ocean Bay."

"More like three hours to Ocean Bay from St. Diablo," advised Eula as she placed an LP record album on her turntable.

Long playing vinyl record albums - nicknamed the LP - were recorded in an analog microgroove format and would revolve on a turntable at a speed of $33\frac{1}{3}$ revolutions per minute when played.

"Hold it!" commanded Carolyn. "Almost four hours there and then back again? That's almost eight hours of drive time, plus driving around once we get there! And gas just went up this last year. It was 38¢ a gallon when we got here and now it's over 55¢ a gallon!"

"You know who you sound like?" laughed Eula as she pulled a twenty-dollar bill from her purse and laid it on Carolyn's desk.

"If she'll take Professor Krain's money, I'm sure she'll take ours," smirked Karlin as she, too, opened her purse. "All I've got right now is a ten, but I'm good for the rest on payday."

96

"What's your gas mileage on that thing?" quizzed Eula with a raised eyebrow.

"Well, it's supposed to get 15 miles per gallon," answered Carolyn, "but I've never gotten more than 12 out of it."

"Twelve miles per gallon is pretty good," commented Stacia. "My dad's station wagon only gets eight miles per gallon."

"That's nothing to brag about," chuckled Eula. "Anyway, if there's not enough there, I'll have more cash with me. Don't you see? This is the perfect opportunity for you ladies to practice your dancing at a REAL discotheque!"

"I hear they do have some pretty amazing discotheques down in Ocean Bay," agreed Karlin.

"I'm totally broke, but if you'll have me anyway, I'm definitely in," informed Stacia rather excitedly.

"I gotcha covered," assured Eula with a mischievous grin. "Good, it's all settled then. We're goin' to Ocean Bay!"


Located just three hours south of St. Diablo, the huge metropolis of Ocean Bay had a population approaching 700,000 people in 1974. Built around a natural harbor section of the coastline, Ocean Bay was home port to many sailing ships, yachts, barges and oceangoing vessels. Shops and merchants of every kind could be seen along its bustling docks and busy piers. In fact, it had nearly doubled in size since Carolyn's last visit only two years prior.

Sprawled between Ocean Bay and St. Diablo were countless acres of grapes. Several of the more renowned wineries in the area offered guided tours complete with barrel sampling in romantic caves, and catered lunches among the vineyards of their lavish estates. Despite the urging of her friends, Carolyn did not stop until reaching the outskirts of Ocean Bay and then only long enough to use the restroom and refuel her car.

Bright red trolley cars filled with people were expertly guided by an overhead cable support system down various tracks in the center of Ocean Bay's busiest streets. The clanging sound of trolley bells announced each passenger stop.

"Wow! Just look at this place!" marveled Stacia from the backseat of Carolyn's new green Mustang.

Stacia gaped with amazement at the variety of towering skyscrapers, the busy traffic and the never-ending horde of pedestrians dashing all at once in every direction imaginable.

"Is it always this busy?" Stacia finally asked. "I'd heard that this was one of those cities that never sleeps, but I never dreamed it would be like this!"

"I've been here a time or two," grinned Eula.

"You're *from* here!" reminded Karlin with a smile on her face.

"Really?" Carolyn was surprised. "I thought you both went to Hillview Academy together?"

"We did," replied Karlin. "And, we went to Ocean Bay High together before that. I'm from here, too."

After a moment of silence as she drove through the busy city, Carolyn finally asked, "Did either of you happen to know a guy named Lenny Owens?"

Eula, who was in the front passenger seat, turned back to exchange a look of consultation with Karlin, who was seated directly behind Carolyn on the driver's side.

"You did!" realized Carolyn as she gave Eula a sidelong glance. "How come you didn't say anything when I mentioned him before?"

"Calm yourself, girl!" cautioned Eula. "Keep your eyes on the road, and make a left at that next light."

"When was the last time you saw him?" pressed Carolyn as she slowed down for the turn.

"We were in the tenth grade together, at Ocean Bay High," informed Eula matter-of-factly.

"It was not in the best of neighborhoods, either," added Karlin.

"The whole city looks dangerous," opined Stacia.

"Susan tells me there's at least one or two murders in the park by her house each week," recalled Carolyn with trepidation.

"Relax," responded Eula. "There's safety in numbers. Besides, we've got her address right here."

"My yearbook!" recognized Carolyn from her peripheral vision.

"Yeah, for the address," explained Eula as she began to glance through the yearbook and paused on the page with Lenny's picture when she noticed his lengthy handwritten note on it. "You sure did know Lenny, didn't you?"

"Give me that!" demanded Carolyn, nearly driving onto the curb as she reached for the precious book.

"Hey, relax!" chided Eula. "What's wrong with you? Are you trying to get us all killed?"

"I'm sorry, but what Lenny wrote in my yearbook is private," snapped Carolyn as she pulled over, came to a stop, and grabbed her yearbook.

"Sounds like you had it pretty bad for him," recognized Eula.

"So, did either of you actually know him?" pressed Carolyn, as she turned off the engine and turned to face her friends. "We're not goin' anywhere until you tell me."

"Carolyn did mention Lenny earlier, the day we all first met!" reminded Karlin. "It was when we were down in your room, and Carolyn and I were talking about two ships passing in the night."

"Oh, not that again! Okay, yeah. I know who Lenny was," answered Eula, "but never had the chance to talk to him. The guy was always busy studying, no time for anything else, no social life at all."

"He did play basketball, though," remembered Karlin. "That was the only time anyone ever saw him with his nose outside a book. I never had a chance to talk to him, either, but oh, if only I had!"

"He looked mighty fine in that yearbook photo," apprised Stacia with a mischievous grin. She had managed to lean forward in time to get a glimpse of the photo of Lenny, while the yearbook had still been open to that page on Eula's lap – before Carolyn snatched it away.

"Yes, he was," agreed Carolyn, rather distantly.

"And you let that fella go?" chastised Eula. "Shame on you!"

"It's complicated," replied Carolyn as she slowly handed the closed yearbook back to Eula, started the car up again, and pulled back onto the road. "Turned out, his parents were even more prejudiced than mine, especially his dad."

"You *let* your families keep you apart?" quizzed Karlin. "You know, my dad was prejudiced, too, except Kyle was a white guy and my dad is an old-school Mexican."

"Kyle Monagan?" recalled Carolyn. "Isn't he the guy that was always studying for his chemistry class while you were busy studying for your English Literature class, just like those two ships passing in the night?"

"That was him," confirmed Karlin, impressed that Carolyn had remembered his last name.

"Well, Lenny Owens was the guy I was crazy about at Oceanview who was always busy studying for his chemistry class while I was over in my room studying for my English Literature class."

"Oh, brother!" Eula rolled her eyes. "You two aren't going to recite that 'ships passing in the night' thing again are you?"

"Humph!" snorted Karlin.

"Sounds romantic," sighed Stacia.

"Well, Kyle and I both defied our parents' wishes and were planning to run away and elope," explained Karlin. "He was killed that very night, on his way over to get me, when his motorcycle went off the road and crashed into a tree!"

An awkward silence pervaded the vehicle for several moments as Carolyn drove along in silence. Only the sound of Karlin sniffing and blowing her nose could be heard.

"So, what did happen with you and Lenny, anyway?" Eula suddenly asked.

"Lenny had promised his mother on her deathbed that he would go to medical school and become a doctor," described Carolyn. "It was his dad who threatened to pull the plug on his studies at Oceanview if he dared to continue seeing 'that white girl.'"

"You?" Eula was stunned. "Just how serious was it?"

"Lenny told me that when he finished medical school someday, he hoped our paths would cross again," answered Carolyn as a tear escaped the corner of one eye and began to roll down her cheek. "That was the day he kissed me goodbye, but it was just on the cheek because his dad was watching."

"That's just lame!" opined Eula. "Has he tried to contact you?"

"I'm not sure," replied Carolyn rather sadly.

"Excuse me?" sniggered Eula. "You're not sure?"

"I think he may have tried to write to me," added Carolyn.

"And what, your dad intercepted his letter?" questioned Eula.

"My dad actually did intercept two of Susan's letters," related Carolyn. "I found them in his desk drawer one afternoon when I was looking for a paperclip."

"You're kidding?" interjected Karlin.

"That's not right," agreed Stacia.

"Now, that's lame!" commented Eula as she shook her head.

"So, who knows," added Carolyn rather sadly as she shrugged her shoulders.

"Then Lenny very well could have tried to write to her," guessed Karlin. "That really is like two ships passing in the night. Hey, maybe while we're here we should stop by and look him up?"

"And risk having his dad pull the plug on Lenny's medical school?" rebutted Carolyn. "No way!"

"She really does care about him," recognized Stacia.

"Sounds like love to me," assessed Eula with a knowing smile.

"You *did* read what he wrote, didn't you?" accused Carolyn as she slowed to a stop for a yellow light.

"You'll want to turn right at the next corner," advised Eula. "Susan's house should be just a few blocks up from there."

Carolyn suddenly noticed a peculiar looking church that she and Susan had fled to for safety two years earlier while visiting Susan's parents for the weekend. The entire three-story structure was painted bright red with black trim. Attached, but set back from it, was a Painted Lady residence that was also painted red with black trim. Small black gargoyles sat menacingly around the base of the building's tall spiraled steeples.

"That's where Susan and I went to hide the night some band roadie named Steve gave us a harrowing ride down the sidewalk on his modified golf cart," pointed out Carolyn.

"Really?" Eula was surprised.

"It had a high-powered racing engine on it, and a really loud air horn that he would sound to warn frightened pedestrians, just in time so they could leap out of the way," continued Carolyn.

"He actually drove on the sidewalk?" questioned Stacia. "Where people were walking?"

"He sure did," confirmed Carolyn. "I'll never forget the shocked and frightened looks on their faces. Or, the sidewalk tables with chairs that were bumped out of the way, too, along with several trash cans."

"Sounds like a maniac," assumed Stacia.

"Well, whatever he was, Steve certainly was not someone Susan wanted knowing where she lived," chuckled Carolyn sardonically.

"Just how did you get there?" Karlin suddenly asked.

"We walked," replied Carolyn. "At least at first. Then, when we noticed some people with dark hoods following us, we started walking faster, but then so did they."

"Hopefully it was during the day!" remarked Eula. "This is one of the most dangerous neighborhoods in the entire city."

"It was late at night," answered Carolyn.

"Did you get away from them all right?" quizzed Stacia.

"We finally broke into a run, went behind that row of Painted Ladies, right over there, climbed over the fences in each back yard, and came in through the back at Susan's house," described Carolyn.

"So they wouldn't find out exactly where you were going?" guessed Eula with a knowing nod.

Most of the homes in the meandering hillside area where the Rives family lived consisted of whimsical looking three-story homes.

"Those are called Painted Ladies," indicated Eula, for Stacia's benefit. "Even though they are all connected, each one is owned by a different family and each is painted a different color."

"That's fascinating," remarked Stacia as she studied the various color combinations used throughout the block. "Kind of reminds me of Copacabana. They use color combinations like that on their homes."

"Well, this is Susan's house here," indicated Carolyn as she pulled to a stop in front of it.

The Rives home was painted white with dark green trim, while the homes on its right side were painted pastel pink, pale green, light blue, lavender and yellow. The homes on its other side were beige, yellow, gray and mauve, respectively. Each had trim painted in a contrasting yet complimentary color for that particular house.

"I hope there's room in their garage," added Carolyn. "I'm sure not leaving my car out on the street in this neighborhood!"

"Amen to that, sister!" agreed Eula.


"Carolyn!" screamed Susan as she threw open the front door, rushed outside, and embraced her high school friend and former roommate. "Come in, all of you!"

"What about my car?" questioned Carolyn as she hugged her old friend Susan. "Is there a place I can leave it in the garage?"

102

"Carolyn!" called Susan's mother as she raced to the front entryway and gave her a crushing hug before pushing back just enough to kiss her on each cheek before repeating the process. "And these must be your new roommates?"

"I'm Karlin."

"Karlin!" exclaimed Mrs. Rives as she gave her a warm embrace and then kissed her on each cheek. "Welcome!"

"This is Stacia," introduced Eula as she took a step back, not anxious to receive one of Mrs. Rives' crushing hugs.

"I'm so pleased you could come," beamed Mrs. Rives as she hugged and embraced her before turning her attention to Eula. "And a woman of color!"

"Eula," informed Eula as she braced herself for the inevitable greeting. "Thank you for having us," added Eula as Mrs. Rives hugged her, but then stopped short of kissing her cheeks.

"Susan did not tell you?" frowned Mrs. Rives.

"Mom, they just got here," reminded Susan.

"Oh, forgive me!" apologized Susan's mother as she motioned for them to come inside and sit down before dashing to the kitchen.

"We will be spending the night at the Moranga residence," informed Susan with a mysterious smile as they all sat down.

"At the winery?" Carolyn asked.

"Here you are," indicated Mrs. Rives as she returned with a huge platter of chocolate chip cookies and placed it on the coffee table.

"Don't we have any milk?" quizzed Susan.

"I'll be right back," indicated her mother as she hurried to the kitchen again before returning with a large bottle of milk, several small mugs and a roll of paper towels. "Please, help yourself! You must be famished after your long journey."

"At the winery, there will be plenty of space to safely park your car, as well as guest rooms for all of us to comfortably stay," explained Susan. "And, we'll be having dinner there."

"Will we go disco dancing after that?" asked Stacia.

"Oh, may the saints preserve us!" exclaimed Mrs. Rives as she drew the symbol of a cross by touching her right hand sequentially to her forehead, her lower chest, and then to each shoulder. "You'll end up with the St. Vitus' Dance!"

"Mother, we won't be dancing at a discotheque," assured Susan. "We'll just be dancing up at the winery."

"We won't be going to a discotheque?" Stacia was crestfallen.

"Your mom actually knows we're going to a winery, then?" questioned Eula with disbelief.

"Oh, the winery is fine," assured Mrs. Rives. Jorge is Susan's betrothed, and it's his winery."

"Moranga Vineyards," clarified Susan.

"It's *his* now?" quizzed Carolyn. "What about his parents?"

"His papa passed away last year," interjected Mrs. Rives.

"He would have been a hundred in just three more days," added Susan. "They had already planned an elaborate birthday celebration for him anyway, so they just turned it into a celebration of life instead."

"He sure was a nice old guy," recalled Carolyn.

"Uh, he was old," Mrs. Rives shrugged her shoulders. "What are you gonna do?"

"What about his mama?" pressed Carolyn.

"She's eighty-four years old now," informed Susan.

"That's what happens when you marry an older fellow like that," commented Mrs. Rives with a knowing nod.

"She says that because I'm so much younger than Jorge, I could end up alone someday, like his mother did," chuckled Susan.

"It's no laughing matter!" chided her mother.

"Well, I'm only twelve years younger than Jorge," reminded Susan. "I think there's some time yet before I have to worry about it."

"And just look at Jorge's mama! She was only sixteen years younger than his papa," reiterated Mrs. Rives. "I know, I know, but it's the same, don't you see?"

"Forgive my mother," apologized Susan, who was clearly embarrassed by the entire exchange.

"That's quite all right," grinned Eula, quite entertained by it.

"We should get going, then," advised Susan. "Let me get my suitcase. I'll be right back."

"How big is it?" Carolyn suddenly asked.

"How much room do you have?" smirked Susan.

"If it's that big one you had in high school, it will never fit," assured Carolyn. "In fact, each of us brought only a small tote bag along. So, there's probably only room for one more tote in the back."

"One small tote bag?" frowned Susan.

"And probably one more person in the backseat, if we're lucky," agreed Carolyn. "But, it will be a tight fit."

"That's for sure!" agreed Karlin.

"Well, since I'll be sitting in the front seat with Carolyn," responded Susan, "I'm fine with that. You do have bucket seats in the front, right?"

"Yes, indeed," confirmed Carolyn with a smile.

"Is she always like that?" wondered Karlin as they watched Susan dash upstairs to get her things.

"Always," sighed Mrs. Rives as she rolled her eyes.

"Will you and your husband be bringing Damien over to the winery when he gets home?" quizzed Carolyn.

"My husband is in the hospital," explained Susan's mother, almost apologetically. "He just had a major bypass surgery. Damien will be taking me over to the hospital when he gets back."

"Oh, I'm so sorry!" commented Carolyn.

"Damien is actually out at the park with his girlfriend right now," informed Susan as she descended the stairs with a green Army duffel bag. "It's the closest thing to a tote bag that I own."

"We could always tie it on top," suggested Eula as she noticed that the duffel bag was literally stuffed to the gills.

"It'll fit in the back," assured Susan. "Trust me!"


Once they had said their farewells to Mrs. Rives and were on their way, with Susan sitting in the front seat beside Carolyn, Susan turned to the others. "Have all of you been down Zigzag Hill? If not, we should definitely do that on the way."

"Oh, not there!" objected Carolyn as she recalled the treacherous drive that Jorge and Susan had taken her down during her last visit, mainly so Jorge could show off the street racing technology and expert maneuvering capabilities of his little yellow sports car.

Zigzag Hill had originally been designed to make it easier for its many residents to traverse the steep 29% grade on which it was built, and was definitely too steep for most vehicles. Its one-way series of sharp hairpin turns meandered back and forth down a less-steep grade of only 7% that was manageable at a slow pace.

"We *will* be observing the five mile-per-hour speed limit if we do go there in this car," advised Carolyn. "We're not going down that road at ten miles-an-hour without our seatbelts on like Jorge did!"

"Where's the fun in that?" laughed Eula.

"I like her!" approved Susan as she grinned at Eula.

Karlin and Stacia remained silent.

"Well, maybe on the way back tomorrow," relented Susan. "We probably do need to try to get to the winery pretty soon, to set up for the party."

"Party?" questioned Carolyn with a raised eyebrow.

"A disco party," enlightened Susan as she grinned at Stacia and the others in the backseat. "With an open no-host bar."

"What's that?" queried Stacia.

"None of us will be getting snockered, anyway, so you don't need to worry about it," assured Eula.

"Suit yourself." Susan shrugged her shoulders. "But, you should know that Moranga Vineyards produces some of the finest wines anywhere, second to none, even those up by St. Diablo!"

"So, did you know Lenny Owens, too?" Karlin suddenly asked.

"Lenny Owens?" repeated Susan with surprise.

"Yeah, the guy Carolyn was sweet on back in high school, when you were her roommate," reminded Eula.

"You're still not holding out for Lenny are you?" demanded Susan as she turned to Carolyn.

"Carolyn thinks her dad may have intercepted Lenny's letters to her," explained Stacia from the middle of the backseat where she was squeezed in-between Eula and Karlin.

"He did intercept *your* letters to me," interjected Carolyn.

"My letters to you?" Susan was astonished.

"Yeah, I found them in his desk drawer, just two weeks before coming up here," described Carolyn.

"Turn left on the next street," directed Susan. "Do you think he read them?"

"They had been opened," revealed Carolyn. "And believe me, I wasn't very happy about it! That was actually the final straw that led to me going away to boarding school again."

"Ouch! How humiliating!" Susan angrily shook her head.

"What'd you say in the letters?" grilled Eula.

"Nothing against the law," replied Susan. "At least I hope not!"

Everyone but Carolyn then laughed, finding Susan's remark quite humorous.

"Was there anything in the letters about Lenny?" quizzed Karlin.

"Probably just that I never did get a chance to talk to him," recalled Susan. "Even though he and I both ended up back at Ocean Bay High for our senior year, it's a pretty big school."

"That's true," acknowledged Eula. "There were over 1,200 students there during our sophomore year. In fact, I think I remember seeing you there that year."

"You may have," supposed Susan. "My junior year at Oceanview Academy was the only year I didn't go to Ocean Bay High."

"We both went there our freshman and sophomore years, but were at Hillview Academy after that until we graduated," described Eula.

"I hear they're a lot like Oceanview with their rules," commented Susan.

"Am I the only one who didn't know the Church had other schools like that?" Carolyn suddenly asked.

"You always did lead a sheltered life," chuckled Susan.

"Not as sheltered as Stacia!" informed Eula. "Trust me!"

Susan and Carolyn exchanged a meaningful glance and stifled a giggle as they silently mouthed the words, "Trust me?"

Carolyn's green Mustang slowed as it reached the very outskirts of Ocean Bay. A meandering hillside district of expensive villas with spacious yards could be seen above. These were definitely not Painted Ladies and most certainly were not connected. It was clearly a neighborhood for the very well-to-do. The winding road they were ascending began to climb through a hillside vineyard to an extravagant villa and matching winery at the very top.

Views of the entire city and the bayside harbor below were unparalleled. Various boats and ships could be seen nestled along its alcove. The entire west-facing slope on the steep hill had long since been denuded of its ancient old growth forest, to make room for the various varieties of grapes in the huge vineyard now growing down its side. What was left of the tall conifers and other deciduous trees surrounding them remained only on the east facing slope in the background.

"There it is," pointed out Carolyn as she slowed her vehicle.

"Moranga Vineyards," read an arched wooden sign over its entrance. Its hand-crafted lettering had been carefully carved into the wooden sign. The sign itself was mounted on top of an arch-shaped opening in a wrought iron trellis to which well-manicured grape vines clung.

"Wow!" admired Eula. "Impressive!"

"I think I've been here before," recalled Karlin. "My dad used to do a lot of picking when he was younger, and one time he brought us up here to help him pick during harvest season. I was about ten."

"Your dad was a picker?" Susan tried not to sound too condescending.

"Yes, he was!" informed Karlin, rather proudly. "And now days he's head foreman of the entire work crew!"

"I only meant ...," began Susan.

"I know what you meant!" snapped Karlin. "How could someone like him afford to send two daughters to a private school like Powell Mountain University?"

"Well, the thought had crossed my mind," answered Susan, uncomfortably.

"Scholarships!" announced Karlin with pride.

"She is one sharp cookie," added Eula.

"So is her older sister Ruby," added Stacia.

"Hey, I apologize," said Susan.

"No problem," accepted Karlin, but rather curtly.

"Just look at this place!" marveled Eula, to change the subject.

The sand colored brickwork on the villa and winery was identical in shape, size and layout pattern, as were their red tile roofs. A fifty foot long corridor connecting the winery to the house was held up by wrought iron posts, and the corridor's roof of red tiles matched those on the villa and winery exactly. On either side of the connecting walkway was a waist-high wrought iron trellis on which more of the highly manicured grape vines were trained to grow, with access openings on either side at intermittent locations that led to connecting walkways into a huge rose garden where two white marble benches were strategically placed to enjoy it. An aging sundial stood in the midst of the rose garden that had been brought over from the old country when the Moranga family had first come to Ocean Bay three generations earlier. A solitary oak tree had been left near the garden benches to provide shade when necessary on hot sunny days. Beside it was a huge memorial headstone commemorating the life and accomplishments of Jorge Moranga, Sr.

Behind the winery was a large parking area, where its full-time staff would park each day. During his lifetime, Jorge's father had insisted that the winery be closed on weekends so its workers could spend more time with their families. Since his death, the winery had remained open seven days each week. Its facilities included ample room for visitors as well as seasonal workers and additional staff during harvest season, which was now concluded for the year.

The front entryway courtyard of the villa itself was surrounded by a four foot high wrought iron fence on which yet another variety of carefully maintained grape vines grew. A marble fountain in the middle of the courtyard was graced with a half nude maiden holding a large decanter from which water actually flowed out and into the pool below her. The water would then recycle itself back up through the statue and into the container for another round. Carefully placed accent lights were mounted at ground level around the base of the statue that pointed to it from three different angles. The lights themselves were equipped with automatic sensors that would come on when they detected an insufficient level of light, such as at dusk or in the evenings.

"This reminds me so much of one of the wineries back home," commented Stacia with excitement.

"Then you oughta feel right at home here," assumed Karlin.

Jorge was a tall, slender Italian man, with a clean shaven but handsome face and shoulder-length wavy hair. Though thirty years old already, Jorge appeared several years younger than he actually was. He was standing on the front porch waiting for his guests to arrive.

"That's Jorge," Susan informed the others as Carolyn brought her new car to a stop in front of the elaborate courtyard.

"Susan!" greeted Jorge with a warm smile as he rushed over, held the car door open for her, helped her out, and then passionately hugged and kissed her on the lips.

"Betrothed, indeed!" smirked Karlin.

"Just go with it," advised Eula. "It's not like we get to come someplace like *this* every day!"

"Carolyn!" noticed Jorge when he was finished greeting Susan.

"Hello!" smiled Carolyn as Jorge rushed over to the driver's side to help her from the car and then gave her a hug. "This is Eula, Karlin and Stacia."

"Welcome!" beamed Jorge as he helped each of them from the car's backseat and then gallantly kissed each of them on the hand. Jorge then stood to one side and motioned for them enter the Moranga home.

"Beautiful place," complimented Eula, and she meant it.

"I think you'll be surprised when you see the inside," warned Carolyn, with a wry smile.

"Not as surprised as you're gonna be!" chuckled Susan as she took Carolyn by the arm and led her inside.

"Oh my!" exclaimed Carolyn.

"After papa passed, we had the inside redone," grinned Jorge.

"Unbelievable!" mumbled Carolyn. "This place used to be just like stepping back in time."

"With no television, no phone, no microwave, or any other modern appliances anywhere," laughed Susan. "And all the interior lighting was managed with oil lamps and candles!"

"Papa hated modern conveniences," explained Jorge. "It would only upset him when we suggested that mama give up the wood burning stove, or get a refrigerator."

"She even had to make all her own bread, churn her own butter, wash all the clothes on a scrub board, the whole deal," elaborated Susan.

"We both felt that being 84 years old finally entitled poor mama to an easier lifestyle," smiled Jorge as he put his arm around Susan.

"Everything looks state-of-the-art now," admired Eula.

"It certainly is!" answered Susan. "And just wait until you see the disco room tonight. You're gonna love it!"

"Disco room?" repeated Stacia with a smile.

"And a few friends that we've invited to help us celebrate your visit to our humble home," beamed Jorge.

"Who needs a discotheque, anyway?" approved Eula.

"Jorge!" exclaimed Mrs. Moranga as she rushed into the room to greet their guests. "Welcome! Welcome! Jorge will show you to your rooms. We eat at six."

"Wow! Your English is amazing!" marveled Carolyn.

"I learn," grinned Jorge's mama. Then, turning to Jorge, "Sicuramente lei non sono facendoli dormire in baracche di lavoratore?"

"Mama, abbiamo appena finito di mettere dei fogli di pulizia su tutti i letti, non vi ricordate?" objected Jorge. "Si tratta di giovani ragazze! Essi hanno bisogno della loro privacy."

"Essi possono dormire nel vostro padre della vecchia camera," insisted Jorge's mama. "Esso dispone di un letto matrimoniale king size."

"Essi non vogliono dormire nello stesso letto, mama. Fidatevi di me su questo," persisted Jorge.

"Is there a problem here?" demanded Susan.

"Mi dispiace!" apologized Mrs. Moranga as she shook her head with dismay. "Jorge does not think you should sleep here in the house."

"Where will we be staying, then?" questioned Carolyn.

"In worker shacks," described Jorge's mama as she shook her head again. "Mi dispiace."

"Mama doesn't seem to understand that the five of you wouldn't want to sleep in the same bed," elaborated Jorge.

"But, they should stay here with us," opined Mrs. Moranga. "Not out there!"

"We just put clean sheets on five of the beds out in the crew quarters, and thoroughly cleaned the entire place," described Jorge. "There are no workers this time of year, anyway."

"Papa never stand for this," added Jorge's mother with dismay.

"Forse dovremmo far loro decidere?" suggested Jorge.

"Yes, they decide," agreed his mother with a nod of her head.

"As lovely as your home is," prefaced Eula, "I think I'd be happier in my own bed."

"Me, too," agreed Karlin.

"Our entire family used to share a single bed," revealed Stacia, "but I've gotten pretty used to having my own now, too."

"That settles it then," pronounced Susan. "And I already know that Carolyn wants her own bed."

"I'm afraid so," smiled Carolyn. "But, perhaps we could draw straws to see which one of us gets the big bed in here?"

"Nothin' doing!" replied Susan as she slipped her arm through Jorge's. "That's ours!"

"They are betrothed," agreed Mrs. Moranga with a flush of embarrassment, suddenly realizing why Jorge and Susan had wanted the others to sleep elsewhere.

"And, as much as I'd love having five lovely ladies in my bed ...," began Jorge with a sly grin.

"We get the idea," interrupted Karlin, rather curtly. She was still upset by Susan's condescending attitude toward her father's occupation as a picker and was finding it hard to be cordial.

"What's wrong with you?" whispered Carolyn to Karlin.

"She's obviously still upset with me because of how I reacted to her father being a picker," whispered Susan from behind them.

"Well, can you blame me?" demanded Karlin. "My father worked hard all his life to make a better life for us, and just about the only thing that Ruby and I do agree on is that we are proud of him!"

"Hey, my dad picked crops, too," advised Susan with a shrug of her shoulders. "Until he became a professional investor in the stock market. Now he's worth millions."

"He's even got his own Rolls Royce," mentioned Carolyn.

"Nevertheless," added Susan, "I am sorry. I hope we can put this behind us and not let it ruin what promises to be an amazing night."

"Even I picked crops for a while," chuckled Carolyn.

"I thought it was daisies?" razzed Susan.

"That job only lasted for three hours," reminded Carolyn. "It was my Spanish teacher's idea for me to work there so I could improve my communication skills, if you will remember."

"You worked on an all-Spanish-speaking picking crew?" Karlin suddenly laughed quite heartily.

"For three whole hours!" roared Susan.

"But, I made it for almost three weeks in squash, until they put me back in the lumber mill," added Carolyn.

By then, everyone was laughing, including Jorge's mother.

"Hey, I had to work in the dairy at Hillview," informed Eula.

"At least you didn't have to do chickens!" recalled Karlin.

"You two worked in the dairy?" Carolyn and Susan both began a renewed round of laughter at the very thought of it.

"That reminds me," interjected Mrs. Moranga. "Avete portato le uova ancora?"

"Mama still keeps a few hens for their eggs," explained Jorge. "I'll be right back. Make yourselves at home."

"I'll show 'em to their rooms," offered Susan. "You're gonna love 'em. Trust me!"

In anticipation of seeing Jorge's disco room later that evening, Carolyn and her friends from Powell Mountain University had taken the liberty of changing into their disco clothes before coming to dinner.

Eula was dressed in an extremely low cut one-piece black swimsuit with a wrap-around miniskirt over it, not unlike the tutus often worn by figure skaters. Her black fishnet stockings and high heeled go-go boots were definitely a show-stopper!

Carolyn and Karlin had each elected to wear dress jeans with fancy tops and platform sandals. Naturally, each pair of jeans was bell-bottomed and floor length, kept only from dragging on the floor by the very height of their platform sandals. Carolyn's platform sandals were made of blue denim and had three-foot-long shoelaces that wrapped up her leg underneath the jeans. Her bright red top with black trim and matching black sweater jacket were low-cut and stunning.

Karlin's platform sandals were made of wood with leather tops and straps with buckles to hold them on. Her elegant sequined tube top had three wide rows of color, the top being black, the middle purple, and the bottom entirely silver. The sheer lavender blouse she wore over it gave the entire outfit a bold but classy look.

Stacia, however, had declined to wear the stunning blue polyester evening gown Eula had brought along for her and insisted instead upon wearing her plain white blouse, red cardigan sweater, and green and red plaid skirt. It had taken some doing, but Eula had finally convinced Stacia to fold down the waistband on her skirt several times by "rolling it up" to make it shorter. Stacia's two-toned hushpuppy shoes and dark blue knee-high wool socks did go rather well with her outfit as it was, again despite Eula's protests.

The evening meal had been simple but delicious, complete with hand-made pizza, fresh salad and home-made ice cream for dessert.

"Thank you so much for such a lovely meal," Carolyn mentioned to Mrs. Moranga. "Everything was so delicious!"

"Grazie," nodded Jorge's mother.

"Is everything ready?" Susan suddenly inquired of Jorge.

"Come with me," instructed Jorge. "All of you."

"I'll be along shortly," promised Susan. "I just need to help mama with the dishes first. She goes to bed rather early these days."

"We can help," offered Karlin. Her attitude toward Susan had softened considerably.

"I appreciate it," acknowledged Susan, "but Jorge has something very special that he wants all of you to see. So please, go ahead."

"Okay," Karlin finally agreed as she followed Jorge, Carolyn, Eula and Stacia from the Moranga residence, down the covered walkway and toward the huge winery across from it.

"Where did all those cars come from?" Carolyn suddenly noticed. "Those weren't here earlier."

"You'll see," smiled Jorge, rather mysteriously.

"There's at least thirty cars over there in the parking lot," Eula whispered to Karlin.

"Oh, look!" observed Stacia. "There's a van that says 'The Ocean Bay Gang' on the side."

"The Ocean Bay Gang?" squealed Eula and Karlin together as they craned their necks to see where Stacia was pointing.

"Oh, man!" sighed Jorge. "You can't tell Susan you saw the van before you saw the band, okay?"

"The Ocean Bay Gang is *here*?" Eula was flabbergasted.

"Who?" frowned Carolyn. She obviously had never heard of The Ocean Bay Gang.

"They're only one of the best disco bands in the entire city," opined Karlin. "I had tickets once to see them over at the Ocean Bay Coliseum, but then Ruby found out and told my dad about it!"

"Isn't that where you took us to see the Doobie Brothers?" Carolyn gave Jorge an inquiring glance.

"It was," smiled Jorge.

"You and Susan went to see the Doobie Brothers?" asked Karlin with amazement. "Don't tell me that was when you and Susan were still roommates?"

"It was," confirmed Carolyn. "In fact, it was their roadie that gave us that wild ride down the sidewalk on his modified golf cart."

"Oh, yeah. I remember Steve." recalled Jorge. "Nice enough guy, but haven't seen him since. I was just glad you and Susan made it home okay."

"That's an understatement!" acknowledged Carolyn.

"We're here," whispered Jorge as he put his finger to his lips to indicate silence. "Please try and act surprised when we go inside."

"Oh, we are surprised, that's for sure," promised Eula. "We won't have to pretend."

Jorge then gingerly opened the door to his tasting room and turned on the lights inside. Carolyn, Eula, Karlin and Stacia followed.

"This is the tasting room," indicated Jorge with a devious grin.

"Where is everyone?" Carolyn silently mouthed the words so Jorge could see what she was saying.

Jorge merely smiled in return.

"Oh, look!" noticed Stacia. "They even have a little gift shop over there."

"And, over here," continued Jorge in a loud voice, "is one of our aging rooms. In fact, Carolyn is finally going to get that private tour, since she didn't get to see any of this when she was here before."

"Aging room?" questioned Stacia.

"Not all wines age in the same way," began Jorge. "Wine is a living and breathing entity, which basically means the flavor and texture of wine will not stay constant over long periods of time. Therefore, understanding what happens to wine during long-term aging is one of the first steps to determining whether or not to cellar a bottle."

"Say what?" questioned Eula.

"Most wines begin to soften over time and lose their youthful sharpness as they age," described Jorge. "Another consideration is the effect of oxygen. Even sealed bottles will oxidize over long periods of time and with oxidation comes nutty flavors and browning. But, this can also cause a wine's quality to deteriorate with age, too."

"So, older isn't necessarily better?" asked Karlin.

"Exactly," confirmed Jorge. "Wines with greater levels of tannin and higher acid levels will usually hold up best during the aging process and are less likely to become oxidized or to spoil over time."

"There must be thousands of bottles of wine in here!" marveled Carolyn as she studied the vast collection.

"It would be terrible if there was ever an earthquake here," assessed Stacia.

"Do ya think?" smirked Karlin.

"Oh, give her a break," chastised Eula.

"Sorry," apologized Karlin with a smile.

"No problem," replied Stacia, oblivious to the intended sarcasm.

"And down at the end of that hall is our special event room," nodded Jorge with a mischievous twinkle in his eyes. Both sides of the hallway were lined from floor to ceiling with bottle after bottle of wine, many of them actually quite dusty.

"What kind of events?" questioned Stacia.

"Well, let me see. There are wedding receptions, bar mitzvahs, quinceaneras, engagement celebrations, anniversary dinners, private parties, and even celebrations of life following funerals," described Jorge. "You name it."

Eula smiled and nodded with approval. "May we see the special event room?"

"After you," invited Jorge with a flirtatious smile.

"Surprise!" came the voices of at least two dozen people as Eula and the others entered the room.

Immediately, the song *Lady Marmalade* began playing.

"They're not bad," approved Carolyn as she studied The Ocean Bay Gang more closely.

"Check out that floor!" instructed Eula as she admired the illuminated disco floor.

"We sometimes bring that out for special celebrations that involve disco music," grinned Jorge.

"So, what, you just store it somewhere else the rest of the time?" quizzed Eula.

"Something like that," answered Jorge.

"Look at that light!" pointed Stacia as she stared with awe at the rotating mirrored disco ball suspended from the ceiling above the lighted dance floor.

"Wanna give it a whirl?" offered a handsome, well-dressed young black man in his late twenties as he offered Stacia his arm.

"You wanna dance with *me*?" questioned Stacia. She was unaccustomed to such attention from perfect strangers.

"Name's Harlan," added the man with a flirtatious smile.

"Sure!" agreed Stacia without further persuasion.

Just then the song *Jungle Boogie* began playing.

"May I interest you ladies in a taste of the grape?" asked a tall, good-looking Italian man by the no-host bar.

"We're good," assured Carolyn.

"No thanks," added Karlin.

"Allow me," offered Jorge as he extended his hand to Karlin. "You're next," warned Jorge as he smiled flirtatiously at Carolyn.

It was just then that Susan entered the special events room, filled with well-dressed couples disco dancing and enjoying themselves immensely. And, although Susan and Jorge had what they considered to be an open relationship where each of them were free to see other people, she could not help but feel a tinge of jealousy when she saw her fiancé dancing with Karlin. There was just something about Karlin that seemed to rub Susan the wrong way, though she couldn't say precisely what it was.

"Wanna dance?" flirted a well-built blonde man who obviously lifted weights.

"Me?" questioned Carolyn with surprise.

"You go, girl!" encouraged Susan.

Just then *Dancing Machine* began playing. Surprised at how well Carolyn was dancing, Susan decided to seat herself at the no-host bar to watch.

"Eula taught her how," mentioned Karlin as she came to the sidelines to rest.

"*Shake Your Body to the Ground* is next!" advised Eula as she joined Karlin by the sidelines to catch her breath.

"And how would you know that?" asked Karlin suspiciously.

"Because I asked the band to play it," answered Eula.

"They'll play anything you want," advised Susan as she took a sip of wine.

"Should you be drinking that?" questioned Carolyn as she joined them. "I didn't know you drank."

"Just a glass of wine after dinner isn't actually considered drinking," argued Susan as she set the glass down on the bar counter behind her. "But, I've probably had enough."

"Where's Stacia?" Eula suddenly asked.

"She's over there," indicated Susan.

"With some guy named Harlan," added Karlin with disdain.

"What is your problem?" demanded Susan, suddenly taking offense at Karlin's attitude. "Harlan just happens to be a close friend of ours! In fact, all of these people are."

"Stacia's drinking from a glass of wine!" realized Eula with dismay. "She has no idea what it will do to her."

"Perhaps just one might help loosen her up," chuckled Susan.

"You don't understand," replied Eula. "Stacia just got done telling me after dinner that her brother Alfredo is coming up to visit her tomorrow night. In fact, he flew all the way up from the Dominican Republic. Right now, he's on a 350 Honda motorcycle that he rented for the rest of his journey. I wasn't going to mention it until later, but now that she's over there getting sozzled, that changes everything. Stacia could very well still be snockered when he gets here!"

"So?" Susan shrugged her shoulders. "Surely he'll wait until she's ready to see him, especially after coming all that way. I think you guys could leave first thing in the morning and still make it in plenty of time."

"That's another problem," responded Eula. "He could be on Dominican Republic Time."

"Aren't they supposed to be in the same time zone as we are?" questioned Susan.

"No," replied Eula. "They're actually three hours ahead of us."

"That means that even though it's only eight o'clock here," explained Karlin, "it's already eleven o'clock there."

"If anyone finds those coats and wigs in our beds," worried Eula, "we're sunk!"

"No one else is even in your room," Carolyn reminded Eula.

"Not unless a visitor shows up!" replied Eula. "Then, when no one answers the door, they will go in and check."

"We actually stand a better chance than they do," opined Karlin. "Rachel and Sarah would most likely be there to cover for us."

"This is not good," Eula shook her head with dismay.

"Well, somebody better get her away from that glass of wine," recommended Carolyn.

"Especially if she's never had any before," agreed Susan. "She could very well still be sauced when her brother shows up."

"This is terrible," muttered Carolyn as she and her friends headed toward Stacia and Harlan.

118

"Something has come up," explained Eula to Stacia. "We are going to have to go back tonight."

"Hey, just when we were getting to know one another!" objected Harlan with a flirtatious grin at Stacia.

"I'm sure you'll survive it," informed Eula with a forced smile as she grabbed Stacia by one arm. "I'm going to need some help here."

"Good heavens!" exclaimed Susan from behind them. "How many has she had?"

"Just the one glass of wine," lied Harlan. "Doesn't look like the lady holds her liquor very well, though."

"That's an understatement," agreed Karlin as she grabbed Stacia's other arm.

"Just get her to the car," instructed Carolyn. "Susan can help me get our things."

"Are you sure you won't reconsider?" pressed Susan. "You just barely got here! When will I see you again?"

"We'll get together again soon, I promise," replied Carolyn as she and Susan started for the guest rooms to gather up all their things.

"Hold it!" commanded Jorge. "You're not leaving already are you? Not without saying goodbye!"

"Thank you so much for everything," Carolyn smiled weakly as she gave Jorge a hug. "Something unexpected has come up and we absolutely must get Stacia back as soon as possible. Susan will tell you all about it after we're gone. Please thank your mama for her hospitality, as well. It was a lovely meal."

"They really do need to get back," corroborated Susan, rather sadly as she turned to follow Carolyn to the guest rooms. "Perhaps I should come up there to Powell Mountain University for a visit sometime?"

"That would be great!" beamed Carolyn. "We even have an extra bed in our room."

"Yeah, I know," replied Susan. "It had been reserved for me."

"For you?" Carolyn was astounded.

"Until my dad found out that you and I would have been roommates again, had I gone there," explained Susan.

"You're kidding?" Carolyn could not believe it.

"That's my dad for you," shrugged Susan. "It's absolutely amazing the lengths our dads will go through to try to keep us apart, isn't it?"

"That may be true, but we will keep in touch," promised Carolyn as she and Susan hugged farewell.

"We will, trust me!" Susan smiled a crooked smile.


Carolyn had already begun the return trip to Powell Mountain University. Her friends rode in silence.

"Hold it!" Eula suddenly spoke up. "We have until eight o'clock tomorrow morning before Stacia's brother can get into the dorm anyway, right?"

"So, what's your point?" asked Carolyn as she proceeded toward the main connecting road that would eventually lead them to the freeway.

"Don't you see?" replied Eula. "We can't take Stacia back like this! She can't even walk straight."

"Not to mention how she smells!" opined Karlin.

"And we'd never make it there by the nine o'clock curfew," pointed out Eula.

"Which means we'd have to climb the fire escape stairs to get back inside the dorm," explained Karlin.

"I don't think I could make it," moaned Stacia, who was clearly dizzy and sick to her stomach.

"Here, just hang onto this," offered Karlin as she dumped the things from Stacia's tote bag onto the seat between them and handed it to her to use as a barf bag, in case she needed it.

"So," continued Eula, "we have just enough time to try to find the Owens residence while we're waiting for Eula to sober up."

"What?" Carolyn became alarmed. "We can't just stop by their house unannounced, especially late at night like this! Not to mention Stacia being drunk like she is!"

"Not to stop or anything, but it really isn't all that late," countered Eula. "Just to see where the house is. Haven't you always wondered where Lenny lives, and what the house looks like?"

"Or, we could just go to a park somewhere and let her walk it off," suggested Karlin.

Carolyn breathed in deeply and then exhaled quickly. "You're right. You're absolutely right. We do need to wait for her to sober up before we try and take her up those fire escape stairs."

"And we can't very well lurk around the parking lot at the dormitory for very long once we get there," added Karlin. "Otherwise, the campus security guy would spot us and we'd still end up busted."

"That would be very bad," recognized Carolyn. "Especially with Stacia like she is."

"Just where's that yearbook again?" grinned Eula with a mischievous twinkle in her eyes.

"In the back with the other tote bags," described Carolyn as she slowed to a stop beneath a street light so they could look up the address.

"Here it is!" mentioned Karlin as she located and grabbed the precious yearbook from the back.

"Let me see that," instructed Carolyn as she reached for and took the book from Karlin.

"It says here that they live at 323 Southwest Diamond Street," read Carolyn aloud. "I should have that memorized by now."

"Just how many letters have you sent him, anyway?" asked Eula.

"Only two," revealed Carolyn as she handed the yearbook back to Eula to hold for her while she put the car back into drive and pulled out onto the roadway. "Though who only knows if he ever got 'em."

"I think I'm gonna be sick," moaned Stacia from the backseat behind Eula.

"Don't you even face yourself this way, child!" instructed Eula.

"Here, keep this handy," instructed Karlin as she again showed Stacia the empty tote bag.

"No, not in my tote bag," objected Stacia as she started to push it away.

"Maybe you'd better hold it open for her," recommended Carolyn to Karlin.

"I ain't holding that thing while she pukes in it!" informed Karlin. "She can hold it herself!"

"Ohhh!" muttered Stacia as she finally grabbed the empty tote bag to hold it open, but then just took a deep breath and set it back down again without throwing up.

"She's gonna throw up, I just know it," feared Karlin.

"Well, until she does, let's talk about something else," suggested Carolyn. "Tell me how you know Woody the Woodcutter?"

"Actually, Ruby told me about him," clarified Karlin.

"Ruby?" Carolyn seemed surprised.

"Well, I know him, too," added Karlin. "But Ruby met him first when she had a flat tire last year. It was Woody who stopped to help her out. Wouldn't take a dime for helping her, either."

"He sure is a nice man," remarked Carolyn as she thought of how Woody had gone out of his way to help tow the Bennett family car, and even with hauling and unloading her own things that first day.

"Not too many people like that these days," mentioned Eula. "I'm just surprised he keeps doing business with them Crusading Knight people over there at the University!"

"Probably because he cares about helping out the students," assumed Karlin. "That's what it seemed like to me, the day I met him."

"When was that?" asked Carolyn as she pulled to a stop for another red light.

"It was the day I'd gone over there to meet John after class," recalled Karlin. "John introduced me to Woody when he stopped by with some parts for the car they're building in class right now."

"The one they're auctioning off?" asked Eula.

"That would have to be the one," opined Carolyn. "I knew it was from Woody's salvage yard after seeing an invoice for it on my desk at work. Did you know that Woody actually sold the entire car to them for only twenty-five dollars?"

"Really?" Eula was surprised.

"I was actually thinking of buying it myself, at one point," added Carolyn. "But I don't recall seeing any invoices for the extra parts."

"He probably just donated them," assumed Karlin.

"You know, that just makes me sick," began Eula. "That poor old woodcutter being taken advantage of like that by those creeps!"

"There must be a reason why he doesn't ask them for more?" speculated Carolyn.

"I'll tell you why," fumed Eula. "He's afraid of 'em. It was only two years ago that Woody's entire family was burned from their home by those people! Most folks around Powell Mountain know all about how the Crusading Knights lit up a burning cross in front of Woody's place and then it caught his house on fire! TURN, right there!"

"Right?" questioned Carolyn.

"No, LEFT!" corrected Eula. "Turn left, right here."

"How much farther is it?" asked Carolyn as she managed to make the left turn in time before traveling past it.

"Just a few more blocks," assured Eula.

"So, what's this about Woody and his family being burned from their home?" demanded Carolyn. "I've never heard about that."

"Me neither," interjected Karlin.

"Professor Sandut may have mentioned it to me," revealed Eula uncomfortably. "One reason I dropped his class was because I just didn't have time for it. The other was that he has a strict policy against dating any of the students in his class."

"You *are* going out with him, aren't you?" accused Karlin with a knowing grin. "I knew it!"

"Well, we'd rather it not become general knowledge," insisted Eula uncomfortably. "Perhaps I shouldn't have said anything."

"Your secret is safe with us," assured Carolyn as she pulled to a stop at a four-way intersection. "Oh! This is Diamond Street! Which way?"

"What was that number again?" quizzed Eula as she rolled down the window on her side to get a better look at the house on the corner beside her. "This one says 323."

"Oh my god!" exclaimed Carolyn. "That's it! They'll see us, just sitting here under this streetlight."

"Turn right and pull up a couple of houses," suggested Eula.

"And turn off your lights," recommended Karlin.

Without further comment, Carolyn turned right, pulled up past the next house, and parked in front.

"Your lights," muttered Stacia.

"Shhh!" whispered Karlin.

Carolyn immediately shut off her lights. "Now what?"

"There actually is a light on inside the house," noticed Eula.

"No way are we getting out!" Carolyn shook her head decisively. "Besides, Lenny's away at school. If anyone's there, it would be his dad."

"May I help you ladies?" came a melodic deep voice from the curb on Eula's side of the car.

The handsome young black man standing there was probably in his early twenties. His black leather pants, boots, vest and cap appeared to be all he had on. The hair on his well-built chest was visible where the vest came to a V in front, and his huge muscular arms had exotic, tribal-looking tattoos on them. His huge black afro glistened in the rays of the streetlight. Even though it was dark out, he had on sunglasses. A bright silver chain belt accentuated his trim, muscular waistline, and a gaudy silver chain hung around his neck.

"We're good," assured Eula as she rolled down her window and flirted shamelessly with the stranger.

"You lost?" quizzed the man.

"I'm Eula," she replied.

"Well, I'm Calvin," informed the man. "You ladies shouldn't be here alone in a neighborhood like this, especially at night."

"Is that the Owens place over there on the corner?" Eula suddenly asked.

"Humph," nodded the stranger with an almost sinister smile. "You know the Owens family?"

"Could be," replied Eula, realizing at once that mentioning their name might have been a mistake.

"Hey!" called another young man as he approached. "What's goin' on? Who are these people?"

"Pete?" called Carolyn as she rolled down her window.

Pete was about five feet, five inches tall, well-built and clean shaven with a close-cut afro. From the dark blue dress slacks and matching suit coat he had on, Pete appeared to have just gotten home from a church meeting. Pete's maroon colored necktie was neatly framed against the clean white dress shirt he had on beneath it.

"Carolyn?" Pete hurried over to the driver's side of the green Mustang. "How are you?"

Carolyn climbed from the car and gave Pete a quick hug of greeting. "My roommates and I were down here visiting Susan and decided to stop by and say hello while we were in the neighborhood."

"This here is our neighbor Calvin," introduced Pete. "But, he's right, this is a very dangerous neighborhood. You shouldn't be here."

"How's Lenny?" Carolyn quickly asked.

"He's got his own place, over by Ocean Bay University," informed Pete. "Never was able to get enough studying done around here. Anyway, Dad's actually dropping him off at his apartment now, but should be back any minute. We were finally able to pull Lenny away from his books long enough to get him to come to one of the crusade meetings they're having over at the church this week. But, if dad were to see *you* here ...."

"There ain't been a white person in this neighborhood in years," interjected Calvin. "Pete's right. If his daddy were to see the likes of you here, there's no tellin' what he might do."

"Ask him about the letters," whispered Karlin from the backseat. "Did Lenny get your letters?"

"That's Karlin, Stacia and Eula," introduced Carolyn.

"Eula," repeated Calvin with a big grin. "Now, that's what I'm talkin' about!"

"My mama didn't raise no fool!" informed Eula. "You be barkin' up the wrong tree!"

"Well, excuse me!" retorted Calvin in an exaggerated voice as he shook one hand back and forth. "Miss Eula's obviously grown accustomed to hanging out with the hoity-toity sort."

"Calvin, that's enough!" instructed Pete.

"Did Lenny get my letters?" Carolyn hurriedly asked.

"I don't think so," frowned Pete. "I'm sure he would have mentioned it if he had."

"Here comes trouble," smirked Calvin as he noticed a rickety blue van approach.

"It's Dad," realized Pete. "You'd better go, quick like, before he sees you here. We'll have to catch up later. It was good to see you!"

"Please tell Lenny hello for me," pleaded Carolyn as a tear escaped from one eye and began to trickle down that cheek.

"I will," promised Pete as he gave Carolyn a quick hug of farewell. "Now hurry, go!"

Carolyn swiftly got back into her car, shut the door, started up the engine and drove away without looking back.

"Girl! Why on earth did you do that?" demanded Eula. "That old man couldn't do anything to us."

"You don't understand," replied Carolyn as she wiped more tears from her face. "What if my being here were to cause Mr. Owens to pull the plug on Lenny's education for good?"

"Are you serious? Maybe Lenny should get a job," opined Eula.

"Lenny's studying to become a doctor," explained Carolyn. "It was his final promise to his mother on her deathbed, and it would just kill him not to keep his promise to her, don't you see?"

"So, let me get this straight. You think Lenny's dad would stand in the way of his own son's education, just for dating a white girl?" doubted Eula.

"If he thought Lenny was seeing me, yes," assured Carolyn.

"Oh, you poor naive girl," Eula sadly shook her head.

Quiet until now, Stacia suddenly threw up onto the floor of the backseat where her things had been dumped from the tote bag by Karlin, and all over Karlin's lap.

"Eeew! Gross!" screamed Karlin. "Stop the car! Stacia's throwing up all over the place back here!"

"There's just got to be a gas station up ahead," replied Carolyn as she kept on driving. "We'll have to stop there."

"After all that, and you didn't even get Lenny's new address?" chastised Karlin as she grabbed a sweater from Stacia's pile of things to use as she wiped the vomit from her lap but then discovered it, too, was drenched in the foul smelling substance. "How are you going to find Lenny now?"

"What are you doing?" mumbled Stacia, who was so drunk she could barely speak.

"Here, next time use this!" commanded Karlin as she again handed the empty tote bag to Stacia and placed her hands on either side of it to hold it open.

Carolyn sniffed and wiped her eyes and nose on her sleeve. "I can't believe I didn't even ask Pete for Lenny's address, but there just wasn't time. Everything happened so fast, and there's no way we can go back there now! Not with his dad lurking around."

"It's okay," assured Eula. "Maybe we can come back another time. I'm sure Pete will tell Lenny you came by."

"Perhaps Lenny will still write to you yet," pointed out Karlin. "Even without our room number on it, anything addressed to you at the University should eventually find its way."

"But I didn't even mention to Pete that I'm going to Powell Mountain University now!" lamented Carolyn.

"You could always write a letter to Pete," suggested Karlin, "and then put another letter inside for Lenny."

"His dad would still get it somehow," believed Carolyn. "He's worse than my dad!"

"Just don't put a name on the return address," added Karlin.

Stacia suddenly heaved again, this time managing to get most of it into her empty tote bag.

"God Almighty!" exclaimed Eula as she wrinkled her nose from the smell. "There's a 7-Eleven on the next corner. You've got to stop!"

"Maybe they'll have a hose we can use," hoped Karlin. She was anxious to hose herself off.

Carolyn and Eula each rolled down their windows again as the green Mustang pulled into the parking lot of the 7-Eleven gas station and mini-mart. "Look, there's a faucet with a hose on it, over on the side of the building!" pointed out Eula.

"You really need to get a four-door," advised Karlin, who was extremely anxious for Carolyn to get out of the driver's seat in front of her so she could push the seat forward to climb out.

"Careful!" cautioned Carolyn as she climbed from the car. "See if you can keep most of it on the floor mats. That way, we can just take them out and hose 'em off over there on the sidewalk."

"Help Stacia get out of the car!" Karlin instructed Eula and Carolyn as she sprung from the car and raced for the faucet to turn it on.

"I'm gonna be sick again," mumbled Stacia as Eula and Carolyn tried to pull her from the backseat of the car.

"Don't you DARE throw up on me, girl!" cautioned Eula.

"Come on, you can do it," encouraged Carolyn.

"I don't believe it!" wailed Karlin. "The faucet needs a key! I can't go inside like this."

"You'd better let me go in, girl," advised Eula. "Especially in this neighborhood. Wait here."

Carolyn put her arm around Stacia and slowly guided her toward the faucet to wait with Karlin for Eula to return with the key.

"This is the worst!" Karlin shook her head with despair.

"No," corrected Carolyn, "the worst will be if we don't manage to get back inside the dorm undetected before eight o'clock tomorrow morning."

"Actually," realized Karlin, "we'll have to get there before five o'clock when the security guy begins his morning sweep of that area."

"Well, it's only eleven o'clock now," assured Carolyn. "We can do this."

"We'll obviously have to take showers when we get back, too," pointed out Karlin. "Before anyone smells us!"

"I know," sighed Carolyn as she readjusted her weight to keep Stacia from falling down. "And we'll need to wash our clothes, too, and all the washing machines are down on the first floor by the Dean's apartment."

"Then we'll just have to stash everything in a laundry bag and wash it later," planned Karlin.

"I'm so sorry!" stammered Stacia as she suddenly bent over and puked on Carolyn's feet.

"Oh, yuck!" scowled Carolyn.

Eula could not help but grin as she approached with the faucet key and saw her friends covered with Stacia's vomit.

"If you DARE laugh," warned Karlin, "I'm gonna squirt YOU with the hose!"

"I meant to tell you before," slurred Stacia, "but I actually had some champagne, too." Stacia then burped. "I had to see if it tasted any better than the wine. Harlan said not to tell."

"I didn't think she could get so snockered on just a glass of wine!" Karlin shook her head with dismay. "Now what?"

"Here," Eula tossed Karlin the key. "I'm gonna get Ms. Stacia a cup of coffee. "We gotta get her sobered up."

"Do they have any Twinkies or anything?" asked Carolyn. "Perhaps she should have something to eat, too."

It was two o'clock in the morning by the time Carolyn and her friends were finally on their way again.

"I cannot believe you actually hosed out the car!" scolded Carolyn. "This is my parents' brand new car! How could you do such a thing? What were you thinking? My dad will KILL me for this!"

"Hey, I'm sorry," replied Karlin, "but there was no other way to get the vomit out of here, and it will eventually dry. At least you don't have to sit back here in wet clothes on a wet seat for three hours with someone who might vomit on you again at any given moment!"

"No, but I get to drive with wet shoes!" snapped Carolyn.

"Take 'em off," suggested Eula.

"You're right," realized Carolyn as she pulled over to the side of the road and came to a stop so she could remove her drenched blue denim platform sandals. "These were my favorite pair of shoes, by the way, and now they're completely ruined!"

Stacia suddenly began to sob.

"Oh, now look what you did," chided Eula. "Stacia's crying!"

"We're all gonna get kicked out of school, and it's *my* fault!" wailed Stacia.

"No, we're not!" differed Carolyn.

"But it's a three-hour drive," stammered Stacia, who was still quite drunk. "It'll be five when we get there!"

"Just when the security guy does," grasped Karlin as she shook her head. "Stacia's right, we'll never make it."

"Then we'd better hustle," recommended Eula.

"You got that right," agreed Carolyn as she resumed the drive with bare feet. "And we *are* gonna make it! Trust me!"

# 4. Rendezvous with Destiny

While Jim busied himself loading everyone's things into the luggage compartment of his Learjet aircraft, Carolyn, Sherry, Susan and Janette climbed onboard.

"Nice aircraft," remarked Sherry as she sat down in the first seat behind the pilot's cabin.

Not only was Jim's Learjet aircraft fully equipped with the best-in-class ease of mobility available with ample leg and headroom, but also included seating for up to eight passengers.

The first four luxury seats immediately behind Jim's cockpit faced one another, with small retractable wall tables beside each one. Also, included near each seat was a customized personal light and an electrical outlet, as well as internet access and various charger outlets for carry-on devices.

The seating quadrant beyond them was arranged differently. Two of the seats faced one another while a long couch across the aisle from them could seat two or more persons quite comfortably.

The entire passenger section was decorated entirely in white, with plush white leather seats and a forest green rug. The cockpit, however, was decorated entirely in forest green, with soft forest green leather seats.

"Now, this is the life!" nodded Janette with approval. "Sure beats driving there in a car!"

"And not only that," interjected Jim as he climbed onboard, "There's a small kitchenette in the back, fully stocked, just this side of the luggage compartment. Feel free to walk about the cabin, once we've reached cruising altitude. The restrooms are back there, as well."

"The man certainly knows how to travel," grinned Janette.

"And all so we can get Carolyn there before two o'clock this afternoon," chuckled Jim.

"Oh, joy," muttered Carolyn as she rolled her eyes and headed for the couch in the rear portion of the craft. She did not feel like sitting with Susan, Janette or Sherry just now, who were all seated immediately behind Jim in the first section.

"MIRA, secure craft," commanded Jim as he seated himself in the pilot's seat.

MIRA was an acronym for "Modulated Interfacing Resonance Assistant" and also the name Jim's onboard computer was programmed to respond to.

"Good morning Jim," replied MIRA. "Securing craft now."

The sound of doors and windows locking could be heard from throughout the craft.

"Wait a minute!" called Carolyn from where she was. "Don't you have to do one of those walk-around inspections for this, too? Just like you do for your Cessna?"

"Already done, while you were down on the beach with Lenny, Jr.," informed Jim with just a bit of sarcasm.

"Humph!" snorted Carolyn as she folded her arms and frowned.

"What's up with her?" wondered Susan.

"Everyone buckle up!" called Jim, ignoring Susan's question. "MIRA, skip control tower sequence."

"Why would we skip the control tower sequence?" questioned Sherry, suddenly concerned about it.

"Because there's no control tower here at this private airport," smiled Jim as he studied his passengers in the large rearview mirror installed above his complicated-looking instrument panel. "But, we do have a flight plan and will be cruising at 19,000 feet."

"Aren't the cockpit voice and flight data recorders supposed to start up automatically in one of these things?" asked Susan.

"This one is programmed to respond specifically to my own personal commands and her name is MIRA," bragged Jim, proud of his accomplishment. "Thanks to my research and development in the field of avionic voice recognition, the feature has become standard industry-wide. In fact, individual pilots may now choose whether to have the computer respond automatically or only when commanded to do so."

"Does he always keep his cockpit door open like that?" whispered Janette to Susan.

"Always," responded Jim, who was able to hear quite well. Then, returning his attention to his piloting duties, Jim commanded, "MIRA, begin data recorder."

"Data recorder engaged," verified MIRA.

"Today is March the 23rd, 2023, at 10:45 a.m., Pacific Standard Time," stated Jim for the recorder. "Departing from Oceanview Academy Airport, destination Powell Lake Airport."

"Confirmed. Aircraft system and flight parameters have been uplinked to satellite relay," stated MIRA.

"Wait a minute!" objected Janette as she glanced out the window and noticed that Jim had repositioned the Learjet so that it was headed toward the bluffs. "There's not enough runway for a plane like this!"

"That runway does seem to end pretty suddenly on the far edge of that bluff over there," agreed Sherry. "What if we aren't able to get up into the air before you reach it?"

"Then we'd most likely sail over the edge and crash onto the boulders below it," laughed Jim, half-jokingly.

"That's not funny!" scowled Janette. "Maybe this isn't such a good idea after all. You can just stop right here and let me off!"

"Too late," smirked Jim as he finished double checking his instrument settings. "MIRA, initiate takeoff sequence."

"Takeoff sequence initiated," responded MIRA.

Without further warning, the engines began to spool. "We are waiting for the engines to stabilize for a symmetrical thrust," described Jim. "Don't worry, we'll be fine."

"You really won't have time to stop if anything goes wrong!" estimated Susan. Although she had been offered countless opportunities to fly in Jim's private Learjet during the past seven years, this actually was her first ride.

"Well, I haven't crashed it yet, but I would recommend you hang on," smirked Jim. "Seriously, though, one of the great things about this particular aircraft is its ability to negotiate even short, rough and unimproved airstrips."

"Oh, Mother of Mary!" muttered Janette as she drew the symbol of a cross on her chest.

"You'll be fine," chuckled Jim as he set his flaps, aligned his aircraft with the runway centerline, and advanced his throttles. "Just be sure your seatbelts are buckled."

"Symmetrical stabilization acquired," verified MIRA.

"MIRA, fire thrusters," ordered Jim. Then for his passengers, Jim advised, "Don't worry, we won't be doing a vertical takeoff or anything like that."

"We're all gonna die!" moaned Janette as she closed her eyes and braced for the inevitable ascent.

"Thrusters firing now," confirmed MIRA.

"We're not gonna die," laughed Jim as his Learjet suddenly thrust off and began to accelerate at a rapid speed down the private runway at Oceanview Academy.

"146 knots indicated airspeed," advised MIRA.

"What does that mean?" questioned Sherry as the precipice ahead raced toward them with finality.

"That means the aircraft has reached its minimum takeoff safety speed," grinned Jim. "This is the speed we will hold until we have a positive rate of climb."

"Positive rate of climb attained," announced MIRA. "Landing gear retracting."

The sound of landing gear being retracted could be heard and felt by Jim's passengers. The craggy ocean-top bluffs below quickly disappeared from beneath them as Jim's Learjet ascended into the airspace above the expansive ocean.

"Whew!" exhaled Susan with relief. "You can open your eyes now, Janette."

"We made it?" asked Janette as she opened her eyes and looked out the window.

"What a beautiful campus," noticed Sherry as Jim's aircraft circled back and flew over Oceanview Academy one last time before veering its course toward Powell Lake Airport.

"It is," agreed Susan as she thought about the many adventures she and Carolyn had experienced there, both good and bad.

"Flap reduction speed attained," reported MIRA.

"Continue to flight level one niner zero, MIRA," instructed Jim.

"Flight level one niner zero?" Janette's eyes opened wide.

"Haven't you flown before?" asked Sherry.

"No, not really," answered Janette. "The one time I did come up to visit Carolyn was by train."

"That takes just as long as traveling by car," interjected Susan.

"Course plotted for Powell Lake Airport," announced MIRA. "Estimated arrival time in 23 minutes."

"Thank you, MIRA," added Jim.

"You are welcome, Jim," responded MIRA.

"One niner zero is pilot talk for 19,000 feet," informed Jim for Janette's benefit. "The extra zeros are not spoken in altitudes of 18,000 or above, which are called flight levels."

"That's just weird," opined Janette as she shook her head.

"Not as weird as you might think," differed Jim. "Pilots and air traffic controllers have their own language so there is no misunderstanding in communications. For example, at altitudes below 18,000 feet, the thousands are spoken as 'climb and maintain niner thousand' or 'descend and maintain one two thousand,' but at flight levels altitudes are spoken by saying something like 'climb and maintain flight level two niner zero.'"

"Say what?" frowned Janette.

"Just leave the flying to MIRA and me," grinned Jim.

"At least MIRA understands you, right?" snickered Susan.

"She ought to. Designed her myself," bragged Jim. "Right along with several other improvements that are now considered standard industry-wide."

"Yes, I believe you've mentioned that before," Susan rolled her eyes. "Jim's been bragging about his many accomplishments for as long as I can remember."

"You should have seen the older jets," continued Jim. "Even in 2016, the interiors were very cramped, and not all of them had the advanced voice recognition technology that most pilots enjoy today. In fact, my first jet was technically classified as an experimental design."

"Has he always been this humble?" joked Janette.

"Even when Susan and I were partners in biology class together back in 1972," reminisced Jim with a wicked smile.

"Something I try to forget," bantered Susan with a placating smile. "But, Jim is actually rather brilliant, at times."

"Why, thank you!" grinned Jim.

"Leveling off for cruising altitude now," announced MIRA.

"What does that mean?" questioned Janette.

"It means you'll be able to unbuckle your seatbelt, just as soon as we reach cruising altitude," explained Jim.

"Cruising altitude attained," verified MIRA.

"Well, it was technically 10:50 when we finally took off," pointed out Jim. "So, that should put us there at the Powell Lake Airport at 11:13, give or take a minute or two for wind turbulence."

"Wind turbulence?" repeated Janette with a frightened look on her face. "What'll that do? Is it dangerous?"

"Oh, just shake us up a bit," laughed Jim. "Probably not too bad, though. Just enough to keep anyone from dozing off."

"Will you please stop frightening her like that?" requested Carolyn from where she sat on the couch in the rear seating portion of Jim's Learjet.

"MIRA, engage autopilot," directed Jim as he unbuckled his seatbelt, got up, and headed toward Carolyn.

"Autopilot engaged," confirmed MIRA.

"Just wait a minute!" objected Janette. "Don't tell me that MIRA thing is going to fly this all by herself? What if another airplane crosses our path?"

"She can handle it," assured Jim as he seated himself beside Carolyn. "Hey, what's the deal? Are you not speaking to your friends, either? You don't really hate me, do you?"

"No, of course not," muttered Carolyn. "I was just upset."

"And you're not now?" pressed Jim.

"What do you think?" Carolyn finally turned to face him. "It's not like you gave me a choice about flying up there like this."

"You wouldn't have made it in time on your own," reminded Jim as he, too, folded his arms.

"Look, I do appreciate your help," Carolyn finally said. "I just don't like the way you went about it."

"Sorry about that," apologized Jim with a wry smile.

"And, if you ever threaten to arrest me like that again, or try and confiscate my personal belongings ....," began Carolyn.

"So, that's why you're so upset?" laughed Jim as he cut her off.

"Ooooh!" fumed Carolyn through gritted teeth as she got up to head for the restroom so she could escape Jim's continuous prying.

"Hold it!" commanded Jim as he grabbed Carolyn's arm and pulled her back onto the side couch. Then whispering so only Carolyn could hear, Jim reminded her, "I could have said something about Lenny's letter to your friends, but I didn't."

Carolyn turned to stare at Jim with disbelief. How could he know that the letter was from Lenny?

"It was pretty obvious what it was," continued Jim with a raised eyebrow. "Have you read it yet?"

"No, I haven't," replied Carolyn as she clutched her purse more closely to her chest, in which Lenny's long overdue letter was stashed.

"Your secret is safe with me," promised Jim. "Whatever you decide to do with it." Then loud enough for the others to hear, Jim invited, "Ladies, please join us back here, if you will."

Jim then grabbed and pulled out a retractable table from the wall and pressed a button on the edge of it. The surface of the table suddenly became a computer display.

"Yes, I designed this, too," smirked Jim as Susan, Janette and Sherry joined them. "This is the entire case file on *The Powell Mountain Matter*."

"*The Powell Mountain Matter*?" frowned Susan.

"Carolyn's idea," mentioned Jim. "To call it that."

"*The Powell Mountain Matter*?" repeated Sherry with surprise.

"And we're gonna solve it!" committed Jim. "Together."

"Oh, great!" remarked Janette. "Just like in *Nancy Drew*?"

"No, not quite like that," assured Jim. "This matter is quite real, and the facts are overwhelming."

"Fill us in," urged Sherry, already curious what Jim was going to share with them.

"Okay," began Jim as Susan and Janette sat in the two seats across from them and Sherry sat down beside Carolyn and Jim. "This is what we know. Woodrow Wilson, aka Woody the Woodcutter, was arrested on March 23, 1975, for the brutal murder of a young coed from Powell Mountain University."

"The girl's name was Lydia Cain," recalled Carolyn, rather distantly as she thought of her former classmate.

"Lydia Cain was allegedly dating her roommate's boyfriend, Paul Johnson, and having a romantic tryst with him up at Powell Lake on the afternoon Paul Johnson was run down by a green Mustang," described Jim as he studied the table monitor and used his hand to push it to the next screen. "Lydia must have jumped out of the way in time if she was with him as alleged, but was later hit over the head with something hard, perhaps while trying to escape."

"I do remember hearing about that," admitted Carolyn. "But, it was some *other* green Mustang, not mine!"

"We know," assured Jim. "Anyway, when Paul's body was found, forensic evidence proved conclusively that he was run down and killed by a green Mustang, and obviously not yours. It says here that your vehicle was brought in for minor fender damage just after that and forensically investigated before ruling it out as the suspect vehicle. The blood on your bumper was analyzed, too, and found to be animal, not human."

"That's what the guy at the auto place finally told me," revealed Carolyn. "But not until I came to pick it up. I actually did run over a squirrel, and while trying to miss him I ended up with minor fender damage. Anyway, that's obviously why it took so long for them to make the necessary repairs."

"That's just creepy," opined Janette.

"Woody obviously was arrested after that, then?" delved Sherry.

"Yes, ma'am," confirmed Jim.

"That's incredible," marveled Susan.

"Oh, it gets better," assured Carolyn. "It was Woody who gave me a ride into town to pick up my car when it was finally ready."

"No kidding?" Sherry furled her brow.

"That means you would have ridden alone with Woody on an isolated mountain road for at least 45 minutes to get there," calculated Susan. "Sometime after the alleged crime."

"Imagine how I felt after learning that he had murdered that couple like that?" Carolyn sadly shook her head. "It just didn't seem possible that he could do such a thing! He was always so nice to everyone, going out of his way to help people."

"Those are always the ones you gotta watch out for," mentioned Janette, with a knowing look.

"Not necessarily," differed Jim. "And what makes you so sure Woody was guilty?"

"What happened to them, then?" questioned Sherry.

"That's where it gets really interesting," advised Jim. "Forensic evidence proved that Lydia had been at Powell Lake with her roommate's boyfriend Paul when he was run down – but was not run down herself – and seemingly disappeared without a trace from the scene. Her remains were discovered four months later on Woody's property."

"If she disappeared during Thanksgiving weekend," calculated Sherry, "then that means her body would have been exposed to some rather severe winter weather during that time."

"The worst," agreed Jim. "At least two months of snow."

"I always thought both of them were found up at the lake, right after Thanksgiving," frowned Carolyn. "I'm certain that's what I heard on the news. I still remember the news people saying that Woody had been involved in a romantic triangle with them."

"What?" Jim merely shook his head. "That's not what happened, at least not according to the Deputy DAs who investigated the case."

"Why else would Woody have killed them like that?" pressed Carolyn.

"Well, you can't believe everything you hear on the news," replied Jim. "Only Paul's body was found up at Powell Lake. Lydia apparently was still alive when her assailant clobbered her over the head with something. Probably to knock her unconscious so he or she could transport Lydia to the location on Woody's property where she was eventually found."

"How horrible!" exclaimed Janette.

"Then why would Woody have been convicted for something he didn't do?" demanded Carolyn. "That was on the news, too. And he was sentenced to prison for life for it."

"So, what does any of this have to do with Carolyn's former roommate Karlin?" Sherry finally asked.

"That's what we hope to find out," replied Jim. "What we do know is that her skeletal remains were recently discovered at a long-abandoned winery site near Powell Mountain University, and that Carolyn's long lost wallet was discovered there, too. We also know that there were some similarities between the two crimes."

"Such as?" grilled Sherry.

"Well," sighed Jim as he again advanced the screen on his tabletop computer with his hand, "it says here that Karlin's skull showed signs of blunt force trauma to the back of her head – similar in manner to the way Lydia had been struck – and that her hands had also been tied behind her back."

"Really?" Sherry raised an eyebrow and gave Carolyn a questioning look.

"That's why Carolyn is now wanted for questioning up at the St. Diablo Sheriff's Office," interjected Jim as he pursed his lips and studied the screen on his tabletop computer monitor.

"But I didn't do it!" exclaimed Carolyn indignantly.

"We *know*," assured Jim. "And that's why we're doing this."

"Weren't there rumors of other people that have disappeared up there, too?" pressed Susan.

"I don't think they ever found some of 'em," recalled Carolyn. "But, I really don't think Woody was responsible for Karlin. That was an entirely separate matter and would have had nothing to do with what happened to Paul Johnson or Lydia Cain."

"Why not? How can you be so sure?" pressed Susan.

"Well," added Carolyn, "because students have actually been disappearing up there for years. Some as far back as 1956. And, Woody just wasn't that kind of a guy. Plus, he wouldn't have been old enough."

"It says here that he had three children in 1975," read Jim.

"Didn't you tell me once that Woody was only in his twenties?" Susan suddenly asked. "Even so, he still could have had kids, though."

"Wait a minute!" Carolyn finally responded. "That's right! He *was* older than that! I don't know why, but I always thought of him as being in his twenties. Still, he couldn't possibly have been! If you'd ever met him, you'd know what I mean. He was old school. But I do remember Woody mentioning to my mom that he had a family."

"Your mom knew him, too?" Susan was stunned.

"Oh yes," confirmed Carolyn. "Didn't I mention it? When my dad's car broke down on the way up there to drop me off, Woody stopped and gave us a tow over to Mike's Auto Shop. In fact, he even helped me bring all my stuff up to the dorm that night in his truck, while my dad waited for Mike over at the auto place."

"No way!" exclaimed Janette.

"Oh, yeah," continued Carolyn. "It was Woody who helped me carry all my suitcases and other stuff into the dorm that night, too. The Dean had to unlock the door to let him in because it was after curfew."

"Where was your mom while you and Woody were carrying in all your stuff?" grilled Sherry.

"In Dean Forrest's office, trying to figure out a place for my parents to stay that night," recalled Carolyn. "But, my dad ended up staying over at Mike's Auto Shop with his car while my mom spent the night with me and my new roommates up on the fifth floor."

"So, you definitely knew Woody, then," Jim shook his head. "Well, here's what else we know. Even though the forensic and circumstantial evidence convinced the Deputy DAs assigned to the case that Woody was innocent of the crimes against Lydia Cain, all attempts on their part to recuse the judge who presided over Woody's trial were in vain. Significant, because Woody was a black man and Judge Jonathan Lorik was Head Knight of the Crusading Knights of Powell Mountain at that time!"

"You're kidding?" Carolyn was flabbergasted.

"Who knows, perhaps Woody confessed to the crimes so the Knights wouldn't go after his family?" deduced Sherry.

"What ever happened to Woody?" Carolyn suddenly asked. "Is he still in prison for a crime he didn't commit?"

Jim advanced the screen on his tabletop computer again before answering. "No. In fact, he died in prison in 1978."

"That's just sad!" exclaimed Janette.

"Unbelievable," Carolyn shook her head. "What ever happened to Judge Lorik?"

"Alzheimer's," answered Jim. "Died of a heart attack in a nursing home back in 1994."

"Whatever happened to Woody's family?" pressed Carolyn. "I seem to remember his wife was in a nursing home or something, where Karlin worked. Woody would come in to visit her."

"His wife died of a stroke back in 1978, just months after learning of her husband's death," informed Jim. "No one knows what happened to any of their kids."

"How did Woody die, anyway?" delved Sherry.

"The records don't say. All it indicates is that he was found dead in his cell, cause undetermined," read Jim.

"That sure sounds suspicious to me!" opined Susan.

"What if the Crusading Knights had him killed so he wouldn't talk?" speculated Carolyn. "Perhaps it was an inside job?"

"All very good questions," recognized Jim, "but we just don't know yet."

"What else do we know?" questioned Sherry.

"Well, we know that someone hit Lydia over the head, put her in a green Mustang, and transported her to Woody's property," began Jim. "The forensic evidence shows, however, that Lydia was still alive at the time. She died of exposure to the elements sometime after being left in a small ravine between two logs on Woody's property, where brush was thrown on top of her to prevent discovery. It was less than a

140

mile from his house, but snow over the site would have kept it from discovery until the spring melt. Her body was not found until March 23, 1975. Now, that is creepy."

"March 23rd again," repeated Susan as she shook her head.

"So, you're telling me that someone just brought Lydia there and left her to die like that?" Carolyn was horrified. "Wouldn't she have at least tried to get away?"

"Not only were her hands tied behind her back with some baling wire, but the restraints were tightly secured to the logs on either side of her from behind," explained Jim. "Even worse, the baling wire was forensically matched to a roll of it Woody kept there on his property for securing bundles of firewood. And, one end of the American flag Woody always kept on the antenna of his old pickup truck was stuffed into Lydia's mouth, while the remainder of it was draped around her head. Over that was a handmade hood fashioned from an old Army bag matched to the Woodcutter by the serial numbers on it."

"I do remember his flag being missing the day he gave me that ride," Carolyn suddenly realized. "I even asked him about it!"

"What did he say?" asked Sherry.

"He was upset that someone would steal something like that, but figured it best not to make waves," remembered Carolyn.

"Waves with who?" demanded Janette. "Those creepy old Crusading Knight people?"

"Obviously, since the local judge was a Crusading Knight," deduced Sherry, "the police probably were, too. No wonder Woody didn't bother to report it."

"Sounds like Woody was framed," suspected Susan. "That's pretty sad."

"It would also explain why he never reported that one of the cars from his salvage yard was stolen," added Jim. "A green Mustang."

"I think I remember Woody mentioning once that some kids had been stealing parts, tools, and even cars," frowned Carolyn. "But, I don't think he specifically mentioned to me that it was a *green* Mustang. That was something I heard from someone else."

"Having a salvage yard like that, Woody could have had several green Mustangs, for all we know," pointed out Sherry.

"True," acknowledged Jim. "It also says here that Woody's house and salvage yard were on the site of a historic brothel. However, it was considered haunted and eventually sold for a nominal fee to anyone who would buy it after his wife's death."

"How sad!" frowned Carolyn.

"Finally," concluded Jim, "it says here that Woody came out here with his young wife Harriet back in 1956. They were originally from the deep south, and both were descended from slaves on the Josiah Smith plantation in Charleston, South Carolina."

"That's impossible!" objected Carolyn.

"Why is that impossible?" questioned Jim.

"Because I have a Josiah Smith in my family tree who owned slaves on a plantation in Charleston, South Carolina! Your daughter Ann and I came across it when we were working on our genealogy together," revealed Carolyn.

"I thought you had a crusading look about you," teased Jim.

"Guess we can't help who our ancestors are," chuckled Susan. "Jim's wife is descended from Lizzie Borden."

"Oh yeah, the axe murderer," recalled Sherry.

"No way!" marveled Janette.

"Well, I also have a famous Union soldier on one of my other lines," interjected Carolyn. "Private James Grey, Sr. fought in one of the bloodiest battles of the entire civil war. He and his platoon fought at Dutch Gap and even served in the trenches during the Siege of Petersburg throughout the winter until the spring of 1865. In fact, when they finally recaptured Petersburg ...."

"Uh, ladies," interrupted Jim. "Can we discuss genealogy later?"

"Sorry," apologized Carolyn.

"Didn't you say that 1956 was when the students began disappearing up at Powell Mountain University?" reminded Sherry.

"That was my understanding," answered Carolyn.

"Yes," confirmed Jim, "that's what the file says, too."

"I still don't think Woody would have had anything to do with something like that," persisted Carolyn. "He just wasn't like that."

"Well, it's 11:10 now," advised Jim as he turned off the tabletop computer monitor, released the small lever lock holding it up, and then slid it back into its receptacle. "We need to prepare for landing."

Janette and Susan got up and returned to their seats in the front when suddenly a loud alarm began to sound.

"What's that alarm?" demanded Janette. "What's going on?"

"I'm not sure," claimed Jim as he hurried to the cockpit, careful not to let his passengers see the slight smirk on his face. "MIRA, please explain alarm?"

There was no response.

"MIRA?" shouted Jim, as if doing so would help the onboard computer system to hear him any better.

Jim suddenly seemed serious as he put on his pilot's headset, sat down in his chair, put on his oxygen mask, and began checking the various settings on his instrument panels.

"I'll be right back," Carolyn mentioned to Sherry as she hurried toward the cockpit.

"This can't be good!" Janette now had tears streaming down her face. "I'm never gonna see my family again!"

"You'll see 'em again," assured Susan, unconvincingly.

"I was kind of hoping to do it in this life!" replied Janette.

Carolyn poked her head inside the cockpit and questioned, "What's wrong? Are we going to be okay?"

"Please have everyone put on their oxygen masks and buckle up," instructed Jim as he quickly fastened his seatbelt.

"Everyone hear that?" inquired Carolyn from the doorway of the cockpit. "Sit down, put on your oxygen masks and buckle up!"

"I knew we shouldn't have flown on March 23rd," fretted Susan.

"And now we're all gonna die!" moaned Janette as she and Susan put on their oxygen masks and fastened their seatbelts.

"Well, we're not dead yet," reminded Sherry as she, too, sat down, put on her oxygen mask and secured her seatbelt.

"Hey, where are the life vests?" yelled Janette as she temporarily pulled away her mask to speak.

"Under the seats," pointed out Susan as she pulled away her mask long enough to reply. "Don't worry, we'll be fine. Trust me!"

"Oh, God! Now I know we're gonna die," wailed Janette as she put her oxygen mask back on. She, too, was quite familiar with Susan's infamous expression of "trust me" and it was the last thing she needed to hear at that moment.

"We really are going to be fine," reassured Sherry as she pushed aside her mask to talk, but not very believably.

"Better sit down, put on that mask and buckle up," Jim instructed Carolyn, who was still standing in the doorway of the cockpit, watching to make sure her friends were all secure.

"Up here?" Carolyn asked with surprise.

"Why not?" responded Jim as he pushed his mask part-way aside to converse with Carolyn. "With MIRA out, I just might need another set of eyes."

"Oh, my," muttered Carolyn as she sat in the co-pilot's chair and fastened the safety belt.

"You should've let me show you how to fly back in '73," joked Jim, to lighten the mood of an already serious situation.

"That was fifty years ago!" Carolyn laughed sardonically. "I doubt it would have done you much good now."

"Touché," agreed Jim. "Hey, can you please close the cabin door, too? And before you do, just tell the others to stay buckled until we let them know otherwise. We're expecting some wind turbulence up ahead."

Carolyn seemed frozen with fear for a moment.

"Go on!" urged Jim before putting his mask back in place.

Carolyn hurriedly unbuckled her seatbelt, stood up and announced to the others, "Please remain seated until the all clear, and keep your oxygen masks on. Oh yes, we're also expecting some sort of wind turbulence up ahead."

Janette shook her head with despair.

"We'll be okay, really," promised Carolyn before closing the cabin door and returning to the co-pilot seat.

"Emergency simulation complete," sounded the voice of MIRA.

"WHAT?" demanded Carolyn. "Are you seriously kidding me? My friends are back there scared out of their wits! And poor Janette thinks she is going to die and will never see her family again!"

Jim took off his mask and began laughing quite heartily.

"I can't believe you!" fumed Carolyn as she pulled off her mask, unbuckled her seatbelt, and started to get up.

"Wait, I'm sorry," apologized Jim as he reached for Carolyn's arm to pull her back into the co-pilot chair.

"Why on earth would you do such a thing?" quizzed Carolyn, rather angrily.

"I needed to see how each of you would react in an emergency situation," explained Jim, now serious. "There's no telling what awaits us when we get there, including dangerous people."

"Dangerous people?" frowned Carolyn.

"The Crusading Knights," reminded Jim. "Remember them?"

"Still, that was a pretty unkind thing to put them through," opined Carolyn.

"And just as I predicted, it was YOU who came through with flying colors," informed Jim. "You even came up here to see what you could do to help *me*, of all people."

"Shall I tell the others you were finally able to get MIRA back on line?" Carolyn was a bit snide.

"Perhaps you might want a few minutes to just sit there and read your letter first?" suggested Jim with a crooked grin. "You certainly can't take it out in front of your friends – unless, that is, you don't mind them wanting to know what it is and what it says."

"I'll tell you what," agreed Carolyn. "I won't tell them about your EMERGENCY SIMULATION if you won't mention anything to any of them about my letter!"

"Shhh!" responded Jim. "We don't want them hearing the words 'emergency simulation' spoken so loudly, now do we?"

Carolyn pursed her lips and studied Jim for several moments.

"So, are you gonna read your letter or not?" pressed Jim. "Aren't you the least bit curious what it says?"

"Of course I am," replied Carolyn.

"I know if I were to receive an old letter from someone special like that, I'd sure want to know what it said! Especially a letter written fifty years ago," related Jim.

"Actually," admitted Carolyn, "I'm almost afraid to read it. I know that sounds crazy, but what if it's disappointing in some way?"

"There's only one way to find out," prompted Jim.

"I'm just not ready yet," answered Carolyn. "I need to be completely alone when I read that letter. Besides, you probably have hidden surveillance cameras here in your cockpit somewhere and are just waiting for me to pull out that letter so you can get a photo of it!"

"Well, it was worth a try," grinned Jim as he winked at Carolyn.

"Oooh!" snapped Carolyn as she got back up.

"Remember our deal," cautioned Jim.

"Mum's the word," Carolyn responded with a forced smile.

Meanwhile, over in St. Diablo, Detective Charles Priest (aka Chip) was busy looking over his old case file, in preparation for an interview at two o'clock that afternoon in the Karlin Gomez case. Jim Otterman from Ocean Bluff would hopefully arrive by then with an important new witness.

Priest's partner, Detective Ron Telluric, was busy making a fresh pot of coffee. Both men were in their late sixties but retirement was not even a consideration at this point for either of them. No one else in the St. Diablo Police Department was as knowledgeable or experienced enough to take on the reopening of this particular cold case. And, even though it had been nearly half a century since either of the Detectives had worked the Karlin Gomez or Lydia Cain cases, both knew every detail of them by heart from when they had formerly worked as Deputy District Attorneys.

When Lydia Cain's body was first discovered on the property of the local woodcutter on March 23, 1975, it had been Deputy DAs Chip Priest and Ron Telluric who arranged for an arrest warrant to be served upon Woodrow Wilson, aka Woody the Woodcutter, only hours after the gruesome discovery.

Bit by damning bit, the carefully staged evidence seemed convincing at first, though an independent investigation after the fact ultimately created more than a reasonable doubt as to the woodcutter's involvement – at least as far as Priest and Telluric were concerned. Sadly, all attempts on their part to convince anyone else of their findings – or to have the judge recused who presided over Woody's trial – had been in vain.

Not only was Judge Jonathan Lorik Head Knight of the Crusading Knights of Powell Mountain back in 1975, but Woody was a black man. Times being what they were, Woody was convicted in spite of any reasonable doubt that should have prevented it. Deputy DA Priest, in particular, had made adamant objections to the entire proceedings and requested a mistrial, but the threats that were received by his family finally convinced him to hold his silence. Deputy DA Telluric's family received similar intimidations, causing him to likewise cease his efforts.

Nevertheless, it was because of the stance they had taken during their involvement with the Woodrow Wilson trial in 1975, that both Chip Priest and Ron Telluric had been forced to resign as Deputy DAs from the St. Diablo District Attorney's office.

Most of Chip and Ron's files and notes on the case had been seized at that time and destroyed. Thankfully, Chip had managed to secrete a backup copy of the file among his personal possessions when leaving.

Lucky to be employed now, even as Detectives with the St. Diablo Police Department, neither Priest or Telluric had been in any hurry to make waves in regard to the old case or to make any new or unnecessary trouble for themselves. At least not until now. The discovery of the Gomez girl's skeletal remains had hit a sensitive nerve of conscience for both men.

Detective Priest thought of how the poor woodcutter had languished and died in prison in 1978. The news of his death had been heart wrenching for the woodcutter's ailing widow Harriet, who was in a nursing home at the time, where she died only six months later. The case had haunted Chip for years and was particularly personal to him. What more could he have done to prevent the imprisonment and death of an innocent man for something he clearly hadn't done? Would the Crusading Knights have harmed Chip's family if he had done more?

"Do you really think the two cases are connected?" Ron suddenly asked, rousing him from his thoughts.

"I believe they are," responded Chip as he turned to a particular page in his thick paper file. "See how the blunt force trauma on the back of Karlin's head exactly matches that of Lydia's?"

"And we're sure this one is Karlin Gomez?" questioned Chip as he poured some cream into his thick black coffee and stirred it with a previously-used stir stick before attempting to take a sip.

"Oh, absolutely," replied Ron. "The dental records are conclusive, too. There's no doubt about it."

"Poor girl," Chip shook his head. "I wonder if she ever knew what hit her?"

"I'm hoping her old roommate, Carolyn Bennett, can tell us whether the two victims knew each other," revealed Chip.

"That could explain a lot," agreed Ron.

"Or very little," added Chip. "We do know now that the Gomez girl worked at the same nursing home that Lydia Cain worked at."

"But Gomez didn't start there until after Cain's disappearance," pointed out Ron. "Heck, for all we know, Gomez was hired to take Cain's place after she disappeared."

"The Bennett girl might very well know," hoped Chip. "I can't believe no one bothered to interview her back then, but when her car came up clean, there didn't seem to be any need."

"Do you ever miss practicing law?" Ron suddenly asked.

"Actually, I prefer detective work," admitted Chip. "Especially when there's not a group of vitriolic hypocrites running around committing subterfuge at every turn!"

"Most of 'em are probably dead by now," figured Ron.

"Regardless," replied Chip, "we are going to get to the bottom of this matter once and for all! No more cowering in the shadows."

"It's time for lunch," mentioned Ron, who was always anxious to enjoy a good meal.

Ron Telluric had first met Chip Priest when they were students together at Harvard University. He had originally enrolled at Yale, but then received a better scholarship from Harvard. Ironic that a highly-educated man such as himself should now be working as a second-rate detective in an obscure police department in an out-of-the-way place like St. Diablo. Ron shook his head with dismay as he pondered what he might have done with his life instead.

Ron usually wore over-the-counter reading glasses from a local drugstore, which he referred to as his "cheaters." He tried his best to keep them in his front shirt pocket when not wearing them. Still, they would frequently fall out onto the floor whenever Ron bent over for anything at all, which was less often now than in the past due to his substantial waistline. Nevertheless, Ron was constantly losing or breaking each successive pair. Meanwhile, the clip-on glasses case Chip had gotten him for his last birthday lay unused somewhere in his top desk drawer.

Ron's pale bald head gave no indication of his previous dark brown hair color, and his clean-shaven though plump face was indeed one of his better features. His piercing blue eyes had a rather penetrating quality about them that tended to put potential witnesses on edge when they were questioned by him. Ron was six feet, two inches tall, about 230 pounds, and dressed in a rather average-looking brown men's suit. His suit jacket was currently hanging on a coat tree near his desk with his clip-on necktie, and both sleeves of his white shirt were unbuttoned and rolled up to his elbows. "Sure you won't have some coffee?"

"I'm good," declined Chip. "But, you're right, it's time for lunch. Let's head over to Maria's."

Maria's Mexican Restaurant had been a long-time favorite in St. Diablo since 1965, renowned for its delicious homemade Mexican food. Best of all, it was located right across the street from the St. Diablo Police Department.

"What if Otterman calls while we're over there?" asked Ron.

"We do have an answering machine," reminded Chip.

Though neither man was particularly fond of modern-day technology, they did have an old cassette style answering machine plugged into Chip Priest's aging black desk phone. The antiquated rotary dial phone had seen better days. The very fact that Chip had actually scanned and emailed an electronic copy of his paper file to Jim Otterman was an uncharacteristic act of faith in technology on his part.

"Take our file with us?" asked Ron.

"Absolutely," replied Chip as he grabbed his thick paper file and stuffed it into his tattered brown leather briefcase, along with an empty notepad and a couple of number two pencils.

"Do you think they've eaten yet?" quizzed Ron, referring to Jim Otterman and his party. "They should be here any time."

"If not, we can always take 'em back over to Maria's," suggested Chip as he closed his briefcase and secured the latch.

"It's only been a week and a half since daylight savings time began," reminded Ron as he followed Chip to the door while putting on his suit coat but leaving his necktie behind. "What if they happen to get here early?"

"The man's a pilot," stated Chip. "I think he would know what time it is. Hey Maggie, we'll be back after lunch."

"Yes, sir," nodded their secretary Maggie, who usually ate her lunch at her desk while reading a romance novel. With the other police officers either at lunch or out on patrol already, Maggie could take full advantage of the opportunity.

"Besides," Detective Priest mentioned to his partner as they stepped outside and crossed the street on foot, "they still have an hour and a half of driving ahead of them after they land."

"And if they're late?" asked Detective Telluric as he shuffled along beside his partner toward the Mexican restaurant.

"Well, it's not like we can issue a warrant for anyone's arrest without someone here to sign it, now can we?" chuckled Chip. "Judge Krain is never in on Thursdays. It's his golf day."

"One of 'em," snorted Ron, with obvious disdain. Judge Michael Krain's father, Ronald Krain, had *never* been one of Ron Telluric's favorite people! Not only had Ronald Krain been the Head Professor over at Powell Mountain University when he was alive, but also an active member of the Crusading Knights of Powell Mountain. It was in that capacity that Ronald Krain had managed to influence the DA's office to railroad both Telluric and Priest from their jobs as Deputy DAs following the Wilson trial.

"Unless Michael Krain is out appreciating one of the many local wineries around here, like his father used to," grinned Chip.

"If only we should be so lucky as to find him like that and be able to arrest him," mumbled Ron while he grabbed and held open the door to Maria's for his partner.

Over at Powell Lake Airport, Jim's Learjet was safely parked and secured near the black 2021 Honda Odyssey minivan that Mark Kraven had waiting for them at the single-hangar facility. Mark's late father Jim Kraven had been the Welding Professor at Powell Mountain University back in 1974, so his name immediately caught Carolyn's attention.

"I used to work with your dad when I was the secretary over there at the Industrial Education Department," explained Carolyn as she shook hands with Mark. "Sorry to hear about your loss."

"Thanks," nodded Mark Kraven as he quickly scanned Jim Otterman's smartwatch. "Just have it back before closing time on Saturday. That would be five o'clock."

"Can't we just rent it for an entire week instead?" posed Jim, not willing to be bound by the constraints of a two-day deadline at a time like this.

"Oh, sure," agreed Mark. "But, it'll cost you more. You know, we only began renting cars out here last year."

"No problem," smiled Jim. "Money's no object."

"Really?" Mark Kraven took a second look at Jim Otterman but then just shrugged his shoulders and rescanned his wrist. "The access code has just been downloaded to your smartwatch."

Still upset with Jim for making her promise to be silent about the emergency simulation stunt he had pulled just prior to landing, Carolyn merely rolled her eyes and shook her head.

"Does it have all-wheel-drive?" Janette whispered to Susan.

"It does," confirmed Jim, after easily having overheard. "The Honda Odyssey first came out with all-wheel-drive in 2017. It's one of the few minivans that comes with standard seating for eight."

"Good, then there's room for our luggage!" approved Susan.

"You ladies go ahead and get in," instructed Jim. "We'll take care of the luggage."

"We will?" questioned Mark, who was not as old-school as Jim when it came to assisting women or handling their luggage, especially when some of them happened to be minorities.

"I will take care of the luggage," corrected Jim with a forced smile as he gave Mark Kraven a look of disapproval.

At Maria's, Detectives Priest and Telluric had just finished a leisurely, gut-stuffing lunch and were ready to head back over to the Police Department.

"Hey, look outside," advised Ron Telluric.

"I see," smiled Chip Priest as he glanced out the restaurant's front window. "It's a black Honda Odyssey minivan, probably about two years old."

"Think that's Otterman?" questioned his partner.

"Sure looks like it," assumed Detective Priest as he watched a slightly stooped man with graying red hair in his mid-sixties climb from the vehicle. Chip continued to watch with interest as the man walked around to assist his passengers from the vehicle.

"He's got four women with him!" noted Ron.

"One of 'em has to be Carolyn," supposed Chip. "Probably the tall blonde woman. Nice looking for her age, too!"

"They're heading this way!" observed Ron.

"Perhaps they haven't eaten yet?" wondered Chip.

"We could always order dessert and have an informal interview over here, in the back room," suggested Ron.

"The banquet room is at your disposal," smiled Maria as Detective Priest handed her two twenty-dollar bills. "Not many people pay with cash anymore."

"Well, I ain't even got one of them new-fangled smartwatches," joked Chip, "so that's not about to change anytime soon."

"Here's to the paper generation!" added Ron as he handed Maria a five-dollar bill as her tip.

"Thank you, gentlemen," beamed Maria as she quickly put the cash tip into her apron pocket.

"Always a pleasure," smiled Ron in return.

Just then the door to Maria's Mexican Restaurant opened and in walked Jim Otterman with Carolyn, Sherry, Janette and Susan.

"Will there be five for lunch?" questioned Maria as Jim Otterman approached.

"Yes, ma'am," acknowledged Jim.

"I'm starved!" announced Janette.

"We all are," whispered Susan.

"I'm Detective Priest," Chip introduced himself to the new arrivals. "You must be Jim Otterman?"

Jim merely nodded. He had been caught off guard.

"We can begin Carolyn's interview over here in the back room while you folks get some lunch," added the Detective.

"You read my mind," approved Jim as he shook hands with Detective Priest. "We didn't have time to stop for lunch when we landed, so none of us has eaten yet. And, we were hoping to eat first before the interview."

"Then we can do both at the same time," smiled Chip.

"I'm his partner, Detective Telluric," Ron added as he shook hands with Jim. "You can call me Ron."

"I'm Carolyn," remarked the tall blonde woman as she shook hands with each of the detectives.

Waiting until Jim Otterman and his group had placed their orders, Detective Priest finally turned to Carolyn and asked, "Mind if I go ahead and ask you some questions?"

"Apparently, that's why I'm here," responded Carolyn.

"I've already shared what you sent me with the ladies while we were en route," interjected Jim.

"Very good," approved Chip. "And again, I apologize that we failed to properly question you back in 1975."

"It was exactly 48 years ago today that the body of Lydia Cain was found, on March 23, 1975," reminded Ron.

"I was under the impression that this was about Karlin," frowned Carolyn. "You found my missing wallet with her remains?"

"That is correct," verified Detective Priest. "Can you describe your wallet for us?"

"Well," Carolyn took in a deep breath and then quickly let it out, "it was a sky blue folding leather wallet with my driver's license, Social Security card, personal photos, and a twenty-dollar bill inside. There may have been other stuff, too, but after all these years I just can't remember exactly what."

"Did you have any trouble getting your driver's license and Social Security card re-issued after reporting them lost or stolen?" probed Detective Priest.

"Uh, no, not really," answered Carolyn.

"Does this mean anything to you?" asked the Detective as he pulled an enlarged photo from his briefcase and laid it on the table where Carolyn could see it.

"Socky!" exclaimed Carolyn excitedly. "That's of my cat Socky that I used to have back then. It looks like a copy of the one that was in my wallet."

"The original photo did have 'Socky' written on the back of it," verified Detective Telluric.

"Would there be any chance I might be getting my wallet back?" wondered Carolyn as she suddenly thought of the long-missing photo of Lenny Owens that had also been inside her wallet.

"I'm sorry, ma'am, but the wallet is now evidence in an active murder investigation, so we're going to have to hang onto it for a while," apologized Detective Priest. "Perhaps when this is over."

"Well," sighed Carolyn, "I've done without it for 48 years, so I guess a little longer won't matter. I never expected to see it again, anyway."

"Would you happen to know why it was with the skeletal remains of Karlin Gomez?" asked Detective Priest.

"I can only speculate," advised Carolyn.

"Let's move on and then come back to that question," suggested Ron. "To your knowledge, did Karlin Gomez or Lydia Cain know one another?"

"Of course they did," replied Carolyn. "I knew her, too. We were all in the same Bible History class together."

"Bible History?" repeated the Detective.

"The New Testament," clarified Carolyn. "We were studying about the life of Christ that semester."

"And did either you or Karlin associate with Lydia outside of class?" delved Chip Priest. "Were either of you friends with her?"

"No, not really," responded Carolyn. "But, we did eat at the same table with her in the cafeteria sometimes. Lydia really loved those vegetarian tacos they served there."

"That doesn't sound very appetizing," opined Janette as she took a bite of her pulled pork burrito.

"Indeed," agreed Ron Telluric.

"Did Karlin have a job at the school?" continued Chip Priest.

"No," answered Carolyn. "I was the only one of us who worked at the school."

"What did you do there?" inquired the Detective.

"I was the secretary at the Industrial Education Department for Professors Krain, Kox, Kraven and Kollins," informed Carolyn. "And for Professor Sandut, too, though he wasn't part of their Crusading Knights group."

"You actually *knew* that your bosses were Crusading Knights?" questioned Detective Priest.

"That's what they told me," confirmed Carolyn. "They all wore those little white knight lapel pins, too. All except for Professor Sandut, that is."

"Understandable," frowned Detective Priest. He was well aware of Professor Sandut's reputation as an artist within the community, and with the fact that Al Sandut was originally from India.

"Did you have any interaction with the Crusading Knights as an organization, or associate with any of its members outside your capacity as secretary there at the school?" grilled Chip Priest.

"Absolutely not!" Carolyn was indignant.

"So, you *were* aware that the Crusading Knights are a white supremacist organization?" questioned Detective Priest.

"Of course! Even my friend Eula knew about them," revealed Carolyn uncomfortably. "Eula was black."

Detective Priest suddenly laughed quite heartily. "I'll just bet your bosses were overjoyed about that!"

"Not particularly," frowned Carolyn.

"Can you think of any other possible connection between Karlin Gomez and Lydia Cain?" interjected Ron Telluric.

"Well, I don't know if it's a connection," began Carolyn, "but I do know that Karlin was finally offered a job at the Powell Mountain Nursing Home sometime after Lydia disappeared."

"Really?" Ron Telluric did not seem surprised.

"When Lydia didn't show up for work, they needed someone to fill the position," explained Carolyn. "But, it wasn't an official school job, it was just a job out in the community."

"Anything else about it?" urged Detective Telluric.

"Well," recalled Carolyn, "Lydia's roommate Martha gave Karlin one of Lydia's extra white nursing uniforms when Karlin got the job at the nursing home, since it required its employees to wear them while at work and Karlin didn't have one. Anyway, Martha said she figured Lydia wouldn't be needing it anymore."

Ron and Chip exchanged a meaningful glance. They had indeed questioned Martha Krain 48 years ago, but the information gathered had been seized and placed under seal by the court at the request of her father, Professor Ronald Krain.

"Just how well did you know Martha?" asked Ron Telluric.

"Martha Krain?" confirmed Carolyn. "Not very well at all."

"Did you associate with her outside of classes or hang out with her on a social basis?" pressed Detective Telluric.

"Are you kidding?" snorted Carolyn. "She was such a snob! Always thought she was better than everyone else, and definitely wouldn't have hung out with me or my friends!"

"Because some of them weren't white?" inquired Detective Priest.

"How should I know?" Carolyn shrugged her shoulders.

"Is there anything else you can tell us about Lydia?" grilled Detective Priest.

"Well, I had always assumed that Lydia was originally found up at the lake with her roommate's boyfriend Paul. That's what the media always implied," mentioned Carolyn. "But, Jim Otterman told us on the flight up here that Lydia was not actually discovered until four months later, on Woody's property."

"That is correct," responded Detective Priest, rather sadly.

"You were going to speculate for us why your wallet was with the skeletal remains of Karlin Gomez?" reminded Detective Priest.

"Oh, yeah," sighed Carolyn as she took a bite of rice and refried beans and quickly washed them down with a gulp of water before continuing. "That was the night that Karlin and I had dinner here."

"Here, at this restaurant?" interjected Jim Otterman.

"Yes, after Woody dropped us off here," recalled Carolyn, "then the two guys who were supposed to meet us had a flat tire, so we had to find another way back up the mountain in order to get back to the dormitory before curfew."

"Wait a minute!" requested Detective Priest. "You knew Woody the Woodcutter? On a social basis?"

"She was telling us about that on the way up here," interjected Jim Otterman again. "Apparently, her dad's car broke down on the way up to the girls' dormitory back in 1974 when Woody stopped to give them a tow."

"I think Carolyn can tell us about it," advised Detective Priest.

"It's just like Jim said," corroborated Carolyn. "And after he dropped my dad off at Mike's Auto Shop, Woody drove me and my mother over to the girls' dormitory."

"Tell 'em about bringing in your stuff," suggested Janette as she grabbed another handful of chips for her plate.

"Woody tried to get my dad to come back with him, but my dad insisted on staying there with his car," continued Carolyn. "So, Woody loaded all my stuff onto his truck and brought it to the girls' dormitory. But, it was after curfew, so the Dean had to unlock the door to let him in."

"Really?" marveled Detective Priest.

"Oh yes," assured Carolyn. "Woody even helped me carry it all inside. Anytime anyone needed anything from him, Woody was always there. Like the times he gave Karlin and me rides to town, and the time he brought me in to pick up my car when it was finally ready!"

"The green Mustang?" questioned Detective Priest.

"Yes, and that's another thing I learned about on the way up here," added Carolyn. "Jim mentioned to me that YOU were the ones who ordered a complete forensic investigation be done on my car, and that was why it had taken so long for the auto repair place to get it back to me!"

"Squirrel blood and vomit," muttered Detective Telluric.

"Say what?" interjected Janette. "That's not a very nice thing to say when someone is eating!"

"We were looking for a vehicle with fender or bumper damage that had blood on it," informed Chip Priest. "The vehicle that ran down Paul Johnson was a green Mustang. And not only that, we were also looking for a vehicle that had possible traces of blood in the backseat, from the transport of Lydia Cain's body. Perhaps one that had been recently cleaned out, to remove the blood."

"Oh, my God!" exclaimed Carolyn. "The night I damaged my fender while trying to avoid that poor squirrel was the same night Stacia threw up all over the backseat of my car! That was why we had to clean it out. Or, at least we tried to!"

"Like I said," chuckled Ron Telluric as he shook his head. "Squirrel blood and vomit."

"It was the weekend that Eula, Karlin, Stacia and I drove down to Susan's house in Ocean Bay," described Carolyn.

"But they had to leave early," informed Susan, who had been quiet until now, "because Stacia had gotten herself drunk on wine and champagne."

"Stacia had never had alcohol before," explained Carolyn. "Then, when she threw up in the backseat of my car on the way back, it was Karlin's bright idea to hose it out when we stopped at that 7-Eleven. I really was quite upset with her for that."

"Squirrel blood and vomit!" Jim Otterman began to laugh.

"Well, it sure did look like the right car at first blush," recalled Detective Priest. "We were absolutely certain of it until the forensic results came back."

"So, it was Woody who actually gave you a ride into town to pick up your car when it was ready?" continued Detective Priest.

"Yes," replied Carolyn. "I've already told you that!"

"And you were alone with him, on a lonely, mountain road, for about 45 minutes?" reminded Chip Priest.

"Yes, I was completely alone with him," assured Carolyn.

"According to our notes, your car was taken in after Thanksgiving weekend, and finally released to you on February 17, 1975," recounted Ron Telluric.

"That sounds right," agreed Carolyn. "I didn't even get to go home for Christmas that year, because I was without my car!"

"Sorry about that," apologized Detective Priest, "but we had to be absolutely sure."

"I understand," nodded Carolyn.

"And it was just a few short weeks later, on March 23, 1975, that Ron and I made one last sweep of a remote part of Woody's property, near the location where Woody's stolen Mustang had been abandoned," described Chip Priest.

"The Mustang with the human blood on the bumper and in the backseat?" Carolyn suddenly asked.

"That would be correct," verified Ron Telluric.

"Anyway," continued Chip Priest, "it was during that sweep, while we were searching that section on the Woodcutter's property, when we actually made the discovery."

"You two are the ones who found Lydia Cain, then, aren't you?" inquired Sherry.

"Yes, ma'am," responded Detective Priest.

"And it was not a pretty sight," added Ron Telluric.

"Was that when you actually arrested Woody, then?" asked Carolyn.

"We obtained an arrest warrant within the hour; but it was the Sheriff who met us there and actually served it on him," clarified Detective Telluric. "DAs and their Deputies can't arrest people."

There were several moments of silence while Carolyn took a few more bites of her belated lunch.

"So, just how did you and Karlin get back to the dormitory that night?" pressed Detective Priest. "The night you had dinner here, and those two guys stood you up?"

"The old winemaker gave us a ride," revealed Carolyn as she gulped down another sip of water. "He was here having dinner, too."

"The old winemaker?" frowned Detective Priest.

"From the Shady Brook Winery," clarified Carolyn as she took another bite from her burrito.

Another awkward moment of silence pervaded the room as Detectives Priest and Telluric exchanged a surprised look.

"What about the Shady Brook Winery?" Jim suddenly pressed. "Is that the abandoned winery where ...."

"Where Karlin's skeletal remains were found," Chip Priest cut him off. "With Carolyn's blue wallet."

Carolyn suddenly stopped eating and set down her fork. "I knew it! That had to be where I lost it!"

"The wallet?" quizzed Ron Telluric.

"The old guy was really creepy, if you know what I mean," explained Carolyn. "He was just about to drop us off by the entrance to Powell Mountain University when he finally convinced us to come see his old winery first. He was going to bring us back after that."

"You went with him to the winery?" Susan suddenly asked.

"We even went on a tour of his old winery with him," recalled Carolyn. "He told us stories of how some of the kids from the school used to come up there on Friday and Saturday nights to play their rock 'n roll records and dance, and even showed us an old record player from back in the day. But then when he wanted us to stay for eggs, things got a little weird."

"What do you mean?" frowned Detective Priest.

"Well, he had these old eggs, but they hadn't been refrigerated," elaborated Carolyn. "He said he had gathered them earlier that day from his hen house."

"And?" urged the Detective.

"He didn't appear to have a hen house," replied Carolyn. "And, the eggs looked all rotten."

"Why would he offer you rotten eggs?" frowned Janette.

"I have no idea," answered Carolyn, "but there was no way he was gonna let us leave unless we tried his eggs. Then, he was trying to show us how alcohol can cook an egg without the need for cooking it."

"That's pretty weird," agreed Susan.

"Karlin and I both felt there was something almost sinister about the man," continued Carolyn. "Perhaps it was the way he kept handling the knife he was using to stir the eggs with, but whatever it was, we both decided to just go ahead and make a run for it."

"How did you get back to the school after that?" quizzed Detective Priest. "That's several miles beyond it."

"We walked for quite a while before Woody happened along, saw us, and gave us a ride," replied Carolyn. "And we were never so glad to see anyone in our lives!"

"Was Woody ever romantically involved with either of you?" Detective Priest unexpectedly asked.

"Certainly not!" Carolyn was indignant. "Woody was a married man! In fact, his ailing wife was a patient at the same nursing home where Karlin worked, and Woody would come and visit his wife there every Sunday and sit for hours reading the Bible to her."

"Was Woody ever romantically involved with Lydia Cain?" continued Detective Priest. "We have to ask."

"Of course not," answered Carolyn. "Woody was very much in love with his wife and would never have cheated on her!"

"I do have one more question," added Detective Telluric. "What time did you leave Ocean Bay, the night you hit that squirrel?"

"It was between eight thirty and nine o'clock when they left," Susan answered for her.

"Yes, but Stacia was so drunk, that we needed to give her time to sober up before getting back," explained Carolyn. "That was when Eula decided we should try to drive around and find the address listed for Lenny in my yearbook."

"Lenny?" prompted the Detective, who was already fatigued and wanted the interview to be over with already.

"Lenny Owens," replied Carolyn.

"He was Carolyn's high school sweetheart," interjected Susan.

"Isn't that an odd thing to do?" frowned Detective Priest. "Driving around at night with a drunk girl in your car while you're looking up an old flame from high school?"

"It wasn't like that," justified Carolyn. "Lenny and I had each written to each other, but there was reason to believe our dads had destroyed our letters. It was Eula who convinced me to just drive by and see what his house looked like. We weren't even going to stop."

"Why would your dads have destroyed your letters?" wondered Detective Priest.

Carolyn remained silent and took another sip of water.

"Lenny was a man of color," informed Jim Otterman.

"Oh," nodded Chip Priest, suddenly understanding. "What did Lenny have to say about you just showing up unannounced like that?"

"He wasn't even there," answered Carolyn. "It was his cousin Pete that we spoke with that night, but just briefly."

"Was there ever any proof that Lenny did try and write to you?" Detective Priest finally asked.

"And just what would that have to do with any of this?" demanded Carolyn, suddenly becoming defensive.

"Well, you did have Karlin with you that night, and it is her death that we are investigating," explained Detective Priest. "Perhaps Lenny may have mentioned something – anything at all – that would be helpful in solving this case?"

Jim and Carolyn exchanged a meaningful glance but remained silent. Carolyn then shook her head in the negative while Jim imperceptibly nodded in silent agreement. Nothing would be said about the letter from Lenny Owens that Carolyn had stashed in her purse.

"When did you first notice your blue wallet was missing?" Jim Otterman unexpectedly asked.

"Not until the next day," remembered Carolyn. "It was when I needed my food card to pay for a late breakfast that I actually realized my wallet was gone."

"What did you do then?" pressed Jim.

"Karlin paid for both of us and put it on her card," recalled Carolyn. "And she kept saying something about going back up there and getting my wallet back from that old geezer, but that we needed to take reinforcements with us when we did."

"Would Karlin have gone up there alone?" questioned Jim.

"I seriously doubt it," scowled Carolyn. "But, what if she did?"

"Perhaps she saw the old winemaker somewhere else and confronted him?" speculated Susan.

"Yeah, and maybe he forced her into his truck and took her back up there to the winery," imagined Janette.

"Perhaps if Carolyn were to actually go to the winery, it might jog anything else she has forgotten?" suggested Sherry.

"Kind of like retracing her steps," recognized Janette.

"Is Karlin's skeleton still there?" inquired Carolyn, suddenly feeling sick as she recalled what it felt like when finding Joyce's and Veronica's skeletons in the bunker tunnel alcove at Oceanview Academy back in 2016.

"Along with several others," informed Ron Telluric. "The place almost looks like an archaeological dig site."

"We are going to find out what happened up there," promised Detective Priest. "Trust me!"

# 5. The Squirrel Incident

"**H**ow much farther is it?" mumbled Stacia. "I think I'm going to be sick again."

"No, you're not!" informed Karlin as she found the empty tote bag and placed it again on Stacia's lap.

"It's all wet," objected Stacia as she tried to push it away.

"That's what happens when you have to rinse something off after someone vomits in it," described Karlin as she put the wet tote bag back on Stacia's lap.

"Here, give her some more coffee," suggested Eula as she handed a lidded Styrofoam cup of coffee back to Karlin. "I can't finish it, anyway."

"So, tell us again what you were saying about Woody's family being burned from their home?" asked Carolyn as she glanced at Eula.

"Humph! As I said, the Crusading Knights lit up a burning cross on Woody's property one night to scare him," recalled Eula, "but it got out of hand and ended up catching the entire first floor of his house on fire."

"That's unthinkable!" remarked Carolyn, angry that someone could do such a thing.

"He was lucky to get his family out alive," added Eula.

"Aren't they afraid someone might try to do something like that again?" wondered Carolyn.

"Well, of course they are, child," replied Eula. "Good thing the place they got is built mostly of stone."

"Stone?" questioned Karlin from the backseat. "What kind of place is it?"

"Al – or should I say Professor Sandut – was telling me that it's a historic brothel," revealed Eula. "Most folks 'round here think it's haunted."

"Why in the world would Woody and his family want to live somewhere like that?" questioned Carolyn.

"Probably because it was the only place they could afford when they first came here," guessed Eula. "Haunted places usually sell for pretty cheap, since no one wants to live there."

"Poor Woody," Carolyn shook her head.

"What time is it?" muttered Stacia. "Are we gonna make it?"

"I think so," replied Carolyn. "We're just now starting up the mountain, so we're right on schedule."

"Good," slurred Stacia as she slumped back down in the seat and leaned her head against the headrest.

"It is 3:30 now," noted Karlin as she looked at her watch.

"We'll be fine," assured Eula. "Trust me!"

"Did we ever find Lenny?" Stacia suddenly asked.

"Oh, girl!" Eula just shook her head.

"Don't you remember?" grinned Karlin.

"He didn't see me throw up, did he?" worried Stacia.

"No, he didn't," assured Karlin.

Karlin didn't bother to try to explain to Stacia that Lenny hadn't even been there when they finally found his house.

"Good," nodded Stacia. "I wouldn't wanna mess things up any worse than I already have."

"Give it time," commented Eula with a knowing glance at Carolyn. "I'm sure you can think of something."

The looming oak trees beside Powell Mountain Road were almost completely denuded of leaves for the season, though still covered in many places with a thick layer of moss. Various Ponderosa pines and Douglas fir trees were interspersed among them. A thick covering of red, yellow and gold leaves covered the emerald carpet of manzanita, ceanothus, poison oak and other dense shrubs on the forest floor.

"Hey, we're in the woods," noticed Stacia as she glanced out the window again. "Are we almost back?"

"Pretty soon," informed Carolyn as she slowed to negotiate the first of many treacherous hairpin turns that Powell Mountain Road was known for.

"I hate roads like this," mentioned Karlin.

"Me, too," agreed Carolyn. "It's always kind of scary when there's a steep mountain on one side and a sheer drop-off on the other. Especially at night when you can't even see how far down it goes."

"More like the edge of a cliff," opined Eula as she checked to be sure her seatbelt was fastened.

"I wonder where Alfredo is now?" slurred Stacia. "Do you think he got there ahead of us?"

"Girl, you better hope not!" answered Eula.

Just then, a squirrel scurried in front of the car and came to an abrupt stop on the roadway when it noticed the bright headlights of the oncoming vehicle.

"Look out!" warned Eula. "You're gonna hit him!"

"Oh, no!" exclaimed Carolyn as she swerved toward the mountain on her right to try to miss hitting the unfortunate creature.

"I think you hit him!" yelled Karlin from the backseat when she felt the jolt of the impact.

Carolyn looked in vain for a place to stop so she could check on the animal and survey the damage to her right front fender.

"That's not all she hit, child," responded Eula. "That fender's gotta be damaged after that, too! You definitely hit the embankment!"

"Well, I can't very well get out here to check on it – or the squirrel – not with that drop-off there!" realized Carolyn as she proceeded forward at a crawl.

"That poor little thing," lamented Stacia from the backseat.

"Better him than us," opined Eula.

"The tires still seem to rotate okay," noticed Carolyn. She was worried that the damage to her right front fender might somehow prevent them from turning.

"Still better not go too fast after that," advised Karlin. "That happened to my dad once, and he ended up with a blowout after the bent fender stripped all the tread from his tires until they were bald."

"That's a lovely thought!" fumed Carolyn. "My dad will absolutely kill me now – that is, unless we all die first!"

"We're not gonna die!" differed Karlin. "Hey, perhaps you can get it fixed without your dad finding out about it?"

"Mike's Auto Shop already has my father's contact information," reminded Carolyn as she carefully negotiated the next hairpin turn. "There's no way they're not gonna call and tell him."

"I hear a scraping sound," cautioned Eula.

"Sounds like it is scraping, but maybe it's just when I turn the wheel," hoped Carolyn as she cautiously straightened out the tires after the turn. The scraping sound immediately subsided.

"It does sound okay on the straightaways," agreed Karlin.

"I'm so sorry!" wailed Stacia as she began to cry again.

"Hey, listen to me, girl," commanded Eula from the front seat. "This is not your fault! Do you hear me? We all feel bad about the little squirrel and especially about Carolyn's car, but it was just one of those things. We can't do anything about it right now, can we?"

Stacia nodded as she wiped her tear-stained face with one sleeve and blew her nose on the other one.

"Eeew!" Karlin made a face.

"At least she seems to be more coherent now," observed Carolyn.

"About time! Anyway," continued Karlin, "I know a guy down in St. Diablo who has a small auto shop. His name is Ron."

"Hey, there you go!" approved Eula. "There's no way your dad would know Ron."

"And what am I going to do for funds to pay for it?" questioned Carolyn as she came to the last of the hairpin turns.

"Maybe Ron will let you pay over time," suggested Karlin. "I'll be glad to talk to him."

"Just how do you know Ron, anyway?" pressed Carolyn as she finally turned into the front entrance of Powell Mountain University and proceeded toward the dormitory parking lot at the far end of the campus.

"We've gone out a couple of times," replied Karlin. "I first met him when he brought some auto parts and dropped 'em off at the automotive class when I was hanging out with John that day."

"Does John know you went out with Ron?" Eula raised one eyebrow and gave Karlin a crooked smile.

"Are you kidding?" laughed Karlin. "Of course not! But, let me finish. Anyhow, Ron's mother works at the Powell Mountain Nursing Home, and is going to try to get me a job there, just as soon as they have another opening."

"Well, we'll have to worry about the car later today," replied Carolyn. "Right now, we just need to try to make it back inside."

"Without anyone seeing us!" added Karlin.

"Ya think?" Eula said sarcastically.

"It's 4:35 right now," informed Carolyn as she pulled into her assigned parking space and shut off the engine. "We should be able to do this in 25 minutes."

"I vote for leaving the tote bags here in the car," suggested Karlin. "We can get 'em tomorrow. Then the only stuff we'll have to stash in the dorm until we can wash it later is what we have on."

"Agreed!" replied Eula and Carolyn together as they got out of the car and pushed the front seats forward for Karlin and Stacia to climb out from the back.

"Oh, this is horrible!" exclaimed Carolyn when she got her first good look at the right front fender. "What if someone sees this? Perhaps I should park it somewhere else?"

"Even if someone sees it, what are they gonna do?" asked Karlin as she helped Stacia from the car. "Who would they tell?"

"Good thing it's Thanksgiving weekend and hardly anyone is still here," pointed out Eula.

"Which makes it all that much more noticeable," reminded Carolyn. "At least if there was a car parked next to it, someone would be less likely to see it."

"One thing at a time," suggested Eula as they rolled up the windows, locked and closed the car doors.

"Today is Friday, right?" questioned Karlin as she and Carolyn each put an arm around Stacia to help steady her.

"Yes, it is," replied Carolyn.

"Ron's place could be open later today," believed Karlin.

"But a lot of places are closed the day after Thanksgiving," pointed out Eula. "Hey, you guys look way too obvious with both of you helping her. If someone sees you, we'll all be busted for sure!"

"I can help her by myself," offered Karlin.

"Okay," agreed Carolyn as she let go of Stacia and left the burden to Karlin.

"Let's go then," urged Eula as she and Carolyn traversed the parking lot, started past the girls' dormitory, and approached the back end of the building.

"Where are they?" demanded Carolyn when she noticed that Karlin and Stacia had fallen behind.

"Maybe we'd better help," realized Eula.

"Even if we have to pick Stacia up and carry her!" agreed Carolyn. The last thing they needed right now was for the campus security guy to show up early for his rounds!

"We're coming!" hollered the slurred voice of Stacia.

"Shhhh!" replied Eula, as loudly as she dared.

Carolyn quickly surveyed the various dormitory windows overlooking the landscaped area behind the dormitory, to be sure no one had been awakened by the noise or was looking outside.

166

"Oops!" cried Stacia as she suddenly fell into the dirt flowerbed.

"Oh, no!" exclaimed Karlin in a low whisper. "I think Stacia's sprained her ankle!"

"How can someone trip in a pair of hushpuppies?" growled Eula.

"I don't care if both legs are broken!" snapped Carolyn. "Just get her over here!"

Eula and Carolyn then raced back to help Karlin. All three of them grabbed Stacia and half carried her the rest of the way, about a hundred feet.

"What if someone notices all the tracks we just left behind in the flowerbed?" Carolyn suddenly worried as they approached the end of the building. The permanent fire escape stairs mounted to the east side of the girls' dormitory were just around the corner.

"Just go!" commanded Eula as she let go of Stacia and broke a small branch from a nearby Ponderosa tree. Eula then began using it to rub away all traces of their tracks in the dirt behind them.

"That should work," approved Carolyn as she and Karlin struggled to get Stacia to their destination.

"I'm sorry!" sobbed Stacia as she hopped along and tried her best to assist them in their efforts to get her there.

As the group finally rounded the southeast corner of the girls' dormitory and came face-to-face with the permanent fire escape stairs mounted there, they stopped and stared with disbelief.

"The bottom one doesn't even come all the way to the ground! It's at least twelve feet up!" Carolyn suddenly realized. "What are we going to do?"

"We just need something to grab the bottom section with," advised Karlin. "It should pull right down. They're all built like that, where the bottom one is retractable."

"We'd better hope so!" snapped Carolyn.

"Maybe that branch will work," suggested Eula as she raced back to find it.

"What time is it?" questioned Karlin.

"Ten minutes until five," advised Carolyn, rather nervously.

"We're not gonna make it," predicted Karlin.

"We will!" determined Carolyn.

Just then Eula raced up with a 30-inch steel sprinkler control valve key. "This is all I could find."

"That's not long enough!" wailed Karlin, who was becoming more agitated by the moment.

"Climb on my shoulders!" commanded Eula.

"I'll do it," offered Carolyn as she hastily climbed onto Eula's shoulders and waited for Eula to stand back up.

"Looks like it'll work!" Karlin sighed with relief.

"Hang on, I got this!" advised Carolyn as she carefully hooked the handle end of the sprinkler control valve key onto the bottom leg of the retractable fire escape ladder.

"Pull!" urged Karlin as she repositioned her weight to keep Stacia from falling back down again.

"Here it comes!" mumbled Stacia. "You got it!"

The moment the bottom leg of the retractable fire escape ladder was within reach, Carolyn grabbed it with both hands and tossed the steel sprinkler control valve key onto the ground below.

"Watch that thing!" cautioned Karlin. "You almost hit us!"

"Sorry!" whispered Carolyn as Eula lowered herself back into a squatting position so Carolyn could climb off.

"Don't let go!" slurred Stacia.

"I got you," assured Karlin.

"Of the ladder," clarified Stacia, who was becoming more lucid by the moment and well aware of their dire situation.

"Once we get up to the first landing, the other sections are permanent," Karlin informed Stacia. "Let's go!"

"Uh, why don't you let us go first," suggested Eula. "That way Carolyn and I can make sure the window to your room is open by the time you get there."

"Do you think they might have it locked?" worried Carolyn.

"Guess we'll find out when *we* get there," replied Eula. "One thing at a time."

Eula and Carolyn rapidly ascended the four flights of fire escape stairs and then waited on the roof of the dormitory for Karlin and Stacia to follow.

"Better get down, just in case the security guy shows up with his surveillance light," recommended Carolyn.

"No kidding!" agreed Eula as she and Carolyn both flattened themselves down onto their stomachs and waited until they were certain that Karlin and Stacia had begun their ascent up the fire escape stairs.

"They're good," advised Carolyn after peeking over the edge and noticing that Karlin and Stacia had managed to arrive at the first landing. "Uh-oh!" muttered Carolyn. "Stacia's puking over the edge."

"That's just great," sighed Eula.

"We'd better go get that window open," recommended Carolyn.

Eula merely nodded as she and Carolyn carefully tiptoed across the roof of the fourth floor and up to the dormitory's solitary fifth-floor section poking up at its far end.

"The windows are both closed," whispered Eula.

"Did you see a light just now?" panicked Carolyn.

"The security guy's right below us," realized Eula. "Get back down!"

Both Carolyn and Eula flattened themselves onto their stomachs where they were and waited. The first rays of daybreak could be seen over the tops of the eastern tree line in the distance.

"There's no way he's not gonna see *them* on that fire escape!" feared Eula. "We're so busted!"

"Not necessarily. He didn't stop," noticed Carolyn. "Come on!"

"What time is sunrise?" questioned Eula in a soft voice.

"Probably not until about seven thirty," guessed Carolyn, "and it's only five o'clock now."

"That gives us half an hour from sunup until the front doors of the dormitory are unlocked for the day," mentioned Eula as they tried the north window but found it locked. "And then we get to go deal with all that stuff in the car, not to mention the car itself!"

"Right now, we'd better just worry about getting off this roof before the security guy comes back," reminded Carolyn as she cautiously tiptoed over to the south window. "It's locked, too!"

"You're gonna have to tap on the window and get Rachel or Sarah to let us in," urged Eula. "They know about us being gone, anyway."

"What if they said something already?" feared Carolyn.

"Then we're busted, either way," replied Eula as she gently rapped on the window.

"They're sound asleep," assessed Carolyn.

Eula then knocked a little louder on the window.

"Shhh!" cautioned Carolyn. "Someone else will hear us!"

Just then, Karlin and Stacia finally made their way onto the roof and began walking across it.

"Tiptoe!" called Eula as loudly as she dared.

Stacia suddenly lost her balance and sat down with a thud.

"Oh, my God!" moaned Karlin. "Everyone on the fourth floor's gonna hear us!"

"Just crawl," called Carolyn in a loud whisper.

"What in the world are you guys doing out here?" questioned Sarah from the window.

"Be quiet!" commanded Eula in a soft voice. "We just need to get back inside and the windows were both locked."

"I'll unlock the other one," agreed Sarah. "That way we won't have to worry about trying to take the screen off of this one."

"Good idea," approved Carolyn.

"Lucky thing they never bothered to replace the screen on that north window," recognized Eula.

Once Carolyn, Eula, Karlin and Stacia were safely inside the fifth-floor dormitory room, Sarah abruptly closed the window after them before returning to her bed over on the south half of the room. "It's absolutely freezing out there!"

"You guys are lucky no one discovered your coats and wigs!" added Rachel after sitting up in her bed. "This is absolutely the last time we are covering for you guys!"

"That's right," nodded Sarah. "No matter what you do to us!"

"Fair enough," agreed Eula as she quickly helped Stacia across the big room. "Sprained her ankle."

"Better have someone look at it first thing," suggested Rachel.

"I will," called Stacia as she and Eula hurriedly exited the room.

"Thanks, guys," acknowledged Carolyn. "We appreciate it."

"Let's get to the showers right now!" whispered Karlin as she quickly grabbed both wigs and tossed them into her closet.

"Do you think they can smell anything?" asked Carolyn, as she silently mouthed the words.

Karlin merely shrugged her shoulders as she grabbed a towel, a bottle of shampoo, and her bathrobe. "Come on!"

Not surprisingly, Stacia and Eula were already in the shower room when Carolyn and Karlin got there.

"We can use this to put our clothes in," indicated Karlin as she grabbed one of the extra cloth laundry sacks from the janitorial closet.

"Better grab an extra one for the stuff in the car," suggested Eula as she exited her shower stall dressing room in her bathrobe with a towel wrapped around her head. "Maybe even two! Too bad they don't have plastic ones. Then, at least it wouldn't be as easy to smell!"

"Or as likely to soak through and drip," mumbled Karlin as she hurriedly took her shower.

"They should have plastic laundry sacks," agreed Stacia, as she hobbled from her shower stall dressing room, also in her bathrobe but with her dripping wet hair hanging down on a towel over her shoulders. "It doesn't seem like it would be all that hard for them to come up with something like that. After all, they do have Ziplock bags." Stacia had finally sobered up.

Though plastic garbage bags were invented in 1959, followed shortly thereafter by plastic laundry sacks in 1963, neither were sold commercially until the late sixties and mostly just to businesses and hospitals. The introduction of such specialty items to grocery stores in 1977 was surpassed in popularity only by the introduction of the first drawstring bags in 1984.

"Hey, I'll get Stacia down to the nurse's office just as soon as the dorm doors are open for the day," volunteered Eula. "Can you guys take care of all the laundry? We really should get that stuff washed before anybody figures out what it is. We can all meet at the cafeteria and have breakfast after that."

"I can go to the nurse's office by myself," offered Stacia as she began to swoon and suddenly had to sit down on a bench.

"Like I said," Eula sighed deeply and shook her head.

"Well, I need to get my car down to that auto place right away," informed Carolyn from her shower stall dressing room where she was busy drying herself off. "Before anyone sees it and asks questions."

"She's right," acknowledged Karlin as she joined them. "I guess I'm on laundry detail?"

"Don't forget all the stuff in the car, too," reminded Eula with an amused grin. "Unless, of course, you'd like to walk Stacia down to the nurse's office."

"Nice try, but I think it's your turn now!" grinned Karlin. "Just let me get dressed and then I'll go down and try to reach Ron on the phone. I'll get the laundry started after that."

"What time is it?" asked Carolyn.

"About six o'clock," advised Eula. "And by the time we're all dressed, it'll probably be closer to seven."

"Is anyone else as tired as I am?" Carolyn suddenly asked.

"Exhausted," admitted Karlin.

"Amen, sister!" added Eula. "But, there's apparently no rest for the wicked. Right, Miss Anastacia?"

"Oh, my ankle hurts so bad!" moaned Stacia from the wall bench where she sat with her leg propped up on it beside her.

"What about Alfredo?" Carolyn reminded them. "What if he shows up while you're down at the nurse's office? And what if he asks you how it happened?"

"I tripped on my granny skirt while walking down the stairs this morning," decided Stacia.

"Works for me," approved Eula.

"You can always leave a note for him at the front desk on your way out and let him know where you are," recommended Karlin.

"Well, I'm coming down with you when you go to use the phones so I can call Woody," informed Carolyn. "Then you can follow me out to the car and grab all the laundry before I leave. By then, Woody can hopefully be here to follow me down the hill."

"Not a bad idea," commended Eula. "I'm sure he would do that if you ask him. Hopefully he can give you a ride back, too."

"I can't imagine he would just leave me there," responded Carolyn. "I just know one thing for sure."

"What's that?" frowned Eula.

"That I'll be even more starved when I get back than I am now!" answered Carolyn.

The four friends chuckled at Carolyn's remark.


Martha Krain was already up and starting a load of laundry by the time that Karlin got to the laundry room on the first floor of the girls' dormitory.

"You're sure up early," commented Karlin as she hurriedly stuffed all three sacks of dirty laundry into three of the four machines.

"Hey, can't you save at least one of those until later?" objected Martha. "I still have two more to do!"

"What happened to you?" asked Karlin when she noticed fresh blood on the sleeve of Martha's white peasant top.

"Uh," Martha suddenly became quite edgy. "I had a bad nosebleed and got some of it on my blouse. How embarrassing! I also got some of it on my sheets and want to wash them right away, before they become permanently stained."

"Well, I've already started my loads," Karlin shrugged her shoulders. "Sorry! But, at least I don't have any more."

"I guess I'll just have to wait, then. Say, what's that smell?" noticed Martha as she wrinkled up her nose.

"One of my roommates has the stomach flu," lied Karlin. "Hopefully it's not contagious."

"Definitely go ahead," agreed Martha as she nervously stuffed the remainder of her unwashed laundry into a basket and started to leave.

"Hey, you can just leave that stuff here if you like," offered Karlin. "I'll be happy to start it for you when mine's done. Just leave me some quarters."

"That's all right," responded Martha as she nervously left with her basket of blood-soaked laundry.

"That was odd," noticed Carolyn as she entered the laundry room. "Do you think she'll say anything about our stuff? I can still kind of smell it."

"I don't think so," decided Karlin. "Something else was going on with her. Oh, well. Guess we weren't the only ones that didn't get to go home for Thanksgiving."

"That's Lydia's roommate, by the way," advised Carolyn. "Martha seems like somewhat of a snob, if you ask me."

"Isn't Lydia the girl that's in our Bible History class?" asked Karlin. "That we had lunch with that time?"

"That's her," confirmed Carolyn. "I always did think it was odd that Lydia's roommate would be living over here in the dorm."

"What's so odd about that?" queried Karlin. "Where else would she live?"

"With her parents," responded Carolyn. "That was Martha Krain. Her father's my boss, and I'm pretty sure her parents live nearby. I met her one day when she stopped by to ask her dad for some money."

"You're kidding?" Karlin was surprised.

"It just seems strange that Martha would be washing her laundry over here when she could just take it to her parents' house and wash it for free, don't you think?" queried Carolyn.

"Maybe she was just too embarrassed about all the blood on it," guessed Karlin. "From her nosebleed."

"That makes sense," nodded Carolyn. "Well, anyway, I finally got ahold of Woody, and he says he can be here by nine o'clock."

"Then let's race over to the cafeteria and at least get a bowl of cereal," suggested Karlin. "We've got just enough time."

Just one day earlier, on Thanksgiving morning, Martha Krain had thought about calling her boyfriend Paul to invite him to go with her to have Thanksgiving lunch at the Krain residence. Unfortunately, she hadn't reached Paul in time, and he had already gone fishing for the day without her. Martha and her parents just did not get along, so she dreaded the prospect of going there alone. Perhaps she could come up with an excuse to get out of it?

The stormy relationship with her father was but one of the many reasons Martha had chosen to live over at the girls' dormitory instead of at home. She also did not approve of her father's association with or participation in activities relating to the Crusading Knights of Powell Mountain. Martha had long suspected that her real mother's untimely disappearance might have been involuntary, but could never prove her suspicions that her father – the great Professor Krain – was somehow involved. Worst of all, Martha's stepmother was absolutely horrible to her and had made it clear that there was not enough room in the Krain household for both of them!

Fair complexioned and freckled with strawberry blonde hair, Martha tended to sunburn easily so usually avoided activities that placed her in the sun for very long. Martha was not unattractive, but just not spectacular in any way. Weighing only 123 pounds and being only five feet, six inches in height, Martha was also slight in frame. In fact, most who knew her thought of Martha as a stuck-up delicate wallflower who felt she was better than everyone else, especially with her father being the Head Professor of the Industrial Education Department there at Powell Mountain University. Insecure and self-conscious, Martha tended to be clingy and possessive of her boyfriend Paul and suddenly found herself wishing that she had not turned down his invitation to join him for the day up at Powell Lake.

Paul Johnson had his own vehicle and would occasionally give Martha and her roommate Lydia rides into town, but his old blue Volkswagen was not in its assigned parking place at the moment. Martha knew that because she had already walked out to the parking lot behind the boys' dormitory to see if it was there. Martha frowned as she thought of how Paul would give Lydia rides over to her job at the Powell Mountain Nursing Home each afternoon after her last class, and how much it bothered her. Naturally, Lydia had denied having any interest whatsoever in Paul, but Martha just did not believe her.

More than likely, Paul would go up to Powell Lake alone, realized Martha. She was fairly certain of it. Paul was known to go fishing whenever he had the opportunity, even if no one else was available to go with him. Should she abandon her plans to have lunch with her parents altogether and just to go the Lake to surprise him? Perhaps she should take a picnic basket along? Paul would inevitably decide to catch, cook and eat his freshly caught fish at the Lake, so she would need to bring something that went well with fish. A loaf of French bread with some fresh grapes and cheese might be nice. And some barbecue chips! Those were his favorite. She just happened to have those things on hand. Martha could also bring a cast-iron skillet and a spatula along, and definitely a blanket! Her father kept a cast-iron skillet in his shed, along with various other camping items. She could walk over to her parents' house – which was less than a quarter of a mile from the school – and borrow it. Her father would be none the wiser.

Martha unfortunately did not have a vehicle of her own to make the ten-mile drive to Powell Lake. But, she did have a standing arrangement with her father that she could borrow the extra Krain family car when needed. It was a dark green 1965 Chevy Impala. She even had her own key. But, she wouldn't dare take her father's car onto the gravel road leading into Powell Lake! Even if it was just an extra vehicle that was seldom used.

Martha suddenly came to a decision. She would walk over to her parents' house, make her apologies and tell them she already had a previous lunch date with Paul.

Martha knew that her stepmother would be fine with any arrangement that took her someplace else, particularly on a family holiday. Then she would slip into the shed, borrow the cast-iron skillet and whatever else might be appropriate for a surprise rendezvous with Paul. Finally, Martha would drive over to the local Woodcutter's salvage yard and park her father's car there while she used one of Woody's old cars for her trip to Powell Lake.

Martha also just happened to have a standing arrangement with the Woodcutter that she was free to borrow any of the extra vehicles from his salvage yard – the ones that ran – as long as she returned them with a full tank of gas. Naturally, that involved having a way to get there and then home again afterwards. She certainly hoped that she would be able to find a gas station open on Thanksgiving Day. In any event, her agreement with Woody was definitely *not* something her father needed to know about! But, what if Woody wasn't home when she got there? He probably wouldn't mind, she reasoned.

Actually, Martha hated to bother him at all on Thanksgiving Day, especially when Woody would be busy spending time with his family. After all, she already knew exactly where Woody kept a special large keyring in a small shack at the salvage yard where there were keys to each of the extra cars available, at least to the ones that ran. That's what she would do!

Martha had secretly had a crush on Woody the Woodcutter since she was 13 years old. Woody faithfully brought and stacked a load of firewood at the Krain residence each Sunday afternoon and Martha had always made it a point to be around whenever Woody came, even after her recent move to the girls' dormitory. Martha did think it curious that she had never actually seen her father pay Woody for any of the firewood he brought, but assumed her father must send Woody the money by mail for convenience. Martha then smiled to herself as she thought of what her father might think, had he known of her feelings for Woody, especially with Woody being a man of color. But, since Woody was her father's age and married already, the matter was moot.

If only her father was as kind and thoughtful as Woody always was! Martha was sure Woody would be fine with her borrowing one of his extra cars. Perhaps the green Mustang?

That's exactly what she would do, Martha finally decided. She felt certain that Paul would be surprised to see her when she showed up at Powell Lake for an unexpected romantic tryst with him in the Woodcutter's old green Mustang. Martha smiled with excitement at the very thought of seeing the look on Paul's face when she arrived.

Paul Johnson was an outdoorsy type of guy who not only loved to go fishing up at Powell Lake whenever the opportunity presented itself, but also enjoyed hiking and mountain biking. Paul was majoring in Accounting with a minor in Abnormal Psychology. Paul was also in excellent physical condition from jogging each day for his physical education class, where students would always run together in groups on the nearby mountain trails. Powell Mountain University had made it clear that none of the students should be wandering off alone, especially with the Powell Mountain Killer still at large.

Paul was six foot, two inches tall, had auburn colored hair, hazel eyes, and a contagious smile that was definitely noticed by members of the fairer sex. In fact, Paul was well liked by everyone, though most of his friends thought it odd that he would waste his time with someone like Martha Krain. That included Martha's roommate Lydia, who had a definite interest in Paul Johnson herself.

Lydia had come from a small-town farming community. Her father's orange grove kept the entire family busy year-round, especially during cold spells when there was danger of the precious crop having frost damage. Lydia's earliest winter memories involved lighting up smudge pots in the orange grove at night with her parents and two sisters. Thankfully, the Cain Family Orchard had continued to be successful enough that her parents were finally able to send her to Powell Mountain University for her first year of college.

Lydia Cain had fair skin with dark brown chin-length hair that she wore parted in the middle and curled under on the ends in a pageboy style. Her keen blue eyes were alert and sensitive, nicely complimented by the midnight blue eyeliner she wore. Lydia was about five feet, eight inches tall, and in excellent shape. She was an English Major with a minor in Physical Education. Gymnastics was one of Lydia's favorite pastimes when she wasn't busy studying or working to help contribute to the cost of her tuition. Lydia's after-school job at the Powell Mountain Nursing Home left her little free time, so she was quite pleased when Paul Johnson had called her that morning and invited her to accompany him to Powell Lake for an impromptu fishing trip. Too bad her roommate Martha would be busy having Thanksgiving lunch with her parents, thought Lydia with a smile of satisfaction.

It was one of those surprisingly pleasant late fall days. The sun was out and the few clouds to be seen were fluffy and white. An occasional light breeze could be both felt and seen as it lightly assaulted the forest surrounding them.

"Are you going to be warm enough?" flirted Paul as he shifted his old blue Volkswagen into first gear for a particularly steep hairpin turn just ahead.

"I'm fine," assured Lydia with a flirtatious grin. Though she had her white cardigan sweater with her, the lowcut yellow cotton top and blue denim miniskirt she had on hardly seemed adequate.

"I did ask Martha first, you know," admitted Paul rather sheepishly, "but as usual, she had no interest in coming along."

"Her parents do expect her to be at their house for Thanksgiving lunch today," reminded Lydia as she absentmindedly ran one hand through her smooth shiny hair from the inside outward. Light glistened momentarily on the tips of her sensuous long fingernails. Her midnight blue nail polish exactly matched the color of her eyeliner.

"Is it too windy?" Paul suddenly asked as he shifted back down to second gear. Lydia's subtle smile of suggestion was not lost on him, and her dark red lips were enticing.

"Not at all," assured Lydia as she unexpectedly rolled her window down a little further. "This is probably the last truly nice day we'll see before winter."

Even the tallest of the oak trees surrounding Powell Mountain Road were almost completely void of leaves for the season, though still quite green with thick clumps of moss clinging to their trunks and limbs. Occasional gusts of chilly wind served as a reminder that the entire forest would soon be blanketed with a soft white layer of snow for the winter. Colorful leaves carpeted the soft green forest floor while low-lying shrubs became increasingly interwoven with blackberry canes as they neared the lake.

"You may wish you'd worn your jeans," predicted Paul as he pulled into a dirt turnout near the lake.

"We're not walking in *there* are we?" Lydia suddenly became concerned when she noticed some poison oak nearby.

"I was thinking the fishing might be better down at the lake," teased Paul. "From the beach."

"Oh, of course," laughed Lydia.

"I even brought an extra sheet along," offered Paul with a playful smile. "You might want a clean place to sit down while I fish."

"I thought both of us would be fishing," Lydia feigned disappointment.

"Without a fishing license?" Paul raised an eyebrow.

"I guess I would need one of those, wouldn't I?" grinned Lydia.

"I even brought a bag of barbecue chips along," pointed out Paul. "To go with the fish."

"Fish and chips," approved Lydia. "I like it!"

"Or just chips if I don't catch anything," added Paul with a crooked smile.

"Soda?" asked Lydia.

"Dr. Pepper," answered Paul.

"My favorite," replied Lydia as she reached over and put her hand on Paul's leg. "Too bad these have bucket seats."

"Come on," beckoned Paul as he opened his door and climbed from the old blue Volkswagen. "We can spread the sheet down there on the sand."

"What if someone else shows up?" worried Lydia. "That road does lead straight onto the beach."

"Nobody else is gonna come up here on Thanksgiving Day," laughed Paul as he quickly walked around the car, opened Lydia's door and extended his hand to her.

"Have you had a chance to tell Martha about us yet?" Lydia suddenly questioned as she climbed from the Volkswagen and stood close to Paul, facing him.

"I didn't want to spoil her holiday," explained Paul. "But, I will tell her. I promise."

"When?" pressed Lydia as she put her arms around Paul and began kissing him on the mouth.

"Soon," promised Paul as he gently grabbed Lydia's wrists and wriggled free from her grasp. "Come on!" Paul then snatched up the extra sheet, grabbed Lydia by the hand, and headed for the beach.

"Wait!" requested Lydia as she stopped to remove her sandals.

"Are you sure you're going to be warm enough?" quizzed Paul.

"Absolutely!" Lydia smiled flirtatiously at Paul as she grabbed her sandals in one hand and grabbed his hand with the other.

"What about here?" suggested Paul when they came to a clean-looking flat stretch of sand.

"It is pretty close to the water," objected Lydia.

"What about back there, then?" pointed out Paul as he nodded toward a similar portion of beach that was just a few feet farther away from the lake.

"Perfect!" approved Lydia as she tossed down her sandals and began helping Paul spread out the sheet. "What about your fishing?"

"Oh, I don't think the fish are going anywhere," flirted Paul as he sat down on the sheet and began removing his rubber-soled hiking boots. "What I really need is a pair of waders."

"Waders?" frowned Lydia.

"A pair of waders is a special waterproof outfit for fishing that comes all the way up to the chest," described Paul as he tossed his hiking boots onto the ground beside the sheet.

"Like a one-piece pair of pajamas with footies?" teased Lydia.

"Kind of like that, but made of *rubber*," emphasized Paul with a mischievous smile as he grabbed Lydia by the hand and pulled her down onto the sheet beside him.

"You certainly seem warm enough," commented Lydia as she began unbuttoning Paul's green plaid flannel shirt.

"Are you sure about this?" Paul suddenly asked.

"As long as you plan to make an honest woman out of me," responded Lydia as she finished unbuttoning his shirt and began to push it down over his arms.

"I really should break it off with Martha first, don't you think?" hesitated Paul.

"You've already promised to do that," reminded Lydia as she paused to study him. "You weren't just saying that, were you?"

"Of course not," assured Paul as he suddenly grabbed Lydia and pulled her close. "Lydia Cain, will you marry me?"

"Yes! I will!" beamed Lydia as she hugged him tightly. "Hold on a minute."

Paul then waited with great anticipation as Lydia carefully removed her under panties, folded them, and neatly stashed them in the pocket of her blue denim miniskirt. She considered whether or not to remove her skirt and top, as well, but decided against it.

Then, just as Paul and Lydia began kissing most passionately, the faint sound of a car engine approaching could be heard.

"Did you hear something?" Lydia suddenly asked.

"You're just being paranoid," chided Paul as he unbuckled his belt, unzipped his blue jeans, and stood to remove them.

"Look out!" screamed Lydia as she suddenly noticed an approaching green Mustang that picked up speed as it headed directly for Paul.

Realizing at once that he was in danger, Paul started to try to run but tripped over his hiking boots and fell into the path of the oncoming car.

"Martha?" recognized Lydia as she leaped out of the way. "What are you doing? STOP!"

Martha floored the gas pedal and continued toward Paul. The horrible sound of the impact nearly drowned out Paul's screams of pain as he was drug for several yards and into a thicket of blackberries.

"Martha!" screamed Lydia. "Why are you doing this?"

"How dare you!" fumed Martha as she grabbed the cast-iron skillet from the basket of things in the front passenger seat beside her, flung open the car door, and started toward Lydia.

"Have you lost your mind?" questioned Lydia as she stared at Martha with disbelief. "We need to get Paul to a hospital!"

"Didn't think I'd find out, did you?" snapped Martha.

"Look, I know you didn't mean to hurt him," advised Lydia as she quickly considered what she might say to try to reason with her.

"You could have had any guy you wanted!" screamed Martha. "But you thought you'd try and steal *mine*!"

"He was going to break up with you, anyway," informed Lydia, a little too defiantly for Martha's liking.

"Well, if you're so worried, then perhaps *you'd* better check on him," suggested Martha, oblivious to the fact that the car engine was still running.

"What are you going to do with that skillet?" asked Lydia.

"Well, I certainly won't be cooking any fish with it, now will I?" growled Martha.

"I'm going to check on Paul now," advised Lydia. Afraid to turn her back on Martha, Lydia cautiously glanced in Paul's direction.

The very moment Lydia did so, Martha swung the skillet with all her might, smacking Lydia so hard on the back of the head that she knocked her unconscious.

Meanwhile, at the Krain residence, Professor Ronald Krain had glanced through the kitchen window and noticed his shed door was ajar.

"Where is Martha?" he asked. "Shouldn't she be here by now?"

"She won't be joining us for lunch today," replied Mrs. Krain with a barely noticeable smile of triumph.

"What did you say to her?" demanded her husband.

"Nothing," sneered his wife. "She stopped by earlier to let us know she already had a lunch date with that Johnson boy. At least that's what she said."

"And, of course, you waited until now to mention it?" retorted the Professor. "Isn't it bad enough that Michael can't be here today? And why is that shed door open?"

"Perhaps you should ask Martha?" snickered Mrs. Krain.

"You know what?" hollered her husband. "You can just have Thanksgiving lunch by yourself! I'm going to eat at the school cafeteria. That's probably where Martha is, anyway."

"Fine!" snapped Mrs. Krain, who really didn't seem to care one way or the other what her husband did.

"Don't wait up," advised Ronald Krain as he put on his coat, grabbed his car keys, and slammed the door behind him.

Upon checking the shed, Professor Krain noticed at once that his cast-iron skillet, camping blanket, and a large basket were missing. Had his daughter gone up to Powell Lake with that Johnson boy?

Shaking his head with dismay, Ronald Krain headed toward the stand-alone garage, where his Dodge Ram pickup truck was kept. Just as he reached for the handle of the garage door to open it, he glanced toward the covered carport adjoining his garage. His dark green 1965 Chevy Impala was missing!

Seething with rage, Professor Krain yanked open the garage door, climbed inside his pickup, started it up, and peeled out of the driveway as he headed for Powell Lake. *If that boy so much as lays a hand on my daughter, I'm going to kill him!* decided Ronald Krain.

Over at Powell Lake, Martha sat on the small beach, staring absently at the water. She was in a mild state of shock and disbelief.

"Please let me go?" pleaded Lydia from the nearby tree where Martha had tied her up while she was unconscious. In fact, Lydia's arms were stretched behind her, around the trunk of the tree, and tightly fastened together behind it with a section of baling wire from the back of Woody's green Mustang. "The wire is cutting my wrists and my hands are getting numb! Martha, *please* untie me? I won't tell anyone, I promise! *Please!*"

The lifeless body of Paul Johnson remained in the blackberry thicket, where his head had slammed into a hidden boulder. His death had been painful but quick. The engine of the green Mustang was still running.

Tears of regret began to stream down Martha's cheeks, though she continued to ignore the cries for help from her estranged roommate. Most likely it would be necessary to do away with Lydia, too. Perhaps if she just left her where she was, Lydia might eventually die of exposure to the elements.

Startled to see her father's Dodge Ram pickup truck approach, Martha began to panic. Hurriedly, she ran toward the green Mustang, climbed inside, slammed the door shut, and shifted the still-running car into reverse. It was her plan to flee.

Screeching to a sudden halt behind her, her father's pickup suddenly blocked any possible avenue of escape.

"What in the hell is going on here?" hollered Ronald Krain as he leapt from his pickup, stormed over to the Mustang, and threw open its door. "What have you done?"

Martha froze for a moment before responding. Tears streamed down her cheeks as she replied, "I was going to surprise Paul with a picnic lunch."

"But instead, she found us together," came the voice of Lydia from nearby. "I'm pretty sure Paul is dead now, but your daughter wouldn't let me check on him. And if he is still alive, he needs immediate medical attention."

Professor Krain carefully approached the lifeless body of Paul Johnson and checked it for a pulse. He then checked for any other possible signs of life but found none. Sadly shaking his head, Ronald Krain backed away from the body.

"No!" wailed Lydia. "Maybe if you give him CPR, you could bring him back?"

"And have him testify?" scoffed Professor Krain. "I think not, young lady. I'm sorry, but we must leave him where he is."

"I've already told your daughter that I won't say anything!" assured Lydia, suddenly afraid of what might happen next.

"Where is the Impala?" questioned the Professor as he turned to Martha for a response.

"On a dirt turnout off the small access road on the edge of Woody's property," answered Martha uncomfortably.

"And why would it be there?" pressed her father.

"Because I drove it there when I went to borrow Woody's green Mustang," revealed Martha.

"And Woody knows you have it?" her father seemed surprised.

"Absolutely not!" assured Martha. "I just happened to know where he kept the keys and decided to borrow it."

"Why?" quizzed her father.

"Because I knew you wouldn't want me to drive the Impala on a road like this," responded Martha.

Professor Krain merely shook his head in response. Then, after several moments of awkward silence, he continued.

"This is what we are going to do," informed her father as he pulled out a pocket knife and cut a small branch from a nearby pine tree and began wiping away his tracks from the sand by Paul's body. "Lydia is going to get into the backseat of that Mustang. And then Martha, you are going to drive back to where the Impala is parked. Make sure no one sees you. Stay inside the Mustang until I get there. Can you do that for me?"

"Yes, sir," Martha swallowed hard.

"Lydia, I'm going to untie you from the tree, but will have to secure your hands behind you," explained the Professor. "Martha, if she makes any attempt to escape while I'm doing this, I want you to hit her over the head with that skillet."

Martha weakly nodded her head in response.

"She's already hit me once with that thing," informed Lydia. "That's how she was able to tie me up like this in the first place, while I was unconscious!"

"Give me that!" ordered Professor Krain as he reached for the skillet, took it from Martha, and whacked Lydia on the head with it.

"Is she dead?" questioned Martha as she watched her father untie Lydia from the tree.

"No," replied her father. "But, she'll probably wish she was when she wakes up."

"What are you going to do with her?" delved Martha.

"Plausible deniability is what you will have," answered her father as he secured Lydia's hands behind her with some of the baling wire, wrapped her in the nearby sheet, and carefully placed Lydia into the backseat of the Mustang.

"What if it won't drive like it is, with the bumper all messed up like that?" worried Martha.

After squatting near the front bumper to inspect its damage, Professor Krain informed her, "It's drivable."

"What if someone sees me?" feared Martha.

"You'd better hope they don't. Just drive carefully," bid her father as he got back into his Dodge Ram pickup truck and closed the door without so much as a second glance back at the lifeless body of Paul Johnson. If he had, he might have noticed Lydia's sandals on the ground nearby. "And do not stop anywhere else along the way or speak to anyone!" he added through his open truck window. "I'll meet you at the Impala."

When Martha finally arrived where her father's Impala was parked, she slowly pulled in behind it and shut off the Mustang's engine. Only one other car had passed her during the entire ten-mile journey from Powell Lake to Powell Mountain University. Thankfully, it had not been anyone familiar. No other cars had passed her during the additional miles from there to the Woodcutter's property.

The sound of moaning could be heard from the backseat of the Mustang. Lydia was regaining consciousness! What would Martha do now? If Lydia did call out, someone might hear her! Martha quickly searched for something to stuff into Lydia's mouth, but there was nothing readily available. Unknown to her, Lydia's under panties were neatly folded and inside the pocket of her blue denim miniskirt. Had she known they were there, she would no doubt have used them for that purpose. And, Martha didn't dare use any of her own clothing to gag Lydia with. Who only knew where it might end up!

Martha quickly glanced inside the glovebox but saw nothing promising. She had to act quickly! Martha then thought of the American flag that Woody always kept fastened to the radio antenna of his beat-up old pickup truck. Perhaps on foot, she could stealthily approach without being seen to grab it? It was only 250 yards away from where she was, so she felt certain she could make it.

Despite her father's mandate to remain inside the car, Martha cautiously opened the Mustang door and climbed out. Careful not to slam it, she left the door ajar as she embarked upon her mission.

Angry at herself for wearing her new white peasant top, Martha continued picking her way through the dense manzanita brush that stood in her way. Should she have waited for her father? Tears of remorse flowed freely down Martha's cheeks as she thought of Paul Johnson, the handsome young man she had planned to marry someday. Whatever made him turn to Lydia, of all people? And why had she felt such unbridled rage when seeing Lydia and Paul together? Perhaps she was more like her father than she cared to admit – that is, if her suspicions about him were true. But, after watching Ronald Krain step in and handle the situation at the lake like he did, little doubt remained that her father was capable of just about anything.

Woody and his wife were seated on bar stools at what looked like a rather long curved bar counter, along with their three young children. All of them were seated with their backs to the window – including the little girl, who was in a highchair.

Martha kept low as she scurried toward Woody's pickup truck, pausing often to make sure none of them had turned around or were glancing outside.

The flag did not come off of the antenna as easily as she had anticipated. Woody had tightly fastened it with more of that baling wire he seemed to keep everywhere. Noticing that Mrs. Wilson was getting up from the table, Martha hastily ducked down. After waiting for a few moments, Martha glanced again at Woody and his family. At least they were getting something to eat for Thanksgiving!

Finally prying the end of the baling wire loose with her thumbnail, Martha proceeded to unwind it from the antenna without

186

being seen. At last, the American flag slid free from Woody's antenna and was in her grasp.

Martha hurried as fast as she dared on her return to the damaged green Mustang. What would poor Woody do when he finally saw it?

"There you are!" came the voice of her father as she arrived. "What in the world are you doing, going over there like that?"

"She's waking up and I needed something to put in her mouth," stammered Martha.

"Give me that!" snapped the Professor as he snatched the flag from his daughter. "Good choice, actually. Everyone around here knows that flag belongs to Woody."

"Maybe that's not such a good idea after all," realized Martha.

"Nonsense," smirked Ronald Krain. "It would seem that great minds think alike, after all."

"What's that supposed to mean?" pressed Martha as she watched her father stuff one end of the flag into Lydia's mouth before draping the remainder of it around her head."

"Hand me some more of that baling wire," instructed her father as he held the flag in place.

Martha grabbed the remainder of the baling wire from the back of Woody's wrecked green Mustang and handed it to her father.

"You've got gloves on?" noticed Martha.

"As should you," responded Ronald Krain as he removed a pair of women's green gardening gloves from his pocket and handed them to his daughter. "Put these on. Now, break me off a piece of that wire. Be sure to run your gloves along it first to wipe away any fingerprints."

"What are you going to do with her?" persisted Martha as she put on the gloves.

"Plausible deniability," answered her father with an almost sinister grin on his face. "Your basket and things are in the trunk of the Impala, in a blue duffel bag. Every inch of the Mustang has been wiped free of fingerprints – except the back where you just now retrieved this baling wire. Go wipe it down with the palm of your gloves. Then, get into the Impala, and drive home. I'll be there shortly."

"You aren't going to kill her, are you?" worried Martha.

"What are you so worried about?" countered her father. "After the way you ran down that young man, I should think you'd be relieved to be rid of the one witness who could put you away for life – or worse."

"Worse?" frowned Martha.

"Maybe the gas chamber," speculated Professor Krain.

"I must know what you plan to do with her," insisted Martha. "I'm as much to blame for this as you are!"

"Probably more, I should think," snickered her father as he reached into the backseat of the car, picked up Lydia's semi-conscious body, and hoisted it onto his shoulder.

"She might suffocate with that flag tied over her head," pointed out Martha. "And people will know that's Woody's flag when they finally find her."

"I'm counting on it," replied Ronald Krain, rather evenly. "This charade with the Woodcutter has gone on long enough, anyway."

"What charade?" questioned Martha.

Ignoring her inquiry, Professor Krain added, "If your stepmother asks you anything at all, just tell her you got stood up, and had lunch by yourself at the cafeteria."

"What if they check the receipts and learn that my card wasn't even used there today?" posed Martha.

"You brought your own lunch with you," described her father as he adjusted the weight of Lydia's body. "Lots of kids do that. Now go! We never saw one another today. Understood?"

"Yes, sir," Martha swallowed hard as she watched her father head up the nearby hogback with his unwieldy load.

The following morning, Professor Krain pulled up in front of the girls' dormitory to personally drop off his daughter.

"If anyone asks where your roommate is?" tested Ronald Krain.

"Spending Thanksgiving with her parents at their orange grove," answered Martha. "There was danger of an early frost, and they needed her there to help them light up the smudge pots."

"Very good," approved her father. "And when she doesn't show up Sunday night?"

"Perhaps she was detained, and that I have no idea how much longer she will be," replied Martha, rather nervously.

"You need to sound more convincing than that," pointed out Professor Krain. "Work on it."

"What if someone sees all the blood on this laundry?" feared Martha. "This might not be so easy to explain!"

"Simple, you had a bad nosebleed and got it on your things," replied her father, "though I can't imagine anyone would ask you about it. Besides, if you go straight to the laundry room first and get that stuff started, no one else will even be up yet. Besides, there's no way we dare wash it at the house where your stepmother might see it."

"I sure hope you're right," mumbled Martha Krain as she got out of her father's pickup truck with her basketful of bloody laundry and quickly ascended the dormitory steps. After cautiously checking to be sure no one else was in the first-floor lobby, Martha headed straight for the laundry room.

Thankful that she had remembered to bring enough quarters with her, Martha started her first load of laundry with some extra laundry detergent someone had left behind. Just then, Karlin Gomez rushed into the laundry room and hurriedly stuffed three entire sacks of dirty laundry into the remaining three machines.

"Hey, can't you save at least one of those until later?" objected Martha. "I still have two more to do!"

"What happened to you?" asked Karlin when she noticed fresh blood on the sleeve of Martha's white peasant top.

"Uh," Martha suddenly became quite edgy. "I had a bad nosebleed and got some of it on my blouse. How embarrassing! I also got some of it on my sheets and want to wash them right away, before they become permanently stained."

"Well, I've already started my loads," Karlin shrugged her shoulders. "Sorry! But, at least I don't have any more."

"I guess I'll just have to wait, then. Say, what's that smell?" noticed Martha as she wrinkled up her nose.

"One of my roommates has the stomach flu," lied Karlin. "Hopefully it's not contagious."

"Definitely go ahead," agreed Martha as she nervously stuffed the remainder of her unwashed laundry back into her basket and started to leave.

"Hey, you can just leave that stuff here if you like," offered Karlin. "I'll be happy to start it for you when mine's done. Just leave me some quarters."

"That's all right," responded Martha as she nervously left with the basket of blood-soaked laundry.

Fresh tears began to stream down Martha's cheeks as she raced up the stairwell toward her room. She wept as she thought of her boyfriend Paul Johnson, whose half-dressed body lay dead in a blackberry thicket up at Powell Lake. It almost seemed unreal. Thankfully, his death had been quick, she reasoned. At least with his car parked there, he would no doubt be found sooner rather than later.

Lydia was another story, considered Martha rather sadly. If only she knew what her father had actually done with Lydia's unconscious body. Had her father finished Lydia off, or just left her there to die from exposure to the elements? Would the Woodcutter be blamed for Lydia's death when she finally was found? And, why on earth would her father want that to happen? She felt certain that her father and the Woodcutter had history, and that it involved far more than just Woody being a man of color.

Up on the fifth floor, Carolyn and Karlin had just returned from having breakfast. Woody had not yet arrived.

"Perhaps we should wait downstairs," recommended Carolyn.

"That's not a bad idea," recognized Karlin. "Let me just put on my earrings. I forgot them earlier."

Unlike Carolyn, Karlin never bothered to soak her earrings in alcohol before putting them on. Karlin would put them on first and then hold the bottle of alcohol tightly against each earlobe after putting on her earrings, and with a quick movement of her head would splash on just enough to do the job.

"Aren't you worried about getting an ear infection?" asked Carolyn as she watched the process.

"Not really," shrugged Karlin. "I usually turn them after that, too." Karlin then demonstrated.

"Pretty ingenious," realized Carolyn.

"Why, thank you!" grinned Karlin as she and Carolyn headed from their dormitory room and for the first-floor lobby.

"I sure hope Stacia will be all right," mentioned Carolyn.

"Oh, that's right!" remembered Karlin. "Her brother Alfred is supposed to arrive any time."

"Alfredo," corrected Carolyn.

"Whatever!" shrugged Karlin as they descended the steps.

"Hey, I'm really sorry the weekend turned out like it did," apologized Carolyn.

"It's not your fault Stacia ended up drunk and threw up all over me," assured Karlin in a whisper. "She probably had no idea what alcohol even was."

"I'll bet she does now!" grinned Carolyn. "Hopefully, she learned a lesson from it."

"No kidding! Say, I'm going to try to call Ron again," promised Karlin.

"The guy with the small auto shop down in St. Diablo?" recalled Carolyn. "What if he isn't open today?"

"Perhaps Woody can let you borrow one of his cars for a few days?" suggested Karlin.

"I suppose I can ask him," responded Carolyn, though not sure she wanted to impose so much upon the poor Woodcutter, especially after all he had done to help Carolyn and her family already.

"Karlin?" called the Dean's assistant as they arrived on the first floor. "There's a phone call for you."

"For me?" Karlin was surprised.

"Anyone show up or call for me?" asked Carolyn.

"Not yet," informed the assistant. "I'll let you know."

"Thanks," muttered Carolyn as she sat down on a bench in the lobby to wait for Karlin.


Several minutes later, Karlin approached with a scowl on her face and shook her head with dismay.

"What is it?" pressed Carolyn.

"Karl," spat Karlin.

"Karl?" frowned Carolyn. "Who is Karl?"

"Karl Simpson," Karlin said the name vehemently. "The Security Guard who saw us on the fire escape steps!"

"You're kidding?" exclaimed Carolyn.

"I wish I were!" spat Karlin.

Carolyn put a finger to her lips to caution silence, just in case the Dean's assistant might be eavesdropping.

"Come on," suggested Karlin. "Let's go over into the visiting room. There's no one else in there right now."

Once Carolyn and Karlin were comfortably seated in a far corner of the room, Carolyn turned to Karlin with a worried look on her face. "What are we going to do?"

"He didn't see you or Eula, so *you* have nothing to worry about," revealed Karlin. "But he did see both Stacia and me on the fire escape steps."

"That light that we saw, once Eula and I were on the roof?" recalled Carolyn.

"Yeah, that light," confirmed Karlin. "That was Karl."

"Why did he bother to call you instead of just turning you in?" Carolyn suddenly wanted to know.

"Because, the creep is trying to blackmail me into going out with him!" fumed Karlin. "I've managed to avoid him all year, until now."

"Blackmail you?" repeated Carolyn. "I don't understand."

"It's simple," explained Karlin. "Either I go out with Karl, or he'll tattle on us."

"Then it would only be a matter of time before Stacia opens up her big mouth and says something," predicted Carolyn.

"No, she won't!" assured Karlin. "I have a date with Karl for tomorrow night. He'll be driving me down to St. Diablo where we'll be attending the Saturday night movie of the week."

"It could be worse," consoled Carolyn.

"How?" scowled Karlin.

"You could be worrying about how to get your parents' car repaired without them finding out about it," reminded Carolyn.

"Oh, my gosh! I'll go call Ron right now," replied Karlin as she raced for the first-floor lobby phones.

"Carolyn?" called the Dean's assistant as she poked her head into the visiting area. "There is a Woodrow Wilson here to see you."

"Thank you," acknowledged Carolyn as she raced back into the lobby where Woody the Woodcutter stood waiting.

"Miss Carolyn?" greeted the woodcutter.

"Oh, Woody! Thank you so much for coming!" responded Carolyn. "Something horrible has happened to my father's green Mustang, and I was hoping you might be able to help?"

"Must be da season for it," replied Woody.

"The season for it?" clarified Carolyn.

"Neva mind," smiled Woody. "After you, perty lady."

"Ron said he will meet you there," Karlin informed her as she raced up to where Carolyn and Woody were standing.

"Thank you so much!" replied Carolyn.

"No problem," assured Karlin. "Hey, if you don't mind, I need to get back to the room and get some rest."

Carolyn merely smiled and nodded.

"I take it we's goin' to Ron's, down it St. Diablo?" asked Woody. "Mike's is a mite bit closer."

Carolyn and Woody stepped outside and continued their conversation alone as they walked down the dormitory steps.

"I was afraid Mike might say something to my dad," explained Carolyn as they continued toward the parking lot where her damaged green Mustang was parked.

"And Ron wudn't?" grinned Woody as he shook his head with amusement. "You sure?"

"I'm not sure about anything right now," admitted Carolyn, "but was hoping you could follow me into town and then give me a ride back. I'll pay you."

"Nah, yer money's no good here, perty lady," refused Woody. "It wud be my pleasure to help ya out."

"Well, here it is," motioned Carolyn as they approached the vehicle. "I wasn't sure if it's even safe to drive, or if it needs a tow."

Woody bent down to inspect the damaged front right fender of the Bennett vehicle. "Shudn't be too hard to fix."

"Will it be very expensive?" questioned Carolyn.

"I wud hope not," answered Woody, "but only Ron kin tell ya dat. He just mite be cheeper den Mike."

"Okay, then, where's your truck?" inquired Carolyn.

"Rite over der," motioned Woody with his head. "Say, what'd ya hit, anyway?"

"A squirrel ran across the road," Carolyn replied rather sadly as she fought back a tear. "And, as you know, there is a mountain on one side of that road and a drop-off on the other."

"Mountain wuz probly the best choice," agreed Woody. "Bad break for da squirrel, tho."

"Indeed," nodded Carolyn as she opened the door and climbed into her parents' green Mustang.

The trip into St. Diablo took well over an hour, due to the slower speed Carolyn needed to travel in the damaged vehicle, especially on each hairpin turn.

Upon reaching town, Woody motioned for Carolyn to pull over and then took the lead, since he already knew right where Ron's Auto Shop was located.

After a short trip through the main part of quaint old-town St. Diablo, Woody turned down several smaller streets before finally reaching Ron's Auto Shop. Carolyn was grateful, as she might never have found the place without Woody's help.

Carolyn then pulled into the parking area in front of the two auto bays at the small auto shop while Woody parked his truck out front on the street, took out and lit up his white corncob pipe to smoke while he waited. The aroma of Woody's special brand of "tobacco" wafted gently across the parking lot.

"Hello!" greeted Ron as he approached to get a better look at his potential customer. "You Karlin's friend?"

"I sure am," replied Carolyn through her open window as she parked and started to get out of the car.

"Wait! Start her back up and pull in there," directed Ron as he made a motion with his hand for Carolyn to drive into the auto bay on the right.

"I was kind of hoping to find out what your prices are first," advised Carolyn, rather cautiously.

"This is the cheapest you're gonna get around these parts," chuckled Ron. "Especially with Mike being my only competitor."

"Hang on just a moment," indicated Carolyn as she got out of the Mustang and walked over to Woody's parked truck.

"Well, I ain't got all day," called Ron behind her, half teasingly.

"I just need to ask Woody something," replied Carolyn. Then, lowering her voice so only Woody could hear her, Carolyn whispered, "Is this something you might be able to fix? As long as I have to pay someone, I'd just as soon give the money to you."

"Uh, me wishes I kud," replied Woody as he took another long drag on his pipe. "Even if I fixed de fender, ders no way I kud match de paint color on dat fender fer ya, perty lady. Ron'll do ya rite. He's good people."

Carolyn merely nodded and then returned to where Ron was waiting. "Apparently, you come highly recommended."

"But, of course," grinned Ron, who patiently waited while Carolyn got back into the damaged car and drove it into his auto bay.

Carolyn then glanced around the inside of the car to be sure nothing vital had been left behind that she needed to keep in her possession.

"I'll need the key, too," indicated Ron as he held out his hand.

"When will you know how much it will be?" quizzed Carolyn as she gingerly removed the key from her keyring. The only other key on it was her key from home, since keys were not used at the dormitory.

"A couple days, at least," replied Ron apologetically. "I may need to order some new parts, too, you never know. And, then however long it takes to do the body work, and then to match up and repaint the right front fender."

Ron was about 25 years old, nice looking in a rugged western sort of way, but was definitely not Carolyn's type. His curly red hair was just past his chin and the baseball cap he wore to keep the front portion out of his face was smudged with axle grease. In fact, Ron's blue denim coveralls were also covered with grease and grime, as were his worn-looking work boots. Carolyn tried not to stare with disapproval.

"Say, how's Karlin?" Ron suddenly asked. "I was kind of hoping she might be available tomorrow night."

"Saturday night?" Carolyn swallowed uncomfortably. She knew that Karlin already had agreed to go out with Karl the security guard – though not willingly – but kept silent. "You'd have to ask her."

"Indeed, I will," grinned Ron as he put Carolyn's key on his clipboard before handing it to her. "I'll need you to sign here before I can get your estimate. And, I can just call Mike for his. I promise mine will be lower, whatever it is."

"This says it's an insurance form?" noticed Carolyn.

"Required," replied Ron. "Any time there's an accident. In fact, most insurance companies require at least two, and preferably three estimates, before they'll even touch a claim."

"I was hoping to pay for it in cash, so my father wouldn't find out about it," Carolyn finally admitted.

Ron laughed quite heartily and then became serious. "No can do. They could pull my license if it turns out your vehicle was involved in something like, say, a hit-and-run, or something like that."

"I hit a squirrel," informed Carolyn, saddened by the memory.

"At night?" doubted Ron. "I've never seen a squirrel at night."

"Well, he *was* there, right in front of me, in the headlights of my car!" argued Carolyn. "And just how did you know it was at night?"

"Karlin mentioned it," smiled Ron. "You'd be surprised the stuff people tell me. But, I believe you. Maybe it got spooked by a bobcat or something."

"What else did Karlin say?" probed Carolyn.

"Well," grinned Ron, "Karlin told me about your little accident, the condition your friend Stacia was in, and about you not wanting to get in trouble for coming back late to the dorm."

Ron had her over a barrel, and Carolyn knew it. "My father will kill me."

"Well, look at it this way," laughed Ron, "at least you have a nine-and-a-half-hour head start. You are from Ashton, right?"

"How did you know that?" frowned Carolyn as she finally got out of the green Mustang and stood up.

"License plate frames," pointed out Ron. "Ashton Auto Sales."

Carolyn sighed deeply, nodded, and took the clipboard from Ron. "Can you wait until tomorrow to make any phone calls? I would like a chance to call my parents first."

"Not a bad plan," agreed Ron as he watched Carolyn sign the form and then hand it back to him. "Will Woody be giving you a ride back to the school, then?"

"Uh, yes, he will," answered Carolyn as she approached a nearby paper towel dispenser and tore one off to wipe her hands on.

"I was just gonna say, I am heading up to the Powell Mountain Nursing Home at three o'clock to pick up my mom when her shift ends, and she does live pretty close to the University," described Ron. "I'd be happy to take you back. Besides, it might give me a chance to drop by and see that roommate of yours."

"I think you should call Karlin first," advised Carolyn. "Just to make sure she's there."

"Where else would she be?" frowned Ron.

196

"Oh, maybe over in study hall, or down in Eula's room," replied Carolyn, though she knew her explanation sounded lame.

"She's not seeing someone else, is she?" probed Ron.

"Not that I know of," Carolyn shrugged her shoulders as she turned to leave. "Hey, I hope to hear from you soon – about the car."

"Don't forget to call your father tonight," reminded Ron as he watched Carolyn head for Woody's waiting truck.

"Mind if I stops at me place fer a quik load 'fore we head up de hill?" questioned Woody as he helped Carolyn into his truck and closed the door for her.

"Oh, of course not!" replied Carolyn. "I'm just grateful for the ride. Today's not a school day, anyway."


Carolyn offered more than once to help Woody load the firewood into his truck as she waited, but he would not hear of it. In no time, Woody had filled his truck bed with a fresh load of firewood.

"Sorry 'bout da delay," apologized Woody as he climbed into the old blue pickup truck.

"No problem. Say, didn't you used to have a flag on your antenna?" Carolyn suddenly asked.

"Dem kids," Woody shook his head. "Dey keep stealin' stuff!"

"Oh, really?" Carolyn was surprised. "Like what?"

"Mostly parts, tools, even cars," described Woody.

"How awful!" replied Carolyn. "It seems people would have more respect, especially after all you do for everyone!"

"I dunno. Me don't do dat much," Woody shrugged his shoulders as he pulled his bad leg – the one with the wooden foot – into his truck and then closed its door.

"Nonsense," differed Carolyn. "You practically donated an entire car to the auto class up there at the school! And parts to go with it."

"Humph," mumbled Woody as he set his white corncob pipe in the ashtray and started up his engine. "Just how wudya know dat?"

"Well," explained Carolyn, "I'm the secretary at the Industrial Education Department, and just happened to see an invoice for it."

"Ya don't say," frowned Woody as he shifted into gear, pulled out onto Powell Mountain Road, and began the ascent.

"What's wrong?" questioned Carolyn.

After several moments of silence, Woody finally asked, "Ya wudn't know a fella named Krain, wudya?"

"Professor Krain?" questioned Carolyn. "Yes, he's my boss."

"Oh, Lord Almighty!" Woody shook his head. "Very bad man."

"Professor Krain? Why would you say that?" pressed Carolyn.

"Oh, perty lady," cautioned Woody. "Be careful o' dat man."

"Oh, my goodness! I'd forgotten completely about the fact that he belongs to the Crusading Knights of Powell Mountain! I'm so sorry I mentioned it," apologized Carolyn.

"Woody knows yer not like dem folk," assured Woody. "Ya just shudn't mention to 'em dat we's friends, specially to yer boss man."

"What could he do?" Carolyn shrugged her shoulders.

"He kin do much," replied Woody as he slowed for an upcoming hairpin turn. "Looks like de perty weather be 'bout over."

"It does look like it could rain," noticed Carolyn. "And it was so nice out yesterday."

"Mite even snow, if it gets cold enuf," predicted Woody.

"Can I ask you something?" wondered Carolyn.

"Anythin' perty lady," smiled Woody.

"My friend Eula tells me that the Crusading Knights lit up a burning cross at your place one night, and that it got out of control and caught your house on fire?" delved Carolyn.

Woody's face took on a sad expression and he was silent for several moments before responding.

"I shouldn't have said anything," Carolyn apologized again.

"Nonsense," assured Woody. "What yer friend Eula says is true. Folks like Mister Krain wanna git folks like me and my family off de face of de Earth. But we shows 'em! We just turned 'round 'n repaired de damage. Wuz mostly just de first floor, anyhow. Dey ain't gettin' rid of old Woody ner his kin all dat easily!"

Carolyn suddenly thought of her friend Lenny Owens and of his father. Lenny had mentioned once that his family had relocated to a new home following the Watts riots back in the 1960s. Had they been through something like this?

"Penny fer yer thoughts," offered Woody, in an effort to lighten the mood.

"I was just thinking of a young man I cared about back in high school," mentioned Carolyn. "Lenny was a man of color."

"Really?" grinned Woody. "I bet yer dad just loved dat!"

"Quite the contrary," assured Carolyn. "He forbade me to see Lenny because of his color. And, Lenny's father forbade him to see me, for the same reason."

"Perhaps you two is better off?" Woody sadly shook his head. "De world is unforgivin' of things like dat."

"Lenny promised his mother on her death bed that he would stay in school and become a doctor," added Carolyn. "But his father threatened to pull the plug on his education if Lenny dared to keep seeing 'that *white* girl'!"

"You?" Woody nodded with understanding. "Perhaps sumday yer paths kin cross again?"

Unbidden tears began to escape onto Carolyn's cheeks as she remembered Lenny telling her how much he hoped that their paths would cross again someday.

"Ya shudn't mention any o' dat to yer boss man, either," added Woody as he pulled into the entrance of Powell Mountain University.

"That sounds like good advice! And thanks so much for the ride," commented Carolyn as Woody drove toward the girls' dormitory, pulled up in front of it and came to a stop.

"My pleasure, perty lady," beamed Woody as he got out, hobbled around his truck, and opened the door for Carolyn. "Let me know plez, when ya needs a ride back to Ron's to pik 'er up?"

"I will," promised Carolyn as she walked away and ascended the dormitory steps.

Carolyn was deep in thought as she ascended the stairs which led to the fifth floor of the girls' dormitory.

"Carolyn!" called Stacia from the doorway of her fourth-floor room when she happened to see Carolyn on the landing.

Roused from her thoughts, Carolyn came over to Stacia and Eula's room. "Stacia! How are you? How's your ankle?"

"Hurts like hell!" informed Stacia as she hobbled back into her room to sit down on her bed so she could elevate her leg again.

"I see you have a cast on it?" noticed Carolyn as she followed Stacia inside the room and closed the door.

"And strict orders to stay off of it for at least a week," added Stacia. "I don't know what I'm going to do about classes, either."

"What were you doing up on it just now?" asked Carolyn.

"Actually, I was looking for you," admitted Stacia. "Thankfully, it wasn't necessary to hobble all the way up to your room to wait for you there!"

"For me?" frowned Carolyn.

"Alfredo is down in the lobby," advised Stacia.

"You haven't seen him yet?" Carolyn seemed surprised.

"Oh, yes, and I've had a chance to visit with him," assured Stacia. "It's not that. My ankle began swelling so badly that he insisted I come up here and lay down."

"So, he's just sitting down there waiting for you?" Carolyn was puzzled.

"I have a favor to ask," hesitated Stacia.

Carolyn raised an eyebrow and waited for Stacia to continue.

"I need someone to hang out with Alfredo, show him around, take him over to the cafeteria to eat, that kind of thing," described Stacia. "Here's my food card."

"Why me?" Carolyn was skeptical.

"Well, Eula already has a date with Al Sandut tonight, and Karl Simpson managed to talk Karlin into going out with him tonight, too," informed Stacia. "So, neither of them is available."

"I thought Karlin was going out with Karl tomorrow, for the Saturday night movie thing," mentioned Carolyn. "Wait a minute! She actually told you about Karl blackmailing her to go out with him?"

"I feel horrible about it, too! It's all my fault," lamented Stacia.

"I'm curious why Karlin would even tell you?" queried Carolyn. "Last I heard, she wasn't gonna say anything."

"I kind of forced it out of her when I tried to get her to go out with Alfredo," confessed Stacia. "I insisted upon a good explanation why she couldn't."

"Well, maybe Karl won't be all that bad," hoped Carolyn.

"He's a total dweeb, and you know it," smiled Stacia. "And, I want you to know how horrible I feel for throwing up in your car, too! I owe both you and Karlin bigtime!"

"You owe me nothing," assured Carolyn, "but I will use your food card for whatever your brother decides to eat."

"Then you'll do it?" Stacia seemed relieved.

"Of course," agreed Carolyn. "Do you want me to bring you anything back?"

"Alfredo already went over to the market and bought me a huge basket of things to tide me over," indicated Stacia with a nod of her head at the large basket of non-perishable food items on her desk.

"That was thoughtful of him," approved Carolyn.

"Alfredo is a very thoughtful guy," Stacia smiled with a slight twinkle in her eyes as she grabbed her food card from the table beside her bed and handed it to Carolyn. "Anyway, he's down there waiting for you."

After quickly changing into her best pair of jeans and a warmer top, Carolyn grabbed her beaded handbag – the one that matched her sisal rope platform sandals – and fastidiously checked her hair and makeup one last time. Just in case, Carolyn also grabbed a sweater.

Carolyn tried to imagine what Alfredo might look like as she descended the various flights of stairs. He definitely would have dark skin like Stacia, and most likely would have straight, dark hair. Would he be tall, too, or just average in size like Stacia?

What am I worried about? Carolyn suddenly chided herself. The guy lives all the way in the Dominican Republic, and is only here for the weekend! I'll probably never see him again.

When Carolyn entered the visiting room, she was stunned by the incredibly handsome, dark stranger there, and stared with disbelief. He was not extremely tall, but at least six foot two and probably about 28 years old! Surely that can't be Alfredo? His hair was not straight – anything but – yet it was not worn in the traditional afro hairstyle that most black people sported back in the 1970s, either. Kinky but close-cropped, his hair was very neat looking. His blue denim jeans were straight-legged and fit snuggly over the tops of his steel-tipped cowboy boots. Most people in the 1970s wore bell-bottomed pants that came down to at least the ankle, but he was from another country and probably didn't know that. Alfredo also wore a light blue polo shirt and a rather nice looking black leather jacket. A black and maroon colored motorcycle helmet was tucked under his left arm.

"Miss Carolyn?" greeted the stranger with a warm smile as he approached and extended his right hand.

"Alfredo McFerson?" smiled Carolyn, a little more flirtatiously than she had intended.

"My apologies that you're stuck with me for the day," Alfredo flirted back as he gallantly kissed the back of Carolyn's hand. "And hopefully for the evening, too," added Alfredo as he admired Carolyn, causing her to blush.

Alfredo's thick Dominican Republic accent almost sounded Spanish to Carolyn, yet somehow different. In spite of it, Alfredo was well-versed in the English language and quite articulate.

"Not at all," replied Carolyn. "The pleasure is all mine! I'm only sorry you weren't able to spend more time with your sister."

"Perhaps you can show me around in her stead?" suggested Alfredo. "I would be delighted to see where my baby sister attends her classes, and whatever other sights on your beautiful campus you think I might like to see."

Carolyn merely nodded as she stared at the striking foreigner.

"Would that be all right?" Alfredo had an alluring smile.

"Oh, yes, absolutely!" beamed Carolyn. She could not believe Stacia had failed to mention how handsome her brother actually was.

Alfredo then extended his right arm to Carolyn, for her to grab onto as they left the visiting room. "Shall we?"

"Have you had lunch yet?" Carolyn suddenly asked.

"We are actually three hours ahead of your time in the Dominican Republic," informed Alfredo as they exited the girls' dormitory, "so instead of noon there it would be mid-afternoon already."

"Oh." Carolyn seemed disappointed.

"But, that doesn't mean I'm not hungry," smiled Alfredo. His remark almost seemed to encompass more than just food, but Carolyn decided to feign naiveté. After all, she really knew nothing about him.

"Is that your motorcycle?" wondered Carolyn when she saw it parked out front.

"It's a rental," advised Alfredo. "Have you ever ridden one?"

"Only once." Carolyn frowned at the memory.

"Was it not a pleasant ride?" questioned Alfredo as they descended the front steps of the girls' dormitory.

"It was at a church picnic, when I was in the eighth grade," remembered Carolyn. "The man who had it gave all the kids a ride around the cow pasture there."

"A cow pasture?" laughed Alfredo. "No wonder you didn't enjoy the ride!"

"It would probably be easier to just walk over to the cafeteria." Carolyn hoped to change the subject.

"Tell me please, what kind of a man would make kids ride on the back of a motorcycle through a cow pasture?" pressed Alfredo.

"It was only for fun," replied Carolyn. "He actually let the older kids try it on their own."

"Uh, and you were one of them?" perceived Alfredo with a sly grin. "On which leg did the motorcycle land when you fell?"

"My right one." Carolyn flushed with embarrassment.

"First of all," teased Alfredo, "I promise not to let you drive the motorcycle by yourself, and most certainly will not be driving it through a cow pasture!"

"That's good to know," laughed Carolyn, finally seeing the humor in his response.

"What is that building over there?" inquired Alfredo. "The one with all the fancy gargoyles on it?"

Carolyn glanced up at the building indicated, where tiny cement figures engaging in lascivious acts of pleasure, frolicking, eating grapes, or playing small harps, adorned its front soffits. "That's the Administrative Building, though I'm not sure those are actually gargoyles. This place used to be some sort of exclusive resort back in the 1800s, and last I heard the school eventually plans to remove them due to their inappropriate subject matter."

Alfredo and Carolyn then laughed together as they walked arm-in-arm past the imposing gray and tan brick structure.

"This place reminds me of a scene from Camelot," decided Alfredo as he studied the black spired rooftops on most of the older buildings surrounding them.

"Yeah, it does," agreed Carolyn. "Usually, my view of it is from the window of the fifth floor in the girls' dormitory, and when I'm rushing to and from classes I rarely take the time to admire any of the buildings."

"That one over there seems much newer," assessed Alfredo. "The one with the open courtyard and the water feature in front of it."

"That's the cafeteria," replied Carolyn. "Sometimes the kids just bring their food outside and sit on the cement bench beside it – at least when it's nice out."

"The sun still could come out again today," hoped Alfredo. "It was really quite beautiful driving up here yesterday."

"And that building over there is the Industrial Education Building," indicated Carolyn. "That's where I'm assigned to work as a secretary for the professors there."

"Sounds boring," smiled Alfredo as they approached the cafeteria. He immediately rushed ahead to open the door.

"Thank you." Carolyn was quite impressed with Alfredo's manners, so far.

"Is it all vegetarian?" asked Alfredo as they got in line to get their food.

"I'm afraid so," apologized Carolyn. "But, they've come a long way with imitation meat. Some of it's not all that bad."

"Suppose I take you to a restaurant somewhere?" offered Alfredo. "One that serves real food."

"Really?" Carolyn was surprised. "I had planned on paying for our meal with my food card." She decided not to mention that she also had Stacia's food card in her possession.

"My treat," grinned Alfredo.

"Okay, sure, why not?" Carolyn finally agreed.

"It will mean riding on the back of the motorcycle," reminded Alfredo as they exited the cafeteria.

Carolyn seemed to waffle in a moment of indecision but then finally shrugged her shoulders. "Perhaps it's time I rode a motorcycle somewhere else besides a cow pasture."

Both Alfredo and Carolyn laughed quite heartily as they made their way back across the campus to where the 350 Honda motorcycle was parked. Unseen by them, the scowling face of Professor Ronald Krain observed them with disapproval from his office window at the Industrial Education Department.

"You will need these," advised Alfredo as he reached into a compartment on the motorcycle, brought out a pair of pant leg cuff clips, and handed them to Carolyn.

"I used to have a pair of those for my bicycle," recognized Carolyn. "Before someone stole it."

"Do they have much problem with theft around here?" worried Alfredo as he checked the locks on the motorcycle compartments.

"Not around here. Mostly just murders," added Carolyn as she put the cuff clips on her pant legs.

"Murders?" Alfredo was shocked by the revelation.

"The Powell Mountain killer has killed at least two people this year – that they've told us about – so the school has a very strict policy about any of us wandering off alone," described Carolyn.

"I should hope so!" exclaimed Alfredo. "I would not want anything to happen to Miss Anastacia. She's the only sister I have."

"How old were you when she was born?" probed Carolyn.

"Uh, you wish to know how old I am?" flirted Alfredo with his irresistible smile. "Americans never cease to amaze me with their round-about way of asking questions."

"So, is it the Dominican Republic way to avoid answering them?" teased Carolyn as she stood back up to see how her bell-bottomed pants looked with the pant leg cuff clips on them.

"I'm 28 years old, next-in-line to inherit my father's tobacco plantation, and currently looking for the right woman to share the rest of my life with," described Alfredo as he put on his helmet and climbed onto his motorcycle. "Is that direct enough?"

Carolyn stood for a long moment before climbing onto the motorcycle behind him, but did not answer.

"You must hang on tight, and whatever you do, do not let go!" instructed Alfredo.

Carolyn nodded that she understood as she put her arms around him. His shoulders were too broad to hang onto very well, so she moved in closer and put her arms around his muscular chest instead.

"Do you like Mexican food?" shouted Alfredo, to be heard above the roar of the motorcycle.

"Yes!" answered Carolyn.

"Me, too! I saw this place down in St. Diablo that looked pretty good." recalled Alfredo.

"Maria's?" queried Carolyn.

"I think that was it," nodded Alfredo. "Hang on!"

Carolyn hung on for all she was worth as Alfredo negotiated the treacherous hairpin turns. Near the bottom of the mountain, she suddenly recognized the place where she had hit the poor squirrel and damaged the right front fender on her parents' green Mustang earlier that same morning. No wonder she was so tired!

Down in St. Diablo, Carolyn and Alfredo were just finishing up their meal at Maria's Mexican Restaurant when Karlin walked in with Karl Simpson.

"Karlin!" greeted Carolyn when she saw her.

"Carolyn?" noticed Karlin as she hurried over to say hello.

"This is Stacia's brother, Alfredo," introduced Carolyn. "This is my roommate, Karlin."

Alfredo immediately stood up, took Karlin's hand in greeting, and chivalrously kissed it. "The pleasure is all mine."

Karlin blushed slightly but then smirked with satisfaction when she noticed the jealous look on Karl's face.

"I'm her date, Karl Simpson." He introduced himself rather curtly. "Security guard up at Powell Mountain University." He then gave Karlin a meaningful glance which did not go unnoticed by Carolyn or Alfredo as he headed toward a different table.

Karlin leaned close to Carolyn and whispered, "Trade you dates?"

Carolyn whispered back with an amused look on her face. "You wish!"

"See you later, then," bid Karlin as she followed Karl Simpson over to the table where he was already standing and waiting behind a chair that he had pulled out for Karlin.

"They should join us?" offered Alfredo as he started to get back up. "Is she not also one of Anastacia's close friends?"

"She is one of Stacia's close friends," responded Carolyn, "but I think they want to be alone together."

Alfredo furled his brow and sat back down. "Strange, but Miss Karlin did not seem very enthused with her date."

"No, she didn't, did she?" agreed Carolyn.

"Perhaps we should rescue her?" Alfredo raised one eyebrow.

Carolyn merely shook her head.

"I would love to know why such a beautiful young lady would go out with a guy she clearly does not like?" urged Alfredo with a persuasive smile. "There must be a good reason."

"I'm afraid you would have to ask her about that," suggested Carolyn. "It would not be my place to gossip about it." She was not about to be drawn into a conversation that would lead to telling Alfredo about Karlin and his sister being seen on the fire escape stairs, or that Stacia had been drunk at the time.

Alfredo slowly nodded. "Very well, shall we go for a ride someplace more private where we can get to know one another better?"

"What do you have in mind?" Carolyn became suspicious of his motives. "It took me twenty minutes just to brush the snarls from my hair when we got here, but then you already know that!"

"You will wear my helmet," insisted Alfredo as he took her hands in his and gazed into Carolyn's eyes.

"Plus, it's getting cold out there," added Carolyn. "It will probably rain before we get back."

"Then you will wear my jacket, as well," persisted Alfredo as he stood to take it off before walking over to where Carolyn was seated and tenderly draped it over her shoulders.

"What about you?" argued Carolyn. "Won't you be cold?"

"It is not important," assured Alfredo as he laid a twenty-dollar bill on the table before extending his hand to Carolyn.

Realizing she was out of excuses, Carolyn slowly took Alfredo's hand as she got up. "Thank you for lunch, by the way."

"My pleasure." Alfredo's gaze seemed to envelop Carolyn as he helped her put on his jacket. He then extended one of his muscular brown arms to her while he grabbed his helmet with the other. It had been sitting on one of the other chairs at the table. Carolyn could not help but stare at Alfredo's well-built physique, especially without his jacket on! She hoped fervently that his good manners would continue once he had her alone.

"See you soon!" called Carolyn to her friend Karlin from across the room.

"Count on it!" replied Karlin, who did not appear to be having an enjoyable time with her date.

"Sir, your change," offered the waitress as she hurried to give it to Alfredo before he left.

Alfredo merely smiled and waved her away. "Everything was splendid, thank you so much!"

"Thank YOU!" beamed the waitress, stunned that a perfect stranger would leave such a large tip for a six-dollar meal.

"Are you always so generous?" asked Carolyn as they left and approached the motorcycle.

"Only with my friends and people that I like," responded Alfredo as he gently placed his helmet on Carolyn's head and fastened the chinstrap. "I would like to see Powell Lake while I'm here. Are you up for it?"

"Powell Lake?" frowned Carolyn. She was becoming more exhausted by the minute from being up all night. Plus, she still needed to call her parents before it got too late.

"It is still early," reminded Alfredo, as if he could read her thoughts.

"Sure, why not?" Carolyn finally agreed. "As long as you can promise to have me back before curfew." Carolyn frowned when she thought of how she and her friends had snuck into the dormitory early that morning.

"Curfew?" Alfredo seemed surprised. "When might that be?"

"Nine o'clock," informed Carolyn.

"Absolutely, I promise!" Alfredo and Carolyn then climbed onto the motorcycle where she quickly put her arms around him as he revved up the engine before taking off with Carolyn hanging on for dear life.


Some sun managed to stream through the surrounding forest as Alfredo and Carolyn sped up Powell Mountain Road on the motorcycle, yet the sky was turning dark. It was going to rain, that much was certain!

"That's where the Woodcutter lives," pointed out Carolyn as they passed an older looking two-story stone building that was set back from the road.

Alfredo slowed to admire a rickety but eye-catching wooden roadside sign that rested in the hands of a hand-carved, life-sized wooden statue of an ornately decorated woodcutter. It was clearly intended to depict a man of color. On his head was a white hardhat and in his mouth was a white corncob pipe. The black sign's gold lettering simply read, "Woody's Salvage Yard and Woodcutting." There was no way of knowing when the place might be open for business, as no phone or other contact information was listed. On one side of the gravel entrance road was a quarter acre salvage yard of older cars and parts in various degrees of usability. On the other side of the old stone building where the Woodcutter and his family now lived was a huge stack of firewood, with a well-used axe stuck into an old tree stump beside it. Most of the surrounding clutter was hidden from view of the main road by dense manzanita brush, scrub oaks and

208

various other trees. It was therefore somewhat of a relief to local residents that only the top part of the Woodcutter's two-story stone residence was easily visible from Powell Mountain Road.

Carolyn had mentioned during her late lunch with Alfredo that Woody had driven her back from town earlier that day, after she had dropped off her car for minor fender work. She had even mentioned that it was the result of an unfortunate squirrel who had crossed her path, but the rest of her tale remained untold.

Alfredo slowed as he prepared to negotiate the next hairpin turn but then came to a stop. "Nice car!"

Carolyn turned in time to see a well-kept, dark green 1965 Chevy Impala that had been parked in a dirt turnout, just off the road. "That is a nice car. Odd place to leave it."

"Who knows, maybe they broke down." Alfredo shrugged his shoulders as he revved up his engine and took off again.

Unseen by either of them, Martha Krain had been inside of the Impala, having ducked in the nick of time to avoid being visible when she heard the motorcycle approach. Martha had been absolutely beside herself since the horrible events of the previous day. How could she have done such a thing? She still could not believe that she had actually run down and killed Paul Johnson, the love of her life, the man she had intended to marry. "Oh, Paul, I'm so sorry!" sobbed Martha as she tried to regain her composure.

Martha felt sick as she thought not only of Paul, but of her roommate Lydia, and that horrible load of bloody laundry her father had insisted she take and wash! Tears of grief and remorse streamed down Martha's cheeks as the knot in her stomach grew. On the seat beside her was the bottle of Valium she had taken from her stepmother's top dresser drawer. Unable to cope with the guilt and despair any longer, Martha had decided she would end her own life. She could not go on like this! But first, she would find Lydia. She must know for herself whether Lydia was still alive, or not. She also hoped that her father would not notice right away that his precious Chevy Impala was missing – again!

It was her plan to try to rescue Lydia – if she were still alive. Hopefully, she would be able to discover where her father had secreted the unconscious girl. Time would be of the essence now, especially with it ready to rain. Any tracks he had left behind would surely be eradicated after that! "Oh Lydia!" wept Martha. "Forgive me!"

Waiting until the sound of the motorcycle was gone, Martha stealthily climbed from the Impala, lightly closed its door, and made her way through the Manzanita brush toward the Woodcutter's shed. She would need to find something from which to construct a stretcher she could drag. Martha would not be able to carry Lydia by herself.

But, what if Lydia were no longer alive? Once the body was found, the Woodcutter's flag would point directly back to him, and it was all her fault! Why had she ever taken it? Martha decided right then that she was not about to let the poor Woodcutter be blamed for something he hadn't done! She would need to be prepared for whatever she might find, though. If Lydia was already dead – as she suspected – she would need to torch the body, including the flag, as it undoubtedly was soaked with blood from Lydia's head wounds. There was an extra can of gas in the Woodcutter's shed and she knew right where it was.

Martha managed again to sneak past the Woodcutter's residence without being seen. Silently, she opened the door to his shed and slipped inside. After commandeering the nearly-full can of gas, Martha started to leave but then noticed an old green Army bag. It was one of those top loading ones, so if she cut it down both sides with her Swiss Army knife and then spread it out lengthwise, it would make an excellent stretcher! All she would need to do is fasten a pole onto either side of it. She could use some of that baling wire Woody kept everywhere and weave it back and forth through the sides of the fabric. Before going to all that trouble, though, she would wait to see if Lydia were still alive. At least she would have the Army bag and some bailing wire with her. In fact, she could carry both the gas can and the baling wire inside the old green Army bag.

"Oh, please let me find her!" muttered Martha as she returned to where the wrecked green Mustang had been left. The brush pulled around and over the vehicle would make it most difficult to find, of that she had no doubt. It could be months or even years before its discovery.

The Army bag and its contents were becoming quite heavy, but that did not matter. She must find Lydia before it was too late.

Carefully following the exact same route she had seen her father take, Martha searched for any signs of broken branches or other disturbances that might signal the way. He had done a rather thorough job of wiping away most of his tracks, but not all. There were also other telltale signs that finally led her to the shallow ravine where the body of Lydia Cain had been left beneath a huge brush pile, including a torn piece of her father's jacket on one of its branches. Martha carefully retrieved and pocketed it.

"Lydia?" called Martha, hoping against hope that her roommate might still be alive. But, there was only silence.

Martha cautiously moved aside the entire brush pile, piece by damning piece, until uncovering the lifeless body of Lydia Cain.

"Oh, Lydia!" wailed Martha as she dropped the green Army bag and sank to her knees in the dirt. "What have I done?" sobbed Martha as she held her face in her hands.

Unsure how long she had knelt there staring at the horrific scene, Martha realized she must hurry if she was going to burn Lydia's body before it began to rain. The flag would need to be made less noticeable, too. That was it! She could fashion a head-sized hood from the Army bag, and put it over Lydia's head. First, she would weave the baling wire through the edges of it, so it could be pulled taut and stay in place. Then, if her attempts to torch the body were unsuccessful, perhaps the gasoline might at least keep predators away. Martha could not bear the thought of vultures or other wild creatures feeding upon Lydia's carcass.

Martha carefully poured gasoline over the entire scene, concentrating in particular upon the crudely fashioned green hood over Lydia's head. All at once, a clap of thunder could be heard. The rain began pouring down quite heavily. It would be impossible to complete what she had begun, and Martha knew it. She would have to pull the brush pile back over Lydia's body and just leave her there, along with the gas can. Thankfully, she had remembered to bring and wear the green gardening gloves she had worn earlier. At least there would be no fingerprints of her own left behind. Not that it would matter anyway after she ended her own life, which was next on her list. Then, in one last act of generosity toward her undeserving father, Martha grabbed a pine branch and tried her utmost – despite the heavy rain – to wipe away all tracks from the area, including those behind her as she left.

Meanwhile, up at Powell Lake, Alfredo and Carolyn had finally found a secluded beach with a log on it where they could sit to continue their conversation. The first secluded beach area they had come across before that had already been taken by someone else, as evidenced by the old blue Volkswagen parked at its entrance. Had they only ventured into it, they might have discovered the lifeless body of Paul Johnson lying face up in the blackberry canes.

As it was, they were now on the complete opposite side of the lake, seated on a log overlooking it. "Did you hear that?" questioned Carolyn. "That sounds like thunder."

Alfredo sighed deeply with frustration. He had finally managed to get Carolyn alone in the perfect setting and now would be forced to take her back. "Perhaps it is farther away than it sounds?"

"At the first sign of rain, we need to head back," insisted Carolyn. "Plus, it's absolutely freezing up here!"

"Tell me about it," smiled Alfredo as he glanced at his warm leather jacket, that Carolyn was wearing.

"I'm so sorry!" apologized Carolyn as she started to take it off.

"Nonsense," refused Alfredo as he scooted over and put his arm around her. "Tell me more about yourself."

"That's all I've been doing all afternoon," objected Carolyn. "Now it's my turn to learn about you!"

"What would you like to know?" Alfredo's eyes seemed to envelop her with an inescapable magnetic pull. "May I kiss you?"

Carolyn hesitated. "This is only our first date."

"You must surely feel the magic between us?" Alfredo tenderly touched the side of Carolyn's face as he wiped away a stray hair. "You are so beautiful!"

Carolyn suddenly stood up, hoping that would put her in a safer position to ward off Alfredo's advances, should they get out of hand.

"What's wrong? Is the log uncomfortable?" worried Alfredo.

"Uh, it was a little hard," muttered Carolyn rather nervously.

Alfredo then stood up, too, and pulled Carolyn against him. She could feel the hardness of his body against her, and his desire for her was unmistakable.

"Please take me back," insisted Carolyn.

"May I just kiss you first?" pleaded Alfredo. "I will do nothing you do not want me to, I promise."

"Just a kiss and nothing else?" clarified Carolyn.

Alfredo then kissed her tenderly and passionately on the lips as he pulled her closer still. Carolyn finally closed her eyes and kissed him back, imagining for a moment that he was Lenny. If only he really were, she thought to herself as she allowed herself to be caught up in the moment. An indescribable sort of electricity flowed between them.

"That wasn't so bad, was it?" smiled Alfredo as he stopped kissing Carolyn long enough to study her face more carefully.

Carolyn then opened her eyes and pulled away. "I can't do this."

"Who is he?" demanded Alfredo, half teasingly. "The one you thought of while you were kissing me?"

"What?" Carolyn was stunned. *How could he possibly know?*

"It is in your eyes," replied Alfredo as he gazed into them. "They are like a window to the soul, you know."

Carolyn became overcome with emotion and suddenly unbidden tears escaped the corners of her eyes and began to flow down her cheeks.

"I am so sorry!" apologized Alfredo as he pulled Carolyn close to hug her, this time just to comfort her. "I did not mean to make you cry. And I had no right to expect so much so quickly. I hope you will not think badly of me?"

Carolyn pulled back to look at Alfredo's face. "I'm the one who is sorry. You were up front with me from the very beginning when you told me that you are looking for a wife. But, I can't just marry someone I don't even know and suddenly move to a foreign country."

"Is that what you think this is about?" Alfredo suddenly laughed.

Carolyn raised an eyebrow.

"I was merely hoping that you and I could have an enjoyable day together," explained Alfredo. "And we have."

Carolyn then pulled Alfredo close and kissed him on the lips, but not as passionately as before.

Alfredo then pulled away. "Just who is the man who holds your heart hostage like this? Does he know how lucky he is?"

Carolyn then became sullen and quiet as she glanced wistfully at the darkening sky. "It is like two ships passing in the night."

"Ships that pass in the night, and speak each other in passing?" recited Alfredo with a wry smile.

"You've heard of it?" Carolyn was stunned.

"They have books in my country, too," grinned Alfredo. "*The Theologian's Tale*, from *Tales of a Wayside Inn.* My father has a first edition in his library. It was published in 1873."

"Only a signal shown and a distant voice in the darkness," continued Carolyn.

"So on the ocean of life, we pass and speak one another, only a look and a voice, then darkness again and a silence," finished Alfredo.

Carolyn and Alfredo then stood quietly watching the ducks diving for fish, until they felt the first drops of rain.

"It would seem we must head back now," acknowledged Alfredo rather sadly as he guided Carolyn toward the motorcycle, with his arm still around her. "That is one of the most romantic passages of literature in history, you know. Whatever made you think of it now?"

"You did," smiled Carolyn as she put the helmet back on. "I've never met anyone quite like you before."

"Nor will you again," assured Alfredo as they climbed onto the motorcycle.

Saturday morning was overcast and rain hung heavily in the air. Exhausted from her date with Alfredo the previous day – not to mention everything that happened before that – Carolyn managed to sleep until well after noon.

"Wake up!" urged Karlin. "You're gonna end up sleeping the entire weekend away."

"What time is it?" yawned Carolyn as she slowly stretched and sat up in bed.

"It's almost one o'clock," chuckled Karlin. "That was some hunk you were out with, by the way."

"Stacia's brother?" laughed Carolyn, trying her best to appear nonchalant about it.

"I can't believe she never told us what a stone-cold fox he is!" continued Karlin.

"Well, it's not likely that I'll be leaving all this to go live on a tobacco planation somewhere in the Dominican Republic," assured Carolyn as she sat up to put on her slippers.

"Say what?" pressed Karlin. "He didn't ask you to marry him, did he?"

"Not in so many words." Carolyn decided to be elusive.

214

"Well, he left that for you when he came back by this morning to say goodbye to his sister," indicated Karlin as she nodded toward a beautiful red rose in a glass vase on Carolyn's desk. "He said to 'please give it to Miss Carolyn' for him."

"I see," mumbled Carolyn as she stood up and walked over to smell it. "Did he say anything else?"

"No, not really," answered Karlin. "At least not to me."

"Say, how was your date with Karl?" Carolyn decided to change the subject.

Karlin simply made a sour face and rolled her eyes.

"That good, huh?" chuckled Carolyn as she grabbed her robe from the back of the chair and put it on. "I'll be right back; I need to use the little girls' room."

"I'll go with you," responded Karlin as they both headed for the door to their dorm room. "After our late lunch at Maria's, the creep took me to see *The Exorcist* of all things, can you believe it?"

"*The Exorcist?*" Carolyn shook her head. "Never heard of it."

"It's been out since last year," informed Karlin. "It's a horror movie! Anyway, I can't believe he would have the nerve to take me to see a movie like that!"

"You should've just gotten up and left," responded Carolyn as they reached the fourth-floor landing.

"Actually, that's exactly what I did," admitted Karlin rather sheepishly. "Now, there's no guarantee whether he'll say anything about Stacia and me being on the fire escape stairs, or not."

Carolyn stopped and shook her head. "That's not good."

"Don't worry," assured Karlin. "No matter what Karl says, it's only his word against ours."

"You'd better make sure Stacia knows that," recommended Carolyn as she continued into the restroom. "Perhaps we should stop by and pay her a visit after this?"

"You read my mind," responded Karlin as she and Carolyn proceeded to use the restroom.

As they were washing their hands afterwards, Carolyn suddenly asked, "How in the world did you get back up here to the school after you walked out on Karl?"

"I called the Woodcutter," replied Karlin. "He had a load of firewood to bring up the mountain, anyway. I don't know what any of us would do without that man! Thank goodness he's always willing to help folks out like he does."

"That's for sure!" agreed Carolyn as she dried her hands.

"Did you remember to call your father yet?" reminded Karlin as she dried her hands, too.

"Oh, no!" realized Carolyn. "I completely forgot about it!"

"Well, I need to go see Stacia right now," indicated Karlin.

"I'll call my dad right after that," conceded Carolyn. "A few more minutes probably won't make any difference at this point."

"Guess you'll find out," replied Karlin as they headed for Eula and Stacia's room and briskly knocked on the door.

"It's open," called Stacia.

"How are you?" greeted Carolyn as she and Karlin entered the room. "Do you need anything?"

Stacia then grinned at Carolyn and shook her head.

"What?" demanded Carolyn.

"You broke his heart, you know." Stacia was looking at Carolyn, but had a twinkle in her eyes.

"Explain," frowned Carolyn.

"I'm kidding!" laughed Stacia as Carolyn and Karlin sat down on Eula's bed.

"Where's Eula, anyway?" queried Karlin.

"She went to get me some lunch," answered Stacia.

Carolyn became quiet.

"I was only joking," reassured Stacia. "My brother has left a long list of broken hearts behind, believe me! It's about time he met someone able to give him a run for his money."

"I don't understand." Carolyn truly didn't.

"No woman has ever turned my brother down before," elaborated Stacia. "Until now, of course."

Carolyn flushed deeply as Karlin and Stacia grinned at her.

"You turned him down?" Karlin was flabbergasted.

"I didn't exactly turn him down," clarified Carolyn. "I did let him kiss me, but nothing else."

"And then?" pressed Karlin.

Carolyn shrugged her shoulders.

"And then he probably asked her to give up all this and go live in the Dominican Republic on our tobacco plantation," guessed Stacia with a huge grin.

"You do have a tobacco plantation, don't you?" Carolyn became skeptical.

"We do," confirmed Stacia.

"You're kidding?" Karlin seemed puzzled. "I thought Carolyn was just being facetious. And I'd always assumed you dressed the way you did because your family was hard-pressed financially?"

Neither Karlin nor Carolyn had noticed Eula slip into the room.

"That's what I thought, too," laughed Eula as she tossed her purse onto her desk before bringing Stacia a food tray with a plateful of vegetarian tacos on it."

"Oh, thank you!" beamed Stacia. "I was starving!"

"Then, after giving this young lady half of my sexiest clothes," continued Eula, "I found out that her family's actually quite wealthy!"

"You definitely blew it, then," surmised Karlin as she winked at Carolyn. Then, turning to the others, she added, "He even left a single red rose for her!"

"Oh, girl!" chided Eula.

Carolyn then smiled and shrugged her shoulders.

"There was one other thing my brother did confide to me before he left," added Stacia as she gave Carolyn a sly smile.

Carolyn motioned for her to continue.

"Alfredo felt certain that you were already in love with someone else, but just wouldn't tell him who it was," revealed Stacia.

"Lenny Owens?" interjected Karlin with a knowing nod.

"Well, uh, yeah," stammered Carolyn. "But, I didn't tell Alfredo that! He just seemed to know there was someone else."

"Whatever *did* you say to that man?" demanded Eula as she turned to Carolyn. "I've seen Stacia's brother for myself, and he's absolutely drop-dead gorgeous!"

"Well, it wasn't really what *was* said, but more of what *wasn't*. It was just after we kissed," elaborated Carolyn.

"He's just not used to having any competition," grinned Stacia. "You're probably the best thing that's ever happened to my brother."

"Hold it! Hold it!" interrupted Eula. "Tell me this – just why hasn't Lenny bothered to write to Carolyn yet? She did mention to his cousin Pete that she goes to school here, didn't she?"

"No, I didn't!" reminded Carolyn. "I didn't even have a chance to. There just wasn't enough time."

"That's right," confirmed Karlin. "And you suggested she write to Pete. Remember?"

"Oh, that's right," realized Eula. "Well, it was the day before yesterday, and that seems like a lifetime ago already."

"Not to my ankle, it doesn't!" advised Stacia as she glanced at the ace bandage on her ankle. "It about killed me making the trip downstairs to see my brother off."

"Speaking of killed," Eula redirected the conversation, "I hear they found another body this morning. Al mentioned it to me at lunch today. It was on the morning news. Some fisherman found it."

"None of the coeds on this campus are safe!" assumed Carolyn.

"It wasn't a girl," advised Eula. "This time it was a guy."

"A guy?" Carolyn was stunned.

"The Sheriff won't say who it is yet, though," continued Eula. "They still have to notify the family. But they did say he was a student here."

The room became quiet for several moments.

"Where did they find him?" Karlin suddenly asked.

"Up at Powell Lake," replied Eula. "They also found a blue Volkswagen, probably his."

"A *blue* Volkswagen?" Carolyn became ashen. "Alfredo and I drove right past a blue Volkswagen when we were up at Powell Lake yesterday! It was parked by one of those little beaches."

"Oh, my God!" exclaimed Karlin. "Did you see anyone else while you were up there?"

"I don't think so," believed Carolyn, though she wasn't sure.

# 6. Angie's Secret

"**W**here will you be staying while you're here?" questioned Detective Priest as he turned to Jim Otterman. They had just finished with the informal questioning of Carolyn Bennett-Hunter and were standing at the cash register in the foyer of Maria's Mexican Restaurant.

"At the Powell Mountain Bed and Breakfast," advised Jim as he snatched the bill for lunch from the waitress and quickly swiped his smartwatch over the cash register on the counter.

"Uh, I was going to get that," objected Detective Priest, as he put his small stack of paper money back into his aging leather wallet, folded it back up, and stuck it into his pants pocket.

"Nonsense! You guys paid for your lunch already. There's no need for you to buy ours, too," grinned Jim.

"Thanks," acknowledged Chip Priest. "But, the Department would most likely reimburse us, since it was a business lunch."

"Jim can afford it," assured Susan with a crooked smile. She could tell without looking that Jim was scowling at her with disapproval. While it was true that Jim did have lots of money, he wanted to be the one to mention it – if and when he chose to do so.

"Okay, then." Chip merely raised an eyebrow and nodded.

"Did you say you were staying at The Powell Mountain Bed and Breakfast?" frowned Ron Telluric. "That used to be the Wilson residence, where the Woodcutter lived."

"It also was a historic brothel before that," recalled Jim. "And then, it was a pub for several years after the Wilsons were gone. In fact, it's only been a bed and breakfast since 2013."

"Folks around here say it's haunted," added Chip with a smile as he helped himself to one of the complimentary peppermint candies on the counter beside the cash register. He was impressed that Jim had done his homework.

"So, you already knew about its being the Woodcutter's place when you made the reservations, and that it was *haunted*?" demanded Janette as she turned to Jim. Janette was somewhat superstitious about such things.

"Of course," smirked Jim.

"A haunted B&B?" Susan was intrigued. She was familiar with most bed and breakfasts of any significance, but had never heard of that one. Still, Susan was not overly concerned about the prospect of it being haunted, either, as the house she had once lived in with her parents in Ocean Bay had also been haunted. Indeed, Susan and several of her former house guests over the years had been witness to the apparition of an old German woman in historical-looking attire, circa 1850, slowly making her way down the steps with an empty water bucket before disappearing through the front door. Interestingly, there had once been a street-side watering trough for horses there.

"Actually, that's not a bad idea," approved Carolyn. "Perhaps we just might come across some clue they missed fifty years ago."

"They? Meaning us?" Ron Telluric became defensive.

"No," assured Carolyn. "Just anyone who might have missed something. You two didn't solve the entire case alone, did you?"

"Darn near!" muttered Chip. "For all the good it did."

"Well, it was on March 23, 1975," reminded Ron, "and this is already 2023, so technically it was only forty-eight years ago, not fifty."

"Seriously?" Janette and Susan both rolled their eyes.

"A lot can happen in two extra years," interjected Sherry as she purposely flirted with Ron to soften his attitude. Sherry was a widow and could not help but notice that Ron did not have on a wedding band. Unknown to her, he had stopped wearing it sometime back after gaining so much weight that he could no longer slide it over the knuckle of his ring finger. Ron was flattered, nonetheless.

"Thank you," replied the Detective as he smiled back at Sherry. His piercing blue eyes twinkled with delight.

Jim decided to get things back on track. "So, as soon as we get checked in, I was hoping to have a good look around the old Wilson place. Perhaps you gentlemen might be able to come out there and show us where you found the other Mustang, and also where you found Lydia Cain or any other pertinent evidence?"

"I hope you ladies all have better footwear along?" added Chip.

"Hold it!" interrupted Carolyn. "I thought we were here to find out what happened to Karlin. Shouldn't we be heading up to the old winery first? That should be our first priority!"

"Not today," advised Ron. "There wouldn't be enough daylight left by the time we got there to make it worth the trip. What we need to do is get an early start in the morning."

"Agreed," nodded Jim. "And I'll make sure they all have better footwear when we do."

"What is he gonna do?" Janette asked sarcastically. "Go out and buy us all new hiking boots?"

"What size do you wear?" quizzed Jim as he became serious and folded his arms in front.

"Don't test him," cautioned Susan. "He probably would!"

"I do believe I've found a new subject for my documentary," nodded Sherry with an even smile. "The sharks and boogie boarders can wait until later!"

"Hey, I'm really sorry about that," apologized Carolyn.

"Nonsense," assured Sherry. "This should prove to be a lot more interesting, anyway."

"Not to mention more dangerous!" feared Susan.

"What are you gonna do your story on, anyway?" delved Janette.

"Racial intolerance in the 1970s and how it related to corruption in the judicial system," beamed Sherry.

"Sounds like a best seller to me!" approved Janette.

Detectives Priest and Telluric stared at the women beside them with disbelief. Jim smirked with satisfaction. He was in his element and it showed.

"Hey, I feel as bad as anyone does about Woody dying in prison for something he didn't do," reminded Carolyn, "but how is the Lydia Cain case going to help us find out what happened to Karlin?"

"What if the two cases are related?" proposed Jim.

"That was our thought, too," agreed Chip, though cautiously.

"You really think so?" Carolyn pursed her lips as she considered the possibility.

"Perhaps a fresh set of eyes just might find something we missed out at the Wilson place," conceded Ron. "You never know."

"So, I take it you fellas aren't going to do a formal interview of my client with a court reporter?" questioned Jim as they finally exited the restaurant and began walking towards the black Honda Odyssey minivan parked outside.

"Your client?" interjected Carolyn as she gently grabbed Jim's arm. "Your client?"

"I also happen to be an attorney," smirked Jim.

"He actually is," confirmed Susan with a deep sigh. "I've seen the degrees on his wall, among all his other impressive credentials."

"A well-educated man, too?" Ron Telluric reacted as if he had just been defeated in some way. "Just what other degrees do you have?"

"Well," Jim paused for a moment, "after graduating first in my class at Yale with a Doctor of Jurisprudence, I took and passed the Bar exam for each of the two main states I commonly deal with, including this one, though putting in the practicums did set me back a year or two. Plus, keeping up on all the CLE requirements has had its drawbacks, too. Time waits for no man!"

"I suppose that must cut somewhat into your duties as Sheriff?" scowled Ron. He and Chip were both Harvard men, but did not savor the idea of explaining to a successful Yale man like Jim how they had each been ousted from the DA's office and were now lucky just to be working as Detectives.

"Actually, he's the Mayor of Ocean Bluff now," grinned Susan, finding it strangely exhilarating to be on Jim's side for a change.

"Though they never bothered to officially remove him from his post as Sheriff after the election," added Carolyn.

"But," continued Jim, "besides detective work, my true loves are flying and photography. I'm also partial to biology, mathematics and architecture, and have degrees in each of them."

"You're just quite the accomplished man," muttered Ron.

"And he's humble, too!" snickered Janette.

Jim had not wanted to appear as if he were bragging, so decided against mentioning that he was also sole heir to his late father's multi-million-dollar brokerage firm or that he had an entire regiment of well-paid employees to run it for him. That was something he rarely mentioned to anyone, anyway. Thankfully, it was only necessary for Jim to make an appearance at the home office once or twice each year.

"So, you're a regular super hero?" chuckled Ron, sardonically.

"He sure knows how to fly," informed Sherry. "You should see the Modulated Interfacing Resonance Assistant that Jim invented for his Learjet."

"She answers to MIRA, though," added Jim. "In fact, she's programmed to respond specifically to my own personal voice commands."

"And naturally, you programmed her yourself?" Chip Priest was reaching his limit, too.

"As a matter of fact, I did," Jim informed him, proud of his accomplishment. "Thanks to my research and development in the field of avionic voice recognition, the feature has become standard industry-wide. In fact, individual pilots may now choose whether to have the computer respond automatically or only when commanded to do so."

"Gee, that sounds familiar," interjected Janette.

"We get the idea," informed Detective Priest as he narrowed his eyes at Jim. "But, like it or not, we're all here to help each other solve these cases, and that's exactly what we're going to do!"

"I couldn't agree with you more," assured Jim. "I would like very much to see every scrap of evidence and every single page in your file – I assume it's a paper one?"

"You got something against paper?" challenged Ron Telluric.

"Absolutely not," smiled Jim. He seemed almost amused by the entire situation. "I had a paper file of my own on *The Oceanview Matter* that I carried around with me for over forty years."

"Hey, let's all take this down a notch, guys," intervened Chip. "And no, we won't be doing a formal interview with a court reporter. That's a long story. But, you folks get settled at the old Wilson place and we'll be by later with the file on our way home after work tonight. Let's say about 5:30?"

Jim suddenly perceived that Detectives Priest and Telluric were acting on their own, but decided not to acknowledge it. Not just yet. "Very well then. We'll look forward to seeing you gentlemen later."

Carolyn silently stared out the minivan window at the aging forest surrounding them as Jim drove up the steep mountain road.

"Will we each have our own room?" questioned Janette from the next seat back, where she was seated behind Jim.

"I'm sure *I* will," assured Jim with an amused glance at her in the rearview mirror as he slowed to negotiate a hairpin turn.

"This is quite the road," commented Sherry from the third row of seats where she was seated by herself.

"Just where did you hit that squirrel?" questioned Susan. She was seated in the second row, beside Janette and directly behind Carolyn. "Hey, Carolyn?"

"Oh, I'm sorry." Carolyn had been deep in thought. "I was just remembering some of my previous rides up this road."

"What about the squirrel incident?" pressed Susan.

"The squirrel incident?" repeated Carolyn. "That was at least two turns back from where we are now."

"And you still drove that car all the way up this road, even with major fender damage?" quizzed Susan.

"Very slowly and carefully," assured Carolyn. "But, it only scraped the tire on that side during the turns."

"You're lucky you didn't have a blowout," opined Jim as he slowed to read the numbers on a mailbox.

"It should be the next driveway," indicated Carolyn.

"I think I see it," acknowledged Jim as he approached it.

At the driveway entrance was a quaint but aging sign that read, "Powell Mountain Bed and Breakfast." Its gothic blue lettering was hand painted on a white background with a blue surrounding border, carved to appear as if it were braided. The sign itself rested in the hands of a hand-carved, life-sized wooden statue of an ornately decorated woodcutter which was clearly intended to depict a man of color. On his head was a white hardhat and in his mouth was a white corncob pipe.

"That's neat!" exclaimed Janette.

Carolyn merely nodded while she carefully studied their surroundings. Susan and Sherry became unusually quiet as they, too, tried to do the same.

Jim pursed his lips as he turned onto the gravel driveway that led to the old two-story stone building where the Woodcutter and his family had once lived. He would definitely make arrangements for the road to be paved by an anonymous benefactor following their departure, decided Jim. It would probably be the least he could do after disrupting their operations as he intended to during their stay.

"The salvage yard used to be right over there," advised Carolyn.

"Anything could be in there now," opined Janette when she noticed the dense foliage.

"There's no way we're finding *anything* in there!" judged Susan.

"You never know," replied Jim as he pulled up by an aging fountain in front of the two-story stone building.

"The base of that fountain is mounted right on top of Woody's old chopping stump," realized Carolyn. "He used to keep his axe stuck into the top of it, when he wasn't using it. And over there, on the other side of the building is where his old shed used to be."

"I wonder why they tore it down?" frowned Jim. He had hoped to search it for any possible clues, should any remain after all this time.

"I can't believe how overgrown everything is now," commented Carolyn as Jim shut off the engine and put the minivan's parking brake on.

"We are in a forest," pointed out Jim. The automatic doors then slid open as Jim hurried to assist his passengers from the vehicle.

"A lot of this must have grown up after they removed the old salvage yard," surmised Carolyn as she climbed out of the minivan. "There was quite a bit of manzanita around the edges of it, too, but not out in the middle like it is now."

"Maybe there are still some cars in there?" speculated Janette as she, too, climbed from the vehicle.

"I knew I should have brought different clothes with me!" muttered Susan. "And some hiking boots!"

"Sure glad I brought mine," razzed Carolyn as she gave Susan a crooked smile.

"Well, if there's anything here that we're meant to find," interjected Sherry, "I'm sure we will."

"Touché," agreed Jim with a resigned smile as he scowled at the thick blackberry canes now covering the manzanita and other scrub brush where the salvage yard had been. He would need to make arrangements right away to get an independent forensic team of his own brought in to assist with the investigation, that much was certain. Not only that, they would need to bring in some specialized excavation equipment, as well. Besides, it would most likely be needed up at the winery, too, decided Jim.

"Well, clearly someone is still trying to keep the Woodcutter's memory alive," surmised Carolyn when she noticed another life-sized wooden statue near the front entrance of the bed and breakfast. It was every bit as ornately carved as the one at the front entrance to the gravel road, but more protected from the weather, better maintained, and was holding a real axe.

"Did the Woodcutter actually look like that?" wondered Janette as the five of them approached the front door of the Powell Mountain Bed and Breakfast.

"Just his left foot," chuckled Carolyn as she climbed the rickety wooden porch.

"Why just his left foot?" quizzed Jim as he gingerly rang the old bell hanging beside the front door.

"Woody had a wooden left foot," explained Carolyn. "But, he managed to get around well enough, despite his disability."

"He must have walked with a limp, then?" pressed Jim.

"Indeed, he did," confirmed Carolyn. "But, that never stopped him from coming around to open the door for his passengers."

"That poor man." Janette sadly shook her head.

Suddenly, the front door opened. "Greetings! You must be Jim Otterman?" A middle-aged black woman in her late forties joined them on the front porch. "I'm Luella."

"Luella," acknowledged Jim as he shook her hand. "This is Carolyn, Sherry, Susan and Janette." They each nodded in greeting.

"I've only got three rooms up there," informed Luella. "But, I'm sure we can work it all out."

"I almost feel guilty having my very own room," confessed Jim as he shot Carolyn a flirtatious grin.

Carolyn glared at Jim with disapproval. The interaction did not go unnoticed by Susan or Janette. If Sherry saw it, she feigned ignorance.

"So, what's the deal between *them*, anyway?" Janette whispered so only Susan could hear. "Why is Jim still so obsessed with her, especially after all this time? Carolyn's made it quite clear to him that she's happily married!"

"So is he, to Sheree!" whispered Susan in return as she shot Jim a look of censure.

Jim had seen them whispering and suddenly flushed with embarrassment.

"Please come sign in," invited Luella, who had also observed the whispered and unspoken exchanges between her guests.

"We will be renting the entire compound for at least a week," announced Jim. "For whatever compensation you feel is fair, of course. Name your price."

"Compound?" Luella was perplexed.

"The grounds, the entire property," elaborated Jim as he gestured with his hands toward the landscape behind him. "Not only are we are here to find out what happened up at the old winery where the skeletal remains of a particular young coed were recently discovered - as I mentioned when we spoke on the phone - but we also hope to find out what may have happened to the Cain girl back in 1974, right here on this property."

Luella seemed pale for a moment and visibly shaken. "Just who are you people, anyway?"

"We believe that Mr. Wilson may have been wrongly convicted for a crime he did not commit," interjected Carolyn.

"And you come here only now, forty-eight years later?" Luella shook her head with dismay. "I've heard that the wheels of justice could be slow, but seriously?"

"Did you know Mr. Wilson?" questioned Sherry.

"Before we go another step further," decided Luella, "you folks will tell me exactly who you are and just why you are looking into this only now? Why was nothing done back in 1975, or in 1978, for that matter, when my father died in prison for a crime he had absolutely nothing to do with?"

"Your *father*?" Sherry and the others were stunned.

Tears began to flow down Luella's cheeks as she turned away from her new customers so they wouldn't see her cry.

"Wait!" pleaded Carolyn as she gently put her hand on Luella's arm. "I knew your father. I actually rode with him several times back when I was a student up there at Powell Mountain University, and I do believe he was innocent."

"Carolyn's green Mustang was even forensically investigated by the police at one point," added Susan.

"That's right!" corroborated Janette. "They thought at first it was the one they were looking for, before they finally ruled it out."

"What?" Luella turned to study Carolyn more closely. "I think you folks should come in and sit down."

"May I bring in their luggage first?" questioned Jim.

"Of course," agreed Luella without further persuasion. "I already have your credit card information, so yes, go ahead. The room on the left at the top of the stairs is yours. The one on the right is mine, and you can put Carolyn's things in there. She can stay with me. The rest of you may stay in the middle room, as it's much larger than the other two."

"That works for me," approved Jim as he left to retrieve everyone's luggage. "I'll be right back."

"As you can see, this place was once a pub," apologized Luella as the others got their first good look at the long, curved bar counter lined with stools inside. "Before that, it was a brothel, though it was the Krain family who turned it into a pub when they bought us out. Still, there was always a bar counter here, even in its brothel days. My parents used it as our dining room table, just like I do now."

"The Krain family?" questioned Susan. "Would that be the same Krain family that Carolyn knew when she went to school up there?"

"I worked as a secretary for a Ronald Krain when I was a student," described Carolyn. "Over in the Industrial Education Department."

Luella's face took on an angry expression. "Yes! I know quite well who the late great Professor Ronald Krain thought he was!"

"He never cared for me much, though," Carolyn quickly added, "not after he realized that one of my closest friends was a person of color. Her name was Eula."

"What'd I miss?" inquired Jim as he entered the front door with two of the suitcases.

"That Professor guy Carolyn was telling us about bought this place and turned it into a pub when he was alive," blurted Janette.

"Professor Krain is dead?" Jim was stunned.

"Praise the Lord, yes!" replied Luella. "Too bad the same can't be said for his son, the Honorable Michael Krain, who is now the presiding judge over at the St. Diablo County Courthouse!"

"Diablo means devil, you know," interjected Susan.

"Very appropriate!" acknowledged Janette.

"Who owns this place now?" quizzed Jim as he set down the suitcases. "Is it still the Krain family?"

"Heavens, no!" assured Luella. "It took years to do it, but it now belongs to the Wilson family again!"

"Do you have any plans to convert it to a more conventional floorplan?" asked Sherry.

"Probably not. As I said, it did used to be a brothel." Luella shook her head. "You folks sure ask a lot of questions!"

"Pardon me if I ask another," added Jim, "but why in the world would a black family sell their land to a member of the Crusading Knights of Powell Mountain?"

"From what I understand, we needed the money for our parents' final expenses, and they were the only buyers," replied Luella.

"I take it the Krain family pub was not a smashing success?" perceived Jim.

"No, it wasn't," frowned Luella. "How'd you know?"

"Why else would they sell it back to you?" Jim raised a knowing eyebrow. "Besides, I hear the place is haunted?"

"And yes, there is that," sighed Luella.

Janette's face suddenly took on a worried expression. "That's right! Jim was telling us about that."

"As I told you, this place was originally an infamous brothel," grinned Luella. "Back in the 1800s. Its ghost is rumored to be one of the former residents. Often, following sightings of her, the strong odor of perfume can be smelled for several minutes near an unexplainably cold area."

"Really?" grinned Jim. "I can't wait to meet her!"

"Be careful what you wish for, Mr. Otterman," advised Luella as she motioned for the ladies to follow her up a narrow flight of hardwood stairs. "Our resident ghost is also believed to be the original Madame of this house. Her name was Angie. In fact, it is *her* room in which *you* will be staying."

"Angie?" chuckled Jim.

"And, she has been known to be responsible for a little harmless mischief from time to time, though usually just involving our male guests," winked Luella.

"Yeah, right," scoffed Jim with a wave of his hand as he started for the door, to retrieve the rest of the suitcases.

"Angie has indeed been seen many times in full apparition," Luella assured them. "I've seen her myself."

"I'm *sure* Jim will enjoy having his own room," teased Susan.

"Oh, man," muttered Janette as she shook her head and drew the symbol of a cross on her chest. "Perhaps we should go see if there's somewhere else we can stay, down in St. Diablo?"

"Come on!" chuckled Susan as she grabbed Janette by the arm to keep her from leaving.

"This way, ladies," directed Luella.

Like her late father, Luella was diminutive in size and of slight but shapely build. Her facial features were exotic and beautiful, with an ageless quality about them. Luella's low-cut royal blue sweater showed off her cleavage to its best advantage, and hung gracefully over the top of her black leggings. Neatly arranged in an almost 1960-ish style, her sleek black chin-length hair had been carefully straightened before being curled under at the ends. If there were any gray hairs on her head, they had been eradicated by the miracle of hair dye. Her high-heeled dress slippers had faux black fur across the tops and clearly were not intended to be worn outside.

"What else do you know about Angie?" delved Sherry as the group of women made their way up the stairs.

"That is a rather long and sordid tale," began Luella, "but the short version of it is this. Angie and her girls catered mostly to lumbermen throughout the area."

"That makes sense," nodded Janette.

"Let her finish!" chided Susan.

"Angie naturally kept sixty percent of her girls' hard-gotten earnings, in exchange for their room and board here," continued Luella. "Each girl was allowed to decorate her own area as she wished, so none of the wallpapers in these rooms will match."

"So, she had two other women here, then?" questioned Sherry.

"Actually, there were six women in all," clarified Luella. "Each of the rooms up here had a divider across the middle, though the dividers were nothing more than old sheets hung from a drawstring. That's why you'll see two different types of wallpaper in each of the rooms."

"Now, there's privacy for you!" snickered Janette.

"The girls actually made quite a decent living here," advised Luella with a mischievous grin, "despite the indecency of their occupation."

"Is that Angie?" asked Susan as they reached the top of the stairs and stood by a life-sized oil painting of what looked like an attractive saloon girl, in a surprisingly expensive looking frame.

"She was a black woman?" Carolyn was stunned.

"Indeed, she was," smiled Luella.

"Weren't most of the men living in the area back then all members of the Crusading Knights?" quizzed Sherry.

"That, they were," confirmed Luella. "Even the lumberjacks. Some of them, in fact, were among Angie's more frequent customers."

"Well, I'll be!" remarked Jim from behind them, after overhearing the last bit of their conversation. He had already managed to bring in the rest of the suitcases and had followed them upstairs with the first two. Then, turning to study the huge oil painting, Jim remarked, "She certainly was a beauty!" Jim also noticed an uncanny resemblance between Luella and the woman in the oil painting but refrained from mentioning it just yet.

"He's just trying to get on Angie's good side," jabbed Susan with a crooked smile.

"Let's hope he succeeds," smirked Luella. "As I mentioned earlier, this room here will be yours, Mr. Otterman. It is smaller than the other two rooms because my parents put a bathroom at one end of it. The room was theirs when we were living here as a family. Prior to that, there was just the outhouse."

"Are there any other restrooms inside?" questioned Carolyn, suddenly concerned about it.

"No, there are not," replied Luella. "But, there is a pocket door on either side of it."

"A pocket door?" scowled Jim.

Luella gently inserted her fingers into a small indentation in the natural wood wall and began to pull. "Stand back."

The others watched in amazement as she slid the panel open. Inside was a rather modern-looking restroom, complete with toilet, double sink and ADA accessible shower stall. The powder blue tiled floor and matching throw rugs were immaculate, along with the rest of the room. The white marbled counter and elegant round mirrors above each of its sinks were quite stunning. Complimentary bottles of shampoo and individually wrapped bars of lavender guest soaps sat in an expensive white basket on one corner of the counter. The restroom's white walls had recently been painted, and its white guest towels appeared to be new. There was even a small electric wall heater.

"Whoever gets here first has the pleasure of securing the deadbolt that leads to Jim's room. Unless, of course it is Jim, in which case he would need to secure the inside deadbolt on this door. There are extra towels in that closet by the shower stall, and all dirty towels go in the laundry hamper beside it." Luella then demonstrated how to latch the door.

"So, what you're saying is that I might have my own restroom, but will probably never be lucky enough to even use it?" recapped Jim.

Susan grinned at Jim's predicament. "Guess you'd better have Angie get you up pretty early, then."

"I might just do that," chuckled Jim. "Whose suitcases are these?"

"The big leopard patterned one is mine," grinned Susan.

"And the plain brown one is mine," informed Janette.

Jim gingerly picked up and carried both suitcases into the middle room. "Who are these other paintings supposed to be?"

All along the wooden hallway hung realistic-looking oil paintings of attractive saloon girls, though none as large or as finely done as the painting of Angie.

"These are the various girls who lived and worked here at different times," revealed Luella. "Most either disappeared or died under unusual circumstances."

"How sad!" remarked Sherry. "Most of them were very beautiful, too."

"Nature of the business, I'm afraid." Luella shrugged her shoulders as she headed for the middle room.

"What became of Angie?" pressed Sherry.

"Well, she committed the one unpardonable sin, at least for a Madame of her status, that is," Luella smiled.

"She fell in love?" guessed Carolyn.

"She fell in love," confirmed Luella with a nod of appreciation for Carolyn's astuteness.

"Then what happened?" urged Janette.

"Well, let's save that story for suppertime," decided Luella. "You folks still need to get settled, and I need to get supper started."

"Fair enough," agreed Sherry. "And is all this still the original wallpaper inside the rooms?"

"We could never afford to have it all replaced," admitted Luella. "And the Krain family obviously didn't bother! They probably didn't even come up here, except to use it as a place to crash after drinking too much down in the bar!"

"At least you were able to get it back," pointed out Sherry.

"My two brothers are actually co-owners of it with me," Luella informed them, "though neither of them chose to come back permanently. It's just me now."

"What are their names?" grilled Sherry.

"Matthew and Mark," replied Luella. "My name was supposed to be Luke, but when I turned out to be a girl, my parents decided to name me Luella. My parents were very religious."

"That's true!" corroborated Carolyn. "When I knew him, Woody always carried a beat-up old Bible around with him, and kept it on the dashboard of his truck."

"That, he did," reminisced Luella.

"What about your husband?" wondered Sherry.

"He was a truck driver, so I never really saw him much anyway," explained Luella. "He was killed last year in that big crash on I-5, just out of Ocean Bay."

"Oh, I'm so sorry!" apologized Sherry.

"And, as you can guess, I don't get out much," added Luella, "so the prospects of another man in my life are virtually nil."

"Woody told me once that he wanted to make sure all his kids got an education someday," mentioned Carolyn. "He seemed quite proud of you. And, if you don't mind my saying so, your grammar is quite impressive compared to his."

"Yeah, I suppose it is," nodded Luella. "After having nothing more than a fourth-grade education himself, my daddy would have wanted to make sure we stayed in school."

"I'm just gonna grab the rest of the suitcases," announced Jim as he quickly headed toward the stairs.

"Very sweet man," approved Luella as she watched Jim go.

"He can be," agreed Carolyn, which surprised the others.

"Jim can also be a royal pain in the butt!" chuckled Susan.

"As can we all," rebutted Luella. "Anyway, the furniture is old, but the rooms are clean, the bedding is fresh, and the hardwood floors were just waxed yesterday. There are two sets of bunkbeds here in the middle room, four small dressers, four wooden chairs, and one large closet down there at the end. No frills."

"Not even an area rug," frowned Janette.

"What about Jim's room?" questioned Susan as she poked her head inside and noticed the extravagant Queen Anne furniture and Tiffany floor lamp inside.

"That room originally belonged to Madame Angie," reminded Luella. "The red velvet fabric on the overstuffed armchair is the only thing that isn't original. It finally wore out and had to be replaced."

"What about *your* room?" frowned Susan.

"Utilitarian, like yours," replied Luella, "though it has only two single beds. Unlike your room, however, it does have a nice writing desk. It also has a small sitting room at one end, with a wall mounted flat screen television, and a small collection of old movies. You ladies are welcome to use it anytime. There's a comfortable couch in there, too."

"I like the nice big window on that end," complimented Sherry.

"There is one just like it in each of the three rooms," described Luella. "They all face east, overlooking the front entrance below."

"No curtains?" queried Sherry.

"Who would be out there to see you, anyway?" laughed Luella.

"Is there a patio, where people can go to smoke if they like?" asked Janette. "I quit after giving it up for Lent last year, but all this talk of ghosts has got me kind of jumpy."

"Right behind you," indicated Luella with a nod of her head as she walked over to yet another hidden door panel and pulled it open. A narrow staircase leading to the roof could be seen inside.

"Just how many of those secret doors have you got around here, anyway?" asked Janette.

"Who knows." Luella merely shrugged her shoulders. "Those stairs lead to a rooftop patio where the girls could quickly escape and hide whenever the law showed up."

"Too late, here I am," grinned Jim as he arrived with the last of the suitcases. "And I believe this is Carolyn's?"

"Thanks," nodded Carolyn as she took it from him and began wheeling it toward Luella's room.

"Allow me," insisted Jim as he grabbed the suitcase handle.

"So, he's the law, is he? Just how long have you two been separated, honey?" questioned Luella as she turned to Carolyn.

"Excuse me?" Carolyn was flabbergasted.

"Jim is not your husband, then?" pressed Luella.

"Carolyn's been married for 40 years now, but certainly not to *him*!" howled Janette as she slapped her knee.

"Jim has had a crush on Carolyn since high school, though," added Susan with a crooked smile.

"I see," nodded Luella. "So, Jim is available, then?"

"Oooh!" chuckled Janette as she shook her head.

"I'm afraid Jim's married, too," informed Susan as she became serious. "But not to me, either! Her name is Sheree – with two e's – and they've been married for seven years now."

"And I'm Sherry with a y," added Sherry, so there would be no misunderstanding about it.

"Humph," muttered Luella as she proceeded into the large middle room without commenting further on Jim's marital status. "And this is the room where my two brothers used to stay, when they were living here."

"So, the other room was always yours?" asked Carolyn.

"Except during the Krain occupation," spat Luella with obvious bitterness.

"How do you afford to stay here?" Jim was standing directly behind Luella and briefly startled her.

"You're just all detective, aren't you, Carrot Top?" Luella flirted mildly but guardedly with Jim.

"Carrot Top?" pouted Jim.

"Very fitting," snickered Susan.

"I get by," assured Luella as she winked at Jim.

In truth, Luella had no idea where the anonymous stipend payments originated from each month that she had been living on since the death of her parents back in 1978, and she certainly wasn't about to jinx the process now! And, although Luella had her suspicions about who the initial benefactor might have been, she was not so sure his heirs would approve of the continuing payments from their estate if the matter was openly brought to their attention.

"Hey, if you ladies will be okay," remarked Jim, "I'm going to go try to get some rest before those two flatfoots show up."

"Flatfoots?" repeated Luella.

"Detectives Priest and Telluric," clarified Jim. "They're stopping by here with their old case file tonight, on their way home from work. And while they're here, I was hoping they could walk me around the property and bring me up to speed on where everything was."

"I see," grinned Luella. "So, they really *are* reopening the old case on their own?"

"What makes you say that?" frowned Jim.

"Honey, you should've seen the way them Crusading Knights ousted those poor men from their jobs at the DA's office," revealed Luella. "Very sad business there."

"Ousted from their jobs?" Sherry had begun making notes with her cellphone's memo app but had finally given up and was using a paper notepad and pencil instead whenever something important was said. This was one of those times.

"They were lucky just to get jobs as beat cops with the St. Diablo Police Department after all that business of sticking up for my daddy like they did! Took 'em years to work their way up to the rank of Detective, but I'm sure they can tell you all about it when they get here," replied Luella. "Make yourselves at home." With that, she turned and left to go begin preparations for the evening meal but paused half way down the stairs. "Will your detective friends be joining us for supper?"

"Absolutely, yes. On me," called Jim. "See you ladies later."

With that, Jim went into his assigned room, closed the door and removed his boots. He then lay down on the bed on his back with his hands folded behind his head and crossed his feet. He had not noticed it before, but there was also wallpaper on the ceiling above him, a rather intricate pattern of miniature roses. The ceiling on the other half of the room had wallpaper on it, too, but was more of a lilac pattern that ended abruptly at the edge of the updated restroom that had been added on.

It was with great effort that Jim finally managed to relax enough to drift off to sleep. In his dream, a rather beautiful young black woman had come into the room and approached. She was elegant and demure, yet voluptuous and provocative, all at the same time. Her penetrating gaze seemed to envelop him. Her old-fashioned red and black dress was cut particularly low in the front. Her puffy red sleeves covered just her shoulders, leaving her sensuous arms exposed. Jim sleepily turned over onto his stomach, at her behest, so she could massage his back. He could feel her sitting down on the bed beside him. Her slow and deliberate fingers began to soothe him, almost from the inside out, unlike anything he had ever felt before. Strange that he should be having such a dream.

*If only you were real*, he thought. Jim was well aware of the fact that he was probably dreaming but enjoyed himself immensely nonetheless. "You do know that I'm here to try to find out what happened to those girls?" mumbled Jim out loud.

*Are you?* came the thought. Had someone just asked him that? It was as if the voice was speaking to him from inside his head. Jim slowly turned onto his side, opened his eyes, and glanced around the room. He was suddenly overwhelmed by the sickening smell of jasmine perfume and felt unusually cold.

Could the legend really be true? Had Angie been the one massaging his back? Jim slowly reached for a folded quilt at the foot of the bed, picked it up, and wrapped it around his shoulders.

"Okay, I'm also here to prove that Woodrow Wilson was innocent, and that he had absolutely nothing to do with the murder of Lydia Cain," added Jim, though suddenly feeling ridiculous for trying to communicate with a ghost.

"Angie?" Jim cautiously asked. "Look, if you're the real deal, I really could use some help here."

Without warning a small panel in the wall beneath the windowsill slid open, startling Jim quite badly. He slowly got up and cautiously approached the secret drawer. Jim then stared at its contents with amazement. The small pile of official looking documents was clipped together with a solid gold money clip that was inscribed with the official insignia of the Crusading Knights. Soldered onto it was a small white knight fashioned from mother of pearl and holding a tiny sterling silver sword. "Unbelievable!" Jim started to reach for it.

"Fingerprints!" Jim reminded himself. "I can't touch any of it until it has been dusted for prints, though there probably aren't any after all this time, anyway. Unless ...."

Jim then raced over to the bed, took off the quilt that had been draped around his shoulders, and laid it on the bed. Jim then removed the pillow case from its pillow and quickly returned to the windowsill to retrieve the little drawer. There could be fingerprints on the drawer itself, as well, realized Jim as he gingerly used the pillow case to remove the drawer from the wall and then brought it over to the bed where he carefully set it down.

"Jim?" called Luella as she briskly knocked on the door to his room. "Your detective friends are here."

Jim immediately raced over and opened the door to acknowledge Luella's announcement but then stopped and stared past her with disbelief. Directly behind her was the large oil painting of Angie. "It's her!"

Understanding immediately what Jim meant, Luella then sniffed the air and noticed the smell of jasmine perfume and how cold it was in the area. "Land sakes alive! Where did you find that?" Luella raced over to the bed and was about to touch the mysterious drawer.

"Stop!" commanded Jim. "We need to have it dusted for fingerprints first!"

"Fingerprints?" scoffed Luella. "After all this time? The people who left that there are long dead, Mr. Carrot Top."

"Would you *please* quit calling me that?" frowned Jim. "My name is Jim, or Mr. Otterman. And, what if someone else did touch it recently? Some fingerprints can still be viable for up to two years."

"Sorry," grinned Luella. "Looks like you're a believer now?"

"Oh, yeah," assured Jim as he glanced again at the oil painting in the hall. Jim felt as if it were watching him.

Downstairs, Detectives Chip Priest and Ron Telluric were seated at the bar, visiting with Sherry, Susan and Janette.

"You'll never believe what old Carrot Top just found," announced Luella as she and Jim came down the stairs together. Jim was carefully holding the mysterious drawer, using the pillow case to avoid touching it.

"Carrot Top?" chuckled Ron. "I like it."

"The name's Jim Otterman, thank you very much," replied Jim as he approached the bar to set down his treasure. "The drawer and everything inside MUST be dusted for prints, and the sooner the better."

"Fingerprints do fade over time and ultimately disappear from most surfaces completely," advised Chip. "That drawer looks like it's pretty old."

"Unless someone touched it recently," remarked Jim. "I know, it's highly unlikely. But, fingerprints can sometimes survive for up to two and a half years on a non-porous surface, even after being subjected to inclement weather conditions in an external environment."

"How do you figure?" frowned Chip.

"There actually was a case where identifiable fingerprints were found on a plastic carrier bag after seven years," informed Jim.

"I doubt it," differed Chip.

"You've never heard of the Elemental Fingerprint Comparison Study done at the Otterman Forensic Laboratories?"

"Don't tell me!" laughed Chip. "OFL is yours?"

"Well," blushed Jim, "yes. It's one of my investments."

"You really have your own forensic laboratory?" doubted Chip. "I suppose you did the study yourself?"

"It was done at my request," grinned Jim with a shrug of his shoulders. "But, even the lack of a person's fingerprint on something doesn't demonstrate that they didn't touch it, either, especially over time."

"How could a fingerprint survive for seven years?" grilled Sherry. "That's pretty hard to believe."

"That was in a protected environment," described Jim. "Usually two and a half years is the longest a fingerprint can survive, especially when subjected to inclement weather conditions."

"How do you figure?" scowled Chip.

"Well, one of our technicians ran an independent comparison of various substances," elaborated Jim. "Eccrine sweat, sebaceous and apocrine sweat, soda pop, insect repellant, linseed oil, sausage and even chips. The results of each were examined after exposure to various conditions and after different periods of time, with the linseed oil, sausage and chips most easily visible before powdering, even after two and a half years. After that, the prints all began to degrade."

"How long did the prints on some of the other items survive?" probed Chip, suddenly quite intrigued.

"Anywhere from a couple months to a year," answered Jim. "The point is, we need to check for anything that might be in this drawer. Including hair and skin samples, if there are any."

"I have my kit out in the car," advised Ron. "I'm sure it's nothing like yours, but I can go get it."

"That would be great, thanks," smiled Jim.

"We really should get started if we're going to do a walk-through of the old crime scene," recommended Chip. "Before it gets dark."

"Perhaps Ron can do the dusting while you two get started?" suggested Sherry.

"You have *no idea* how long people have been looking for that little drawer or the things that are inside!" advised Luella. "Probably for over a hundred years now."

"Did they even have fingerprint technology back then?" asked Janette rather skeptically.

"Oh, absolutely," confirmed Jim. "In fact, fingerprints were used for identification purposes as far back as 1686. They were even used on clay tablets and seals as signatures in ancient Babylon and China. But, Chip's right, there probably aren't any surviving prints on this drawer or the items inside. Still, we need to check."

"Ancient China and Babylon?" doubted Susan.

"You can look it up if you don't believe me," suggested Jim. "It was a physiologist named Marcello Malpighi who first examined fingerprints under a microscope and noted the unique series of ridges and loops in them in 1686. Then in 1823, physiologist Jan Purkinje noted at least nine different fingerprint patterns."

"That's true," corroborated Ron as he came back inside with his fingerprint kit. "But, it wasn't until the 1880s that it was scientifically demonstrated how the uniqueness of fingerprints could be used to identify specific people."

"By Sir Francis Galton," interjected Jim with satisfaction. "Not only was he the first to determine that no two fingerprints are exactly alike, but that fingerprints remain constant throughout a person's lifetime. I even have a personally autographed copy of his first book in my library."

"You actually have an 1892 edition of Galton's first book?" Chip was now in awe. "Isn't that the one where he lists the three most common fingerprint types: loop, whorl, and arch?"

"Yes, indeed," answered Jim rather proudly. "And those same classifications are still used by forensic technicians today."

"Enough already!" insisted Susan. "We get the idea."

"I think it's actually quite interesting," differed Sherry. "So, when were fingerprints first used by law enforcement?"

"These two gentlemen aren't the only ones who went to law school," advised Chip with a mischievous grin. "Once Galton published his findings, law enforcement officials were all over it. Sir Edward Richard Henry was a British official stationed in India, and it was he who first began to develop a system of fingerprint identification for Indian criminals."

"But, it was an Argentinian police official named Juan Vucetich, who first used the technology to solve an actual murder in 1892," interjected Jim. It had been far too long since he'd had the opportunity to show off his knowledge with equally-educated cohorts who could truly appreciate it.

"Then, in the United States," continued Chip, "it was the New York Police Department and State Prison System, along with the Federal Bureau of Prisons, who first instituted a standard fingerprint system in 1903."

"Finally, in 1905," added Ron for good measure, "the U.S. Army began using fingerprint identification, as well."

"Are you gentlemen done ponying up all your knowledge, or do I need to go get a yardstick?" inquired Luella with her hands on her hips.

"My thoughts exactly!" agreed Janette with a nod of her head.

"So, even if there are any fingerprints on this drawer, what if they aren't in your database?" posed Carolyn.

"Guess we'll find out, won't we?" shrugged Jim.

"Come on," Chip urged Jim. "Let's let Ron do his thing while we go look around."

"I'll come with you," offered Carolyn, who already had her hiking boots on.

"You might wanna leave your purse here," suggested Jim.

"I'll just keep it with me, thanks," advised Carolyn as she met Jim's even gaze with one of her own. Inside the purse was Lenny's precious letter, and she was not about to let it out of her possession.

"Suit yourself," agreed Jim. "Sure hope it doesn't rain."

"Why honey, there's not a cloud in the sky out there," pointed out Luella. "If Miss Carolyn feels best keeping her purse close at hand, that should be her business."

"Thanks." Carolyn smiled weakly at Luella as she followed Chip and Jim outside, tightly clutching her shoulder bag.

"What do you have in that thing, anyway?" razzed Chip. He could tell that whatever Carolyn had in the purse was of great value.

"Nothing," assured Carolyn as she and Jim exchanged another meaningful glance that did not go unnoticed by Detective Priest.

"Well, we can look at the old case file when we get back, but over here is where the Woodcutter's shed used to be." Chip motioned with his hand.

"Carolyn pointed that out to me already, when we first got here," replied Jim. "I had hoped to go over it for evidence."

"Coulda, woulda, shouda," laughed Chip. "That's what my mama always used to say."

"What did happen to the shed?" asked Carolyn.

"Who knows," shrugged Chip. "It was kind of an eyesore. Maybe someone tore it down for firewood."

"What about over here where all the brush is?" nodded Jim. "Carolyn mentioned that it used to be the salvage yard?"

"That would be correct," verified Chip. "In fact, there could still be some cars in there."

"Do you think Luella would have any objection if I had a team of forensic specialists come tear all this out so we can see?" questioned Jim.

"Just how big of a team are we talking about?" queried Chip.

"I don't know," pondered Jim. "Maybe twenty, thirty guys."

"An expense like that would never get approved by the Department's budget committee," predicted Chip.

"What about all the overtime you two are putting in up here?" posed Jim as he gave Chip a crooked smile.

Chip Priest pursed his lips as the three of them trudged along in silence, past the overgrown manzanita bushes covered with half dead blackberry canes. He had no intention of answering Jim's question about the budget. Jim already knew the answer, anyway.

"Luella mentioned to us that you and your partner were ousted from the DA's office for sticking up for Woody," Carolyn suddenly mentioned. "That was very brave of you."

"And also very stupid!" snapped Chip.

"But, you tried to do what was right," reminded Carolyn.

"For all the good it did poor Woody!" fumed Chip, still angry at the thought of it.

"And yet you're still troubled by it?" pressed Carolyn.

"Yes!" confirmed Chip. "And not a day goes by that I don't think about it and wonder what we could have done differently." Chip then picked up a rock and threw it as hard as he could at an overgrown blackberry thicket.

Late rays of afternoon sun shone through the forest surrounding them, a reminder that they needed to hurry if they were going to finish their survey of the crime scene before dark. The screech of a hawk could be heard from somewhere close by.

"I don't imagine the Knights were particularly keen on your national origin, either?" guessed Jim.

"Excuse me for saying so," apologized Carolyn as she turned to Chip, "but I didn't realize you were a man of color?"

"I'm not," chuckled Chip, rather sardonically. "I'm Jewish."

"Then why would it matter?" frowned Carolyn.

Jim sighed deeply and then advised Carolyn, "The Crusading Knights are a white supremacist group who believes that *all* other races should be eradicated from the face of the earth. People of color aren't their only targets."

"I think I did hear that once," recalled Carolyn as she shook her head rather sadly. "That's horrible!"

"Indeed!" agreed Chip. "Over here is where we found the green Mustang – not yours, but the other one. It was covered with so much brush that no one found it until February of '75."

"And your report indicated that you thought it had been here since Thanksgiving of '74?" reminded Jim.

"That's what we believed, and still do," answered Chip as he relived the moment in his mind that the car had finally been discovered forty-eight years ago. "Searchers spent days sifting through every rock, pebble and grain of dirt in this entire area for any other possible clues."

"So, both the DA and the police were out here searching?" quizzed Jim. "Isn't that unusual?"

"Perhaps," answered Chip, "but this particular case was also very personal, especially for me."

"That doesn't make sense," countered Jim.

"Does hating someone because of their race ever make any sense?" demanded Chip. "Perhaps knowing that the CKPM had as little regard for me as they did for someone like Woody was why it was so important for me to try to prove his innocence, especially with everyone searching his property like they were."

The three of them stood and stared at the location in silence for several moments, listening to the sounds of the forest.

"And over here," motioned Chip, "is where we found several sets of old tire tracks, though there's no way of knowing if they were made at the same time the Mustang was left here, or who left them."

"Did you take any impressions of the tire tracks?" probed Jim.

"Oh, absolutely," replied Chip. "Those are in the file. The strange thing was, none of the tracks matched any known cars in the area at the time. One set seemed to belong to an older Chevy, and another to a motorcycle."

"A motorcycle?" Carolyn suddenly asked.

"Why?" Chip narrowed his eyes.

"Oh, it's probably nothing," responded Carolyn.

"Tell us anyway," urged Jim.

"Well, it was the same day Woody followed me into town to leave my car there to be worked on," remembered Carolyn. "It was afterwards that I went on a date with my friend Stacia's brother Alfredo."

"And?" Jim was quite anxious to hear more.

"As I think I mentioned to you before, we had a late lunch at Maria's Mexican Restaurant," recounted Carolyn. "Then, on our way up to Powell Lake, we saw a dark green low-rider type of car, and I could swear this is where we saw it!"

"What kind of a low-rider car?" pressed Chip. "And how can you be so sure it was here?"

"I'm pretty sure it was a Chevy," answered Carolyn. "The reason Alfredo slowed down to get a better look at it was because it was in such excellent condition for car from the '60s. And, I'm quite familiar with this road! This is not too far past the place where I had my little fender bender with the squirrel."

"What year would you say the car was?" coaxed Chip.

"Definitely mid-sixties," nodded Carolyn.

"I knew it!" fumed Chip as he put his hands on his hips and shook his head with dismay.

"Is that significant?" questioned Jim.

"Professor Ronald Krain had a dark green 1965 Chevy Impala at the time," revealed Chip, "though we didn't learn of it until several years later when it was finally auctioned off at his estate sale."

"Really?" Jim was most interested. "We are definitely going to have to locate and acquire that car."

"What, and just buy it?" scoffed Chip.

"Why not?" shrugged Jim.

"There wouldn't be any evidence in it after all this time," objected Chip.

"Perhaps inside the trunk, there very well could be," differed Jim. "How many people do you know who even bother to clean out their trunks to that degree?"

"Just why would that be significant?" wondered Carolyn.

"Because it could have been used as a getaway car by whoever left the Mustang here," Chip patiently explained. "Perhaps a roll of duct tape or a spool of wire in the trunk of that car could match what we found with the body and already have in our file."

"We just need to find that car," added Jim.

"Well, I'm sure you can afford it," assured Carolyn with a knowing smirk. "Anyway - and I think I mentioned this before also - it was during that same motorcycle ride with Alfredo that we drove right past a blue Volkswagen up at Powell Lake. It was parked by one of those little beaches."

"Oh, my God! Are you kidding me?" Chip shook his head with disbelief. "And to think we never even bothered to question you!"

"What did you guys do when you saw the blue Volkswagen up at the lake?" grilled Jim. "Did you see anything else while you were there? Anything at all?"

"No, absolutely nothing," sighed Carolyn. "We were looking for a private place to be alone together and when we saw that spot was already taken, we just kept going."

"Really?" Jim's eyes narrowed. "And just what did you and Alfredo do up at the lake when you finally did find such a place?"

"Nothing!" snapped Carolyn.

"Wait a minute!" interjected Chip. "That would have nothing to do with this investigation."

"Sorry," apologized Jim. "It's just that Carolyn and I have some personal history."

"In a pig's eye!" retorted Carolyn. "You wish we did! But, I can assure you, that I have no more history with Alfredo than I do with you, except of course for the romantic goodbye kiss he gave me!"

Jim took a deep breath and folded his arms.

"Up that hogback is where we finally discovered the body," indicated Chip with a nod of his head, in an effort to redirect the conversation. "We should have just enough time to go take a look before we need to head back."

"After you," motioned Jim. He was clearly upset.

"Hey, I'm sorry," whispered Carolyn, "but you did have that coming."

Jim merely nodded as he followed Carolyn and Chip up the rugged hogback and to the place where Lydia Cain's body had finally been discovered in a shallow, brush covered trench.

"It was exactly forty-eight years ago today, on March 23rd," muttered Chip. "Ron and I decided to take one last look around the area before throwing in the towel."

"Hadn't this area been searched already?" recalled Jim.

"Oh yes," sniggered Chip. "One of the rescuers who combed this area actually sat on a log not more than two feet from the body, but never even saw it!"

"That's pretty hard to believe," remarked Jim.

"Not with all this brush here!" differed Carolyn as she nearly sprained her ankle in a small hole.

"Hey, I'm sorry, too!" apologized Jim as he reached out to help her. "Here, let me take that for you."

"My purse?" Carolyn raised an eyebrow. "Nothin' doing!"

"Perhaps you two should have gotten married," joked Chip. "Then you could get a divorce!"

"Very funny!" Jim forced a smile.

"So, this is where they found her?" Carolyn changed the subject.

"Right here," assured Chip as he sadly stared at the spot. "It was her half-rotted foot that caught our attention first, as it was sticking out from the huge brush pile that had been stacked on top of her. The snow had just recently melted."

"You mentioned in your writeup that Lydia might have been alive when she was left here?" recalled Jim.

"The weather from late November to February can be brutal in these parts, especially when it snows." Chip could never erase the memory from his mind of what he had seen that day and fought the tears he felt welling up in his eyes. "The forensic analysis of her corpse indicated a 95% probability that she was left here to die from her injuries and/or exposure to the elements."

"Why would someone do such a thing?" muttered Carolyn.

"We think that whoever ran down Paul Johnson – that was the young man whose body was found just feet from the blue Volkswagen up at the lake – also tried to run down Lydia but missed. That must have been when they came after her and whacked her on the head hard enough to knock her out before bringing her here." Chip took a white handkerchief from his pocket and wiped his cheeks with it before blowing his nose.

"Then there had to be more than one person involved!" realized Carolyn. "One of them drove the Mustang here and left the body, but someone else would have had to drive the other car!"

"That's what we think, too," sniffed Chip. "You never get used to something like this."

"Didn't the file say they put Woody's flag over her head?" pressed Jim.

"That's right," confirmed Chip. "And on top of that was a head-sized hood fashioned from an old Army bag. Someone actually took the time to weave baling wire through the edges of it, so it could be pulled taut and stay in place. We also think they considered burning the body at one point, but were interrupted. Most likely, it rained before they had a chance to finish it."

"Why do you think that?" questioned Carolyn.

"Because there were traces of gasoline poured over the entire scene," recounted Chip. "Most of it was poured on and around the crudely fashioned green hood over Lydia's head. The empty gas can was left right over there. We could tell that the can belonged to Woody, because his fingerprints were all over it, but there were also traces of green fabric on the can, as well. Probably gloves of some kind."

"Were there any tracks?" delved Jim.

"Nothing recognizable," regretted Chip. "Someone went to a great deal of effort to wipe as many of them away as they could with tree limbs, that kind of thing."

"What other evidence was collected from the scene?" Carolyn suddenly wanted to know.

"Well," sighed Chip, "Lydia's hands were tied behind her with some baling wire, which unfortunately matched against a roll of baling wire we found in Woody's shed."

"Someone obviously stole it to try to frame him!" Carolyn was becoming angrier by the minute.

"That's what we think, too," assured Chip. "The duct tape used to reinforce her restraints also matched a roll from his shed. And of course, the flag from his truck was clearly used to try to incriminate him. Even the green hood from the Army bag was traced back to Woody using serial numbers from the bag itself."

"Was there any sign of a struggle?" Jim frowned as he studied the shallow trench again for any telltale sign of evidence that might still remain, however insignificant.

"Lydia did have a pretty bad head injury," reminded Chip. "She was most likely unconscious when her killers first brought her here. Whatever they hit her with was extremely flat and hard. Not round like a rock, but flat. And they hit her more than once with it."

"Humph," muttered Jim as he put one hand on his chin and grabbed the elbow of that arm with his other hand.

"One other thing our forensic team found was a neatly folded pair of women's underwear in her pocket," added Chip. "And there was absolutely no sign of sexual activity of any kind. Forensics ruled that out completely."

"Perhaps she put them there herself?" guessed Carolyn. "When she was up at the lake with Paul Johnson?"

"And that her jealous roommate Martha Krain saw them there together and then tried to run both of them down?" added Chip. "We've mentioned that theory before, but nobody would listen to us, and the Krain girl was eventually ruled out as a suspect."

"I just remembered something else!" Carolyn suddenly realized. "The morning we came back with the Mustang, and this was before I took it in, Martha Krain was trying to wash a load of blood-soaked laundry there in the laundry room of the girls' dormitory. She

248

had only managed to start one load when Karlin raced in and started washing all of our stuff."

"Karlin? The Gomez girl?" scowled Chip.

"Yes!" replied Carolyn. "And she – Martha – told us she had a bad nosebleed, so she wanted to wash her stuff right away, before it had a chance to soak in."

"I'll just bet she did!" fumed Detective Priest.

"And that was on Friday morning, the day after Thanksgiving?" pressed Jim.

"Yes! I just told you that!" snapped Carolyn. "We just thought it was rather odd for her to be staying there at the dormitory when her parents lived so close."

"Where is the Krain girl now?" Jim turned to Chip with a raised eyebrow.

"In an institution," replied Chip. "The poor girl had a complete mental breakdown after they discovered the body of her boyfriend up at the lake. Between that, and her roommate Lydia disappearing – obviously before she was found – Martha tried to kill herself with a bottle of pills that she stole from her stepmother. Valium, I believe."

"And she's still there at the institution, then?" quizzed Jim.

"Yes, she is!" Chip suddenly appeared hopeful. "Her father would never allow anyone to see her after that when he was alive."

"Good thing he's not around anymore then, isn't it?" smirked Jim. "That's another thing we need to do. We need to interview Martha Krain at the first possible opportunity."

"It's back east somewhere," revealed Chip.

"Not a problem," assured Jim as the three of them slowly turned to head back to the Powell Mountain Bed and Breakfast.

"You're not planning to fly back there, are you?" asked Carolyn.

"Why not?" shrugged Jim. "I could fly back there, question Martha, and be back by tomorrow night. Perhaps I can get Susan and Janette to come with me. Besides, staying in that haunted room has lost its appeal for me."

"What about the case here?" reminded Chip.

"Carolyn and Sherry can accompany you up to the winery," suggested Jim. "I need to make arrangements to find that green Chevy, as well. Not to mention getting some men up here to go through that brush pile! And I probably will have a motorhome brought in for me to stay in when I return. I don't believe I want to sleep in that room again, if I can help it."

"Do you think they found any usable fingerprints on that drawer or the stuff inside it?" Carolyn suddenly asked.

"Probably not, but let's go find out," urged Jim as the three of them slowly made their way back down the hogback.

"Greetings!" called Luella as Jim, Carolyn and Chip entered the room. "Supper is ready."

"Smells great," complimented Jim as he approached the long, curved bar and sat down on a stool.

"Beans and cornbread with coleslaw," replied Luella.

"Is that the only thing on the menu?" questioned Chip. "I'm still enjoying that large lunch we had down at Maria's."

"There is no menu!" advised Luella rather coldly.

"I just meant that I can't eat very much right now," clarified Chip. "Acid indigestion from lunch."

"Well, there is ice cream for dessert," informed Luella, "but it will not be served until everyone has eaten their supper first."

"I definitely will have some of that!" grinned Chip.

"Very well," Luella smiled again. "I've already eaten more than my share while preparing this lovely meal, so I'll be telling you Angie's secret while you eat yours."

"Angie's secret?" Jim raised an eyebrow.

"I have a feeling it's a doozy, too!" guessed Sherry.

"Especially if it explains those papers!" agreed Ron.

"What *was* in that drawer, anyway?" Jim suddenly was curious. "And were there any prints?"

"No prints," advised Ron. "But, there certainly are some pretty interesting items!"

"I will tell you about those things as I tell you Angie's story," assured Luella with an even gaze.

"Very well, let's hear it then," agreed Jim.

"Plates are at the end of the bar, with the silverware and napkins," indicated Luella with a wave of her hand. "The food is beside it. Please help yourselves."

Luella then quickly began pouring glasses of water for each of her guests as they went to get their food.

"It does smell pretty good," remarked Janette as she put a second helping of coleslaw onto her plate.

"Save some for the rest of us!" teased Susan.

"You do see the size of those serving bowls, right?" bantered Janette. "There's enough here to feed a small army!"

Once everyone had finished dishing up their food and returned to their stools at the bar, Luella directed, "everyone hold hands please." She patiently waited until they complied before blessing the food. "Dear God, we thank you with all our hearts for this bounteous meal, and for sending Angie here to help us. We thank you also for these detectives and pray you will guide them in their efforts. And please give Angie our regards. Amen!"

"Amen!" repeated several of the others.

"First, I wish to thank old Carrot Top for his part in all this," grinned Luella as she held up an old black and white photo and walked down the bar past each of her customers so everyone could see it.

"Wait!" requested Janette. "It's Jim!"

"Let me see!" insisted Susan as she took the photo from Luella and carefully turned it over. "Wilbur Krain?"

"Taken in 1895," assured Luella. "And this is a photo of him with his wife Angie. As you can see, she is expecting her first child at the time."

Jim could no longer wait for the photo to come down to his end of the bar, so he got up and came to look at it over Susan's and Janette's shoulders. "Well, I'll be."

"It says 'old Carrot Top' on the back of it," chuckled Susan.

"And *THIS* is their marriage license," Luella proudly announced as she held it up.

"That was one of the things in the drawer," confirmed Ron. "Even though there were no prints, we can always check to see if the handwriting on their signatures is a match – that is, if we locate anything to compare it against."

"Oh, it's the real deal, all right," assured Luella.

"It probably is," agreed Jim as he continued to stare at the wedding photo. "This is incredible. I can't believe how much this guy looks like me!"

"Actually, it is *you* who looks like *him*," corrected Luella with an amused grin.

Carolyn suddenly pulled out her cellphone and took several close-up shots of the wedding photo, and the marriage license. "I'm sending these to Ann."

"Whatever for?" frowned Jim.

"Because she recently started working on *your* family tree," reminded Carolyn. "Didn't you know?"

"No, I didn't," replied Jim. "I thought she was still working on the Roth line. Or, should I say, the Lizzie Borden line?"

"Lizzie Borden?" questioned Detective Telluric. "Isn't she the girl who murdered her parents with a hatchet back in the 1800s?"

"Yes, that would be her," sighed Jim. "My wife and stepdaughter Ann are direct descendants of hers."

"Oh, God Almighty!" exclaimed Luella. "No wonder you have such a restless spirit, you poor man. You must live in constant fear for your very life."

"Not as much as here," assured Jim as he recalled his experience with Angie's ghost earlier that day.

"At least Angie likes you, honey," grinned Luella.

"Of course she does," nodded Jim. "She probably thinks I'm old Carrot Top."

"Please continue with your story?" requested Sherry.

"Well," began Luella, "this story actually begins with Josiah Smith, a slave owner ...."

"From Charleston, South Carolina?" interrupted Carolyn.

"You know of him?" glowered Luella.

"I have a Josiah Smith in my family tree who owned slaves on a plantation in Charleston, South Carolina," revealed Carolyn. "Jim's daughter Ann and I came across it when we were working on our genealogy together."

"You don't say?" Luella folded her arms, narrowed her eyes and pursed her lips.

"But, I also have a famous Union soldier on one of my other lines," assured Carolyn. "Private James Grey, Sr. and his platoon fought at Dutch Gap and even served in the trenches during the Siege of Petersburg throughout the winter until the spring of 1865."

"That was one of the bloodiest battles of the entire civil war," recognized Luella, more softly. "But, none of us can choose who our ancestors are, now can we?"

"What if it turns out you're a Krain?" Janette teased Jim as she poked him in the side with her elbow.

"Ann will find out," promised Carolyn.

"So, was Angie a Krain, then?" nodded Sherry. "Was that Angie's secret?"

"No dear, but she certainly was married to one," smiled Luella.

"That would make *you* a Krain?" realized Sherry.

"Technically, yes," admitted Luella with a sad look on her face.

"Did Ronald Krain realize he and Woody were related?" Carolyn suddenly asked.

"That's a good question!" remarked Detective Telluric.

Jim and Chip merely exchanged surprised looks.

"Anyway," Luella continued, "it was at the conclusion of the Civil War in 1865 when Josiah Smith granted freedom to the 300 some slaves that had been working on his plantation."

"Three hundred?" repeated Sherry with surprise.

"Yes, ma'am," confirmed Luella. "Andrew Wilson was one of Josiah Smith's most trusted slaves and had even worked in his house. That was where Andrew met and fell in love with his master's half-white daughter, Angie Smith."

"Excuse me?" Sherry furled her brow.

"Josiah Smith had once forced himself upon a beautiful young slave girl who worked in his kitchen," explained Luella. "She later became pregnant and Angie was the result."

"What a horrible man!" commented Susan.

"So, even though Angie had a white daddy, she was actually an exotic black beauty in her own right, as you can see from that painting of her at the top of the stairs."

"I just knew this would be a juicy story!" grinned Janette as she took another bite of cornbread.

"Naturally, Josiah Smith did not approve of the relationship between Andrew Wilson and his daughter," continued Luella. "But, Angie Smith truly loved Andrew Wilson, so she moved to Powell Mountain with him anyway. That was in 1867. Times being what they were, no one would marry them at first, until a traveling moonshine distributor happened along who also was a preacher. He married them right here in this room, and this is their marriage license – not to be confused with that other marriage license you just saw, from when she married Wilbur Krain later on." Luella proudly held up both licenses for everyone to see and compare.

Sherry was furiously writing down the information in her little notepad while Carolyn was busy photographing and texting information to Ann.

"And here with it is a copy of the emancipation certificate presented to Andrew Wilson by Josiah Smith when he finally freed him." Luella then held that up for everyone to see, too. "This was in that drawer, as well."

"Wow!" exclaimed Susan. "Two marriage licenses! No wonder everyone was looking for the stuff in that drawer like they were."

"It was in 1873 that Andrew Wilson died in a logging accident," recounted Luella. "And, unable to obtain gainful employment on her own after the death of her husband, Angie finally converted this place into a brothel in 1875."

"So, where does Wilbur Krain come into the picture?" pressed Sherry.

"In 1895, of course," smiled Luella. "Wilbur Krain just happened to be one of the widow Angie's best customers. He had been coming to see her for years by then."

Janette and Susan nodded knowingly at one another.

"It was when she finally became pregnant that Angie threatened to reveal the secret publicly if Mr. Krain did not marry and make an honest woman of her," narrated Luella.

"So, did any of their friends know about their marriage?" confirmed Sherry.

"Not at first," replied Luella.

"That must be why she needed a safe place to keep the marriage certificate," assumed Jim.

"Right with her other one," nodded Luella. "But, Wilbur Krain was also one to hit the bottle quite frequently, and one night while playing cards with his friends, he managed to blab the secret."

"What happened then?" urged Susan.

"Wilbur was then blackmailed by a man named Mark Dalton, who was the Head Knight of this area at the time," revealed Luella. "When Wilbur had finally turned over the last of Angie's hard earned savings to him – unbeknownst to Angie until it was too late to do anything about it – Mr. Dalton threatened to expose Wilbur to the

Crusading Knights if he didn't keep paying up. That would, of course, have resulted in a trial."

"By the Knights?" quizzed Sherry.

"Oh, yes," assured Luella. "Absolutely."

"So, what'd Wilbur do then?" pressed Janette.

"He shot himself," informed Luella. "That was when Angie took back the name of Wilson, even knowing that folks might think her son William was a bastard child. She then traveled back to South Carolina to throw herself on the mercy of her estranged father."

"I'll bet that went as expected," sniggered Carolyn.

"She was finally hired as a cleaning woman at a local bank," revealed Luella, without responding to Carolyn's comment. "Angie was about my age when they found her body, slumped over the bucket and mop she had been using to clean with at the time of her death. A very sad ending."

"What happened to her son William?" questioned Sherry.

"Poor little William was raised in an orphanage, from the age of five, until he finally ran away," described Luella.

"That's so sad," remarked Carolyn.

"He was only 15 years old when he fathered Woodrow Wilson, who was my daddy," added Luella. "That was in 1909."

"Were there any siblings?" coaxed Sherry.

"My dad's brother Walter Wilson was born in 1915, but died during the Spanish flu epidemic of 1920. He was only five." Luella fought back the tears as she held up a tattered black and white photo of the little flower-covered casket for the others to see.

"So, how did Woody end up back at Powell Mountain, then?" wondered Sherry. "Did his father come back out here?"

"My Grandpa William just up and took off, leaving Woody at the same orphanage he had once run away from," related Luella. "And according to my daddy, the man never even bothered to look back!"

Carolyn, Sherry, Janette and Susan each had tears streaming down their cheeks by this point.

Chip sadly shook his head. Jim and Ron exchanged a doleful look and shook their heads.

"My daddy was eventually taken in by a Christian black family there in South Carolina," revealed Luella. "It was finally as an adult that he and my mama Harriet decided to come back out here and try to reclaim this property. That was in 1956, when my daddy was 47 years old. His first job was as a lumberman, until the accident when he lost his foot."

"That's just sad." Janette shook her head.

"And you three kids were still living at home at the time?" quizzed Sherry.

"Goodness, no!" chuckled Luella. "We weren't even a twinkle in their eyes yet, not then."

"When did they have you?" asked Sherry.

"My brother Matthew was born in 1965," began Luella, "and Mark was born in 1969."

"Making them 58 and 54 years old now," calculated Sherry as she documented it.

"And just what year were *you* born?" interjected Jim with a mischievous smile.

"Okay, you got me, I was born in 1972," admitted Luella, "but don't tell anyone!"

Sherry then flipped back several pages in her notebook and began to erase something.

"What are you doing?" frowned Luella.

"I had you down as being about 45 years old," informed Sherry as she corrected the entry to reflect Luella's true age of 51.

"Had me fooled, too," flirted Jim.

"Humph!" grinned Luella as she flirted back with him.

"So, just how long did you kids actually live here, then?" interrogated Sherry as she flipped back to the current page in her notebook.

"You know about the fire, I presume?" questioned Luella.

"That's right!" realized Carolyn. "My friend Eula was telling me about it. She said it was pretty common knowledge around these parts that the Crusading Knights had lit up a burning cross out here to scare you guys, but that it got out of hand and ended up catching all this on fire. Your daddy mentioned it to me, too, one time while I was riding with him."

"Some of the wood up there looks older than 1972," pointed out Jim. "Especially in Angie's room."

"Well, it didn't exactly catch the entire place on fire, but it did do significant damage, especially down here," clarified Luella.

"Eula also mentioned that all of you were lucky to get out with your very lives," added Carolyn with a cautionary look at Jim.

"This bar looks newer than that, too," pointed out Jim, ignoring Carolyn's warning glance.

"That's because it was rebuilt after the fire!" snapped Luella. "And yes, our family barely got out in the nick of time when it happened! At least that's what they told me."

"I'm so sorry!" Carolyn said to Luella as she shot Jim another look of disapproval.

"Me, too!" mentioned Jim, suddenly feeling foolish. "Hey, what can you expect from an old Carrot Top like me, anyway?"

"I expect you won't mind when I call you that from now on," Luella finally smiled again.

"How old were you when they set the fire?" questioned Sherry.

"Oh, honey, I was just a baby, probably no more than six months old at the time," informed Luella, "so I really don't recall the fire. That was in 1972."

"That would have made Matthew seven years old and Mark about three years old at the time," figured Sherry.

"Sounds right," nodded Luella.

"I remember Woody telling me that all his kids would be going to school down in St. Diablo, and then would most likely attend the Junior College down in Ocean Bay," interjected Carolyn.

"Well, my brothers did go to school in St. Diablo, but the only schools I went to were down in Ocean Bay," admitted Luella. "I was privileged to live in a fairly decent foster home following my daddy's incarceration, since mama was in a nursing home at the time. Then after their deaths, the Greens adopted me permanently. But, none of us kids ever could afford to attend that school of privilege up on the hill!"

"You were only six years old when your daddy passed in 1978?" continued Sherry.

"Murdered is more like it!" Luella suddenly fumed. "And I do remember my foster mom taking me there to the prison where I got to see my daddy one last time before that."

"What about your mother?" quizzed Sherry. "Did you get to see her, too? Which nursing home was she in?"

"Her mother was at the Powell Mountain Nursing Home." Carolyn spoke up. "That's where Karlin used to work."

"That's right," recalled Detective Telluric. "And you mentioned that Woody would come visit Harriet each Sunday afternoon and would read to her from the scriptures?"

"Yes, he did, before they arrested him." Luella folded her arms and her face took on a distant expression. "The day my foster mom took me to the prison to visit him was the same day she took me to the nursing home to visit my mama."

"What did your mama die of?" delved Sherry.

"Some kind of cancer of the blood," replied Luella, rather sadly. "At least that's what they told me. I think she just plain died of a broken heart! She took the news of my daddy's death pretty hard and it was just six months later that she passed."

"Have you ever thought of taking up detective work?" Ron suddenly asked Sherry. "You're a natural."

"Well, I do have to ask lots of questions for the documentaries I put together," blushed Sherry. She still did not realize that Ron was married, or that he didn't wear his wedding band because it no longer fit on his fat stubby finger.

"What did your brothers think of Angie when you were all living here?" Jim suddenly asked. He was serious and not joking.

"Matthew and Mark each told me once that they were none too fond of Angie's pranks," admitted Luella. "I suppose that's one reason they refuse to spend the night here when they come to visit, which isn't too often now that they both have kids of their own."

"What about you, do you have any kids?" asked Sherry.

"No, I don't," replied Luella with a sad expression on her face. "The good Lord never saw fit to bless me with any."

"Me, neither," mentioned Carolyn.

"Okay, what about that money clip?" Jim suddenly asked, to try to steer the conversation back on track.

"This here?" Luella suddenly beamed as she grabbed and held it up for everyone to see.

"It looks expensive," assessed Janette.

"Let's hope it is," nodded Luella. "I'm sure the Krain family would pay dearly to get it back."

"Now, let's not go tempting fate," cautioned Jim. "Besides, technically you're a Krain, aren't you?"

"You got me again," shrugged Luella. "Yes, I suppose I am."

"And most likely I am, too," grinned Jim, "so, more than likely we're family."

"What's your point?" Luella narrowed her eyes at him.

"The point is, you need my help, and for me, money is no object," explained Jim. "I think you should keep the money clip as a souvenir."

"Is this guy for real?" Luella turned to the others with a questioning look as she pointed her thumb at Jim.

"Yes, he's for real, all right," assured Susan most seriously.

"Old Carrot Top, you're all right!" Luella finally broke into a big smile. "You're all right."

"I could sure use some of that ice cream," reminded Chip.

"You got it, honey," smiled Luella as she pulled some ice cream from the freezer and began dishing some up for everyone.

Once everyone had eaten their ice cream, Jim suddenly announced, "I will be flying back east tonight to try to find an important witness in this case." He did not want to spend the night in Angie's room, and was glad to have an excuse not to.

"You can't fly back there alone!" objected Janette, who also was reluctant to spend the night at the Powell Mountain Bed and Breakfast.

"Jim is a married man," pointed out Sherry. "You can't just hop alone on a Learjet with him and fly back east like that."

"A Learjet?" repeated Luella with surprise.

"Well, it's a way to get around," Jim shrugged his shoulders. "But, Carolyn definitely needs to stay here, in case she remembers anything else up at the winery tomorrow."

"I couldn't agree with you more!" assured Chip.

"And you'll probably want Sherry here to take notes?" pointed out Ron Telluric as he flirted with Sherry. His piercing blue eyes met their mark as Sherry blushed and smiled back at him.

"I guess that leaves me?" assumed Susan.

"Well, it's not like you brought along the right clothes for something like this, anyway," chastised Jim with a teasing sneer.

"Where we goin', anyway?" Janette suddenly asked.

"Chicago," answered Jim as he finally found something on his smartwatch. "Yep, that's where she is."

"Who?" demanded Janette.

"Martha Krain, of course," replied Jim with a subtle nod.

"You're really serious, aren't you?" realized Luella.

"And, by the time I get back, there should be a motorhome parked outside where I can stay," added Jim. "I do need to have my own restroom."

"What about me?" Janette began to panic. "I can't stay here in this place, not with it being haunted like it is!"

"Okay, make that two motorhomes," corrected Jim. "And, whoever wants is welcome to stay in the other one with Janette when we get back."

"Just like that?" Luella shook her head and chuckled.

"Oh, yes," added Jim. "A dark green 1965 Chevy Impala will hopefully be waiting for me when I get back, too. Chip will know what to do with it. It should be treated as a crime scene and touched only with rubber gloves by the forensic team, especially the trunk. Even though there are probably no viable fingerprints, there could be bits of hair or other useful evidence."

"You found it?" Chip was surprised.

"I believe so," responded Jim. "I sent a request to one of my people to try to locate it and just heard back from them that they think they have it. Some man down in Ashton has it now."

"That's quite a way to bring it," assessed Chip.

"Do we know what ever happened to the green Mustang?" added Jim, ignoring Chip's comment completely.

"We can probably find out," hoped Chip.

"May I leave that one task to you, then?" asked Jim.

"Sure, I can do that," agreed Chip.

"Excellent. The other equipment should get here sooner, though," assured Jim. "Excuse me, but I've got a Learjet to fly. Susan and Janette, may I get your suitcases?"

"You gotta go back in that room for yours, too, don't you?" razzed Janette. "That's okay, we can get our own."

"What equipment?" questioned Luella as she watched them head upstairs for their luggage.

"Excavation equipment for the old salvage yard," explained Chip. "And a crew of twenty or thirty guys."

"What!" Luella raised her voice. "I can't feed that many people!"

"You won't have to," assured Jim as he raced past her toward the door with his suitcase. "I'll have a caterer brought in for the crew, and a couple of Honey Buckets, too. And thanks for a great dinner!"

"Amen to that!" agreed Janette as she hurried to keep up with Jim, despite her heavy suitcase.

"Everything was wonderful, thanks!" called Susan as she hurried out the door after them with the wheels of her leopard patterned suitcase spiraling out of control behind her.

"Is old Carrot Top always like that?" Luella stood staring after them in disbelief with her hands on her hips.

"He certainly is," assured Carolyn. "Trust me!"

The morning of Friday, March 24, 2023, proved to be a bright, sunny one. Sunlight streamed through the old growth forest and danced tantalizingly on the brush-covered salvage yard beside them. Even the old dead blackberry canes seemed to glow in the early morning light, with gossamer spider webs shimmering across the tops of them. Beads of morning dew gently dripped from a towering Redwood tree nearby. The screech of a hawk could be heard in the morning stillness as it circled high above in search of its morning meal below.

The two-story stone building where Carolyn and Sherry had just spent the night somehow seemed less haunted than it had the night before. The three round-arched windows above its front entrance seemed to beckon visitors to look up to where saloon girls would once have been perched on its windowsills, waiting for customers to arrive. Strangely, the ornately carved wooden statue of the Woodcutter seemed to blend right in with its surroundings, though the fountain perched on top of his old chopping block appeared out of place.

The unmarked patrol car of Chip Priest and Ron Telluric was waiting for them.

"Guess you ladies will need to ride with us," apologized Ron as Carolyn and Sherry climbed into the backseat of their vehicle for the journey to the Shady Brook Winery.

"Got your notepad?" Carolyn asked Sherry, half teasingly.

"Absolutely!" smirked Sherry as she flirted with Ron.

"You gonna tell her?" Chip whispered to Ron.

"Tell who what?" frowned Ron.

"That you're a happily married man?" spelled out Chip.

261

"There's nothing going on between me and her," assured Ron in a whisper, so only Chip could hear.

"I certainly hope not!" responded Chip with an even gaze.

The two detectives and their wives had been close friends for many years, often celebrating holidays and special occasions together, and Chip was not about to let Ron step out on his lovely wife, Andrea. They had been through too much together. Besides, it wouldn't be fair to Sherry not to tell her, since she did seem to be getting her hopes up over Ron.

"Penny for your thoughts," interrupted Sherry from behind them in the backseat.

"Oh, nothing," apologized Chip. "I was just thinking of what lies ahead of us up at the winery. Are you ladies sure you're ready for this? Even though all of the corpses are skeletons now, it's still a pretty sobering crime scene. They each had to be extracted from wine barrels full of concrete."

"How in the world would they extract them from concrete?" quizzed Sherry.

"With a very specialized new type of forensic laser beam cutting torch," answered Ron. "Very high tech stuff."

Carolyn merely nodded, though she wasn't at all sure whether she was ready to see yet another of her friends reduced to skeletal form so soon. The discovery of Veronica Jensen's and Joyce Troglite's skeletal remains in the bunker tunnel at Oceanview Academy's beach just seven years earlier still haunted her.

Chip started up the engine of the unmarked patrol car and slowly made his way down the gravel road. "Do you think your friend Karlin might have confronted Martha Krain later on about the bloody laundry she saw her with that morning?"

"I have no idea," responded Carolyn as she began to think of Karlin. *What had happened to Karlin, anyway?* wondered Carolyn.

"Remind me again. What bloody laundry?" Sherry pulled out her notepad at once and began writing.

"It was the morning I ran over the squirrel with the Mustang, but before I took it in to the auto shop," related Carolyn. "Karlin and I had cleaned what was left of Stacia's vomit from the backseat. I wanted to get it as clean as possible before taking the car in to be worked on."

"That's understandable," nodded Sherry.

"Anyway, when Karlin went down there to wash our stuff, Martha Krain was already there starting a blood-soaked pile of laundry. That was in the laundry room at the girls' dormitory. But, Karlin managed to get to the other three washing machines first, so Martha was only able to start one of her loads right then. And, she seemed really put out about it, too."

"Really?" Sherry was intrigued.

"When Karlin noticed the blood on Martha's sleeve, she gave Karlin some lame excuse about having a bad nosebleed and getting it all over her stuff," added Carolyn. "But, it did seem like an excessive amount of blood, now that I think about it."

"How excessive?" Chip suddenly asked as he turned onto Powell Mountain Road.

"Probably more than there would have been for something like that," assessed Carolyn as she tried to visualize it in her mind.

"What did Martha do with the rest of her laundry?" asked Ron.

"She took it back upstairs to her room, I guess," shrugged Carolyn. "Karlin offered to get it started for her when our loads were done, if she would just leave some quarters, but Martha clearly wasn't interested in doing that."

"I see." Chip pursed his lips as he thought of the repeated times he had tried to get a follow-up interview with Martha Krain, following her commitment. He hoped that Jim Otterman would be more successful, and that Martha was coherent.

"There's where that dark green Chevy was parked," Carolyn pointed out for Sherry's benefit as they approached it.

"That's also the place where the other green Mustang was found," added Ron. "Just beyond it, covered by a pile of brush on that logging road."

Sherry then craned her neck to get a better look at the area as they drove past it.

"It's still a marvelous forest, though," commented Sherry.

"Wish the same could be said for this road!" muttered Chip as he slowed for yet another hairpin turn.

"We got enough gas?" Ron suddenly asked.

"Of course not!" realized Chip. "They do have a gas station up at the school, though."

"For only $8.23 a gallon," muttered Ron. "And they probably don't even take old fashioned credit cards at a place like that!"

"We better hope they do," responded Chip.

"How much is the gas down in St. Diablo?" wondered Sherry.

"Oh, I don't know, about $6.12 a gallon." Chip was clearly agitated about it, especially since he would be using his own credit card for the transaction, and not the Department's.

"They will reimburse you, won't they?" Sherry suddenly asked.

"Yeah, probably at the end of the month," sighed Chip.

"Good thing the case up there is official business," reminded Carolyn as she studied Chip Priest's eyes in the rearview mirror in front of him. "I'm sure Jim will be more than happy to make it right."

"Just what is the deal between you two, anyway?" grilled Chip.

"It's just like we've told you already," promised Carolyn. "The guy has been obsessed with me since high school. But, he is married to someone else, and so am I – quite happily, I might add."

"Hey, I'm sorry about that crack I made yesterday," apologized Chip. "I was out of line."

"What crack?" questioned Carolyn. She knew full well what Chip was talking about but chose to feign ignorance.

"You know, when I said you guys should have gotten married, so now you could get a divorce?" reminded Chip rather sheepishly.

Carolyn, Sherry and Ron then began to laugh most heartily.

"It's not that funny!" scowled Chip before he finally saw the humor in it and began laughing, too.


The Shady Brook Winery had been magnificent in its heyday, attracting customers from miles around. That was in the mid-1950s. Not only casual wine tasters, but also important vendors had sought out its business. Naturally, the Shady Brook Winery offered the best brunch on the mountain, and was quite popular on Mother's Day. Its fabulous gift shop offered gourmet cheeses and other specialty food items, gifts and souvenirs – not to mention its highly sought after wines. Its romantic Shakespearean architecture would seemingly transport guests into a distant time. Of special interest to many of the students at Powell Mountain University were its Friday and Saturday night barn dances, where they were able to listen to and enjoy popular music and performers of the day. Such activities were not condoned by the school but nevertheless quite well attended.

264

Its long-time owner Jerry Krain had been a faithful member of the Crusading Knights from his home town in Texas until finally moving to Powell Mountain. In fact, it was Jerry who was responsible initially for enlisting his cousin Ronald to their cause.

Like his cousin Ronald, Jerry Krain had been born in Texas, but was two years older. Jerry had been offered a permanent job at his uncle's Texas cattle ranch more than once, but had elected instead to head out to Powell Mountain where he could fulfill his true interest in becoming a Wine Master with his own vineyard. It was in 1953, when Jerry was 45 years old, that his dream came true.

The Crusading Knights of Powell Mountain were quick to enlist Jerry in their local chapter, especially due to his prior affiliation with their organization. In his younger years, Jerry was rather well liked by all who knew him, especially the young people who came out to the barn dances that were held each weekend at the winery. Most of them, however, knew nothing of his involvement with the Crusading Knights.

But, since Jerry's uncelebrated death sometime in December of 2022, the once great Shady Brook Winery now stood in shambles. At least that's what forensic experts estimated as the approximate time of Jerry's death. The cause was yet to be determined. Having been a loner in his old age, Jerry had no real friends. At least none that were still alive. The only family members to succeed him were his late cousin Ronald's two children, Michael and Martha. Both had become alienated from him due to his disagreeable temperament, and wanted nothing to do with him anyway. Jerry's participation in Crusading Knight activities had also been limited during the months preceding his death due to his failing health. As a result, his absence from the world had gone virtually unnoticed until a bill collector for the local power company finally stopped by to pay him a visit, to find out why the account was delinquent.

The overgrown wrought iron entrance gate to Shady Brook Winery was now rusted and hung at an angle. The once elegant benches by its entrance were so dilapidated from wear that many of their boards had fallen through, leaving only the frames behind. The huge barn where dances had been held - when not being used to age barrels of expensive wine - stood ruined by the ravages of time.

"Are you sure this is the place?" questioned Sherry with a look of trepidation on her face as Detective Chip Priest stopped his vehicle so Detective Ron Telluric could get out to move the rusted gate to one side, thus enabling them to drive through its entrance.

"This is it, all right," confirmed Carolyn with a shudder. The place actually looked creepier now than she had envisioned it might.

"You said it was already rundown back in 1975?" verified Sherry as she made some notes in her little pad.

"Very much so, but *nothing* like this!" replied Carolyn. "And it was creepy enough back then!"

"I wish I could tell you it gets better," advised Chip, "but what you're about to see is shocking, even to old detectives like us."

"Understood," nodded Carolyn, though nothing could be further from the truth.

"At least now you might find out what actually happened to her," consoled Sherry as she put a comforting hand on Carolyn's shoulder.

"Thanks," Carolyn smiled weakly.

"So, this is where old Jerry Krain brought you ladies?" questioned Ron.

"Yes," confirmed Carolyn.

"The old buzzard!" muttered Chip as he pulled to a stop by the large, rickety barn.

"Are you sure it's safe to go inside?" Sherry stared at the dilapidated building with concern as Carolyn pulled out her cellphone and took a few photos of the area, after climbing from the unmarked patrol car.

"Does kind of look like a good windstorm might just do her in," opined Ron rather sardonically.

"I've got hardhats in the trunk for each of us," informed Chip as he went back to retrieve them.

"I doubt those are gonna save us if the entire building decides to collapse," assessed Carolyn, who was also quite worried about it.

"Where's the rest of your forensic team, anyway?" quizzed Sherry as she climbed from the vehicle and approached the huge opening where the barn's front doors had once hung, but now lay on their sides by the entrance.

Chip and Ron exchanged a meaningful glance. The barn's huge front doors had been locked and tightly bolted following their last visit to the site several days ago, not like they were now! How could something like this happen? Had the various crime scenes

266

inside been compromised in some way? And by whom? Or, was the breach due to natural causes? Neither detective was in any hurry to mention their suspicions just yet, so they kept silent about it.

"You're it?" Sherry was flabbergasted.

"For reasons we can only speculate about," explained Chip rather nervously, "the Department does not seem to be in any hurry to work this particular crime scene, especially with it being a cold case like it is."

"Oh, my God!" exclaimed Carolyn as they entered the building after putting on their hardhats.

At least a dozen sets of skeletal remains had been carefully placed on the aging wooden floor, each beside the now-empty wine barrels in which they had been encased in concrete for untold numbers of years. Beside each barrel were various chunks of cement that had been carefully removed from that victim's skeletal remains by a special forensic laser cutting torch.

"I think I'm going to be sick," informed Sherry as she turned away and took several deep breaths from outside.

After taking a few photos, Carolyn then stood there and stared with disbelief at the entire scene. "Which one is Karlin?"

"Hang on, let me get the file," apologized Ron. "I left it in the car." He then raced out to retrieve it.

Small plastic A-framed evidence tent markers sat beside each skeleton. They were bright yellow with black numbers on them. Wooden stakes with caution tape surrounded each individual skeleton and its corresponding barrel and cement fragments. Sprawled on the ground out in front of the barn, where its heavy fallen doors lay was a strip of bright yellow crime scene tape with black letters that read, "Police Line Do Not Cross."

"Why does this marker say twenty-three?" demanded Carolyn, refusing at first to accept the ramifications of it.

"Because that's how many there are," Chip sadly answered.

"What about those other barrels?" quizzed Sherry. "Over there in the alcove? Are there bodies in those, as well?"

"Just rancid wine in those ones," replied Chip.

"How horrible this place is!" muttered Sherry, who had finally forced herself to take out her notepad and begin taking notes again.

"Just how on earth did the police first learn about all of this?" questioned Carolyn.

"Some debt collector came out to see why the old guy hadn't paid his electric bill," revealed Chip.

"Here it is!" called Ron as he returned with the file. "Karlin Gomez is number thirteen."

"Are they numbered in the order of when each crime was committed?" Sherry managed to ask, though she still felt shaky.

"It's okay," assured Ron as he put a supporting arm around her. "It never gets any easier, either."

"Thanks," Sherry smiled at Ron's reassuring blue eyes. Having him nearby was comforting.

"No, they are not numbered sequentially of when the crimes were committed," advised Chip as he shot Ron a glance of disapproval upon noticing his continued interest in Sherry. "That has yet to be determined, as well. These are just in the order they were each processed by the original forensic teams."

Carolyn silently walked over to the skeleton labeled "13" and reverently knelt on the splintered wooden floor beside it, just beyond the crime scene tape. Tears streamed down her cheeks as she studied the skeleton. Finally, she forced herself to take some photos of it.

"Interesting that the old guy would use barrels like that," pointed out Chip, "since most wineries began using the twenty and forty-foot containers in 1956, that hold 885 and 324½ gallons respectively. They were invented by a trucking business owner named Malcom P. McLean to reduce delays at cargo ports by loading directly from ship to truck."

"Before that," added Ron, "most wineries were using the old fashioned wooden barrels like the ones you see here, though some used 55-gallon stainless steel drums instead. But, around 91 million barrels were manufactured in the United States alone in 1910."

Both Sherry and Carolyn frowned at the two detectives with disapproval.

"It was in 1901 that a 63-year-old woman named Annie Edson Taylor became the first person to survive a plunge over Niagara Falls in a barrel like this," babbled Chip. "As you can see by the other barrels over there that are still intact, there is plenty of room inside for a human body. The barrels are 4½ feet tall and 3 feet in diameter."

"Virtually indestructible, too," reminded Ron. "Heck, these barrels probably all came with the place when Krain first bought it."

"Do you mind?" Carolyn was clearly shaken, and the last thing she needed right then was to hear about the history of wine barrels!

"Oh, sorry!" apologized Ron.

"Forgive us," Chip held out his hand to Carolyn to help her back up. "Everything here will be treated with the utmost respect and care, we assure you."

"As long as we have anything to say about it, anyway," added Ron when his gaze wandered to the fallen barn doors.

"Does her family know?" inquired Carolyn as she allowed Detective Priest to help her to her feet.

"They are being notified," he replied.

"Just where was my wallet found?" Carolyn suddenly wanted to know. She sadly surveyed Karlin's skeletal remains and took a couple more photos of them as she waited for the detective to respond.

"I have photos here in this file of what the barrel looked like inside when it was first found, both before and after the forensic team managed to laser away the concrete," described Ron. "Would you like to see?"

Carolyn merely nodded her assent while Ron Telluric thumbed through the file and then stopped.

"Perhaps you might want to sit down first?" offered Chip.

An old wooden church pew sat along one wall near the former dance area. The bales of hay that had also been used for people to sit on by the other walls were long since reduced to piles of aging straw on the floor. A large spool of rusted baling wire sat nearby.

After Ron removed a clean handkerchief from his pocket and wiped off the pew, the four of them sat down on it. Carolyn and Sherry were in the middle, with Ron seated beside Sherry and his partner beside Carolyn. Carolyn took the file from Ron and silently studied the gruesome photo. The skeleton had been in kneeling position inside the barrel, with its hands wired together behind its back. Indistinguishable remnants of fabric and hair, along with the badly damaged blue leather wallet inside the skeleton's hands, were clearly visible in the photo.

"Oh, Karlin! Why did you do it?" wept Carolyn. "I told you not to come back here for that wallet by yourself!"

Sherry put her arm around Carolyn and let her cry for several minutes as the detectives patiently waited.

"Just what made the bill collector start poking around inside the barrels, anyway?" quizzed Sherry.

"From what we can tell, at least one of the old wooden racks that was used here managed to crab-walk off the ends of the barrels that were stacked beneath it – probably due to seismic activity or settling of the earth beneath all of it over time. That would then have caused one or more stacks of barrels to fall or roll off and crash onto the floor below," elaborated Chip. "Especially with them stacked six high like that."

"What do you mean by crab-walk?" quizzed Sherry.

"Crab-walking is something that usually occurs when a two-rack system like this is used," explained Chip. "The two-rack system has a known weakness where all racks higher than level two need to slide only a few inches before they slip or 'crab-walk' off the barrels below them. And, all it takes is one rack to slip off one barrel to trigger the domino effect on all the other barrel stacks. That is known as crab-walking."

"What about all the rest of those barrels?" Carolyn became alarmed. "Are we safe here?"

"Don't worry," assured Chip. "They've been secured." He certainly hoped so, anyway.

"So, I see the defective barrel stacking rack has its own number, too?" noticed Sherry. Carolyn then went over and took a photo of it.

"It does," confirmed Ron. "Plenty of photos were taken of the entire group of wrecked barrels, before they were each processed."

"Naturally, seeing skeletal remains protruding from broken chunks of concrete that had been inside one of the broken barrels out here was more than just a little suspicious," recounted Chip. "So, the guy called the police at once."

"All other barrels became suspect at that time and were subsequently searched," added Ron. "This was the result. The ones you see still stacked over there in the alcove were forensically confirmed to contain only liquid inside them. X-rays were taken of all of them."

"What if there are more?" Carolyn suddenly asked.

"As far as we know, the only remaining barrels are over there in that alcove," indicated Ron.

"Not barrels," clarified Carolyn. "What if there are more skeletal remains? Somewhere else on the property?"

"Let's certainly hope not!" exclaimed Sherry.

"There actually were twenty-nine missing coeds in all between 1956 and 1975, when the Woodcutter was finally arrested," informed Chip. "So, not all of them have been recovered yet. There are six missing people still unaccounted for, that we are aware of."

"And Woody did move out here to Powell Mountain in 1956," reminded Ron.

"There's no way he did this!" Carolyn angrily stood back up and walked toward the large opening to go outside but then stopped and turned to face them. "Absolutely not!"

"You're preaching to the choir," informed Chip. "The two of us were ousted from our jobs at the DA's office for trying to convince those people Woody was innocent! And just look at us now!"

"At least we aren't beat cops anymore." Ron shrugged his shoulders and shook his head. "Took us years just to make detective."

"I don't understand," frowned Sherry.

"Well, it's simple," answered Chip. "The judge who heard Woody's case was also the head of the Crusading Knights of Powell Mountain at that time. Worse still, Woody was a black man. Nothing we said or did made any difference, not even the forensic evidence – or lack thereof – that should have proven him innocent. At the very least, it should have created a reasonable doubt in the minds of the jurors. Some of it even proved that the crime scene was staged."

"That's just wrong!" Sherry angrily shook her head.

"As I recall, Chip being a Jewish guy didn't help matters much, either," reminded Ron. "Not only that, we each came home to burning crosses on our lawns during the trial, and threats were made to our families. That's when we were still Deputy DAs."

"You're Jewish, too?" asked Carolyn as she looked more closely at Ron's piercing blue eyes.

"Goodness, no!" laughed Ron. "My terrible sin was being best buddies with one and then sticking up for him." Ron gently grabbed Chip's shoulder and let his hand rest there for a moment.

"Hey, we need to level with you," advised Chip as his face took on a somber expression. "There's a reason we're handling this case on our own like this."

"And not involving the rest of the Department?" perceived Sherry with a knowing nod as she made more notes.

"The long arm of the Crusading Knights still reaches not only into the Department, but also into the local judicial system, as well," informed Chip. "Michael Krain, who just happens to be son of the late great Ronald Krain, is currently the Presiding Judge over St. Diablo County. He succeeded Judge Jonathan Lorik, who presided over the Woodcutter's trial when he was alive."

"And Michael Krain's a member of the Crusading Knights, as well?" delved Carolyn.

"Head member these days," Chip pursed his lips to keep from cursing. "He and his sister Martha are the late Jerry Krain's only living relatives."

"Martha Krain, the one with the bloody laundry that Jim went to Chicago to interview?" Sherry began writing in her notepad again.

"That would be her," confirmed Chip with a deep sigh. "Sure hope Jim gets what he needs from her while he's out there."

"Hopefully so," muttered Carolyn.

"I just hope he gets back soon," admitted Ron. "Those barn doors were tightly sealed when we left here last week."

"What?" Carolyn came back over to where they were. "Someone just came out here and pulled down those big heavy doors?"

"There do appear to be tractor tracks outside in the dirt by that caution tape," realized Sherry, who had not fully comprehended their significance until now. "I take it that was on the doors?"

"That would be correct," confirmed Ron.

"We're definitely on our own, then," recognized Sherry.

"So, do you have any ideas who did this?" pressed Carolyn.

"We've got our suspicions," replied Chip. "Nothing we'd ever be able to prove."

"Are we safe here?" Carolyn finally asked.

"During the daytime with us, probably," replied Chip as he began to walk around and study everything in the room more closely.

"While we're here," interjected Ron, "we would like you to try to remember exactly what happened the night you were here in 1975. Every little detail, no matter how insignificant, even if you've mentioned it already. Let us decide what may or may not be important."

272

Carolyn took in a deep breath and then let it out. "Valentine's Day was on a Friday night in 1975. These two guys were supposed to meet Karlin and me at Maria's Mexican Restaurant for dinner and then take us to the movies."

"How did you get there?" quizzed Ron.

"Woody brought us down," replied Carolyn.

"So, the Woodcutter drove you and Karlin from Powell Mountain University down to Maria's Mexican Restaurant in St. Diablo on February 14, 1975, and dropped you off?"

"Yes, at about 6:00 p.m." Carolyn seemed sad as she thought of it. "That was where we met Jerry Krain."

"What about your dates, who were they?" pressed Ron.

"I honestly can't even remember their names now. Just that they stood us up," answered Carolyn. "We didn't find out until later that they had a flat tire and were late, but we were already gone by the time they got there anyway."

"Did you have dinner with Jerry?" continued Ron.

"No, but we were at the cash register paying for our meal at the same time he was paying for his," remembered Carolyn. "That's when we first spoke."

"Then what?" urged Chip.

"He asked us what two nice young girls like ourselves were doing out alone on a Friday night," recounted Carolyn. "That was when we explained to him that we'd been stood up and had no idea how we were going to get back up the mountain."

"And that was when he offered you a ride?" assumed Chip.

"Actually, it was Karlin who asked him if he was headed that way," revealed Carolyn. "And if he could take us along."

"Which he gladly did, no doubt." Chip shook his head with dismay. His memories of Jerry Krain were not pleasant.

"It was on our way up the mountain that he told us about his old winery – this place – and made it sound like a grand ballroom," continued Carolyn. "He went on and on about how all the kids from the school used to come out here on Friday and Saturday nights for the big barn dances and that we should come see it for ourselves."

"Which you obviously did," noted Chip.

"What happened when you first got here?" coached Ron.

"Well, the first thing he did was turn on the lights," described Carolyn. "The switch was right over there by the entrance."

"Where were the lights?" frowned Ron.

"It was a big chandelier, right up there." Carolyn pointed at the rafters above them.

"Well, there's nothing there now," observed Chip. "And no light switch, either."

"He had a long extension cord strung up over the rafters leading from the chandelier over to the wall, and then down to where the switch was," elaborated Carolyn.

"That sounds safe," Sherry chuckled sarcastically.

"What next?" encouraged Ron.

"That was when he took us on a tour of the place," continued Carolyn. "First, he showed us the barrels out here and went on and on about the wine inside, how great it was, that kind of thing."

"Did he give you any of it to drink?" pressed Ron.

"He tried to persuade us to try some," replied Carolyn, "but it smelled weird, so even if we were people that drank, we wouldn't have tried it. Something was wrong with it. It smelled rancid."

"It probably was!" interjected Chip.

"Do you think some of the barrels out here could have had bodies in cement inside them, even back then?" Sherry suddenly asked.

"There's no way of knowing for sure at this point," replied Chip.

"And what did he show you next?" urged Ron.

"He had a rickety old wooden table here in the middle of the room with a cast-iron skillet on it," described Carolyn. "That was where he mixed the wine with the rotten eggs he tried to get us to eat. He said it had something to do with the chemical reaction, or something like that, and claimed it would actually cook them."

"Rotten eggs?" frowned Chip.

"Yes, but first he took us over into the alcove area, and showed us where his old hen house used to be," remembered Carolyn. "Apparently, he had chickens at one point, but there certainly weren't any live ones around here that we could see! The place was already pretty run down, even then."

"Very creepy!" muttered Sherry.

"Then he grabbed a handful of unrefrigerated eggs from a bowl back there and a bottle of his rancid wine that had already been opened, and came out here to the table. Then he proceeded to crack the eggs into the pan, and poured the wine into it," elaborated Carolyn. "He kept telling us we were gonna love it."

"And that's when you made a run for it?" assumed Chip.

"You bet it was!" assured Carolyn. "The man had a wild look in his eyes, like he thought he was gonna try and poison us or something. We weren't taking any chances, though."

"Did he run after you?" asked Ron.

"Well, he did grab the big knife he was using to stir the egg mixture with and had it in his hand when he followed us to the door, trying to persuade us to stay," recalled Carolyn. "Actually, it may have been a bowie knife. A pretty big one, too!"

"Did he try and swing it at you, or anything like that?" grilled Ron. "And did he continue to follow you after you left?"

"No, he didn't," remembered Carolyn, "but just the fact that he had it in his hand when he followed us to the door made us very uncomfortable. That was when he finally told us, 'fine, just leave, but don't expect me to take you back!'"

"How did you get back then?" continued Ron.

"We walked for at least a mile," answered Carolyn.

"And that was when the Woodcutter happened along to give you a ride back?" reminded Chip.

"Yes, it was!" confirmed Carolyn. "And we were never so glad to see anyone in our lives!"

"How was it that Woody just happened to be up here, right when you needed a ride?" pressed Ron.

"He said he had delivered an unexpected order to the Krain residence, and was on his way back," explained Carolyn.

"But, this is farther up the hill than the Ronald Krain residence," pointed out Ron. "Why was he all the way up here?"

"I honestly don't know," admitted Carolyn. "Perhaps this was the Krain residence he was delivering to? He did deliver to just about everybody on the mountain."

"That would make sense," nodded Chip. "The Jerry Krain residence."

"Is there anything else at all you can recall, like when you would have lost your wallet?" persisted Ron.

"It was in the alcove, when I bent down to pick up a beautiful rooster feather that was just lying there on the floor," described Carolyn. "Jerry said I could keep it."

"You wouldn't still have it, would you?" asked Ron.

"No," responded Carolyn. "And I have no idea what I might have done with it. That was forty-eight years ago."

"Anything else?" Ron was like a vicious little dog that had ahold of someone's pantleg and wouldn't let go.

"Like what?" Carolyn was frustrated.

"Any other unusual smells or noises or unusual temperature variances, anything at all?" listed Ron.

Carolyn was silent for several moments before responding. "There was an unusual dripping sound when we were in the alcove, but there wasn't a sink."

"But you have no idea what it might have been?" confirmed Ron. "Was there any unusual smell in there by the dripping sound that was stronger than the smell out here?"

"It did smell pretty bad in there," admitted Carolyn. "Almost like something had died."

All four of them became deathly quiet as they glanced toward the alcove. "I think we need to have another look in there," suggested Ron. "The forensics team worked mostly out here."


Meanwhile, at the Chicago O'Hare International Airport, Jim, Janette and Susan had stopped for a late-morning breakfast at a small bistro in the airport's expansive mall. Jim's Learjet was safely secured inside a private hangar that he had managed to rent on-the-spot after their arrival. Janette stared with amazement at the various gift shops, restaurants and even department stores located in the airport mall. Waiting areas along its various hangars were filled to capacity with travel weary passengers and their luggage.

"If it weren't for all those people with their suitcases," commented Janette, "I'd swear this was just a regular shopping mall! Just look at all those stores!"

"It is an international airport," reminded Jim as he studied the online L Train pamphlet on his Smartwatch.

"Perhaps I should try and pick up a pair of hiking boots and some jeans while we're here?" suggested Susan. "If we see a place like that."

"That's fine," muttered Jim as he continued trying to decipher the L Train pamphlet.

276

"How can you even read that?" scowled Janette as she glanced at the tiny print. "Can't you make it any larger?"

"Are we sure that the L Train even goes out that far?" questioned Susan. "I show the address we need as being pretty far out."

"So, you have one of those Smartwatches, too?" Janette shook her head. "Here, use mine!" Janette then took out her outdated cellphone and set it on the table. "At least you can read the print on it! Well, kind of. Even that's too small for my liking."

"Excuse me, ma'am." Jim flagged down a woman wiping off one of the tables nearby. "Ma'am?"

"You'll need to bus your own dirty dishes," advised the cross worker. She was a middle-aged black woman with a bad attitude and clearly wanted to be anywhere else.

Jim immediately pulled out a twenty-dollar bill and handed it to her. "All I need is some information on where we need to catch the L Train to get to the Shady Brook Research Center over on North Lake Shore Drive."

"At the train terminal," replied the woman as she quickly stuffed the twenty-dollar bill into her pocket without bothering to thank him.

"Excuse me?" Jim was losing his patience. "Which train?"

"Ask them," the worker shrugged her shoulders and resumed wiping off tables.

"Thank you," sighed Jim as he returned to the table to finish his coffee. "Hopefully the people at the L Train terminal will be of more help!" He said it loud enough for the worker to hear him, though she gave no indication one way or the other.

"Nice town," Susan commented sarcastically, also loud enough for the woman to overhear.

"Can you believe her?" Janette was stunned by the woman's rudeness. "You shouldn't let her get away with that!"

"Come on, you two ready?" prompted Jim as he stood to leave. He had paid for their meal when first placing their order by using his Smartwatch, so there was no need to wait around. Besides, Jim was anxious to get where they were going before it got any later and had no desire to get into an argument with the restaurant worker.

"Hang on!" called Susan. She was studying Janette's cellphone screen. "The train runs 24/7, we should be okay."

"That's a relief," nodded Jim, though not too worried about it.

"It says here that we need to take train number 206 to get to the 2300 block of North Lake Shore Drive," added Susan.

"Train number 206?" Janette could not believe it. "How in the world can there be 206 trains in one city? A person could get lost in a place like this!"

"It's probably a good thing we left our luggage on the jet," pointed out Jim with a slight smile. "I didn't think we'd want to be hauling it around with us."

"That's for sure!" Susan rolled her eyes.

"Good thing we slept on the jet, too!" added Janette. "One thing I haven't seen yet is a decent place to stay."

"Don't worry, we'll be back to the jet by tonight," assured Jim as he started to leave the bistro without putting a tip on the table.

"I've never seen Jim leave someplace without giving 'em a tip," Susan whispered to Janette.

"Seems to me like he already gave her a tip!" replied Janette, loudly enough for the woman to hear.

Jim then came back to where Janette and Susan were still standing near the table and suddenly put one arm around each of them and began gently guiding them toward the door. "Come on, ladies, let's go. We've got a train to catch."


Once Jim, Susan and Janette had managed to locate and board train number 206, they settled into their seats. Janette stared at the snarled tangle of skyscrapers outside in silence as both Jim and Susan dozed where they sat.

"Stop 17 on North Lake Shore Drive," came an automated voice overhead as the train began to slow.

"We're here already?" Janette was surprised at how quickly they had made their way across the huge city. "Hey, you guys, wake up!"

Jim and Susan were on their feet almost immediately, well aware that the train paused for no more than 60 seconds at each stop.

"Hurry!" urged Jim as he grabbed Janette by the hand and pulled her up. "They only stop for 60 seconds."

"Oh, my goodness!" exclaimed Janette as she followed Jim and Susan from the L Train and out onto the pedestrian ramp outside.

"MIRA, what block of North Lake Shore Drive are we in?" Jim asked of his Smartwatch, which was paired to his Learjet's mainframe via satellite.

"You are in the 1900 block of North Lake Shore Drive," indicated MIRA.

"Which way is the 2300 block?" grilled Jim.

"Turn north," answered the voice of MIRA on Jim's Smartwatch.

"Which way is north?" demanded Janette. "How can you stand that thing? It's exasperating!"

"I think this way is north," indicated Susan with a nod.

"Well, if it's not, we can always turn around and go the other way," decided Jim. "After you."

"Hey, what lake is this?" Janette suddenly wanted to know as she paused to admire the huge lake beside them.

Jim and Susan both stared at her with disbelief for several moments without responding.

"I think it might be Lake Michigan," snickered a nice looking Jamaican man that was sitting on a brick ledge nearby.

His shoulder-length dreadlocks were neatly tied back with a red bandana, and his black leather vest and riding pants did not seem unduly worn. His pointy-toed leather boots almost looked new.

"You sure about that?" laughed Jim, unable to help himself.

"Lake Michigan is one of the five Great Lakes of North America and happens to be the only one located entirely within the United States," replied the man.

"You seem like a well-educated person," commented Jim as he pulled a twenty-dollar bill from his pocket and handed it to him. "How'd you like to be our tour guide for the day? There's more where that came from when we're done."

Susan and Janette both shot Jim daggerous looks but remained silent to see what the man would say.

The man was about fifty years old and had a strong Jamaican accent. He flirted shamelessly with Susan as he stood to face his potential employer. "Name's Rupert." He then smiled as he held out his hand to Jim. "How much more?"

"Rupert?" acknowledged Jim as he shook his hand. "How 'bout a hundred bucks?"

"You've definitely got my attention," grinned Rupert. "Okay, sure, why not?"

"We are trying to find the Shady Brook Research Center," informed Jim.

"The looney bin?" Rupert seemed surprised.

"Someone we're trying to locate might be there," explained Jim.

"To each his own," Rupert shrugged his shoulders as he carefully deposited the twenty-dollar bill into his pocket. "Lunch might not hurt, either."

"It would be our pleasure if you join us for some lunch," added Jim. "Perhaps there's a place along the way?"

"I think I might know just the place," nodded Rupert as he continued to flirt with Susan, despite her efforts to appear as if she didn't notice. After all, she was a married woman.

"Just how do you know so much about this lake?" Janette finally decided to ask.

"I live here," replied Rupert. "This is one huge lake, though. Besides Chicago, it has ports in Milwaukee and Green Bay, Wisconsin, Gary, Indiana, and even Benton Harbor in Michigan."

"Just how big is it?" challenged Susan.

"How big would you like it to be?" responded Rupert as he undressed Susan with his eyes.

"The lake!" snapped Susan.

Jim tried in vain to suppress a chuckle as he enjoyed Susan's predicament.

"Word is, she's 307 miles long and 118 miles wide," answered Rupert, more seriously. "She's also the third largest of the Great Lakes."

"So, how does a homeless guy like you just happen to know so much?" tested Susan as they all began walking along the pedestrian ramp toward their destination.

"What makes you so sure I'm homeless?" asked Rupert.

"What's your story, then?" challenged Susan.

"I used to be a professor at Chicago State University," informed Rupert. "Before I was forced into an early retirement."

"Why was that?" pressed Susan.

"Drinking problem," shrugged Rupert. "It wasn't too long after that when I lost the house and then my family took off, too."

"Didn't you ever even try to stop drinking?" interjected Janette.

"Oh yeah," assured Rupert. "I've tried countless times."

Jim silently hoped the money he had promised Rupert would not be frivolously wasted on booze but remained silent about it.

Rupert then nodded toward a sidewalk hotdog vendor. "Best food on the block."

Jim then approached the vendor and indicated, "Hotdogs for everyone, and whatever they want to go with it."

"Cash only," indicated the vendor as he suspiciously narrowed his eyes at Jim.

Jim then pulled a hundred-dollar bill from his wallet and handed it to the man. "I assume this will cover the drinks, as well?"

"Yes, sir!" grinned the man as he began filling everyone's orders.

Jim then sat on the continuous brick wall that bordered the pedestrian ramp, facing Lake Michigan.

"Kind of grows on you, doesn't it?" asked Rupert as he sat beside Jim on the wall and began eating his hotdog.

"What would you like on yours, sir?" the vendor called to Jim.

"Surprise me," answered Jim. He was not overly thrilled about the prospect of eating a hotdog, but realized the others needed to eat.

"Hey, thanks!" mentioned Rupert with his mouth still full as he continued to devour his hotdog.

"You must be staying somewhere?" pried Jim. "I can tell you've had a shower recently, and you don't seem like most street people."

"I actually have a room at the Y," admitted Rupert.

"Ever thought about starting over, somewhere else?" grilled Jim.

"Like where?" Rupert turned to study Jim more closely.

"I'll tell you what," proposed Jim. "When we fly out of here tonight on my Learjet, we'll be going to Powell Mountain University. I can't promise anything, but who knows, they might have an opening there for a man with credentials like yours. In the meantime, I'm needing a crew of men to help me with some excavation work and it's not too far from the school."

"Well, I actually taught Sociology and Economics," Rupert laughed sardonically. "But just look at me now!"

"You any good at running a forklift or a digger?" quizzed Jim.

"I actually did use them during a summer job at a construction site when I was working my way through college," described Rupert.

"Then you have until the end of the day to decide," indicated Jim as he took the hotdog from the vendor and began to eat it while he walked away. "Right now, we need to get to Shady Brook Research Center."

Rupert hopped up to walk alongside Jim as he wolfed down the rest of his hotdog.

"Can you believe it?" Susan whispered to Janette. She was extremely displeased by the whole affair.

"I'm with you, girlfriend!" assured Janette as they got up to follow after Jim and Rupert.

Neither Susan nor Janette had eaten yet, but carried their hotdogs with them and slowly began to nibble on them as they walked.

"There it is!" pointed out Rupert as they finally neared the large, five-story brick building.

The well-manicured grounds surrounding it were park-like in their appearance. Neatly arranged daffodils were just beginning to come up in some of the flowerbeds. Several mature oak trees were interspersed throughout the grounds. A handful of cement benches had been placed in strategic locations where views of Lake Michigan could be enjoyed. Above the building's grand entrance was a large tile mosaic of a white horse with an amour-clad knight on its back holding a silver sword. Above it in large gold letters were the words "Shady Brook Research Center."

"God Almighty!" Rupert shook his head. He immediately recognized the all-too-familiar insignia of the Crusading Knights of Lake Michigan.

"Is that what I think it is?" Susan was surprised.

"The Crusading Knights own this building?" questioned Janette with alarm.

"Perhaps you might want to go inside without us," suggested Rupert. "I can wait here with these lovely Latin beauties."

"Nonsense," differed Jim. "In fact, the three of you may be my ticket in."

"How do you figure?" questioned Susan.

"Simple," replied Jim. "According to the information that I have, Martha Krain did not approve of her father's affiliation with the Crusading Knights."

282

"I still think I might like to wait outside," informed Rupert.

"Not if you want to get paid," countered Jim. "Besides, it's highly unlikely that Ms. Krain would be willing to see me if she suspected I was a member of the Crusading Knights, which I'm *not*, by the way."

"And of course, with all of us along, she'll be certain you're not?" realized Susan.

"Something like that," hoped Jim.

# 7. Air Show

"Christmas will be on a Wednesday this year," mentioned Karlin as she studied the 1974 wall calendar hanging above her desk in the fifth-floor dormitory room.

"At least we have the whole week off," reminded Rachel, who was busy packing her things for a trip home to visit with her family.

"At least some of us get to go home!" snapped Carolyn as she stood gazing out the north window, where she and her friends had snuck into the dorm the previous month.

"Perhaps you should call Ron's Auto Shop again," suggested Karlin. "It does seem odd they would be taking so long to fix it."

"It does," agreed Carolyn. "What kind of part could they possibly need just to repair a small ding in the fender, anyway? And why would it be on backorder for so long?"

"Could it have something to do with your dad's insurance?" guessed Sarah, who usually didn't get involved in conversations with her roommates, though she did empathize with Carolyn's inability to go home to see her parents for Christmas. "Perhaps it's not covered and your dad is in no hurry to pay for it?"

Carolyn and Karlin exchanged a surprised look at Sarah's suggestion. *What if she was right?*

Karlin had already made plans to ride home with her sister Ruby for the holidays, and Eula would be headed down to Ocean Bay to spend the holiday with her family.

"I suppose you're going home, too?" Carolyn suddenly asked Sarah as she watched her carefully place her various school books into a sturdy brown Samsonite suitcase. "Aren't you taking any clothes with you? Just books?"

Sarah paused to refasten one of the barrettes that she used to keep her long, straight, strawberry blonde hair off her pale face. "I already have plenty of clothes at home, back on the farm."

"That's handy," recognized Carolyn, though Sarah was so thin and frail that it was doubtful her clothes at home fit her any better than the ones she already had with her at school.

"Stacia will be here," mentioned Eula as she turned to head back to her own room.

Carolyn suddenly realized that all of her roommates would be gone for an entire week and could not help but feel a sense of sadness.

"Cheer up," grinned Rachel with her southern drawl. "I'll be here until Monday the 23rd before I take off. I'm just getting some things ready now, in case I can persuade my brother to take me sooner."

"That is odd that he'd want to hang around here for the weekend," agreed Carolyn. "Is he dating someone here at the school?"

"No, nothing like that. It's because my brother plans to be in some stupid air show while he's here," Rachel rolled her eyes with disapproval. "And of course, we can't head home until it's over."

"When is the air show?" asked Carolyn.

"The show takes place on Saturday and Sunday up at Powell Lake, but he won't know until tomorrow morning which day they have him scheduled to actually fly," revealed Rachel.

"An air show?" Karlin was intrigued. "I didn't know they had air shows up there."

"Oh yes, every year," replied Rachel. "They have all kinds of historic planes doing fly-overs, and even aerobatic planes – that would be where my brother comes in."

"That actually might be fun to see," nodded Karlin.

"They even have parachute jumpers doing synchronized jumping routines for the event," added Rachel. "It's quite a big deal."

"Your brother's not flying you home in a stunt plane, is he?" Karlin suddenly asked.

"Goodness, no!" drawled Rachel with her southern chortle. "Dennis has a Piper Cherokee 180. It's a four-seater with a single engine. My brother likes to live on the edge."

Carolyn's mind drifted to thoughts of the Piper Cherokee 180 she had ridden in with Jim Otterman and Bart Higbee during her junior year of high school and her face took on a sad expression.

"Well, not that much on the edge," assured Rachel. "He's actually a very careful and conscientious pilot."

"I'm sorry," apologized Carolyn. "I was just thinking of something else."

"Hey, I know what might cheer you up," proposed Rachel.

"What?" Carolyn became suspicious of Rachel's motives.

"Have you ever gotten to ride in an aerobatic plane before?" Rachel's eyes twinkled as she suggested it. "It can be very exciting."

"Why?" frowned Carolyn.

"Okay, here's the deal," Rachel decided to go ahead and spell it out. "My brother wants me to ride with him in the air show, and frankly, I just don't think I'm up to it. I'm having my monthly right now."

"Why would that make any difference?" pressed Carolyn.

"Well, they do nose-dives, stalls, spins, you name it," described Rachel. "I even threw up once while my brother was doing his routine."

"And so, you want *me* to go up with him?" laughed Carolyn.

"I'm leaving tonight," reminded Karlin with a mischievous grin.

"Me, too," added Sarah.

"Please?" begged Rachel.

"I don't think so," Carolyn shook her head with trepidation.

"It will ensure that I never tell anyone about your little adventure last month," promised Rachel. "The night you guys came in through that window in the middle of the night?"

"Yes, I remember!" snapped Carolyn, realizing at once that Rachel was attempting to blackmail her.

"It will buy my continued silence, as well," assured Sarah with a twinkle in her light blue eyes.

"I thought we already resolved this issue!" growled Karlin, clearly unhappy about what they were trying to pull.

"That was before we heard on the news that the police are on the lookout for a green car involved in the hit-and-run death of Paul Johnson up at Powell Lake," answered Rachel rather smugly.

"What?" Carolyn could not believe it.

"It was on the news last week," corroborated Sarah. "We saw it on the little black-and-white news television they keep down at the library. It also mentioned that his girlfriend's roommate Lydia Cain has been missing ever since, as well."

"That's preposterous!" exclaimed Karlin. "Eula, Stacia and I were all with Carolyn when she ran over that squirrel!"

"How do *we* know that?" Rachel shrugged her shoulders.

"And, it would sure be a shame if your car were to fall under suspicion, wouldn't it?" suggested Sarah.

"You wouldn't!" fumed Carolyn.

"Of course, if that happened, you'd all be forced to tell them about your little squirrel incident in order to clear yourselves - that is, if they knew about it," added Rachel rather smugly.

After several awkward moments, Carolyn finally agreed. "Okay, I'll do it." Her father had been angry enough about the car as it was. She was not about to have him find out that she and the other girls had sneaked into the dormitory, too! Not to mention what the dean might do if she ever found out.

"I thought perhaps you could be persuaded," Rachel smiled triumphantly.

"I can't wait," mumbled Carolyn, unenthusiastically.

The next morning was one of those crisp clear winter days, and usually would have involved sleeping in, since it was a Saturday. Today, however, Carolyn would be meeting Rachel's brother Dennis. Rachel had already gone downstairs to make the arrangements with him for Carolyn to take her place in the air show.

Carolyn frowned as she stared out the north window of the fifth-floor dormitory room at the campus below. Then she thought of Alfredo and could hear his voice in her mind saying, "This place reminds me of a scene from Camelot."

It really does, realized Carolyn as she studied the black spired rooftops on most of the older buildings below. And, even though it was cold outside, the bright sun made it seem less so, even with the window open as it was now.

"Are you ready?" prompted Rachel as she entered the room.

"Can't he just go up alone?" pleaded Carolyn.

"The aerobatic planes must be properly balanced weight-wise in order for the stunts to work," explained Rachel. "The show is carefully choreographed, so any abrupt changes in weight distribution would be hard on the airframe and the engine."

"Couldn't they just put a dummy in the backseat?" Carolyn asked with a piteous expression on her face.

"Against regulations," smirked Rachel. "Both the pilot and his passenger must be coherent and ready to act in the event of an emergency."

"What kind of emergency?" scowled Carolyn as she followed Rachel down the stairs.

"The kind that might require evacuating the plane by parachute in the event of something unexpected," snickered Rachel. "Who knows."

"I can't do that!" objected Carolyn.

"I'm just kidding about that part," laughed Rachel, though she actually wasn't.

"And your brother will show me everything I need to know before going up?" grilled Carolyn.

"Oh, absolutely," promised Rachel as they hurried down to the visiting room on the first floor where Dennis Pierson was waiting.

Dennis was about six foot three, strikingly handsome, and bore a remarkable resemblance to actor Paul Newman. His smooth sandy blonde hair was neatly parted in the middle and feathered back on the sides. And although Dennis was not as muscular as Alfredo had been, he certainly was tanned and well-built. In fact, his self-confident green eyes sparkled with immediate interest when he saw Carolyn.

"This is my roommate Carolyn," introduced Rachel, displeased at once by the obvious attraction her brother had shown toward Carolyn.

"Dennis Pierson," flirted Rachel's brother as he took Carolyn's hand and warmly held it for several moments before letting go.

"Carolyn Bennett," replied Carolyn, who was equally attracted to Dennis. She could hardly believe he was Rachel's brother!

Dennis was outfitted in western boots, jeans, and dress shirt with a bolo tie. He held his ten-gallon cowboy hat in his other hand. It was a beige colored Stetson. His disarming smile and smooth southern accent were somehow compelling.

"My brother is twenty-five years old!" Rachel whispered to Carolyn, as a warning of some sort.

"Our flight isn't until two o'clock this afternoon," grinned Dennis, "so might I take you ladies to lunch first?"

"Absolutely," accepted Carolyn without hesitation.

"Why don't you two go on without me," insisted Rachel. "I still have some packing to do. We can meet back here at one o'clock and drive over to the air show together."

"Works for me," answered Dennis, without taking his eyes off of Carolyn for a single instant.

After eating far more than she had planned to for lunch, Carolyn accompanied Dennis and his sister Rachel as they drove in her small white Toyota Corolla over to Powell Lake.

"We're lucky it hasn't snowed yet this year," commented Rachel as she drove up the steep hill.

"Indeed," agreed Dennis from the back seat behind her. His attention was focused almost completely on Carolyn, however, who was in the front passenger seat.

"It is quite beautiful up here," added Carolyn. "Especially with all these trees. That school really will look like Camelot once it has snow on all the steeples."

"That it might," grinned Dennis. His heavy southern drawl was fascinating, and not irritating at all like Rachel's was.

Rachel merely rolled her eyes and shook her head.

"Have you ever been up in a plane before?" questioned Dennis.

"Only once," answered Carolyn. "It was a Piper Cherokee 180, just a small four-seater."

"Really?" Dennis was interested at once. "That's the exact same model I have!"

Carolyn suddenly seemed distant and a bit sad.

"I take it your flight was less than expected?" assumed Dennis.

"You could say that," replied Carolyn. She was not about to get into the details of her flight with Bart Higbee and Jim Otterman. That was the same day Steve Fredrickson had died on the beach as the result of his shark bite injuries, while she had tried in vain to save him on March 23, 1973. Carolyn also still thought of Veronica Jensen and Joyce Troglite and how they had mysteriously disappeared that day as well, and how she had vowed that one day she would return to Oceanview Academy to try to find out what had happened to them.

"A penny for your thoughts," interjected Dennis.

"Oh, I'm sorry," apologized Carolyn. "It's just that the pilot did try to scare us during that flight."

"That wasn't very nice of him," opined Dennis with his disarming southern accent.

"It was also the runway," added Carolyn. "It was pretty short and headed straight toward the edge of a cliff."

"Not Oceanview Academy?" Dennis suddenly asked.

"Yes, actually, it was," confirmed Carolyn.

"Well, you won't have anything like that to worry about at Powell Lake," assured Dennis. "There's plenty of runway, and no cliffs, Scout's honor!" Dennis promptly held up his right hand in the Scout pledge position.

Carolyn chuckled. Dennis did have a charming way about him and it was undeniable that he was nothing like his sister Rachel.

"Did you bring your flight suit with you?" Rachel suddenly asked. "And an extra one for your passenger?"

"What kind of flight suit?" worried Carolyn. "Why would he and his passenger need flight suits?"

"Don't pay any mind to her," laughed Dennis. "She's just trying to scare you."

"She should be scared," smirked Rachel as she gave Carolyn an even glance.

"Why?" demanded Carolyn.

"Don't listen to her," chuckled Dennis. "Wearing a Nomex flight suit is fairly standard when performing in an airshow. The fabric is built to military specifications and is actually worn by all its flight crews."

"I don't understand," admitted Carolyn.

"The suit is fire proof," explained Rachel with a wicked grin.

"The term is flame resistant," corrected Dennis as he gave his sister a warning glance.

"In case the plane should catch on fire while you're up there," chuckled Rachel, ignoring her brother completely.

"Do stunt planes catch on fire very often?" Carolyn was becoming alarmed.

"Sometimes," persisted Rachel.

"It would be extremely rare if it did," clarified Dennis. "Besides, we'll be equipped with parachutes – in case we should need to abandon the craft for some reason, though that's highly unlikely."

"You weren't kidding, were you?" Carolyn angrily turned toward Rachel.

"No, not so much," grinned Rachel.

"I will get you for this!" promised Carolyn.

"Remember our arrangement," warned Rachel.

"Did my sister somehow get you to do this against your will?" Dennis was not pleased.

290

Carolyn was silent for several moments before responding but maintained eye contact with Rachel as she did. "No, I wasn't coerced against my will, was I?"

"Absolutely not," agreed Rachel with a subtle nod of triumph.

"Hey, you don't have to do this if you don't want to," informed Dennis, who was not about to take Carolyn up against her will. "It won't be the end of the world if I don't go up today."

"Humph!" snorted Rachel, who was well aware of how much the air show meant to her brother.

"I could take you up in my Piper Cherokee 180 instead," offered Dennis. "Perhaps I could fly you to some romantic location for dinner tonight? Just the two of us?"

Rachel then shot Carolyn a cautionary look and imperceptibly shook her head no.

"Let's wait and see if I'm up to it after the air show," replied Carolyn. "And yes, I would love to go up with you. Who knows when I'll ever get another opportunity to be in an air show, right?"

"Atta girl!" chuckled Dennis as he gently put his hand on Carolyn's shoulder. "I think you'll do fine."


Once Carolyn finished filling out and signing a waiver, which she had been reluctant at first to do, everything seemed to happen rather rapidly. So fast, in fact, that she could barely take it all in.

"The first thing you will need to do is put this on," advised Dennis as he handed her a neatly folded flight suit.

"Where do I change?" questioned Carolyn.

"Just put it on here, over what you have on," indicated the other man. "Right over your other clothes."

"Thanks," mumbled Carolyn as she unfolded the flight suit and then stared at it with a perplexed look on her face. "Do the pant legs go inside or outside of my boots?"

"Outside," grinned the man. "You'd better hurry, too. We go up in five minutes."

Carolyn then stepped into the flight suit but noticed at once that it was at least three sizes too big in width, though not nearly tall enough.

"You're gonna need a different size!" laughed the man.

"Ya think?" sighed Carolyn.

"Something a little taller but not as big around, I'd say," grinned Dennis as he flirted with Carolyn.

"It's only a 15-minute flight," reminded the other man.

"I'll be fine," assured Carolyn. "This will do."

"Suit yourself," shrugged the other man. "No pun intended!"

Dennis and the other man laughed.

Carolyn got it, but didn't think it was funny. She was trying not to think of what the ride would be like. All at once, someone was putting a parachute on her back. It was Dennis. The other man began strapping it into place.

"Are you sure it will work?" Carolyn was clearly alarmed.

"Absolutely!" assured Dennis. "Don't worry, I'll be right there with you, all the way, if anything like that should happen – which it won't – but right here is where the rip cord is located. And do NOT pull it under any circumstances unless I tell you to. Understood?"

Carolyn merely nodded as the other man led her to the plane where she would be riding with Dennis in the air show and pointed toward the backseat.

"Won't I be sitting in the front?" questioned Carolyn.

"Not unless you plan to fly this thing," snickered Dennis.

"Passengers always sit in the back," confirmed the other man. "Up front is where all the instruments and fancy gadgets are. You're just along for the ride."

"The only thing you'll probably need to know is where the barf bag is," chuckled Dennis as he waved his hand toward the seat.

"Where?" questioned Carolyn.

"Under the seat," indicated the other man. "Don't worry, if you do need one, they're just right there."

"What about head gear?" asked Carolyn rather nervously.

"Yes, ma'am," nodded the other man as he placed a helmet with built-in ear muffs and microphone onto her head and then fastened the chin strap. He had not bothered to show her the actual microphone button, as most of his customers usually knew where it was.

Noticing at once that it left her face exposed, Carolyn then quizzed, "What about if we need oxygen?"

"The oxygen masks are right there," pointed the man. "Just like on a commercial airplane, where you grab it and put it over your face."

"What if I need my hands free for the parachute?" Carolyn actually had tears streaming down her cheeks at that point.

"Hey, you don't have to do this," advised Dennis, suddenly aware of how afraid Carolyn really was. "Wearing a parachute is just a precaution. Plus, it's regulation that we wear them in a plane like this. But, I've been up dozens of times and have never had to parachute out of one yet."

"I'm just being silly," Carolyn tried to force a convincing laugh.

"It's normal to be afraid your first time," assured the other man as he helped Carolyn into the back seat and strapped her securely inside.

Dennis then immediately hopped into the front seat, strapped himself in, and tested the various straps while the other man closed and secured the door.

"What about the pre-flight check?" reminded Carolyn.

"Already done," replied Dennis as he started up the CT-133 Silver Star training aircraft and let the engine run for a few moments before speaking into his mouthpiece. "Victor Zulu Tango Charlie Delta Seven, ready for take-off."

"Victor Zulu Tango Charlie Delta Seven, you are cleared for take-off."

"Copy that," responded Dennis.

All at once, the plane began accelerating forward, down the runway, picking up speed at an alarming rate.

"How will I open the parachute if I need to?" called Carolyn, though unheard above sudden acceleration of the engine, and because she had no clue that she needed to actually depress the microphone button on her helmet.

Realizing at once that she should not have eaten so much for lunch, Carolyn fought to control the nausea. She had been on rides at the fair that had made her sick in the past, but nothing like this! It made Bart Higbee's little plane look like a mere toy in comparison.

Upward, upward the plane went, straight up. Carolyn felt as if she were en route to the moon. Then, without warning, the nose of the plane leveled out, the engine stalled, and they were spinning downward, straight toward the ground!

Carolyn didn't even realize it at first, but she had already thrown up, all over the pilot, all over the inside of the cockpit.

"Use your barf bag!" scolded Dennis as he tried to wipe himself off in the few moments he had available. His voice came through loud and clear in her helmet.

"I'm sorry!" apologized Carolyn as she began groping the bottom of her seat in vain for something that might be a barf bag. "I don't want to die!" She still had no inkling that she needed to use the microphone button to communicate, so her cries went unheard.

Just short of crashing into the ground, the plane immediately leveled off and began another ascent. People on the ground could be seen clapping and craning their necks to get a better view.

Carolyn felt light-headed, almost as if she would pass out.

"Are you all right?" questioned Dennis as he suddenly flipped the plane upside down for a straight pass over the crowd below. "There's a microphone button on your helmet." He then pointed to his with one hand, hoping she would understand.

Carolyn then felt herself throwing up again! She still had not managed to locate the barf bag. "Where is it?" hollered Carolyn as she fumbled with the microphone button on her helmet.

"That's it! Now I can hear you. Here, use mine!" offered Dennis as he handed a barf bag to Carolyn over his shoulder with one hand.

Carolyn started to reach for it, but the plane's sudden horizontal roll pulled it from her grasp. Carolyn then threw up yet again.

"I'm so sorry!" wailed Carolyn, this time using the microphone button.

"Don't worry about it!" replied Dennis. He had heard her loud and clear that time.

Carolyn again felt as if she was losing consciousness when the plane joined formation with two other planes that were flying over the crowd. Everyone below shouted and cheered, though Carolyn would not have cared if she had been able to hear them.

Then all at once, the unsettling plane ride was finally over and Dennis was landing the plane. Carolyn felt like a ragdoll that had been run over by a Mack Truck at that point.

"You all right?" grilled Dennis as he taxied the plane back up to the loading area.

"I'm alive," muttered Carolyn as she wiped the remaining vomit from her face. "Remind me to NEVER do this again!"

"Flying isn't for everyone," advised Dennis as he brought the plane to a stop and finally handed her the barf bag. "You did fine."

"Good thing for these flight suits!" Carolyn suddenly laughed, realizing that they had kept her vomit from soaking into their clothes.

"That's for sure!" chuckled Dennis as the other man came and opened the door to the plane for them.

"Naturally, you vomited on the parachutes?" chided the man.

"That means he'll need to take them apart and re-do them," explained Dennis.

"That will cost ya extra," smirked the other man.

"No problem," replied Dennis as he unfastened himself and climbed from the plane before unbuckling and helping Carolyn out, too.

"Thanks!" mentioned Carolyn as she struggled for a moment to stand steadily on her feet.

"You'll get your land legs back in no time," assured Dennis as he took off his parachute and unzipped his flight suit.

The other man had already removed Carolyn's parachute before Dennis could begin helping her from the flight suit.

"I guess I shouldn't have eaten so much for lunch," apologized Carolyn. "Sorry about that."

"Not a problem, really," insisted Dennis as they rejoined his sister Rachel by her car.

"Never again!" Carolyn whispered to Rachel. "No matter what you threaten to do to me, not ever!"

Rachel then beamed with satisfaction as the three of them climbed into her white Toyota Corolla for the drive back to Powell Mountain University.

"Hey, maybe I can fly you somewhere nice for dinner," proposed Dennis. "To make up for all of this."

"No thanks," declined Carolyn. "I dare say it will be quite some time before I ever go up in a plane again!"

"What about dinner somewhere nearby?" persisted Dennis. "I'm sure my sister will let us borrow her car?"

Rachel merely glared at her brother in the rearview mirror as she continued the drive.

"I did cosign for you," reminded Dennis, "so technically the car's still part mine until it's paid for."

"How 'bout the cafeteria?" suggested Carolyn. "That is, if I'm able to eat again by then."

"So, it's a date?" beamed Dennis as he flirted with Carolyn, much to his sister's obvious disapproval.

Knowing how much it would upset her, and partly to get back at Rachel for forcing her to ride in the air show, Carolyn agreed. "You can pick me up at six o'clock at the girls' dormitory."

Exhausted and queasy from the air show flight, Carolyn had laid down to rest until her dinner date with Dennis. His sister Rachel was the only one of her roommates that had not yet left to go home for Christmas vacation, and was currently over at the campus chapel attending one of the worship services offered there. Students who failed to turn in enough of their computerized worship service cards prior to the end of the semester ran the risk of having their grades withheld. But, Carolyn had the entire next week in which to turn in the three cards that remained in her stack, so she wasn't too worried about it at that particular time.

"Carolyn!" Stacia knocked as she entered the room. She would be the only one left in Carolyn's close circle of friends who would be there the entire week.

"How's your ankle doing?" asked Carolyn when she noticed that Stacia still had a slight limp.

"Much better," replied Stacia as she walked over to Carolyn's side of the fifth-floor dormitory room.

"Hey, you should stay up here this week," suggested Carolyn as she nodded toward the extra bed on the north wall.

"That's not a bad idea!" beamed Stacia. "But that's not why I'm here. Guess what?"

"Tell me," shrugged Carolyn, amused by how animated Stacia got when she was excited.

"Alfredo is back!" blurted Stacia.

"Alfredo?" Carolyn suddenly sat up. "He's back? Here?"

"Yes!" exclaimed Stacia. "He said he felt so bad about my not being able to come home for Christmas, that he came all the way back out here so I would have family here that day. Isn't that great?"

"He's actually here now?" pressed Carolyn.

"Well, he's staying over at the boys' dorm in one of their extra rooms so he can be close by," explained Stacia, "but yes, he's here at

Powell Mountain University and he plans to be here the entire week! And you know what else?"

"What?" prompted Carolyn with a worried look on her face.

"I don't think I'm the only reason he's here!" Stacia then winked at Carolyn with a knowing grin.

"Does Alfredo know I wasn't able to go home for Christmas?" asked Carolyn, though already suspecting the answer.

"Of course," smirked Stacia. "And he plans to surprise you by showing up here at the girls' dormitory at six o'clock tonight, to see if you will go out to dinner with him. Isn't that great? Who knows, maybe we really will be sisters someday!"

"Just hold on," indicated Carolyn. "There's no way I'd just drop everything and suddenly move to the Dominican Republic!"

"You never did hear from Lenny Owens, did you?" challenged Stacia. "Don't you think he would have written by now if he was going to? And Alfredo is absolutely crazy about you!"

"Well, there's another problem," sighed Carolyn.

"What do you mean?" scowled Stacia.

"Rachel's brother Dennis has asked me to go to dinner with him tonight, to make up for my horrible experience in the air show earlier today," elaborated Carolyn. "In fact, he plans to show up here at the girls' dormitory at six o'clock."

"Oh, that's terrible!" recognized Stacia. "What are you going to do? That means they will both be down there waiting for you at the same time!"

"I have an idea," decided Carolyn. "Trust me!"

At six o'clock that evening – on Saturday night, December 21, 1974 – Alfredo McFerson and Dennis Pierson were seated together in the waiting room of the girls' dormitory at Powell Mountain University. Though not much had been said between them, the two had engaged in some polite conversation and useless chitchat as they waited for their dates. Unknown to them, they were both waiting for the same person.

"Alfredo!" greeted Stacia as she entered the visiting room and gave her brother a hug. "I need to see you outside for a moment."

"Excuse me," Alfredo nodded politely at Dennis. "Nice to meet you. Have a good evening."

"You, too," acknowledged Dennis as he reached for and picked up a magazine to read from the coffee table as he continued to wait.

"Where's Carolyn?" frowned Alfredo. "Is she coming?"

"She was very surprised to learn you are here," responded Stacia, rather nervously as she glanced through the open door of the visiting room at Dennis.

"I must see her!" persisted Alfredo.

"She actually was a little queasy earlier and is laying down resting," continued Stacia.

"Is she ill?" Alfredo became concerned.

"No, not exactly," hedged Stacia. "She rode along as a passenger in an air show today and it made her quite sick."

"In an airshow?" Alfredo loudly asked.

"Shhh!" indicated Stacia. "That's the guy she rode with."

"That guy in there?" Alfredo's face took on a jealous expression.

"It's not what you think," assured Stacia as she grabbed her brother's arm to restrain him. "Carolyn is not the least bit interested in that guy, and she only went up with him because his sister Rachel threatened her if she didn't."

"Threatened her? In what way? I'm getting to the bottom of this right now!" announced Alfredo as he turned to confront his rival.

"Stop!" commanded Stacia. "Dennis was planning to take her out to dinner, but only to make up for everything he put her through earlier today. There's *nothing* between them, I promise! I only brought you out here to try to avoid an embarrassing situation. After all, Carolyn did have *no idea* you were coming!"

"And which of us does she now choose?" demanded Alfredo.

"You, of course!" laughed Stacia as she playfully slapped her brother on the arm. "But, we need to find a graceful way to get rid of Dennis without hurting his feelings or making him feel small. Just think how you would feel if the roles were reversed."

"I have an easy solution," offered Alfredo. "We just tell him the truth. Carolyn will be going out with me tonight, not him."

"You can't just go in there and tell him that!" objected Stacia. "This isn't the Dominican Republic. They do things differently here."

"I've always found that honesty is the best policy," insisted Alfredo. "The man needs to be told."

"Why don't you and I go to the cafeteria and let Carolyn be the one to tell him?" persisted Stacia. "I'm certain she will be along to join us in no time, and then you and she will be free to go wherever you wish for dinner. Okay?"

Alfredo breathed in deeply and then let out a heavy breath. "This is not to my liking."

"Would you want Carolyn to feel humiliated?" challenged Stacia with a raised eyebrow.

"Well, no, of course not," Alfredo finally gave in. "All right, let's go wait for her at the cafeteria then."

Unknown to Alfredo, Carolyn had secreted herself in the first-floor lobby behind one of the wooden phone booth dividers and had been waiting for Stacia to convince him to leave. She knew she must work quickly to get rid of Dennis.

Waiting for several minutes after Stacia and Alfredo had left, Carolyn casually slipped into the visiting room and approached Dennis.

"Well, hello!" flirted Dennis, pleased to see that Carolyn was feeling better.

"Thank you again for the ride today," began Carolyn.

"Nonsense," replied Dennis. "I'm not sure how my sister coerced you into doing that, but I wish to extend my deepest apologies right now before we go another step farther."

"Apology accepted," laughed Carolyn. Dennis truly was nice and she almost wished she could go out with him, but she didn't dare. By now, Stacia would have blurted the truth to Alfredo, and who knew what might happen next. He could very well decide to turn around and come back to confront them.

"So, have you decided yet where you would like to go for dinner?" questioned Dennis in his almost-innocent sounding southern drawl. "Perhaps I can fly you down to Ocean Bay for the evening? I know this marvelous seafood place ...."

"Dennis," interrupted Carolyn. "I'm not going to be able to go out with you tonight, or any other night, for that matter."

He suddenly appeared crestfallen.

"And you are right," continued Carolyn. "Your sister did coerce me into going on that flight with you earlier."

"I don't understand," pouted Dennis. "You did lead me to believe that I had a chance with you?"

"Then it's my turn to apologize," replied Carolyn, "but there is someone else."

"And this must be him now?" Dennis raised an eyebrow when he noticed Alfredo and his sister Stacia enter the visiting room.

"Uh, yes, this is him," informed Carolyn as she hurried over to give Alfredo a hug and a romantic greeting kiss.

"I see," shrugged Dennis with a deep sigh of defeat as he picked up his hat to leave. "If you see her, tell my sister Rachel that I'll be down in the cafeteria, by myself."

"She'll do that," Alfredo answered for her as he pulled Carolyn close to give her another kiss.

Stacia then cleared her throat to get their attention. "You two shouldn't do that in here."

"Indeed," agreed Alfredo as he put his arm around Carolyn to escort her from the building. "We should definitely find another place to continue where we left off. It's a good thing I got here when I did!"

"I'll be down in the cafeteria," mumbled Stacia as she started to leave. "Maybe I'll have dinner with Dennis."

"Nonsense!" protested Carolyn. "I think you should join us. After all, you haven't had a chance to see each other for quite a while, and it wouldn't be fair for me to keep you two apart. Why don't the three of us go to dinner together tonight?"

"When will I get a chance to be alone with you?" pressed Alfredo as he enveloped Carolyn with his hungry eyes.

"Stacia was telling me that you plan to be here all week," replied Carolyn with an enticing smile.

"Well, yes, that is true," confirmed Alfredo. He had been caught off guard and certainly didn't want his sister to feel left out.

"Let me just go get my coat, then," replied Carolyn as she gently pulled away from his grasp. "I'll be right back. Would you like me to get your coat for you, too, Stacia?"

"Oh, that would be great!" beamed Stacia. "Thanks!"

Carolyn chided herself as she hurried up the stairs for using Alfredo as she had to rid herself of Dennis. What was she going to do now? And how was she going to rid herself of Alfredo without breaking his heart, or Stacia's? Had he really come all the way back from the Dominican Republic just to see her, and not his sister?

One thing was certain! Carolyn was not in any hurry to marry anyone, especially someone from another country that might possibly be marrying her just to acquire United States citizenship! She had heard of people doing that. True, there was definitely chemistry between them, but he just was *not* Lenny Owens!

Had Pete remembered to tell Lenny that she had tried to see him when she was in Ocean Bay last month? These and other thoughts spiraled out of control in her mind as Carolyn finally reached the fifth-floor dormitory room to grab her coat. Oh, yes, she would need to stop by Stacia's room and grab hers, too.

Carolyn was still deep in thought when she returned to the first-floor visiting room with the two coats, and could tell that Stacia and Alfredo had been having some sort of disagreement. Was he trying to convince his sister not to join them? Carolyn hoped not!

"Hello again, beautiful lady," greeted Alfredo as he gallantly took Carolyn's hand in his to kiss it.

"My ankle is bothering me again," Stacia suddenly mentioned, "so I probably won't be joining you."

"Actually, I'm still feeling somewhat queasy myself from that airplane ride today," informed Carolyn with an even gaze. "Perhaps we should just wait until tomorrow to do this when we're all feeling up to it and we can go to dinner together?"

"Surely you must be hungry?" questioned Alfredo with surprise.

"Stacia must be too, but we do have food upstairs in our room," advised Carolyn with finality.

"Actually, my car for the week is right out front," revealed Alfredo, "and it shouldn't be too far for Stacia to walk?"

"Are you *sure*?" Stacia appeared hopeful.

"Absolutely!" assured Alfredo. "I think the three of us should head down to Maria's Mexican Restaurant for dinner right now. How does that sound? I purposely rented a car instead of a motorcycle this time. I wouldn't want my passengers to be cold or wind-blown like they were during my last visit."

"I was your *only* passenger during your last visit," reminded Carolyn with a slight grin. "Well, okay, I suppose I could manage to eat something."

Alfredo's plan to be alone with Carolyn that night had been foiled, but the week was young. After helping Carolyn and Stacia put on their coats, Alfredo escorted them out front to the black 1974 Chevy Impala rental car he had managed to obtain.

"It's almost like the one we saw that day," mentioned Alfredo rather proudly as he helped Carolyn into the front passenger seat before bothering to open the rear passenger door for his sister.

"Oh, okay," nodded Carolyn. "It is kind of like the car we saw parked on the side of the road down near Woody's."

"But newer," pointed out Alfredo, disappointed that Carolyn was not as impressed with it as he'd hoped.

The next few days passed much too slowly for Carolyn's liking. It was a continual challenge to make sure that Stacia was included whenever she and Alfredo went anywhere together.

Alfredo was near the end of his rope with being put off like he was and beginning to show signs of impatience. Why was Carolyn unwilling to be alone with him? He had shown her nothing but respect and kindness during his last visit. She surely must know he wouldn't do anything inappropriate towards her?

Carolyn had managed to convince Alfredo how important it was that both she and Stacia turn in their remaining computerized worship service cards, so that their grades would not be withheld.

After attending two such consecutive 45-minute worship services with Carolyn and Stacia, Alfredo made it clear that Carolyn would have to turn in her final card without him. He had endured all the worship services he could take. But, with him leaving on Saturday, Carolyn would still have Sunday – the final day – in which to unload herself of her only remaining card. She reflected for a moment upon Dean Forrest's advice that she not wait until the last moment to turn them in. That's for sure, thought Carolyn. Not only had she worried about those remaining three cards during finals but was now struggling to unburden herself of them during Christmas break!

"Merry Christmas!" greeted Stacia as she entered the fifth-floor dormitory room where she had been staying with Carolyn for the week. "Well, Alfredo is downstairs waiting for us."

"You know, since it's Christmas, and you two are family," prefaced Carolyn, "perhaps you should spend the day together without me. I feel as if I've been in the way all week."

"It's only Wednesday," reminded Stacia with a mischievous grin. "And you're not gonna be able to put him off forever."

"What do you mean, put him off?" frowned Carolyn. If ever there were a time to feign ignorance, this was it.

"Girl, he's crazy in love with you!" pointed out Stacia. "The more you play hard to get, the more of a challenge it becomes for him."

"A challenge?" disapproved Carolyn.

"I think Alfredo's going to ask you something very important today," hinted Stacia, "but don't let on like you know anything."

"I won't!" assured Carolyn.

"No woman has *ever* turned him down before, or played so hard to get," added Stacia. "He actually asked me if I knew whether you are a virgin or not."

"And what did you tell him?" Carolyn pursed her lips.

"That I thought you were," Stacia replied honestly.

"Well, you are right," Carolyn confirmed, almost embarrassed about it. "And that's not about to change until I'm married someday, either!"

"Would you marry him if he asked you?" pressed Stacia.

Carolyn was silent for several moments before responding. "Things are different here in this country, Stacia. Woman are not considered as possessions or tokens of conquest."

"Oh, I'm sure that's not what he has in mind!" believed Stacia.

"Nevertheless," persisted Carolyn, "I have my education to consider, as well. Your brother has made it quite clear that a woman's place is in the home, and how pointless it was for them to send you here in the first place, as that's where you'll end up eventually, anyway."

"There may be some truth to that," admitted Stacia. "They probably just sent me here to get me to stop pestering them about it. I guess they figured a year of school would get it out of my system."

"Well, that's not happening to me, I can assure you!" promised Carolyn. "And, although it's never been mentioned, what if your brother only wants to marry me so he can gain his citizenship here? Tell me you think he's beyond trying something like that?"

Stacia became somber and quiet.

"Well?" pressed Carolyn.

"I don't know," admitted Stacia. "That would never have crossed my mind."

"Well, it has been done before," pointed out Carolyn. "A girl I knew in high school married some foreign guy when she turned eighteen, only to find out too late that his ulterior motive was to become an American citizen! Then, and as soon as the wedding vows were over, that was it. He took off and she never saw him again."

"How could someone do something like that?" Stacia was shocked. "What did she do then? Get it annulled?"

"She had to," replied Carolyn. "No one could even find the guy to serve divorce papers on him."

"Alfredo would NEVER do something like that!" informed Stacia indignantly.

"I'm not saying he would," assured Carolyn, "but the fact remains that he *is* a foreigner, and so are you, for that matter. In fact, another girl I know was approached by a guy from the Middle East who wanted to marry her so he could become a citizen, but at least he was up front about his intentions! He presented it to her as a business arrangement."

"What kind of a business arrangement?" frowned Stacia.

"Well," described Carolyn, "all she had to do was marry him and then he would pay her a predetermined amount of cash, under the table. She would not even be expected to consummate the marriage or even live with him! Then, when the year was over, they would get a quiet divorce and she'd be free to go on with her life."

"That's unconscionable!" exclaimed Stacia, repulsed by the idea. "Did she actually do it?"

"I'm not sure," admitted Carolyn, "but I'm pretty sure doing something like that is not altogether legal."

"If it's not illegal, it sure ought to be!" exclaimed Stacia. "But, I promise you, my brother would never be a party to something like that, not ever!"

"So, how do you propose I bring up the subject without making him angry with me?" questioned Carolyn with a raised eyebrow.

"Oh, Carolyn, I don't know," Stacia shook her head. "I'll tell you what, let me go talk to him and explain that is the reason you've had reservations about him, and then see what he says."

"You can't just tell him that," objected Carolyn. "He'll go through the roof!" One thing Carolyn had managed to learn about Alfredo during the past two days was that he had a volatile temperament and could only be pushed so far.

304

"Better that he gets mad at me than at you," pointed out Stacia. "Besides, I know how to handle him. Trust me!"

Carolyn sighed deeply at hearing the words "trust me" and thought briefly of her friend Susan, who always used to say that at the most inopportune times.

"Well?" pressed Stacia.

"Go ahead," agreed Carolyn. "I'll wait here."

Carolyn decided to make good use of her time as she waited for Stacia, so she began writing a letter to Susan. Just as she was describing what had happened during the squirrel incident, Stacia finally returned. It had been over an hour.

"Alfredo insists upon seeing you," informed Stacia. "Alone."

Carolyn suddenly felt the same sort of trepidation she would have felt while on her way to be chewed out by her father for something - were she still at home. Carolyn slowly stood up.

"It'll be okay," grinned Stacia. "I don't think he's mad or anything, just disappointed."

"Disappointed, how?" quizzed Carolyn.

"Go! He's waiting," urged Stacia. "I'll see you tonight."

Carolyn stopped to grab her coat on the way out, just in case. "Merry Christmas!"

"You, too!" called Stacia as she watched Carolyn leave.

Carolyn had become quite adept at negotiating the various flights of stairs in record time and was usually able to travel from the fifth floor down to ground level in about six minutes or less. Each flight of stairs had a mid-level landing.

"Merry Christmas!" greeted Alfredo as Carolyn approached him in the first-floor visiting room. "I see you brought your coat." He smiled with approval.

"Merry Christmas," smiled Carolyn, rather nervously. *What had Stacia told him during the past hour, anyway?*

"May I have the honor of spending the day with you?" Alfredo asked cautiously. "*Alone* for a change? You have gone out alone with me before, you know, and *I have not tried to bite your neck*." Alfredo tried to mimic the way Dracula might speak during his last remark.

Carolyn blushed deeply but could not help laughing.

"Excellent!" beamed Alfredo as he helped Carolyn put on her coat before extending his arm to her.

"Thanks," replied Carolyn rather timidly as she and Alfredo headed for the front door.

The Dean's assistant, who was well aware that Carolyn had also been out with Rachel's brother Dennis only days before, glared at Carolyn with disapproval. The Dean's assistant had also been there when both Dennis and Alfredo had been in the waiting room at the same time on Saturday night and shook her head with condemnation.

"Friend of yours?" whispered Alfredo.

"No way," assured Carolyn.

"Good," chuckled Alfredo while he opened the door and winked at the Dean's assistant before they left.

"You're terrible!" chuckled Carolyn.

"I have my moments," replied Alfredo as he put one of his well-built muscular arms around Carolyn.

"Where are we going?" questioned Carolyn.

"It's a surprise," informed Alfredo with a mysterious smile.


Half way to Powell Lake, Carolyn began to worry that it might be their destination. "Did Stacia tell you that they found some guy dead up there at the lake last month?"

"Really?" frowned Alfredo.

"Remember the blue Volkswagen we saw that night?" added Carolyn. "Well, the guy they found was by a blue Volkswagen!"

"That's terrible!" exclaimed Alfredo.

"The poor guy was probably laying there dead when we stopped," muttered Carolyn. "It had to be him!"

"Would you feel more comfortable going somewhere else?" Alfredo became concerned. He had actually planned on going to that very spot but decided not to mention it.

"I think they still have search parties all over the place up there at the lake, looking for the girl that was with him," elaborated Carolyn. "She's still missing."

"And they're sure she was with him that day?" Alfredo was clearly disturbed by what Carolyn had told him.

"That's what they said on the news," answered Carolyn.

"What if she did it?" speculated Alfredo as he slowed the car and pulled into a wide turnout on the side of the road, beside an old growth stand of trees at the entrance to a logging road. "Perhaps we should just stop here, rather than go all the way up to Powell Lake?"

306

"Well, I suppose you could pull off the road just a little bit," agreed Carolyn. "Maybe down there?"

"My thoughts exactly," approved Alfredo.

"On the other hand," Carolyn suddenly worried, "perhaps we're fine where we are."

"Wherever you would feel more comfortable," agreed Alfredo. "All we will be doing is talking, anyway, and enjoying the picnic lunch I have in the trunk, so it doesn't matter."

"I guess the logging road would be fine," Carolyn agreed.

Alfredo then pulled onto the logging road and drove several yards before finding another turnout, in a more secluded place.

Though the sun was out, the weather was brisk, and felt as if it could snow at any time. No sooner than Alfredo had shut off the engine, the windows began to fog up. Alfredo then rolled down his window just an inch. "Is that too cold for you?"

"I'll be fine," promised Carolyn. "As long as I leave my coat on. You don't think it will snow do you?"

Alfredo then pulled Carolyn close and put one arm around her. "We are not here to discuss the weather."

Carolyn blushed deeply and felt her breathing become shallow.

"I have come to a decision, Miss Carolyn," announced Alfredo. "I had planned on asking you to marry me today, but after speaking with Stacia, have changed my mind."

"You have?" Carolyn swallowed uncomfortably.

"I am a man of honor," explained Alfredo, "and I would not dishonor you by asking you to marry someone whose motives are in question."

Carolyn silently waited for Alfredo to continue.

"That is why I plan to become an American citizen first before I dare to request the honor of your hand in marriage," revealed Alfredo with finality. "And only then will my fair princess from the fifth-floor dormitory tower finally be rescued from all of this." Alfredo then waved his free hand as if to encompass it all.

"But, what if I don't want to be rescued?" protested Carolyn. "Getting an education is important to me."

"Ah yes," sighed Alfredo. "The American woman and her independence."

"There is that, too," shrugged Carolyn, not the least bit apologetic about it.

"Nevertheless, I am leaving tomorrow," informed Alfredo, "and you will not see me again after this – that is, not until I am an American citizen. But, I give you my sincere promise that I *will* be back. You may count on it."

Carolyn suddenly felt ashamed for mentioning the citizenship issue to Stacia, and was speechless.

Alfredo tenderly put his free hand under Carolyn's chin and studied her carefully. "You do realize that you hold my heart captive, dear lady? And not just like two ships passing in the night?"

Carolyn silently wondered to herself whether she could learn to love someone like Alfredo? Would they be able to overcome their cultural differences and be happy if she did agree to marry him? Would his attitude toward women and their so-called place in society ever change from what it was now? And most importantly, could she ever force herself to forget about Lenny Owens? Did Lenny still plan to contact her again, or had he met someone else? If only she knew!

"What troubles you so greatly?" delved Alfredo as he tenderly stroked the sides of Carolyn's face and wiped a stray hair from her cheek. Tears began to escape from the corners of Carolyn's eyes.

"You asked me once before, when we kissed, who I was thinking of at the time?" reminded Carolyn rather hesitantly.

"Go on." Alfredo became serious as he waited.

"His name is Lenny." Carolyn spoke barely above a whisper.

"Lenny *who?*" demanded Alfredo.

"Lenny Owens," informed Carolyn as she finally looked Alfredo in the eyes. "He and I went to school together our junior year, at Oceanview Academy."

"Have you seen him since?" questioned Alfredo.

"No, I haven't," Carolyn sadly shook her head.

"What is *wrong* with him?" Alfredo was indignant. "How could someone you care for so much simply abandon you and break your heart like this?"

Carolyn looked away, unable to withstand Alfredo's probing gaze any longer. Tears now streamed down her face.

"Does Lenny *know* that you still care for him?" At least Alfredo was direct.

Carolyn folded her arms in front of her and stared at the dashboard of Alfredo's rental car for several moments before responding. "I'm just not sure anymore."

"You will tell me about this Lenny," insisted Alfredo. "I would like to know more."

"Well," began Carolyn, "we first met when our names were matched up by a computer for a blind date."

"A blind date?" frowned Alfredo. He was unfamiliar with the term.

"It's where people fill out questionnaires, answering honestly about their likes, dislikes, beliefs, that kind of thing," described Carolyn. "After that, the results are analyzed and compared for compatibility. Then, those whose answers match most closely are selected."

"So, this Lenny was selected by a *computer* to be your date?" Alfredo suddenly began to laugh until he noticed the look on Carolyn's tear-stained face.

"Okay, so a computer thought the two of you were a perfect match, then what?" urged Alfredo, who was trying now to remain serious.

"We both were very shy," added Carolyn, "but he *did* hold my hand during the movie when we had our date that night."

"That's it?" chuckled Alfredo. "All he did was hold your hand? This Lenny must have been very shy indeed."

"Male and female students were not even allowed to hold hands with one another at all, there at that school," recalled Carolyn. "So, it was actually rather brave of both of us to even try it."

"And you got away with it, I presume?" Alfredo was almost being flippant at this point.

"Only because the lights were out during the movie!" snapped Carolyn. "And what difference would any of this make to you, anyway?"

"I'm sorry," apologized Alfredo more seriously. "Please, tell me more."

"No." Carolyn then turned away and began to stare out the passenger window of the black Chevy Impala.

"Hey," urged Alfredo as he put his arms around Carolyn and pulled her close again, gently forcing her to turn back around to face him. "I can see how important this Lenny is to you, and I apologize."

"We really were like two ships passing in the night, you know," Carolyn finally continued. "Me, with my English Literature class, and Lenny with his Chemistry and Biology classes. Each of us always locked away in our rooms studying all the time. Just about the only times we ever saw one another was in the cafeteria, and usually just for breakfast. Lenny's goal was to become a doctor someday."

"A doctor?" Alfredo raised an eyebrow in surprise.

"Lenny promised his dying mother on her deathbed that he would do it, too!" added Carolyn as she wiped the tears from her cheeks with her sleeve.

Alfredo then reached into the glove box and removed a small packet of Kleenex that he handed to Carolyn.

"Thanks," sniffed Carolyn as she removed a couple of them and proceeded to wipe her eyes and blow her nose.

"What type of medicine did Lenny intend to go into?" asked Alfredo.

"Probably something that had to do with Biochemistry, if I know him," opined Carolyn. "The biggest problem was our fathers."

"Your fathers?" scowled Alfredo.

"Like you, Lenny was a person of color," revealed Carolyn rather hesitantly as she waited to see how Alfredo would react.

"Lenny was black?" Alfredo began to snicker.

"Is that somehow *funny*?" Carolyn was becoming more annoyed each time Alfredo would smile or laugh.

"I take it your father did not approve of his daughter dating a black man?" smirked Alfredo.

"Not nearly as much as Lenny's father objected to him dating a white woman!" clarified Carolyn. "In fact, Mr. Owens literally threatened to pull the financial rug out from under Lenny's educational feet unless he complied."

"I don't understand." Alfredo found it incomprehensible that a parent would do something like that.

"In other words," spelled out Carolyn, "either Lenny would stop dating me, or else his father would make sure Lenny did not become a doctor, as he had promised his dying mother he would."

"I get that part," assured Alfredo. "I just do not understand how his father could not want him to succeed in his educational goals."

Carolyn then calmed down and merely nodded.

"Has Lenny written to you?" Alfredo then asked.

"I have reason to believe that my father destroyed his letters," Carolyn informed him. "I do know for a fact that my father confiscated two of my friend Susan's letters because I actually found them in his desk drawer! Otherwise, I probably never would have seen them."

"That is terrible," agreed Alfredo, "but what if Lenny *hasn't* written to you? How would you even know?"

"I think you should take me back now," requested Carolyn. Her arms were still crossed.

"Not until you make me a promise," replied Alfredo.

"What?" Carolyn had not intended to be so sharp with him but was becoming highly agitated by Alfredo's flip attitude about Lenny.

"Promise me you *will* contact this Lenny," insisted Alfredo, "and find out whether or not there is still something between you."

Carolyn suddenly felt exposed and vulnerable as she silently considered Alfredo's request.

"Then, once I am an American citizen, and you are free to give your heart to someone else," described Alfredo, "it is my earnest prayer that you will choose to give it to me."

Carolyn then turned to look at Alfredo again and was suddenly enveloped by his dark, pleading eyes. His longing gaze became a powerful magnet, drawing her towards him. Carolyn finally allowed herself to kiss Alfredo's waiting lips once again. The electricity that flowed between them was overwhelming and undeniable.


By mid-morning on Saturday, December 28, 1974, Carolyn's roommates were busy returning from their week-long Christmas break. Stacia had moved her things back to the room she shared with Eula on the fourth floor.

"Hey, girl, how goes it?" greeted Karlin as she entered the fifth-floor dormitory room with her overstuffed suitcase.

"It's been a long week!" informed Carolyn, as she set aside the letter she was still trying to write to Susan.

"So, how was the plane ride?" wondered Karlin as she tossed her suitcase on the vacant bed between them where Stacia had slept during the past week.

"I threw up three times," mentioned Carolyn.

"Who threw up? Is someone sick up here?" It was Eula.

"Eula!" shouted Carolyn as she and Karlin raced over to hug their friend.

"Hey, I don't want it, if someone's got the flu," advised Eula as she held them both at arm's distance.

"I threw up during a plane ride in an air show," clarified Carolyn. "No one has the flu!"

"In that case, come here!" Eula then hugged her two friends.

Just then Stacia followed her into the room and stood there waiting until the friends were done embracing.

"Check out this rock, girl!" Eula then grabbed Stacia's hand and held it where both Carolyn and Karlin could get a better look at the ring on her hand.

"What's this?" questioned Carolyn.

"This is the ring my brother gave me to *keep* for you," informed Stacia with a sly wink at Carolyn. "It belonged to our mother when she was alive."

"Then it definitely should be *yours*, not mine!" opined Carolyn.

"You don't get it," grinned Stacia. "This will be your engagement ring someday, once you agree to accept his proposal of marriage."

"Okay, let's start from the beginning," interrupted Eula. "I definitely gotta hear all about your week, 'Miss Carolyn.'" Eula was deliberately mimicking Alfredo's way of saying Miss Carolyn, accent and all.

"Carolyn threw up three times in the stunt plane she went up in with Dennis," interjected Karlin.

"Who in the world is Dennis?" demanded Eula.

"Dennis just happens to be *my* older brother!" advised Rachel from behind them with her hands on her hips. No one had heard her or Sarah come in. "And how dare you make a date with my brother and then embarrass him like that!"

"How was I to know Alfredo would show up right when Dennis was down there waiting for me like that?" asked Carolyn with feigned indignance for Rachel's benefit.

"You should've seen 'em, too," added Stacia with a mischievous smile. "They were just sitting there, side by side in the visiting room, when Carolyn sent me down there to distract Alfredo long enough for her to get rid of Dennis."

"Get *rid* of Dennis?" Rachel's southern drawl was stronger than usual, especially after spending a week at home. "I can't believe you people!"

"Then, before Carolyn could manage it," continued Stacia, "Alfredo realized what was going on and came back to confront him."

"Alfredo came back to confront Dennis?" laughed Eula as she shot Rachel an amused look.

"That was when Carolyn rushed over and gave my brother a welcome hug and a romantic kiss of greeting," described Stacia triumphantly. "To keep him from challenging Dennis."

"That was when Dennis grabbed his hat and left, I'm afraid," finished Carolyn. "But, I hardly expected him to fly me somewhere else for dinner, especially after taking me up for the other flight earlier that day. Besides, I was still kind of queasy from all those stunts during the air show."

"Yeah! She threw up three times!" reminded Rachel as she picked up and angrily tossed her suitcase on her bed.

"That sounds like a good time," commented Sarah rather smugly as she opened her large brown Samsonite suitcase on the floor and began removing all the books she had taken home during Christmas break.

"Wanna try it on to see how it will look someday?" questioned Stacia as she took off the beautiful diamond engagement ring and held it out to Carolyn. "This will be Carolyn's someday, when she and my brother become engaged!" Stacia smirked at Rachel.

"Did you remember to hand in the rest of your computerized worship service cards?" questioned Sarah from where she was busy unpacking her books on the south side of the room.

"All but one," informed Carolyn.

"The last service starts in ten minutes," advised Rachel with a smug grin. "And they've cancelled the service for tomorrow since nearly everyone has turned in all their cards already."

"They *what*?" Carolyn became alarmed.

"She's right," confirmed Karlin. "I just saw a notice about it posted up by the mail slots on my way in."

Rachel and Sarah merely laughed as they watched Carolyn hurry to put on a granny skirt - since there wasn't time enough to put on a pair of panty hose - before scurrying from the room with her final computerized worship service card.

Eula, Stacia and Karlin simply glared at them with disapproval. The line of demarcation between the north and south sides of the fifth-floor dormitory room had clearly been reestablished.

Carolyn usually tried to negotiate the five flights of stairs more slowly when wearing one of her floor-length granny skirts, just to be sure she would not trip on the edge of the fabric, but time was of the essence. She needed to get to that worship service in time, or her grades would be withheld for the semester!

That was when it happened – Carolyn somehow managed to step on the hem of her granny skirt, causing her feet to slide out from beneath her. Even while tumbling down the flight of stairs leading from the fourth floor to the third, all Carolyn could think of was getting to the campus chapel in time! Thankfully, Carolyn had tucked and rolled during her fall and was otherwise unhurt, save for a few minor bruises, but had managed to tear open the skin on her right kneecap quite badly. Blood began oozing down her leg. Carolyn suspected she would probably need stitches, but would have to wait until after the 45-minute worship service was over before taking the time to stop at the nurse's office. Would she make it in time?

# 8. Perfect Match

Carolyn and Sherry slowly followed Chip and Ron toward the alcove at Shady Brook Winery on Powell Mountain Road.

"Maybe we should wait for backup," suggested Sherry. "I think it still smells bad in there, even after forty-eight years!"

"It does smell," recognized Carolyn as she made a face. "How could it still smell like that, after all this time?"

"Jim and the others may not be back until tomorrow, for all we know," reminded Ron.

"Shouldn't we be worried at all about the fact that those big heavy barn doors were pulled down so easily?" questioned Carolyn. "It's obvious that whoever did it had no regard for your bright yellow crime scene tape."

"Or the big black letters on it that read, 'Police Line Do Not Cross,'" added Sherry. "What if they come back while we're here?"

"Perhaps we should just call it a day," recommended Chip.

"It's broad daylight," differed Ron. "They're not gonna come here now. Besides, it's not even lunchtime yet. And, we're armed. I think we'll be fine. That is, unless you ladies would like us to take you back first before we return to continue our investigation?"

"It would be a shame for you to lose at least an hour of time you could have spent up here investigating," admitted Carolyn.

"Sherry?" Chip turned to her for consensus.

"Fine," Sherry shrugged her shoulders, though she did have some reservations about staying.

"Good!" Ron smiled at Sherry with his piercing blue eyes. "You'll be safe with us."

The four of them then made their way to the alcove. Though only twelve feet wide and high, it continued for at least fifty feet in length. At least two-dozen of the unopened 55-gallon wine barrels filled with rancid wine were carefully stacked along its inside wall, using the two-rack system.

"Let's hope none of those barrels decide to go for a crab-walk," mentioned Sherry.

"This is the old wooden table that used to be in the other area," Carolyn suddenly recognized it. "It was against the outside wall."

"Are you sure?" quizzed Chip.

"See that gouge on the tabletop?" nodded Carolyn. "That's where Jerry Krain stuck his bowie knife, point-first, when he came over here to get the eggs."

"Exactly where were the eggs?" grilled Chip.

"In a small cupboard that was fastened to that outside wall above it," indicated Carolyn. The outline from where a wall cupboard had been could be seen on the wall, emphasized by a less-worn layer of paint inside the area.

"What kind of a cupboard was it?" asked Ron.

"Just the kind you'd have on the wall in your kitchen, with two shelves, and a single door that opens from one side," described Carolyn. "It was painted the same dark green color as the walls."

"There's nothing like that out there in the main area," mentioned Chip. "Or in here, either, that I can see."

"Maybe someone used it for firewood, or something else?" speculated Sherry.

"Not with paint on it," differed Chip. "That would cause fumes while burning it."

"Maybe it was burned outside," countered Sherry. "And, for some other reason."

"Could something with a painted surface still retain trace evidence of blood splatter?" Carolyn unexpectedly asked.

"It would depend upon how well it was scrubbed or cleaned afterwards," replied Chip as he began studying the walls more carefully. "This entire room needs to be analyzed for trace evidence. The walls, and especially that table. But, scientists have determined that under ideal conditions, some DNA evidence can persist for up to a million years. The short answer, though, is that it usually survives for only a number of weeks, depending upon all sorts of unpredictable factors such as weather, that kind of thing. So, there's no way of really knowing until we test it."

Carolyn then took several photos of the room to include those things. "That is odd that they would just take down a cupboard like that, but not even bother to do something else with the wall."

Ron and Sherry began walking the length of barrels that were stacked two-high, carefully searching for any other evidence in or around them while Chip and Carolyn remained near the alcove entrance.

"Is there another way out down there?" called Chip.

"Not that I can see," responded Ron. Chip frowned with disapproval when he noticed Ron put his arm around Sherry again, presumably to share the light from his flashlight as they walked.

"What's this on the ceiling here?" wondered Carolyn when she looked up and noticed the remnants of something that had once splattered onto it. Chip then shined his flashlight on the area while Carolyn proceeded to take a couple photos of it, one with her zoom lens.

The ceiling in the alcove was only twelve feet high, and not thirty feet high, as in the main barn area where the chandelier had once hung from its rafters at the center peak. The alcove's ceiling was likewise unfinished pressure-treated wood with only its rafters showing, once lit by seven equidistantly spaced outdoor patio lights whose frames still hung on the wall. The two that still contained light bulbs appeared to be broken or smashed by something.

"You'd think they would have put some windows in here," muttered Chip as he pointed his flashlight down the long row of barrels before starting after Sherry and Ron.

"And you're absolutely positive that they x-rayed all these barrels?" pressed Carolyn.

"Yes," answered Chip.

"So, there's still wine in them, then?" grilled Carolyn.

"Allegedly," replied Chip.

"And you're positive there's no danger of them going for a crab-walk?" persisted Carolyn.

"It would be highly unlikely," sighed Chip, not willing to admit that he shared Carolyn's concern.

"Does wine always smell so bad?" frowned Carolyn as they continued past the aging wine barrels. The splintered wooden floor creaked as they walked on it, causing an undeniable shift of weight on its surface.

Both Chip and Carolyn stopped where they were and exchanged a concerned glance upon hearing another unusual sound.

"What is that?" demanded Carolyn.

"Come on you guys!" shouted Chip. "I think the barrels may be starting to move! Hurry, we gotta get out of here!"

Carolyn and Chip immediately turned and began to run toward the alcove entrance and into the main barn area.

"Keep going!" instructed Chip. "We need to get all the way outside! Once those barrels do collapse, there's no telling what might happen. The whole barn could come down!"

"Sherry!" screamed Carolyn. "Come on!"

"Ron!" hollered Chip.

The sound Chip and Carolyn had heard was the cave-in of an aging trap door. Its rotting wood had given way under the weight when Ron Telluric crossed its surface. Sherry had immediately tried to grab Ron's arms to prevent him from falling inside the space beneath it, but had been pulled in after him. Their screams went unheard above the sound of thirty-three wine barrels launched into an imminent collapse. The domino event had triggered a path of travel directly towards them!

Drenched by rancid-smelling wine that began pouring into the cellar at an alarming rate where they lay, Ron and Sherry immediately tried to get up. Ron was unable to move.

"I think I've broken my back," moaned Ron. He was in agony, though the pain was unexplainably beginning to diminish.

Sherry immediately located his flashlight but discovered it had broken during their fall. "You've got to try to sit up! If that wine keeps pouring in here like this, we'll both be drowned!"

Though Sherry had no way of knowing that thirty-three 55-gallon wine barrels could potentially contain 1,800 gallons or more of wine, she felt certain that the small narrow cellar in which she and Ron were now trapped could never contain whatever amount of the foul substance might find its way in.

"There are cement steps leading up to the entrance where the trap door was," shouted Sherry excitedly after groping the floor of the dark cellar with her bare hands. "We are going to have to try to climb back out of here while we can!"

"Just leave me," groaned Ron. "Perhaps there's a chance you can make it out and get help?"

The rancid wine was already up to Ron's chin and deepening by the moment.

"Sit up!" screamed Sherry as she got behind Ron, removed his hardhat, and forced him into a sitting position. "I'm not leaving you here to die!" Sherry then found one of the boards from the trap door and wedged it between Ron and the wall to keep him in sitting position while she continued to search the liquid darkness surrounding them.

Sherry suddenly felt something squirm beneath her hand and screamed as it scurried up the cement steps, squealing as it went.

"Are you all right?" called Ron.

"I think it was a mouse," stammered Sherry. "Or a rat!"

"Which way did it go?" questioned Ron. "Perhaps there is a way out of here. For you, that is."

The foul-smelling wine was already at least a foot deeper than it had been moments ago. "For *both* of us!" persisted Sherry. "We are getting out of here, together. I've waited a long time to meet someone like you, and I'm not about to let you die now!"

Ron suddenly realized that he had unintentionally led Sherry to believe he was available, but fearful of telling her that he was already happily married to someone else, especially now.

"Do you hear me?" screamed Sherry, as she checked to be sure the liquid level had not yet reached Ron's head where it might drown him. "You need to tell me at once if it gets up to your chin again."

"Yeah, okay," promised Ron. He could no longer feel his legs and was beginning to give up. Ron knew that he would rather die than become a burden to someone else for the rest of his life. It was intolerable to think of such an existence!

Sherry had been a widow for several years, and her two adult daughters now had families of their own. Her hopes of finding an acceptable prospect for her next husband had been tenuous at best, until finally meeting Ron.

"You must leave me here!" pleaded Ron. He did not want Sherry to die with him.

Sherry carefully made her way to the top of the slippery cement steps, only to find wreckage from broken wine barrels that were tightly wedged across its opening. "The opening is blocked by the broken wine barrels."

"Can you squeeze past any of it?" called Ron. The wine level had already reached his chin once more.

"Only if I were a mouse!" replied Sherry as she crawled down the steps and then splashed her way back over to Ron.

"There's something I need to tell you," mentioned Ron.

"You can tell me later, when we get out of here," insisted Sherry. Then, discovering that the wine level had reached Ron's chin again, she chided, "Why didn't you say something?"

"I'm sorry!" Ron was grateful for the darkness that hid the tears flowing down his cheeks. He was going to die down here, and there was nothing he could do about it. The least he could do was give Sherry a message for his family. "Sherry, listen to me."

"We've got to try to tread water as it gets deeper," instructed Sherry, refusing to listen to what Ron was trying to say.

"Sherry! I can't move my legs," moaned Ron. At least the initial intense pain was gone.

Sherry then put her arms around Ron, using his armpits to hold him up. The buoyancy of his body in the reeking pool of wine was working to her advantage. "You are NOT giving up on me, do you hear me?" Their one best hope was that part of the excess wine spillage had found its way elsewhere.

"It's not getting any deeper now," noticed Ron.

"I think you're right," agreed Sherry. "When I count to three, we both need to scream for help, as loud as we can."


Rupert Williams had been born on March 23, 1973, in Chicago, Illinois. Originally an immigrant from Jamaica, his mother had given birth to him out-of-wedlock after coming to America where she had hoped to find a better life for herself and her unborn child.

Sadly, Rupert's mother was also a drug addict and had been found dead in an alley when he was only three years old. Rupert's cries for attention eventually gained the notice of a next-door neighbor, but not until the unfortunate child had spent two days alone in the filthy one-bedroom apartment. Rupert was then seized by the child-welfare system and placed in one foster home after another.

Determined to have a better life for himself and his future family, Rupert had earned a football scholarship and put himself through college doing construction work on the side, eventually becoming a college professor himself.

The distinguished Professor Rupert Williams had taught Sociology and Economics at Chicago State University for almost twenty years before learning that his beautiful wife Gina had been stepping out on him. It was not long afterwards that Rupert had begun imbibing in a glass of wine to calm his nerves and forget his troubles each day after work. One thing led to another, and Rupert's drinking became a problem that spiraled out of control.

After being forced into an early retirement, Rupert soon lacked sufficient funds to pay the many creditors to whom Gina had managed to indebt him, ultimately leading to bankruptcy and loss of their home. Gina divorced him immediately thereafter, taking custody of their only remaining child at home – a sixteen-year-old girl named Matilda.

More than half of Rupert's meager retirement payments were pre-distributed to his ex-wife Gina as spousal support, by order of the court. What little remained was barely enough for him to afford a small room at the Y. Rupert continued to drown his sorrows with alcohol and had done so for the past three years.

Rupert finally reached the absolute bottom of his life on his fiftieth birthday. That was on March 23, 2023. Rupert knelt and prayed for help, promising Jesus that he would quit drinking and somehow turn his life around, if only he had the help to succeed. He knew he could not do it on his own and would definitely be looking for a sign.

The following day, Rupert had been prompted to go for a walk down by Lake Michigan. He finally sat down to rest on the wall by the L Train stop, and was thoroughly enjoying his first sober day in three years. That was when he first met Jim Otterman, Susan Rives and Janette Manza.

Just why had Jim Otterman suddenly been prompted to give Rupert - who was a perfect stranger to him - a new lease on life? Rupert knew in his heart that it was indeed a sign from the Almighty. Determined that he would not allow it to slip through his fingers, as he had so many other things in his life, Rupert made his decision. He would go with these people to Powell Mountain to start a new life, no matter what it took!

"Hey, Rupert?" Susan snapped her fingers in front of his face.

"Sorry," apologized Rupert. "I seem to be getting a really bad headache. It might even be a migraine."

"I've got some Advil, if you'd like some," offered Janette.

"That's no good for a migraine," differed Susan. Even though her initial reaction to Rupert's appearance had been one of disgust – mostly because of how he was dressed – there was something undeniably appealing about him, as well. "Here, try this."

"Thanks," nodded Rupert as he took the two Excedrin from Susan that she had removed from her purse. Rupert then walked over to a drinking fountain nearby to wash them down.

"Bad news," informed Jim as he rejoined them in the lobby of the Shady Brook Research Institute where they had been waiting for him. "Suicide."

"Suicide?" Janette drew the symbol of a cross on her chest and shook her head with dismay.

"Yesterday," added Jim. "And of course Martha Krain would pick March 23rd to do it, too! If only she could have waited one more day!"

"Now what?" questioned Susan.

"Sir, wait!" called an orderly who had followed Jim Otterman from Martha Krain's old room. "Martha was a friend of mine, and left this in my care." The man was holding a small metal box with a lid and a handle on top. "She did not want her brother to get ahold of it, but had no other family. May I give it to you? I don't think she would mind. There is no one else."

"Uh, sure, thanks!" accepted Jim as he took the box from the man. "I'll take good care of it."

The man then leaned close and whispered, "You might want to take your friends and leave here before the two o'clock shift change. Most of my associates are not as understanding as I am about having people like that in here. Me, I'm good with it, but them – not so much."

"People like what?" challenged Rupert after overhearing the remark. "People with dreadlocks?"

"You do realize that this facility is run by the Crusading Knights?" questioned the man in hushed tones as he studied Rupert, Susan and Janette.

"We got ya," informed Jim as he cordially slapped the man on his shoulder in farewell before shaking his hand. "Thanks again."

Jim then indicated to the others, "Let's go."

Rupert merely shrugged his shoulders, but Janette and Susan were less than pleased by the man's remark and paused to glare at him for a moment first.

"Ladies, come on," prompted Jim.

Without further comment, Janette and Susan followed Jim and Rupert from the building.

"So, what was that all about?" demanded Susan as she hurried to catch up with Jim.

"I'm not even sure yet," replied Jim, "but I have a feeling that whatever's in this box might be pretty important. I think we should try and get back to the jet first before we open it up."

"Hey, the Y is right on the way," pointed out Rupert. "Is there any way I could stop by there, just long enough to grab a small suitcase and some personal things?"

"We can always get you new things," offered Jim.

"My college diploma is something I'd really hate to leave behind," replied Rupert. "But, I definitely want to go with you folks."

"Sure, we can stop by the Y on our way," agreed Jim.

"There is something else you should know," added Rupert as they continued their walk down the pedestrian ramp. "I'm not even sure if it matters, but this is my first official day as a sober man in three years. I'm going cold turkey."

Jim stopped where he was to study Rupert more closely. "How are you feeling right now?"

"He's got a migraine coming on," interjected Janette. "Susan just gave him two Excedrin."

"That might not be all he'll need," sighed Jim. "We really should hurry before he has any other symptoms."

"Symptoms?" frowned Janette.

"What Jim is trying to tell you," elaborated Rupert, "is that the signs of alcohol withdrawal can start anywhere from two hours to two days after someone's last drink."

"So, a migraine is one of the symptoms, then?" quizzed Janette as they all began walking again.

"Along with mild anxiety, shakiness and a host of other things," answered Rupert.

"Not to mention severe complications in some people such as seizures and delirium tremens," muttered Jim. "You know, maybe this wasn't such a great idea." Jim then stopped again to face Rupert.

"Yes, and some people have even died from the complications of alcohol withdrawal," verified Rupert. "I know it! But I swear to you, as God is my witness, that I am determined to remain sober, no matter what, even if it kills me!"

"Even if it kills you?" doubted Jim.

"Yes, even if it kills me!" asserted Rupert. "It was my fiftieth birthday yesterday when I got down on my knees and prayed to the good man upstairs for His help with this. And I truly do believe he has answered that prayer! He sent you, didn't he?"

"That may be true, but ....," began Jim.

"Then tell me who in their right mind would even consider giving a perfect stranger like me a second chance to make something of himself in this life?" interjected Rupert. "Tell me this isn't a sign!"

"Hold it!" indicated Susan. "Did you say yesterday was your fiftieth birthday?"

"March 23, 1973," verified Rupert. "Why?"

"You were born on March 23, 1973?" Jim was stunned.

"Yes, that's what I just said," confirmed Rupert, uncertain why the others were staring at him so peculiarly.

"I'd say that's a sign, all right," Susan finally managed to say.

Jim and Janette merely shook their heads.

"I can't help when my birthday is," apologized Rupert. "Does that day hold some sort of special significance for you people?"

"You could say that," responded Jim, with more empathy. "All right, you can still come with us."

"Oh, thank you!" Rupert sighed with relief. "You won't regret it, Mr. Otterman, I promise!"

"But," stipulated Jim, "if you do start having any serious symptoms at all, I'm flying you straight to the nearest hospital. Is that understood?"

"I have no health insurance," answered Rupert apologetically.

"It would be on me, of course," promised Jim. "I'll pay for any expenses you might have."

"Hey, thanks, man," beamed Rupert as they all began walking again. "Whatever it takes."

Rupert was well aware that the initial symptoms of alcohol withdrawal could include not only headaches, but also tremors, sweating, agitation, anxiety and irritability, nausea and vomiting, heightened sensitivity to light and sound, disorientation, difficulty concentrating, and, in more serious cases, transient hallucinations. Still, it was his sincere hope that the migraine headache would be the worst of it. Perhaps he might not have any of the other symptoms this time.

Jim was equally aware of the possible symptoms Rupert might experience during the next couple of days but decided not to mention it to Susan or Janette just yet. Who knew, perhaps Rupert might get lucky and recover okay on his own. Still, Rupert would not only need to be watched carefully, but would need to be kept hydrated to help restore his water and electrolyte balance, and receive plenty of healthy foods to prevent anemia or vitamin deficiency.

The four of them walked along in silence, each lost in his or her own thoughts as they approached the Y where Rupert had been staying. "Perhaps you might want to come help me?"

"We'll be right here," assured Jim.

Rupert did not want to chance the fact that Jim and his friends might decide to take off or leave without him, so again suggested that Jim help him. "Not them, just you. Perhaps you can help me decide which things might be most appropriate for me to bring along, being that you're familiar with where we're going?"

"We can wait here in the lobby," suggested Susan.

Jim merely nodded and then followed Rupert toward the narrow staircase at the opposite end of the lobby.

"So, Rupert was actually born on the exact same day all that stuff happened on the beach at Oceanview Academy?" whispered Janette to Susan. "When Joyce and Veronica went missing, and also when that other guy died from shark bites?"

"Apparently so," responded Susan as the two of them sat down on a hard wooden bench to wait. "And his name was Steve Fredrickson, by the way. The guy who died."

"That's just creepy!" Janette shook her head.

"Yeah, it is, isn't it?" scowled Susan.

"And, despite the clothes," added Janette in an attempt to change the subject, "Rupert's one fine looking man! Don't deny it!"

Susan blushed slightly but then reminded Janette, "Don't forget, I'm a married woman!"

"I thought you were wed, not dead!" joked Janette as she playfully jabbed Susan in the side with her elbow. "You'd have to be blind not to notice a looker like Rupert."

"And, in case you can't add," chided Susan, "the fact that he was born in 1973 also happens to make me sixteen years older than him."

"Didn't you say Ray is 81 years old now?" questioned Janette with a raised eyebrow.

"Yeah, so, what about it?" Susan became defensive.

"And yet you're only 66 years old now," pointed out Janette. "That would make Ray fifteen years older than *you*!"

"So, what's your point?" Susan was becoming irritated.

"Never hurts to have an iron in the fire," replied Janette with a sly grin. "Just in case."

"What's that supposed to mean?" demanded Susan.

"Well, you said it yourself," reminded Janette. "Ray is getting older. Didn't you say he has a heart condition now?"

"He does," scowled Susan.

"That must mean he can't be allowed to get too excited or anything," persisted Janette. "Must be awful hard on you?"

"That's none of your business!" snapped Susan.

"Hey, you're right. It's none of my business if you're stuck with some old man who might keel over and die after a good roll in the sack," retorted Janette, "but you're still young and beautiful! Just look at you! And don't try and tell me Rupert hasn't noticed! I've seen him checking you out, girl!"

Susan and Janette became silent as they watched Rupert and Jim return. Rupert was dressed in a rather expensive-looking black suit with a white shirt and red paisley necktie. Rupert's black patent leather shoes also looked as if they might be new. In one hand was a small black leather briefcase, and with the other hand he pulled a small silver Samsonite "Hardside Spinner" suitcase. Without the dreadlocks, Rupert might actually have passed as a typical business executive on his way to an out-of-town business convention somewhere.

"Now, that's what I'm talkin' about, girl!" grinned Janette as she gently jabbed Susan in the side with her elbow again.

"Would you stop that?" requested Susan as she moved away from Janette's elbow and slowly stood up. The attraction she suddenly felt for Rupert was undeniable.

"Let's go," smiled Jim. He, too, was well aware of the effect Rupert's new appearance was having on Susan.

"Hey, isn't that your Smartwatch?" Janette questioned Susan.

Susan's Smartwatch was set to ring in an unmistakably haunting melody played on the Theremin.

Patented in 1928 by Russian inventor, Léon Theremin, the Theremin was an early electronic musical instrument controlled without any physical contact by the musician playing it.

"Hang on!" requested Susan. "It's from Ann."

326

Jim and the others then paused to wait while Susan activated her phone's earpiece and took the call. "Hello? Ann? How are you?"

After listening for several moments, Susan's face took on a serious expression. "Are you sure?"

"What is it?" whispered Janette.

"Shhh!" instructed Susan as she continued to listen to what Ann had to say. "How long do they think he has?" Unbidden tears began to escape the corners of Susan's eyes.

"It's Ray," Susan finally revealed to the others. "Ann says he's in the hospital up at Ocean Bay."

"His heart?" guessed Jim.

Susan nodded affirmatively as tears streamed down her lovely cheeks.

"Tell Ann we'll be there within four hours, tops," instructed Jim.

"We're still half an hour away from the airport by L Train," reminded Janette.

"That we are," agreed Jim, "but it's only a three-and-a-half-hour flight by jet."

"Who's Ray?" questioned Rupert. He could not help but be concerned that whatever was happening might cause Jim to change his mind again about taking him along.

"Ray is her husband," informed Jim with a sly look.

"Oh, I see," nodded Rupert. He had not been aware of Susan's marital status before and was clearly disappointed.

Then, to Ann over the phone, Susan advised, "Jim said we can be there in about four hours."

"Are you still in Chicago?" questioned Ann.

"Yeah, we are," confirmed Susan. "We're about half an hour away from the airport where Jim's Learjet is parked in a private hangar."

"Okay, we'll see you soon then," replied Ann. "We love you."

"We love you, too." Susan then pressed the app on the face of her Smartwatch to end the call.

"We will be swinging by Ocean Bay on our way to Powell Mountain," described Jim to Rupert. "Our first stop will be the hospital there. Who knows, perhaps it will be perfect timing for you."

"Let's just hope we make it there in time to see Ray before it's too late!" muttered Susan as she exited the Y and began walking down the pedestrian ramp toward the L Train stop.

"We will!" assured Jim as he and the others followed after her. "Trust me!"


Meanwhile, at the Shady Brook Winery, Detective Chip Priest and Carolyn stood staring with disbelief at the massive scene of destruction before them. The entire 30 by 50-foot barn had entirely collapsed, literally imploding upon itself as it did. Amazingly, part of the 12 by 50-foot alcove hallway built along its side still stood, though at least 30 feet of it had also been destroyed, along with the two-dozen 55-gallon wine barrels that had been inside. The stench of rancid wine spilling in all directions was overwhelming.

"We've got to help them!" advised Carolyn with finality.

"Are you sure that's wise?" asked Chip. "Perhaps we should call for help first?"

"You still have no idea who pulled down those barn doors, do you?" questioned Carolyn, as she and Chip both removed their hardhats.

"No," sighed Chip with frustration.

"Well, I'm getting them out of there now, before it's too late, if it isn't already! Besides, we don't have time to wait for someone else to get here, even if we knew we could trust them."

Chip waffled, but only for a moment. Perhaps Carolyn was right. "All right, come on!"

Chip and Carolyn raced around the outside of the old barn, to the back end where Ron and Sherry hopefully were before putting their hardhats back on.

"I've got a crowbar in the car," remembered Chip. "I'll be right back. Please wait for me before you try and move anything!"

"Humph," muttered Carolyn as she began calling. "Sherry? Ron? Can you hear me? Sherry! Ron!"

All at once, Carolyn could hear a mild thumping sound from somewhere below where the alcove had stood. "I think they're over here, on the end that collapsed!"

Chip arrived just then with the crowbar and began using it to pull away some of the loose boards. "We've got to be careful we don't make it worse. If they are trapped in an air pocket somewhere, we don't want what's left to come crashing down on them."

Carolyn began grabbing and pulling away any small or loose boards that could easily be moved while Chip continued to pry against the larger ones with his crowbar.

"Sherry? Ron?" Carolyn continued to call. "We're trying to dig you out. Can you hear me?"

Then, finally, Carolyn could hear the muffled sound again. "Chip, stop for a moment! I hear something."

Both Chip and Carolyn listened for several moments, but only silence could be heard. Chip then picked the crowbar back up.

"Help!" came a muffled scream from below them.

"It's Sherry!" screamed Carolyn. "Sherry! We're right here!"

Chip then began removing the debris immediately in front of him with renewed zeal. "Ouch!" He paused to remove a large splinter from his hand before continuing.

Carolyn, too, had acquired several splinters but remained silent about it. Their first priority was rescuing Sherry and Ron, before it was too late. "Sherry? Are you still there?" called Carolyn.

"Down here!" yelled Sherry. Her voice was suddenly louder. "Ron is hurt! He can't move! He thinks his back is broken."

"Understood," called Chip. "Just hang on!"

It took Chip and Carolyn almost another two hours to finally reach the entrance to the wine-filled cellar where Sherry and Ron were trapped.

"Oh, thank God!" cried Sherry. "I've been holding Ron up by his armpits all this time, so he wouldn't drown down here!"

"Oh, how horrid!" Carolyn made a face and nearly gagged from the stench of the rancid wine in which Sherry and Ron were trapped. Suddenly realizing that she should be snapping photos of what was going on so she could send them to Jim, Carolyn proceeded to do so.

"Thank God he floats in this stuff!" commented Sherry. "But, you guys will have to help me lift him out of here, once you figure out a way to clear the opening. And, when we try and lift him out of the liquid ...."

"Understood," interrupted Chip. He was well aware of how overweight his partner had become over the years, and how difficult it would be to lift Ron once they got him to the open air.

"He's been drifting in and out of consciousness, but still has a pulse," added Sherry. "I removed his hardhat so he could breathe more easily, but it's probably submerged by now. I can't find it."

"We're gonna need a flat board to put him on," Chip advised Carolyn. "Most of these boards are from the wine barrels and are curved, so none of them will do."

Carolyn quickly put her cellphone away and made sure the opening to her purse was tightly zipped. She then secured the purse over her shoulder by slipping the strap over her head on one side.

"We really should hurry," urged Chip. Then to Sherry, Chip remarked, "You guys are lucky you were down there when this all collapsed. Otherwise, you'd probably both be dead right now."

Just then a creaking sound from the surrounding rubble could be heard. "Faster, please!" Chip mentioned to Carolyn as he finally managed to heave the last obstructing piece of debris from the cellar opening and was able to get his first good look at his unconscious partner below.

"Here's a flat one that's long enough to use as a stretcher," indicated Carolyn as she hurriedly grabbed onto what was left of a two by twelve-foot plank and managed to drag it over to Chip. Fortunately, it had broken almost exactly in half, so its remainder was only about six feet long. Still, it was rather heavy for Carolyn and it was with great difficulty that she had struggled to move it at all.

"Can you hang onto this end?" questioned Chip.

"I sure hope so!" answered Carolyn as she watched Detective Priest step into the rancid-smelling wine and make his way down the cement steps and into the murky malodor.

Sherry held the bottom end of the board steady while Chip hoisted Ron onto it. Chip then removed his belt and wrapped it around the board, but quickly realized it was not quite long enough to reach around Ron, as well.

"What if you tie his belt onto yours?" suggested Sherry.

Chip nodded and then removed Ron's belt from him so he could attach it to his own. "Let's hope this will be enough."

Once Ron was securely strapped onto the board, Sherry and Chip began pushing the bottom end of it while Carolyn guided it past the top step. There was no way she would have been able to help lift it, though, and was only able to help steer its direction of travel.

Finally managing to shove Ron's makeshift stretcher onto the floor above, Sherry and Chip pushed with all their might while Carolyn grabbed and yanked loose boards from its oncoming path.

"Let's move him away from the building," instructed Chip. "I can get this end if you two ladies can get the other end."

Sherry began hobbling over to where Carolyn was. "I think I may have sprained my ankle down there."

"I think I've got an ace bandage in the car," replied Chip. "Let's just get him moved first, if we can."

"Let's do this," encouraged Sherry.

"On three," directed Chip. "One, two, three!"

Chip made a guttural animal-like groaning sound as he heaved to lift his end of the stretcher, realizing at once that Sherry and Carolyn had been unable to lift their end at all.

"Move out of the way, ladies," commanded Chip. "I'm going to try to drag it over there."

Carolyn quickly got her cellphone back out and took a couple more photos. "I'm sending these to Jim right now, and hopefully he can get life flight out here."

"My thoughts exactly," approved Chip.

"Why don't you just call 911?" questioned Sherry as she hobbled over to a nearby boulder to sit down so she could get the weight off her ankle.

"Because whoever dragged down those barn doors could be dangerous, and because we have no idea who it was," explained Carolyn as she began texting the photos to Jim.

"I'm afraid she's right," agreed Chip. "Alerting them to our condition could put us all in more danger than we are already."

Ron began to awaken and then moaned incoherently.

"I'm not getting a signal right here," advised Carolyn. "It looks like my other texts never went through, either. I'm going to head up that ridge over there."

"Not alone, you're not!" informed Chip.

"I'll just stay here with Ron, then," agreed Sherry, though Chip and Carolyn were already several yards away by the time she said it.

Ron took out his old-fashioned cellphone and also checked to see if there was a signal. "Does Sherry at least have a Smartwatch?"

"I'm afraid not," answered Carolyn as she continued up the hogback for several more yards. "Both of us just have cellphones, like you. Hey, this almost looks like a trail here."

"There's a building of some sort up there, too," realized Chip. "I don't think anyone went up there when we were out here before, probably because no one knew about it."

Carolyn and Chip hurried to the small shed. Beside it were seven large wine barrels, neatly stacked on their sides. Huge boulders were braced against them at either end. Surrounding them were several tall cedar and oak trees. Beneath those grew manzanita, ceanothus and rhododendron bushes, many just beginning to bloom. Most of the surrounding area had once been nothing but a sprawling hillside grape vineyard, though now overcome in large part by trees and other native vegetation. The sound of a high mountain brook could be heard in the distance, as well. An unexpected icy blast of early spring breeze against Chip's damp clothing caused him to momentarily shiver.

"These are filled with something," noted Carolyn as she rapped on one of them with her knuckle.

"Something rather solid, I would say," opined Chip as he banged the crowbar he still held against the side of another one. "Probably cement, just like the others."

"That almost looks like cement on the edge of this one," realized Carolyn. "Could more of the victims be in these?"

Chip then banged on each of the other barrels, also with the crowbar. "Every single one of 'em is filled with something solid, that's for sure. We need to get some GPR equipment out here so we can see what else might be inside."

"GPR?" questioned Carolyn. She was unfamiliar with the term.

"Ground-penetrating radar," interpreted Chip. "Equipment that is normally used to transmit high-frequency radio waves into the ground, but it would also work for these. With GPR, when the electromagnetic energy encounters a buried object or a boundary between materials having different permittivities, it then reflects those back to the surface."

"Kind of like an x-ray?" asked Carolyn.

"Somewhat," answered Chip. "It has a receiving antenna that can record the variations in the return signal. It's actually more similar to a seismograph – like the kind used to measure earthquakes – except GPR methods utilize electromagnetic energy rather than acoustic energy, and energy may be reflected using electrical properties rather than mechanical properties as is the case with seismic energy."

"I'll have Jim send us some GPR equipment, too," promised Carolyn as she snapped some photos of the barrels.

"Just what's the deal between you two, really?" quizzed Chip. "You and Jim?"

"As I've told you before, there's no 'deal' between us," asserted Carolyn as she turned to take a photo of the shed, as well. Then, noticing that the shed door was ajar, Carolyn approached to get a look inside.

"Allow me," insisted Chip when he noticed what she planned to do. "It's doubtful there's any viable prints, but like Jim said, we still need to check." Chip then carefully hooked the edge of the shed door with his crowbar and pulled it open. Inside was a beat-up wooden table into which an old bowie knife was stuck, point first.

"THAT'S THE KNIFE!" recognized Carolyn. "See that insignia of the Crusading Knights on its handle?"

"You didn't mention that when you were describing the knife to us earlier," mentioned Chip as he stared at it with disbelief.

"Oh, my God!" exclaimed Carolyn as she looked up and noticed an old green cupboard on the wall above. "There must have been more than one table like this! But, I'm pretty sure that's the cupboard that was on the wall in the alcove – unless there's another one of those, too."

"We're NOT going inside this shed until a forensic team gets here!" announced Chip. "Make sure that Jim of yours sends us one of those, too, while he's at it."

"He's not *my* Jim," countered Carolyn.

"Well, it sure seems like it to me!" snapped Chip. He was tired and hungry, as it was nearly three o'clock. "Some lunch might not hurt anything, either."

Carolyn then reached into her purse and pulled out a granola bar. "I'll split it with you?"

Chip then shook his head and laughed. "Sure, why not? Hey, sorry about that. I'm just worried about Ron."

"I know," advised Carolyn. "Me, too." She then opened the wrapper and split the granola bar in half, handing the part with the wrapper to Chip. They both paused to devour their halves.

Chip then pulled his cellphone back out and began testing again for a signal.

"Over here!" called Carolyn. She had climbed onto the wine barrels and was now standing on top of one.

"Hey, be careful!" admonished Chip.

"No kidding!" Carolyn laughed sardonically as she proceeded to send Jim Otterman a series of text messages. "These will certainly get his attention."

"Of that I have no doubt," agreed Chip.

After climbing down from the barrels, Carolyn then frowned. "Didn't you say that there were twenty-nine missing coeds in all between 1956 and 1975, when the Woodcutter was finally arrested?"

"Yeah, why?" wondered Chip.

"And there were only twenty-three of them found in the barn?" continued Carolyn.

"Leaving six of them unaccounted for," reiterated Chip as he turned to stare at the barrels more carefully.

"That you knew of," reminded Carolyn. "There are seven barrels here."

"Why in the world would anyone do something like this?" Chip's question was more rhetorical than anything. He certainly did not expect a response. It was almost certain that the other missing coeds were inside these barrels, though. He felt sure of it.

"We also need to try to recover that roll of baling wire that was inside the barn," added Carolyn. "So it can be compared against the baling wire from the Lydia Cain location, and also against the victims here – once they can be removed from all of this, that is."

Chip shook his head with trepidation. Why hadn't he recognized the significance of the baling wire before? It had been sitting right there in front of him in the barn the whole time! "You know, the old guy at that hardware store did tell us back in 1975 that he sold several rolls of baling wire from the same manufacturer's lot, but was unsure to whom all of them went. Most of his customers were cash only. And, few people used credit back in those days, so the sales would be virtually untraceable. Not only that, the man's probably dead by now. He was about 90 years old at the time."

"Perhaps the ends of the wire used on Lydia Cain and how they were cut would match the roll of baling wire from the barn up here?" suggested Carolyn.

"Actually, we did test the baling wire on the victims in the barn," revealed Chip. "And it was a perfect match against the baling wire from Woody's shed. But, it still could have come from the roll here in the barn."

"Then all of the murders must have been committed by whoever stole Woody's flag!" reasoned Carolyn. "There's no way Woody would have hurt someone."

"I know," assured Chip. "Oh, no! The FILE! We left it on that old wooden pew, inside the barn!"

"One of us probably needs to wait here for a response from Jim," pointed out Carolyn, "since there's not a signal down there."

"I'll be right back," promised Chip. "I'm just going to let Sherry know what's going on so they don't worry, and check on Ron."

Ray Killingham drifted in and out of consciousness as he lay on his hospital bed at the Ocean Bay Memorial Hospital. The steady drip of an IV – plus the constant blip of the heart rate monitor beside him – were almost hypnotic. Even with the drugs he knew they had given him, the pain was excruciating. Was the oxygen mask really necessary?

Where was Susan, anyway? wondered Ray. Why isn't she here? After waiting for most of his life to finally marry the woman of his dreams, it was unbearable to think that he might slip away like this without the chance to even tell her goodbye. Ray loved Susan with all his heart. An unbidden tear escaped one eye as he thought of what her life might be like without him. What would she do?

Ray was lucky to even be alive, but the damage to his heart had been so extensive that the surgery had only served to prolong his life until, if, and when a suitable donor match could be found. At 81 years of age, his prospects of surviving a transplant surgery were also in question. And, there was the financial burden to consider, as well, not to mention the recovery time it would involve. There was no way he could ask Jim Otterman to spring for this! The man had done enough for them already. It would be too much to ask.

"Time for your medication," informed an overly cheerful young nurse in her mid-twenties as she entered the room with a small tray with a liquid-filled syringe on it. She then proceeded to inject some unknown substance into his IV tube.

"What are you giving me?" mumbled Ray from inside his oxygen mask.

"There, there," reassured the nurse. "This will help you rest a little easier."

*But I don't want to rest easier!* thought Ray. He could barely keep his eyes open as it was!

"You need to remain quiet and still," added the nurse as she gently patted his arm with her hand in an accommodating manner. "Your wife should be here soon. Just close your eyes and get some rest."

Ray merely nodded his thanks before trying to relax and let the drugs take effect again. He felt so useless! Ray had not felt this helpless since he was in Vietnam and learned of the raid on Sơn Mỹ village where his common-law wife and unborn child had lived at the time. Ray had been sent on a fool's errand to supposedly participate in another mission over at Da Nang, which was about 70 kilometers north of Sơn Mỹ village. It was not until learning of the tragedy afterwards that Ray realized he had only been sent there to get him out of the way.

Ray began to shed silent tears as he thought of the horrible tragedy that had generally come to be known in America as the "My Lai Massacre." Just why had he been forced to endure such an endless facade of government bureaucracy and red tape before even being allowed to come and identify Minh Chau's body on March 23, 1968, when he was finally allowed to take her for burial?

That was fifty-five years ago yesterday, assuming today was still March 24th. Ray was no longer sure what day it was, actually. After major heart surgery and drifting in and out of consciousness, it could even be the 25th by now for all he knew.

Ray finally fell into a fitful sleep, suddenly finding himself in the jungles of Vietnam, crawling on his belly through the jungle at night. After smearing more mud on his face for camouflage, Ray inched his way forward. The sticky hot sweat from his forehead kept washing the mud away, some of it into his eyes. The bandana he wore under his helmet was completely soaked, yet this was not the time to stop and try to wring it out. All movement must be kept to a minimum to avoid detection by the enemy. Not only was the jungle unbearably humid this time of year, but completely infested with snakes, rodents, and insect life of every imaginable variety. The sound of crickets, frogs, and nocturnal predators sounded out in the night while the constant steady hum of mosquitos persisted in the background. In his dream, Ray and his comrades were slowly working their way toward a makeshift holding cell where several American prisoners were being held hostage. In a flicker of light from one of the guard's hand-held torches, he suddenly noticed that Susan was inside the bamboo cage. "Susan!" whispered Ray as he began crawling forward again, as fast as he dared.

The guard had ripped off Susan's blouse and no doubt intended to force himself upon her! Ray knew he must get there in time to prevent it! Try as he might, Ray suddenly seemed unable to move any farther. It was as if the vines around him had come to life and wrapped themselves around his hands and feet, preventing his escape.

"Susan!" Ray finally hollered, as loud as he dared. Tears were now streaming down his cheeks, rinsing away whatever mud his own sweat had not already removed.

"Yes, my husband has had PTSD in the past," confirmed Susan, "but it's been years since his last episode. I *must* see him now!"

"Not in his condition," argued the nurse, "not without a doctor's order. Besides, there's absolutely nothing in his chart about post-traumatic stress disorder, not that I can see."

"Perhaps we should just take this down a notch," interjected Jim. "I've known Ray for years, and have never known him to have an episode during that time. He's not a violent man."

"Nevertheless, he could possibly be dangerous in his condition, and that could pose a liability issue," persisted the nurse. "Not only that, we've already given him all the medication we dare, especially with his heart like it is."

"I'll give you a liability issue!" threatened Susan through gritted teeth. "I demand that you let me see my husband at once!"

"We've had to strap him down," added the nurse. "Plus, he may not even recognize you with all the medication he's on."

"I'll take my chances!" snapped Susan, enraged that she should be kept from seeing Ray at a time like this.

"Are you Mrs. Killingham?" asked a handsome young doctor from behind them, a regular Dr. Kildare type if ever there was one. At least he was more pleasant than the old biddy at the nurse's station! "I'm Ray Killingham's doctor, Dr. Blair."

"For now you are," muttered Jim, who also was upset by the treatment they had received from the nurse.

"Yes, I'm Susan Killingham," replied Susan, suddenly hopeful that she might be allowed to finally see her husband.

"Who are these other people with you?" questioned the doctor.

"This is my, uh, my brother-in-law, Jim Otterman," lied Susan. She knew it would be the only way she could get Jim approved to go in with her, and she could not bear to face what might await her alone.

"Jim?" acknowledged the doctor as he shook Jim's hand.

"Janette Manzo and Rupert Williams are close friends of ours," explained Jim.

"I'm afraid only family can go in," apologized the doctor, "but you two may see him if you keep it brief."

"Thank you, sir," nodded Jim as he put a comforting arm around Susan while they walked toward the cardiac unit. "You'll be fine," he whispered to Susan. "Trust me."

"Please don't say that!" whispered Susan rather sharply as they entered the room. They then stood there for several moments watching Ray sleep. "Oh, my God!" exclaimed Susan. "They've got him hooked up to everything but the kitchen sink!"

"Shhh!" advised Jim as he gently pushed Susan forward with his hand on her back.

"Ray?" whispered Susan as she approached and tenderly put one hand on his arm, fearful of bumping any of the tubes to which he was attached.

Ray's eyes fluttered open at her touch and a smile of relief suddenly crossed his lips. "Susan!" Ray felt as if he were shouting, but inside the oxygen mask his words were inaudible. Still, Susan had been able to read his lips.

"Don't try to talk!" advised Susan as she tenderly stroked Ray's forehead with her other hand. "Are these straps really necessary?"

"I'm afraid so," apologized Dr. Blair, who had followed them into the room as a precaution.

Susan then glared at the doctor for an eternal moment before turning her focus back on Ray. "Just know that I love you and I'm here for you. Everything will be okay."

338

Ray weakly nodded that he understood.

"Ray?" greeted Jim. "You've had heart surgery, but they don't expect you to make it without a transplant."

Ray sadly pursed his lips and then looked at Susan with pleading eyes. He loved her so much and was not ready to lose her so soon.

"Ray?" It was Jim again. "We've got a donor for you, but need your consent. According to an independent doctor I've hired to come on board – if you agree – it's a perfect match. They've already done all the blood typing, cross-match and tissue typing."

Susan had already unfastened the wrist restraint on Ray's hand so she could hold it, without the doctor noticing.

Ray then loosened his hand from hers, reached up, and pulled away his oxygen mask part way so he could converse with them. "A heart donor?"

Dr. Blair suddenly noticed that the restraint had been removed from Ray's right wrist and started to intervene, but was held back by Jim as he continued his conversation with Ray.

"Yes," confirmed Jim. "A man in his sixties who just died of severe injuries following a horrible fall."

"What about his family?" mumbled Ray with concern.

"They're completely on board with it," reassured Jim. "The man was an official organ donor, and his heart is in perfect condition."

"What will this cost me?" worried Ray.

"Nothing!" insisted Jim. "That is his family's wish. They want only to see you get better again and enjoy what's left of your life with the woman of your dreams. And, they wish to remain anonymous."

"Please say yes?" Susan gazed at Ray with pleading eyes, the look he could never refuse. "I just can't lose you now!"

Ray finally nodded and tried to smile. "Okay. I'll do it."

Susan then gave Ray a kiss on the cheek. "I love you so much!"

"We'll be back shortly with your NEW doctor and the final paperwork," advised Jim as he finally let go of Dr. Blair's arm.

"I trust you will have clearance with the hospital administrator?" reminded Dr. Blair, rather snidely.

"You can depend upon it," returned Jim with an even gaze.

Only three hours earlier, at the Shady Brook Winery, Sherry had hurried up the hogback to get Chip and Carolyn, limping on her injured ankle as she went. "Hurry! It's Ron! I don't think he's going to make it. Do either of you know CPR?"

Carolyn and Chip exchanged a look of concern but quickly followed Sherry to where Ron lay on the wooden plank they had used as a stretcher for him. Ron opened his eyes and tried to speak.

"Help will be here soon," assured Sherry as she took Ron's hand in hers to comfort him.

"Tell my family that I love them," whispered Ron, with great effort. "And Sherry, I'm sorry!" Ron then took his last breath and died.

"Ron!" screamed Sherry. "Come on, you two! Let's give him CPR. There's got to be something we can do."

Chip then knelt by his partner, checked for obstructions in his airway, tilted his head back, and blew two breaths of air into his mouth.

By now, Carolyn was kneeling by Ron's chest and proceeded to give him five compressions. Both she and Chip knew their method was obsolete, but it was what they knew and were comfortable with. They had taken off their hardhats and left them on the ground by Sherry.

"All we do is alternate," Chip advised Sherry as he waited his turn to give the two breaths.

"Someone needs to get back up there and wait for Jim's response," added Carolyn as she waited for her turn to give the next five compressions.

"Can you take Carolyn's phone up there and do that, Sherry, or would you rather take over for her?" grilled Chip before giving the next two breaths.

"Go!" instructed Sherry as she knelt on the other side of Ron and took over giving the next five compressions.

Carolyn then got up, grabbed her cellphone from a nearby rock, and hurried up the hogback with her tightly zipped purse still carefully draped over her head and across one shoulder.

The moment she reached the shed area, Carolyn climbed onto the first of the nearby wine barrels and sat down to wait. Almost immediately, her cellphone began to ring. "Hello?"

"This is Jim, I got your texts," advised the voice at the other end.

"Ron is dying," informed Carolyn. "Chip and Sherry are giving him CPR, but I had to come up here by the wine barrels for a cell signal."

"Bart Higbee is on his way right now," assured Jim. "He should be there very soon."

"Jim?" Carolyn hesitated.

"Yes?" prompted Jim.

"I don't think Ron's gonna make it." Carolyn's voice was shaky and Jim could tell she was upset. "I'm pretty sure he's already dead."

"I have an idea," Jim suddenly proposed. "Go ask Chip if he knows whether Ron is an organ donor. Ray Killingham just had major heart surgery following a heart attack, and without a transplant in the next twelve hours, he's probably going to die."

Carolyn was stunned by the news and by Jim's suggestion.

"Carolyn, are you still there?" grilled Jim.

"Uh, yes, I will ask," agreed Carolyn. "And if Ron is an organ donor, then what?"

"Then have Bart fly his body at once to the Ocean Bay Memorial Hospital," instructed Jim. "I'll be here waiting for him. Of course, Chip will need to get Ron's wife to sign off on it in the meantime, and find out his blood type, that kind of thing, if they know it. Plus, anything else he knows about Ron's health history, too. We need to make sure the organ is a match."

"I can do that. Say, did you get the other texts I sent you about someone dragging down the barn doors?" questioned Carolyn. "We may not be safe here."

"Understood," answered Jim. "Other help is on the way, too; you'll know it when they get there. It won't be long, I promise."

"Thank you so much!" sniffed Carolyn.

"Not a problem. And, Carolyn, I don't like the idea of you hanging out alone by those wine barrels," added Jim. "Please get back down to where Chip and Sherry are. We can talk more when I get there. I've got news about Martha Krain, too."

"Okay, see you then," responded Carolyn before hanging up.

Carolyn then hurried back to where Sherry and Chip sat on either side of Ron's body, absently staring at it. They were no longer giving him CPR. Tears were streaming down both their cheeks. Chip had already closed Ron's eyes with one hand and then put his coat over him.

"Is Ron an organ donor?" Carolyn got straight to the point. The sound of a helicopter was already approaching in the distance.

"What?" Chip could not believe what he was hearing.

"Susan's husband has had a major heart attack and just got out of surgery," continued Carolyn. "Without a transplant in the next twelve hours, he will die. Jim will pay whatever costs are involved, I'm sure. All he wants is for you to get Ron's wife to sign off on it, and get whatever other medical history on him you can. They'll need it to confirm whether he's a match. The man in that helicopter can take Ron's body over to the Ocean Bay Memorial Hospital where Jim is waiting for him. Chip, do you hear me?"

It had become necessary for all of them to speak quite loudly due to the noise from the approaching helicopter.

"Uh, sure," nodded Chip. "Let me call his wife right now. I'll be right back." Chip then raced up to where the wine barrels were to make the call.

"His wife?" repeated Sherry with disbelief.

"I suspected that Ron might be married," mentioned Carolyn as she tenderly put an arm around Sherry to comfort her.

"Ron did try to tell me something when we were down there," recalled Sherry. "More than once, but I just wouldn't listen. I kept promising him he would be all right, if only we got him out of there." Sherry then began to sob on Carolyn's shoulder.

"Hey," interjected Carolyn. "You'd better stop crying, or my clothes will end up as wet as yours!"

"Just not as smelly," hollered Sherry as she tried to force a smile. "At least Ron won't have to be a burden on his family for the rest of his life. He didn't seem like the kind of a man who would have wanted that."

"Touché," shouted Chip as he joined them. "My wife is on her way over to the Telluric residence now, and the consent forms will be sent to Jim within the hour."

"Carolyn?" greeted Bart Higbee, after stepping from his helicopter and approaching them from several yards away. The engine was still running and the whir of the spinning blade on top created a strong breeze that could easily be felt, especially by Sherry and Chip in their wet clothing.

"Bart!" exclaimed Carolyn as she raced over to give him a quick embrace. "How are you?"

"Still bailing you and Jim out of these life-and-death situations you seem to keep getting yourselves into," teased Bart. "What's it been, seven years?"

"Yes, indeed." Carolyn became serious as she thought of the harrowing rescue Bart had managed when saving her from the bunker tunnel opening in which she had been trapped behind a locked iron gate at high tide, along with Ray Killingham (formerly known as Ray Dixon) and Sheree Otterman (formerly known as Sheree Wilkins and then Sheree Roth – until the untimely suicide death of her first husband Jon).

"This is my friend Sherry Collingsworth, and Detective Charles Priest," introduced Carolyn. "This is Bart Higbee, pilot extraordinaire!"

They briefly shook hands to acknowledge the introductions.

"I taught Jim Otterman everything he knows about flying," grinned Bart.

"Bart used to be Jim's roommate at Oceanview Academy," explained Carolyn. "And he's also the one who flew us over the beach at Oceanview, the day of the tragedy there."

"Don't tell me," interjected Sherry. "March 23, 1973?"

"In fact, it was." Bart shrugged his shoulders.

"Well, the 24th wasn't too lucky for my friend Ron." Chip became glum as he motioned toward the body. "His wife Andrea is wiring all the permission forms to Jim now, and yes, Ron was an organ donor. Apparently, all we need to do now is make sure he's a match for the guy at Ocean Bay who needs a new heart."

"That would be Ray," Carolyn mentioned to Bart.

"No kidding?" Bart raised an eyebrow. "The man that was trapped in that cave with you and Sheree over at Oceanview in 2016?"

"Yes," confirmed Carolyn, rather sadly.

"Well, let's get going then," urged Bart as he approached the makeshift wooden plank stretcher but then saw how heavy it was. "I've got a regular stretcher in the copter. I'll be right back. The doctor's in there, too, but needs to remain sterile – he's already scrubbed so he can get started on the match for compatibility once we're in flight."

"Unbelievable." Chip shook his head. He had never seen anything so intricately orchestrated before in his life, or so quickly.

Bart was back in a flash with a lightweight aluminum stretcher. "Detective? Can you get his feet for me, sir?"

Chip merely nodded in response as he walked toward Ron's lifeless feet. He thought it curious that Bart hadn't commented at all on the rancid stench of rotten wine.

"On three," instructed Bart. "One, two, three." The two men quickly picked up and hoisted Ron Telluric's body onto the new looking stretcher. Chip groaned from the weight as he did.

"Let's hope his heart is the right one," commented Bart as they each picked up an end of the stretcher and began carrying him toward the helicopter.

"Indeed," agreed Chip as he felt an unbidden tear begin to roll down his cheek.

"I can't believe all this has happened!" Sherry began sobbing again as she watched them load Ron's body through the open door of the helicopter and slide it inside. Within moments, Bart was back on board and Chip ran over to stand by Carolyn and Sherry as the helicopter became airborne and zoomed away.

Jim Otterman was close to wearing a hole in the waiting room carpet of the cardiac unit at Ocean Bay Memorial Hospital. Janette and Rupert sat on a hard vinyl couch nearby. "Bart, where are you?" muttered Jim.

"Is he always like that?" Rupert asked Janette.

"Since I only met him two days ago, it's hard to say," Janette shrugged her shoulders. "But I have known his friend Carolyn since 1976. She and I used to work at a hospital together, not much different than this one here."

"Really?" Rupert was interested in learning more about the people he would soon be meeting up at Powell Mountain.

"What did you two do there?" asked Rupert.

"Me?" laughed Janette. "I was housekeeping."

"That doesn't sound like much fun," flirted Rupert.

"Well, my husband thinks I do a pretty good job of it," informed Janette, just to let Rupert know she was married.

"Lucky guy," smiled Rupert. "What about Carolyn?"

"She's married," volunteered Janette. "For forty years now. Her husband's a lucky guy, too."

"I was just trying to make casual conversation," pointed out Rupert with a mischievous grin. "You certainly don't have to tell me about her if you don't want to."

"Okay, I'm sorry," laughed Janette. She suddenly felt foolish for overreacting to Rupert's natural charm. "Well, Carolyn was a medical unit clerk at the Ashton Valley Medical Center."

"What does a medical unit clerk do?" prompted Rupert.

"I don't know." Janette shrugged her shoulders. "Transcribe doctors' orders, make sure the patients get whatever they need, that kind of thing, I guess."

"That sounds like a rather important job," acknowledged Rupert. "How long has your friend been in the medical field?"

"Oh, she quit years ago," replied Janette. "She became a legal secretary after that."

"That sounds kind of interesting, too," nodded Rupert.

"But, I'll never forget the night Carolyn decided to quit being a medical unit clerk," reminisced Janette.

"What happened?" urged Rupert. The sweat was beginning to pour from his body, but he was trying to keep his mind off of it.

"Well, it was late one night when Carolyn and I were working together on the critical and contagious floor – and for half the rooms you had to wear a mask and gown just to go into them. It was horrible!" described Janette.

"So, did everyone have to wear masks and gowns?" asked Rupert. "Not just the housekeeping staff?"

"Absolutely! Nobody wanted to die from any of that stuff," confirmed Janette. "Anyway, that was the night that some guy Carolyn had been out with got killed in a motorcycle accident. He'd just dropped her off at her apartment right before that – and this was when she was single, of course. But on his way home, he got into a horrible accident. His body was all mangled."

"I get the idea," assured Rupert.

"Well, when the City started laying off all the lab runners and transport orderlies at the Ashton Valley Medical Center," continued Janette, "the medical unit clerks had to do their jobs, too."

"The point of all this?" questioned Rupert.

"When Carolyn went to wheel a body down to the basement where the morgue was – which normally would not have been her job," revealed Janette, "the body lying on the slab next to it was that guy – the one she had been out with."

"Oh, that's awful!" exclaimed Rupert. "And she had no idea before that he was down there?"

"No, not a clue." Janette sadly shook her head. "So, that was when she quit. She just couldn't take it anymore."

"I can't say I blame her," opined Rupert. "But yet the two of you kept in touch?"

"Oh, sure," nodded Janette. "Carolyn and I have been dear friends for years. We even climbed Half Dome together, over at Yosemite one summer."

"That sounds like fun." Rupert was relieved at the change in subject matter.

"And, when we were camped on top one night," elaborated Janette, "we actually saw a flying saucer hovering over us."

"Okay, then," Rupert rolled his eyes and shook his head with disbelief as he got up. "I need to use the men's room. I'll be right back."

"We really did see a flying saucer up there!" assured Janette as she watched Rupert head for the men's room.

"I believe you," grinned Jim as he approached and sat down. "The government has spy surveillance equipment that is often tested in high mountainous areas like that, usually assumed by witnesses to be flying saucers."

Janette folded her arms and narrowed her eyes at Jim, not sure what to make of his comment.

"I do believe you," reassured Jim, more seriously.

"So, will Rupert be checking in here at the hospital?" asked Janette, to change the subject.

"He may be in for a tough time of it for the next few days," acknowledged Jim, "but he definitely wants to do it on his own."

"He sure keeps sweating and going to the bathroom a lot," commented Janette. "And, he's starting to get irritable!"

"Well, we need to make sure he drinks plenty of water," advised Jim. "Can you make sure he does?"

"Me?" frowned Janette. "Why is that my job?"

"Okay, we both need to keep an eye on him," corrected Jim. "Rupert is going to need all the looking after he can get."

"Do you always go around picking up perfect strangers like that?" Janette suddenly asked.

"Actually, this might be the first time I've ever done anything like that before." Jim then folded his arms in front and raised one hand to his chin to consider it.

"That's a relief," razzed Janette, to lighten the mood.

"Honestly, I'm really not sure why I did it," added Jim. "It was almost as if I was compelled to help Rupert when I first saw him, for reasons I can't even begin to explain."

Jim's Smartwatch suddenly began buzzing. "It's Bart!" Jim then got up and walked over to a corner of the waiting room to take the call. "Bart?"

"It's a perfect match." It was Bart.

"Where are you?" demanded Jim.

"Already back in flight," apologized Bart. "Sorry I didn't get to see you, old man, but have to be in Ketchikan as soon as I can get there, for another delivery."

"Hey, thanks for doing this one," replied Jim. "I can't tell you how much I appreciate it."

"That's what old friends are for," advised Bart. "Gotta go now. Say hello to Ray for me, when he's up to it. He'll be in my prayers for a speedy recovery."

"Thanks again," mentioned Jim before ending the call.

"Well?" Janette was standing beside him.

"It's a go," Jim informed Janette as he turned to approach the desk at the nurse's station.

"Yes?" snapped the unpleasant woman.

"If Mrs. Killingham comes back out of her husband's room, please let her know that Jim Otterman has gone to tie up some loose ends with the hospital administrator," requested Jim with an even smile.

"What kind of loose ends?" demanded the woman.

"That, my dear, is something you will soon find out," smirked Jim as he walked away. *It could also include a change in hospital staff*, Jim thought to himself with a wicked smirk. Perhaps a new hospital wing donated by an anonymous benefactor couldn't hurt either.

Less than an hour later, Jim, Janette and Rupert were on board Jim's Learjet, on their way to Powell Lake Airport.

"You sure told her!" laughed Janette, as she thought of the old biddy at the nurse's station and the look on her face when they left.

"At least she still has a job." Jim shrugged his shoulders as he walked back to the rear section of his jet to pull out the conference table.

"Housekeeping!" roared Janette. "I love it!"

"You must," interjected Rupert, "to be doing it for so many years." It was a poor attempt at humor on his part, but Rupert was feeling anything but fine at the moment.

"I'm just grateful that Ray is getting his new heart," pointed out Jim as he opened a small cabinet and removed the metal box that had once belonged to Martha Krain.

"You're gonna open that now?" Janette was surprised.

"Any reason we should wait?" Jim raised an eyebrow.

"Heck, no!" grinned Janette as she came over and sat in the chair beside him. Then, looking at Rupert – who was laying on the couch seat across from them – Janette asked, "Comfortable?"

"I suppose you two are going to make me drink more water?" muttered Rupert.

"Probably so," nodded Jim, "but not until we see what's inside this box. I'm only sorry Ron Telluric didn't live to see this, too."

"Just how do they know for sure his heart won't be rejected by Ray's body, once they transplant it?" Janette was serious.

"Well," sighed Jim, "there are actually three tests they do to evaluate donors. The first is blood type where they determine the blood types of both the donor and the recipient. Then, once that is established, they do what is called a crossmatch. For example, anyone with type O blood can donate to someone with type O, A, B, or AB."

"Even if the recipient is different?" doubted Janette.

"Well, those are the guidelines," described Jim. "For anyone with type A, though, they can only donate to type A or AB. And B can only donate to type B or AB."

"What about someone like me, with AB?" quizzed Rupert.

"If you were the donor," stipulated Jim, "you could only donate to another AB.

348

"And they did all this on your friend Bart's helicopter while they were on their way down there?" Janette found it hard to believe.

"Well, it's a pretty specialized helicopter," responded Jim with a patronizing smile. "It even has an operating room."

"Like a self-contained MASH unit?" quizzed Rupert.

"Precisely," confirmed Jim. "Bart routinely flies missions of mercy to third world countries, assists in dangerous rescue situations, and of course transports vital organs for transplants when there is a critical need."

"I'll bet that cost you plenty," opined Rupert.

"More than a little, and less than too much," answered Jim with a look of satisfaction on his face.

"What about the third thing you mentioned?" reminded Rupert. "You said there was a third test they do to evaluate donors?"

"You were listening." Jim was pleased to see that Rupert was trying to keep his mind occupied. "That would be HLA typing."

"Huh?" frowned Janette.

"HLA stands for 'human leukocyte antigen' but is often referred to as just 'tissue typing,'" explained Jim. "Of the hundred or so different antigens we know of, there are six vital ones for each organ transplant. And of those six antigens, we inherit three from each parent."

"Say what?" Rupert was sorry now that he had asked.

"And, except in cases of identical twins and some siblings," rambled Jim, "it is truly rare to get a six-antigen match between two people, especially if they are unrelated. But, even with a perfect HLA match, there is no way to predict who will experience a rejection episode. In short, even if the surgery goes like clockwork, Ray's still not out of the woods just yet. He will need considerable care for quite some time to come."

"It's a good thing Susan decided to stay there with him," nodded Janette as she shot Rupert a reproving glance. "Ray's gonna need her now more than ever."

"What was that for?" scowled Rupert.

"Just for good measure," smirked Janette. She was beginning to enjoy giving Rupert a hard time.

"Don't worry, I think she means well," assured Jim. "Don't you, Janette?"

"Oh, absolutely," guaranteed Janette with a spirited grin. "Guess I just can't help myself."

"You know, most women find me irresistible," Rupert tried again to flirt with Janette to smooth things over and then changed his mind. "I know! All of Jim's lady friends are already married, so I'm just wasting my time."

Jim then slapped his knee and began laughing quite heartily. "I like this guy! And I think I know someone else who will, too."

"Luella?" guessed Janette.

"Heck, maybe even her great-grandmother," heckled Jim.

Janette then drew the symbol of a cross on her chest.

"What's wrong with Luella's grandmother?" questioned Rupert.

"That would be great-grandmother," corrected Jim with a chuckle, "and absolutely nothing's wrong with her, not for someone who's been dead for well over a hundred years!"

"Phew!" Rupert sighed with relief. "You had me worried there for a minute."

Janette was about to say something about Angie, but was quickly silenced by a warning glance from Jim.

"So, what about that metal box?" Janette nodded toward Martha Krain's metal box.

"Well, on second thought, perhaps we should just wait until we get there," decided Jim. "We're really not that far away."

"Now, that's good news," Rupert smiled weakly. It was obvious he was miserable.

"Here," Jim offered Rupert another bottle of water and a barf bag. "Please keep this handy."

"Thanks, man," acknowledged Rupert as he unscrewed the lid on the bottle of water and took a deep drink.

Janette then turned to Jim. "Any news on whether they got your motorhomes put in okay?"

"Let's take a look," suggested Jim. He unexpectedly pressed a button on the edge of the retractable wall table they were seated at. The surface of the table suddenly became a computer display.

"Whoa!" exclaimed Rupert as he sat back up to get a closer look. "I sure hope I'm not having hallucinations now, too!"

"MIRA, please engage satellite imaging mode," commanded Jim with a sly smile as he deftly secured the small metal box that had belonged to Martha Krain back inside the wall compartment.

"Satellite imaging mode engaged," replied a pleasant female voice. "Specify target."

"MIRA, please display a real-time image of The Powell Mountain Bed and Breakfast in ultra-zoom," answered Jim.

Immediately, a real time moving image of The Powell Mountain Bed and Breakfast appeared on the tabletop. Two new forty-foot motorhomes could be seen parked a short distance from the Wilson residence, where manzanita and other brush had already been cleared away to accommodate them. Several workers with orange vests and hardhats could be seen performing various tasks. One man was busy operating a backhoe and leveling an area for the two new outhouses that still sat in the trailer of the delivery truck nearby.

"Which motorhome's yours?" pressed Janette.

"Whichever one you don't want," conceded Jim. "It doesn't matter. As long as I have my own place while I'm there."

"Where will I be staying? With you?" Rupert gave Jim a questioning look.

"Actually, you'll be staying over in my old room at the B&B," informed Jim.

Janette then crossed herself again.

"Would you *please* stop doing that?" requested Jim as he gently grabbed Janette's forearm and carefully lowered it to her lap before letting go.

"What's wrong with the room at the B&B?" asked Rupert, rather suspiciously.

"Nothing's wrong with the room," assured Jim.

"Is this the crew of guys you were wanting me to work with?" Rupert suddenly asked.

"Not until you're up to it," responded Jim. "Perhaps in a couple more days. They are currently clearing away several years of overgrowth from an old salvage yard so that forensic experts can go over what's left."

"Forensics experts?" Rupert appeared worried. "What do they expect to find there?"

"We won't know that until they find it," answered Jim.

"So, they will need to clear away a good deal of it by hand, then?" realized Rupert. "That's going to be a hell of a lot of work!"

"That's only one of two sites," added Jim. "MIRA, please display a real-time image of the Shady Brook Winery. This is the other site where Carolyn should be right now, along with her friend Sherry and Detective Priest."

"A detective?" repeated Rupert. "I think you'd better tell me what's going on. Why is there a detective there?"

"Because it's a crime scene," replied Jim as he watched the tabletop screen change.

"Oh, my God!" exclaimed Janette as she stared with disbelief at the collapsed barn.

"Is that Carolyn?" pointed out Rupert.

"No, that's Sherry," muttered Jim as he searched in vain to determine where Carolyn might be.

"Looks like Sherry is limping pretty badly," noticed Rupert.

"Is that Detective Priest?" gasped Janette. "Look at his suit! It looks like someone tossed him into one of those wine barrels. And Sherry, too!"

"MIRA, please locate Carolyn Bennett-Hunter," commanded Jim. The screen panned over to a small out building several yards away.

"What is that beside it?" asked Janette as she tried to make it out.

"MIRA, zoom in closer," ordered Jim.

"Maximum zoom established," replied MIRA as the screen zoomed in one last time.

"Looks like a row of wine barrels," noted Rupert. "Odd place to stack them outside like that."

"Indeed," agreed Jim as he suddenly noticed Carolyn walking beside them with a man in an orange vest and hardhat and pointing toward the out building.

"There's gotta be fifty guys down there," estimated Rupert.

"Seventy-five, actually," revealed Jim.

Forklifts, backhoes, utility trailers and other equipment could be seen near the collapsed barn. Rakes, hand shovels, wheelbarrows, pickaxes, sledge hammers, crowbars and even a couple of handheld chainsaws could be seen either sitting on the ground or being used by the workers. A huge tractor trailer with wooden slatted sides was being used to load black plastic bags that were sealed at the top with bright yellow crime scene tape.

"What's in those bags?" queried Rupert.

"Probably evidence," assumed Jim. "There were twenty-three individual crime scenes inside that barn before it collapsed, and now they need to be removed, transported, and processed again."

Rupert was stunned.

"The seven wine barrels by the out building are believed to contain additional evidence," Jim finally mentioned. "Looks like that guy with Carolyn is setting up some GPR equipment now."

"Ground-penetrating radar?" questioned Rupert.

"To check for more skeletal remains," clarified Jim. "There were actually twenty-nine missing coeds between 1956 and 1975 in that area, so we're hoping the last of them have finally been located."

"Twenty-three from twenty-nine leaves six," perceived Rupert, "and there's *seven* barrels there."

"Don't they have to have the property owner's permission first to do all that stuff?" Janette suddenly asked.

"Most definitely," answered Jim with a slight smile.

"You didn't? You bought the place, did you?" grilled Janette.

Jim merely shrugged his shoulders as he powered down the computer display on the table's surface before sliding it back into its holder.

"What about probate?" questioned Rupert.

"Not everything automatically goes through probate," replied Jim. "Customarily, a decedent's probate assets are administered and distributed directly to the decedent's heirs, who is then free to sell them to whomever he or she chooses."

"I don't understand," scowled Janette. "You mean to tell me that *you* somehow got that man's heirs to sell you their property? What about the fact that it's a crime scene?"

"Tainted property is seldom something heirs wish to be strapped with," reminded Jim.

"Why on earth would you buy such a place?" demanded Janette.

"So I can eventually turn it into a wildlife refuge," described Jim. "I think Carolyn will like that, once all the debris is cleared away."

"Isn't there a waiting period of some kind before a purchaser can just step in and acquire possession of property that could potentially be subject to probate?" grilled Rupert.

"Technically, yes," confirmed Jim, "but on paper only. If property is titled correctly, it wouldn't have to go through probate at all. For example, if there were two owners who held the property 'by the entirety' each would own the property 100% (as if there were 200% of the property). Then, when one died, the other would automatically own the full 100% and it wouldn't pass through probate at all."

"Huh?" muttered Janette.

"Conversely," continued Jim, "if the property was held 'in common' each of the two would own only 50% and then when one died his/her share would pass through their will (or intestacy) which would almost certainly mean probate."

"I take it this particular property was 'by the entirety' then?" assumed Rupert.

"Exactly!" smiled Jim. "Still, there can be some issues if the person who automatically owns the 100% is the killer of the other owner, which we do not believe is the case here."

"That makes sense," nodded Rupert.

"And of course," elaborated Jim, "there are public policy reasons that legislatures don't want this to go unchallenged. In some states, a person can transfer their ownership before death, but not tell the other owner. Once person A dies, person B learns they only own 50% - that she/he has unexpectedly become a tenant 'in common' instead of 'by the entirety' as assumed."

"So, does that mean that Martha Krain and her brother owned the property they inherited 'by the entirety' then?" questioned Janette.

"By George, I think she's got it!" chuckled Jim.

"Just 'cause I'm not some overly educated big shot like you, doesn't give you the right to talk down to me like that!" snapped Janette.

"The girl's got spunk, too!" grinned Rupert with a subtle nod of appreciation.

"And don't you forget it, either!" smirked Janette.

"The bottom line," particularized Jim, "is that Otterman Enterprises is currently excavating the property with the written permission of its technical owner, the Honorable Michael Krain."

354

"Now, wait a minute!" Janette had become confused again.

"With Martha Krain being declared *non compos mentis* – which means mentally incompetent – at the time of Jerry Krain's death, her brother Michael became his sole heir 'in the entirety.'"

"She's the one that's dead now, whose metal box you have?" verified Rupert.

"That would be correct," confirmed Jim. "And, Michael and Martha were Jerry Krain's *only* remaining relatives when he died, so there would be no one else to step in and challenge anything."

"Just what is Otterman Enterprises, anyway?" pressed Rupert.

"Why, it's mine, of course," smiled Jim. He was not about to divulge to Rupert or Janette that it was a multi-million-dollar brokerage firm, or that he was its exclusive owner. Jim thought for a moment of the topnotch staff of trusted employees who had been hired to run his business for him and how grateful he was that it was only necessary for him to show up once or twice a year for board meetings.

"So, is that some kind of an investment firm or something, then?" guessed Rupert.

"Well, yes, I guess you could call it that," Jim finally admitted, "but it can also be whatever I need it to be at the time."

"It's not some kind of mafia organization, is it?" asked Janette suspiciously.

"No, of course not," laughed Jim as he leaned back to put his hands behind his head and interlocked his fingers.

"What about the other site you're having excavated, where the B&B is?" reminded Rupert. "Is that yours now, too?"

"That is not very likely," smirked Jim. Clearly, he was not interested in it.

Janette then crossed herself and shook her head as she thought of the Powell Mountain Bed and Breakfast.

"Is the B&B a crime scene, too?" Rupert suddenly asked.

"Unfortunately, yes," informed Jim as he got up to stretch before heading toward the pilot's seat. "It's time to fasten your seatbelts." Then to Janette, Jim smirked as he said, "You'll be all right. Trust me!"

# 9. The Shady Brook

**M**usic could be heard blaring from a cheap transistor radio inside the new barn where Jerry Krain was busy getting everything ready for the barn dance that night. The country-western music station was playing Jerry's favorite Slim Whitman song, though it was somewhat fuzzy sounding and slightly out of range. The students from Powell Mountain University who ventured out to attend the Friday and Saturday night barn dances at his winery, however, tended to favor a more upbeat repertoire. Frankie Avalon, Bobby Darin, Paul Anka, Ritchie Valens and Dodie Stevens were among some of the more popular choices from Jerry's handy stack of 45 record singles. Lloyd Price and Brook Benton were also popular selections, much to Jerry's consternation, since those particular vocal artists were people of color. Jerry always kept an RCA turntable available that exclusively played seven-inch 45 records. Its internal speakers were wearing out and starting to become tinny sounding, but were still loud enough to serve their purpose.

It was Friday afternoon on March 20, 1959, the last weekend of spring break. Many students had returned a day or two early from home leave, just to attend the weekend barn dances out at the Shady Brook Winery before resuming the usual drudgery of classes the following Monday morning.

"Hey cuz," greeted Ronald.

"Ronald!" Jerry was delighted to see him. "I didn't hear you pull up. How's my favorite cousin doin'?" The two men slapped one another on the back and shook hands.

"Just great, daddy-o," replied Ronald. "This is some crazy place you got here. I can dig it."

"Thanks, man." Jerry grinned with amusement. It was just like his cousin to try to use the vernacular of the young people he taught, even though Ronald Krain was 49 years old.

"Hard to believe all of this was nothin' but an overgrown thicket of forest land back in 1953." Ronald nodded with approval as he motioned with his hand at the sprawling hillside grape vineyard surrounding them.

"Well, yeah, it is." Jerry shrugged his shoulders in an attempt to appear modest about it, though it had been a tremendous task initially to fell the area now being used for his vineyard and to rid it of the many trees and underbrush that had once called it home. The remaining old growth forest surrounding his vineyard served as a constant reminder of his evil deed and threatened to once again reclaim its territory at some future date.

"Slim Whitman?" Ronald raised an eyebrow. "Better change that radio station in case some of your little groupies decide to show up early."

"Groupies?" scoffed Jerry. "I'm 51 years old already, hardly the type of man some beautiful young coed might take a fancy to."

"The power of the almighty dollar, daddy-o," reminded Ronald as he rubbed his fingers together on one hand.

"Don't call me that," requested Jerry. "Do you realize how ridiculous it sounds for a man your age to be talking like that?"

"At least I managed to get hitched before the big five-O, cousin! Better find yourself a little woman to mind the store before it's too late," advised Ronald. "Otherwise, you might just end up alone."

"Oh, I think I'd rather enjoy the bachelor life," chuckled Jerry.

"Say, what gives in there?" Ronald was suddenly interested in the improvements Jerry had made to the new alcove he had helped his cousin install over the winter months. "Olive green, really? And why that color?"

"Atmosphere, my boy," grinned Jerry as the two men walked over to his new alcove. "This is where the gift shop will be. It will feature everything from gourmet cheeses and other specialty food items to gifts and souvenirs – not to mention its highly sought after wines, of course. It will also have a small table at this end for tasting after tours, and a small cupboard up on the wall to keep the clean wine glasses and cocktail napkins."

"We can still cut you out some windows," offered Ronald. "It's total doom and gloomsville in here, man."

"Nonsense," differed Jerry. "It's supposed to be romantic, like a night in Paris. Check out the light fixtures I just got done putting up along the inside wall in here. All they still need is a little electrical work and then I can put in some low wattage bulbs. Those will be more wine-friendly than regular bulbs would be for this area. Besides, we wouldn't want to unwittingly damage the merchandise with radiation from exposure to too much light, now would we?"

Ronald glanced at the seven equidistantly spaced outdoor style patio lights on the alcove's inside wall. "You're gonna need 'em, daddy-o," smirked Ronald as he shook his head. "It just don't rock for me. And what about the ceiling? You gonna leave it as is? Unpainted like that? And what about the floor?"

"I wanted the ceiling and floor in the new alcove to match the ones in the barn," explained Jerry. "I kind of like the look of unfinished pressure-treated wood with only its rafters showing overhead and the rustic wooden floor. Gives it a practical look, too."

"I'll say!" laughed Ronald. "Right down to that gothic-looking chandelier you got hanging from the center peak of that thirty-foot ceiling over the dance floor in the barn. You gonna put a chandelier in here, too?"

"No, but I am going to start offering brunches on Saturday mornings again," described Jerry. "Empty wooden spools on their sides will serve as the new tables, and blocks from a large tree trunk can be cut into stools to put on either side of each one. Then, they can easily be dragged out of the way on dance nights."

"How many do you need?" questioned Ronald. "I can probably get you some of each."

"Maybe fifteen or twenty spools and twice that many stools?" proposed Jerry.

"Only if you agree to let me have the seats sanded," agreed Ronald. "The fairer sex in particular just hate getting splinters in their derrieres."

The two men then howled with raucous laughter.

"Daddy, daddy!" called three-year-old Martha Krain as she ran inside the barn and over to the alcove to join them.

"I thought I told you to wait in the truck!" Ronald Krain was displeased that she had disobeyed him.

"But, I'm hungry, daddy," pouted Martha as she stamped her feet and folded her arms to wait where she was.

"Just what do ya got in there, a hollow leg?" razzed her father. Ronald Krain sometimes wished he had not waited until so late in life to start a family, but there was little he could do about it now.

"No!" answered little Martha as she shook her head and tried to look pitiful at the same time.

"All right, then, we'd better go feed you," agreed her father. "But, not until we drop off the surprise we brought for my cousin Jerry."

"Will you be back for the dance tonight?" Jerry suddenly asked. "Perhaps you can just bring it then?"

"Oh, not this!" Ronald shook his head. "You'll definitely want time to try to get it set up before then."

"What is it?" Jerry was intrigued. "A new record player? I've been thinking about getting one that plays 33s."

"It's in the back of the truck." Ronald smiled mysteriously. "Plus, I'll probably need you to help me carry it in."

Jerry followed Ronald over to the forest green 1956 Dodge pickup truck parked outside. Not wanting to be left out of the excitement, Martha followed.

"Is that what I think it is?" Jerry stared with disbelief as his cousin Ronald lowered the back gate of his pickup truck. "A console television! How can you afford something like this?"

"Actually, it's our old one," grinned Ronald. "Just got Misty a new one for her birthday."

"A new television?" questioned Jerry. "That must have run you at least a hundred and fifty dollars!"

"Well, considering that I make $2.05 an hour, it should only take me about 73½ hours of work time to pay for it!" laughed Ronald.

"That's insane," objected Jerry. "Seriously, how long do you get to pay it off?"

"Not your concern," persisted Ronald. "Besides, I make more than twice minimum wage."

"What about your house payment?" reminded Jerry, concerned for his cousin's financial welfare. "Not just anyone can afford to live in a $25,000 home! Do you know how fortunate you are? What if you run short now?"

"Good thing gas is still just 30 cents a gallon," chuckled Ronald. He was not too worried about it.

"Well, I don't know what to say." Jerry was overcome by emotion. "This will be my very first television, you know."

The television was a 1957 RCA 21-inch "Flip Top" model with a large speaker on one side.

"I know!" smiled Ronald. "Maybe now those groupies of yours can enjoy watching some of the shows that come on when they're here. I've heard there's a show called American Bandstand where they play popular dance music and broadcast it live."

"I've seen that advertised in the newspaper," nodded Jerry as he helped his cousin unload the heavy console television from the back of his truck and begin carrying it towards the barn. "But, I think it only comes on in the afternoons. One of the kids was telling me about it."

"Well, there's gotta be something good on while they're here," countered Ronald. "They do show Walt Disney movies at 8:00 on ABC, but the kids would probably need to leave before it's over just to make it back to their dormitories before curfew."

"There is that," huffed Jerry, who was unaccustomed to carrying heavy furniture.

"Of course, you'll need to put up a pretty high antenna to get any kind of reception, especially way out here," pointed out Ronald.

"Probably so," agreed Jerry as he struggled to see where he was going, since he was the one walking backwards.

"Misty's mother sent her $25.00 spending money for her birthday, too," muttered Ronald, obviously displeased about it.

"For clothes?" presumed Jerry as he and Ronald set the television down over near the alcove entrance, but facing toward the barn area.

"What I don't understand is how one woman can have so many clothes and still think she needs more!" Ronald shook his head.

"That kind of cash could buy half a dozen bags of groceries," calculated Jerry. "Or fill up a 25-gallon gas tank at least three times!"

"Yes, I know," sighed Ronald, "but it is her birthday money to do with as she pleases."

"Mommy said she might get me a new dress to match one of hers," bragged Martha.

The men had clearly forgotten about Martha until now.

"I really need to get down to St. Diablo to pick Misty up," mentioned Ronald, "before it gets any later."

Just then, Jerry Krain's black rotary dial wall phone began ringing. "Maybe that's her now, wondering where you are?"

Ronald waited while Jerry walked over to answer the phone, to see who it was.

"Misty?" greeted Jerry. "Yes, he's here."

Ronald started over to where Jerry was, expecting to take the phone's mouthpiece from him so he could talk with his wife.

"Okay, I'll tell him," agreed Jerry as he hung up before Ronald could get there.

"Tell me what?" frowned Ronald, upset that Misty had not wanted to speak with him.

"She said to tell you she's riding back with her friend Ginger," informed Jerry with a disapproving look. "That woodcutter guy is headed up to your place with a load of firewood, anyway, so it's right on his way to bring the two of 'em back."

Ronald Krain's nostrils flared with silent rage. How dare his wife and her friend be seen riding with a black man! Especially around these parts! What if someone they knew saw them?

"Like I said, cousin," reminded Jerry, "I'm thinkin' bachelor life agrees with me just fine!"

"I can't believe she would do something like that!" fumed Ronald.

"Misty did say she would come to help chaperone the dance tonight," reminded Jerry.

"We'll be here," informed Ronald Krain rather coldly as he grabbed little Martha's hand and started for his truck.

"Hey, thanks again for the television!" called Jerry. "I'll see what I can do about getting it set up before tonight."

Misty Chadwick (Krain) had once been a student of Ronald Krain's, sweeping him off his feet from the moment he first laid eyes on her. Though only half his age, Misty had easily managed to turn his head. She knew absolutely nothing about woodworking, but had decided to take the class anyway, just so she could expand the selection of eligible male prospects in her life.

Misty had been 20 years old at the time of her marriage to Professor Ronald Krain, a marriage of necessity due to her untimely pregnancy. Although Ronald had never been completely convinced that the child was his, he married her anyway, just in case. After all, he did have his reputation to protect. That was three short years ago, in 1956.

Though only five feet, five inches in height, Misty seemed much taller than she was. Perhaps it was her slender build, tight clothes and high heeled shoes, but Misty definitely was tall on southern charm. Her bleach blonde hair was worn in a pageboy style, curled inward at the bottom, just above her shoulders, with overgrown bangs combed neatly over to one side in the front.

Obsessed with wearing the latest clothing styles, Misty had become quite an expense for Professor Krain. Needless to say, her stunning wardrobe continued to turn many heads, and often. The blouse dress she wore on the afternoon of March 20, 1959, was hot pink, lowcut in the front, and sleeveless. Its matching hot pink belt showed off her long slender waist quite nicely. The short white sweater she wore over her shoulders did little to keep off the chill of the early spring weather, even though the sun was out. And, though it was not officially summer just yet, Misty wore white high heeled shoes with pink and white tennis socks neatly turned down at the top. Her well-tanned legs were clean-shaven and bare. Misty's hot pink nail polish and lipstick were as noticeable as the false eyelashes and heavy eye makeup she wore.

Misty's friend Ginger Martin was also considered by most male conquests from the area to be somewhat less than choosy, always trying her best to entice and seduce any unsuspecting prey with her charms. Ginger was one year younger than Misty, and they were virtually inseparable, especially when it came to shopping excursions.

Woody had hesitated at first to give Misty and Ginger a ride, but it was not in his nature to refuse anyone in need of his help. After carefully putting their packages in the back, he helped each of them into the passenger side of his truck, gingerly closed the door, and hobbled around the beat-up old pickup to climb in from the driver's side.

"Ya sure yer mister ain't gonna mind me takin' y'all back up der?" questioned Woody as he carefully pulled his bad leg - the one with the wooden foot - into his truck and closed its door.

"Why should he mind?" flirted Misty, who was sitting in the middle, closest to Woody. She had tried for the past two years to get Woody to notice her, without success.

"I dunno," shrugged Woody as he started up his pickup and shifted it into gear before taking off. "De Professor did seem a mite bit put out de last time I dun did a delivery up der. After all, you is his woman. Can't say as I blame him."

"Oh, I'm sorry," apologized Misty with a big Cheshire grin as she deliberately rubbed her leg against his. "He must have seen me noticing how handsome you are."

Woody nervously grabbed his white corncob pipe and put it into his mouth, mostly out of habit.

"Here, let me help you with that," offered Misty as she grabbed the book of matches on his dashboard and pulled out a match.

"You gonna put anything in it first?" chuckled Ginger upon noticing the pipe was empty.

"In de glovebox," muttered Woody. "'Tis an old home grown remedee frum de south."

Ginger opened the glovebox and removed a small leather pouch. "Uh, what have we here?"

"Can we try some, too?" grinned Misty. She was well aware of what it was but had never tried any before.

"'Tis a very bad idea, ma'am," pointed out Woody as he slowed down and shifted the truck into low gear for the first hairpin turn. "De reefer pipe, it ain't for you."

"Nonsense," differed Misty as she carefully reached for Woody's pipe and removed it from his mouth. She then grabbed the pouch from Ginger, removed some of the special tobacco inside, and stuffed it into Woody's pipe.

"Maybe later," insisted Woody as he grabbed his pipe from Misty and carefully placed it inside his ashtray.

"It sure would be a shame if anyone else found out about your special tobacco," razzed Ginger, intimating that his secret might no longer be safe unless he gave in to their request.

Woody drove in silence for several moments before realizing that the two voluptuous women beside him were not about to give up. "Ya got me," Woody finally said. "Go ahead."

Misty smiled in triumph as she snatched Woody's white corncob pipe from the ashtray, lit it up, and began smoking from it.

Ginger suddenly grabbed the pipe from Misty and smoked some, too, relighting the contents with another match as she did.

"Ya'll shud slow down a bit on dat," cautioned Woody, "'til ya know how it does ya."

"Oh, it does me just fine," assured Misty with a wicked smile, suddenly feeling the intoxicating effects of it.

"Me, too!" giggled Ginger as she smoked yet more.

"De Professor," reminded Woody, "he'll be most upset if old Woody takes y'all home like this."

"He already knows you're dropping us off when you bring up this load of firewood," advised Misty as she took the pipe from Ginger and finished off what was left inside.

"Plez, ladies," implored Woody. "Don't do dis."

"We probably have had enough," agreed Misty as she suddenly thought of her husband and how he might react. Ronald Krain would be angry enough as it was that she and Ginger had dared to ride with Woody! But, if he were ever to find out they had smoked Woody's special tobacco, there was no telling what he might do.

"I'm starved!" announced Ginger as she looked again in Woody's glovebox to see if there was anything to eat.

"Ain't got nothin' fer ya to eat, ma'am," apologized Woody as he slowed the truck again for the next hairpin turn.

"Let's see what's on the radio," suggested Misty as she turned on Woody's old dashboard radio and began turning the channel knob.

"Wait! Turn it the other way!" directed Ginger. "*Personality*, by Lloyd Price! I love that song!"

"Isn't he the one that did *Stagger Lee*?" questioned Misty.

"That's him," nodded Ginger as she began singing along with the song on the radio.

Woody finally smiled and shook his head. Music was his one true weaknesses and before he knew it, he was singing along with them.

After singing several popular songs together, Misty suddenly asked, "What would you think about coming up to one of the barn dances to sing for us?"

"I'm perty sure de folk up there wudn't want my kind der," reminded Woody.

"Oh, come on!" pleaded Ginger. "I hear you've even got your own band."

"He does?" questioned Misty with excitement.

"Woody and the Woodcutters," mentioned Ginger with a sly grin. "Word gets around."

"Deys jus sum o' de boys I used to work with," replied Woody, clearly uncomfortable to be put in such a situation. "When I first lost me foot, dey would stop by fir a visit now 'n den. Fore' long, we was jammin' on sum tunes, just to pass de time."

"I hear you guys are quite good," challenged Ginger. "My friend Ronda told me she heard you guys play at a pub down in town one Friday night."

"Dat was just fir fun," grinned Woody as he slowed for yet another hairpin turn.

"What kind of songs do you do?" persisted Misty as she again rubbed her leg against Woody's and shamelessly flirted with him.

"Well," began Woody, who was beginning to feel most uncomfortable, "just sum older songs."

"How old?" quizzed Misty.

"*Old Man River* wud be one of 'em," revealed Woody.

"Anything more recent?" asked Misty.

"Sum stuff by de Platters and den a few Elvis songs," admitted Woody rather reluctantly.

"Oh!" sighed Misty. "I absolutely adore both of 'em! You absolutely must come perform for the dance tonight. Besides, it's my birthday! I insist."

"Perhaps we shud see what de Professor thinks o' dat," cautioned Woody as he slowed to pull into the driveway leading up to the Krain residence.

"Oh!" screamed Ginger. "*The Great Pretender*! I love that song!" She then turned up the radio so she and Misty could sing along with it. Woody merely smiled and shook his head.

Professor Ronald Krain had easily heard them coming and managed to be in the driveway waiting when they got there, with his hands on his hips. The scowl of disapproval on his face when they pulled up went unnoticed by Misty and Ginger, but caused Woody to reach over and turn off the radio immediately.

"Oh, don't turn it off!" objected Ginger.

"We's here, ladies," mentioned Woody as he pulled to a stop.

Misty smiled and waved at her husband from inside Woody's truck while she and Ginger waited for the woodcutter to come around and open the door for them.

Woody grabbed their various shopping bags from the back and carefully handed them to Ginger and Misty as he helped each of them from the truck.

Professor Krain glared with particular disapproval as his wife took Woody's hand before stepping down from the truck, and gazed at

Woodrow Wilson as if he were an undesirable insect of some sort that needed to be squashed.

"Oh, Ronald!" beamed Misty as she came over to give her husband a hug while trying to juggle the various shopping bags she was carrying. "Wait until you see the new shirt I got you to wear to the dance tonight!"

"I can't wait," replied her husband, rather unemotionally. "Your daughter is just finishing up a late lunch, perhaps you should go inside and check on her."

"Oh, before I do," interjected Misty, "I've asked Woody if he and his band can come perform at the dance tonight. Do you think that would be all right?"

"It *is* her birthday," reminded Ginger as she winked at the Professor with a crooked smile.

"We'll see what we can work out," promised Ronald. "You ladies go inside now. I'll be along shortly."

Woody swallowed uncomfortably as Mr. Krain approached him.

After waiting to be sure the ladies were inside, Ronald Krain put his hands back on his hips and shook his head with displeasure.

"I kin explain, sir," began Woody.

"Don't you EVER give my wife or her friend a ride like that again!" interrupted the professor. "She was supposed to call me and she knew it! How dare you! What will people think?"

"I's sorry, sir," apologized Woody, as he looked down to avert Ronald Krain's penetrating glare and uncomfortably shifted the weight from his wooden foot to his good one. "It'll never happen again, sir."

"You got that right!" fumed Mr. Krain as he grabbed Woody by the front of his shirt and shoved him up against his truck and continued to hold him there for what seemed like an eternity to the woodcutter.

"I'll tell you what," proposed the professor. "We'll forget about it this time, provided this load's on the house."

"Oh, yes, sir!" agreed Woody. He silently wondered how he could afford to go without being paid for an entire load of firewood, but held his silence about it. He was well aware that Ronald Krain belonged to the Crusading Knights of Powell Mountain.

"Good!" smirked Ronald Krain as he let go of Woody's shirt and gave him another little push against the truck for good measure as

366

he did. "And when you're done here, you can go round up your band. I'll expect to see the whole lot of you up at the barn tonight. Be there at seven o'clock sharp. That way you'll have time to get all set up before the kids start showing up."

"What if de rest o' de band ain't all around?" feared Woody.

"Oh, I think you can manage to locate them," smirked Ronald Krain. "After all, it is my wife's birthday tonight, and we wouldn't want to disappoint her, now would we?"

"No sir," replied Woody. "Me 'n de boys, we'll be der."

"Chop, chop," prompted Ronald Krain as he clapped his hands together and then motioned toward the covered storage area where his firewood was normally kept.

Woody immediately grabbed the first armload of firewood and hurried over to it.

Professor Krain watched with folded arms as Woody made several more trips, hobbling as fast as he dared without losing his balance on his wooden foot.

"And another thing," added Ronald Krain.

"Yes, sir, anythin', sir," promised Woody as he reached into the back of his truck to grab more firewood.

"If I *ever* see you touch my wife again," threatened Ronald Krain, "I may just have to round up some of *my* boys so we can string us up some Mississippi windchimes. Do I make myself clear?"

Woody momentarily glared with unbridled rage at the professor but then forced himself to look away.

"I didn't hear you, boy," taunted the professor.

"Good thing den dat old Woody's frum South Carolina," muttered Woody as he forced himself not to give in to the desire he suddenly had to rip off his wooden foot and beat Ronald Krain to within an inch of his life with it.

"See you tonight, then," smirked Ronald Krain as he turned to slowly saunter into his house.

Woody fought back his rage with great difficulty. How dare Ronald Krain treat him like that! And what would he do if the professor's young wife continued her unwelcome advances toward him at the dance that night? Was the professor deliberately setting him up?

Woody had been born on New Year's Day in 1909 and was now 50 years old. He sadly thought of his wife Harriet and wished there were more he could offer her. At forty-seven years of age, her dream of having children someday was growing slim. After three miscarriages already, it was hard to tell what the future might bring. In any event, Woody determined that any children he and Harriet might have would get schooled. None of them was going to end up like him, with only a fourth-grade education to fall back on! And especially, having to grovel for a living to the likes of someone like Ronald Krain!

Still, the Wilsons had successfully reclaimed the original family homestead – but only because it was haunted and no one else wanted it. Woody finally finished unloading the rest of the firewood from his truck and sadly shook his head as he thought again of the financial loss. How would he explain it to Harriet? The three dollars he would have made might have been used to buy milk, bread, eggs, vegetables, and even a package of ground meat! Why had he allowed Ronald Krain to take advantage of him like that?

Woody climbed inside his truck and angrily slammed the door shut. How would he convince his friends to come give what would undoubtedly be a "free" performance for one or more members of the Crusading Knights that evening? Woody shook his head with chagrin as he started the engine of his rickety old pickup truck.

Thankfully, the professor had not even noticed the fact that Misty and Ginger had smoked some of his special tobacco! Woody smiled with relief as he grabbed his white corncob pipe, stuffed more of the special tobacco inside, and lit it up for another toke.

Inside the Krain residence, Misty and Ginger had already managed to devour an entire platter of chocolate chip cookies. Little Martha had helped them, of course.

"How about some milk with your cookies?" offered Ronald Krain rather sarcastically when he came inside.

"Don't mind if I do," grinned Ginger as she grabbed a glass from the cupboard, opened the refrigerator, and quickly located the bottle of milk inside.

"I'll have some, too," requested Misty.

"Me three!" laughed Martha as she devoured the last cookie in her possession.

"You do realize those were for the dance tonight?" questioned Ronald with a sigh of frustration.

"Oops!" laughed Ginger as she wiped the remaining cookie crumbs from her face before gulping down the glass of milk.

"Hollow legs must run in the family," muttered Ronald as he started for his study.

"Wait!" called Misty as she hurried to the couch where her shopping bags still sat, grabbed one of them and brought it to her husband. "Here's the shirt I was telling you about!"

"Ginger?" called Ronald. "Can you watch Martha for a few minutes. I'd like to have a word with my wife alone."

"Sure!" agreed Ginger as she sauntered over to the refrigerator to see what else there was to eat inside.

"Yes, dear?" flirted Misty as she put her arms around her husband's neck and tried to kiss him.

"Later," responded Ronald as he grabbed her arms and pulled them away. He then abruptly tossed the shopping bag onto a nearby chair. "Follow me."

"Anywhere!" agreed Misty as she took his hand and allowed herself to be led upstairs and into their bedroom.

"Close the door," instructed her husband.

"Absolutely!" grinned Misty as she closed the door and then began undressing.

"We're not doing that right now!" advised Ronald rather curtly.

"What's wrong?" pouted Misty as she slowly began to rebutton her hot pink blouse dress back up again.

"I'll tell you what's wrong!" shouted Ronald Krain. "I saw the way that negro was holding your hand when he helped you out of his truck! And the way you were looking at him!"

"What?" Misty feigned surprise. "You've got to be kidding me? Woody's a married man!"

"And you're a married woman! At least when it suits you! Tell me, just why did you ask the woodcutter for a ride home, rather than calling me as agreed?" persisted her husband.

"Well, he was right there," argued Misty. "It just seemed easier at the time. Besides, I didn't want you to have to go out of your way if you didn't need to."

"You don't think being strapped with a three-year old to watch for the day was going out of my way?" hollered Ronald.

"Martha is a good girl," pointed out Misty. She was now afraid. Her husband's temper could easily get out of hand if provoked.

Ronald Krain thought about mentioning the fact that he was not even sure the child was his, but decided against it – for now. The important matter at hand was his wife's inappropriate association with a black man, and the fact that she potentially could have been seen by anyone in the community!

Shaken by her husband's unexpected outburst, Misty sat on the bed and nervously waited to see what he would say next.

Finally satisfied that Misty had been appropriately put in her place, Ronald softened. "Hey, I know it's your birthday, and I'm sorry if I overreacted, okay?" Ronald then sat on the bed beside Misty and put an arm around her. "It's just that we do have our reputations to protect, especially with my job as professor over at the school. Do you understand how important that is?"

Crocodile tears began streaming down Misty's cheeks, smearing her makeup. Her lower lip quivered as she sniffed and slowly nodded.

"Good girl," smiled Ronald. "Now, go fix your makeup and put on something more appropriate for the dance tonight. And perhaps Ginger can help you make up another batch of cookies before we leave?"

"You don't like the dress I have on?" frowned Misty, ignoring her husband's remark about the cookies.

"I'm sure there's probably a new one somewhere in one of those bags on the couch?" snickered Ronald Krain.

"Maybe there is," replied Misty, trying to appear timid about it.

"So, what kind of shirt did you get me?" asked Ronald.

"One of those western ones," described Misty. "It should go great with your turquoise bolo tie – the one with the knight in shining armor on it."

"Okay, I'll be sure and wear it. Thanks," mentioned Ronald as he kissed his wife on the cheek before leaving to go back downstairs.

At seven o'clock sharp, Woody and the Woodcutters arrived at the Shady Brook Winery in Woodrow Wilson's beat up old pickup truck. Woody's home-made wooden flute sat on the seat beside him. His buddy Rolo rode shotgun, holding his banjo on his lap.

Leon and Mike rode in the back, and had been practicing during the drive. Leon was mostly a vocalist, but also played the harmonica. Mike played the accordion. The unlikely group of musicians was well rehearsed and their eclectic collection of instruments blended nicely together to produce a most unique sound.

Jerry Krain had just finished installing the antenna for his new television set but had not been told of the band's performance that evening. Surprised to hear the sound of *Why Do Fools Fall in Love?* emanating from the front of his barn, Jerry came to see who was there.

"Gud evenin' Mister Krain, sir," greeted Woody as he climbed from his truck. "De professor said we shud be here rite at seven."

Jerry stared with disbelief at the four black men. Didn't they know that this was the main meeting place for the Crusading Knights of Powell Mountain where they held their annual rally each year?

"Dis is Rolo," introduced Woody. "He be de banjo man."

"Howdy, sir," grinned Rolo as he stuck out his hand.

"Humph!" snorted Jerry, without bothering to shake it.

"And dis be Leon and Mike," added Woody as his other two friends jumped from the back of his truck with their instruments and approached. All of them were younger and taller than Woody, and well-muscled from their daytime jobs as lumbermen.

Rolo was only 25 years old and still single. Leon and Mike were 30 and 45 years old, respectively, and both were married. They all had on the very best clothes available to them, though obviously worn and out of style.

"May I assume that the good professor intends for you boys to perform at the dance tonight?" questioned Jerry. He clearly was displeased about the arrangement. Having the woodcutter deliver his firewood each week was one thing, but this was another matter entirely!

"Yes, sir!" smirked Woody. "He said we shud be all set up before de kids start showin' up for de dance."

"Indeed!" grunted Jerry. "Right in there, then."

Woody and his friends exchanged interesting but silent glances as they grabbed their instruments and went inside the Shakespearean style barn. "Nice place," mentioned Rolo.

"The kids usually dance right out there in the middle," indicated Jerry, "so anywhere on the side will work."

"How 'bout over there?" nodded Mike at the refurbished wooden church pew along one wall. "Woody'll need a place to sit down when he plays, and I kud use one, too. De accordion kin get pretty heavy after a while."

"I kin get by," differed Woody.

"I take it the professor plans to be here shortly?" presumed Jerry.

"Dat wud be my guess," responded Woody as he and his band walked over to the pew to sit down and practice.

How dare his cousin pull a stunt like this! Jerry scowled at Woody and the Woodcutters as if they were a small army of cockroaches that needed to be vanquished from the premises. Hopefully, he would be able to get the television hooked up and working soon. Perhaps then, the band would not be needed!

Mike had dabbled in electronics before joining the lumber crew and had once considered becoming an electrician. Unfortunately, the racial prejudice of the day had been a factor in ruling out that possibility.

Jerry Krain cursed under his breath as he tried unsuccessfully to hook up the television.

"May I?" questioned Mike as he approached.

"You think *you* can hook this thing up?" doubted Jerry.

"I kin try," offered Mike, unwilling to allow Jerry's sour attitude to dissuade him from showing off his expertise.

"Go for it," insisted Jerry as he backed away and waved his hand toward the troublesome television.

In less than ten minutes, Mike had managed to hook up and get the television working. The local news was being broadcast on all four channels. During a commercial, it was announced that *The Adventures of Rin Tin Tin* would be on next on ABC.

"What's on the other channels?" demanded Jerry. "How does this thing work?"

"Just turn dis knob right here, sir," demonstrated Mike.

Rolo had picked up the newspaper laying on Jerry's future tasting table and read, "*Your Hit Parade* starts at 7:30 on CBS."

"Let me see that!" demanded Jerry, unhappy that Rolo had touched his newspaper. "What's *Buckskin*? That's on NBC."

"A western," informed Rolo.

"What about *Man Without a Gun*?" frowned Jerry.

"Dat's a western, too," advised Rolo. "On de NTA channel."

"Humph!" snorted Jerry. "I suppose all of you have televisions already, too?"

"Not me, sir," advised Woody. "But, de rest of 'em do."

"Duzn't *Walt Disney* come on at 8:00 on ABC?" asked Leon.

"What's the world coming to?" Jerry shook his head with disdain. It was inconceivable that three of the four black men here in *his* barn had managed to acquire television sets before he had!

"Hey, cuz!" greeted Ronald from the doorway. "I see you've met the band?"

"We've met," confirmed Jerry.

"Good thing we was here, too," mentioned Rolo.

"Thank you, boys, for hooking up the television for me," acknowledged Jerry as he shot Ronald Krain a look of disapproval.

Ronald raised his eyebrow with surprise and then smiled with amusement at his cousin's predicament.

"Misty, always a pleasure," nodded Jerry as he noticed her approaching with a platter of cookies.

"Thanks for having us here," replied Misty as she walked over to the *tasting* table to set the platter down.

"Those are for our other guests," advised Jerry as he noticed Rolo eyeing the delicious cookies. "If there's any left over, you boys are of course welcome to help yourselves."

"Yes, sir," frowned Rolo, displeased by the conditions.

"Where's your friend Ginger?" wondered Jerry.

"She's at our place, watching Martha," Ronald answered for her.

"Oh, turn on *Your Hit Parade*," requested Misty. "It's on CBS."

"Go ahead," Jerry shrugged his shoulders in resignation. "It is her birthday."

Rolo smiled in silent triumph as he walked over and changed the channel on Jerry Krain's television. "Happy birthday, Miss."

"That's Mrs. to you," advised Ronald Krain.

"Yes, sir!" acknowledged Rolo, almost sarcastically.

"I guess *they* still need to show you how your new television works?" Ronald razzed his cousin Jerry.

"I'll get you for this," promised Jerry.

"For what?" Ronald affected innocence.

"You know full well what I'm talking about," differed Jerry. "I like your bolo tie, by the way. Especially the shining knight on it. That's a symbol that used to mean something to you!"

"Let's take this outside, cousin," directed Ronald. "We wouldn't want to upset our guests."

"Our *guests*?" scoffed Jerry as he followed his cousin outside. "As far as I can see, you and Misty are the only two that have arrived so far. The others are nothing but a bunch of uninvited interlopers! I can't even imagine what the guys would think if they saw *them* here!"

"Well, they aren't going to, daddy-o," assured Ronald. "And the only other guests stormin' this joint will be nothing but a bunch of liberal college students who couldn't care less."

"Very well, then," replied Jerry. "I sure hope so, for both our sakes. We could get ousted from the order for something like this."

"We'll be fine," differed Ronald. "Trust me."

By eight o'clock, nearly two dozen college students had arrived to attend the barn dance. The new television was not as much of a novelty as Jerry or Ronald had hoped it would be, but the band was an instant success. Woody and the Woodcutters played one popular tune after another, including *Why Do Fools Fall in Love, Blue Suede Shoes, The Great Pretender, Heartbreak Hotel* and *Only You (And You Alone)*.

Misty Krain danced with one young man after another, flirting shamelessly with each of them. Her husband sat on the sidelines watching her every move. Then, when Misty began flirting with the members of the band – Woody in particular – Ronald Krain reached his breaking point.

The hour passed quickly and it was soon time for the students to return to the school so they would get there before curfew. Several of them had made the trek to the outhouse already, several yards up the hogback outside. Except when in use, the lantern Jerry kept handy for such trips was customarily located by the main door, along with a pack of matches.

Misty suddenly had to use the outhouse most desperately and grabbed the lantern from a student returning from the outhouse. Thankfully, it was already lit.

"Ya'll kin't go up der by yerself," reminded Woody, who just happened to approach from behind her. "'Tisn't safe."

"Come with me?" pleaded Misty. She was nearly hopping up and down to keep from wetting on herself.

"I dunno," objected Woody. "Yer man wud be most upset about dat. Lemme see if I kin find him. Me thinks he's in de alcove."

"I can't wait!" informed Misty with finality as she adjusted the flame on the lantern and headed for the hogback.

"Lord Almighty!" muttered Woody as he hobbled after her. He knew there were wild animals in the forest and that it would be unwise for Misty to travel to the outhouse by herself. Hopefully, her husband would be none the wiser and they would both make it back unnoticed, especially by the professor!

Misty nearly ran the last half of the way, leaving Woody to shuffle along after her in the dark. Twice, he nearly stumbled and fell.

Realizing he had to relieve himself also, the woodcutter decided to make use of a nearby tree as he waited for Misty to emerge from the outhouse. There was no "colored" outhouse on the property, anyway. He was nearly done when she came back out, and flushed deeply with embarrassment when she saw him.

Misty grinned with unabandoned delight as she watched Woody tuck himself in and zip his pants back up. She had not even had the courtesy to look away!

"I's most sorry, ma'am," apologized Woody. "Guess I kudn't wait, nether."

"Say, what's in there?" Misty suddenly asked as she noticed the nearby shed.

"We must git back," advised Woody.

"Nonsense," differed Misty as she headed for the shed with the lantern. "I just wanna take a look inside."

Woody had no choice but to stay with her, in order to see, since Misty had the lantern, but was most uncomfortable about it. What if the professor were to notice them missing and follow after them?

"Check it out," called Misty from inside.

"Misty, plez," urged the woodcutter as he stepped inside the shed. "We shudn't be here."

"Tell me you haven't dreamed of this moment?" challenged Misty as she slipped her arms around Woody and began kissing him on the mouth.

"We jus' kinnot do dis!" objected Woody as he struggled to push Misty away. "I's a married man!"

"So's my husband," purred Misty as she tried again to force herself upon him.

Meanwhile, down in the barn, most of the students had departed already. It was almost nine o'clock. Ronald Krain and his cousin Jerry were now quite anxious for the band to leave, as well, though none of them seemed to be in any hurry. Suddenly it was obvious that they were waiting for Woody, who was nowhere to be seen.

"Where's the lantern?" Ronald demanded of Jerry. Misty was nowhere to be seen, either, and he had not observed her slip out.

"You lookin' for Mrs. Krain?" asked a handsome young college student who was outside by his old jalopy.

"Yes, have you seen her?" quizzed the professor.

"I saw her headed up to the outhouse," volunteered the young man's date. "With the lame guy, from the band."

"The lame guy? From the band?" Ronald Krain flushed with rage. "Thank you!"

Unable to think of anything else but Misty being with Woody, Ronald made his way up the hogback in the dark. Why in the world would they be up there together? The only thing there besides the outhouse was an old shed his cousin used mostly for storing gardening tools or for sorting and preparing grapevine starts, if there were any.

"Hey, where you going?" questioned Jerry as he hurried to catch up with him. "You'll need this."

"Thanks," muttered Ronald as he absentmindedly took his cousin's flashlight from him. "What about you? How will you get back?"

"Always keep a spare," grinned Jerry as he pulled another flashlight from his coat pocket. "Hey, if you see Woody, tell him the band is looking for him. They're anxious to be on their way."

"I will certainly do that," promised Ronald as he continued alone up the hogback.

"See ya soon," grinned Jerry as he watched his cousin storm up the hillside.

Ronald Krain had worked himself into a frenzy by the time he finally arrived at the outhouse, but no one was there! He then headed for the old shed nearby.

Without warning, he grabbed and yanked open the door. Inside was his wife Misty, with her arms around the woodcutter's neck. They appeared at first to be kissing, but instantly it was apparent that she

376

had been trying to force herself upon Woody, and that he was attempting to shove her away.

"Oh, how could you?" Ronald made a face of disgust.

"'Tis not how it looks," Woody tried to explain. He was still busy trying to fend off Misty's unwanted advances, just as he had been prior to Ronald Krain's arrival, but without success. "She won't listen to me, sir. Plez make her stop!"

"He's lying!" claimed Misty, to save face. In truth, she was angry that Woody had rejected her attempts to be intimate with him, and that he'd been trying to shove her away when Ronald Krain had shown up.

"You little tramp!" hollered Ronald Krain as he grabbed Misty by the front of her new baby blue dress, causing the fabric to rip.

"What are you doing?" screamed Misty.

"First, you go riding around town with this man, and now you try and force yourself upon him?" yelled her husband. "A *black* man, no less? How could you do something like this?"

Misty began sobbing and babbling incoherently.

"I want nothing more to do with you!" informed Ronald Krain. "Not ever!" He then shoved her away with all his might, causing Misty to stumble and hit her head on the corner of the gardening table. She quickly lost consciousness and fell onto the concrete floor with a loud thud. Blood gushed from an open wound near her left temple.

"And YOU!" growled Ronald Krain as he glared at Woody. "It would sure be a shame if you were to go to prison for the rest of your life for this, wouldn't it?"

"But ...," Woody stopped in midsentence.

Ronald Krain suddenly grabbed an old bowie knife with the insignia of the Crusading Knights on its handle. It had been stuck point first into the gardening table. He then brandished it toward the woodcutter. "If you say anything about this to anyone, anyone at all, you will live to regret it, boy. And, your wife might get mighty lonely with you in prison."

"Please, sir, I knows nothin'! I swears, not ever will I say a word, not to anyone!" promised Woody, most solemnly.

"Then take that band of yours and skedaddle!" ordered Ronald Krain. "And best you be quick about it, too, boy."

Tears of anger and rage had begun to stream down Woody's cheeks as he glanced one last time at the limp body of Misty Krain on the floor in the lantern light. Was she still alive? Woody's hand shook as he picked up the lantern to leave. He and the professor locked eyes for an eternal moment, and what passed between them was inexplicable. The incident Woody had just witnessed would never be mentioned again by either of them, but would always be there, between them.

"Was sure a shame that she took off and left town with that vacuum cleaner salesman," muttered Ronald Krain, intending for Woody to overhear his every word.

"A horrible shame," agreed Woody as he hurriedly left the old shed and made his way back to the huge new barn below.

"Der you are," grinned Leon. "We was gonna send de cavalry after ya."

"What's up?" demanded Mike. It was clear that the woodcutter was extremely upset about something.

"Nothin' at all. 'Tis fine," assured Woody. "We best be movin' out now."

"Aren't dey gonna pay us?" questioned Rolo.

"That's Ronald Krain's department," laughed Jerry, who had overheard their conversation.

"Me 'n de professor, we kin work it out later," promised Woody.

"You sure you're okay?" asked Mike again.

"Never better," lied Woody as he and his friends climbed into his old pickup truck.

Jerry watched in silence as Woody started up the old pickup truck and slowly drove away. What was keeping his cousin? Something clearly was wrong. The remaining guests were finally gone. Quickly pulling his flashlight back out, Jerry hurried up the hogback to see what might be amiss. Was Ronald alright? Had his cousin and the woodcutter had a confrontation of some sort about Misty?

Even suspecting the worst, Jerry was ill prepared for what met him when he arrived at the shed.

Woody drove in silence as he took his friends to their homes. Though none of them had any idea what had happened, they knew better than to press Woody about it. He would tell them in his own good time.

378

It had taken Woody longer than expected to finally get home, and it was nearly midnight by the time he pulled into the long drive leading to his place. Stunned by what he saw, Woody came to a sudden stop. Silhouetted against the old two-story stone building where the Woodcutter and his wife Harriet lived was a burning cross! Thankfully, the burning ground cover surrounding it had not yet reached the residence!

With no thought for himself, Woody scrambled from his truck and hobbled as fast as he could past the burning cross and into his home. "Harriet!" screamed Woody. "Harriet?"

His wife had been asleep upstairs and was unaware of the burning cross out front. "Woody?" called Harriet as she stretched, put on her bathrobe and started for the stairs in her bare feet.

"Der's a fire out front!" hollered Woody. "Hurry!"

Harriet raced down the stairs at once and followed her husband outside. The two of them began grabbing handfuls of dirt and tossing as much of it as they could at the area around the burning cross. Harriet then took off her bathrobe and began beating at the flames with it while Woody hurried to his shed and returned with an old bucket and a shovel.

"Ders no time to fetch any wader frum de well," muttered Woody angrily as he continued to shovel dirt directly onto the fire until finally managing to extinguish most of it. Only then did he take the time to kick down the cross before fetching a bucket of water to pour on what remained of the embers around it, and on the cross itself. Woody then dug through them again with his shovel to stamp out any remaining danger from the charred wooden cross that now lay on its side in front of his home. *How dare the professor do this!*

"Who could be responsible?" questioned Harriet. She was quite shaken and sadly picked up her bathrobe to assess the damage to it – it had been a gift from her late mother.

Woody considered telling her what had happened with Misty and the professor, but decided against it. Harriet would be enraged and demand justice. There would be no convincing her that his continued silence was all that stood between him and an unjust prison sentence for something he hadn't done.

This was not the first time Woody had seen a burning cross in front of his home, nor would it be the last. And, Woody was no stranger to what it meant, either. Clearly, it was a reminder from the professor that Woody had best keep his mouth shut about what he had seen.

*Was Misty still alive?* If only Woody knew, but he couldn't afford to concern himself with it any longer. The safety of his own dear wife Harriet would be in serious jeopardy if he dared.

On Saturday evening, March 21, 1959, several of the same students from the previous night had returned to the Shady Brook. Any who had witnessed or knew of Misty Krain's trip up the hill with Woodrow Wilson would need to be eliminated.

"Are you sure about this?" questioned Jerry. "If we just come clean about the whole thing now, it will be over, especially with it being an accident like that!"

"And have the entire community know that *my* wife was in a compromising situation with a *black* man?" argued Ronald. "Absolutely not! Can you even imagine what the brethren would do to us?"

"Well," sighed Jerry with despair, "at the very least we'd probably each find burning crosses in front of our homes."

"Or go to trial," pointed out Ronald. "With my only witness being the woodcutter!"

"He'd no doubt testify any way you tell him to," smirked Jerry.

"And do you really think they'd accept testimony from one of his kind in a white court?" scoffed Ronald.

"Hey, I'm really sorry about Misty," mentioned Jerry.

"Well, I'm not!" growled Ronald. "As far as I'm concerned, that little tramp got exactly what she had coming to her!"

"You don't really mean that?" challenged Jerry.

"There's no way she's going to continue making a fool out of me," differed Ronald. "As far as people will know, she left town with a vacuum cleaner salesman. We did have one stop by the house on Thursday. How should I know where they went?"

"So, you really do intend to eliminate whoever was at the dance last night?" Jerry shook his head with trepidation.

"Not everyone," assured Ronald. "Just the ones who might say anything, or any who become a threat in the future. Definitely the kid with the jalopy that left after the others, and that girl who was with him. They knew for sure that Misty had gone up there with the woodcutter, and were actually the ones to tell me about it."

"I can't believe you're even thinking about doing something like this!" Jerry continued to oppose Ronald's suggestion.

"And I suppose YOU would like to go to prison for the rest of your life?" posed Ronald. "As an accomplice? Why didn't YOU go to the authorities when you first found out about this? Won't they want to know?"

Jerry pursed his lips with anger and glared at his cousin. "I want no part of it."

"Well, you're already a part of it! You've got one dead body, cemented inside a wine barrel up by your shed!" reminded his cousin. "And the shoes you wore when you helped me mix up the cement are still inside your shed!"

"We can't kill all those people," persisted Jerry. "We just can't! What would little Martha do if she ever found out what you've done?"

"Technically, it was an accident," justified Ronald, rather coldly.

"That one was," muttered Jerry. "What about the others?"

"Collateral damage," assured Ronald. "No one will ever be any the wiser, if we do this as planned. Why heck, we can probably make 'em all look like accidents. Everything will be okay. Trust me!"

## 1975

Karlin and Carolyn were enjoying a scrumptious meal at Maria's Mexican Restaurant. Neither of them had been invited to the Valentine's Day activity on Friday evening, February 14, 1975, so had made dates instead with two young men from their English Literature class, who had promised to meet them at the restaurant.

"Did you say Eula actually went to the banquet with Al?" questioned Karlin.

"That's what she told me," related Carolyn.

"I thought she didn't want any of the students or faculty to know she was dating him," mentioned Karlin as she scarfed down another bite of her enchilada.

"Well, now that they're engaged, perhaps that changes things," assumed Carolyn. "At least she has a date."

"That's too bad we couldn't get Stacia to come down here with us," remarked Karlin. "She really needs to get her mind off things, especially now."

"Can you blame her?" replied Carolyn as she sadly shook her head. "I still can't believe it myself."

"Are you sure Alfredo was on board that flight when it went down?" grilled Karlin. "Perhaps it was a mistake?"

"If only it were, but there's no mistake. They even recovered the body," reminded Carolyn. "The dental records verified it was him."

"What a loss!" frowned Karlin. "Such a nice-looking guy, with his whole life still ahead of him."

"Good thing he made Stacia hang onto that ring he wanted to give me," added Carolyn. "Otherwise, it would have been lost forever."

"Didn't Stacia still try to give it to you, even after that?" pressed Karlin as she grabbed a handful of tortilla chips from a basket on the table between them.

"Yeah, she did," confirmed Carolyn, "but I insisted she keep it. After all, it did belong to her mother and grandmother. It should stay in their family."

"Would you have actually married him?" Karlin raised an eyebrow out of curiosity as she dipped one of her chips in a small bowl of salsa before devouring it.

"I'll take the Fifth on that," replied Carolyn with a slight smile as she, too, grabbed some of the delicious chips and put them on her plate. "Who knows?"

"He was absolutely crazy about you, you know," reminded Karlin. "That guy would have walked on water for you."

"Unfortunately, that's exactly what he did," replied Carolyn, more seriously. "Say, shouldn't those guys be here by now?"

"They did say they'd meet us here at six," confirmed Karlin.

"Well, it's half past seven now," pointed out Carolyn.

"Good thing we brought enough money with us to pay for it," muttered Karlin. She was not happy about being stood up.

"Hopefully, they have a good excuse," Carolyn laughed sardonically. "Good thing we went ahead and ordered."

"Tell me about it! Hey, did I mention that I finally got a nurse's uniform?" asked Karlin. "It used to belong to Lydia, the girl that went missing after Thanksgiving."

"Lydia Cain?" scowled Carolyn. "Does that mean they've given up the search?" Carolyn then took a bite of rice.

"Quite some time ago," revealed Karlin. "Her roommate Martha finally decided to clear out Lydia's stuff. Most of it was sent back to Lydia's parents, but Martha remembered that I'm working at the nursing home now so offered it to me."

"Isn't *your* job the one that used to be Lydia's?" grilled Carolyn.

"Actually, it is," shrugged Karlin.

"That's kind of creepy," opined Carolyn.

"It's a job." Karlin shrugged her shoulders. "Say, how's your knee doing these days, anyway? Even being roommates, we hardly get to talk much anymore. It seems like one of us is always busy studying and going to classes, or working!"

"My knee?" Carolyn was puzzled for a moment.

"From when you fell down that flight of stairs on your way to worship service last semester?" reminded Karlin.

"Oh yes, right at the end of Christmas break," recalled Carolyn. "That was when I managed to step on the hem of my granny skirt, and slipped down that flight of stairs."

"At least you still made it to the chapel in time to turn in your last worship card," reminded Karlin.

"I did get quite a lecture from the school nurse, though," informed Carolyn. "She couldn't believe I went to the service with blood oozing down my leg like that. She said that if I'd only gone in right when it happened, they could have put stitches in my knee."

"They didn't?" Karlin was surprised.

"Apparently, if you wait too long to get stitches when something like that happens, it becomes too late," remembered Carolyn. "I sure got a heck of a scar on it now, though."

"Humph," nodded Karlin. "Say, shouldn't we call Woody to come take us back? He did say to let him know if those guys didn't show up."

"Let's pay first," suggested Carolyn. "Then he won't have to wait for us – in case he gets here right away."

383

"Okay," agreed Karlin as the two of them got up and headed for the cash register.

"Hey, what are two nice young ladies like yourselves doing out alone on a Friday night?" questioned another customer who was also at the cash register paying for his meal. He was a clean-cut older gentleman about sixty-five years of age.

"Looks like we're in the same boat," laughed Karlin as she reached for a mint from a small bowl by the cash register.

"Let me get that," offered the man, as he started to take Karlin's receipt from her.

"We got it," declined Karlin as she handed a ten-dollar bill to the woman at the register. "But, we were stood up by our dates and have no idea how we're going to get back up the mountain."

"Hey, I'm going that way," informed the man as he handed an extra five-dollar bill to the waitress as a tip.

"Are you going as far as the school?" Karlin hopefully asked. "Perhaps you could drop us off?"

"It would be my pleasure, ladies," smiled the man.

"Hey, thanks!" beamed Karlin.

Carolyn remained silent but followed the two of them outside. The man drove an older pickup truck, probably from the 1950s, but it was clean. Something about the man made Carolyn uncomfortable, but hopefully it was just her imagination.

"Jerry Krain," the man introduced himself as he shook hands with Karlin and then with Carolyn before opening his passenger door for them. "Owner of the Shady Brook Winery."

Karlin and Carolyn exchanged a look of surprise. Would the owner of a prestigious winery be driving an older vehicle like he was?

"You both students at the school?" questioned Mr. Krain as he started up the engine.

"Freshman year," revealed Karlin.

"I was your age once," grinned the man as he put the truck into gear and took off.

"If this is any trouble at all ...," began Carolyn.

"And you are?" asked the man.

"Oh, I'm sorry!" apologized Karlin. "I'm Karlin Gomez, and this is my roommate, Carolyn Bennett."

Carolyn scowled ever so slightly at Karlin, but she did not notice. Why was it necessary for her to give the man their last names?

"Nice to meet you both," nodded Jerry Krain, "and no, it's no trouble at all."

Jerry was actually less than pleased that one of his passengers was of Hispanic descent, but gave no indication of it in his expression. Perhaps her association with a white girl rendered her to be of some redeeming value. Unknown to his passengers, Jerry had spent the past sixteen years ridding the area of what he and his cousin Ronald considered to be undesirables.

"How long has your winery been there?" wondered Carolyn. She knew of an old abandoned winery farther up Powell Mountain Road, but had not seen any others.

"Well, it's actually been closed for a while now," admitted Jerry, "but it was something in its day."

"The Shady Brook?" recalled Carolyn, suddenly realizing that was the name she had seen on the road sign while previously driving past it.

"Yes, ma'am," confirmed Jerry. "And you should have seen her in the day, all shiny and new. Lots of kids from the school used to come out there on Friday and Saturday nights for the big barn dances."

"Barn dances?" frowned Karlin, immediately visualizing a square dance.

"Top songs from the day," advised Jerry. "Songs like *Blue Suede Shoes, Heartbreak Hotel* and *Only You (And You Alone)*."

"Oh, Elvis songs," recognized Carolyn.

"The Platters, too," recounted Jerry, "and others."

"Did you have live performances, then?" grilled Carolyn.

"Only once," revealed Jerry, more seriously. "Just some local band. For most of the dances, the kids played 45s on a turntable. Bet you don't know what those even are?"

"My grandparents used to play the seven-inch 45s on an old RCA turntable they had," recalled Carolyn.

Jerry nodded with approval. "Say, if you girls don't have to be back right away, I could show you the place. What do you say?"

"I don't know," Carolyn started to decline.

"We'd love to!" accepted Karlin, despite the glance of disapproval Carolyn had given her.

"We do have some homework we need to finish up," reminded Carolyn, hoping to persuade Karlin otherwise.

"Then I'll just drop you off at the school then," Jerry easily agreed. "But, I can certainly have you back before curfew if you would like to come up for a spell. Is it still at nine o'clock?"

"Yeah, it is," verified Karlin.

"And you could brighten the life of a lonely old man, even if only for an hour or so," persuaded Jerry Krain.

"Oh, all right," Carolyn finally acceded.

"Great, you're gonna love it!" beamed Jerry. "Trust me!"

One hour later, Carolyn and Karlin were walking down Powell Mountain Road on foot in the dark, after fleeing in fear from the Shady Brook Winery. They were still at least six miles away from reaching Powell Mountain University, and would probably miss curfew. But, there was nothing they could do about it now.

"How'd I know he'd turn out to be some kind of weirdo?" asked Karlin as she caught herself in time to avoid stepping into a pothole on the side of the road.

"What if he comes after us?" worried Carolyn. "There was seriously something wrong with that man, and I wouldn't put it past him. Did you see the look in his eyes when he came toward us with that bowie knife? He was totally wacked!"

"Is that the feather you picked up in his chicken-less chicken room?" scowled Karlin when she noticed it still in Carolyn's hand.

"Yeah, why?" questioned Carolyn.

"How do you know it doesn't have lice on it?" posed Karlin.

"Eeew!" scowled Carolyn as she tossed the feather down onto the side of the road and wiped her hands on the sides of her blue jeans.

"Better be sure and wash your jeans when you get back, too!" Karlin laughed to relieve the tension.

"No kidding!" agreed Carolyn.

"Say, you don't think he was trying to poison us, do you?" Karlin was serious.

"That's a good question," recognized Carolyn. "That wine smelled rancid, that's for sure! I can't imagine anyone drinking something like that, even if they drank!"

"I don't believe a person can cook eggs with alcohol alone and then make 'em safe to eat," added Karlin. "That's bunk!"

"Even if the wine weren't rotten, that would still be bunk!" laughed Carolyn. "Thank goodness we got away from him! Please don't ever put me in a situation like that again, okay?"

"Deal!" agreed Karlin without hesitation. "Hey, I'm really sorry about that. He seemed like a pretty decent man when we first met him at the restaurant."

"I know," nodded Carolyn.

All at once, a rickety old pickup truck pulled up beside them, traveling in the same direction they were headed. "Hey ladies, what you doin' way up here?"

"Woody!" exclaimed Carolyn and Karlin together.

"'Tisn't safe for y'all to be roamin' around up here like dis," pointed out Woody as he got out of his truck, hobbled to the passenger side, and opened the door for them.

"Oh, Woody! Thank you!" Karlin sighed with relief as she gave him a brief hug before getting inside his truck.

"Yes, thank you!" Carolyn smiled with relief and nodded at him as she climbed in after her.

Woody quickly circled the truck and got back inside. The engine was still running. "Really, what in de world wud you ladies be doin' up here? De Powell Mountain Killer kud be up here sumwhere."

"Our dates stood us up at the restaurant," revealed Karlin, rather timorously. "So, we met this man at the restaurant and he seemed really nice, at first."

"And den what?" frowned Woody.

"He was telling us about this old winery he has," volunteered Carolyn. "The Shady Brook."

Woody seemed visibly shaken for a moment but refrained from comment.

"I was the one who asked him to show us his winery," confessed Karlin. "He really made it sound like something grand, some historical thing we needed to see."

"Ya'll were at de winery?" questioned Woody with surprise. "Dats where I wuz, making a delivery. Wish I'd known ya wuz der!"

"I was just thinking the same thing!" exclaimed Karlin. "But, we weren't there for long."

"Only until the old guy tried to poison us and then came after us with a bowie knife!" mentioned Carolyn.

"Say what?" Woody furled his brow with indignation.

"After he got done giving us a tour of the place," clarified Carolyn, "the man told us he wanted to show us how to cook eggs with alcohol alone – rancid alcohol. Then, when we wouldn't eat any of it, he got all weird. So, we decided to leave, but then he picked up this big bowie knife and started coming after us, trying to persuade us to stay."

"Did he try 'n hurt ya wid it?" pressed Woody.

"Well, he didn't swipe it at us or anything," replied Carolyn. "It was just the menacing way he held it – and the way he looked at us – that made us afraid."

"Naturally we didn't go back to try to ask him for a ride," Karlin pointed out.

"Next time, plez call old Woody," offered the woodcutter. "Anytime, no matter de time."

Woody pulled up in front of the girls' dormitory, got out of his truck with the engine still running, and again hobbled around to open the door for his passengers. "Ya'll got ten more minutes 'fore curfew."

"Hey, thanks again," responded Karlin. "I don't know what we would have done if you hadn't shown up."

"Yes, thank you so much!" mentioned Carolyn as she got out of the truck, with Woody's help. "I think I'll take you up on that. It's just too bad we didn't know earlier that you were at the winery making a delivery!"

"Praise be to de good man upstairs dat I seen ya when I did," responded Woody.

*What if something really had happened to them without him knowing it?* wondered Woody as he watched them hurry up the dormitory steps. Woody silently thanked the Almighty that he had been able to give them a safe ride back!

Woody was very near the end of his rope with the Krain cousins and the horrible secret they had forced him to keep for all those years! Woody had no proof, but also suspected that other disappearances in the area over the years were somehow related to the original incident. Particularly, when several of the other young people that had been at the Shady Brook the night of Misty's demise had also mysteriously disappeared without a trace. Woody was not about to let any more victims fall prey to those monsters! Not if he could help it!

On Saturday, February 15, 1975, both Carolyn and Karlin had decided to sleep in after their harrowing ordeal the previous evening. It was already ten thirty in the morning.

"Hey, you two!" called Eula. "It'll be lunch pretty soon."

"Eula?" Carolyn yawned and stretched before sitting up. "What time is it, anyway?"

"Ten thirty," laughed Eula.

"Hey, you guys," greeted Stacia. "Where were you? We waited for you at breakfast."

"Speaking of food," interjected Karlin, who was now awake, "I'm famished!"

"How 'bout an early lunch?" proposed Carolyn. "I can be ready in no time."

"Mind if we play some tunes while we wait?" asked Stacia.

"Go for it," mumbled Karlin as she put on her bathrobe, and grabbed a towel and her toiletry kit before following after Carolyn. "We won't be long."

"Oh, hey you guys," called Eula as she followed after them and walked with them to the fourth-floor shower room. "Remember those two guys who were supposed to meet you last night?"

"What about 'em?" frowned Karlin. She definitely intended to have a word with them about not showing up for their so-called date!

"Steve and Mike, was it?" questioned Carolyn as she entered the shower stall dressing room and took off her robe.

"Yeah, that's them!" snorted Karlin as she entered the shower stall dressing room beside Carolyn's to prepare for her shower.

"They said to tell you how sorry they are," called Eula, who stood in the restroom's outer area nearby.

"I'll just bet they are!" fumed Karlin as she turned on the water and began to take her shower.

"They had a flat tire!" informed Eula. "They were gonna tell you at breakfast, but you never showed up."

"A flat tire, huh?" scoffed Carolyn. Like Karlin, she was still quite upset about their experience with Jerry Krain at the Shady Brook.

"How did you get back, anyway?" questioned Eula, who had decided to sit down on a bench nearby to wait for them. Undoubtedly, Stacia was up in the fifth-floor dormitory room listening to disco music and practicing her dancing skills.

"Hang on!" advised Carolyn, who was in the midst of washing her hair, and would not be able to continue the conversation until she was done.

Eula used the restroom while she waited and was also anxious to tell them about her date with Al Sandut the previous evening.

After fifteen minutes, both Carolyn and Karlin emerged from their shower stalls with towels wrapped around their heads, and wearing their bathrobes and slippers.

"It's about time!" chastised Eula with a teasing grin.

"So, what were you saying?" prompted Karlin as she walked over to the nearby sinks so she could use the mirror above them.

"How did you get back from town?" repeated Eula, as she came to stand beside them.

"We met this old guy at the restaurant," began Karlin as she spread the towel down onto her shoulders and began combing out her hair. "He really seemed nice at first."

"Huh!" scoffed Carolyn, who was also combing out her long, golden blonde hair.

"And?" urged Eula.

"He turned out to be a real creep!" informed Karlin as she turned on her blow dryer and began drying her hair.

"I'll say!" shouted Carolyn, who was also drying her hair already.

"What'd he do?" pressed Eula.

"First, he tried to poison us," advised Carolyn rather loudly, to be heard above the sound of the hair dryers.

"And then he came after us with a bowie knife!" added Karlin.

"What?" exclaimed Eula as she reached over and grabbed Karlin by the arm. "Just what did happen to you guys last night?"

"Well," explained Karlin as she turned off her hair dryer, "we made a run for it and got away unscathed."

"Seriously?" Eula was flabbergasted.

"Thankfully, Woody happened along and gave us a ride back," mentioned Carolyn, as she turned off her hair dryer, too.

"It was ten minutes before curfew when we got here, too!" added Karlin as she finally wrapped the cord around her hair dryer before stuffing it back into her toiletry bag.

"Did you call the police?" grilled Eula. "About the old guy?"

"No, we didn't," advised Carolyn as she put away her hair dryer and pulled out her makeup kit.

"Let's just put on our makeup in the room," suggested Karlin. "You never know who might be listening down here."

Carolyn merely nodded in agreement before the three of them walked back up to the fifth-floor dormitory room.

"So?" pressed Eula as Carolyn and Karlin got dressed before sitting down at their "makeup table" desk to finish getting ready.

"What would we say if we did call the police?" asked Karlin as she put on her eye makeup.

"If some old guy tried to poison you and then came after you with a bowie knife, why wouldn't you call the police?" demanded Eula.

"First of all," interjected Carolyn, who was also putting on her eye makeup, "we have no proof that he actually was trying to poison us. It would just be our word against his."

"He was trying to tell us that you can cook eggs without heat by merely putting alcohol on them," elaborated Karlin as she put on her lipstick and rubbed her lips together.

"I do remember hearing something like that is possible, from my high school chemistry class," recalled Eula.

"Nevertheless," continued Karlin, "the alcohol he was using was rancid wine!"

"The stench was unbelievable!" corroborated Carolyn.

"And then he got all mad and offended when we wouldn't try any of it," described Karlin as she put on her earrings.

"How do you know he was offended?" frowned Eula.

"Gee, I don't know," interjected Carolyn. "Maybe it was the way he brandished that bowie knife at us when he followed us to the door and tried to convince us to stay."

"Yikes!" Eula shook her head with understanding. "No wonder you decided to leave! Where was this, anyway?"

"Oh, that's the best part!" laughed Carolyn. "Remember that rundown old winery up the road?"

"That's half way to Powell Lake," recalled Eula. "Yeah, I've seen it while driving by."

"The Shady Brook Winery," described Karlin, "was apparently some hotspot for college students to go to back in the 1950s, where they would play 45 records and have barn dances."

"Square dancing?" assumed Eula.

"That's what I thought, too." Karlin rolled her eyes. "But, the old guy said they played popular stuff, like Elvis and others from the day, and made it sound like some historical landmark we just had to see. That's how he convinced us to go there."

"But it's just a rundown old winery that's been closed for years," added Carolyn. "And the whole place stunk like rotten wine, probably the same stuff he tried to poison us with!"

"So, he really didn't try and poison you?" snickered Eula, after hearing the rest of their tale.

"You really need to smell something like that for yourself," persisted Carolyn. "That wine would have killed us! It was completely rancid and stunk worse than anything you can imagine!"

"She's right," agreed Karlin. "And there was something very creepy and sinister about that man, especially the look in his eyes when he was waving that knife around!"

"Sounds like you did the right thing to leave, then," nodded Eula.

"Oh, no!" muttered Carolyn as she began frantically digging through her purse.

"What is it?" asked Karlin.

"My wallet!" moaned Carolyn. "I know it was here when we were at the restaurant last night, when I gave you that ten-dollar bill to pay for our meal! And I know I put my wallet back in my purse after that, before we got in that guy's truck!"

"What does it look like?" questioned Eula as she and the others began looking around the room, to try to help Carolyn find it.

"It was a blue folding wallet!" Carolyn was quite upset. "How am I going to pay for my food? My food card was in there, too!"

"Could you have dropped it in the parking lot at the restaurant?" wondered Stacia.

"Absolutely not!" insisted Carolyn. "I remember seeing it in my purse while we were riding with him.

"What if you dropped it in his truck?" feared Karlin.

"Oh, God, I hope not!" worried Carolyn. "I have no desire to ever see that man again!"

"No worries," assured Karlin. "I'll buy your late breakfast. Then, after we find your wallet, you can buy the next meal for me."

"Perhaps you should eat first, before you continue your search," suggested Eula. "Maybe you'll remember where it is."

"Oh, no," fretted Carolyn. "I think I do know where it is!"

"Where?" pressed Karlin.

"Remember when I bent down to pick up that feather?" frowned Carolyn. "At the winery?"

"No way!" Karlin shook her head with trepidation.

"I'm pretty sure it fell out, right there," recalled Carolyn. "I remember hearing something at the time, and it must have been my wallet falling out onto that filthy floor!"

"Maybe Woody can take us back up there?" proposed Karlin.

"I sure hate to keep taking advantage of that man," differed Carolyn. "I know! Right after we eat, I'm calling Ron's Auto Shop to see if my car is ready yet."

"You'll still need to call Woody, to take you to get your car," pointed out Karlin. "And that's if it's even ready. What's it been, ten weeks now?"

"More than that," advised Carolyn. "That was right after Thanksgiving weekend, and yesterday was Valentine's Day already."

"That's just wrong!" opined Eula. "Perhaps you can get your car and have it towed someplace else? There's no way it should take anyone that long just to repair a ding in the fender!"

"You got that right!" Carolyn sighed with frustration

"Was there any money in your wallet?" queried Stacia.

Carolyn became sullen. "Probably twenty dollars, but that's not the worst of it! My driver's license, Social Security card, and other stuff was in there too! Including my picture of Lenny, where he wrote me a special note on the back!"

"Seriously?" Eula rolled her eyes. She had heard all she cared to about Lenny Owens.

"That's terrible!" sympathized Karlin, who understood how much the photo must mean to Carolyn, and how important it was.

"What if that guy at the winery is some kind of psychopath?" speculated Stacia. "And now he knows who you are, where you live, and everything about you!"

"You're not helping!" chastised Karlin. "Don't worry, we will find your wallet, somehow, even if we have to go back up there to that winery to get it. I know how much that photo of Lenny means to you."

On Monday, February 17, 1975, Deputy DAs Chip Priest and Ron Telluric decided to make one last sweep of the area that had previously been searched by other local authorities on the Wilson property. It was time to try to close their file on the Cain case, and no one else seemed interested in helping.

For Ron Telluric, it had been more of a hunch than anything. The snow had finally melted, even in the area of the hogback near the old logging road, and it made sense that anything hidden before might be more visible in the bright morning sunlight.

Songbirds could be heard overhead in the dense forest surrounding them. The intermittent sound of trickling snowmelt in the distance echoed across the mountain landscape.

"We really should be searching up by the lake," advised Chip. "Whoever murdered the Johnson boy probably just stashed the Cain girl's body nearby and we missed it somehow. The green Mustang we're looking for is probably up there, too."

"I disagree," replied Ron. "Literally dozens of searchers combed that area for weeks. Lydia's body is somewhere else, and so is the car."

"Why here?" pressed Chip.

"Just humor me," entreated Ron. "If we don't find anything by noon, we can go back up to the lake again."

"Okay," sighed Chip. "That sounds reasonable."

The two men finally agreed to start with the old logging road at the edge of the local woodcutter's property, carefully searching both sides of the road as they went. True, they did not have a search warrant, but the road itself was considered public domain by virtue of an easement held by the county.

"I'll take this side," volunteered Ron, "since I did that side when we were here before. Maybe one of us will see something the other one didn't. You never know."

"All right," agreed Chip as he reached down to pick up a stick so he could poke at things along the way as he went.

Ron suddenly stopped and stared with disbelief. "Hey, Chip, check this out!"

"Are you seriously kidding me?" demanded Chip, when he realized what Ron was looking at.

Ron bent down to grab a dried manzanita branch that had been stacked onto a pile of other dead brush. Seeing that the branch refused to loosen its hold, Chip came over to help. The two of them pulled with all their might before the branch finally gave way. Both of them fell butt-first onto the muddy road in the process. They sat there gaping with amazement at what had been uncovered.

"It's the car!" Ron shouted excitedly. "The green Mustang!"

"I see it," assured Chip, as the two of them got up and brushed themselves off. "Unbelievable!"

"I suppose we need to get a search warrant before we do anything else," realized Ron.

"Well, we probably do," agreed Chip, "since most of it is over the woodcutter's property line."

"Do you see anything like a body inside?" questioned Ron as he walked back and forth, trying to see what he could from the road.

"No, not really," replied Chip. "Let's call the local police and get a forensic team out here, too. We need to do this one by the book."

After taking what photographs they could of the long-missing green Mustang, the two lawyers hurried to get in their car and make the drive to town. The reception on their dashboard-mounted radio was completely blocked by the mountainous landscape in the area, so they would have to wait until returning to the St. Diablo District Attorney's office to share the news of their discovery.

"Hey, let's stop by that auto shop on the way," suggested Ron Telluric. "We can let the other Ron know it's okay to release the Bennett girl's car."

"Oh, yeah, good idea," recognized Chip.

"She's probably wondering by now why it took so long for him to repair that ding in her fender," laughed Ron.

"Who knows." Chip smiled as he shrugged his shoulders. "Women don't know much about cars anyway."

"I think he did tell her he needed to order a part or something," chuckled Ron. "But she didn't buy it."

"Well, we did find animal blood on her bumper, so naturally we wanted to run a second test to be sure," reminded Chip.

"That's just the way it goes," agreed Ron. "We did have to be sure. Now, there's no doubt whatsoever."

Later that afternoon, Carolyn received a phone call from Ron's Auto Shop, letting her know that the green Mustang was *finally* ready!

Woody had just picked Carolyn up from in front of the girls' dormitory and was giving her a ride into town.

"I's so glad to hear yer car be ready, Miss Carolyn," remarked Woody as he lit up his white corncob pipe and took a long drag from it.

"Me, too!" assured Carolyn. "Hey, I really appreciate all the rides you've given us lately. Especially that night you brought us back from up by that creepy old winery!"

"'Tis my pleasure," smiled Woody. "Old Woody is grateful fer Miss Karlin takin' de time to read de good book to my Harriet when she kin. I's only able to be der fer a short time each nite, specially wid de kids der at home waitin' fer me to cum fix 'em sumthin' to eat."

"What are their ages again?" asked Carolyn.

"Matthew, he born in '65," began Woody.

"That would make him ten?" calculated Carolyn.

"Yep, dat sounds right," agreed Woody. "And Mark, he goes to skool next year."

"Six?" guessed Carolyn.

"Yes'um," nodded Woody. "And Luella, me princess, she be walkin' for a while now, into everythin' she is."

"Eighteen months?" surmised Carolyn.

"Almost three," Woody smiled with pride. It was obvious that Luella was very important to him, and that he was proud of her.

"That's too bad they won't let the kids come visit their mother at that place," mentioned Carolyn.

Woody merely nodded in agreement as he took another toke from his white corncob pipe.

Each night after Karlin's evening shift at the Powell Mountain Nursing Home, she would visit with Harriet Wilson while waiting for Woody to come pick her up and drive her back to the school. It was not long until Harriet had asked if Karlin would read from the scriptures to her, as Harriet's eyesight was failing. Harriet had not wanted to mention to Woody that she needed glasses, for fear that it would strain the family's meager budget even farther than it already was, especially since she had been in the nursing home for nearly two months already.

"How long has your wife been in the nursing home now?" questioned Carolyn.

"Lemme see." Woody slowed for the next hairpin turn before answering. "Since right before Christmas."

"I'm so sorry." Carolyn could tell how much Woody loved his wife and that it was a touchy subject for him. "Hopefully, she'll be better soon."

"Dey just don't know." Woody sadly shook his head.

"If you don't mind my asking," questioned Carolyn, "do they know what's wrong with her?"

"Sumthin' with her blood," revealed Woody. "Blood cancer."

"That's awful!" Carolyn fought back tears after seeing the pained look on Woody's face.

"But, as de good book says," replied Woody, "I knows I will see her again sumday. Dey say she ain't got long."

Carolyn picked up and began thumbing through a tattered old Bible that Woody had laying on his dashboard. It was called *Good News for Modern Man* with a subtitle indicating that it was *the New Testament in Today's English Version.*

"'Tis easier to read den de old King Jimmy's version," advised Woody most seriously.

"It does seem easier to read," realized Carolyn as she opened the book to a page that was bookmarked.

"Dat be Mark," informed Woody after glancing to see what Carolyn was looking at. "It tells how de good man healed de sick."

Carolyn noticed that Mark 1:29-34 was underlined in red pen.

"Woody prays much, fer de good man's will fer Harriet," advised Woody as an unbidden tear escaped the corner of one eye.

Woody wanted to go on and say more – to confide in someone of his secret fear that the great Almighty had allowed this to happen to Harriet as punishment for him not telling anyone about what had happened to Misty Krain, and possibly to the others. But, he had three small children at home now, and had their safety to consider, as well. What would they do if another burning cross were to show up while he was out working? The last one had shown up when Luella was only six months old. Thankfully, he had been there at the time, but had barely gotten his family out in time. It had taken months to repair the damage to his home after that, including most of the first-floor furniture.

After riding in silence until reaching St. Diablo, Carolyn finally offered, "Please tell me what I owe you for all your help, Woody. I know you've gone out of your way."

"Yer money's no good here," advised Woody as he slowed to turn into the driveway at Ron's Auto Shop. "Just do somethin' kind for sumone else sumday."

"I will," promised Carolyn as Woody climbed from his truck one last time to come and open the door for Carolyn. "Thanks so much!"

"My pleasure, Miss Carolyn," bid Woody as he helped her from the truck. That was the very last time Carolyn ever saw Woody.

After a heated discussion with Ron about why it had taken so long for him to finally finish repairing the green Mustang's right front fender, Carolyn finally took a deep breath, sighed, and shook her head.

"I really should not be telling you this," stipulated Ron.

"You do owe me some sort of explanation," insisted Carolyn.

"Very well," agreed Ron, "but you must promise to keep this to yourself. I could get into trouble if anyone finds out I told you."

"Tell me what?" demanded Carolyn.

Ron merely waited for Carolyn to promise.

"Okay, fine, I promise," agreed Carolyn.

"Well," Ron leaned close and spoke in nearly a whisper, even though no one else was there. "The police did a complete forensic investigation on your car."

"What?" responded Carolyn, quite loudly.

"Shhh!" Ron looked furtively around. "For all I know, the place is bugged. "Those cops were all over this place."

"Why would the police do a forensic investigation on my car?" Carolyn was indignant.

"Remember that kid they found up at Powell Lake last November?" reminded Ron.

Carolyn suddenly felt as if she had been hit by a bolt of lightning. "Oh, my God! I do seem to remember something on the news about the police looking for a green Mustang after that happened. But, it wasn't mine!"

"Shhh!" Ron looked around again, and was obviously very nervous. "They know that now. The blood on your bumper was from some kind of animal or something."

"It was from a squirrel," muttered Carolyn. "And I felt badly about it, too! But, there was a mountain on one side of the road and a drop-off on the other! You've been up Powell Mountain Road, you know how it is."

"So, that's *really* how you dinged up your fender, then?" nodded Ron.

"I already mentioned that to you when I brought it in," reminded Carolyn.

"Well, it wasn't just that," continued Ron. "They were also looking for a car that might have been used to transport a body. The missing girl – and they still haven't found her yet."

"I don't understand?" frowned Carolyn.

"Well, someone had hosed out the back of your car," mentioned Ron. "It was still wet when you brought it in."

"Oh, how embarrassing!" flushed Carolyn. "My friend Stacia was drunk that night and threw up in the back seat. We did our best to clean it out before bringing the car in. But, I thought Karlin had already mentioned that to you." Carolyn was in no mood for playing games.

"Were *you* drunk when you hit that squirrel?" Ron raised an eyebrow and began to grin.

"Absolutely not!" informed Carolyn.

"Well, sorry it took so long," apologized Ron. "But, it was only today that the DA's office released their hold on your car."

"Why now?" wondered Carolyn.

"Hey, look, I've already said too much," replied Ron. "Just watch the news tonight."

"Oh, come on, tell me?" pleaded Carolyn. "You know how hard it is for students up there to see the news! They only have one small black and white television set down in the library."

"Oh, all right," agreed Ron, "but you didn't hear it from me."

"Absolutely not," promised Carolyn.

"Word is, they *found* the other green Mustang today," whispered Ron as he again looked suspiciously around to make sure no one else was listening.

"Really?" Carolyn was surprised. "What about Lydia Cain?"

"Is that her name?" frowned Ron. "Well, that I don't know. Guess you'll just have to watch the news anyway."

"I'll do that," agreed Carolyn as she signed the work order and took her car key from Ron. "Hopefully, I'll never see you again. No offense intended."

"None taken," grinned Ron. "Good luck! And watch more carefully for those pesky little rodents next time."

"Count on it," replied Carolyn as she got into the green Ford Mustang, started up the engine, and drove away.

"Where's Karlin?" questioned Carolyn as she entered the fifth-floor dormitory room.

"Last I saw her, she went looking for you," advised Rachel, rather tartly. She and Karlin had never gotten along and she couldn't care less where Karlin might be at the moment.

"Didn't you tell her I went into town to get my car?" pressed Carolyn.

"What are we, your personal secretaries?" snorted Sarah, as she looked up from the homework she was trying to do at her desk.

"Perhaps she figured you were over at your job," sniggered Rachel. "After all, it is a Monday, and a regular school day for the rest of us."

"I had permission from the Dean to miss the rest of my classes this morning, and you know it!" informed Carolyn, rather angrily. "And I did go to my first one, by the way."

"Well, it's afternoon now," grinned Rachel. "Won't Professor Krain wonder where you are if you don't show up for work?"

"Dean Forrest said she would let him know I might be late," countered Carolyn.

"Then he no doubt knows you'll be there any moment." Rachel was smug and Carolyn did not like her demeanor. Ever since the incident with Rachel's brother Dennis, things had not been the same.

"Fine!" snapped Carolyn as she grabbed her purse and left to walk over to the Industrial Education Building.

Carolyn had taken a risk driving back from town without her driver's license, but at least she finally had the Mustang back in her possession. Hopefully, she would locate her wallet, and soon! If not, she would need to get a new driver's license and Social Security card right away. Fortunately, the school had already issued her a replacement food card after cancelling the other one. Interestingly, no one had tried to use it.

Carolyn glanced sadly at the black spired rooftops on most of the older buildings towering above her as she walked across the campus, and suddenly thought of Alfredo. Could she have been happy with someone so dominant and possessive, had she agreed to marry him? Would he then have stayed longer and not been on that plane? Or, was his destiny to die in that plane crash? Tears began to stream down Carolyn's cheeks as she thought of the tragedy.

This place really does look like Camelot, considered Carolyn. And, the fifth-floor dormitory window towering above it all was not unlike the tower in which a young woman named Elaine had been trapped when Lancelot came to that town and begged the inhabitants to let him rescue her. Carolyn then frowned as she thought of the Crusading Knights of Powell Mountain. Would she one day be rescued by her *black* knight? wondered Carolyn as she thought of Lenny Owens.

Would she ever get her wallet back, that contained the precious signed photo of him? Strange that something she had taken for granted would suddenly mean so much. Carolyn vowed to find out why Lenny had not written or called as expected. Surely he must have tried to contact her at the Ashton address – unless, as she suspected, her letters had been intercepted and destroyed by her father!

The Industrial Education Building loomed ahead, reminding Carolyn almost of a prison. Why had she ever agreed to accept such a job? If she had known of her bosses' affiliation with the Crusading Knights before accepting it, she probably would not have. Still, she did need the money.

"There you are!" greeted Professor Kraven when he noticed Carolyn walking up the steps toward Professor Krain's office.

"Sorry I'm late," apologized Carolyn.

"Ronald mentioned that the Dean called," assured Professor Kraven. "Did you get your car back alright?"

"Finally, yes," smiled Carolyn.

"Well, it's about time!" chuckled Jim Kraven. "Next time, better find a quicker shop."

"I'll do that," promised Carolyn as she opened the door and went into Professor Krain's office, where her desk was located over to one side. An entire stack of student test sheets sat on the desk, waiting to be processed, along with other miscellaneous invoices and bills.

"Ronald said not to worry about it, if you can't get to 'em today," related Professor Kraven. He had followed her into the office.

"Okay, thanks," nodded Carolyn as she began straightening the papers into neater stacks. "Where is the Professor, anyway?"

"I'm not sure, but I did see him chatting earlier with some friend of yours - Karlee, is it?" Jim couldn't remember the name.

"Karlin?" questioned Carolyn.

"Yeah, that's it," confirmed Jim. "That Mexican gal." Jim's expression took on an air of disapproval at that point.

"Did they leave together?" grilled Carolyn, rather suspiciously.

"How would I know?" replied Jim with a shrug of his shoulders. Professor Kraven's poker face was hard to read, so Carolyn was unsure whether to believe him.

"Hey, would you mind if I took the rest of the afternoon off?" Carolyn suddenly asked. "I have some personal business I need to attend to."

"Sure, I see no reason why not," agreed Jim Kraven. "You may want to leave a quick note for Professor Krain, though, in case I'm gone by the time he returns."

"Okay, thanks," smiled Carolyn, doing her best to seem sincere. Her dislike for the Crusading Knights she was forced to work for was difficult to disguise.

Carolyn then wrote a quick note to Ronald Krain, letting him know that Jim Kraven had given her permission to take the rest of the afternoon off, and left it on his desk.

Should she have Woody give her a ride up to the Shady Brook? Or, should she go ahead and drive the Mustang, even if she didn't have her license back yet? Hopefully, she would find it at the winery. She couldn't bring herself to bother Woody again that day, so Carolyn decided instead to drive to the Shady Brook on her own.

Once she was behind the wheel again, Carolyn realized how much she had missed the freedom of being able to come and go as she chose. The old growth forest on either side of the windy mountainous road was lush, green and compelling.

Carolyn felt a tinge of sadness as she drove past the road where she and Alfredo had once parked to talk of their relationship, and she had let him passionately kiss her. Would her dad have been as disapproving of Alfredo as he had been of Lenny? Sadly, she would never know.

Just why was she going to the old winery by herself? What if the old guy really was crazy? What would she do if he came after her with that knife? Carolyn decided she would grab the crowbar from the back of her car before going inside, and use it to defend herself if necessary.

Carolyn thought of many things as she drove, including Joyce and Veronica, and how they had disappeared without a trace just two years earlier from the beach at Oceanview Academy. She was not about to let another one of her friends vanish from the face of the earth without doing her utmost to prevent it! She hoped earnestly that Karlin was not in trouble. And, try as she might to shake it, Carolyn continued to have a feeling of foreboding. Had Karlin gone back to the winery on her own to try to retrieve Carolyn's wallet? Did Karlin feel responsible for the loss of it, and her picture of Lenny?

Before long, Carolyn arrived at the Shady Brook Winery and slowed as she pulled onto its overgrown gravel road. Tall weeds scraped against the undercarriage of the green Mustang as Carolyn negotiated the various ruts and potholes. Even in daylight, the old winery was just downright creepy. The sinister-looking structure was in desperate need of repair. Why in the world would Jerry Krain have thought anyone might want to see it? Carolyn pulled to a stop in front of the old barn and cautiously got out of the car. Glancing around to be sure she was alone, Carolyn quickly went to the back of the car and opened the hatch. The rear cargo section beneath the hatch was lined with a green rug held down by large snaps. Beneath it lay the tire jack, wrench, crowbar, and a small tool kit. Without hesitation, Carolyn grabbed the crowbar before closing the hatch.

"Well, hello again!" greeted Jerry Krain as he approached. He actually seemed friendly and unthreatening at the moment. "What's the crowbar for?"

"After the way you were waving that knife around the other night," reminded Carolyn, "I wasn't sure whether I'd need something to defend myself with."

Jerry Krain thought that was incredibly funny, slapped his knee and laughed quite heartily. "At least that was honest. Well, come on in, I won't bite. And please, bring the crowbar if it makes you feel any better."

Carolyn continued to stand where she was, carefully studying Mr. Krain before saying anything else. She had already tightened and loosened her grip on the crowbar several times. "Have you seen my friend Karlin? The girl who was with me that night?"

"Not that I know of," grinned Jerry, almost making Carolyn feel foolish for asking. He did seem sincere.

"Well, the reason I'm here," revealed Carolyn, "is that I think I may have dropped my wallet when I was here. I thought perhaps Karlin might have come up here looking for it."

"No, sorry," chuckled Jerry. "But, you're sure welcome to come on in and look around. With your crowbar, of course."

Carolyn merely nodded as she approached the barn with her crowbar, keeping an eye on Jerry as she did, and giving him a wide berth at the same time. Carolyn proceeded to walk over to the table where Jerry had been mixing the foul-smelling eggs with rancid wine three nights ago. The remnants of it still sat in the cast-iron skillet and were absolutely putrid. Carolyn made a face as she passed by it and headed for the alcove where she had picked up the feather. After carefully searching every square inch of floor surface with her eyes, Carolyn sighed with disappointment.

"Is there a number where I can call you if I find it?" Jerry Krain had somehow managed to sneak up behind her and was calmly standing quite close. The easy-going smile on his face seemed to contradict a more sinister look in his eyes. Carolyn suddenly felt a cold chill; the hairs on the back of her neck and arms literally stood on end. It was as if she were in the presence of evil itself. Carolyn tightened her grip on the crowbar as she slowly backed away from Jerry Krain.

"Told you I wouldn't bite," chuckled Jerry. The grin on his face slowly began to match the ominous look in his eyes.

"Thank you for letting me look," mentioned Carolyn as she tried to appear calm and forced herself to smile nonchalantly. "I'm sure I must have dropped it somewhere else."

"And if I find the wallet?" grilled Jerry as he watched Carolyn work her way toward the barn door.

"Then if you would, please call Dean Forrest at the girls' dormitory," suggested Carolyn.

"I'll certainly do that," agreed Jerry as his entire countenance became more threatening.

404

Carolyn suddenly turned, ran to the green Mustang and climbed inside as fast as she could. The crowbar sat on the passenger seat beside her as she fumbled with the keys before starting the engine.

"Do come back, anytime," called Jerry Krain from the large doorway of the rundown barn.

"Thanks again!" called Carolyn as she put the car into gear and drove away. Returning to the Shady Brook Winery was definitely not on her list of things to do at some future time!

The queasy feeling in Carolyn's stomach stayed with her, even after getting back onto Powell Mountain Road. Was Karlin still there at the Shady Brook Winery? Had something happened to her? And, did Jerry Krain actually have Carolyn's wallet stashed away someplace?

# 10. Letters from Beyond

Luella had just finished putting away the food from the evening meal, and Carolyn was helping her dry off and put the dishes away. Meanwhile, Sherry was upstairs with ice on her sprained ankle, watching an old episode of *Downton Abbey* on Luella's wall mounted flat screen television. It was Friday evening, March 24, 2023.

Carolyn and Sherry had long-since changed and showered, after being dropped off by Chip Priest two hours earlier.

"You really don't have to do this," Luella reminded Carolyn. "Don't get me wrong, I'm grateful for your help, but you are a guest."

"Well, it's too early to go to bed," smiled Carolyn. "Besides, I'm one of those people that just needs to be doing something all the time. I never was very good at just sitting around and doing nothing."

"Girl, we definitely need to work on that while you're here!" chuckled Luella.

Five quick knocks on the front door suddenly caught both of them by surprise.

"I didn't hear anybody pull up, did you?" frowned Luella.

"Maybe it's Jim and Janette?" guessed Carolyn. "They probably had to park down by the road, what with all that construction equipment blocking the way."

"And that's another thing!" frowned Luella as she reached for a nearby broom with a heavy wooden handle before answering the door. "Jim will need to do something about that for sure!"

Luella then slowly opened the door, cautiously peering through the crack to see who it was before opening it any wider.

"Detective Priest?" Luella then pulled the door open wide.

"Jim back yet?" questioned Chip.

"Oh, honey, get on in here and let me help you with that suit!" instructed Luella. "That's the same one you were wearin' before! I can't believe you still got that stinky thing on!"

"Well, it's not like I have anything else handy to change into," advised Chip. "I just stopped by to make sure this was here for Jim to look at when he arrives. It's my case file. I expect you to guard it with your life, Carolyn. They finally uncovered it from that pile of rubble!"

"You went back up there?" Carolyn was surprised.

"I just had to make sure this file was okay," replied Chip. "Believe it or not, that was the first time in forty-eight years that file has *ever* been out of my possession! This will be the second."

"So much for the chain of custody," teased Carolyn. "Hey, that's the same way Jim Otterman was with his Oceanview file for all those years, too. Don't worry, I'll take good care of it."

"Jim's actually a pretty decent guy, you know," commented Chip. "I'm looking forward to sitting down with him tomorrow and comparing information. But, I need to get back to town now. My wife will be expecting me to pick her up. She's over with Andrea Telluric."

"I'm really sorry about Ron," mentioned Carolyn as she put a comforting hand on Chip's shoulder.

"Detective, have you even eaten anything yet tonight?" grilled Luella. "We got lots of leftovers."

"I was thinking of taking my wife and Mrs. Telluric out to Maria's," advised Chip.

"Not in that stinky old suit, you're not!" insisted Luella. "I have an old suit upstairs, and it's just about your size. You can take a shower while I dig it out for you."

"Your clothes do smell pretty bad," agreed Carolyn. "Sherry was trying to decide earlier whether or not to just burn the clothes she had on today. They're in the wash now."

"Mr. Priest, I can have your suit all clean and ready for you by tomorrow," offered Luella.

"Chip," corrected the detective. "Just call me Chip. Sure, why not? I guess I could use a good shower at that."

"And I can give you an extra blanket to spread down on the seats of your vehicle," added Luella. "Just in case."

"That's not a bad idea," realized Chip. "Thanks!"

"This way, Chip honey," indicated Luella as she nodded toward the stairs. "Follow me."

Aside from the past two days, this was Chip Priest's first social call to the Powell Mountain Bed and Breakfast after hours. His last visit before that had been on March 23, 1975, when he and Ron Telluric had witnessed the local Sheriff serve an arrest warrant upon Woodrow Wilson for the murder of Lydia Cain. Chip paused to study the large oil painting of Angie Wilson at the top of the stairs.

"That isn't you, is it?" questioned Chip.

"Heavens, no! That's my great-grandmother," informed Luella with a mischievous smile. "Hopefully, Angie won't bother you much."

"Angie, huh?" chuckled Chip. "Beautiful lady."

"Thank you," grinned Luella. "This room here was Jim Otterman's. For now, it's yours, and the shower is right in there. Just leave your dirty clothes on the floor. Clean ones will be waiting for you on the bed."

"I'll hurry and make sure I'm done before Jim gets back, then," assured Chip. "He'll no doubt want his room back."

"Actually, Jim will be staying in one of those new motorhomes outside," revealed Luella. "Said he needed more privacy than he was able to get here, with all us women folk hanging around. So, take your time." Luella then gave Chip a flirtatious grin and undressed him with her eyes before leaving.

"Okay then." Chip raised an eyebrow as he stepped into the bathroom and locked its doors. He sincerely hoped clean clothes would indeed be waiting for him, especially after having been the subject of a college prank once when some of his classmates had stolen his clothes from the locker room while he was taking a shower after gym class.

Meanwhile, Carolyn had taken Chip's file with her to the room she was sharing with Luella upstairs, and was seated at Luella's desk examining it. In fact, Carolyn was so engrossed by what she was reading in the file, that she did not hear Luella approach.

"The switch for the desk light is on the back," recommended Luella. "You'll hurt your eyes like that."

"Oh, thanks!" smiled Carolyn as she found and flipped the switch on. "Much better."

"Land sakes alive!" exclaimed Luella upon seeing one of the crime scene photos laying on the desk.

"Sorry about that," apologized Carolyn as she quickly turned the photo over so Luella would not have to see it.

"I think I'll just go watch some *Downton Abbey* with Miss Sherry," remarked Luella. "I need to stay up until Jim gets here, anyway. Old Carrot Top'll probably be starving by then."

"Please let me know when he gets here," requested Carolyn. "I need to show him this file."

"Humph!" Luella just shook her head as she started to leave.

"Luella?" called Carolyn.

"Yes 'um?" Luella stood at the doorway with her hands on her hips, waiting to hear what Carolyn had to say.

"I truly believe your father was innocent," commented Carolyn. "I still remember that last time he gave me a ride into town, to pick up my car."

Luella came over and sat down on the bed nearby.

"Woody had an old tattered Bible on the dashboard of his truck," remembered Carolyn. "Actually, it was one of those modern new testament ones, with everything marked and underlined. And, I still remember that he had a bookmark on a page in the book of Mark, where it talked about Jesus healing the sick."

"Daddy never let anyone touch that book," reminisced Luella. "It was very special to him."

"Well, he didn't seem to mind at the time," recalled Carolyn. "That was when your mother was in that nursing home, and my friend Karlin would read to her from the scriptures each night while she waited for Woody to come pick her up and give her a ride back to the school."

"So, you two really knew my daddy better than most folk, then?" realized Luella.

"Oh, I wouldn't say that, necessarily," differed Carolyn. "Let's just say we knew what kind of a man he was, and we were always grateful for his generosity in giving us rides when we needed it."

"That was Daddy, all right," nodded Luella. "I can barely visualize what he even looked like now, but I'll never forget that Daddy would've given anyone the shirt off his back. That's just the way he was, helping anyone who asked, even though we were dirt poor."

"I know," assured Carolyn. "And, if there's anyone who can find the evidence that will finally exonerate his name, Jim Otterman will be the one."

"Old Carrot Top," whispered Luella with a smile. "You know, I believe he will. Just a feeling."

"This was my friend Karlin," pointed out Carolyn as she turned the photo back over again. "I have a feeling that Jerry and Ronald Krain may have been responsible, but nothing will bring her back."

"Those nasty Krain folk!" spat Luella as she angrily studied the photo of Karlin's skeletal remains beside the wine barrel in which they had been encased. "They and those other Knights were all responsible for my daddy's death, too! I just know it. The head judge was a Knight, most of the cops were Knights, and even the prison guards where my daddy was kept were Knights!"

"The prison guards were Knights?" Carolyn asked with alarm. "But, why would they want to hurt Woody, if he was already in prison?"

"To keep him from telling anyone else what he knew," answered Luella. "There were terrible secrets between them Knights and my daddy, things that could be very damaging to them, if only there were proof, that is."

"But, you were only two years old at the time, when they arrested him," realized Carolyn. "How could you know that?"

"I have an old letter, written to me by my mama," revealed Luella. "It was in her things when she died. My foster mother gave it to me when I turned twelve. Said she figured I was finally old enough to have it."

"Do you still have the letter?" Carolyn hardly dared to hope.

"I do," assured Luella. "Perhaps my mama wouldn't mind if I let you read it, too."

"I would like very much to read it," advised Carolyn.

"Let me just get some clean clothes for Chip to put on, and I'll be right back," informed Luella.


After locating an old suit that had belonged to her late husband, Luella then found some clean socks, underwear and a shirt.

"Chip?" called Luella as she gently knocked on the door to the room where she had promised to have the clothes waiting.

"There you are!" replied Chip with relief. He was wearing nothing but a towel wrapped around his waist when he opened the door for Luella, and was just about ready to put his dirty clothes back on. "It's absolutely freezing in here!"

"Here I am," flirted Luella as she handed Chip Priest the stack of clothing. "Sorry it took me so long."

"I could have sworn I saw you in here earlier," mentioned Chip, "but you were wearing something else."

410

"Something like that?" smirked Luella as she nodded at the oil painting of Angie on the wall behind her.

"Actually," stammered Chip, "that's exactly what you had on. And the perfume you had on, strange that I don't smell it now."

"That was Angie, my great-grandmother." Luella grinned mischievously. "Sounds like she likes you."

Chip suddenly became solemn. "I heard once that this place was haunted, but seriously?" Chip then slowly glanced again at the oil painting on the wall and suddenly it seemed to lock eyes with him. It was almost as if Angie was trying to seduce him! Chip was again overwhelmed by the sickening smell of jasmine perfume and felt an involuntary chill run through his body.

"Better get dressed before you catch your death of cold," recommended Luella as she turned to leave. "I'll have a hot cup of coffee waiting for you when you get downstairs."

"Thanks!" Chip was so rattled by the realization that he had just seen a ghost that he had forgotten all about the fact that he was wearing nothing but a towel. Chip then flushed with embarrassment.

"See you downstairs, Chip honey," called Luella's melodic voice as she left.


Meanwhile, at the Killingham Lighthouse Bed and Breakfast, Sheree Otterman was pacing the floor. The guests had all gone to their rooms for the night.

"I'm sure Ray will be all right," comforted Ann as she brought her mother a warm cup of tea.

"We're just gonna have to close for the week," decided Sheree aloud as she stood up and walked over to the window to look outside. "We should be there at the hospital with Susan."

"We can't just send guests away that are already here, or that have paid for their rooms and expect to stay here next week! Susan will let us know if there's any change with Ray," assured Ann.

"Maybe Ted can get the Murrays to help out for a couple of days, while you and I drive up to Ocean Bay?" proposed Sheree.

"John and Jeon already have their hands full with all the animals at the wildlife center," reminded Ann. "And Ted has an enormous job, just maintaining and running the golf course!"

"Well, someone needs to run the bed and breakfast for two days!" Sheree had made up her mind. "At least the Roth House next door has an automated donation box and the tours are self-guided."

"There is that, but how can Ted and the Murrays possibly help with all of this on top of what they're already doing?" argued Ann.

Ann was worried not only about the injured and orphaned wildlife that needed constant care at the wildlife center, but also about the colony of feral cats she fed on campus near the dairy each day. Worse still, Professor John Murray was kept quite busy teaching Marine Biology at Oceanview Academy. Every other spare moment of his time was usually spent assisting his wife Jeon with the administrative responsibilities pertaining to the Killingham Wildlife Center nearby. And, her husband Ted was nearly at his breaking point without Ray around to help him with all of the yard maintenance and golf course responsibilities.

"I'm sorry," maintained Sheree, "but it's either that or send people away and close it down for a few days! I'm near my breaking point, too!"

"You're worried about Dad?" grinned Ann.

"Well, it's not like he's about to turn Carolyn's head and talk her into running off with him," muttered Sheree, "but I do believe he still has feelings for her, even after all these years."

"Good thing she's crazy about her husband, then!" laughed Ann.

"I guess I am just being silly," realized Sheree.

"The worst thing you probably have to worry about is whether he crashes that Learjet," teased Ann, "or ends up trapped in some cave somewhere."

"Being trapped in a cave is no laughing matter!" exclaimed Sheree as she thought of the time she and Ray were trapped in the bunker tunnel with Carolyn.

"I'm sure they're all fine!" smiled Ann as she gave her mother a hug. "But, I will ask Ted and the Murrays if they can look after things for a couple of days, okay?"

"Thanks!" Sheree put an arm around her daughter and stood there with her looking out the large dining room window at the setting sun in the distance as it spread its dying tentacles of light across the ocean's surface.

Over at the Ocean Bay Memorial Hospital, Ray Killingham continued to drift in and out of consciousness as he lay on his hospital bed. The ceaseless sounds of the IV drip and the constant blip of the heart rate monitor beside him had become nothing less than annoying. Waves of pain swept over him with every breath, and the oxygen mask was beginning to make Ray feel claustrophobic.

"Susan?" muttered Ray as he finally managed to open his eyes again. *Where was she?*

"I'm right here, sweetheart," reassured Susan as she squeezed his hand. She had been holding it all along.

Ray reached up with great effort to pull his oxygen mask aside so he could speak. "Please thank them for what they tried to do for me?"

"You can thank them yourself," smiled Susan as she gently put his oxygen mask back into place for him.

Ray then pushed it aside again. "Susan, I love you with all my heart! Thank you for being a part of my life!"

Tears were trickling down Ray's cheeks as he studied his beautiful wife Susan for what he knew would be the last time.

Susan suddenly began to cry, too. *Why was Ray acting as if he weren't going to make it?*

"There's something else you should know," added Ray, with great difficulty.

"Perhaps you should just try and rest right now," suggested Susan. "You can tell me later."

Ray then tightly gripped Susan's hand to prevent her from putting his oxygen mask back on just yet. "Susan, I'm dying! I can feel it. My body is rejecting this heart."

"That's nonsense!" scolded Susan as she put his oxygen mask back on with her other hand.

Ray sadly shook his head as he again pulled aside his oxygen mask. "Please have me cremated and sprinkle the ashes out into the ocean by the lighthouse?"

"What about your heart?" objected Susan. "Won't they want it for someone else, if you don't make it?" She was half joking, of course.

Ray merely nodded and then managed to add, "after that."

"Ray, you're going to be all right!" persisted Susan as she started to put his oxygen mask back on.

All at once the instruments surrounding Ray's bed began beeping loudly, and the on-duty nurse came rushing into the room.

"I'm sorry, ma'am, but you'll need to wait out in the hall," instructed the nurse. "I can't let you be in here right now."

A voice overhead announced the words, "Dr. Phillips to 23B. Dr. Phillips, please report to 23B."

Susan was numb with shock and grief, but all she could do was sit there and stare at the limp body of her husband Ray. How could this be happening? Especially after getting the new heart!

"Mrs. Killingham?" prompted the nurse as she carefully unwrapped Susan's fingers from Ray's unmoving hand before helping her up. "We need you to wait in the hall."

Susan numbly allowed herself to be led out into the hall before walking over to and slumping onto one of the waiting room chairs.

After what seemed an eternity, Dr. Phillips emerged from Ray's room. Susan looked up at him with hopeful eyes, disappointed at once by the expression on his face as the doctor shook his head in the negative. "I'm so sorry! There's nothing more I can do."

Unable to hold back the flood of tears any longer, Susan began to sob uncontrollably. The handsome young doctor came over by Susan and put a comforting arm around her while Susan continued to cry on his shoulder. Then, all at once, Susan asked, "Will he ever regain consciousness?"

After a moment of hesitation, the doctor explained, "Your husband signed a 'DNR order' in the presence of two witnesses, right before his surgery. I thought you knew."

"Excuse me?" Susan could not believe it.

"DNR stands for 'do not resuscitate' and is a legal order to withhold CPR or advanced cardiac life support, in respect of the wishes of a patient in case their heart were to stop or they were to stop breathing," the doctor patiently explained.

"I know what it is!" snapped Susan. "What I want to know is why I wasn't told?"

"It was what your husband wanted," advised Dr. Phillips. "He also signed an agreement that his transplanted heart could be taken and used for someone else, were his body to reject it."

"I suppose he donated his entire body to science?" Susan was angry now.

"There is no directive beyond what I've already mentioned," informed the doctor.

Susan dabbed her cheeks on the back of her hands and then reached for a nearby box of Kleenex. After wiping her eyes and blowing her nose, she took a deep breath and then turned to Dr. Phillips. "Just moments before he passed, Ray mentioned to me that he wanted to be cremated, and asked that I sprinkle his ashes into the ocean by our lighthouse." Susan's lower lip began quivering as she burst into a new round of tears.

The woman from the nurse's station approached with a clipboard and a pen. "We're going to need her signature."

"I'll take care of it," advised the doctor as he took the clipboard and pen from the woman with one hand.

"They need to remove the heart as soon as possible," persisted the irritating woman.

Susan stopped weeping long enough to glare at the woman with unbridled rage. She then grabbed the clipboard from the doctor, signed the consent form, and shoved both of them at the nurse so hard that the woman nearly fell over backwards. Susan then stood to face the woman and advised through gritted teeth, "Karma will get you for this! Trust me!" Susan abruptly grabbed her purse and started to leave but then turned back. "Thank you, doctor, I do appreciate you letting me know. Please have Ray's ashes sent to the lighthouse when they're ready. You can reach me on my smartwatch."

"Mrs. Killingham, please accept our apologies," requested the doctor as he gave the nurse a stern look. "And our condolences."

Susan slowly nodded and then left. Before she reached the elevator, her smartwatch sounded. After quickly activating the earpiece for privacy, Susan answered it. "Hello?"

"Susan, this is Ann, how are you?" Her voice seemed very clear, almost as if she were right there in Ocean Bay.

"Where are you?" questioned Susan as she walked over to a secluded corner to finish her conversation before getting onto the elevator.

"We're at the front desk," revealed Ann. "Here at the hospital. What floor are you on?"

"You're here? At the hospital?" sniffed Susan.

"Are you all right?" Ann could tell that Susan had been crying.

"Stay where you are," instructed Susan. "I'll be right down."

It was nearly midnight before Susan, Sheree and Ann began their drive to Powell Mountain from Ocean Bay. They were in Jim Otterman's bright red 2023 AWD Jeep Cherokee.

"At least we have the first two and a half hours behind us," mentioned Ann from the backseat.

"At least," agreed Susan, who was in the front passenger seat.

"How do you figure?" frowned Sheree, who was driving.

"Well, it's a 30-minute drive from the lighthouse over to Ocean Bluff, and then two more hours from there to Ocean Bay," elaborated Ann. "Now, it will be three hours from Ocean Bay over to St. Diablo, and probably another half hour up Powell Mountain Road to the B&B. At least we're not going all the way to the University."

"You two really need to get some rest if you plan to spell me," reminded Sheree. "Especially if we're driving straight through."

"Hey, thanks for bringing more clothes for me," mentioned Susan. "A woman can never have enough clean clothes to wear."

"Maybe we should let them know we're coming," suggested Ann as she stretched out on the back seat and pulled a car blanket over herself so she could get some rest. Her small overnight bag was not the softest pillow, but it would do.

"Jim has enough to worry about right now," differed Susan. "Besides, there's already a room there at the Powell Mountain B&B, so it shouldn't be a problem. We should be there by morning. Trust me!"

Both Sheree and Ann rolled their eyes upon hearing Susan's familiar epithet.

"And you're sure Ted and the Murrays are okay with taking care of *our* B&B at the lighthouse?" Susan suddenly asked.

"Ted's going to hire a couple of ladies to come in and help out while we're away," revealed Ann. "No worries."

"Susan, I'm really sorry about Ray." Sheree wished there was something else she could do or say to comfort Susan, but there really wasn't. Sheree suddenly thought of her first husband's horrible suicide death - right in front of her - and felt an involuntary chill. Was signing a DNR any less infuriating? "How could Ray even think of signing an order like that without your consent?"

"Perhaps Ray felt guilty about being too old to, uh, well, you know," Susan flushed with embarrassment, "to keep up with me anymore. You know what I mean."

"In the sack?" Sheree forced a crooked smile.

"Well, yeah, exactly." Susan sighed deeply and wiped another tear from her cheek. "But, I still think I should have had some say in it! I don't like being angry with him, especially at a time like this."

"Can you imagine how angry I was with Jon, when he shot himself in front of me?" reminded Sheree. "In fact, I still find myself having feelings of anger about it, and often wonder whether he could have been helped. Perhaps with the right medication and psychiatric counseling, who knows."

"Jim really loves you, you know," reminded Susan.

"I know," smiled Sheree.

"Who knows, Susan," piped in Ann from the backseat. "Maybe there's someone else in store for you?"

Susan suddenly thought of Rupert but then dismissed it from her mind. The last thing she needed was to get involved with a recovering alcoholic. Who knew what kind of other problems he might have.

"How's Carolyn doing?" asked Ann.

"I'm not sure." Susan became serious. "Ever since she was on the beach with Lenny, Jr., she's been kind of distant."

"What do you think they talked about?" pressed Ann.

"Get some rest!" interjected Sheree. "Otherwise, we're stopping at the first hotel we come across."

"Good night," bid Ann as she closed her eyes and tried to sleep.


Meanwhile, at the Powell Mountain Bed and Breakfast, Jim had just arrived with Janette and Rupert. After shutting off the engine of the black 2021 Honda Odyssey minivan rental, Jim grabbed a half-full bottle of water from the holder on his armrest and finished it off.

"What time is it?" yawned Janette as she put her seat back up. She was sitting in the front passenger seat.

"Probably too late to disturb the others," decided Jim. "You two wait here while I make sure the motorhomes are secure, and that none of the work crew decided to sleep inside either of 'em."

Janette and Rupert then watched with surprise as Jim opened his door manually to avoid making any unnecessary noise, got out of the vehicle, and removed a concealed handgun from his boot holster.

"You've been packing all this time?" Janette was astounded.

"Two best friends a guy ever had," grinned Jim as he leaned down to look inside the minivan while checking the safety on his gun. "Smith & Wesson. Never leave home without 'em."

"What are you gonna do?" Rupert was half serious. "Shoot the construction workers? I'm not sure now whether I wanna work on your crew or not!"

Jim and Janette both chuckled at Rupert's remark.

"It's not the construction workers I'm worried about," advised Jim in whispered tones as he quietly closed his door most of the way, but then left it slightly ajar on purpose after switching off the dome light. "You just can't be too careful, coming into a place unannounced in the middle of the night like this. Anyone could be in there."

Janette merely nodded in agreement. The City of Ashton where she lived had also become a rather dangerous place to live as of late, especially with all the increased gang activity. So, one never really did know for sure whether a place was safe without checking it out first.

"Guess I'll be staying with Jim, then?" assumed Rupert as he leaned forward to get a better view of where Jim was headed.

"Well, you sure ain't staying with me!" smirked Janette.

"Why do you enjoy giving me such a hard time?" asked Rupert.

"Somethin' to do," chuckled Janette as she shrugged her shoulders. "I don't know, you're just fun to give a hard time to."

"Too bad you're not single," flirted Rupert. "I'd show you a hard time." His statement was meant to be interpreted any way Janette cared to take it.

"Rupert!" objected Janette as she blushed, though it was obvious she enjoyed the banter.

"Come on, you two." Jim startled both of them. "MIRA, open passenger doors."

"I thought MIRA was parked back at the Powell Lake Airport," recalled Rupert.

"She is." Jim grinned a crooked smile. "But, she's also paired to my Smartwatch via satellite."

"Ah ha," nodded Rupert as he climbed from the minivan after grabbing his small briefcase and single suitcase.

"Maybe you can steam some of the wrinkles out of that suit," Jim suggested to Rupert. "Before we go over there for breakfast in the morning?"

"I'll do that," responded Rupert as he glanced at the thick dark forest surrounding them. Thankfully, Jim had turned on the porch lights on both motorhomes. Otherwise, the entire area was extremely dark. Even the porchlight on the B&B had been shut off for the night.

"I'm definitely going to have a chat with Luella about lighting and security!" muttered Jim. Then, to Rupert, "Go ahead, I'll be right there. The door's open now. There was a key under the mat."

Janette then tried unsuccessfully to remove her giant suitcase from the seat behind her.

"May I help you with that?" offered Jim as he grabbed it with ease. "MIRA, please close all doors and secure the vehicle."

Janette then watched with interest as the doors closed and clicked into locking position. "We definitely need to get something like this! Ours is a 2016 model."

"I'm a Jeep man, myself," advised Jim as he carried Janette's suitcase to the other motorhome and took it inside.

"What time do we go over there for breakfast?" asked Janette, suddenly nervous about being alone in the motorhome.

Jim then removed one of his business cards from his wallet and handed it to Janette. "I'm just a phone call away. In fact, let me just copy the contact information to your Smartwatch for you."

"All I got is a cellphone," advised Janette, "and I tried calling my hubby from the B&B when we were here earlier, but there's no reception."

"Oh, that's right. I take it you don't have a satellite phone either, then?" Jim merely shook his head with amazement.

"You don't think that Angie thing would come over here, do you?" Janette was serious.

"I don't know." Jim had not considered that possibility but found it interesting. "Well, just scream if you do need anything. I'll most likely be able to hear you."

"Uh, maybe I should stay with you and Rupert instead?" Janette suddenly suggested, as she gingerly grabbed Jim by the arm to stop him from leaving. "I can sleep on the couch."

"If it would make you feel any safer, sure. But, I'll sleep on the couch." Jim then picked up her suitcase and carried it back outside again and over to the other motorhome where he and Rupert would be sleeping.

Janette followed close behind, furtively glancing at the dense forest around them. The sound of an owl hooting nearby was closely trailed by the echoing cry of some other nocturnal animal in the distance, causing Janette to become more nervous than she already was.

"Let me just make sure Rupert is decent first," advised Jim.

"You're not gonna leave me out here alone, are you?" Janette was clearly terrified at the prospect. "I'll just close my eyes, and then you can let me know if it's safe to open them when we get inside, okay?"

"Very well," Jim finally agreed as he opened the door first and then stepped aside for Janette to enter. Jim grabbed her suitcase and followed her inside.

"What's this?" questioned Rupert, who had on nothing but his boxer shorts.

"She was afraid to stay over there by herself," smirked Jim as he set down Janette's suitcase.

"Is it safe to open my eyes now?" prompted Janette.

"Fine by me," agreed Rupert. He was too tired to care whether Janette saw him in his boxer shorts or not.

Janette then opened her eyes and blushed deeply upon seeing him. Rupert was not only extremely handsome, but also well-built, especially for a man of fifty years!

"Sorry, but I still got the sweats and was hot." Rupert shrugged his shoulders as he headed for one of the beds, which had already been made up by someone.

Janette merely crossed herself and shook her head while Rupert smiled at her flirtatiously before laying down on top of the bed he planned to sleep in.

Rupert then put his hands behind his head and crossed his legs.

"You wanted to stay over here," smirked Jim as he checked the refrigerator. Jim then nodded with approval. Undoubtedly, it was Luella who had taken the time to make sure everything was ready for them. Everything but the outside lights, that is!

"Rupert's gonna catch cold like that," Janette pointed out to Jim as she took off her shoes before climbing into the other bed with her clothes still on and pulled the covers up to her neck.

"Wanna come keep me warm?" teased Rupert.

"I'll give you warm! Just keep it up and I'll tell my hubby about you!" threatened Janette.

"You two sound like an old married couple," laughed Jim as he removed his boots and carefully stashed his handgun between the couch cushions before making himself comfortable.

"He started it!" snapped Janette.

"And she's right," pointed out Jim to Rupert, "you need to cover up. The last thing we need is to have you catch a cold, especially with everything else you're going through."

"He needs to drink more water, too!" added Janette for good measure before turning on her side with her back to Rupert.

"You gonna turn off that light?" questioned Rupert.

"Just as soon as you drink another bottle of water and then cover yourself up," answered Jim. The light switch was right by Jim's head, so it would not be necessary for him to get up to turn it off.

"Okay, fine!" sighed Rupert as he got up to comply, deliberately taking his time for Janette's benefit, especially since the two beds were only an arm's length apart.

"I know you're there, but my eyes are closed," mumbled Janette.

Rupert quickly finished drinking the bottle of water and then went into the restroom.

"Oh, no!" remembered Jim. "I left that metal box from Martha Krain out in the minivan. I'll be right back."

"You're not leaving me alone in here with him?" Janette was not sure she trusted Rupert to behave himself in Jim's absence.

"Would you like to go get it?" offered Jim.

"Just hurry, before he comes back out," urged Janette.

Jim quickly put on his boots and grabbed his handgun before heading back outside.

Rupert had overheard their conversation, even from inside the restroom, so decided to sneak up on Janette and say "boo!"

Just as Janette screamed, Jim came back inside.

"Oh, that's great!" objected Jim. "Now, you've probably managed to wake up everyone over at the B&B."

"I don't see any lights coming on," reported Rupert as he pulled the blinds apart just enough to look outside.

Jim rapidly removed his boots again, stashed his handgun, and pulled an afghan over himself on the couch. Like Janette, he would sleep in his clothes. With one hand on the light switch, Jim advised, "Cover up."

Rupert finally complied, though he had every intention of shoving the covers aside as soon as the lights were out.

Saturday morning, March 25, 2023, brought with it a brilliant sunrise. Birdsong echoed through the budding forest surrounding Powell Mountain Bed and Breakfast. Delicate fingers of light danced on the forest floor through every penetrable opening while morning dew quickly evaporated on gossamer wings of mist, ascending into the heavens.

Luella was an early riser, especially when there were guests to tend to, so naturally she was the first one up. It was already eight o'clock, but Carolyn and Sherry were still sound asleep upstairs. Thankfully, the noisy construction workers would not be there until after nine o'clock, since it was a weekend.

Oddly, neither Carolyn nor Sherry seemed bothered in the least by the fact that the B&B was allegedly haunted. Carolyn, in particular, had been up quite late pouring over the case file entrusted to her by Detective Priest. Determined to read as much of it as possible before having to turn it over to Jim Otterman, Carolyn had actually fallen asleep at Luella's writing desk, slumped over the file. Luella had finally persuaded Carolyn to go lay down on the bed nearby and get some badly needed rest.

As Luella pulled back the blinds for the day, she stopped and stared with disbelief. The minivan was parked outside! And, the porch lights on the motorhomes were both on! She was certain she had turned them off before retiring for the night, to save electricity. How could she have slept through their arrival? Luella was usually a light sleeper.

It was obvious to her that Jim and the others had not wanted to wake anyone when arriving during the night. Luella quickly made a mental note to herself that breakfast would be for at least two additional people. What time had they arrived, anyway? And, how long should she wait to check on them to make sure they had everything they needed?

A rapid series of knocks on the front door caught Luella by surprise. No one else had driven up, so it must be old Carrot Top! Luella quickly checked the large antique armchair mirror near the front door, to be sure she was presentable. Her hair and makeup were perfect, and her bright red sweater fit perfectly in all the right places. She smiled to herself as she imagined Jim's reaction.

Putting on her sexiest smile first, Luella opened the front door with a deliberate casualness. She did not want to appear too anxious.

Upon opening the door, Luella stared with disbelief at the tall, dark, well-built and extremely handsome black man standing before her in an unexpectedly wrinkled suit. Other than the dreadlocks he wore, the man could easily have been mistaken for a professional businessman of some sort. Perhaps a lawyer, or something like that.

Rupert was likewise overwhelmed upon seeing Luella for the first time. She looked *exactly* like the woman he had dreamed about the night before. How could this even be possible?

An immediate chemistry passed between them, and the mutual attraction was undeniable. Both stood staring at one another for what seemed like a frozen moment in time.

"Are you Luella?" the man finally asked.

"Tell me I haven't died and gone to heaven!" exclaimed Luella as she looked Rupert over with her hands on her hips. "But, since this is the second day in a row some man in a wrinkled, smelly old suit has shown up at my door, I've more than likely gone the other direction."

Rupert then laughed and introduced himself as he extended his hand. "I'm Rupert."

"Pleased to meet you, Rupert," acknowledged Luella as she shook hands with him, "but if you don't mind my asking, where in the world did you come from?"

"Jim brought me here from Chicago," advised Rupert. "He and Janette are still asleep and I didn't want to wake 'em. I hear you have a shower over here? Jim said I could stay in his old room."

"Really?" Luella slowly began to smile. "Only if you let me spiff up that suit for you while you're in the shower."

"Deal," flirted Rupert as he admired Luella. "So, this is the Powell Mountain Bed and Breakfast? I like your sign, by the way."

"Daddy made the statue holding it himself, when he was alive," advised Luella as she stopped to admire the hand-carved, life-sized wooden statue by her door. "It was a self-portrait."

"It really is very well done," complimented Rupert as he ran his hand across the top edge of the sign the statue held.

"The lettering used to be gold on black, when this was just a salvage yard and firewood place," reminisced Luella, "but blue letters on a white background seem to give it more character. Plus, it's easier to read."

"I take it your daddy was a woodcutter?" noticed Rupert as he observed the fact that the woodcutter portrayed by the statue was wearing a white hardhat and holding a real axe.

"Indeed, he was," confirmed Luella. "Folks hereabouts used to call him 'Woody the Woodcutter.'"

"Humph," nodded Rupert. "Interesting that a lumberman would risk smoking a pipe, what with the risk of forest fires and all."

"Come on in, Rupert," invited Luella as she stood back and opened the door. "Daddy never smoked when he was on the lumber crew. He didn't even take up smoking that special tobacco of his until after the accident – the one where he lost his foot. At least that's what my mama once told me."

"Oh, I'm terribly sorry to hear that," frowned Rupert as he picked up his small black leather briefcase with one hand, and grabbed the handle of his small silver Samsonite "Hardside Spinner" suitcase with his other hand.

"Daddy couldn't afford a real prosthetic," added Luella, "so he carved his own. That's how he got his name. Plus, he would chop leftover lumber scraps that his friends would leave behind and deliver it as firewood, all over the mountain."

"Where's your daddy now?" questioned Rupert.

"Jim really didn't bother to tell you anything about this place, did he?" guessed Luella as she slowly and sensuously climbed the stairs ahead of Rupert. Her tight-fitting black leggings revealed her excellent physique, while the black pompoms on top of her high-heeled bedroom slippers gently swayed as she walked.

"Jim did say something about meeting your great-grandmother, if you can imagine such a thing," chuckled Rupert.

424

Luella stopped when she arrived at the top of the staircase and motioned toward the wall behind her. "Rupert, this is Angie, my great-grandmother."

Rupert looked as if he had been hit by a bolt of lightning upon seeing the oil painting. "That's what you had on in my dream last night! Or, was it her?"

"Probably her," assumed Luella with a mischievous grin. "You might call her a 'seductive spirit' of sorts, but she's harmless enough. Angie was the original Madame here, back when it was a brothel. Now, it's just a haunted B&B."

"So, that's why Janette was crossing herself." Rupert suddenly understood why Jim had not wanted him to know about Angie at the time. Though, he probably wouldn't have believed it anyway.

"This here is the room Jim was staying in," motioned Luella. "It used to be Angie's, when she was alive. But, she's with my daddy and his mother now."

"I see." Rupert swallowed uncomfortably as he studied the portrait of Angie. It was as if she were undressing him with her eyes. "You're sure she's actually with them?"

"You don't seem like the type that rattles easily," appraised Luella with a crooked smile. "The shower's in there. Just leave your suit on that chair and I'll take care of it later. You do have something else to wear?"

"Just a pair of jeans, a t-shirt, and two changes of underwear," revealed Rupert. "Left everything else behind."

"You're not in some kind of trouble with the law, are you?" Luella narrowed her eyes at Rupert and tilted her head back as she looked at him more closely.

"Heavens, no!" laughed Rupert. "I'm a recovering alcoholic, and have been going through DTs for the past two days. I think the worst is behind me now, though."

"Well, you can tell me all about it after your shower," replied Luella, "while I re-braid those locks for you."

"Thanks, that would be great!" agreed Rupert as he walked into the room. "Nice place."

"Angie thinks so, too," smirked Luella as she turned to leave. "Everything you need should be in there. If not, just let me know."

At the St. Diablo Roadside Inn, Sheree, Ann and Susan had finally decided to stop for the night after a close call when Sheree had drifted off to sleep while driving. They were now up and on their way again, planning to have breakfast upon their arrival.

"Jim's absolutely gonna kill me!" fretted Sheree as she steered his bright red 2023 AWD Jeep Cherokee from the hotel's parking lot onto the main road.

"Hey, it could happen to anyone," assured Susan. "At least you woke up in time before crashing head-on into the median!"

"That's right!" exclaimed Ann. "We all could have been killed."

"But, what about the fender?" moaned Sheree. "There's no way he won't notice that!"

"There's an auto shop over there," pointed Ann.

"Ron's Auto Body?" read Sheree.

"We could at least stop and get a quick estimate," recommended Susan. "Maybe it's something easy to fix."

"No, we need to just get there," decided Sheree. "If I take it to the wrong place, I'll never hear the end of it."

"That's for sure!" added Ann. "Thank goodness that divider was there!"

"Amen to that!" exclaimed Susan. "But, a minor ding to the fender isn't really all that bad. At least it doesn't scrape on the tires or anything. It should be okay. Besides, Jim's just going to have to understand. You can always tell him I was driving."

"You would do that for me?" Sheree was overcome by emotion.

"Hey, I'm emotionally distraught right now," reasoned Susan. "Plus, he's a lot less likely to be as hard on me at a time like this."

"Then, I'm pulling over right now," decided Sheree. "You should definitely be at the wheel when we pull into that place."

"It's not like he's going to be standing there in the driveway when we pull up," laughed Ann. "Besides, he has no idea we're even coming. It will be a complete surprise."

"It'll be a surprise, all right," nodded Sheree as she pulled Jim's Jeep over so she and Susan could exchange places.

Susan paused to get a closer look at the left front fender as she and Sheree got out to walk around the vehicle and then commented, "Actually, he probably will be quite upset."

"Gee, thanks!" muttered Sheree as she climbed into the passenger side seat.

"At me!" reminded Susan with a crooked smile as she climbed into the driver's seat. "It'll work out. Trust me!"

Sheree and Ann both rolled their eyes at that.

The odor of cooking bacon, eggs and hash browns drifted unceremoniously onto the morning breeze. The pungent odor of fresh squeezed orange juice and hot coffee could also be detected.

"Do you smell that?" asked Janette as she yawned and stretched before sitting up. "Where's Rupert?"

"He left earlier, to go take a shower over there so he wouldn't wake you," explained Jim.

"And you're still here?" Janette suddenly felt uncomfortable.

"You said you didn't feel safe alone," reminded Jim with a crooked smile.

"So, what, you've just been sitting there watching me sleep?" demanded Janette.

"I've had some work to do," informed Jim as he saved his document, closed the lid to his laptop, and set it aside to stand up.

"Anything new?" questioned Janette as she got up and headed for the restroom, still wearing her clothes from yesterday.

"Nothing that can't wait until we share it with the others," replied Jim rather mysteriously. "Say, will you be okay here by yourself, now that it's finally light outside? It's time for me to check out that delicious scent on the wind."

"Oh, that smells good!" exclaimed Janette as Jim opened the door, causing a mild burst of the aromatic breeze to waft inside. "Tell 'em they better save some for me! I'll be right there!"

"Deal," grinned Jim as he grabbed his laptop, tucked it under his arm, and took it with him. "See you over there."

Jim was deep in thought as he made his way toward the B&B. It was already nine o'clock and the construction workers – at least those who could be persuaded to come in on the weekend – would be arriving very soon.

Without warning, a bright red 2023 AWD Jeep Cherokee began making its way down the gravel road towards him. Jim realized almost immediately that it must be his! No one else would have a vehicle like that with a license plate that read "Jim" on it. What in the world were they doing here?

Jim suddenly noticed the damage to his left front fender! *Why was Susan of all people driving his Jeep?*

"We're totally busted," muttered Ann from the backseat.

"Ya think?" Susan laughed sardonically.

"Oh, this is *not* good!" agonized Sheree when she saw the look on her husband's face.

"Let me do the talking," advised Susan as she pulled Jim's vehicle to a stop behind the black 2021 Honda Odyssey minivan.

"This better be good!" fumed Jim as Susan and the others got out and approached him.

"Susan's husband just died," interjected Ann, "and that's all you can say to her?"

"Ray is gone?" Jim was flabbergasted.

"We had planned on waiting until we got here to tell anyone," described Ann, "since we all knew how busy you are working on this new case of yours."

"Oh, Susan, I'm so sorry." Jim suddenly felt as if he had been punched in the gut.

"I'll be all right," assured Susan as she began to cry again.

Sheree and Ann then came and put their arms around Susan to comfort her.

Jim took a deep breath before removing a clean handkerchief from his pocket, that he handed to Susan.

"Thanks!" sniffed Susan as her lip quivered.

"What about the heart?" Jim whispered to Sheree, hoping that Susan could not hear.

"He signed a DNR," blurted Susan as she began a new round of tears. True, she was devastated, but Susan saw no reason to hold back now, especially considering the fender situation involving Jim's Jeep. A few extra tears certainly couldn't hurt!

"They took the heart for someone else," whispered Ann to her father. "Then they are cremating the remainder of his remains and sending the urn to the lighthouse when it's ready. Susan said Ray wants his ashes to be sprinkled out into the ocean there."

"Oh, hell!" cursed Jim as he unexpectedly walked over and kicked the left front tire of his Jeep with frustration. "Why would he go and sign something like that?"

"Jim, I'm so sorry about your Jeep," apologized Sheree. She was actually trembling. "It was my fault. And Susan, I can't let you take the blame for something you didn't do."

Jim then noticed Susan glance at Sheree with surprise and shook his head.

Sheree then described, "We were going to drive straight through, but it got so late that ...."

"You dozed off before drifting over and grazing the median?" guessed Jim. "You're lucky you didn't hit it head-on!"

"Yeah." Sheree hung her head with shame and embarrassment.

"Did you bother to get a police report?" grilled Jim. "The insurance company will probably want one."

"No." Sheree hadn't even thought of it at the time.

Jim shook his head again with disapproval, but said nothing more about it. "Come on, I believe Luella has breakfast ready for us. We can get your luggage after that."

"I'm so sorry!" apologized Sheree as she gave Jim a pathetic look. "We should have stopped sooner."

"Oh, well," muttered Jim. "Stuff happens. At least you're all safe. That's the important thing."

"Susan!" screamed Janette as she emerged from the motorhome and ran over to hug her friend. "How's Ray?"

"Ray didn't make it," revealed Susan as she gave Janette a hug of greeting.

"Really? Oh, girl, I'm so sorry!" exclaimed Janette as she hugged Susan again. "That's so unfair!"

"Uh, if you don't mind my asking," interjected Jim, "but who's running the Killingham Lighthouse B&B right now?"

"Ted hired a couple of women from an agency to help him out," piped in Ann. "John and Jeon Murray are helping, too."

"Well, okay, then." Jim shrugged his shoulders, put his arms around Sheree and Ann, and headed for the front door of the Powell Mountain B&B. "Let's have some breakfast."

Inside, Sherry Collingsworth was already seated at the long bar table with her sprained ankle up on the stool beside her, but Carolyn was busy helping Luella set out plates, napkins and silverware so the others could dish up their food.

Jim was about to knock on the door when it flew open.

"There you are!" greeted Luella. "And this must be Mrs. Carrot Top? And your lovely daughter?"

"Carrot Top?" Sheree tried not to smile at hearing the name.

"This is my wife Sheree – with two 'e's in her name," introduced Jim. He was clearly embarrassed at having been referred to as Carrot Top again. "And yes, this is my lovely stepdaughter, Ann."

"Well, I'm Luella!" greeted the woman at the door. "Please, come in! Breakfast is ready."

The entire room rapidly became silent when a tall, muscular, clean-shaven, smartly dressed, handsome black man began descending the stairs. Every woman in the room became transfixed immediately upon seeing him, a fact that did not go unnoticed by the men.

"Who's *that*?" questioned Janette from behind them.

Unable to retain his poker face any loner, Rupert finally broke into a big grin. His flawless smile and perfect teeth were dazzling, but not as much so as his neatly trimmed hair. The dreadlocks were gone! And, thanks to the miracle of Luella's handy black hair dye, so were any telltale signs of premature gray.

"Rupert?" Janette stared at him with utter disbelief.

"Don't you even recognize the guy you slept with last night?" teased Rupert with a flirtatious look.

"Now, wait just a minute!" objected Janette as her cheeks flushed deeply with discomfiture. "Jim and I both had our clothes on the entire time!"

Sheree then turned to Jim with a raised eyebrow.

"We were in separate beds!" laughed Jim as he shrugged his shoulders, though he was somewhat surprised by Rupert's boldness among perfect strangers.

"Everyone, this is the new Rupert," introduced Luella with a proud smile. "And, it's about time my long-dead husband's wardrobe found such a fine-looking man to wear it!"

Rupert was wearing a lavender, short-sleeved polo shirt, tucked into a nicely fitting pair of black jeans. The black leather work boots he wore appeared new and perfectly matched the black leather belt on his pants. The matching leather jacket was still upstairs.

Susan and Rupert locked eyes at that point. The attraction between them was obvious to everyone, including Luella.

"Perhaps a quick round of introductions might be in order before we eat," suggested Sherry Collingsworth, who had remained quiet until now. "Rupert, I'm Sherry – with a 'y' – as in the drink."

"Nice to meet you," flirted Rupert. That was just his way.

"Humph!" snorted Luella, who was starting to become annoyed by the attention Rupert was showing the other women in the room.

"And I'm Carolyn," informed the tall attractive blonde woman beside Susan. "It looks like you already know Susan and Janette."

"Indeed," nodded Rupert as he again turned to stare at Susan.

"And," interrupted Jim as he grabbed Rupert by the arm to redirect his attention, "this is my lovely wife Sheree – with two 'e's – and her daughter Ann."

"Ladies," flirted Rupert, causing each of them to blush, much to Jim's displeasure.

"Something sure smells good!" It was Chip Priest, who had walked in unnoticed while the introductions were being made. "I'm a Detective with the St. Diablo Police Department."

"Officer, I didn't do it! Whatever it was, I'm innocent," joked Rupert as he put his hands up, causing the others to smile.

"Well, speaking as the only single woman here," began Luella, "I'd like to commend Rupert on his excellent new look and certainly hope to get to know him better!"

"Don't be too hasty about that," countered Sherry, who also found Rupert most compelling. "My husband died several years ago, too, but I've never remarried."

"Well, mine died yesterday," muttered Susan as she fought back a new round of tears.

"Ray didn't make it?" gasped Carolyn. "Oh, Susan, I'm so sorry!" Carolyn then pulled her friend Susan close, and hugged her for several moments as they both cried on each other's shoulders.

Rupert could not hide the sudden glint of hope in his eyes at overhearing Susan's remark about her current marital status.

"I'm sure she's probably still in mourning," Jim whispered to Rupert as he motioned for him to sit on a stool at the bar.

"My second day sober and you bring me to a bar in *Peyton Place*?" Rupert teased Jim, to lighten the mood.

"There's no alcohol here, pretty boy!" informed Luella.

"Hey, what'd I do?" demanded Rupert, aware that he had upset Luella in some way.

"I'm sure you'll figure it out, honey," replied Luella. She was not about to let Rupert – or any other man – make a fool out of her now. Fifty-one years of age was just too late in life to be playing games!

"Hey, give the man a chance to enjoy being single and sober at the same time," suggested Jim. "At least for a day or two, anyway."

"That's it!" hollered Luella. "Quiet, everyone! Jim has offered to bless the food for us. Jim?"

"I did?" Jim was surprised. "Okay, sure."

After waiting for everyone to quit talking, Jim began, "Dear Lord, thank you for this food. Please bless it, and the hands that prepared it."

"Amen!" exclaimed Luella in the background.

"We also ask that you would bless us as we examine the details of these cases, that we will have inspiration to be led to find the truth, and to solve them at last."

"Amen!" came the voices of several more in the room.

"Amen," concluded Jim.

As the others finished dishing up their food and began to eat, Carolyn quietly approached Luella. "Do you have any oatmeal?"

"Oatmeal?" frowned Luella. "Why on earth would you wanna eat something like that?"

"I'd like some, too, if you have any," mentioned Susan.

"No wonder you two is about to waste away!" chastised Luella as she began searching the cupboard behind her for a large pot in which to prepare some oatmeal.

"She's just jealous," whispered Sherry, who was also considering the oatmeal option.

"I only want one bowl of it," advised Carolyn.

"The rest will keep," smirked Luella. "Until you get tired of eating it each day."

"You don't know Carolyn!" laughed Sherry.

"She never eats anything else for breakfast," agreed Susan.

"Which is why she looks so fabulous," complimented Jim, sorry at once for doing so upon receiving a swift jab from Sheree in his side.

"Thanks, guys," smiled Carolyn as she shook her head with amusement at Jim's plight.

After everyone had eaten, Luella quickly cleared the dishes away, wiped off the bar counter, and then tried in vain to get everyone's attention. But, as soon as she banged a large spoon against a kettle, the room became silent.

"Folks, before Jim and Chip begin going through their case files together, there is a matter of importance that I believe will be of interest to you all," described Luella as she gave Carolyn a knowing glance.

"Thanks," nodded Carolyn.

"Miss Carolyn has a letter here that she is going to read out loud, so everyone can hear it," announced Luella.

Jim was clearly interested in the letter that was about to be read, though Carolyn kept her best poker face intact until doing so.

"Thank you, Luella," replied Carolyn with a mysterious glance at Jim before unfolding the tattered and worn letter in her hands.

"Are you sure you want to do this?" Jim suddenly asked.

"She has my permission," assured Luella. "Besides, I think you will find it of great interest to your cases."

Chip Priest was also on the edge of his seat, along with everyone else in the room.

*What could there possibly be in Lenny's letter that would be pertinent to the Cain or Gomez cases?* Jim wondered to himself. *Had he made a mistake in allowing Carolyn to keep the letter private earlier when they were at the restaurant?*

"There are actually two letters here," began Carolyn, still with a neutral expression on her face.

"The first is from my dear mother, Harriet," interjected Luella. "She gave it to my foster mother before she passed, with instructions to wait until my twelfth birthday to give it to me.

The disappointment on Jim's face was obvious to Carolyn, just as the subtle smile on her face was to him. No, it was not the letter from Lenny! When their eyes met, Carolyn merely raised an eyebrow of acknowledgment. Jim then nodded with resignation, though he was still quite anxious to hear the letter from Harriet.

"The second," continued Luella, "is a letter from my late father, written by him while he was in prison."

Chip was bristling with curiosity and it showed. So was Jim.

"Oh yes," added Luella. "I will ask you in advance to please pardon my dear daddy's grammar, but the man only had a fourth-grade education."

"Okay, here goes," began Carolyn. "The first letter reads as follows:

*My Dearest Luella,*

*By de time you read this, I'll be long gone, but pray you never forget me nor yer daddy. We will always love you, our little princess. Do not be upset with Mrs. Green dat she waited so long to give you yer daddy's letter, but it was my wish. It were for de safety of you and yer precious brothers, so it has been kept from you 'till now. Guard it with yer very life, as showing it to de wrong folk could put you in most terrible danger.*

*We looks forward to seeing you again someday, our sweet Luella. My prayer now is dat you be old enough to understand what yer daddy wrote in his letter and pray to de good man upstairs, may He guide you to know what is right. With all my love, Mama"*

Luella wiped a tear from her cheek as Carolyn carefully handed the letter back to her.

"Who is Mrs. Green?" questioned Chip.

"She was the woman who became my permanent foster mom following my parents' deaths, since I wasn't old enough to be on my own yet. Even before that, with my daddy in prison and my mama in the nursing home, I stayed with the Greens."

"Were your brothers in the same foster home with you?" asked Sherry, who was again making notes for her documentary.

"No," replied Luella as she sadly shook her head. "They stayed with some family in St. Diablo, where they also went to school. Even our foster parents knew how important it was to our parents that we all become educated, so we wouldn't end up like them."

"How do you mean?" grilled Chip.

"Having to chop wood, scrub floors, that kind of thing," explained Luella as she took off and folded her apron before laying it on the counter behind her. "And just look at me now!"

"This place has definite possibility," assured Jim.

"Is that an offer?" posed Luella.

"We'll see what we can work out," promised Jim. "I think this would make a great tourist attraction, if nothing else. A haunted brothel. People pay good money to go through places like this. Though it's doubtful you'll get many men willing to spend the night here."

Chip and Jim exchanged a meaningful glance at that.

"Where did your foster family live?" pressed Sherry.

"Down in Ocean Bay," revealed Luella. "That's where I went to school, by the way."

"And you were only six years old when your daddy passed in 1978?" confirmed Sherry.

"Murdered!" corrected Luella. "But, I do remember Mrs. Green taking me there to the prison to see my daddy one last time before that. That was when he gave her that letter to take to my mama. She died only six months after that."

"You think he was murdered?" frowned Chip.

"Absolutely!" insisted Luella. "Every one of them Knights was responsible for my daddy's death! I'm sure of it. As I was telling Carolyn earlier, the head judge was a Knight, most of the cops were Knights, and even the prison guards themselves were Knights, right there where my daddy was kept in his cell until he died!"

"Perhaps it was an inside job?" wondered Chip aloud. He had always considered the possibility but never mentioned it to anyone.

"Maybe they poisoned his food?" guessed Janette.

"Probably to keep him from talking," assumed Sherry.

"But talk he did," mentioned Luella as she nodded at the other letter Carolyn was still holding. "And thank the good Lord that this letter can now tell his story. It is long past time that the terrible secrets between them Knights and my daddy be made known. I feel good about Chip and Jim, that you gentlemen will do the right thing."

"Okay, then," nodded Carolyn. "The letter from Woody to Harriet reads as follows:

*Dear Harriet,*

*I kinnot begin to say how sorry I is fer what I must tell you now. Tho I is innocent of what dey say, old Woody is still as guilty as if he done did it hisself. Sumthin' terrible did happen in 1959, and de professor*

*swore to hurt you and de kids if I told. De burnin'*
*crosses were his reminders of it.*

*Maybe wid de courage back den, old Woody kud*
*have stopped him by tellin' de right folk. Just not*
*knowin' who dat wuz tho, and fearin' for yer safety held*
*me back. Dat evil man murdered Misty before me very*
*eyes, back in 1959. It started wid her.*

*De other kids who disappeared later, dey knew*
*he wuz der when Misty died, but sumhow de professor,*
*he got 'em. All de needless deaths over de years, 'n all*
*because I wuz a coward too much to stand up to him.*
*Wud dey be alive if I had? Duz dat make me as guilty*
*as if I'd murdered dem kids myself?*

*May God forgive old Woody for not speakin'*
*sooner, and dat evil professor Krain be stopped before*
*he hurts anyone else! And, may you forgive me, too!*

*Will love you always, Woody"*

Tears were now streaming down several cheeks as Carolyn reverently handed Woody's letter back to Luella.

"Misty Krain!" exclaimed Chip. "No wonder no one could ever find her. Word was that she'd run off with some vacuum cleaner salesman, and just abandoned her husband and little girl. The guys who worked the original case of her disappearance always thought it was odd that there was no trace of her after that."

"She's probably in one of those other barrels," guessed Jim.

"Too bad Ronald Krain isn't alive to answer for it!" fumed Luella. "I always thought there was something fishy about how he up and bought this place right out from under us after our parents both died, allegedly so we would have enough money to bury them at the time! I've even wondered whether my mama's death was entirely of natural causes. But, being minors in foster homes, there wasn't a blasted thing any of us could do about it!"

"Yet, you managed to finally buy this place back?" pointed out Jim. "That must count for something?"

"Nobody wants to stay at a haunted brothel, though," frowned Luella. "At least not the men. Still, it was a matter of honor. My brothers and I all went in on it together."

436

Luella decided to remain silent about the mysterious stipend she continued to receive each month from an anonymous benefactor. She had been living on the payments from a trust fund established upon the death of her imprisoned father back in 1978, and worried whether the payments might cease if the matter became public knowledge. What if it really was Ronald Krain's estate as she suspected? Perhaps he had set up the trust fund out of guilt for what he had done to the woodcutter's family? And, would Michael Krain – his only surviving heir and current head of the Crusading Knights – approve of the arrangement if it were brought to his attention?

"Do either of your brothers live here?" questioned Rupert, who had been silent until now.

"They both refuse to stay here," replied Luella. "My daddy was an exception. He never seemed to mind Angie hanging around."

"Probably because he was her grandson," surmised Ann. "And, if anyone's interested, I researched those photos and documents Carolyn sent me from your family, Luella, and it turns out that both you and my stepdad share a common ancestor."

"Oh, please! Not the genealogy thing again," complained Jim. "Wasn't the Lizzie Borden thing enough? Those people are long dead!"

"And so are the people in that case file of yours!" argued Ann.

"She's got you there, Carrot Top," smirked Luella.

"What I'm trying to tell you," persisted Ann, "is that you are *both* descended from a Josiah Smith, and so is Carolyn! The three of you are equally related distant cousins! By six degrees of separation!"

"No, kiddin'?" beamed Luella. "See, what'd I tell you? And, you do look exactly like old Carrot Top, Mister Jim. There's no way you can deny it!"

"It's true!" agreed Ann. "I couldn't believe it myself, when I first saw the picture Carolyn sent. They're like twins!"

"Maybe it was Jim in a previous lifetime," teased Luella, though she was actually half serious about it.

"Huh," muttered Jim.

"So, what about that metal box from Martha Krain?" reminded Janette. "When do we get to see what's inside?"

"I suppose I should go get that now," sighed Jim.

"No need," beamed Janette as she walked over and set the small metal box down in front of Jim. "I knew you wouldn't want to just leave it out there unattended in the motorhome like that."

Jim gave Janette a crooked smile of appreciation.

"It's doubtful there are any fingerprints," reminded Chip.

"Probably so, but we still need to follow procedure," replied Jim as he pulled two pairs of latex gloves from his pocket and handed one of them to Chip. "There could be blood or other DNA on whatever's in here. You got any evidence bags?"

"How about some of these?" offered Luella as she pulled out a box of quart-sized Ziploc bags from behind the counter.

"Perfect, thanks!" smiled Jim as he took the box from her.

"Just who is Martha Krain, anyway?" grilled Ann, suddenly quite interested in the mysterious metal box.

"Martha Krain was the only daughter of the 'evil professor' that Woody spoke of in his letter," described Jim. "She committed suicide just two days ago, on March 23rd."

"I hate that day!" exclaimed Ann rather vehemently. "Nothing good ever happens on March 23rd!"

"I was born on March 23rd," Rupert informed them, rather pitifully.

The room became quiet again, and those who did not already know that March 23rd was Rupert's birthday gaped at him with utter astonishment.

"Please say it wasn't in 1973?" requested Carolyn.

"Actually, it was." Rupert was almost apologetic about it.

"You just had your fiftieth birthday, then?" It was Sherry.

"Yes, ma'am," confirmed Rupert.

"You must work out?" Susan suddenly asked. Rupert's well-shaped body was noticeable, to say the least.

"Every day," answered Rupert. "Even when I was drinking. They had a gym at the Y where I stayed."

"You ain't gonna be doing any drinking around here!" advised Luella with finality.

"Absolutely not!" promised Rupert with an amused smile. "I'm done with that life for good! What I've just been through is *not* an experience I'd care to repeat! I was wondering if you had a gym around here, though?"

"Perhaps there's some big heavy logs out there you could use," suggested Luella, somewhat sarcastically. "Does this place even look like it would have a gym?"

"Rupert starts on the construction crew tomorrow," advised Jim, "so I'm sure he'll get in his fair share of physical exercise. That is, if he's up to it by then?"

"I'm looking forward to it, sir," mentioned Rupert. "And, to getting a good recommendation from you, for when I do apply for a job up at that university."

Jim merely nodded as he turned his attention again to the small metal box on the counter in front of him.

"Before you open that," interrupted Luella, "Chip, do you need my daddy's letter for your evidence folder?"

"I can just snap some photos of it," answered Chip as he thought of how his precious file had ended up beneath the collapsed barn the previous day. "I'm sure it holds sentimental value for you, so you should definitely hang onto it."

"Thanks!" beamed Luella as she carefully laid the letter on the bar's counter for Chip to photograph.

"Okay, here goes," announced Jim as he carefully opened the small metal box with his gloved hands.

"I don't believe this!" exclaimed Chip as he saw what was inside. "Are you seeing what I'm seeing?"

The others crowded closer to get a better look.

"Back up! Give us some room!" commanded Jim as he carefully picked up a small stack of drivers' licenses.

"Lord Almighty!" exclaimed Luella. "Are those the missing girls from your file?"

Janette merely crossed herself and shook her head.

Chip and Jim both stared at the first ID for almost a minute before saying anything about it.

"We should photograph these as we go," suggested Chip.

"Agreed," nodded Jim as he carefully held the first ID by the edges while Chip snapped a photo of it.

Chip then opened up a ziplock bag for Jim to drop it into.

"That one belonged to a Ginger Martin," announced Jim.

"She was Misty Krain's best friend, back in 1959," described Chip. "Both of them disappeared about the same time. In fact, the detectives who worked on Misty's case wondered at first whether she and Ginger had left town together – as opposed to the vacuum cleaner salesman story – since neither were ever seen or heard from again."

"They're probably each in one of Jerry Krain's other barrels!" opined Carolyn. "And, how do we know Jerry didn't do it?"

"We'll need a copy of his prints, too, just in case he handled any of these things," nodded Chip as he made a small notation in his file. "Though, again, it's doubtful any prints would have survived, unless he made them recently."

"Perhaps on that roll of baling wire up there at the winery?" suggested Sherry.

"That's not a bad idea," recognized Chip.

"Misty Krain?" muttered Jim with astonishment as he slowly picked up the next ID from the stack, again handling it strictly by the edges to avoid destroying any possible evidence that might be left.

"How sad!" lamented Chip.

"So, everything my daddy said in his letter was true, then," pointed out Luella with a nod of satisfaction.

"And just the letters alone plus the things in this box all prove it!" responded Chip.

"Every one of these probably has Martha's prints on it, if she handled them recently," reminded Jim, "so we'll need to get a copy of her prints for comparison purposes."

"Is Karlin's ID in there, too?" Carolyn suddenly asked.

"No," answered Chip. "That was with *your* wallet and ID, in the barrel with her remains. We have both the wallet and its contents in our evidence locker at the station."

"That does seem rather odd that Karlin's ID wasn't in the metal box with the rest of these," frowned Jim. "Did you manage to lift any evidence from the wallet or its contents?"

"Not after all this time," regretted Chip. "But there's no doubt that her fingerprints would have been on it, since it was still clutched in her skeletal hand. And, we confirmed from the dental records that the skeleton was indeed hers."

Carolyn fought back tears as she thought of Karlin.

"Look!" noticed Ann. "There's a note in there, too! At the very bottom of the stack!"

"Let's take this one step at a time," insisted Jim. "We need to work our way through this stack of ID cards first. That way we can catalogue each one and compare it against the names in Chip's file."

440

The others watched in anxious silence as Jim and Chip methodically examined, photographed, and individually bagged each of the remaining ID cards, until they were all spread out in a row on the bar's counter. All but one of them were female.

"Twenty-nine of them in all!" Chip shook his head with chagrin.

"But, there were thirty victims in all, if you include Karlin," reminded Carolyn rather grimly.

"Yet, there were only twenty-nine missing persons," Chip suddenly realized as he began to study the names again on each of the ID cards laid out on the counter.

"That's right!" exclaimed Carolyn. "There was an extra barrel, up by the shed! Which one of those is not in your file now?"

"Right here," recognized Chip. "A young man named John Hansen. I believe he was one of the original students who disappeared back in 1959, but a phone call from his father to the detectives assured them that John was alive and well, safe at home. Apparently, his parents had pulled him from the school after learning of all the mysterious disappearances up here."

"It was probably one of those Krain boys who called you on the phone, just pretending to be the boy's father!" opined Luella.

"Wow!" Chip shook his head with disbelief as he turned to a page in his file and studied it. "Both John Hansen and his girlfriend – a Nancy Wheaton – attended the same barn dance that Misty Krain and her friend Ginger Martin attended, right before their disappearances."

"No doubt they were all witnesses to the Misty Krain murder," presumed Sherry as she wrote down their names in her notepad.

"Whatever that monster did or said to my daddy to keep him silent all those years, it must have been bad," guessed Luella.

"Perhaps he threatened to have Woody put in prison for the murder of Misty Krain if he told anyone about it," deduced Carolyn.

"Even though he didn't do it?" Luella was indignant.

"Especially if he didn't do it," reasoned Carolyn. "Think about it. Woody sees Ronald Krain murder his wife. The Professor then threatens to tell the authorities it was Woody, if he dares to tell anyone. And, to guarantee his silence, Professor Krain threatens to harm Woody's family if he doesn't comply."

"No wonder my poor daddy was always smoking that special tobacco of his," realized Luella. "It was probably one of the few things he had left to help calm his tortured soul."

"That's just sad!" exclaimed Janette.

"The note?" pressed Carolyn.

"I guess I should be the one to read this one," assumed Jim, "since I have the latex gloves on."

"Go for it," encouraged Chip.

"This appears to be a suicide note written by Martha Krain on March 23, 2023," mentioned Jim. "So, it definitely will have viable prints on it. And, it appears to be addressed to Lydia Cain. Humph. This is what it says:

*Dear Lydia,*

*I have no right to ask you to forgive me for what I did to Paul, or for what my daddy did to you. How could he just leave you there like that – still alive – out in the freezing cold to die alone? I'm so sorry I didn't find you in time! I truly tried my best to keep poor Woody from getting blamed for something he didn't do, but it started to rain before I could burn the evidence!*

*My daddy never knew that I went back and tried to do that, or that I knew of his other crimes. All those innocent people! Even my own dear mother!*

*These ID cards were in my daddy's desk drawer when he died. I found 'em when they let me return home to go through his things. But, I'm such a coward – all I did was put 'em in this box.*

*Jerry Krain is finally gone, but one never knows what the rest of those evil men might try to do. Rather than find out, I'm trying one last time to put an end to my miserable existence. I just can't go on! May the right people know what to do with this.*

*Please forgive me! Martha"*

Chip carefully snapped a photo of the letter with his cellphone before opening another of the quart-sized Ziploc bags for Jim to drop it into.

"Unbelievable!" muttered Luella.

"I think it's safe to say at this point that Woodrow Wilson's name will be cleared," predicted Chip. "Even if it is posthumously."

A sudden knock on the door startled everyone.

"Come in!" yelled Luella.

"Hello," greeted a uniformed officer. "We're here to go over that dark green 1965 Chevy Impala, sir."

"I'll finish up in here," offered Jim.

"Or, I can?" suggested Chip.

"Well, if no one else is going out there," advised Carolyn, "I'll go. I'd like to know what's in that car!"

"Me, too!" informed Janette.

"Definitely!" exclaimed Susan.

"How about I keep watch over the stuff here while I work on my notes?" offered Sherry. "Then you can all go check out that car."

"Uh, Carolyn?" It was Jim. "May I talk with you a moment?"

Janette and Susan paused to wait for her.

"Alone?" added Jim, rather uncomfortably.

"I'll see you guys out there," bid Carolyn.

Carolyn waited until everyone else, except Sherry and Luella, was outside and then followed Jim to a private corner of the room.

"I see you're still carrying your purse around with you?" mentioned Jim.

"I told her it would be safe in the room," commented Luella from behind them. *How had she managed to sneak up on them?*

"Uh, Carolyn and I need to have a word alone, if you don't mind," Jim requested of Luella.

"Suit yourself, honey," snorted Luella as she sauntered back over to where Sherry was, guarding the evidence.

Jim then looked around to make sure they were out of hearing distance before continuing. "I was just curious, have you read Lenny's letter yet?"

"Not yet," replied Carolyn with a slight smile. Just knowing how much it bothered Jim was almost worth the wait.

"How can you stand not knowing what it says?" pressed Jim.

"I plan to read it when we get back to Oceanview," informed Carolyn. "I think I'd like to sit on that special log when I do. That seems appropriate."

Jim gazed at Carolyn with pleading eyes, but only for a moment. "Is there any chance I might read it, too? When you do?"

Carolyn took a deep breath and slowly let it out again before responding. "The thing that has been bothering me is this. It was in

1974 that I last saw his cousin Pete, but Lenny's letter is postmarked August 26, 1979."

"That's quite a while," acknowledged Jim.

"And, it's addressed to my parents' house in Ashton," added Carolyn. "Not to me at Powell Mountain University, where it would have been forwarded to my next address."

"Pete never told him you stopped by to see him," deduced Jim.

"Probably not, though I never really did have a chance to let Pete know I was going to school there. But, I did see Lenny once in 1979," revealed Carolyn. "The very day that letter was written."

"Did he see you at the time?" pressed Jim.

"Yes," replied Carolyn.

"Did you speak to one another?" grilled Jim.

"We had a brief conversation," advised Carolyn.

"Well?" urged Jim.

"Later," insisted Carolyn.

# 11. Kangaroo Court

**K**arlin tightly clutched Carolyn's missing blue wallet in her hands, even though they were tied behind her back. Why in the world had she come alone? Karlin drifted in and out of consciousness from the head wound she had now, but was uncertain how bad it might be.

Was it still Saturday, February 15th? wondered Karlin. And what time was it? Obviously, it was still 1975, but would she live to see 1976? And, where was she? Inside one of the wine barrels? It sure smelled like it!

Karlin grimaced from the stench of rancid wine residue surrounding her as she struggled to try to open Carolyn's wallet in the darkness. Strange that they would have put it in the container with her. Hopefully, there might be something inside the wallet that Karlin could use to cut loose the sharp baling wire on her wrists and ankles!

Just as Karlin began to drift into unconsciousness again, the sound of men's voices caught her attention. One of them sounded like Professor Krain, who she had talked into bringing her to the winery in the first place. Big mistake! Karlin shook her head with dismay and then winced from the pain. It felt as if something sticky was oozing down the back of her neck and onto her shoulders. Was it blood from her headwound? Karlin struggled once more, in vain. Why in the world would Jerry have done this to her? And why wouldn't Professor Krain have tried to stop him? Had he *helped* Jerry tie her up while she was unconscious before putting her inside the reeking barrel?

"Jerry, just what do you think you're doing?" demanded the voice of Professor Ronald Krain. He sounded as if he were standing immediately beside the wine barrel in which she was imprisoned.

"What I should have done a long time ago!" snapped Jerry. "I'm putting an end to this, once and for all! Wasn't it enough for you that I had to close this place down back in '69, following that fiasco? Not to mention covering for YOU back in '59, after what you did to your very own wife, right there in my shed! And now, I'm completely bankrupt!"

"This has still got to stop!" maintained Ronald. "Even if the guys we have in the Department find out about this, we'll still be on our own. This is too big."

"Then they won't find out," assured Jerry.

"What are you gonna do?" scoffed Ronald. "Burn the place down?"

"Don't tempt me!" challenged Jerry.

"With all the bodies in cement, there's no way to hide 'em," pointed out Ronald. "Not even with a fire!"

"Well, you shouldn't have brought that Mexican girl back here, cousin," chastised Jerry.

"And YOU shouldn't have brought her or Carolyn here in the *first* place!" shouted Ronald as he angrily kicked the barrel in which Karlin was bound. "Now it's only a matter of time before Carolyn comes here looking for her! And, if anything happens to her, that's obviously going to point back to me!"

"Help!" muttered Karlin. "I won't tell! Please let me go!"

"You idiot!" screamed Ronald when he heard the sound of Karlin's cries from inside the barrel. "Can't you do anything right?"

"She'll run out of air soon, anyway," pointed out Jerry. "Besides, I don't even know if I have any more of that cement mix!"

"Even an injured animal deserves more compassion than that!" snapped Ronald. "It's time to put her out of her misery."

"No!" moaned Karlin. Tears began to stream down her cheeks. "Don't do this! I'll do anything you ask! Please!"

Karlin soon realized that she must have drifted into unconsciousness again, but the voices were finally gone. "Help!"

Where were they? Karlin struggled uselessly against the baling wire. Her limbs had become numb. Yet, now she could no longer move! "Oh, my God!" exclaimed Karlin when she realized that the barrel was slowly being filled with what smelled like wet cement. "Help!" screamed Karlin.

The gooey substance had reached her chest and continued to rise. It was only a matter of time before it reached her face and she was drowned. "Oh, dear God! Please forgive me for the things I have done! I'm so sorry! And please keep Carolyn safe from these evil men! Do not let her come here!" Karlin could feel the wet cement on her neck now and knew that her demise was inevitable. Thinking of nothing more to say in her final prayer, she concluded with "Amen" and then waited for the welcome release of death.

Karlin tightly closed her eyes and mouth and did actually manage to hold her breath for several minutes, even after the wet cement covered her face, just as she had done in her high school

446

swimming class. Carolyn had taken a swimming class, too, remembered Karlin. Would she have been able to hold her breath for this long?

All at once, Karlin released her last breath and abruptly was overcome by the wet cement. "Please don't let Ruby come here, either!" thought Karlin as she rapidly suffocated and died.

Karlin suddenly found herself in fetal position, traveling backwards at an alarming rate, down a long, dark tunnel. Her eyes were tightly closed, though she could see through her eyelids that it was becoming light around her. "Where am I?"

"I'm sorry, but it was her time," apologized a man's voice. The voice was soothing and kind, not at all like that of Ronald or Jerry Krain.


It was the morning of March 23, 1975. Even though it was a Sunday, Deputy DAs Charles Priest and Ron Telluric, had come into the office.

It was troubling to Chip that six entire weeks had gone by since the disappearance of Karlin Gomez, not to mention that they were still no closer to solving the Lydia Cain murder than they had been when finally finding the missing green Mustang on Monday, February 17, 1975, hidden beneath a pile of brush on an old logging road adjoining Woodrow Wilson's property line. Was it somehow possible that the Powell Mountain Killer could be responsible for both of them?

Following a search warrant for probable cause, a subsequent search of the entire area had revealed absolutely nothing. Over a hundred volunteers had combed every nook and cranny of the woodcutter's property, including the hogback and surrounding hillside.

"We need to go back," advised Chip.

"Go back where?" scowled Ron.

"Back to where we found the green Mustang," replied Chip.

"And, we're just going to magically find something there, when over a hundred volunteers spent two entire weeks combing the area and found nothing?" Ron was frustrated and sarcastic.

"We have to go back," persisted Chip. "I know it sounds crazy, but I keep having this persistent feeling that we need to go look again."

"Sure!" sighed Ron. "Why not? We're going nowhere in solving this thing, anyway."

"Well, it's not like the detectives working on the case are doing anything about it, are they?" demanded Chip.

"Just why is this one so important to you, anyway?" frowned Ron. "We've both done our best."

"Perhaps if we'd been out there with them, when those people were searching, we might have found something!" argued Chip.

"It's no one's fault that you had to be in court that day," reminded Ron. "We're attorneys, and when the court demands us to be there, that's just the way it is."

"I know," Chip responded more softly.

"Heck, I had to be in court, too," reminded Ron. "That's just the nature of the job."

"Well, today is Sunday," persisted Chip. "And, I'm going out there for one more look."

"Let's go." Ron was actually as anxious as Chip to see for himself, especially now that the woodcutter had given permission for his property to be searched.

Chip quickly put on his jacket and stood up to leave.

"We won't need to have another search warrant, in case we do find anything, will we?" Ron hesitated.

"Come on!" urged Chip. "I'm sure we're good."

After changing into footwear more appropriate to the terrain they were about to search, Chip Priest and Ron Telluric started up the old logging road where they had found the missing green Mustang six weeks earlier.

"At least it's a nice day," acknowledged Ron as he pulled a pair of dark glasses from his jacket pocket and put them on. Chip had already put his on. Being out of shape, Ron soon found himself winded as he tried to keep up with Chip. If only he'd remembered to bring a hat with him, too!

Songbirds could be heard overhead, echoing across the dense mountain landscape. Blossoms on some of the foliage and several varieties of early spring flowers were in the process of being pollinated by a rather large mountain bumble bee. Ron was allergic to bee stings and hesitated.

"Come on!" urged Chip. "It's not gonna sting you!"

"Well, if it does," replied Ron, "you're the one who'll have to get me out of here! And look, he's got a friend, right over there!"

Chip bent down to pick up a six-foot branch from the ground and broke several dried limbs from it.

"You gonna fight 'em off with that?" teased Ron.

"A walking stick," informed Chip. "Plus, whatever else I might need it for. You never know."

"We didn't bring any water with us, did we?" questioned Ron as he skirted the area where the bees were, making sure to give them a wide berth. He was starting to feel dehydrated, and they had been ascending the steep landscape for half an hour already!

"Let's just search over there," indicated Chip, "and if we don't find anything, we'll call it good. Okay?"

"Seriously?" scowled Ron.

"Since we are here anyway," added Chip. "In fact, that is the area I've been thinking about."

"That's a long way for someone to carry a body," noted Ron.

"Which would probably rule out Martha Krain," opined Chip.

"Unless she had help," added Ron as he paused to gasp for air.

"You all right?" asked Chip.

"Go ahead!" encouraged Ron. "I'll just wait here." Ron then bent down and put his hands on his knees to catch his breath.

"Very well," agreed Chip as he made his way up the last few yards of the hillside, poking the area around him with his makeshift walking stick as he went.

The startling sound of a ruffed grouse exploding into flight from the bushes nearby prompted Ron to resume his trek up the hill after Chip. Was he responsible for startling it that badly, or had something else frightened it? Ron had no idea what else might be in the thick forest undergrowth surrounding him and did not want to remain behind to find out.

The chiaroscuro of shadows on the forest floor danced before Ron's feet as the early morning sunlight stretched its tentacles of light through the old growth forest. A sharp breeze unexpectedly caused him to pull up the collar on his suit coat as he inhaled the fragrance of wild jasmine mingled with other musty odors.

"Ron!" shouted Chip. "Quick! Come here!"

"Are you alright?" called Ron as he approached.

"I think it's Lydia Cain!" exclaimed Chip as he carefully pulled aside the various pieces of rotting brush covering the body. "Look!

See the American flag sticking out from beneath that green hood? The woodcutter used to drive around with a flag like that on his antenna!"

"He did, didn't he?" realized Ron. "We should check to see if it's there now."

"I don't believe it is," replied Chip. "I noticed it was missing when we were out here before, after we found the green Mustang."

"Which means we have probable cause to get an arrest warrant and have the Sheriff arrest him," deduced Ron.

"Or at least hold him for questioning until we can get a forensic team up here," clarified Chip. "But, let's get the arrest warrant to make it official. And then, if it turns out he's innocent, they can always let him go."

"Too bad we can't even touch anything, now that we're here!" panted Ron. "I didn't even bring any evidence tent markers along."

"I've got my Polaroid with me," advised Chip as he took it out of his coat pocket, unfolded it, and snapped several photos of the scene and of the body. His camera was a folding Model 195.

"What if we can't find this place again?" questioned Ron as he struggled to breathe normally.

"Oh, we'll find it, all right," assured Chip as he pulled out a roll of bright red marking tape from his other pocket, tore off a two-foot strip of it, and tied it around a nearby tree.

"Poor kid," muttered Ron as he studied her half-decomposed bare feet and the inadequate clothing she had on. "Even if she was alive when they left her, she would have died of exposure the first night."

The rumpled white cardigan sweater was irreparably stained with dirt and dried blood, as were the lowcut yellow cotton top and blue denim miniskirt the victim had on.

"I wonder what happened to her shoes?" Chip suddenly asked.

"Didn't they did find a pair of women's sandals by Paul Johnson's body last November?" asked Ron.

"I believe they did," realized Chip. "I'm sure the forensic team can determine if they were hers."

"At any rate, we'd better not touch anything else!" cautioned Ron.

"Agreed." Chip then tore off several more strips of the red marking tape and began tying them to various tree branches along the route they had taken as he started back.

450

Ron continued to stand there for several moments longer before finally following after him.

Back at the St. Diablo District Attorney's office, Ron and Chip anxiously paced the floor while they waited for their secretary to finish typing up the arrest warrant. She had not been happy about being asked to come in on a Sunday.

"Do you think we can get Judge Lorik to sign it today?" asked Ron. "What if we can't find him out on the golf course?"

"We'll find him, but that's not what I'm worried about. What if the woodcutter is innocent?" Chip suddenly asked. "He just doesn't seem like the type of a man who would do something like that."

"What about the American flag we saw?" reminded Ron.

"Something just doesn't feel right about it," mentioned Chip.

"Guess we'll find out soon enough," answered Ron as their secretary brought them the completed warrant.

"I took the liberty of getting Judge Lorik to sign it when he stopped by here on his way to the golf course. He just left here five minutes ago," mentioned their secretary.

"Awesome!" praised Chip as he took the paper from her, though he clearly lacked the expected enthusiasm about it. "Thanks again for coming in on your day off."

"Good job!" grinned Ron as he motioned toward the stale pot of coffee on an unplugged single electric burner nearby. "Have a cup of coffee, on me!"

"Gee, thanks!" chuckled Cindy as she shook her head. "I'll try not to drink it all at once!"

Chip and Ron then hurried from the building with the signed arrest warrant, climbed inside their official business vehicle, and headed at once for the Wilson property.

The Sheriff slated to serve it would meet them there.

Meanwhile, at the Wilson residence, Woody had stopped by home to check on Matthew, Mark and Luella, and to make them some lunch before loading up more firewood in his truck for another delivery.

"Luella's dirty again!" complained Matthew as his father walked through the door.

At only ten years of age, the last thing Matthew wanted to do was be stuck at home changing his baby sister's diaper!  It was spring break and Matthew felt like he should be outside playing instead.  Matthew was only in the fifth grade, but worked hard in school and deserved to enjoy his week off.  Already more literate and articulate than his father, Matthew was frequently embarrassed by the woodcutter's poor grammar when conversing with customers.  Thankfully, most of the folks on his father's delivery route were rarely at home when he stopped by to make the deliveries.  Matthew had often ridden with Woody to help unload firewood at each stop after school, but now that his mama was in the nursing home Matthew was needed to help at home.

"Kin ya change Luella whiltz yer daddy makes sum lunch?" questioned Woody.  He needed to have the children fed and be on his way within the hour to be on time for his next delivery of firewood.

"How come Mark can't change her once in a while?" argued Matthew.  "Why do I always have to be the one?  Besides, Luella should be potty trained by now!"

"Yer little brother kin't do it!  He's only six and barely outa diapers hisself," reminded Woody as he grabbed a can opener and began opening a can of beans.

"And why do we always have to have beans for lunch?" frowned Matthew.  "Can't we ever have anything else?"

"When is mama comin' home?" asked Mark rather loudly. "I'm tired of beans!"

"She's in a nursing home, stupid!" reminded Matthew.  "That means she probably ain't never comin' home!"

"Oh boys!" Woody stopped what he was doing, came over, squatted down, and put an arm around each of them to pull them close. "Yer mama will be home soon.  Dats what dey tell me.  She's just very sick rite now."

"I want mama!" Mark began to snivel and cry.

Matthew wriggled free as Woody pulled Mark close to hug him for a moment longer.

"Is today's delivery to one of your paying customers?" grilled Matthew, rather sarcastically.  He was well aware that certain customers seemed to be exempt from having to pay for their wood.

"More den likely," replied Woody as he let go of Mark and returned to the task of opening the can of beans.

"Good!" responded Matthew. "Maybe then we can have something else to eat for a change!"

"Where's de matches?" grilled Woody as he dumped the open can of beans into an aging sauce pan. "They wuz rite here this mornin'."

"Gone," informed Matthew. He actually had hidden them in his pocket, to avoid having beans for lunch again.

"Dey kin't be gone already," surmised Woody. "We still gots to heat up de food for baby Luella."

"How come she still gets baby food to eat?" pouted Matthew as he finally pulled the matches from his pocket and reluctantly handed them to his father. "She's almost three!"

"Kin ya plez change Luella fer me?" Woody asked again as he lit the stove and began heating the beans.

"Someone's at the door!" informed Mark. He had heard a car pull up and was over at the window, looking outside.

"Here, stir de beans fer me, will ya?" Woody suddenly requested of his son Matthew.

"Sure, why not? At least it beats diaper duty!" smirked Matthew as he took over stirring the beans.

Five loud knocks on the front door had awakened Luella, who now was screaming at the top of her lungs. The hand-made wooden crib where she had been napping was over in one corner of the room. Woody had fashioned and assembled the crib himself.

Woody quickly glanced outside before opening the front door. The two men standing there had been by last month, following the discovery of his missing green Mustang, so Woody was well aware of who they were. Woody cautiously opened the door. "Detectives?"

"Uh, actually, we are Deputy District Attorneys," corrected the tall plump man with the piercing blue eyes. "I'm Deputy DA Ron Telluric."

"And I'm Deputy DA Charles Priest," reminded the other man. Chip was much shorter and slimmer than his partner and his distinct Jewish features were unmistakable.

Neither of them made any effort whatsoever to greet Woody by shaking hands, and both were quite serious and businesslike.

"Have ye had any lunch?" offered Woody. "Wuz just feedin' de kids sum beans."

Ron Telluric made a face of disapproval at the suggestion. As much as he loved to eat, beans were not something he enjoyed.

"Mr. Wilson," informed Chip, "I'm afraid this is official business. Can we please ask you to step outside for a moment?"

"I got this," called Matthew from the old wood-burning stove where he stood on an upside-down wooden crate, stirring the beans.

"You stay der, too," Woody directed little Mark. "Yer daddy'll be right back. Plez check on Luella."

Ron Telluric took the liberty of shutting the front door behind Woody after he stepped outside.

"Where is Mrs. Wilson?" grilled Chip.

"Harriet?" Woody furled his brow. He was certain he had mentioned to them last month that Harriet was at the Powell Mountain Nursing Home. "She still be at de nursin' home."

"When do you expect her back?" pressed Chip.

"She got de blood cancer, sir." Woody was almost apologetic about it, though it really was no one's fault.

"I'm very sorry," acknowledged Chip, more softly.

"Who watches those kids when you are out doing your deliveries?" interrogated Ron.

"Is old Woody in trouble fer dat?" Woody suddenly worried.

"Right now, I'd say that's the least of your worries," assured Ron. "Is there someone who can come here to watch your children for you while we take you downtown for a few questions?"

"But, I gots a delivery to do after lunch," mentioned Woody.

Woody was quite concerned with getting paid for the delivery and wanted to make sure he was there on time. After all, Mr. Finch was one of his few paying customers.

"We can't just leave those kids here alone like that," pointed out Chip to Ron.

"Can we just bring 'em with us?" wondered Ron.

"We'll probably have to," agreed Chip.

"Matthew be a good boy, sir," informed Woody. "He kin watch 'em by hisself."

"Just how old is Matthew?" asked Ron.

"Matthew be ten years old," revealed Woody rather proudly.

"And the others?" pressed Ron.

"Mark, he be six, and de baby – dats Luella – she be almost three," advised Woody. "Why?"

"First of all," explained Chip, "it's technically against the law for children so young to be left alone like that, without adult supervision. So, we obviously must take them with us when we take you in for questioning."

"Ask me what ya will," encouraged Woody. "Kin't we just do it here, plez?"

"I need to show you a photograph." Chip hesitated. He really didn't want to have Woody arrested if it wasn't absolutely necessary. "What's in this photo may upset you, but I need you to tell me whether you can identify anything in the picture. Can you do that for me, Mr. Wilson?"

Woody then stared with disbelief at the horrific photo of Lydia Cain's partially decomposed body. "Oh God, Almighty!" Woody suddenly felt sick and hobbled over to a nearby bench to sit down.

Deputy DA Priest came and sat down beside him, still holding the photo while Deputy DA Telluric stood nearby.

"We are fairly certain this was Lydia Cain," added Chip. "The forensics team is up there now. The place in this photo is here on your property, by the way."

Woody silently stared at the photo as tears began to stream down his cheeks. *How could he not have known she was there all this time? Could he have done something to prevent it, if only he had said something about Misty Krain back in '59? And, was it the work of Ronald Krain, this time to try and frame him?*

"Well?" pressed Chip.

After several moments, Woody finally answered. "De hood on her head, it kinda looks like part of de old Army bag sumone stole frum de shed last year."

"Anything else?" probed Chip.

"I kin't be sure," muttered Woody, "but sum kids, dey stole old Woody's flag 'bout dat time, too. Probly when dey stole de car. At least dats whut I believe."

"Are we talking about the flag that used to be attached to the antenna of your pickup truck?" clarified Chip.

Woody merely nodded.

"And the green Mustang that was stolen from your salvage yard and recovered last month over on that old logging road?" added Chip.

"Yes, sir," answered Woody. He was clearly shaken.

"Does anything else in the photo appear familiar to you, Mr. Wilson?" continued Chip. "Take your time."

"Der wuz a gas can taken frum de shed 'bout den, too," recalled Woody. "Dat der kinda looks like it, layin' on de ground der."

"Good eye," nodded Chip. "Actually, it is a gas can, and they're analyzing it for fingerprints as we speak."

"Was there anything else missing from your shed that you can think of right off hand?" interjected Ron.

Woody paused for several moments to think about it before responding. "Der wuz sum balin' wire. A whole roll of it, plus sum o' dat wuz in the car."

"In the green Mustang?" quizzed Ron.

"Yes, sir," confirmed Woody.

"Here comes the Sheriff now," observed Chip.

"I'm sorry, Mr. Wilson," apologized Ron Telluric, "but we are going to need to take you in for more questioning, and will need to hold you until the forensic evidence can be analyzed, hopefully to prove your innocence."

The dust-covered Sheriff vehicle came to a stop beside them.

"You's arrestin' me?" Woody asked with alarm.

"Greetings, gentlemen," nodded the Sheriff as he climbed from his vehicle and approached.

"Let's not use handcuffs on him in front of his children," requested Chip. "We have to bring them with us."

"Fine by me," consented the Sheriff with a shrug of his shoulders. The small white knight lapel pin on his collar suddenly gleamed in the sunlight.

"Can Mr. Wilson ride to town with us and the children?" requested Chip as he handed the signed arrest warrant to the Sheriff.

"Very well, that's fine by me," agreed the Sheriff as he stuffed the warrant into his pocket without bothering to read it. "Woodrow Wilson, you are being arresting as a suspect in the murder of Lydia Cain. You have the right to remain silent. Anything you say can and will be used against you in a court of law. You have the right to an attorney. If you cannot afford an attorney, one will be provided for you. Do you understand those rights?"

Woody merely nodded.

"I'll get the children," offered Chip.

"I kin get 'em," volunteered Woody as he slowly got up and hobbled toward his front door.

"He needs to remain in your immediate custody," pointed out the Sheriff to Chip and Ron with a smug grin as he turned to leave. "At least until you get him downtown."

"No worries," Chip assured the Sheriff as he followed Woody into the house.

"Kids," began Woody. "We's goin' for a ride." Then, turning to Chip, Woody requested, "Kin I change de baby first?"

"Sure," agreed Chip.

"Matthew," directed Woody, "kin ya plez turn off de stove? De fire'll burn herself out."

"But I thought we were going to eat lunch now!" protested Matthew. Even if it was just beans, he was still famished.

"We'll get you something better to eat downtown," promised Chip. "Okay?"

"Okay, sure," nodded Matthew.

"Better 'n beans?" questioned Mark, rather hopefully.

"Better than beans," assured Chip with an amused but sad smile.

After changing Luella into a clean diaper and fresh outfit, Woody carefully picked her up to carry her. "Let's go, boys."

As Woody watched his two boys exit the house with Ron Telluric and climb into the back of the unmarked detective vehicle out front, the Sheriff vehicle could already be seen driving away. Woody then turned to get one last look around. Would he ever see his home again? Or Harriet?

"You can sit up front with your little girl, by Ron," indicated Chip. "I'll sit in the back with the boys."

Once everyone was seated in the dark blue, four-door 1974 Plymouth Valiant sedan, Ron started the engine, put it into gear, and unhurriedly drove away.

Woody stared out the passenger window at the two-story stone building he and his wife Harriet had called home since 1956. What would become of his salvage yard now, or his firewood business? How would Harriet manage to care for the place on her own, when she finally got out of the nursing home? The huge stack of firewood beside the Wilson residence, along with Woody's well-used axe stuck into an old tree stump beside it, slowly disappeared from view.

It was Saturday, April 5, 1975.  Carolyn had just gotten back from breakfast and come into the fifth-floor dormitory room.  Ever since the disappearance of her friend Karlin, Carolyn had become somewhat withdrawn and tended to keep to herself a good deal of the time.

"Hey there," greeted Rachel.

Carolyn was surprised by the friendly greeting.  It had been quite some time since Rachel had even spoken to her, despite the fact that they were roommates.

"Have you seen the news?" questioned Sarah, who was also unusually friendly for a change.

"Why?" asked Carolyn rather suspiciously as she tossed her purse onto her bed and then seated herself at her desk.  It was Carolyn's intention to get an early start on her latest Bookkeeping assignment so that she might be free to spend the evening with Eula and Stacia.

"Carolyn, you've got to see this!" instructed Rachel as she approached and handed a rumpled newspaper to Carolyn.

At first, Carolyn was slightly irritated by the interruption but then stared with disbelief at the front-page headline.  It read, "Woodcutter Faces Trial for Lydia Cain Murder" followed by a full-page article discussing the case.

"How can this be?" questioned Carolyn, who felt sudden anger at seeing the article.  "This is not possible!"

"It says the trial is slated to begin on Monday, April 14th," pointed out Sarah.

"Does it say anything about Karlin in the article?" demanded Carolyn as she hurried to try to peruse the tiny print.  "Have they found her yet?"

"Not a word," replied Rachel.  "But, I did hear last week that they've given up the search."

Carolyn glanced rather sadly at Karlin's empty bed, and at the closet where her clothes still hung.

"Ms. Forrest told us this morning that the Gomez family will be coming here later today to pick up her things," revealed Rachel.

"I see."  Carolyn pursed her lips with frustration, angry that everyone else seemed to be giving up so easily.  Perhaps she should return to the winery, properly armed, to search again? Maybe she could talk Karl Simpson, the security guard, into accompanying her?

"Do you really think he's the Powell Mountain Killer?" Sarah asked Rachel.

"Who else could it be?" posed Rachel. "There haven't been any more killings since his arrest. Plus, they say the marks on her headwound match exactly to the marks found on the two roadside victims they have found so far this year."

"Except for Paul Johnson, of course," reminded Sarah.

"Well, there's still a whole bunch of missing victims that no one has found yet!" pointed out Carolyn.

"And just what makes you so sure that creepy old woodcutter is innocent?" demanded Rachel.

"He just is," replied Carolyn. "There's no way Woody would have done something like that!"

"Sometimes you never know about people," commented Sarah.

"No, you don't!" snapped Carolyn as she grabbed her purse from the bed and stormed from the room clutching the newspaper.


The Honorable Jonathan Lorik sat at a large mahogany desk in his chambers, carefully studying the *Wilson* file in front of him. It was Monday morning, April 14, 1975.

"Your Honor?" It was his judicial assistant, Beverly Clark.

"Please have counsel join me in my chambers," instructed the judge. "There is an important matter we need to discuss."

"The prospective jurors are already assembled for *voir dire*," reminded Beverly.

"I'm well aware of that, Ms. Clark," barked the judge.

"Yes, sir, right away, sir," responded his judicial assistant as she hurried from his chambers.

Jonathan Lorik had served as Head Knight of the Crusading Knights of Powell Mountain since 1952, and was first elected to serve as presiding judge at the St. Diablo County Courthouse in 1961. Judge Lorik had been reelected during each subsequent election.

After tapping lightly on the chambers door, Ms. Clark entered with Deputy DA Charles Priest and Defense Attorney Phillip Dunbar.

"Gentlemen," acknowledged the judge as he motioned toward the two plush leather armchairs on the other side of his impressively carved mahogany desk. Behind him on the wall hung a plethora of gold-framed degrees and impressive community service awards.

"Will there be anything else, sir?" questioned Ms. Clark from the open doorway.

"That will be all for now," advised Judge Lorik. "Please close the door on your way out. We may be a few minutes."

"Yes, Your Honor," complied Ms. Clark as she tried to close the door as quietly as possible on her way out.

"Phil, let's start with you." While Judge Lorik waited for Phil to begin, he deliberately crossed his feet on top of his desk and interlocked the fingers of his hands behind his head.

"Sir, the defense is ready to present its case," assured his long-time friend Phillip Dunbar.

"And you really intend to defend that negro?" grilled the judge as he removed his feet from his desk before leaning forward in his plush leather chair in an intimidating manner.

"It's my job, sir," reminded Phil, unwaveringly.

"We've been friends for a long time, have we not?" pressed Judge Lorik.

"You know we have," replied Phil. "We've served in the Crusading Knights together for over fifteen years."

"And yet you have decided to defend that creature?" Judge Lorik shook his head with dismay.

"I truly believe he will be found innocent, Your Honor," maintained Phil. "There are too many forensic details and other facts that will create a reasonable doubt in the minds of the jury."

"What about you, Chip?" Judge Lorik suddenly turned his attention to the Deputy DA. "Is the prosecution ready to proceed?"

Chip Priest hesitated before responding.

"Well?" urged the judge.

"Your Honor, sir," answered Chip, "the prosecution also believes the defendant will be found innocent."

"What?" hollered Judge Lorik as he rose halfway from his chair in an angry manner. "What is the meaning of this?"

"Sir, I know it's my job to convince the jury of Mr. Wilson's guilt," acknowledged Chip, "but I would be negligent in my duties as a human being to portray him as a guilty man when there is significant evidence to the contrary."

"Significant evidence to the contrary?" fumed the judge as he slowly sat back down in his comfortable chair and narrowed his eyes at the Deputy DA.

"There's not a jury anywhere who could fairly convict him, based on the known facts and evidence available," assured Chip Priest.

"Well, let's just hope you're wrong," advised the judge with a tight-lipped grin.

"If Your Honor will just indulge me further," continued Chip, "the prosecution has no desire to see these proceedings be turned into a kangaroo court."

"A kangaroo court?" growled the judge.

"Yes," acknowledged the Deputy DA. "A kangaroo court is a judicial tribunal or assembly that blatantly disregards recognized standards of law or justice, and often carries little or no ...."

"I know what a kangaroo court is!" interrupted the judge as he abruptly slammed his open right hand onto the top of his desk while he glared at Chip Priest. "And, I can assure you, the decisions rendered in this courtroom do carry official standing!"

"Would that happen to include the burning crosses the defendant has found by his home over the years?" challenged Chip Priest.

"How dare you!" Jonathan Lorik glared at Charles Priest with undisguised hatred.

"How dare I?" ventured Chip.

"You certainly are NOT a member of the Crusading Knights!" muttered Judge Lorik through gritted teeth.

"And you, sir, certainly are not a Jew," rebutted Chip.

"That's a good one!" laughed Judge Lorik, suddenly finding humor in the Deputy DA's remark. "Well, it's a good thing the eventual verdict is up to the jury, then."

It was well after three o'clock in the afternoon before *voir dire* was complete and the all-white jury had been selected.

"Bring the prisoner in," called Ms. Clark.

Accompanied by two armed Sheriff Deputies, Woodrow Wilson was escorted into the courtroom. The one-piece red jumpsuit he wore was clearly designed for a taller individual. But for the heavy ankle chains he wore, the pantlegs would have dragged on the ground while he walked. The waist chain system used to restrain his hands

461

were intended to keep them secure while allowing him just enough leeway to flip through documents or sign something if necessary.

In spite of his circumstances, Woody had an unusual aura of calmness about him as he struggled to hobble into the courtroom with his heavy restraints on. Thankfully, they had allowed him to keep his wooden foot on so he could walk on his own. In one hand was the tattered old Bible that Woody had previously kept on the dashboard of his pickup truck.

"Over here," indicated the public defender.

"Mister Dunbar," acknowledged Woody with a cordial nod as he made his way to the empty chair at the defense table. "Thanks fer havin' 'em git de Bible fer me."

"No problem," replied Phillip Dunbar rather unemotionally.

Seated at the prosecution table on the opposite side of the room were Chip Priest and Ron Telluric. Neither man looked as if they really wanted to be there.

The court reporter – a middle-aged man with thick round glasses and a rumpled suit – was seated at a small table beside the judge's bench. On the other side of it was the empty witness stand.

The entire courtroom was packed, with bystanders in the lobby, and even crowded against the exterior windows gazing inside.

Serving as both judicial assistant and court clerk, Ms. Clark's courtroom table was located directly in front of the judge's bench.

"All rise," commanded the bailiff as Judge Lorik walked into the courtroom from his chambers, directly behind the judge's bench.

"The St. Diablo County Court is now in session, with the Honorable Jonathan Lorik presiding. Please be seated." The bailiff then motioned for everyone to be seated.

"Good afternoon, ladies and gentlemen," greeted Judge Lorik. "We have just returned from recess following selection of the jury in the matter of the *People of St. Diablo County versus Woodrow Wilson*. Are both sides ready to proceed?"

"Ready for the People, Your Honor," indicated Deputy DA Charles Priest.

"Ready for the Defense, Your Honor," informed Public Defender Phillip Dunbar.

"Will the clerk please swear in the jury?" requested the judge.

Ms. Clark grabbed a clipboard from her table with pre-printed language on it before approaching the jury box. "Will the jury please stand and raise your right hands?"

The all-white jury then stood.

"Do each of you swear that you will fairly try the case before this court, and that you will return a true verdict according to the evidence and the instructions of this court, so help you, God? Please say 'I do.'"

"I do," replied the jurors in unison.

"You may be seated," motioned Ms. Clark before returning to her table.

"Before we go on," advised Judge Lorik, "there is just enough time remaining for the opening statements. We will then recess and continue this trial at nine o'clock tomorrow morning. Is that acceptable to everyone?"

After affirmative nods from each counsel, Judge Lorik motioned for them to proceed.

"Good afternoon, lady and gentlemen," greeted Chip Priest.

Strange that only one woman had been selected to be on the jury, thought Chip as he studied each of them. She was also the only juror without a white knight lapel pin, though that was understandable since the CKPM was an exclusively male organization. Perhaps her husband was a member? That might be just as bad, worried Chip.

"We are here today to determine the guilt or innocence of the defendant, Mr. Woodrow Wilson, who is seated at the defense table over there. He has been accused of a horrific crime, the murder of a nineteen-year-old coed named Lydia Cain, whose body was discovered last month on his property."

Chip paused for effect, again studying each juror for his or her reaction to the information he had just revealed.

"It was on March 23, 1975, that Deputy DA Ron Telluric – who is seated at the prosecution table – accompanied me to the Wilson property where we performed a subsequent search of our own to try to find the victim. That was when we discovered her remains. The initial search that was conducted the month before by over a hundred volunteers had been fruitless, so it was no doubt an act of divine providence that we were successful in finally finding her."

"Council will confine his remarks to the facts," cautioned Judge Lorik. "Divine providence is a matter of pure conjecture, so the jury will disregard Mr. Priest's last remark."

"Yes, Your Honor," apologized Chip. "We do know that whoever was responsible for her demise took the time to carefully bind her hands and feet with baling wire, and to put an American flag over the blunt force wound on her head. On top of that was a carefully fashioned outer hood, created from an old Army bag."

Several of the jurors were clearly disturbed by the information, including the woman.

"We also know that – for whatever reason – the perpetrator or perpetrators doused the body of Ms. Cain with gasoline," added Chip. "But, the body was never burned, perhaps due to the weather."

"Conjecture!" warned Judge Lorik.

"I withdraw that last remark," muttered Chip. "During the course of this trial, you will hear from several experts. Those individuals are qualified to testify and offer their expert opinions on subjects such as weather, fingerprints, entomology, pathology, and possible motive."

"Motive?" Judge Lorik was losing his patience.

"Their opinions, not mine, Your Honor," clarified Chip Priest.

"That should prove interesting," smirked the judge.

"One of the experts you will hear from will explain to you why he believes that Lydia Cain was still alive at the time she was left in the location where she ultimately died," added Chip, rather evenly.

"Anything else?" prompted Judge Lorik with an amused expression on his face.

"There will also be several witnesses called to testify in this matter, including the decedent's roommate at the time of her death, a Miss Martha Krain," revealed Chip with a triumphant glance at Judge Lorik.

The entire courtroom began whispering, and even the bystanders in the lobby began loudly conversing amongst one another.

"Silence!" hollered Judge Lorik as his gavel banged repeatedly against the small wooden sounding block in front of him. "Silence!"

The courtroom slowly came to order, but not nearly as rapidly as Judge Lorik would have liked. "Ladies and gentlemen – and I use the term loosely – you will not disrespect this court like that again! Do

I make myself clear? One more outburst from *anyone* in this courtroom, and that person will be asked to leave here at once!"

The bailiff unexpectedly approached the bench with a handwritten note from a member of the audience. After reading the note, Judge Lorik then directed, "Counsel approach the bench."

"Your Honor," objected Chip Priest. "This is highly irregular. I am still in the midst of my opening remarks to the jury."

"Approach!" commanded the judge. He was not going to ask again and did not appear very happy about being challenged.

Once Chip Priest and Phil Dunbar were standing directly in front of the bench, Judge Lorik took a deep breath and slowly let it out. "Mr. Priest, may I remind you that *you* are the prosecution, and *not* the defense attorney in this case?"

"Yes, sir," replied Chip.

"Does the defense have any objection to the calling of Martha Krain as a witness in this matter?" Judge Lorik glanced at the public defender with a raised eyebrow.

"There are some concerns that I intend to bring to the court's attention," advised Phil.

"And those are?" prompted the judge as he drummed his fingers on the bench table in front of him.

"Well, sir," answered Phil, "As the court is aware, Martha Krain is currently recovering from a recent suicide attempt, and may be unfit to testify in this matter."

"Duly noted," nodded Judge Lorik. "Would the defense care to make a motion in that regard?"

"Yes, Your Honor," replied Phil. "The defense moves that any testimony pertaining to Martha Krain be sequestered from the public until the conclusion of this trial."

"But ...," began Chip.

"This is your last warning, counselor," interrupted the judge. "I'm losing my patience with you. Gentlemen, please return to your tables." After waiting for them to comply, Judge Lorik continued so that everyone else could hear. "It is hereby ordered by this court that any testimony pertaining to Martha Krain, Paul Johnson, or any other third parties be conducted under seal. It is further ordered that this entire proceeding be closed to the public and press at the request of the defense, in order that there not be undue prejudice to his client's rights to a fair trial."

Everyone in the courtroom was stunned by the announcement.

"All spectators and newsmen, including television cameramen, will leave the courtroom now," added the judge. "That includes any other members of the public who are not attorneys, jurors, witnesses or courtroom personnel."

"Your Honor?" It was Chip Priest again.

"Yes, counselor?" acknowledged Judge Lorik.

"What about the people outside, at the windows?" pointed out Deputy DA Priest.

"They can stay," ordered the judge. "Besides, that's bulletproof glass. They can't hear anything from out there, anyway. Is there anything else?"

"Shall I continue with my opening statement?" questioned Chip Priest as the last of the unwelcome spectators finally finished exiting the courtroom.

"Please do," indicated Judge Lorik.

After once again approaching the jury box, Chip Priest straightened his tie before speaking. "Lady and gentlemen of the jury, you will also hear from a forensic specialist that none of the evidence collected at the crime scene can be definitively linked to the defendant, thus creating more than sufficient cause for reasonable doubt as to his guilt. And, if I may be so bold, it is the opinion of the prosecution that the defendant is innocent of the crime of which he has been accused!"

"Well done, counselor," snickered Judge Lorik as he mockingly clapped his hands. "Does the defense have anything to add to that?"

"No, Your Honor," smirked Phillip Dunbar. "I think Mr. Priest has more than sufficiently managed to present our case for us."

"That said, this court is hereby adjourned until nine o'clock tomorrow morning. Court dismissed." Judge Lorik then pounded his gavel against its sounding block.

Angry by the way things had gone in court that day, Chip Priest was deep in thought as he drove toward his home. Truly, it had been a kangaroo court! And, no doubt, his wife Jeri had spent the day with Andrea Telluric, most likely shopping and spending his money again!

Roused immediately from his thoughts by the sight of a flaming cross on the front lawn of his house, Chip Priest hurriedly brought his car to a screeching halt, got out, and raced toward the front door. Were his wife and two children still inside?

"Jeri?" hollered Chip as he unlocked and threw open the front door. "Andy? Johnny? Is anybody home?"

There was no answer. They must still be at Ron's house. Chip next hurried to the outside faucet, quickly turned on the garden hose, and used it to extinguish the flaming cross. Someone had gone to a good deal of trouble to dig the hole where it stood – no doubt with a posthole digger! It had been fashioned from two four-by-four inch wooden fenceposts, the vertical one being eight-feet long and the four-foot "cross" section attached two feet from its top by two six-inch screws! They had done everything but mount the thing in concrete!

The smell of gasoline in which it had been doused before being lit was still quite strong. Chip had no doubt in his mind who had been responsible, and there wasn't a blasted thing he could do about it, either!

He would call Andrea Telluric to make sure Jeri and the boys were okay. After finally managing to kick down the extinguished post, Chip angrily went inside to place the call but soon discovered that his phone lines had been cut, as well. What else had they done?

Not knowing what else to do, Chip climbed back into his car and drove to Ron Telluric's home, just thirteen blocks away.

Judging from the commotion outside, it was obvious that Ron had also come home to a burning cross on his front lawn.

"Oh Chip!" exclaimed Jeri as she hurried into his arms. "Who would do something like this?"

"Where are the kids?" grilled Chip.

"Inside, with little Sharon," interjected Andrea Telluric. Her hands were on her hips and she was clearly quite angry about the entire situation.

Ron and Chip exchanged a meaningful glance that did not go unnoticed by their wives.

Ignoring his wife's question, Chip asked of Ron, "Did they cut your phone lines, too?"

"We hadn't even gotten that far yet," admitted Ron as he hurried inside to check on it.

"Well, I'm calling the Sheriff right now if they're not!" informed Andrea as she followed her husband inside.

"I don't think that's such a good idea," advised Ron as he and Jeri followed after her.

"And just why not?" demanded Andrea.

"Our phone lines have been cut, too," revealed Ron.

"Do you think the place might be bugged?" Chip suddenly whispered to Ron.

"You never know." Ron shook his head with dismay.

"Ladies," invited Chip. "Please show us that new patio set you bought today."

"Patio set?" frowned Andrea.

"Oh, yes, the new patio set!" commented Jeri, who immediately understood that her husband wanted them all to go outside where they could talk freely.

"Okay," nodded Andrea, finally understanding.

"Andy and Johnny, can you please stay here with Sharon?" requested Jeri. "We'll be right back."

Once outside, Chip motioned for Andrea, Ron and Jeri to come close and spoke to them in a whisper. "I'm not sure, but our homes may be bugged."

"But, why?" persisted Jeri.

"We had a burning cross like this at our house, too, by the way," advised Chip, "and our phone lines were cut, as well."

Jeri and Andrea were clearly afraid and glanced nervously at the thick bushes surrounding the Telluric's secluded back yard.

"Chip and I are the prosecuting attorneys in the case against the woodcutter," whispered Ron.

"I don't understand," admitted Jeri. "Even if the Crusading Knights are responsible for this, wouldn't they *want* the woodcutter to be prosecuted?"

"Today in court," added Ron, "and this is strictly confidential, your brilliant husband stated in his opening remarks that he believes the woodcutter is innocent."

"What?" Andrea and Jeri both asked together. "But, you're a Deputy District Attorney!"

"And, of course, there's the fact that I'm Jewish," added Chip.

"What about Ron?" frowned Andrea. "He's not Jewish, and neither am I!"

"But, you are my friends," pointed out Chip.

"And, I think the woodcutter may be innocent, too," added Ron rather sheepishly.

"Some prosecutors you two are," Jeri laughed sardonically.

"We're just gonna have to ride this one out," advised Chip.

Unknown to Chip Priest and Ron Telluric until much later, the lady juror – who also was Jewish – had also come home to a burning cross on her front lawn the evening of April 14, 1975.

Three grueling and emotionally-charged weeks later, on May 5, 1975, the unusual trial of Woodrow Wilson finally came to an abrupt conclusion. The jury had deliberated for an entire week.

"Will the jury foreman please stand?" requested Judge Lorik. After waiting for him to do so, the judge added, "Has the jury reached a unanimous verdict?"

"We have, Your Honor," replied the foreman.

"Ms. Clark, will you please get the verdict form from the foreman?" requested Judge Lorik.

"Yes, sir," nodded Ms. Clark as she got up and walked over to the jury box. After receiving the folded paper from the foreman, Ms. Clark brought it to the judge, who opened and read the verdict first before refolding and handing it back to Ms. Clark to read aloud.

"Will the defendant please stand?" instructed Judge Lorik.

After waiting for Woody to stand, Ms. Clark unfolded the paper and read, "The jury finds the defendant, Mr. Woodrow Wilson, guilty of Murder in the First Degree."

The Woodcutter was clearly shaken and surprised by the verdict.

"Your Honor, please give us a moment?" requested Phil Dunbar.

"Granted," agreed the judge.

After several moments of conversing in whispers with his client, the public defender then turned again to the bench. "Your Honor, Mr. Wilson will accept a life sentence rather than pursue any course of appeal, which might ultimately lead him to the gas chamber."

"Interesting choice," smirked Judge Lorik. "Very well, it is the decision of this court that Mr. Woodrow Wilson be sentenced to life in prison at the St. Diablo Correctional Institution for Murder in the First Degree of Ms. Lydia Cain. There will be no possibility of appeal or parole from this ruling.   Do you understand and agree to that, Mr. Wilson?"

"Yes, sir, Yer Honor, sir," responded Woody.   And, though he was devastated at the prospect of never seeing his wife or children again, Woody truly felt as responsible for Lydia's death as if he had killed her himself.  If only he had spoken up back in 1959 when Misty Krain had first been killed right in front of him!  Perhaps then, the poor Cain girl might still be alive.  Ronald Krain and his Crusading Knights were somehow responsible, and Woody was certain of it!

Ronald Krain had been the one to write the mysterious note to Judge Lorik during Woody's trial, informing him that Martha Krain had been put into a medically induced coma until such time as she was strong enough to endure the necessary surgery to preserve her life. Martha's recent suicide attempt had shaken him quite badly, and caused Ronald Krain to reflect long and hard upon the horrible crimes that he and his cousin Jerry had committed over the years.   Did a person's color *really* make such a difference?  Suppose he himself had been born black or some other color?  Would it have been his fault?

Could he ever be forgiven for the things he had done?  Most certainly not!  He could not even forgive himself!  Especially for what he had done to Martha's mother – and she was white!  Ronald Krain then thought about the night he had caught his first wife Misty trying to force herself upon the poor woodcutter back in 1959.   Woody certainly had been trying to push her away!  That clearly made Woody a far better man than Ronald Krain ever had been or ever would be! Ronald angrily slammed his fist onto the top of his desk before slowly opening the drawer where the drivers' licenses and photo IDs of his various victims were kept.   Perhaps there was some way he could anonymously help some of his victims' families?  No!  That would no doubt be traced back to him.  He would then be arrested, sent to the gas chamber, and left powerless to help poor Martha when she needed him most.

What about *just* the woodcutter's family?  He certainly did owe the poor man for a tremendous amount of free firewood he'd received over the years.  What about a trust fund?  That's what he could do!  He would buy the woodcutter's property under the guise of obtaining more land for the Crusading Knights.  The money paid could then be put into a secret trust fund from which a stipend of monthly payments to each of the woodcutter's children would anonymously be made. The funds could also help with their parents' final expenses someday.

*If there is someone up there*, thought Ronald Krain, *please know how truly sorry I am for all of the horrible things I have done.* Ronald paused to see if lightning might strike him dead at that point before continuing. *Please spare my poor Martha's life, Ronald Krain silently prayed. I promise that if you do, I will never harm another person again!*

It was Saturday, June 7, 1975. Finals were over and most of the students at Powell Mountain University had already vacated their rooms and returned home to spend the summer with their families.

Carolyn had already loaded the last of her possessions into the green Ford Mustang and returned for one last look around the huge fifth-floor dormitory room she had called home during the past school year. The room seemed so empty now that everyone's things were gone, especially Karlin's. Carolyn fought back tears as she thought of her friend. Would she ever see Karlin again? Just what had happened to her? Why did her friends keep disappearing like this? Wasn't it enough that Joyce and Veronica had been taken during her junior year of high school? And now Karlin, too?

Carolyn suddenly burst into tears as she walked over to the room's northern window to gaze out of it one last time. Just like the legendary city of Camelot, three of her dearest friends were now gone! Would she ever find out what had happened to any of them?

An unbidden memory of Alfredo McFerson came to mind as Carolyn studied the spired rooftops below. Would he really have come back for her, had his plane not crashed? And, would she have finally agreed to marry him? Could she have put aside her feelings for Lenny Owens? And, why hadn't Lenny written? Had his letters gone to her parents' house? Had her father destroyed the letters or returned them unopened? If only she knew!

Then, as she turned to leave, Carolyn thought of Woody and all the kind things he had done to help her and her family that first day, and all the other times he had given rides to her and to Karlin. What if Woody really were the Powell Mountain Killer? Carolyn shuddered at the very thought. How could she have been so wrong about him? Woody just didn't seem capable of harming anyone! Still, why would he have been convicted if he were innocent? How sad for his wife and three young children!  Had Woody really been romantically involved with Lydia Cain as the newspapers had claimed?  Was that why he had run down Paul Johnson with his green Mustang and later murdered Lydia?  Carolyn sadly shook her head as she took one last look around the fifth-floor dormitory room before leaving.

It was Tuesday morning, February 14, 1978.  Luella Wilson was six years old already, and anxious to finally see her father Woody again.  Her early childhood memories of his appearance were vague, but his kind gentle manner was clearly engrained upon every fiber of her being.

"I think daddy's innocent!" informed Luella as she folded her arms and nodded her head.  She and her foster mother, Mrs. Green, were on their way by car from Ocean Bay to the St. Diablo Correctional Institution.  Despite the fact that it was still mid-February, the sun had managed to make an appearance in honor of the occasion.

"They usually don't let children into prisons, you know," reminded Mrs. Green as she checked the speedometer to be sure she was within the required limit.  "It took quite some doin' to convince 'em to let me bring you."

"Tell me about my daddy?" Luella suddenly asked.  "Why is he there, anyway?"

"Well," began Mrs. Green, "there was a trial ...."

"What's a trial?" interrupted Luella.

"Sweetie," chastened Mrs. Green, "you need to let me answer one question at a time.  Remember, we talked about that?"

"I'm sorry!" pouted Luella as she swung her little legs back and forth, causing her white patent leather shoes to gently tap against the bottom of the dashboard in front of her.  Her dainty white ankle socks were neatly turned down on the tops.

Luella's short black pigtails were tied off with bright pink ribbons that perfectly matched her pink cotton dress.  Her short puffy sleeves were adorned with the same ruffled white lace that decorated the hem of her full skirt, and the white waist ties sewn to either side of her dress were carefully tied in back into a perfect-looking bow.

"That's okay," laughed Mrs. Green.  It was nearly impossible to remain irritated with Luella for long.  She was so adorable!  And, Luella had an insatiable curiosity about everything around her, constantly asking questions of nearly everyone.

"Well?" prompted Luella as she gave her foster mother an inquisitive look.

"Okay," sighed Mrs. Green. "A trial is when someone is arrested for something, and ...."

"For what?" interrupted Luella.

"Honey, please let me finish answering one question before you ask me another?" pleaded Mrs. Green.

"What was daddy arrested for, then?" grilled Luella.

"There were some folks who thought he had hurt someone," replied Mrs. Green, being careful not to say too much.

"Did he?" pressed Luella. "I don't think Daddy would have hurt anyone! He's not like that."

"That's what your mama thinks, too," interjected Mrs. Green, hopeful that she had successfully managed to steer the conversation in a different direction.

"Will we see Mama while we're there?" questioned Luella.

"Absolutely," promised Mrs. Green.

"Will she be at the prison, where Daddy is?" quizzed Luella.

"No, she won't." Mrs. Green was a patient woman who tried to answer Luella's many inquiries to the best of her ability.

"Where is Mama, then?" frowned Luella.

"Your mama is in a nursing home, not too far from there," explained Mrs. Green. "But, she is very sick. That's the reason you are living with me."

"Will Mama get better?" Luella wanted to know.

"Only God knows that, my dear." Mrs. Green hoped that Luella would not start asking her about what illness Harriet Wilson had, as it was some long unpronounceable name, anyway.

"Will Daddy ever get out of prison?" questioned Luella.

"Girl, you certainly want to know everything all at once, don't you?" laughed Mrs. Green.

"I just want my mama and daddy back!" sniveled Luella as tears began to escape from her beautiful eyes. "And my brothers, too!"

"Oh, child, don't start crying on me," cautioned Mrs. Green. "You wouldn't want your mama or daddy to see your eyes all red, swollen, and puffy, would you?"

"Then tell me why my daddy is in prison?" persisted Luella, somehow managing to shut off the tears as quickly as they had come.

"That is something he will need to tell you himself, when you see him today," replied Mrs. Green with finality. She was not about to get into a discussion about the highly-publicized murder case of Woody the Woodcutter with his six-year old daughter.

"They think he killed someone, don't they?" Luella decided to take another approach.

"Where did you hear that?" demanded Mrs. Green.

"From Henry, the neighbor boy," revealed Luella. "When we were out back playing cars."

"Henry Jones?" Mrs. Green furled her brow. "That's another thing I've been meaning to talk to you about, Miss Luella. It isn't very ladylike for a little girl to be out playing cars in the dirt with little boys."

"We're digging a fort, too," informed Luella.

"Oh, Luella, whatever am I going to do with you?" sighed Mrs. Green. "So, just what did Henry tell you, anyway?"

"His parents said they didn't want him to play with me anymore, because my daddy is a murderer," elaborated Luella.

"Well, they're wrong!" advised Mrs. Green as she checked the speedometer again. The last thing she needed was another ticket.

"Then why is he there, if he didn't do it?" Luella wanted to know.

"Sweetie, I do not have all the answers," replied Mrs. Green, "but we're here now, so you can ask your daddy that yourself."

Even while checking in at the gate and again at the visitor desk, Luella continued to ask questions of everyone she saw – until a scary looking prison guard squatted down beside Luella and warned her with a serious face that if she didn't quit asking so many questions, he would have to lock her up in one of the cells and then throw away the key!

Mrs. Green gave the guard a smile of gratitude, after which he surreptitiously winked back at her in return.

Frightened by the scary looking men in their cells as she and Mrs. Green walked through D-block toward the visiting room, Luella silently clung to her hand.

Several of the prisoners whistled and made catcalls at Mrs. Green and Luella as they passed, as well as lude comments that Luella thankfully did not understand. One particularly creepy inmate

474

stuck his tongue out and wiggled it back and forth at Luella, causing Mrs. Green to glare at him in a harsh manner.

By the time Luella and Mrs. Green reached the visiting room, Luella was literally trembling with fright, and speechless for perhaps the first time in her young life.

"Wait here," instructed the guard as he motioned toward two hard plastic chairs in a small room before closing the door and leaving to stand outside.

"We aren't in a cell, are we?" whispered Luella.

"No, this is a visiting room," assured Mrs. Green as she pointed toward the glass divider beside them. "And here comes your daddy now! He will have to sit over there, on the other side of the glass."

Luella looked up at Mrs. Green with a surprised expression on her face and then turned to watch as her aging daddy was escorted to the hard, plastic chair on the other side of the divider. The ankle chains and wrist shackles he wore could easily be heard as Woody hobbled toward the visiting room to finally see his little Luella. He looked frail and gaunt, not at all as she remembered him.

"Luella!" smiled Woody as he spoke into the telephone headset on his side of the divider.

"You'll need to speak to him on the telephone," directed Mrs. Green. "Otherwise, he won't be able to hear you."

"Daddy?" Luella tried to drink in the sight of him, uncertain whether she would ever see him again.

"Yer daddy loves ya." Woody's eyes had become misty with emotion. *His Luella was so beautiful!*

"When will you get to come home?" questioned Luella with her beautiful, pleading eyes.

Woody suddenly became choked up with emotion and started to cry. He merely shook his head in the negative.

"We'll be stopping by to see Harriet after this," interjected Mrs. Green as she leaned close to the telephone headset Luella was holding, to share it with her. "Is there anything you would like us to tell her for you?"

Woody wiped his cheeks on the upper sleeves of his red jumpsuit and sniffed before responding. "Kin ya give her dis fer me?" Woody then pulled his tattered old Bible from his jumpsuit pocket and slid it under the glass. The guard had already searched Woody quite thoroughly and had allowed him to bring the Bible with him for the visit. On the front, it was titled *Good News for Modern Man* with a subtitle indicating that it was *the New Testament in Today's English Version.*

"I would be happy to," agreed Mrs. Green as she opened the book to a page that had a folded piece of paper stuck inside and noticed that it was at Mark 1:29-34, which was underlined in red pen.

"Dat be where Mark tells how de good man healed de sick," described Woody. "De note is for Harriet."

"Will the good man heal Mama?" Luella suddenly asked.

"Yer daddy prays every day dat he will," replied Woody as he put his hand against the glass. *If only he could hold his little Luella in his arms again!*

"Time's up," advised the guard as he opened the door and came into the tiny room.

"Daddy luvs you!" called Woody as he watched Mrs. Green take Luella by the hand and start to lead her from the room.

Luella suddenly broke free from Mrs. Green and rushed back over to the glass divider, putting her little hand against the glass as she looked one last time at her daddy. "I love you, too!"

Woody and Luella looked deeply into one another's eyes through the divider, each somehow sensing that they would never see each other again in this life.

"Come on, sweetheart," encouraged Mrs. Green as she gently took Luella's other hand and tugged at it. "We need to leave now if we want to see your mama. They have visiting hours at the nursing home, too. If we get there too late, they won't let us see her."

"Goodbye, Daddy!" bid Luella, with tears streaming down her tiny cheeks as she finally left with Mrs. Green.

Luella rode in silence as Mrs. Green drove from the St. Diablo Correctional Institution toward the Powell Mountain Nursing Home.

Mrs. Green shifted into a lower gear as she began the steep ascent up Powell Mountain Road.

Luella stared at the surrounding landscape with amazement. The beautiful old growth forest on the steep hillside next to them was still denuded from the unusually harsh winter that year. Patches of partially melted snow could be seen on the forest floor.

The drop-off on one side of the road was intimidating, to say the least, and it was not someplace Mrs. Green would have driven had she been able to avoid it. After slowing for a hairpin turn, Mrs. Green pointed out, "That's where you used to live, right over there, in that two-story stone building."

Luella gazed at it with awe. It did look familiar! Then, upon noticing the hand-carved wooden statue by the entrance gate, she exclaimed, "Look! It's Daddy!"

Mrs. Green frowned with disapproval at the black and gold lettering on the sign which read, "Powell Mountain Pub." It had formerly read, "Woody's Salvage Yard and Woodcutting."

"I remember that statue!" informed Luella. "There was another one just like it, up by the house!"

"More than likely there still is," acknowledged Mrs. Green.

"What's a pub?" questioned Luella.

"It's a place where people drink alcohol, and NOT a place for little girls!" advised Mrs. Green with finality.

"Does someone else own our house now?" frowned Luella.

"Yes, honey, they do," answered Mrs. Green. "We'll be at the nursing home soon."

Luella then rode in silence again as they made their way up the isolated mountain road. Though the memory was vague, Luella could still recall the time her daddy had let her come along on one of his deliveries, when they had driven up this road together.

"There it is!" pointed Mrs. Green as she turned into the drive leading up to the Powell Mountain Nursing Home.

"Do you think we made it in time to see her?" asked Luella.

"Actually, it's lunchtime," noticed Mrs. Green after consulting her wristwatch. "Perhaps we can have lunch with her."

"Will Mama remember who I am?" Luella suddenly questioned.

"Oh, honey, of course she will," assured Mrs. Green as she pulled the 1965 beige Rambler station wagon into an empty parking space and turned off the engine. "Come on!"

Luella excitedly climbed from the vehicle when Mrs. Green opened the door for her.

"Don't forget your sweater," directed Mrs. Green. "It's still a bit chilly up here on the mountain."

"Yes, ma'am," complied Luella as she reached back into the vehicle, grabbed her little white sweater and quickly put it on.

"There!" smiled Mrs. Green as she squatted in front of Luella to straighten her sweater and make sure the bow on her dress was still tied.

"I'd like a ham sandwich!" informed Luella as she took Mrs. Green's hand and walked with her toward the front door of the nursing home. "And a glass of milk!"

"We'll just have to see what they have," replied Mrs. Green.

Unhappy at being forced to wait in the lobby, Luella sat pouting on an orange vinyl couch with her arms folded. It seemed like she had been waiting forever! Luella had not seen her mother for years and it just wasn't fair! She finally came to a decision. Luella was not about to let the mean old lady at the front desk stop her, either!

Waiting until the receptionist was distracted by an incoming phone call, Luella quickly got up, hurried past her, and down the hall in the direction Mrs. Green had gone.

Stealthily glancing into each room as she made her way down the long hallway, Luella finally spotted Mrs. Green inside one of the rooms and raced inside. "Mama!"

"Luella!" beamed Harriet Wilson.

"Don't get too close!" cautioned Mrs. Green. She was concerned that Luella might unintentionally bump one of the IV tubes hooked up to her mother's arm.

"Why?" Luella asked with alarm. "Will I get what she has?"

"Good heavens, no!" laughed Harriet.

"You just need to be careful not to touch any of the tubes hooked up to your mama," explained Mrs. Green.

Luella nodded with understanding and then cautiously approached her mama. Harriet Wilson looked much older and frailer than Luella had remembered. "Does it hurt?"

"I'm just really weak," replied Harriet.

"Can I give you a hug?" Luella was afraid to do anything that might hurt her mama.

"Oh, yes, honey, come here!" beamed Harriet as she reached for her. "Better come over to this side, though, where I don't have any tubes hooked up. You can just use that there chair to climb right on up here beside me." Harriet gently tapped the bed with her open palm.

Luella carefully came over to where her mama indicated and climbed onto the bed next to her before putting her little arms around her. Luella then rested her head on Harriet's chest while Harriet pulled her close with that arm and then tenderly stroked her pigtails.

"I love you, mama!" sniveled Luella.

"I love you, too!" replied Harriet as she gently put her hand under Luella's chin and pushed up on it. "Let me see you! You look so beautiful today!"

"When do you come home?" grilled Luella.

Harriet and Mrs. Green exchanged a sad glance.

"That's up to God, Luella," advised her mama.

Then, turning to Mrs. Green, Luella asked, "Did you give her Daddy's Bible?"

"She sure did!" interjected Harriet. "It's right over there. And it will be a great comfort for me to have it."

Before Luella had come into the room, Harriet had already read Woody's note, hurriedly written one of her own, and then given both notes to Mrs. Green to keep for Luella for when she was old enough.

"Did you read the note Daddy wrote you?" pressed Luella.

"I will," assured Harriet. She hated to be dishonest, but did not want Luella to know that she already had, or what it said – not just yet.

"Why don't you read it now?" urged Luella.

"Your mama just isn't up to it right now," advised Mrs. Green as a worker in a nurse's uniform came into the room with a food tray.

"Eeew!" exclaimed Luella when she saw the split pea soup. "That looks like vomit!"

"Perhaps we should leave now, so your mama can eat her lunch," suggested Mrs. Green. "Unless you'd like some of that for your lunch, too?"

Luella emphatically shook her head in the negative.

"We'll come back again," promised Mrs. Green, though she wasn't sure if that would even be possible.

"YOU are not supposed to be in here, young lady!" chided the worker. "How did you get back here, anyway?"

"I walked," answered Luella in a sweet and innocent way.

"I'm sorry," apologized Mrs. Green. "The woman at the reception desk said she would watch her."

"No harm," responded the worker. "Just don't let it happen again. We can't have children running around back here."

"Does that mean I won't get to come back?" Luella was near tears again.

"I love you, Luella!" Harriet forced a cheerful smile onto her face as she reached for her daughter to hug her goodbye.

Luella then went back over to embrace her mama one final time. Tears were streaming down her cheeks as Mrs. Green gently took her hand and led her from the room.

Luella paused to look back at her mama once more before allowing herself to finally be led down the long hallway.

"We can get something to eat at that little diner we saw down in St. Diablo," suggested Mrs. Green. "They looked like they might have ham sandwiches."

Meanwhile, back at the St. Diablo Correctional Institution, a new guard arrived at Woody's cell with his noon-time lunch tray.

"Yer new?" acknowledged Woody as he reached for the tray.

"Yes, I am," replied the man with an almost sinister look in his eyes, despite the phony smile on his face. But for a sudden glimmer of sunlight from the window behind him, Woody might never have noticed the white night lapel pin on the guard's collar.

"Word is, you got to see your little girl today," mentioned the man. "Not the healthiest of places for a child to be."

"No, sir," agreed Woody as he grabbed the tray.

"Enjoy!" grinned the man as he started to leave.

"Wuts de occasion?" questioned Woody when he noticed that the food on the tray was not the customary type of food served to prisoners. Instead, it was a nicely cooked steak with a baked potato and steamed broccoli.

"Just a little something special," replied the guard. "I hear the sour cream on the baked potato is to die for."

Woody suddenly wondered whether the food might be poisoned. *Were the Crusading Knights trying to take him out? Were they fearful he might finally say something about what he knew? Had they already done something to Luella and Mrs. Green? Or even to Harriet? Had they somehow managed to intercept his letter to her?*

"Better eat your food," smirked the Guard.

"When duz Frank get back?" questioned Woody.

"He doesn't," replied the Guard. "I'm Ralph, by the way."

Woody glanced at the Guard's name badge and noticed the name Kollins on it. "Didn't yer daddy work in de Industrial Ed building, over at de skool?"

480

"He still does," revealed Ralph with an even gaze.

"I ain't hungry," advised Woody as he pushed aside the tray.

"Listen to me, old man," growled Ralph as he leaned close, reached through the bars of Woody's cell, and grabbed his jumpsuit to pull him close. "You *are* hungry! And you *will* eat this special meal that someone has gone out of their way to prepare for you! Do you understand me? And if you don't eat it, then it can just sit there until it rots – or you do – whichever happens first."

"Fine, it kin just sit der," advised Woody. He had no intention of eating any of it. Besides, whether he died of poison or from starvation, it was obvious that his days were numbered.

On Friday morning, February 17, 1978, Frank Mendez returned from his three-day vacation. If it hadn't been for Ralph Kollins filling in for him, it would not have been possible for him to take the time off.

Frank began his usual routine of delivering food trays to the maximum-security inmates on his cellblock. When arriving at Woodrow Wilson's cell, he could not help but notice that Woody was not up yet. Odd, since Woody was normally an early riser, usually taking advantage of the quiet time to read from his tattered old Bible. At first, it appeared as though Woody were still sleeping on his bed.

"Hey Woody!" called Frank. "Woody?"

There was no answer, even when Frank banged his baton several times against the bars of Woody's cell.

"Woody!" hollered Frank before returning to the guard station for backup. "Something's wrong with the woodcutter."

"He seemed okay to me when I picked up his tray last night," assured Ralph.

"Hey, thanks for filling in for me, by the way," mentioned Frank.

"Not a problem," replied Ralph, who did not seem overly concerned about the woodcutter.

"Well?" prompted Frank.

"Oh, yeah, the woodcutter," snickered Ralph. "I guess we should go check on him."

Returning to the cell, Frank quickly unlocked the cell door while Ralph stood guard. After rushing inside to see whether Woody was still alive, Frank pulled back the single gray wool blanket and tried to take Woody's pulse. Frank sadly shook his head. "He's cold. There's no sign of life."

"Well, what're ya gonna do?" Ralph nonchalantly shrugged his shoulders as he turned to leave, still chewing and popping his bubblegum. "Guess you won't be needing backup anymore, at least not for this one?"

"Apparently not," replied Frank, clearly disturbed by the callous manner in which Ralph had reacted to the inmate's death.

Harriet Wilson had taken the news of her husband's death quite hard, rapidly declining in health thereafter. Just six months later, on August 16, 1978, Harriet passed. The nurse's aide who found her was wearing a white night lapel pin on his uniform. The nursing home had begun hiring male nursing staff as early as 1976.

On Sunday morning, August 26, 1979, Lenny Owens was busy at his Ocean Bay apartment, going through personal papers and getting bills ready to mail on the first of the month.

"Hey, old man!" greeted his cousin Pete as he entered Lenny's small one-bedroom apartment without knocking. "I thought I might find you here."

"What's up?" questioned Lenny. "Forget your key?"

"The door was unlocked," pointed out Pete. "Hey, wanna go over to camp meeting with me?"

"Not particularly," replied Lenny.

"What's wrong with you?" grilled Pete. "You never miss camp meeting!"

"I just don't feel like going this year," frowned Lenny.

It was the second day of the 1979 camp meeting session over in the Oceanview district. Just as in pioneer times, camp meeting was typically held in summer months during favorable weather when people with primitive means of transportation could camp out in tents at or near the revival site. Modern-day camp meeting patrons would try as much as possible to duplicate the event by actually camping in tents. Even the stirring revival meetings would be held in a giant tent, with fellow believers remaining at the site for several days and enjoying spiritual renewal and comradery with one another.

"We don't have to stay for the night, or anything like that," pressed Pete. "We can just drive over for the day! It's only two hours from here. Come on, it'll do you some good to get out for a change. All you ever do is study anymore!"

"*En garde*!" challenged Lenny as he unexpectedly grabbed a nearby sword and swiftly positioned the point of it at Pete's throat.

"Good Lord!" exclaimed Pete. "What are you doing?"

"I lettered in fencing," grinned Lenny as he slowly removed the sword and put it away. "Don't worry, it's not real! This one is just plastic, for practice."

"Okay, so I guess you've been doing something more than just studying," acknowledged Pete, who was still jumpy after being surprised like that – even if it wasn't a real sword!

"I also lettered in basketball," muttered Lenny, "for all the good it did me!"

"What's that's supposed to mean?" pressed Pete. "It got you a scholarship, didn't it?"

"Dad didn't even bother to come to my graduation in June!" snapped Lenny. "After all the sacrifices I've made to make my parents proud of me, that's all the thanks I get!"

"You only have one parent left," reminded Pete.

"You know full well what I mean!" retorted Lenny.

"The promise that you made mama about becoming a doctor?" guessed Pete. He was still nervous that Lenny might draw the practice sword on him again.

"And on her deathbed!" added Lenny.

"So, how is getting to go to college and having a bachelor's degree in chemistry a sacrifice?" frowned Pete. "Plus, now you've got a full scholarship to go to medical school."

"A basketball scholarship?" sniggered Lenny. "That's all I need. So now, I can give up another four years of my life, and for what?"

"Hey, if I were a foot taller," chuckled Pete, "who knows, maybe I'd have a basketball scholarship, too."

"I can't help it if I'm six foot five, and you're not!" grinned Lenny, suddenly seeing the humor in it.

"So, just what's got you so worked up?" pressed Pete.

"Nothing!" assured Lenny as he walked back over to his desk to straighten up his papers.

"What's this?" grinned Pete as he noticed their high school yearbook on the bed nearby, open to the page with Carolyn Bennett's picture on it. "Dear Lenny," Pete started to read.

"That's private!" informed Lenny as he hurriedly snatched the book away and abruptly closed it.

"Is *that* what this is all about?" Pete was stunned. "That was six years ago!"

"Sure, I'll go to camp meeting with you," advised Lenny, without answering Pete's question.

"Who knows," smirked Pete, "maybe Carolyn will be there. You never know!"

"Well, she sure hasn't been at the last five camp meetings," recalled Lenny.

"How would you know?" chuckled Pete. "There are hundreds of people at those things."

Lenny gave Pete a warning glance.

"Okay, so what are you going to wear to this one?" asked Pete. "Just in case she's there?"

"Probably my black suit," decided Lenny. "It's the only one where the legs are long enough."

Two hours later, Lenny and Pete arrived at the annual camp meeting, set up along the blufftops overlooking the ocean beyond. Several miles north of the Oceanview campus, it was basically out in the middle of nowhere. Even Ocean Bluff was a half-hour drive south of the location. Over three hundred tents were set up in sections, surrounding the giant central revival tent.

"I don't know how I let you talk me into these things," muttered Lenny as he steered his shiny black 1978 MGB Roadster onto the dusty dirt road. He was not happy about all the dust.

"How much did this run you, anyway?" delved Pete.

"Got it on time for only $3,900, even though it's worth $4,150," revealed Lenny. "Good thing I left the top up!"

"Better your car than mine!" grinned Pete. "What I don't understand is why such a tall guy would want such a small car!"

"Then it won't be too much trouble for you to wash it for me, will it?" smiled Lenny as he circled the large dirt parking lot until finally finding an empty space.

"We'll see about that!" chuckled Pete as he opened his door to get out.

After climbing out and securing his vehicle, Lenny bent down to check his appearance in the side mirror. His afro was nicely shaped, noted Lenny as he straightened his paisley necktie against the white shirt he had on.

"Gonna check your shoes, too?" razzed Pete.

Lenny glanced down at his black leather shoes and frowned at the dust on them from the parking lot.

"You could go to the men's room up there on the hill and wipe them off," suggested Pete. "But, the whole place is filled with dust."

"I believe I need to go there anyway," replied Lenny. "I might just try that."

"Oh, come on!" teased Pete. "I was only kidding!"

"You go ahead to the big tent and save me a seat," directed Lenny. "I wouldn't want you to miss any of the meeting."

"How will you find me?" scowled Pete.

"I'll find you," assured Lenny.

"Okay." Pete then shrugged his shoulders and started toward the giant revival tent in the middle of the complex. "I'll be in the south section, probably near the front if I can find any seats."

"Duly noted," acknowledged Lenny as he began walking up the hill, to where the portable restroom stalls were located.

*Why in the world had he allowed himself to be talked into coming here?* It was the last place he wanted to be. Lenny had actually been thinking of attempting to write one last letter to Carolyn that day, in the remote chance that she might somehow respond.

He had dated more than one of the attractive young women at Ocean Bay University, but each relationship had ended badly when they had pressed him for a permanent commitment that he just was not ready to make. Lenny needed to know what had become of Carolyn and what her intentions were before he could move on with his life.

Lenny knew for a fact that at least one of Carolyn's letters had been destroyed by his father, learning after-the-fact of it from his cousin Pete. *Had her father done the same with his letters?* If only he knew.

*Had Carolyn found someone else? Was she married, with kids?* Lenny was deep in thought as he made his way up the dusty hill. Then, all at once, there she was! It was Carolyn!

485

Lenny just stood there staring at her, unable to believe his eyes. But, she had two little girls with her! He suddenly felt as if his heart had been pierced with an arrow. It was as if he were frozen to the spot, unable to move. That was when she looked up and saw him. Their eyes locked for an eternal moment of longing and desire.

"Lenny!" exclaimed Carolyn. She was clearly glad to see him.

Lenny merely stood there staring at her. Now that the moment he had dreamed of for six years had finally come, he had no idea what to say or do. *She must be married, with two little girls like that,* assumed Lenny. *And, the oldest one appeared to be about six years old! Carolyn certainly had wasted no time in finding someone else!*

"Lenny, I'd like you to meet my nieces," introduced Carolyn, rather nervously. "This is Teena and Catrina."

Lenny cautiously smiled and nodded. Were they *really* her nieces? If that was true, what was keeping her from running over to embrace him? Why did she just keep standing there, holding hands with the two girls? Had seeing him unexpectedly put Carolyn into an awkward situation? Perhaps they were her children after all, and she just did not want him to know she was married? Lenny nervously swallowed as he tried to see whether Carolyn had on a wedding band, but her ring finger was completely concealed by the older girl's hand.

"Did you finally make it to medical school?" Carolyn asked.

"That's certainly the plan," muttered Lenny.

"So, you will get to become a doctor, then?" pressed Carolyn.

"I sure hope so," replied Lenny, rather awkwardly.

"How about you?" asked Lenny. His sensitive brown eyes seemed to envelop her, though he made no effort whatsoever to come take her into his arms as he wanted to. *Why couldn't he move?*

"I'm having to finish my second year of college by going to night school," revealed Carolyn. She yearned to dash over and throw her arms around him, but was afraid. Perhaps there was someone else in his life? Carolyn tried to see if Lenny was wearing a wedding band, but could not see one.

"I have to go really bad!" reminded Teena as she tugged more urgently at Carolyn's hand.

"Me, too!" whined Catrina.

"Will I see you again?" Carolyn suddenly asked Lenny as her nieces began dragging her toward the portable toilet stalls. Finally,

Carolyn let go of their hands as she opened the door to one of the stalls for them. "Sorry about that!"

"I'll be around," promised Lenny as he unexpectedly turned and walked away. He could see that Carolyn was busy with the girls and was suddenly afraid.

"Me, too!" whispered Carolyn as she stood there watching Lenny walk away, toward the giant revival tent. He never did look back.

As soon as the girls had finished using the restroom, Carolyn made her way to the large revival tent with her two nieces in tow, desperately searching the crowd for any sign of Lenny. She had even asked Teena and Catrina to let her know at once if they saw any sign of the tall man in the black suit with the afro again! Just how could a six foot, five inch black man with an afro be so impossible to find in a seemingly endless sea of white people? Tears streamed down Carolyn's cheeks. *How could she have just let him walk away like that without telling him how she felt? Would there be another opportunity? Would she ever see Lenny again?*

# 12. Final Judgment

Jim Otterman and Chip Priest were seated on the upstairs patio balcony of the Powell Mountain Bed and Breakfast, having a morning cup of coffee as they prepared to review the case evidence gathered so far in the *Powell Mountain Matter*. It was already Thursday, March 30, 2023, and Jim would need to return the minivan rental later that day, so he was anxious to get started.

The flat second-story rooftop had been used as a patio by each of its successive owners. On it was a small round, wrought-iron table, fashioned with swirling floret designs. Open spaces between the florets allowed for drainage when it rained. Painted white, like the table, the matching wrought-iron chairs were in need of comfortable seat cushions. Four of the chairs had been pulled up to the table, while six more of them were arranged in a row next to the railing nearby. Beside them was a large charcoal barbecue grill that had seen better days.

"Think this place will ever make it as a B&B?" chuckled Chip.

"Not a chance," replied Jim as he blew on his coffee to cool it down. "A museum, maybe."

"What kind of museum?" demanded Luella, who had just joined them without being noticed.

"That pocket door of yours is certainly quiet!" noted Jim as he put his coffee cup back down on the table. "Nice view of the property from here, though. I especially like the jasmine you have growing around the railing."

"Angie apparently liked jasmine, too!" interjected Chip as he finally took a sip from his cup.

"Don't evade the question, Carrot Top!" pressed Luella with her hands on her hips.

"Won't you sit down?" invited Chip. "We were just getting ready to go over our files. Perhaps there's something we've forgotten?"

"You two characters ought to open up your own detective agency together," teased Luella as she pulled out a chair and sat down.

"Where's everyone else?" questioned Jim.

"You see what I mean?" bantered Luella. "Just like a good detective, always asking questions but never willing to answer one!"

"What question?" teased Jim.

"Okay, that's it!" Luella pretended to be upset as she started to get back up to leave.

"Sit down!" instructed Jim as he gently grabbed Luella's arm to prevent her from going.

"Priest and Otterman," decided Luella. "I think that's what you should call yourselves."

"Otterman and Priest," corrected Jim.

"I kind of like Priest and Otterman myself," smiled Chip.

"Otterman starts with an O and alphabetically comes before P," differed Jim. "And, if we were to start up a business together, the main stockholder's name would come first anyway."

"He's got a point," agreed Chip as he glanced at Luella. "Jim would definitely be the financial muscle behind it."

"So, tell me, gentlemen," urged Luella, "just why don't you think this place would make it as a B&B?"

"Because it's haunted!" laughed Jim. "I'm nothin' to write home about myself, but that friendly ghost of yours sure seems to have an obsession with me."

"Maybe she just likes has-been detectives!" joked Chip. "Personally, I wouldn't even want to take a nap in that room below us!"

"However," interjected Jim, "with the right publicity, this place might do quite well as a museum. A haunted historic brothel is the kind of thing that tourists like to stop and take tours of. Especially when it's associated with something or someone notorious in some way."

"Like the Lydia Cain murder?" recognized Luella.

"Exactly!" replied Jim. "A nice hunting lodge down there where the old salvage yard used to be might not hurt matters much, either. It is a beautiful setting here in the mountains like this."

"You offerin' to build me one, honey?" quizzed Luella with a frisky grin. She loved the way Jim blushed when she flirted with him.

"You probably will need my help, at that." Jim smiled rather mysteriously as he checked again to see if his coffee was cool enough to drink.

"Actually, I get by," assured Luella with a crooked smile.

"On that stipend you've been receiving from an anonymous benefactor since your parents passed?" mentioned Jim with a raised eyebrow and a smug grin.

"What would you know about that?" demanded Luella.

"Well, I hate to be the one to break it to you," remarked Jim, "but all the poking around I've been doing into the Shady Brook's financial situation also managed to bring your unnamed sponsor's attention to its Wilson Trust."

Luella was clearly upset. Would she lose her home now, and need to find somewhere else to live? How would she get by without the monthly stipend? She had deliberately remained silent about it, for fear of this very thing happening!

"You can relax," beamed Jim. "The Wilson Trust has been taken over by a new investor."

"A new investor?" scowled Luella. "Who, you?"

"Well, it was my fault that Michael Krain found out about your little arrangement with his father in the first place," apologized Jim.

"Michael Krain?" Luella was indignant though not surprised.

"When I took over the Shady Brook property," explained Jim, "it forced Michael Krain to review his remaining assets more closely. After all, he is Ronald Krain's only surviving heir now and free to update any preexisting arrangements his father might have made."

"So, it was Ronald Krain who set the thing up?" nodded Luella. "Probably out of guilt! I suspected as much."

"Well, his son was about to cut you off. But, since you and I are family and all," grinned Jim, "I decided to buy out the Wilson Trust so you wouldn't lose your stipend."

"So, *you* are now my benefactor?" beamed Luella.

"It would seem so," replied Jim. "At least now you know where your money's coming from."

"How can you afford something like that?" quizzed Luella. "Especially after buying the Shady Brook place, plus doing all this?"

"No worries," assured Jim. "Besides, the Shady Brook property will make a great wildlife refuge when they're finished excavating it. There are certain tax write-offs for that type of thing."

"And what about this place?" asked Luella.

"The property itself will remain in your name," confirmed Jim. "You needn't worry. I'll make sure you're on board with it before erecting any permanent structures on it – or before tearing anything down."

"So, I'm nothing more than just an investment now?" Luella raised an eyebrow and feigned disappointment. "Will I still be receiving the same amount each month for my stipend?"

"Nope," replied Jim as he slowly took a sip from his coffee.

Luella frowned with concern.

"I'm afraid you'll be getting a slight increase," informed Jim.

"Carrot Top, you're all right!" beamed Luella as she leaned over and gave Jim a hug and a kiss on the cheek.

"Yeah, yeah," muttered Jim as he blushed with embarrassment and gently pushed her away.

Chip nodded with approval. Perhaps Jim might not be a bad person to go into business with. This could be just the change he needed, to get a fresh start.

"Just how much are you worth, anyway?" Luella suddenly asked.

"*That* is none of your business," replied Jim. "Let's just say you won't need to worry about your stipend again."

"What a shame that Miss Sheree snatched you up first," lamented Luella as she seductively brushed the fingers of one hand against Jim's cheek. "Does she know how fortunate she is?"

"I think she does." Jim became red-faced with embarrassment.

"I can always come back later," suggested Chip.

Jim then gave Chip a warning look. It was clear he did not want him to leave!

"Sorry if I made you uncomfortable," flirted Luella, "but a good-looking man like you is hard to come by. And rich, too!"

"Okay," sighed Jim. "Let's get one thing straight right now."

"Yes?" smirked Luella.

"First of all, I'm married," reminded Jim.

"Me, too!" exclaimed Chip, just to be sure Luella understood.

"Besides," razzed Jim, "you'll probably be hard-pressed for competition against your great-grandmother for any man's attention. At least around here!"

"Point taken. Well, you may as well go ahead and discuss your case, then," prompted Luella as she feigned disappointment, sighed deeply and shrugged her shoulders. "Don't let me stop you."

"Hey, you never did tell us where the others are right now," reminded Jim as he took another sip of coffee. "I think they might like to sit in on this."

"Well, I believe Sheree and Ann went to take your minivan back," began Luella.

"What?" Jim was not pleased about it.

"Relax, Carrot Top!" grinned Luella. "They're just trying to help you out. Ann was the one driving your red Jeep, anyway. Sheree is driving the minivan."

"That's exactly what I was afraid of," frowned Jim. "Sheree's the one who ran the left front fender of my Jeep into that median on the way up here!"

"Think she'll wreck the minivan, too?" asked Chip with a wicked smile.

"She oughta be able to stay awake between just here and Powell Lake," teased Luella.

"Was anyone else with them?" grilled Jim.

"Well, let's see." Luella deliberately took her time. "Oh yes, Susan and Rupert decided to take a hike up to that small fishing lake."

"You actually have a fishing lake right here on the property?" Jim was surprised.

"Sure thing, honey," flirted Luella. "Just a quarter of a mile up that hogback, right beyond where they found Lydia Cain's body."

"Maybe a fishing lodge might be even better than a hunting lodge?" suggested Chip.

"An excellent suggestion," approved Jim.

"The others are probably on their way up here," guessed Luella.

"Including Carolyn?" questioned Jim.

"I'm right here," announced Carolyn from behind them. "That pocket door is great! Say, what did the girls – the ones who used to work here – do if they had to come out here to hide when it rained?"

"I imagine they got wet, dear," answered Luella.

"Good thing it's a nice day, then," nodded Carolyn as she pulled out the fourth chair to join them.

"Let's get started, then," urged Chip as he opened his paper file. "This is what we have so far."

"Hold it!" interrupted Jim. "Before we go any further, did we ever get the forensic results back from that blue duffel bag we found in the trunk of that Impala two days ago?"

"Yes, we did," answered Chip. "You should have received the email from the lab by now."

Jim sighed deeply. He had started to check his email the previous evening but had gotten sidetracked. Jim quickly opened his laptop and advised Chip, "I'll find it. Go ahead."

"Okay, then," responded Chip. "We know from Woody's letter that Misty Krain was killed by her late husband Ronald."

"Hey, wait for us!" greeted Sherry as she hobbled from the pocket doorway. "I'm not as quick with my ankle like this!"

"What'd we miss?" grilled Janette as she ran over to grab a chair for Sherry, and then another one for Sherry to prop her ankle on before grabbing one for herself.

"We were just getting started," advised Jim as he turned his attention back to his laptop. "I got the email, its right here! The report indicates that there were no fingerprints on any of the items inside the blue duffel bag. But, there was some DNA evidence on at least one of the items inside, and on the outside of the duffel bag, caught in the zipper! Human hair?"

"Belonging to Ronald Krain," grinned Chip.

"All rightee, then," muttered Jim. "I just saved the attachment into my copy of the case file. That's great news!"

"That is good news!" agreed Sherry as she took out her paper notepad. "Is there any more coffee?"

"I'll be right back," replied Luella as she left to get some.

"Shall we go over the paper file first?" asked Chip.

"Absolutely," insisted Jim. "I'll just follow along with my laptop, to make sure there's nothing else I missed."

"Well," began Chip. "As I already mentioned, Woody's letter states that it was Ronald Krain who murdered his wife Misty. And, from the DNA evidence found in the blue duffel bag's zipper, we can assume with fair certainty that it was Ronald Krain who placed it in the trunk of the green Chevy Impala at the time of the Lydia Cain murder. We can also assume that he knew who murdered each of the other victims – whether it was him or not – since he had all of their drivers' licenses in his personal desk drawer at the time of his death."

"Correction," interjected Carolyn. "All except Karlin's. And mine, of course."

"That's right," acknowledged Jim. "Those were in her purse and in *your* wallet, respectively, encased in cement in the barrel with Karlin's remains."

Carolyn's face took on a sad expression.

"Do you think Carolyn would have been next?" Janette suddenly asked. "Maybe they were planning to take her out, and just never got around to it?"

"What a horrible thought!" exclaimed Sherry, as she continued to make notes for her documentary.

"Anything's possible," opined Jim.

"Anyway," resumed Chip, "there were no usable prints on Carolyn's wallet or anything in it, but that's no surprise. Not after such a long period of time, and especially being encased in cement like that."

"Well, if there had been any prints, they would have belonged to Jerry Krain, that much is certain!" fumed Carolyn. "If that old geezer wasn't already dead, I'd ...."

"I believe this is yours," interrupted Chip as he pulled the badly damaged blue wallet from his coat pocket and laid it on the table. "We have Karlin's purse, as well, but that's still in the evidence locker at the station, waiting for her family to come claim it."

Carolyn swallowed hard as she stared at the tattered blue wallet, hardly daring to believe her eyes.

"And here are the items that were inside," added Chip as he pulled a snack sized Ziplock bag from his coat pocket and set it beside the wallet.

"There's my twenty-dollar bill," marveled Carolyn as she reached for the snack bag and opened it. Her hands trembled as she began leafing through the stack.

"Clearly, money wasn't a motive," deduced Jim as Luella returned with two more cups of coffee – one for Sherry and one for Janette.

"What'd I miss?" asked Luella as she sat back down at the table.

"That there were no fingerprints on my wallet," advised Carolyn. "Or on anything inside!"

"Who's that?" asked Luella when she noticed the photo of Lenny Owens in Carolyn's stack of photos and came closer. "Now, that's what I'm talkin' about! That guy's a stone-cold fox!"

"Let me see," insisted Janette as she took the cups of coffee from Luella and handed one to Sherry.

"I wanna see, too!" Sherry got up and hobbled closer to the table for a better look. "Wow! Very nice looking guy."

"Absolutely!" nodded Janette with a big grin on her face.

"He sure was," agreed Carolyn as she carefully turned it over to see if what Lenny had written on the back was still there. "His name was Lenny Owens." Carolyn unexpectedly returned the photo of Lenny to the stack of items that had been in her wallet without reading it just then.

"Sorry, but it was necessary to read it," apologized Chip. "And, you should have seen what we went through extracting the contents of your wallet as well as we did. Of course, there was still unavoidable damage to some of the photos, but if it wasn't for the wallet itself protecting them ...."

"May I have a look?" interrupted Jim. "I didn't get to read it."

"Later," promised Carolyn as she opened her purse and carefully put the snack bag inside by her unread letter from Lenny.

Jim was clearly disappointed but didn't press the issue. He eventually would, though, of that much Carolyn was certain.

"Aren't you gonna look through the other things?" Janette was surprised by Carolyn's lack of enthusiasm.

"Very well," conceded Carolyn as she pulled the snack bag back out and opened it again. "As you know, this one is of Lenny Owens." She carefully flipped past it, still without reading the back. "The next photo is of my cat Socky, who died of old age back in 1975."

"That was a bad year," muttered Luella.

"So was 1978," pointed out Carolyn with a sympathetic glance. "The next photo is of me and my parents."

The others gathered close to see.

"What a shame that so many of the photos are damaged," remarked Sherry. "At least you can still see who they are, though."

"Yes, indeed!" agreed Carolyn. "And here is a picture of me with Karlin and Eula, standing by my old green Mustang." Carolyn smiled at the memory. "This picture was taken by Stacia, right out there along the Powell Mountain Road."

"Was that before or after you ran over the squirrel?" asked Chip.

"The day before, because it was actually when we were still on our way to visit Susan that this picture was taken," responded Carolyn. "It wasn't until the next day on our way back that I ran over that poor creature, and I still feel bad about it, even after all these years!"

"Wait a minute!" interrupted Chip again. "That isn't the turnout where we found the other green Mustang, is it?"

Carolyn frowned as she thought about it. "Oh, my goodness! I believe it was!"

"Maybe that's why the tire tracks at the scene were so confusing," guessed Chip as he turned to the page in his file where a photo of the tire tracks was located.

Jim quickly pulled up the slide with the tire tracks on his laptop. "That's incredible! You can see here where the Mustang tracks appear to have pulled in and out of there more than once, though these are probably two entirely separate sets of Mustang tracks!"

"Why didn't we see that before?" marveled Chip as he stared with disbelief at the enlarged version on Jim's laptop. "And you can see there where the Impala tracks are beneath the first set of Mustang tracks, but on top of the other, and finally the motorcycle last, across the tops of all of them?"

"So, the first set of Mustang tracks would have been made by Carolyn's car the morning she and her friends stopped to take this photo?" questioned Jim.

"That's what I think," agreed Chip.

"And then the Impala showed up when Martha and her father arrived on the scene before stealing the other Mustang from Woody's salvage yard?" questioned Sherry.

"No, no, that just doesn't make sense," differed Chip. "There's also a set of pickup tracks just past the area, but not in that photo. Those are in the next shot."

"Oh, okay," noted Jim as he advanced to it. "So, Martha must have acted on her own with the Impala, then."

"How do you figure?" frowned Carolyn.

"Well, like she said in her note," reminded Jim, "Martha came back later to clean up her father's mess, and the pickup tracks are a match to the type of truck Ronald Krain used to drive."

"That does make sense!" realized Carolyn.

"So, this is what I think happened," continued Jim. "Martha shows up with the Impala, steals Woody's Mustang, drives up to the lake, and runs down Paul. She also tries to run down Lydia, but misses. That must have been when she chased Lydia down on foot and whacked her on the head with the skillet. I also believe her father either met her there at the lake, or just showed up unexpectedly."

"I see where you're going with this," nodded Chip. "He probably realized his Impala was missing, had reason to suspect something was up, and went after her?"

"Exactly," nodded Jim. "And then he follows Martha back down to the turnout where the Impala is parked, and pulls in just past the scene with his pickup."

"While Martha drives into the turnout with the stolen Mustang, across the tops of the existing tracks, and waits for her father to unload Lydia's body?" guessed Sherry.

"Precisely," grinned Chip.

"And then," continued Jim, "Ronald Krain has his daughter clean up any evidence in the Mustang while he carries poor Lydia up to the trench."

"Or," interjected Chip, "he does everything himself while Martha hides either inside the Impala or somewhere else in the brush? Maybe even in his pickup? Several of the tree limbs on that Mustang were incredibly heavy!"

"Which would have been when Carolyn and Alfredo stopped by on the motorcycle?" supposed Janette.

"There was no pickup there when we stopped," advised Carolyn.

"So, maybe it was when Martha returned later by herself with the Impala that Carolyn and Alfredo stopped?" guessed Sherry.

"That's the most likely scenario," opined Jim as he studied the photo more closely, "plus, there could be two sets of Impala tracks here, too, so that's definitely a possibility."

"Oh, that's just creepy!" exclaimed Janette as she shook her head and crossed herself.

"Remind me again so I get this straight," requested Sherry. "You actually ran over that squirrel the very same day Paul Johnson was run down by the other green Mustang up at the lake? The same day that Lydia Cain first disappeared?"

"Apparently so," answered Carolyn. "Because it would have been later that same day – after running over the squirrel and then taking my car in to be worked on – that I went on that motorcycle ride with Alfredo and we saw the dark green car at the turnout."

"The Chevy Impala?" clarified Chip.

"Yes!" confirmed Carolyn.

"So, it would seem that the other Mustang must have already been used to transport Lydia's body from the lake to Woody's property, and then secreted beneath that pile of brush by the time Carolyn and Alfredo showed up?" concluded Sherry.

"That's what we think," advised Jim.

"Wow!" Janette shook her head as she crossed herself again.

"So, Martha would have been hiding in that Impala when Carolyn and Alfredo stopped to look at it?" asked Luella.

"Unless, of course, they stopped to look at it while Martha was still up at Powell Lake and hadn't come back yet," proposed Chip.

"In either scenario," continued Jim, "if Ronald Krain did just leave Lydia out there to die, as Martha indicated in her note, then Lydia may very well have still been alive at the time Carolyn and Alfredo stopped, regardless of where she was."

"That's a sobering thought," frowned Carolyn.

"In any event," described Jim, "the forensic evidence we have indicates that Lydia died from eventual loss of blood, internal injuries, and exposure to the elements, not from strangulation as originally determined."

"That is correct," confirmed Chip. "And, it is surprising that a careful man like Ronald Krain would be reckless enough not to notice that he had caught the hairs of his arm in its zipper *before* putting the blue duffel bag into the trunk of his Impala."

"Don't you mean into the compartment *beneath* the rug of the Impala's trunk?" grilled Sherry.

"I stand corrected!" smiled Chip.

"So, what else did you have in your wallet, Carolyn?" questioned Sherry, to get things back on track.

"Okay," continued Carolyn, "here is my driver's license, my Social Security card, my food card from the school cafeteria, and a couple of business cards." Carolyn froze as she glanced at the first one. It read "Woody's Salvage Yard and Woodcutting" with the address and phone number beneath it.

Luella slowly reached for it. "May I?"

"You may have it, if you like," offered Carolyn.

"Thanks!" sniffed Luella as a tear escaped onto her cheek. "I actually don't have one of these."

"And here's Ron's Auto Shop," chuckled Carolyn.

"Maybe Jim would like that one?" grinned Janette.

"If the guy's even still alive." Jim shook his head as he took the card and looked at it.

"He actually is," advised Chip. "Though his automotive skills sure aren't what they used to be, especially with some of the newer vehicles. I sure wouldn't take my car there!"

The others welcomed a laugh to relieve the tension.

"Anyway, that's about it for the stuff from my wallet," concluded Carolyn as she picked up and handed the badly damaged wallet to Jim. "Here, you can have my old wallet if you like. I never want to see it again!"

"Now you can't say she never gave you nothin'!" teased Janette.

"Gee, thanks!" snickered Jim as he took the wallet from Carolyn and set it on the table. Then, wistfully looking at Carolyn's purse, Jim suddenly asked, "Are you sure there's nothing else?"

"I'm afraid that's all for now," smirked Carolyn. She was well aware that he was alluding to the unread letter from Lenny Owens.

Jim merely raised an eyebrow and then nodded.

"What about the ID for Lydia Cain?" Luella suddenly asked. "It wasn't with the other ones in that metal box from Martha Krain."

"That's correct. It was in Lydia's purse, up at Powell Lake," confirmed Chip, "where we found her sandals, near the body of Paul Johnson."

"Plus, we already have Martha Krain's letter telling us what happened to Paul and Lydia, anyway," pointed out Carolyn.

"Indeed, we do," nodded Jim.

Luella furled her brow. "That still means we are no closer to actually *proving* my daddy's innocence than we were before we started this whole thing! All we have is hearsay from those letters."

"That's where you're wrong," smiled Jim. "Let's talk about the individual items that were found *inside* the blue duffel bag. And, as Chip pointed out earlier, the hair caught in its zipper has been confirmed to be Ronald Krain's."

"That sounds like proof to me!" opined Sherry.

"Absolutely!" agreed Jim. "And, if you will recall, it was Carolyn's idea to unsnap the rug in the trunk to see if there was a secret compartment underneath it. So, that's what we did."

"So, everything Martha said in her letter was true!" exclaimed Luella. "It was Ronald Krain that murdered Lydia Cain!"

"No doubt about it," assured Jim. "He was definitely responsible for her death, regardless of the fact that Lydia was still alive when he left her there to die, either from her injuries or from exposure to the elements."

"What a monster!" fumed Luella.

"And speaking of monsters," continued Jim, "Remember that roll of baling wire that was up at the winery?"

"Yeah, I remember it," nodded Carolyn.

"That, of course, was covered with recent prints belonging to Jerry Krain," revealed Jim.

"Really?" Carolyn seemed surprised. "Do you think he may have murdered anyone recently?"

"I doubt it," interjected Chip. "There have not been any missing person reports in this area since the late nineties, but those persons were later recovered and determined to have died during an unfortunate hunting accident. Plus, Jerry could have used the baling wire for just about anything at a place like that."

"Why would the blue duffel bag have gone undiscovered for all that time?" wondered Carolyn. "And why would Ronald Krain have just left it there? It seems like the new owners of the Impala would have at least looked inside the trunk and noticed it."

"He probably just forgot about it," figured Jim. "That's not a place most people even bother to look at, even when they know about it. And, the car changed hands three times."

"Wow!" marveled Carolyn.

"Remind us again what was in the duffel bag?" grilled Sherry.

"A cast-iron skillet, a spatula, a blood-soaked camping blanket, a roll of duct tape, a pair of wire cutters, and miscellaneous pieces of baling wire," described Jim.

"Hold it!" hailed Sherry. "I thought you said the cast-iron skillet was found up at the winery?"

"One just like it, yes," explained Jim.

"Really?" Sherry seemed surprised.

"Not only were the two skillets identical," interjected Chip, "but both had blood residue on them, as well."

"So, whose blood was on which one?" pressed Sherry.

"The blood on the skillet from the blue duffel bag had traces of blood too degraded to test, but also had human hair dried to it that we believe was Lydia's," informed Chip. "In addition to that, there was similar blood on the camping blanket."

"Well, I don't know if it will be of much help," interjected Carolyn, "but don't forget about the pile of bloody laundry Martha Krain had that morning. She was trying to wash it right when Karlin was washing the clothes and stuff from my Mustang, that had Stacia's vomit all over it."

"What?" gasped Luella. "You actually saw Martha Krain with a pile of bloody laundry that same morning? The same morning you ran over that squirrel?"

"Yes!" answered Carolyn. "She told us she had a bad nosebleed and wanted to get everything washed before it became permanently stained."

"And you believed her?" Luella was flabbergasted.

Carolyn apologetically shrugged her shoulders.

"That probably explains why Martha didn't want you guys to wash the rest of her laundry for her," assumed Jim. "You did say she stormed off with the rest of it and refused to let Karlin get it started for her later?"

"That's correct," corroborated Carolyn.

"That's just sad!" Janette shook her head.

"Why in the world would Martha and her father try to cover it all up like that?" Luella was clearly angry.

"Probably because they didn't want to go to prison for the rest of their lives?" guessed Jim.

"Or worse," added Chip.

"What could be worse than that?" asked Janette.

"Spending your entire life in fear for the safety of your family," mentioned Luella. "I can't even begin to imagine the cross my poor daddy had to bear for us. It sure would be nice to clear his name!"

"That's exactly what this is all about," advised Jim. "Now that we have this additional evidence, Chip and I plan to appear before the Honorable Michael Krain and make a petition to the court."

"Before Michael Krain?" scoffed Luella. "Ronald Krain's son? You seriously got to be kidding me!"

"Oh, you'd be surprised what things his son might not want made public," smirked Jim. "To make a long story short, our forensic experts have proved that nearly all of the other victims were hit on the back of the head with a cast-iron skillet. But, because of the vast timeframe involved, the only identifiable blood on the Shady Brook skillet was that of his latest victim."

"Karlin?" assumed Carolyn.

"Yes, ma'am," confirmed Chip. "And, most likely, all of his victims were bound with baling wire while they were still unconscious before being stuffed into the barrels where we found them."

"Do you think any of them were still alive when those evil men started filling 'em up with cement?" asked Janette.

"What a horrible thought!" exclaimed Luella.

"Could that have been the same skillet Jerry Krain had those rotten eggs and rancid wine in, that he wanted Carolyn and Karlin to eat the night she lost her wallet?" speculated Sherry.

"We believe so, yes," informed Jim, "because there were definite traces of egg fragments on the Shady Brook skillet, as well."

Carolyn made a face of disgust and shook her head.

"The good news," added Chip, "is that both of those men are dead, and we should have more than enough evidence here to petition the court to overturn the murder conviction in the Wilson matter."

"Circumstantial evidence alone would convince any jury that Jerry Krain murdered Karlin," mentioned Chip. "No question about it."

"Or that Ronald Krain murdered Lydia!" nodded Janette.

"Correction," interjected Jim. "The late Ronald Krain would unequivocally be found guilty of premeditated murder in the first degree by definite proof, not just by circumstantial evidence."

"Most definitely!" agreed Chip. "Along with his daughter, Martha, as an accomplice, by her own admission in that suicide note.

So, Lydia may or may not have been conscious as she lay there dying, but if she was coherent at the time, she would have suffered immeasurably."

"Poor kid!" sniffed Luella.

"What about the baling wire from Lydia?" questioned Carolyn. "Did they compare it against the roll from the winery?"

"Yes, ma'am," grinned Chip. "It was you and Sherry who noticed it there and gave us the idea to check it out, by the way."

"And?" Luella was anxious to hear the rest.

"The company that manufactures that particular brand of baling wire is based in Ocean Bay." Chip then turned to an enlarged photo of a strand of baling wire in his file. "Each strand is impressed with a highly-individualized marking as it is forced through the narrow opening of the die used in its manufacture. Specific die marks are normally restricted to the limited amount of wire produced during that batch because dies break down under pressure and must be replaced with new dies, which make distinctly different marks."

"What color dye?" questioned Janette.

"Not dye," corrected Jim. "D-i-e, as in *someone died*. Also, a die is a specialized tool used in the manufacturing industry to cut or shape metal or plastic. There is another piece called a die block that is used to hold the metal while it is being stretched, bent, or crimped into place."

"Making the marks comparable," recognized Sherry, "kind of like when you compare the unique striations on a bullet or its casing?"

"Exactly like that!" confirmed Jim. "Not bad!"

"In other words," paraphrased Chip. "When a forensic specialist looks at a sample of wire under a microscope, the die marks peculiar to that particular batch are as distinct as individual fingerprints would be."

"I get it!" snapped Janette.

"Then you'll notice how the die marks on the wire from the winery in Chip's photo match exactly to the marks in this other photo of the wire found in the blue duffel bag," indicated Jim as he turned his laptop around for the others to see.

"But, they look like two photos of the same piece of wire," observed Carolyn.

"That's what I thought at first," replied Jim. "So, I had a double blind forensic comparison done. The photo in Chip's file is of the piece of wire taken from the roll of baling wire at the winery."

"That's amazing!" commented Sherry.

"The photo on my laptop is of a piece of wire found inside the duffel bag," revealed Jim. "It is also identical to the baling wire found on Lydia Cain's body." Jim then advanced to a third photo on his laptop for everyone to see. "All three samples of baling wire are from the exact same die lot."

"I do remember Woody telling us there was a roll of baling wire missing from his shed," recalled Chip. "That obviously is what finally happened to it."

"Could there be yet another roll of baling wire from the same die lot someplace else?" Sherry suddenly asked.

"I like the way she thinks!" smiled Chip. "We may never know if there was another roll. But, as Jim indicated, all three samples we do have were from the same die lot. In any event, we believe Ronald Krain used something to wipe the prints off the baling wire found in the duffel bag and on Lydia Cain's body, because there were traces of green fabric on them, perhaps from a pair of gloves. Though, any evidence of those prints would have disintegrated over time, anyway."

"Yet, he was still careless enough to leave his arm hairs in the zipper of the blue duffel bag?" marveled Sherry.

"You got it!" grinned Chip. "The arm hairs definitely belonged to Ronald Krain. Too bad we didn't have that evidence back in 1975!"

"Didn't you say you had reasonable doubt, though?" reminded Carolyn. "Even back then?"

"It was the lack of Woody's fingerprints on the baling wire that raised the first red flag for me back in 1975," revealed Chip. "The woodcutter never even wore gloves; he didn't own any."

"He's right," realized Carolyn. "In fact, Woody was so poor that he even made his own wooden foot!"

"Plus, there's no way he would have put his own American flag right on the body – a flag that anyone in the community would have recognized as his!" pointed out Chip.

"Don't forget the hood made from the green Army bag with serial numbers on it that were traced back to him," added Sherry.

"You guys have been paying attention!" approved Chip. "But, unfortunately, those facts plus all the other little details that gave Ron and me more than sufficient reason to have reasonable doubt, just weren't enough for the jury."

"What about the gas can?" asked Janette. "Were there any prints on that?"

"That was the most damning evidence of all," sighed Chip. "Woody's fingerprints were all over it. But, tell me this, how could he have left prints on the gas can while NOT leaving any prints on anything else at the scene?"

"Wow!" Janette sadly shook her head.

"Didn't you tell me that one of the jurors came home to a burning cross, too?" reminded Jim.

"Yes, but we didn't find out about it until later," confirmed Chip. "That was after Ron and I had already been ousted from our jobs with the DA's office, and all because we stuck up for what we believed – and still believe – was an innocent man!" Chip then slammed his fist onto the table in frustration.

"I've never forgotten what you tried to do for my daddy," assured Luella. "And I'm so sorry I ever doubted you or thought you'd given up."

Chip merely shrugged his shoulders.

"Were you ousted from your jobs before or after you each came home to a burning cross on your lawn?" asked Jim.

"The burning crosses came first," clarified Chip. "Probably the same day the juror came home to hers. She was Jewish, too, by the way. Apparently, she was the reason the jury deliberated for an entire week before finally reaching their unanimous verdict. Otherwise, they probably would have reached it in ten minutes!"

"All the other jurors were Crusading Knights, then?" confirmed Jim. "In fact, wasn't Judge Lorik the Head Knight back then?"

Chip merely nodded.

"And probably the guards at the prison where my daddy was murdered in his cell were Knights, too!" fumed Luella. "What we need to find is physical evidence of that, as well!"

"That would probably be impossible at this point," Jim admitted regretfully. "However, Chip and I plan to appear before the

Honorable Michael Krain with the new evidence we have on Tuesday morning."

"We do?" Chip was surprised. "Okay, sure! That's excellent. Tuesdays are when *ex parte* arguments are usually heard. But, since you are the only one of us who still has an active membership with the Bar, I assume you will be presenting the case?"

"Oh, absolutely! There is no statute of limitations on murder. And we will get Woody's name cleared!" promised Jim. "Trust me!"

Meanwhile, Susan and Rupert were seated on a log beside the small fishing lake on the Wilson property. The late morning sun reflected brilliant rays of light through the budding forest surrounding them and cast reflective shadows against the calm surface of the water.

"It's hard to believe that something so horrible could have happened in such a beautiful place!" marveled Susan as she admired the scenery. The sound of a chickadee could suddenly be heard.

"They were planning to go over their case file after breakfast," reminded Rupert. "Sure you don't want to go back now?"

"Not particularly," responded Susan. "It's been a long week, and I've had about all I can take. But, don't let me keep you here."

"I'm not leaving you here alone," flirted Rupert. "Besides, they don't need my help."

"Actually," differed Susan, "from what Jim tells me, you've been a tremendous help this past week."

"Too much so, I'm afraid," replied Rupert. "Now that the site has been cleared, those of us working it have literally worked ourselves out of a job."

"Maybe Jim might still need some help up at the winery?" suggested Susan. "Or, if they build something else here?"

"They've got a full crew at the winery already," informed Rupert. "I already checked. But, Jim said he will give me a good recommendation when I go to apply for a job up at the school."

"That's great!" smiled Susan, unable to help staring at Rupert's incredibly handsome face. *Was it wrong for her to be so drawn to him so soon after losing her husband? Was it mere coincidence that he should suddenly drop into her life when he did?*

"Unfortunately," revealed Rupert, "there are no openings at the university right now, at least not for a professor with my qualifications."

"What will you do, then?" frowned Susan.

"Well," sighed Rupert, "Jim did say I could have the old green Chevy Impala if I wanted it. It actually runs good."

Susan began laughing.

"What's so funny?" pressed Rupert.

"Well," explained Susan, "that reminds me of this old junk peddler who used to live down the street from us when I was growing up. He would always have something for sale on the corner in front of his house."

"Your point?" delved Rupert, somehow feeling as if he had been insulted in some way.

"Well, he had two different signs he would use," elaborated Susan. "One sign said 'RUNS GOOD' while the other sign merely said 'RUNS' - so, at least your car *runs good.*"

"Very funny," laughed Rupert. "Here I am, a 50-year old has-been with no job prospects, and all I have in the world is a 58-year old car from a murder investigation that *runs good.*"

"Come work for me," Susan suddenly offered.

"Work for you?" Rupert was bowled over.

"Why not?" Susan rewarded Rupert with one of her crooked smiles as she undressed him with her eyes.

"Doing what?" Rupert raised an eyebrow.

Then, becoming serious, Susan paused to look at Rupert with a sense of longing before turning away with embarrassment. She had not meant for him to get the wrong idea.

"Seriously, doing what?" Rupert put his hand under Susan's chin and forced her to look at him again. His eyes seemed to envelop her.

"We happen to be in need of a groundskeeper at the Killingham Lighthouse Bed and Breakfast," advised Susan rather nervously. "It includes taking care of a golf course."

"Is that what your husband did?" questioned Rupert.

"Among other things," responded Susan as she continued to drink in the sight of Rupert's handsome physique.

"Are you asking me to just step in and *replace* him?" Rupert had a slight smile on his face but tried to remain serious.

"No, it's not like that at all!" blurted out Susan as she got up and walked toward the lake. "It would be just until you find the job you're looking for. Who knows, they could very well be in need of a teacher at Oceanview Academy. That is, if teaching high school isn't beneath someone with your qualifications."

Rupert stood up and walked over to where Susan was, suddenly pulled her close and began kissing her on the mouth.

Susan unexpectedly pushed him away and slapped Rupert across the face. "Is that what you think this is all about? I've just lost my husband, and am still very much in love with him!"

"I'm so sorry!" apologized Rupert. "I just thought ...."

"I know what you thought!" interrupted Susan. Then, more softly, she admitted, "Yes, I am attracted to you! What woman wouldn't be? But, I was also married to another man before Ray, who happened to be an abusive alcoholic that stepped out on me, so you'll pardon me if I'm just a little gun-shy."

"Hey," replied Rupert as he cautiously put one hand on Susan's shoulder. "My wife stepped out on me, too, so I know what it feels like. That was why I allowed myself to become an alcoholic in the first place. But, I'm DONE with that life. Of course, I can't expect you to just take my word for it, but you'll see."

Susan turned to study Rupert more closely. "A professor, huh?"

"Economics and sociology," reminded Rupert.

"And you *never* stepped out on your wife?" grilled Susan.

"I may be a big flirt," admitted Rupert, "but no, I *never* stepped out on my wife, not ever!"

"And, of course, you were born on March 23, 1973," muttered Susan as she shook her head. "There is that."

"I can't help it!" Rupert began to flirt with Susan again, but much more cautiously this time.

"Well," sighed Susan, "I do have a selection of eight rooms to choose from at the lighthouse. Well, actually seven, because one of them is mine."

"Just what would my duties entail?" delved Rupert with a slight grin. "Maintaining an entire golf course all by myself, and what else?"

"Oh, you'd have help," assured Susan. "A young man named Ted Jensen. Ann's husband."

"Really?" nodded Rupert. "The tall skinny woman with pale skin, hooked nose and thick glasses that claims she's a direct descendant of Lizzie Borden?"

"That would be her." Susan began to flirt with Rupert again. She just could not help herself. "But, ask her sometime. Ann can explain to you why Lizzie Borden was entirely sane. She just had tremendous motivation for what she did, even though that didn't make it right."

"What's her husband like?" asked Rupert as he picked up a stone and tossed it, making it skip across the water. "And, is there a gymnasium there?"

"Well," described Susan, "Ted is well-built and muscular, with a firm handshake. His love of surfing and boogie boarding is surpassed only by his love for Ann. He's part Polynesian, has shoulder-length kinky hair, with captivating brown eyes, like yours."

"Really?" grinned Rupert.

"And, his Aunt Veronica was one of the two girls whose skeletal remains were found in the bunker tunnel on the beach at Oceanview Academy on March 23, 2016," related Susan, rather sadly.

"Wow!" remarked Rupert. "At least they weren't found on March 23, 1973!"

"Actually," added Susan, "that was the day they were murdered and put there. It was forty-three years later when they were found."

"Hey, I'm sorry," apologized Rupert.

"Veronica Jensen and Joyce Troglite were two of Carolyn's and my closest friends at the time," continued Susan. "That was also the day that Veronica's boyfriend, Steve Fredrickson, was attacked by a shark while boogie boarding on the beach there."

"Wait a minute!" realized Rupert. "Janette was telling me about this during our flight. Wasn't it Carolyn who tried to save him?"

"She and Bart Higbee gave him CPR, right there on the beach," described Susan. "But, he died anyway. And the clothes Carolyn had on that day – they were literally covered in blood!"

"I'm so sorry!" mentioned Rupert. He could see how painful the memory was for Susan.

"And, as far as a gym," advised Susan, "they do have one over at the school nearby, but not right at the B&B. I've been thinking for a while now that we could use one, though. More than once, I've had customers ask for a workout room."

"I could certainly help you run one," assured Rupert as he purposely flexed his biceps for Susan to admire. Even through the forest green polo shirt he had on, his bulging muscles and trim waistline were compelling. Rupert was well aware of the effect he had on most women and rather enjoyed it.

All at once, a mother beaver with two babies splashed into the lake from the other side.

"Oh look, how cute they are!" smiled Susan.

"It's nice to see wildlife," nodded Rupert. "Especially living in a beautiful place like this."

"Well, they always are needing help over at the wildlife center we have there, too," informed Susan. "Ann is heavily involved with that when she's not helping me clean the rooms or whatever else needs to be done at the B&B. Jim's wife Sheree does most of the cooking."

"It isn't haunted, is it?" Rupert suddenly asked. He was serious.

"The lighthouse?" Susan smiled a crooked smile. "Not that I'm aware of, and I've been living there for seven years now."

"You do make a rather inviting offer, then," admitted Rupert as he again enveloped Susan with his magnetic charm.

"And?" grinned Susan with her hands on her hips.

"I'll take it," agreed Rupert. "Who knows, perhaps it could eventually work into something more permanent?"

"The job?" clarified Susan.

"Look," advised Rupert, "I'm not very good at this kind of thing, but I wouldn't mind it at all if – after you've had an acceptable time to grieve for your loss – you were to consider me as a possibility."

"A possibility, huh?" smirked Susan as she flirted back with Rupert, just a little more than she intended to. "Most definitely!"

"Would you be opposed to my putting my arm around you as we walk?" asked Rupert. "Or even just holding hands?"

"You're not about to give up on me, are you?" realized Susan.

"Probably not," admitted Rupert as Susan extended her hand to him. "Shall we walk around the lake?"

"Sure, why not?" agreed Susan as she and Rupert began to explore the trail that encircled the lake.

After walking along in silence for several minutes, listening to the sounds of the forest, Susan stopped to face him. She wanted him to kiss her again, but would he? "Was there anyone else in your life between then and now?"

"Between my marriage and now?" Rupert was well aware of Susan's intentions, but was not anxious to be rejected again.

Susan merely raised an eyebrow and waited for his reply.

"My wife Gina ran off with our accountant," revealed Rupert, "after running us so deeply into debt that bankruptcy was the only out."

"That's awful!" remarked Susan.

"She took our daughter Matilda with her," continued Rupert, rather sadly. "Matilda was 16 years old at the time, but that was three years ago, and I never saw her again."

"You don't even know where to find her?" Susan was shocked.

"Her mother made sure of it," answered Rupert, rather sadly. "Believe me, I've tried to find her, but nothing. She could even have a different last name by now, for all I know."

"So, this is truly a fresh start for you?" Susan tried to recall what Rupert had looked like before Luella had cut off his dreadlocks but could not even picture it. "You don't plan on growing those dreadful locks again, do you?"

Rupert suddenly started to laugh.

"I went to cosmetology school once," revealed Susan. "So, I can certainly help you maintain your new hairstyle."

"What else did you do?" probed Rupert. He wanted to learn everything he could about her.

"You didn't answer my question," prompted Susan.

"Dreadlocks again?" chuckled Rupert. "No."

"That's a relief! Well, I'm a retired school teacher by trade," admitted Susan with a devious smile. "Grade school."

"A fellow teacher?" flirted Rupert. "I knew there was something I liked about you. Any kids?"

"Two by my first husband, both grown," revealed Susan.

"Grandkids?" grilled Rupert.

"A couple," added Susan.

"And how do they like coming to see their grandma in her lighthouse by the sea?" asked Rupert with a suggestive smile.

Susan then cautiously put her arm around Rupert's waist and looked up at him in an innocent manner. "We'll never make it around the lake at this rate."

Rupert then pulled her closer as they continued to walk. His rippling muscles tenderly brushed against her arm as they made their way. Rupert knew at that moment that Susan was his destiny, and he would do everything in his power to make that happen.

"I am the jealous type," Susan suddenly informed Rupert as she flirted with him again.

Rupert then stopped and turned to face her. "Then, I will make certain you have nothing to be jealous about, but only if I can expect the same in return."

Susan felt her heart rate increase as she looked up into Rupert's eyes. The magnetism between them was undeniable. Susan nervously licked her lips, not meaning to do so in such a suggestive way.

Rupert cautiously put one of his hands on each of her shoulders. "May I kiss you?"

Susan smiled invitingly as she reached up and put her arms around Rupert's neck, pulling him closer.

"Do you know how beautiful you are?" questioned Rupert. He was not about to try to kiss Susan again without her express verbal permission. He did not want to risk being rejected again.

Susan then stood on her tiptoes and sensuously kissed Rupert on the lips, but only for a moment. "What's wrong?"

"You never answered my question," reminded Rupert with a sly but mysterious smile.

"What question?" frowned Susan.

"May I kiss you?" repeated Rupert.

Susan then smiled a crooked smile before answering. "Yes, you may kiss me now, please!"

Rupert took his time, first brushing a stray hair from Susan's cheek with the back of his hand. "You are so beautiful!"

"Perhaps I'm your destiny?" teased Susan.

Rupert became serious upon hearing the word "destiny" and gazed at Susan with such intense longing that it almost frightened her for a moment. *How could she have known that? Could she read his mind?* Rupert then replied, "I certainly hope so!"

He then pulled Susan close and passionately kissed her on the mouth, aroused beyond measure by the feel of her shapely body next to his. She was truly his idea of the perfect woman, and he was powerless to resist her. The magnetism between them was indescribable.

"Hey, you two!" came the voice of Jim Otterman from behind them. "I thought I might find you here."

Both Susan and Rupert turned to glare at Jim with abject disapproval. He had ruined a magic moment.

"Sorry!" blushed Jim, realizing at once what he had interrupted. "Luella has a special lunch for us and asked me to find you."

"You've finished going over your case file already?" questioned Susan, rather tersely.

"We did," answered Jim. "In fact, Chip and I will be filing a petition with the court on Tuesday, to have the murder conviction of Woodrow Wilson overturned."

"He's been dead for forty-five years now," calculated Susan.

"It's important to Luella," advised Jim, "that her father's good name be restored, even if it is posthumously. Besides, a little publicity about the case couldn't hurt when it comes time to open up the new fishing lodge I plan to build down there."

"Fishing lodge?" Rupert seemed surprised.

"And the brothel will be turned into a museum," added Jim. "People will pay good money to come and stay at the Woodcutter's Fishing Lodge and then to tour the haunted brothel next door!"

"That does sound intriguing," acknowledged Susan as she and Rupert began following Jim back down the trail.

"I see you two have become rather friendly," pointed out Jim with a smug grin.

"You jealous?" teased Rupert.

"No, I'm married," smiled Jim. He was not about to get into another philosophical debate with Rupert about that. "Say, we may need some guys who know construction, when it comes time to build."

"No thanks," declined Rupert. "Someone else has made me a better offer."

Jim stopped in his tracks and turned to face Susan and Rupert, who were still walking with their arms around one another.

"Who?" demanded Jim.

"Me," advised Susan with a triumphant smile. "Rupert will be helping with some of Ray's old duties at the lighthouse."

"I'll just bet he will!" snorted Jim as he turned to continue down the trail.

"Hey!" Susan grabbed Jim by the arm, prompting him to stop again and face her. "It's not what you think!"

"Really?" doubted Jim as he gave Rupert a skeptical look. "You do realize who holds the financial purse strings at your lighthouse?"

"You do," acknowledged Susan as she gave Jim a pleading look.

"And, you do realize who Rupert will be working for, if he comes to the lighthouse?" continued Jim.

"For you!" answered Susan with a deep sigh as she put her free hand on her hip.

"In that case," agreed Jim, "Rupert, you're hired! Welcome to the staff of the Killingham Lighthouse Bed and Breakfast."

Jim then held out his hand for Rupert to shake.

"Thank you, sir," smiled Rupert as he shook hands with Jim. Then, letting go of Susan, he suddenly grabbed Jim with both arms to give him a bear hug and actually lifted him off the ground as he did so. "Thank you so much!"

"Yeah, yeah!" muttered Jim. "You can put me down now."

"Sorry, sir," beamed Rupert as he put Jim down but then gave him one more hug and slap on the shoulder before shaking his hand again. "You won't regret this, Mr. Otterman!"

"Just one more thing," added Jim.

"Anything," promised Rupert.

"Please call me Jim," requested Jim.

"Jim." Rupert then turned to hug Susan, lifting her off the ground as he did so, and kissed her on the lips while spinning around in a circle before gently setting her back down again.

"I hope you know what you're getting yourself into," advised Jim as he gave Susan a poignant glance.

"Rupert is obviously our destiny," advised Susan as she flirted shamelessly with Rupert while following Jim back down to the Powell Mountain Bed and Breakfast for lunch.

"*Our* destiny?" doubted Jim. "Because of when his birthday is?"

"It could be a sign," pointed out Susan. "Besides, you're not my father, you know!"

"Well, I'm the closest thing you've got to one," mentioned Jim. "And I do expect you two to do things by the book!"

"By the book?" frowned Rupert.

"By the book!" repeated Jim as he stopped again and turned to face them. "And if I so much as even think you've broken this woman's heart – especially after everything else she's been through already – I'll load you back up onto my Learjet and fly you straight back to Chicago!"

"Why, Jim, I didn't know you cared!" chuckled Susan.

"You have absolutely nothing to worry about," promised Rupert. "Trust me!"

Upon hearing the words "trust me" both Susan and Jim gave Rupert a peculiar look.

"What?" demanded Rupert.

"It's nothing," snickered Jim. "It's just that anytime Susan says that, it usually means just the opposite."

"Trust me?" grinned Rupert.

Jim merely nodded in response.

It was Tuesday morning, April 4, 2023. Jim Otterman and Chip Priest were dressed in black business suits, white shirts and expensive-looking paisley silk neckties. Their black leather shoes literally gleamed. Chip had even polished his briefcase.

Rupert Williams was also dressed in a black business suit, but his shirt was bright yellow. Rupert's necktie was black silk with yellow paisley designs woven into the fabric. The yellow and black men's oxford wingtip shoes he wore were distinctive, with the heels and toes being black while the mid-sections were yellow. Susan took that opportunity to slip her arm through Rupert's as she gave Luella a look of triumph.

"Um, um!" exclaimed Luella as she nodded with approval. "You gentlemen are *all* lookin' fine!"

"How 'bout you?" questioned Jim. "Is that what you're wearing?"

"Why?" scowled Luella.

"Well," Jim cleared his throat. "You may want to wear something a little less suggestive for the courtroom."

"Suggestive?" grinned Luella as she adjusted the hem of her tight red sweater. "Why, Carrot Top, I didn't think you'd notice!"

"He's probably right," agreed Chip. "We all need to look discrete and demure for the courtroom."

"I didn't know we were goin' to a funeral!" remarked Luella. "Very well, I'll be right back. Don't leave without me!"

"We'll definitely need to take both vehicles," realized Jim. "Especially since we don't have the minivan anymore."

"There are ten of us," pointed out Carolyn.

"Sheree, Ann, Susan and Rupert, you're with me," advised Jim.

"Sherry, Janette, Carolyn and Luella will ride with me, then," agreed Chip as he headed for the door.

"We do look like we're all going to a funeral!" laughed Sherry. "But, everyone looks great."

"Why, thank you!" grinned Luella as she descended the staircase. "I want my daddy to be proud of us. I just have a feelin' he may very well be there in spirit, looking in on us."

Janette shook her head and crossed herself as she followed the others outside.


Meanwhile, Judge Michael Krain was seated in his chambers, electronically signing various orders, judgments and other documents from the previous day. A quick knock on his door roused him from his task. He had arrived at eight o'clock; *could it really be nine already?*

"It's time for *ex parte,* Your Honor." It was Avis Hedge, his long-time judicial assistant and court clerk. Due to the small size of the St. Diablo County Court, the two positions had traditionally been combined.

"Thank you, Avis," nodded the judge as he stood to grab his black robe from a nearby coat tree before putting it on and zipping it up.

In some ways, *ex parte* submissions were less complicated than regular court proceedings. In other ways, they were bothersome. Judge Krain much preferred having sufficient time to review a filing in advance rather than being expected to come to an on-the-spot decision in open court. Motions for extension of time, of course, required little effort to decide. It was the unexpected complex matters that he loathed.

"All rise," commanded the bailiff as Judge Krain entered the courtroom from his chambers, directly behind the judge's bench.

"The St. Diablo County Court is now in session this 4th day of April, 2023, with the Honorable Michael Krain presiding. Please be seated." The bailiff then motioned for everyone to be seated.

Ms. Hedge's courtroom table was located directly in front of the judge's bench. Interestingly, the courtroom was relatively empty that particular day, with less than a dozen people in all.

The defense table and jury box both sat empty, as they usually did during *ex parte*. The court reporter's table also was unoccupied, but that was because court reporters had pretty much become a thing of the past now that most proceedings were routinely recorded using advanced video and audio equipment. Often it was used as a place to spread out physical exhibits during trial, if there were any.

Seated at the prosecution table were attorney Jim Otterman and former Deputy DA Charles Priest.

"Good afternoon, ladies and gentlemen," greeted Judge Krain as he pulled up the electronic docket on his desktop. *"Luella Wilson v. The People of St. Diablo County?* Is this some kind of a joke?"

"It's the only case on your docket today, sir," added Ms. Hedge.

Jim Otterman stood before speaking. "Good morning, Your Honor. I am attorney Jim Otterman. Beside me is former Deputy DA Charles Priest, who is here today as my paralegal for purposes of this proceeding."

Judge Michael Krain frowned with disapproval. He knew full well who Jim Otterman was! He had just concluded the final details of a personal real estate transaction with the man, not to mention allowing him to buy out one of his personal financial trust accounts! In truth, his dealings with Jim Otterman had been rather profitable, particularly the opportunity to finally rid himself of the troubling Shady Brook property! *Why, then, was he here now?*

Chip Priest then stood and addressed the court. "Good morning, Your Honor."

"The paralegal may be seated," snickered Judge Krain as he pounded his gavel once for good measure before turning his attention to the *Wilson* file on his desktop computer.

Chip Priest immediately sat back down, pursing his lips with frustration. He had expected a less-than-cordial welcome in court that day, but nothing as humiliating as this!

"Who are these other individuals with you, Mr. Otterman?" questioned the judge as he continued clicking his way through the lengthy complaint on his computer screen.

"The woman on the end is my client, Ms. Luella Wilson," introduced Jim as he motioned for her to stand. "Her father was the late Woodrow Wilson, also known as Woody the Woodcutter."

"Your Honor," acknowledged Luella.

Judge Krain immediately pounded his gavel onto the sounding block in front of him. "You will not address the court unless specifically instructed to do so. Do I make myself clear, Ms. Wilson?"

"Abundantly, sir," replied Luella.

"Then please be seated, Ms. Wilson," directed the judge. "As for the rest of you, you will each stand as Mr. Otterman mentions your name and describes who you are and why you are here. You will immediately be seated thereafter."

Luella's nostrils flared as she glared at Judge Krain.

"Next, Your Honor," continued Jim, "is Carolyn Bennett-Hunter, formerly known as Carolyn Bennett. She was a personal acquaintance of the late Woodrow Wilson, and you will see in the file that her green Mustang was originally seized and forensically analyzed until being ruled out as the suspect vehicle in the *Lydia Cain* and *Paul Johnson* matters back in 1975. She will be testifying on behalf of Woodrow Wilson's character, and ...."

"I get the idea!" interrupted Judge Krain as he again pounded his gavel. "Next?"

Carolyn quickly sat back down and exchanged a worried look with the others.

"The next three individuals are Janette Manza, Susan Killingham, and Rupert Williams," indicated Jim. "These persons were with me during a recent trip to Chicago to visit Martha Krain."

"I'm going to stop you right there, Mr. Otterman," advised the judge upon seeing them stand. "Please approach the bench. You folks may sit down."

Jim Otterman nervously straightened his necktie before approaching. "Your Honor?"

"I'm afraid I'm going to have to recuse myself from this matter," informed the judge. "The Martha Krain you are referring to here is my sister, the one who recently committed suicide."

"She is not actually named in the caption of the complaint, Your Honor, so she technically is not a defendant," pointed out Jim. "Nor is anyone from the Krain family."

Judge Michael Krain carefully studied Jim for several moments before speaking again. "So, you deliberately chose to omit naming anyone from the Krain family as a defendant in your complaint? Was it your intention to avoid creating a possible conflict of interest for me in this matter?"

"That is absolutely correct, Your Honor," replied Jim with a slight hint of triumph.

Judge Krain shook his head with dismay as he continued clicking his way through the 366-page document, dumbfounded upon seeing some of the exhibits, especially the various drivers' licenses. He then paused and stared at one of them, in particular. "Misty Krain?"

"If I may, sir?" asked Jim.

"Your Honor," corrected the judge.

"If I may, Your Honor?" requested Jim.

"I don't believe this!" fumed the judge when he saw the suicide note from Martha Krain. "Just where did you get this?"

"That, Your Honor," replied Jim, "is what Janette, Susan and Rupert will testify to. They were with me when it came into our possession, thus establishing a chain of custody."

"Counsel will return to his table," directed the judge.

"Thank you, Your Honor," acknowledged Jim as he returned to the prosecution table. "Next is my wife and daughter, Sheree Otterman and Ann Jensen. They are here at my request, because my daughter Ann is an expert in genealogy. Ann will be able to testify that the Krain family, the Otterman family, and the Wilson family, are actual blood relatives. You will see a marriage license in your file of the marriage between your great-grandfather and Ms. Wilson's great-grandmother."

Judge Krain closely studied the marriage license of Wilbur Krain and Angie Wilson, frowning with abject disapproval.

"On the next page is a photo taken of them on their wedding day. You will also note the family resemblance between your great-grandfather and myself," smirked Jim. "Your Honor."

Judge Krain stared at the photo with loathing. Clearly, Ms. Angie Wilson was pregnant in the photo!

"Making both of us distant cousins to the late Woodrow Wilson, Your Honor, sir," smirked Jim.

"Blast it!" muttered Judge Krain as he pounded his gavel against the sounding block, for no particular reason other than utter frustration.

"Sir?" prompted Jim.

"Who is the other woman in your group?" barked Judge Krain.

"This is Sherry Collingsworth, Your Honor," introduced Jim. "She was present – as were most of the others here today – during our opening of a hidden wall safe drawer found by me at the Powell Mountain Bed and Breakfast. That was where the Wilson documents you just reviewed were found, making these people all chain-of-custody eyewitnesses."

"Please explain to me the relevance of the Wilson-Krain relationship to the murder of Lydia Cain and Paul Johnson?" grilled the judge. "And, also, how the other alleged murder victims in this file are relevant to the Wilson matter at hand?"

"I'm glad you asked that question, Your Honor." Jim smiled a crooked smile as he turned to give his row of witnesses an assuring nod.

Judge Krain sighed deeply and motioned with his hand for Jim to continue.

"Well, sir," elaborated Jim. "In the letter written by Woodrow Wilson to his wife Harriet before his death, he specifically mentions witnessing the murder of Misty Krain by the late Ronald Krain."

Judge Krain merely nodded. He almost seemed for a few moments as if he were going to be sick.

"It is our belief, Your Honor, that the late Ronald Krain kept Mr. Wilson from saying anything about the 1959 murder for all those years out of fear for his family's safety," described Jim. "That would include the burning crosses on Mr. Wilson's property and the extensive damage caused to his home during one of those episodes."

"Go on!" urged Judge Krain.

"It is also clear from the suicide note written by Martha Krain that she believed her father was guilty of murdering the victims whose ID cards and drivers' licenses were in Ronald Krain's desk drawer at the time of his death," added Jim.

Judge Krain scowled as he clicked his way through the other ID cards pictured in Jim's document.

Careful not to refer to Ronald Krain as Michael Krain's father during his argument, Jim continued. "Would it therefore not make sense that Ronald Krain previously did attempt to finally rid himself of the one remaining individual who could come forward and testify against him for the murder of Misty Krain? And would it not make sense for him to falsify the murder scene of Lydia Cain to make that happen?"

"That's enough!" snapped the judge. "There wasn't a lick of proof in 1975 that my father was guilty of those things, and there isn't any now! This just isn't possible!"

"Oh, yes, it is, Your Honor!" rebutted Jim. "If you will look at page 187 in your document, you will see undisputable forensic evidence that Ronald Krain was indeed the one who secreted the implements used in Lydia Cain's murder inside a blue duffel bag. The bag remained forgotten for years in a secret compartment beneath the carpet in the trunk of his 1965 dark green Chevy Impala."

"This is preposterous!" hollered Judge Krain as he started to pick up his gavel again.

"As preposterous as Ronald Krain's arm hairs being caught in the duffel bag's zipper?" shouted Jim. "Your Honor!"

Judge Michael Krain quickly pulled up page 187 and quietly studied it for several moments.

"Furthermore, Your Honor," continued Jim, "there were verified traces of Lydia Cain's blood and hair on the cast-iron skillet inside the duffel bag itself. No doubt there would have been fingerprint evidence, as well, had the duffel bag been recovered forty-eight years earlier!"

"What about the fact that the woodcutter's fingerprints were found all over the gas can originally found at the scene back in 1975?" questioned the judge. "Explain that one!"

"Well, sir," replied Jim. "It was Mr. Wilson's gas can, one he used to power the only yard tool he owned – a rickety old lawn mower he would mow some of his customers' lawns with. Of course, his fingerprints were on it! But, explain to me, Your Honor, how someone who did not even own a pair of gloves could have left absolutely NO fingerprints at all on anything else at Lydia Cain's murder scene?"

"Hum," muttered the judge as he continued to click his way through the lengthy document.

"Your Honor," continued Jim, "there is more than sufficient forensic evidence to overturn the conviction of Murder in the First Degree against the late Woodrow Wilson."

"I assume the local Sheriff Department has been notified of the items in this file and is in the process of contacting the various families involved with these victims?" questioned the judge.

"Yes, Your Honor," assured Jim.

"Including the letters?" pressed the judge.

"Including the letters, Your Honor," confirmed Jim.

"Mr. Otterman," sighed Judge Krain. "This is a highly complex matter, not at all appropriate for *ex parte*."

"I respectfully disagree, sir," replied Jim. "The exposure of the remaining Krain family to unwanted public attention or unnecessary media coverage would not only be an injustice to them, but it would deprive my client of receiving a fair decision from someone with such unique insight as yourself, Your Honor."

"Cut the crap, Jim," directed Judge Krain. "And this is off the record, Avis. Just tell me what result you're after, plain and simple?"

"Off the record?" confirmed Jim.

"Off the record," assured the judge.

"Well, sir," Jim cleared his throat. "As I mentioned, Ms. Wilson is requesting that her late father's good name be cleared, and that his conviction of Murder in the First Degree be overturned, even if it is posthumously."

"Is that all?" Judge Krain shook his head.

"Unless, of course, Your Honor wishes for there to be a highly-publicized trial concerning the murders committed by Jerry and Ronald Krain," advised Jim as he narrowed his eyes at the judge. "And, I might add, the new wildlife refuge will be an excellent addition to your mountain community, not to mention it being a much better use of the land."

"Are you attempting to blackmail an officer of the court, Mr. Otterman?" accused the judge. "Perhaps you should be recused from this case, as well? It appears to me that both of us have a personal interest in the outcome of this matter, do we not?"

"Not necessarily, Your Honor," argued Jim. "Ms. Wilson is prepared to take this matter to the Supreme Court if necessary, regardless of who represents her. And, not only that, I am personally prepared to offer her whatever financial assistance is necessary to accomplish that goal. In other words, money is no object."

"I hate you!" fumed the judge. "And this is still off the record, Avis! Okay, Mr. Otterman, please give me one good reason why I should decide on this matter in an expeditious manner – perhaps even today – as requested in the closing argument of your complaint?"

"Self-preservation, sir," answered Jim. "To avoid having what's left of the Krain family name being drug through an international media frenzy of mudslinging, not to mention the ramifications that it might have on you personally and professionally."

Jim Otterman had Michael Krain over a barrel and Krain knew it. If he did not do something about it that day, there was no telling what the consequences might be, or if he would have another opportunity, regardless of whether his decision might be challenged. *Worst of all, what would the brethren of the Crusading Knights of Powell Mountain think? And, what would they do about it? Would his own family be in danger after making such a judgment?*

"So, just what's to prevent the other victims' families from going forward with suits of their own?" grilled the judge.

"Probably nothing, sir." replied Jim. "But, as a wise man once said, 'out of sight, out of mind.' Perhaps if their attention is not unduly drawn to the situation – as it would be after a highly-publicized *Wilson* trial – most of them might possibly be content just knowing that their loved ones have finally been located and can put their remains to rest."

"This is highly irregular," muttered the judge.

"And, if I may add something else," requested Jim.

"Oh sure, why not?" Judge Krain shrugged his shoulders and shook his head with dismay. "We're still off the record, Avis."

"Very good, sir," acknowledged Jim. "The witnesses present today are all from out of town, with the exception of Ms. Wilson, and the expense and inconvenience that would be involved in bringing them back at a future date would be unduly burdensome."

"Nothing beyond *your* means, I presume?" snickered the judge. "Very well, we're back on the record now, Avis. After consulting with counsel off the record, it has been carefully determined that the evidence presented this date does indeed exonerate the late Woodrow Wilson of the crime of Murder in the First Degree, for which he was wrongly accused and convicted back in 1975."

"Oh, thank you, sir!" exclaimed Luella as she burst into tears.

"Order!" commanded the judge as he pounded his gavel onto the sounding block several times. "You are welcome, Ms. Wilson! And, on behalf of the People of St. Diablo County, the court wishes to extend its deepest apologies and sympathy to Ms. Wilson and her family. Ms. Hedge will prepare the necessary documents for me to sign, along with a formal letter of apology to Ms. Wilson on behalf of the People of St. Diablo County and this court. Mr. Otterman and his party may remain here in the courtroom if they choose to wait while those documents are prepared by Ms. Hedge and then signed by me. Is there anything else, Mr. Otterman?"

"No, sir! Thank you, Your Honor!" beamed Jim. "And, any court or other costs involved with any of this will be paid by Otterman Enterprises upon presentation of a Cost Bill from the court." Jim then handed one of his business cards to the judge.

"Of that I have no doubt, either," advised the judge as he tossed the business card to Ms. Hedge. Then, pounding his gavel again, he pronounced, "Court adjourned! I'll be in my chambers." Judge Krain then grabbed the portable desktop computer on his way, pausing briefly to survey his courtroom, almost as if for the last time.

Carolyn and Luella embraced, tears streaming down their cheeks. Jim Otterman slapped Chip Priest on the shoulder and vigorously shook his hand. "I'm really sorry that Ron didn't live to see this!"

"He and Woody are probably here right now," joked Chip, though he was actually half serious about it.

"Congratulations!" acknowledged Sherry Collingsworth as she came over to the prosecution table to shake each of their hands. "I loved the way you handled him, Jim. Nice job!"

"Too bad so much of it was off the record," smiled Sheree as she and Ann came over, too. Sheree then gave her husband Jim a hug and a kiss on the cheek before slipping an arm through one of his.

"You should be proud," complimented Ann.

Susan and Rupert, however, were clearly preoccupied and remained seated. Oblivious to everything else, they continued to hold hands and gaze at one another like two love-sick teenagers.

"Hey, you two!" poked Janette as she jabbed Susan in the side with her elbow. "We won!"

"Maybe we need a fire extinguisher?" suggested Luella as she and Carolyn passed by them on their way over to congratulate Jim on his victory.

"Hey, Susan and Rupert?" called Carolyn. "Jim has offered to buy everyone lunch over at Maria's."

"I did?" grinned Jim. "Of course, that would involve getting Susan and Rupert's attention long enough to get them out of here."

"Did someone say lunch?" Rupert suddenly asked, though Susan was evidently foremost on his mind.

"Not until we get those signed papers from the judge!" reminded Luella. "I'm not leaving here without 'em!"

"I don't blame you," agreed Carolyn.

"Shameful!" Janette chidingly whispered to Susan. "You haven't even gotten Ray's ashes back yet!"

"Excuse me?" demanded Susan, suddenly annoyed by Janette's intrusion into her personal business. "They're probably back at the lighthouse waiting for me now. Besides, they'll keep."

Carolyn and Janette exchanged a look of concern. Just how well did they really know Rupert? And, was Susan making a mistake to become involved with someone new this soon? Would Rupert really make Susan happy? Most of all, had Rupert really had his last drink of alcohol? Only time would tell. Luella also shook her head with disapproval at them, disappointed that she had not been the one to turn Rupert's head.

"Mr. Otterman?" It was Avis Hedge. "Before I print this out and take it in for the judge to sign, would you please look this over for me and let me know if it will be adequate?"

Jim took the portable desktop computer from Ms. Hedge and began studying the document. "What about the Judgment?"

"On the next page," indicated Ms. Hedge.

"Luella, what do you think?" questioned Jim as he turned the lightweight computer around and held it for her to see.

Luella then took her time, reading the letter of apology and the Final Judgment. "You're the attorney, is it in order?"

"Uh, I believe the judgment needs to indicate that the dismissal is with prejudice and without costs to any party," pointed out Jim. "That way there will be no question about it, down the road."

"You won't be seeking any compensation for your client or restitution from the court?" questioned Ms. Hedge.

"I've got Ms. Wilson's financial back from here on out," advised Jim. "Everything else looks fine."

"Very well," agreed Ms. Hedge as she took the desktop computer from Jim and sat back down at her table.

Seated at the desk in his chambers, Michael Krain sat staring at his computer screen, carefully studying the entire Wilson complaint and its numerous exhibits again.

Michael kept coming back to his sister's suicide note, and to the letter from Woody, reading them over and over again. Somehow, he had always known the truth about his late father, but had refused to let himself believe. His sister Martha had even come to him once with her suspicions when they were about age thirteen, though he had been unwilling to listen at the time.

Despite being fraternal twins, Michael and Martha were never close. Their mother Misty had been unable to cope with two children to deal with at the same time, so Michael had been sent away to live with close family friends in Texas at the tender age of two. That was in 1958. When finally being told by the family friends that his real mother had run off and abandoned Ronald Krain and little Martha, Michael was embarrassed, angry and ashamed that his mother could do something like that. Then, at age 12, Michael was finally sent back to live with his father and sister again, following Ronald Krain's second marriage. It was then that Ronald had finally told his son Michael how his mother Misty had unexpectedly run off with some vacuum cleaner salesman. From that day on, that was what Michael had believed!

Now, to learn that it had all been a lie, and that his own father had actually murdered his mother, was overwhelming to say the least. Unbidden tears began to well up in his eyes. Michael Krain was not a man who easily cried or allowed himself the luxury of showing his feelings to others. There was no way he could make up to the victims or their families for what his father and second cousin had done to them. And, after signing the Final Judgment reversing the Wilson case, his professional career would be all but over with, not to mention his position with the Crusading Knights of Powell Mountain. Worse still, how would his family react upon learning the truth?

A rapid knock on his door roused him from his thoughts. "Come on in, Avis."

"Here are the documents, sir," indicated Ms. Hedge as she set them on his desk in front of him and handed him a blue pen.

Judge Michael Krain grabbed the pen and signed all of the documents in front of him, without even bothering to read them.

"The date, sir," indicated Ms. Hedge. It's April 4th."

Judge Krain then filled in the date without comment.

"Are you all right, Your Honor?" Avis was concerned by his behavior. "Is there anything I can get you? Perhaps a cup of coffee?"

"How 'bout a new life?" Judge Krain smiled sardonically. "You've been an excellent assistant all these years, Avis. I appreciate you more than I can say. I just wanted you to know that."

"Why, thank you, sir," beamed Avis.

"Goodbye, Avis," bid the judge as she turned to leave. "Give Jim Otterman and the others my best. And, since there's nothing else on the docket, why don't you just go ahead and take the rest of the day off? Go enjoy yourself."

"Well, I do have some things I need to get caught up on," mentioned Avis, "but if you're sure?"

"Go!" insisted the judge as he forced a smile to reassure her.

"Have a good evening then, sir," bid Avis as she left.

"You, too!" replied Judge Krain as he watched her leave and close the door behind her.

Michael Krain then studied Jim's entire pleading yet another time, carefully reviewing each and every one of the exhibits. How could his own father have done such horrible things, *especially* to his mother? Perhaps it was just as well that he had been sent away for all those years as a child. But, how sad that his sister had been forced to remain with that monster! No wonder she turned out like she did. And, had he listened to her, would some of the victims still be alive? Michael was angry now.

It had been on his sixteenth birthday that he and his father had driven up to Jerry Krain's place at the Shady Brook with a truckload of cement bags. Jerry had mentioned at the time that he was building a patio, but no patio had ever been built! That was in 1972.

Michael quickly searched through the ID cards again, this time to see which victims had disappeared in 1972. Renetta Henderson? "Oh, my God!" exclaimed Michael as he finally recognized the photo of a girl he had dated that year. Renetta had been a dark-skinned beauty, but was a nice girl and would never have hurt anyone!

Still, his father had made it quite clear at the time that he was never to disgrace the Krain family name like that again, especially if he planned on becoming a Crusading Knight someday! Wanting to please his father, Michael had complied – strictly dating Caucasian girls from that time on – even though he secretly wondered why dating Renetta had really been so wrong. And, now to learn that either his father or second cousin had actually murdered her? "Why?" muttered Michael as he shook his head with disbelief.

No doubt that was what had become of the very cement that he himself had helped his father unload! Michael angrily hurled his gavel across his chambers with all his might, causing its head to be dented on one side after coming into contact with and bouncing off the bullet-proof window of his chambers.

A series of footsteps could then be heard before Avis Hedge opened his chambers door, this time without knocking. "Are you all right, sir? I heard a noise."

"No, I'm not all right!" snapped the judge as he got up, walked over to where his gavel lay on the floor, picked it up, and tossed it onto his chair. "I thought you left here over an hour ago?"

"Sorry," apologized Avis. "I just had a couple of things to finish up first before I could leave."

"Jim was right, you know," declared the judge. "And, it is my responsibility to help him now in any way that I can! Not just to make sure no one ever challenges my decision today, but also to try to seek some sort of justice for all the other victims, as well. What happened to them is absolutely unthinkable!"

"Yes, it is," agreed Ms. Hedge.

"Have you had lunch yet, Avis?" asked the judge as he took off his robe, flung it onto the coat tree, and put his own suit jacket back on.

"No, sir," admitted Avis.

"How 'bout some lunch at Maria's Mexican Restaurant?" proposed Michael.

"Sir?" questioned Avis. "Do you think that would be appropriate?"

"This is not a date!" laughed Michael Krain as he took a handkerchief from his pocket and wiped the residual moisture from his cheeks. "Just lunch! Besides, we both need to eat."

"I wasn't referring to the fact that you're married, sir," replied Avis uncomfortably.

"Because I'm your boss?" pressed Michael.

"You know full well that's not what I'm talking about, sir!" sighed Avis.

"Could it perhaps be that a respectable young black woman like yourself would rather be caught dead than be seen with a member of the Crusading Knights?" Michael had a wicked grin on his face as he removed the white knight lapel pin from his collar and tossed it into the trash.

"Sir!" objected Avis.

"Well, not to worry, Avis," assured Michael. "I'm done with the Crusading Knights for good! Did I ever tell you about the time my father beat me to within an inch of my life for dating a woman of color? That was when I was in high school."

"No, sir," muttered Avis with disbelief.

"He somehow managed to keep his knight friends from finding out about it, and forced me to join them shortly thereafter. I've always been ashamed to be associated with them!" informed Michael.

"Indeed," acknowledged Avis.

"You didn't think it strange that someone like me would hire you in the first place?" questioned Michael.

"But that was years ago," responded Avis uncomfortably.

"And you're the best judicial assistant I've ever had," informed Michael. "It would be a shame if you don't come with me when I leave."

"You're leaving?" Avis became alarmed. It was doubtful that any of the other judges would want a black woman as their JA, especially since all of them were members of the CKPM.

"After the Wilson case, my career as a judge is finished," reminded Michael. "This is it, the end of the line for me."

"What will you do, sir?" questioned Avis.

"I'm going to see if Jim Otterman is interested in opening up a law firm with me," revealed Michael. "We will need a good legal secretary."

"Me?" Avis was astounded.

"Why not?" asked Michael. "I'm sure Jim can afford it. Perhaps after lunch I can track him down and pitch my idea."

"Actually, while you were in chambers, I overheard the Otterman party mention that they were having lunch at Maria's Mexican Restaurant," revealed Avis.

"Excellent!" approved Michael. "I believe Jim and I have much to discuss. I also owe Ms. Wilson a personal apology, as well, not to mention Chip Priest!"

"In that case," smiled Avis, "I heard a rumor that Jim was buying lunch for everyone."

"Then we'd better hurry," encouraged Michael as he held open his chambers door for Avis.

"Let me just grab my coat and purse," replied Avis. "Are you sure Mr. Otterman won't mind us barging in on them like this?"

"Not once he's heard what I have to say," assured Michael Krain. "Trust me!"

# 13. Epilogue

Carolyn and Luella had become fast friends, so much so that Carolyn had finally persuaded her to fly back with the rest of them to the Killingham Lighthouse Bed and Breakfast for a brief hiatus while the new fishing lodge was being built over the old salvage yard at Powell Mountain Bed and Breakfast. It had been Luella's first Learjet ride.

Janette, Carolyn and Luella were enjoying a late morning walk on the beach at Oceanview. The bright April sun felt warm and inviting. Gentle waves caressed the sandy shoreline beside them, bringing with it an occasional fresh treasure from the sea. In the distance, a faraway ocean liner could be seen making its way toward the horizon. "I can't believe how beautiful it is here!" marveled Luella.

"So, how 'bout that Judge Krain?" Janette suddenly asked. "Who would've seen that coming?"

"Not me, that's for sure!" laughed Luella as she bent down to pick up a seashell. "What kind of a creature would you guess lived in this? And do you think it knew what color it was?"

"That's a good question!" acknowledged Janette.

"It looks like a clam shell," opined Carolyn. "But, it's doubtful that sea creatures think in those terms."

"Do you think Judge Krain will be happy with his new life, now that's he's come out of his shell?" asked Luella.

"That's an understatement!" exclaimed Janette.

"Technically, he's not a judge anymore," reminded Carolyn.

"That part didn't surprise me," commented Luella, "but denouncing his knighthood like that on national television during an hour-long press conference – that certainly was a shock!"

"He clearly wants justice for the families of the other victims," reminded Carolyn. "But, what bothered me was when he told the press he'd had no idea what his father and second cousin had been doing all that time. I'm just not entirely convinced of that part."

"It does seem odd that he wasn't suspicious when that girl disappeared," agreed Janette. "Michael Krain even mentioned to us at lunch that day that one of the victims was someone he'd dated. And, a black girl, too!"

"I'll just bet his father loved that!" Luella laughed sardonically as she shook her head.

"His dad must have kept the other Knights from finding out about it, or else they *never* would have let him join," added Janette.

"Indeed!" agreed Carolyn.

"You know, it really is a shame those men are dead now," lamented Luella. "It's as if all the families of their victims have somehow been cheated out of an opportunity for true justice!"

"At least Michael Krain finally let the world know what they did," reminded Carolyn. "That was pretty brave of him. It was undoubtedly a pretty big step for him to besmirch the reputation of his very *own* father and second cousin like that."

"And to give up his career like that, too," recognized Luella.

"People must certainly know he's not to blame for what his father and second cousin did," pointed out Janette. "Even if he did have his suspicions. Who knows, perhaps he was just afraid to say anything."

"That is a possibility. And, as you pointed out, he did mention at lunch that day that he had suspected something," recalled Carolyn. "Which is probably why he feels responsible for not coming forward until now."

"None of us can go back, though," remarked Luella as she shrugged her shoulders and shook her head. "There are no re-dos in this life, just go-forwards."

"Amen!" agreed Janette.

"Say, what are those pink flowers called?" Luella suddenly asked as she motioned with her head toward the steep bluffs beside them. "Seems like they would need more soil than that. Even the roots on some of those cypress trees are sticking out where there's not enough dirt up there."

"Those are called ice plants," answered Carolyn.

"It must freeze here, then?" asked Luella.

"Not that I know of," chuckled Carolyn. "In fact, ice plants cannot tolerate freezing weather. I tried to plant some at my house once and it all died off after the first frost."

"Then why do they call it that?" wondered Luella.

"I think it gets its name from the small, clear engorged hairs on the surface of its leaves because they look like frozen droplets of water," remembered Carolyn.

"Ah ha," acknowledged Luella.

"They sure do like it here, though," added Carolyn. "They seem to do really well in open sunny places with adequate moisture and plenty of ventilation."

"It does get foggy here, too, doesn't it?" quizzed Janette.

"Sometimes," responded Carolyn.

"So, just what is the deal between you and old Carrot Top, anyway?" Luella unexpectedly asked of Carolyn.

"Yeah!" piped in Janette, anxious to hear what Carolyn would say. "It's almost like you and he had some sort of disagreement, right before we took off to go up there to St. Diablo that day."

Carolyn took a deep breath and then let it out, but remained silent for several moments before responding. Then, turning to Janette, Carolyn questioned, "Remember Lenny, Jr.?"

"Oh, baby!" exclaimed Janette as she grinned. "That guy was so fine, he even put Rupert to shame!"

"Not only that, Lenny, Jr. is literally a carbon copy of his dad," assured Carolyn with a crooked smile.

"No kidding?" Luella was interested at once.

"So, what about Junior?" pressed Janette.

"Remember that day he and I went for a walk here on the beach?" continued Carolyn. "And yes, it was the day we left to fly up to St. Diablo."

"You were acting pretty peculiar on the flight up there," acknowledged Janette.

"Indeed." Carolyn then came to a stop and knelt down in the sand. "It was right here on this very spot where Steve Fredrickson died from his injuries after being attacked by a shark while he was boogie boarding back in 1973. I was with him when he died. That was also the day that Veronica Jensen and Joyce Troglite disappeared."

Janette and Luella then sat down in silence beside her, almost reverently, and waited for her to continue.

"See that bunker tunnel with the barred gate over there?" pointed out Carolyn. "That is where we finally found their skeletal remains, back in 2016." Tears then welled up in Carolyn's eyes as she slowly readjusted her legs and sat down on the warm sand.

Janette and Luella exchanged a look of surprise.

"It was also on this same spot that Lenny, Jr. gave me this," revealed Carolyn as she slowly unzipped her purse and carefully removed the letter from Lenny Owens and handed it to Janette.

"Oh, girl! Are you kidding me?" Janette was stunned.

"Just who was Lenny Owens?" frowned Luella. "Isn't he the guy whose photo was in your old blue wallet?"

"Yes," confirmed Carolyn as she momentarily pulled out and held up the Ziploc bag containing it and the other items that had been with it before putting them back in her purse.

"This letter is postmarked August 26, 1979," noticed Janette.

"What does it say?" inquired Luella.

"I haven't read it yet," responded Carolyn, rather distantly.

"What!" Janette could not believe it. "Tell me you're kidding?"

"Jim has been after me ever since, to read it," added Carolyn. "For whatever reason, he is most anxious to know what it says."

"And you're not?" questioned Luella.

"I didn't say that," corrected Carolyn.

"How did Lenny, Jr. get the letter?" asked Janette.

"He said his mom plans to get married again and was going through some of his dad's old things to clean out and get rid of them," related Carolyn. "When she found a box with some of Lenny's other important papers, she just gave them all to her son to deal with. This was in it."

"How did he know you were going to be here?" grilled Janette.

"He didn't," assured Carolyn. "In fact, he had no idea whether any of his dad's old friends would be here, especially me, but brought it along, just in case."

"That's incredible!" marveled Luella.

"And, he just gave it to you?" pressed Janette. "Just like that?"

"Well, it is addressed to me," pointed out Carolyn. "Lenny Jr. figured that since it has my name on it, he was sure his dad would have wanted me to have it."

"How did Jim find out about it, then?" asked Janette.

"That was when he walked up." Carolyn rolled her eyes and shook her head at the memory. "Jim has a way of doing that."

"That figures!" commented Janette.

"And, naturally, you didn't want to read it in front of him." Luella nodded with understanding.

534

"Wasn't Lenny Jr. curious about what it said?" grilled Janette.

"Actually," admitted Carolyn. "He was going to read it out loud for me, since I'd forgotten my glasses. I'd left them back in the room, like now. But, when Jim walked up, I asked him to merely read it to himself, and that I would read it later."

"Girl, what are you waiting for?" urged Janette. "Let's go get those glasses of yours! In fact, I can read it for you right now, if you like. I got mine!"

"I still would like to read it for myself," replied Carolyn as she took the precious letter back and carefully returned it to her purse.

"And soon, I would hope!" exclaimed Janette as all of them stood up to leave and brushed the sand off their bottoms.

"Hey, I know what it feels like to get a letter from a dead person," informed Luella. "It is kind of scary. What if they say something terrible? Or something you want to respond to and can't, because they're gone now?"

"That would be tough," admitted Janette.

"And not only that," elaborated Luella as the three of them headed back toward the lighthouse, "once I read that letter my mama wrote, it took me about six weeks to work up the courage to read the letter from my daddy."

"You're kidding?" frowned Janette.

"Not surprising," commented Carolyn. "What if it had been a confession of guilt, or something like that? That would have been the last thing you'd want to hear."

"Exactly!" smiled Luella. "And, naturally I was quite relieved when I did finally read it, but it took courage just the same."

"So, why are you so afraid to read Lenny's letter?" demanded Janette.

"I don't know." Carolyn shrugged her shoulders. "Perhaps it's just the finality of it. Once I read it, then that's it. And, what if it says something that's disappointing in some way?"

"Then you *must* read that letter today!" advised Janette. "Then at least you'll know what it says."

"I know I sure felt better after reading my daddy's letter," encouraged Luella. "It's just too bad he had to go through all that he did. But, I can't tell you what it means to me to finally have his name cleared, and if you guys hadn't shown up when you did ...."

Carolyn and Janette each put a comforting arm around Luella as she shed a few tears – she was still quite emotional about the subject of her daddy. The three of them then continued walking along the beach, arm-in-arm, until finally reaching the base of the stairway leading up toward the lighthouse.

"Hey, you guys!" It was Susan.

Luella shook her head disparagingly upon seeing Susan and Rupert cozily snuggled so intimately together on an old log.

"Isn't that *your* log?" questioned Janette. "The one Lenny carved your initials on?"

"Well, it's not actually *mine*," replied Carolyn, "but it does look like the log."

"How romantic!" exclaimed Luella as she unhooked arms with Carolyn and Janette and walked over to where Susan and Rupert were, unconcerned in the least with invading their privacy. "Show me."

"Right there on the end," pointed out Carolyn.

"L.O. and C.B.," read Luella as she bent down to get a better look at the carved initials.

"Lenny Owens and Carolyn Bennett," elaborated Susan.

"I get it," responded Luella, almost snidely.

"Hey Carolyn, look at this!" invited Susan. "Over here on this end. Look what Rupert just carved." Susan was not sure what she'd done to Luella, but refused to allow herself to be upset by it.

"R.W. and S.R.?" read Carolyn out loud. "Rupert Williams and Susan Rives?"

"Now it's official," flirted Rupert, with all of them.

"What ever happened to Susan Killingham?" demanded Janette as she folded her arms. She was still upset that Susan had become involved with someone else so rapidly following Ray's death.

"Uh, let's take this down a notch," suggested Carolyn.

"Thank you!" exclaimed Susan as she gave Janette and Luella a look of displeasure.

"We'd like you three to be the first to know the good news," announced Rupert. "Susan and I plan to be married."

"And from the looks of it, none too soon!" snickered Luella.

"Huh!" snorted Janette.

"I wish you much happiness," bid Carolyn.

"Thanks, we will be," promised Susan. "Trust me!"

Meanwhile, up in the tower room of the lighthouse, Sherry Collingsworth was relentlessly questioning Jim Otterman about first *The Oceanview Matter*, and then *The Powell Mountain Matter*.

"You should have more than enough for both of your documentaries by now, don't you think?" Jim was becoming impatient and wanted the interview to be over with already. "What about Ted or Ann? Or even Sheree?"

"Already questioned 'em," informed Sherry as she paused to glance at a text message on her cellphone.

"What about the Murrays?" suggested Jim. "There must be someone else you still need to question?"

"You're it," smiled Sherry. "And, I was also wanting to know how you plan to set up your new law firm?"

"My new law firm?" Jim furled his brow.

"Otterman and Priest?" reminded Sherry with a sly grin.

"Well," Jim cleared his throat. "It actually will be called Priest and Krain."

"Really? So, will it definitely be a law firm then, as opposed to a detective agency?" beamed Sherry. "With you as a silent partner?"

"Yes," confirmed Jim as he got up and walked over to the window. Below, he could see Carolyn, Janette and Luella standing near the log where Rupert and Susan were seated.

"What area of law will your firm be specializing in?" pressed Sherry. "Civil rights?"

"Actually, everything," advised Jim, distracted as he noticed Carolyn dismiss herself from the others and begin walking down the beach alone.

"Will your firm be filing separate lawsuits on behalf of each of the other victims, or just one consolidated case?" delved Sherry.

"Consolidated," muttered Jim as he watched Carolyn make her way down the beach by herself.

"That won't create a conflict of interest for your partners, will it?" grilled Sherry.

"No, why should it?" demanded Jim, without looking at Sherry.

"You seem preoccupied?" noticed Sherry.

"Uh, what was the question again?" asked Jim.

"Will there be a conflict of interest for Chip because he acted as the prosecution in the Wilson matter back in 1975?" quizzed Sherry. "Or, for you and Michael Krain, due to the 2023 matter?"

Jim sighed with frustration before returning his attention to Sherry. Then, after sitting down beside her again, he responded. "The Wilson matter is resolved, so there would be no conflict. The other case – or cases – is a new matter entirely, one where the families and the public alike will be pleased to see it go forward and eventually be resolved."

"Who do you think they might name as defendants?" pressed Sherry.

"That's something we'll just have to wait and see," advised Jim. He was becoming more agitated by the minute. *Was Sherry deliberately trying to detain him?*

"Just what is it like to have unlimited money and power at your disposal?" probed Sherry. "It must be nice to have anything you want."

"Not anything," differed Jim as he got back up and walked over to the window again. *Carolyn was no longer in sight!*

"She did ask me to keep you occupied for as long as I could," admitted Sherry with a mischievous grin.

"What?" demanded Jim as he came back over to Sherry.

"That was Carolyn," smiled Sherry. "Remember the text I got? That was her."

"Really?" Jim breathed in deeply and then began to laugh as he let it back out. "So, Carolyn asked you to keep me occupied for as long as possible, did she?"

"I did my best, wouldn't you say?" grinned Sherry.

"Where is she?" questioned Jim as he leaned over and put one hand on each arm of Sherry's chair as he looked her squarely in the face.

"I suppose I could show you," smiled Sherry, "but I really need to stay off my ankle as much as possible."

"I could carry you," offered Jim.

"Only if you tell me why this is so important to you," bargained Sherry, though she actually had no intention of giving in now. It had become a personal challenge for Sherry to see if she could best Jim's undaunting determination with some of her own.

"Okay!" agreed Jim as he sat back down again. "Carolyn led me to believe that she would agree to have me present when reading a very important document she has had stashed in her purse this past week. Don't worry, it has nothing to do with *The Powell Mountain Matter*."

"What kind of a document?" Sherry coyly asked. Actually, Carolyn had confided in her already about Lenny's letter before going on her walk with Janette and Luella. But, Sherry wasn't about to let Jim know that. Not just quite yet.

"Something of a personal nature," admitted Jim. "I had promised her I would not tell any of you about it, so I don't feel at liberty to describe what it is."

"The letter from Lenny?" Sherry had a crooked smile.

"You *knew*?" shouted Jim. "All this time, and you knew!"

"You must admit, I certainly did do my best to keep you here," smirked Sherry.

"I can see that Carolyn chooses her friends well," complimented Jim as he got up to leave. "I trust you are finished questioning me?"

"*Au revoir*," bid Sherry.


Upon reaching the narrow footpath near the old bunker tunnel, Carolyn carefully made her way upward, toward the bluffs. It was her plan upon reaching the clifftops to sit on some rock there while she finally read the letter from Lenny. It was taking longer than expected to make the ascent, but the others would not expect her back for at least another hour. It was only eleven o'clock in the morning.

The treacherous switchback trail wound its way up, past loose pebbles, blooming ice plants, Ceanothus, and even sharp manzanita shrubs on the rocky hillside.

The rhythmic sound of ocean waves crashing against the ragged shoreline below was almost hypnotic. A pair of seagulls circled overhead in search of place to mate, but then their cries quickly faded into the distance as they flew farther away. It was enthralling to be part of the scenic landscape. Carolyn squinted against the bright rays of reflective sunlight as they rippled across the water below. Thankfully, she did have a small magnifier in her eyeglass repair kit – which she always kept in her purse – even if she didn't happen to have her reading glasses. One way or the other, she was going to read that letter!

"It really is beautiful here," admired Carolyn out loud. "Lenny wasn't the only one who loved it here. And how sad that neither of our fathers would let us return."

After catching her breath, Carolyn finished the climb. Thirsty but without water, Carolyn found and seated herself on a large flat rock nearby. She would definitely take the blufftop trail for her return trip!

"You really shouldn't be out here by yourself like this," came a familiar voice from behind her. It was Jim Otterman.

"Well, here we are again, on the blufftops," sighed Carolyn as she shook her head with defeat. "What's it been, fifty years since the day you snuck up behind me here, right on this very spot?"

"That was the day you were watching Joyce, Veronica and Steve down there boogie boarding," reminisced Jim. "Right before everything went south, that is."

Carolyn suddenly recalled the long distant scene in her mind's eye. "At times, it barely seems like yesterday."

Jim merely nodded. Then, as he sat down beside Carolyn, Jim handed her an unopened bottle of water. "You must be thirsty?"

"Thanks!" smiled Carolyn as she took the bottle of water, opened the lid, and drank most of it down with a single gulp.

"So, I guess you might need these, too?" offered Jim as he handed Carolyn her reading glasses. "I took the liberty of bringing them along, just in case you might decide to read your letter."

"Why me?' Carolyn suddenly asked. "You know I've been happily married for forty years now, and that's not about to change!"

"I know," assured Jim, rather sadly. "But, maybe it's just knowing that I can't have something – especially with all the money and power at my disposal – that makes me want it that much more."

"Are you sure about that?" laughed Carolyn as she put on her glasses and removed Lenny's letter from her purse.

"No," answered Jim. "But, it sounded good. And, if you don't want me to be here when you read your letter, just say so. I'll leave."

"That would just kill you, wouldn't it?" grinned Carolyn.

"Probably," agreed Jim, "but I'm powerless to refuse you anything. You already know that."

"All right, then," nodded Carolyn. "Before I read this letter, I should tell you that there is a reason why the date on the postmark is so significant."

"Go on," encouraged Jim. He had his arms crossed and resting on his knees as he watched the ocean below.

"It was on August 26, 1979, that my two nieces and I drove over to camp meeting for the day," described Carolyn. "Teena and Catrina were ages four and six at the time, and needed to use the restroom. Have you ever been to camp meeting over there?"

"I have, a couple of times," replied Jim.

"Remember where those portable toilet stalls are, up there on the hill, overlooking the compound below?" questioned Carolyn.

"Okay, I know where you mean," nodded Jim. "Up by that row of eucalyptus trees on the hill, sure."

"Well, the three of us –my nieces and I – were walking along, holding hands, making our way up the hill to where the toilet stalls were. I had promised their mother I would make sure nothing happened to them, and certainly didn't want either of them to get lost," explained Carolyn.

"And?" pressed Jim.

"And that was when I saw him," revealed Carolyn.

"Who, Lenny?" questioned Jim.

"Yes," confirmed Carolyn. "At first, he just stood there staring at me. It was as if he was in shock."

"He probably was," assumed Jim. "So, what did you do?"

"The same thing," admitted Carolyn. "It was terrifying. I wanted with all my being to just run over and embrace him, and tell him how glad I was to see him. But instead, I just stood there. It was as if I was glued to the spot. Plus, I felt obligated to keep a hold of my nieces' hands, especially with both of them struggling like they were to get away. All they wanted to do was get to the toilet stalls."

"Then what happened?" urged Jim.

"I introduced my nieces to Lenny," related Carolyn.

"Maybe he thought they were *yours*?" guessed Jim.

"No, I specifically introduced them as my nieces," recalled Carolyn, "but he did look as if he didn't believe me."

"Wow!" Jim shook his head. "That must have been like a punch in the gut for him. Say, aren't you an only child?"

"Yes, I am," replied Carolyn with a mysterious smile.

"So, how can you have any nieces?" pressed Jim.

"Technically, I don't," advised Carolyn. "But, my friend Linda always insisted that her girls call me Aunt Carolyn."

"Humph," chuckled Jim.

"And, even though it was just an honorary title," explained Carolyn, "the girls really believed I was their aunt."

"I see. So, then what?" urged Jim.

"Well, it was all very awkward," continued Carolyn, "but I did manage to ask Lenny if he finally made it to medical school."

"And obviously, he did, since he became a doctor," interjected Jim. "Perhaps he was seeing someone else at the time?"

"He wasn't wearing a wedding band," remembered Carolyn.

"And naturally you looked?" smiled Jim.

"Of course I looked!" snapped Carolyn. "And I still remember the longing in his eyes as he looked at me, though he made no effort whatsoever to come hug me or tell me how glad he was to see me!"

"Perhaps it was the two little girls you had with you?" guessed Jim. "He probably was afraid."

"Teena did have to go pretty bad," revealed Carolyn. "In fact, both of them were trying the whole time to drag me toward the portable toilet stalls. Then, when Teena started hopping up and down and holding herself, Lenny suddenly left. His last words were 'I'll be around.'"

"And was he?" pressed Jim. "Did you catch up to him later?"

"I certainly looked for him," assured Carolyn. "But no, I never saw him again. That was, in fact, the last time I ever saw him."

"No doubt, he went home and wrote you this letter, that very day?" assumed Jim.

"Most likely," agreed Carolyn as she carefully unfolded it. "Well, here goes:

*Dearest Carolyn,*

*Forgive me! I don't know what came over me when I saw you today, or how I could have just left like that! I feel foolish now. Your nieces are beautiful, and it was nice to meet them, by the way. And you – you looked absolutely stunning! Even prettier than I'd remembered.*

*After coming to my senses, I returned to the spot where you had been. Naturally, you were gone. Even Pete helped me search for you until dusk, but in vain.*

*When you did not answer my other letters before, I'd always assumed you were no longer interested. Then, when one of them did come back, it said you were no longer at that address. What was I to do?*

*It was not until <u>today</u> that Pete finally told me you <u>had</u> written, but that my father destroyed your letter! So, it was in the hope of finding you again that I came to camp meeting today. Guess I really blew it!*

*If, by some miracle, you are willing to give me a second chance, it is my prayer you will let me know!*

*Love always, Lenny"*

Tears were now streaming down Carolyn's cheeks as she carefully folded the letter, put it back in its envelope, and returned it to her purse.

"Are you all right?" Jim finally asked. Even he had been profoundly affected by the letter, more so than anticipated.

"Thank you for bringing my glasses," muttered Carolyn as she leaned over and kissed Jim on the cheek. "And for the water, too!"

"Thank you!" replied Jim, blushing deeply as he stood and offered Carolyn his hand to help her up.

"Guess we just have enough time to get back for lunch," estimated Carolyn as she took Jim's hand and let him help her up, but then quickly pulled her hand away again.

"He certainly did blow it!" remarked Jim as he and Carolyn began walking along the blufftop trail, back toward the lighthouse.

"Well, it's like Luella says," advised Carolyn. "None of us can go back. And not only that, there are no re-dos in this life, just go-forwards."

"Have you ever wondered how your life would have been, though?" pressed Jim. "If things had turned out differently?"

"Don't we all," replied Carolyn. It was clear she had nothing more to say on the subject.

At the lighthouse, Sheree and Ann had just finished making a special lunch. It would be a celebration of life in honor of Ray. Following lunch, Jim would fly Susan out over the ocean in his Cessna, from which she would sprinkle Ray's ashes. A bagpipe recording of *Amazing Grace* would be broadcast from the lighthouse catwalk during the occasion.

Jim and Sheree Otterman, Ted and Ann Jensen, Susan and her fiancé Rupert Williams, John and Jeon Murray, along with Carolyn, Luella, Sherry and Janette, were present in the tower room. The large round, highly shellacked wooden table at which they were seated was surrounded by a continuous round matching bench and was easily able to accommodate them.

Since it had always been Ray's favorite, the menu included shish kabob with rice pilaf and cucumber, tomato and onion salad, and homemade baklava for dessert.

"Is everyone here?" questioned Jim.

"I did invite Tony," informed Ted. "He's the new guy we hired to help out with the grounds while you were gone."

"Tony?" Jim seemed puzzled. "Did I know there was a Tony working for us?"

"Sorry I'm late!" apologized a handsome young Italian man, about forty years of age as he entered the tower room. "That's quite a climb!" Tanned and well-built, he was clearly no stranger to hard, physical labor, but impeccably dressed for the lunch.

"And I'm Luella!" muttered Luella upon seeing him.

Carolyn and Janette exchanged a knowing smile with Ann, who had been the one to suggest they invite Tony in the first place.

"Well, come on in and sit down," invited Jim. "Ann was just about to say grace."

Tony quickly seated himself beside Luella.

"Everyone hold hands," requested Ann. "Dear Lord, thank you for this bounty we are about to enjoy. We are truly grateful for family and friends, and for this occasion to remember Ray Killingham. Please comfort those of us who mourn his loss, and who look forward to seeing him again someday. And please give him our best. Amen."

"Amen!" repeated several of the others as they opened their eyes, began passing around the various dishes, and helping themselves to the delicious food.

Ann unexpectedly got up from the table and walked over to the set of book shelves along one wall of the tower room. Perhaps it was the way the light suddenly shone upon it, she couldn't be sure, but it almost looked like another faux book! None of them had really spent much time in the tower room since opening up the bed and breakfast.

"What is it?" questioned Carolyn, who was also interested in old books.

"It can't be!" muttered Ann as she pulled the book from the shelf and confirmed her suspicions. "It's another faux book!"

"Really?" Sherry Collingsworth was interested, too.

"Well, open it up, honey," encouraged Luella. "Don't keep us all in suspense!"

Ann went over to the built-in, cushion-covered benches opposite the book shelf and sat down to open her find. She didn't want to get any food on her discovery. "I don't believe this! Look! There's an old journal in here!"

Jim frowned but did not say anything. He'd had just about all the adventure he cared for, for a while at least.

"It says here that it belonged to a Jack Killingham," advised Ann. "There's some old photographs in here, too."

"Let's see?" requested Susan.

"It doesn't say who they are," realized Ann. "Perhaps it says something inside the journal!"

"Perhaps we can read it after lunch?" suggested Jim as he took a bite of shish kabob and began to chew.

"The first photo is of a woman with two men – all of them nice looking – standing right outside here on the beach below. They are wearing old-fashioned swimsuits," described Ann. "The two men are each holding a baby, probably twins."

Ann then walked around the table, holding the photo so each of them could see. "And here's another photo of one of those same men – the really tall one – dressed in a safari suit, holding a rifle and a water bag. It looks like it was taken somewhere in the jungles of south America!"

"Ann, please!" Jim sighed deeply.

"And there's a smaller box in here, too!" exclaimed Ann as she took it out and quickly opened it. She then stared at what was inside with utter astonishment.

"Well, what is it?" pressed Carolyn.

Ann then walked around the table with the box, afraid to even touch what was inside.

"Oh, my God!" exclaimed Susan, upon seeing it.

The small round disk was roughly three inches in diameter, and half an inch wide, and appeared to be solid gold!

"There's writing on it, too!" pointed out Ann, excitedly.

"I can see that," replied Susan as she continued to stare at the item. "And you're sure this has been here the whole time?"

"Apparently so," replied Ann as several of the others got up and came over to see the object.

"What do you think it says?" questioned Sherry.

"It looks like Sumerian," assessed Jim, who was now intrigued and reached to take it from the box so he could look at the back of it. "Cuneiform began as a system of pictographs but was eventually replaced by the Phoenician alphabet around the time of the Neo-Assyrian Empire. This reminds me a good deal of the type of characters used on the Code of Hammurabi. See how it continues on the back?"

"Enough with the history lesson already!" requested Janette. "All we need to know is if it's real gold!"

"I think so," replied Jim.

"Actually, it is Sumerian," confirmed Rupert, who had studied it. He, too, was more than casually intrigued.

"Does this mean we're rich?" asked Ann.

"We already are, dear," advised her mother.

"This looks more like a treasure map to me," opined Carolyn.

"It could be," admitted Jim as he studied it more closely.

"Does this mean we're going to south America for our next big adventure?" teased Sherry as she pulled out her notebook and made a few more notations.

"Maybe this is how the Killinghams were able to afford this lighthouse in the first place?" guessed Carolyn.

"And, perhaps there's even more treasure where that came from!" pointed out Susan, rather excitedly as she began to look more closely at the other books in the bookshelf.

"Hey, everybody!" hollered Jim. "Let's finish lunch first, and then we can check out the books. Okay?"

"Perhaps we should go ahead and do the flyover with Ray's ashes first?" suggested Susan, though – like everyone else – treasure was foremost on her mind.

"Don't worry," assured Ann. "If there's anything else here, we'll find it. Trust me!"

62249702R00306

Made in the USA
Lexington, KY
02 April 2017